Genre and Contemporary Hollywood

Genre and Contemporary Hollywood

Edited by
Steve Neale

 Publishing

First published in 2002 by the
British Film Institute
21 Stephen Street, London W1T 1LN

The British Film Institute is the UK national agency with responsibility for encouraging the arts of film
and television and conserving them in the national interest.

Cover design: Barefoot

Set by Fakenham Photosetting, Norfolk
Printed by Bell and Bain, Glasgow

British Library Cataloguing-in-Publication Data

A catalogue record for this book is available from the British Library
ISBN 0–85170–887–0 (pbk)
ISBN 0–85170–886–2 (hbk)

Contents

1. Introduction
    Steve Neale   1

Section One: Genre: Tradition and Innovation

2. Tall Revenue Features: The Genealogy of the Modern Blockbuster
    Sheldon Hall   11

3. Westerns and Gangster Films Since the 1970s
    Steve Neale   27

4. The New Hollywood Musical: From *Saturday Night Fever* to *Footloose*
    J. P. Telotte   48

5. Some Smothering Dreams: The Combat Film in Contemporary Hollywood
    Michael Hammond   62

6. From Female Friends to Literary Ladies: The Contemporary Woman's Film
    Karen Hollinger   77

7. Hollywood Lives: The State of the Biopic at the Turn of the Century
    Carolyn Anderson and John Lupo   91

8. From Paranoia to Postmodernism? The Horror Movie in Late
    Modern Society
    Andrew Tudor   105

9. The Impossibility of Romance: Hollywood Comedy, 1978–99
    William Paul   117

10. Conforming Passions?: Contemporary Romantic Comedy
    Frank Krutnik   130

11. Pleasing the Million: Shakespearean Cinema of the 1990s
    Roberta E. Pearson   148

Section Two: Genre: New Cycles and Trends

12. Hollywood Production Trends in the Era of Globalisation, 1990–99
    Tino Balio   165

13. 'The Best Disney Film Disney Never Made': Children's Films and
    the Family Audience in American Cinema since the 1960s
    Peter Krämer   185

14. Movie Ratings as Genre: The Incontestable R
    Kevin S. Sandler   201

15. Cinema and the Premises of Youth: 'Teen Films' and Their Sites in
    the 1980s and 1990s
    James Hay and Stephen Bailey   218

16. Ghetto Reelness: Hollywood Film Production, Black Popular
    Culture and the Ghetto Action Film Cycle
    S. Craig Watkins   236

17. 'Film Noir Like You've Never Seen': Jim Thompson Adaptations
    and Cycles of Neo-noir
    Peter Stanfield   251

18. Grisham Adaptations and the Legal Thriller
    Keith Bartlett   269

19. Film Parody and the Resuscitation of Genre
    Dan Harries   281

20. '*Gone with the Wind* Plus Fangs': Genre, Taste and Distinction in
    the Assembly, Marketing and Reception of *Bram Stoker's Dracula*
    Thomas Austin   294

Index   309

1

Introduction

Steve Neale

The topics of genre and of 'New' or 'contemporary' Hollywood cinema are very much in vogue at the moment. Individual books such as *Reconfiguring Film Genres*, *Film/Genre* and *Genre and Hollywood* have pioneered new ways of thinking about genre, while the series of books launched by Wallflower and Cambridge University Press have sought to provide updated accounts of traditional genres.[1] At the same time, an interest in Hollywood and its output since the early 1970s has led to at least one seminal essay, Thomas Schatz's 'The New Hollywood', as well as to Jim Hillier's book on the subject, a number of industry-oriented histories and two major collections of essays.[2]

One of the driving forces behind these developments has been the perception of an ever-increasing gap between the accounts of Hollywood and of genre available as starting points for teaching or research on the American film industry and its output since the studio and transitional eras of the 1930s, 1940s, 1950s and 1960s. Tino Balio's *The American Film Industry* and Bordwell, Staiger and Thompson's *The Classical Hollywood Cinema* were for some time the principal texts on Hollywood's aesthetic and institutional history, and, while the former covers the history of the American film industry through to the late 1970s, the latter focuses mainly on the period between 1917 and 1960.[3] Meanwhile most of the pioneering works on genre, including those by Buscombe, Ryall and Tudor, were written in the late 1960s and early 1970s.[4] They therefore inevitably drew for their examples on the films of the studio era or the period of transition in which they were working. Subsequent work on melodrama and the woman's film also focused on the studio and transitional eras, while overviews such as *Genre* and *Hollywood Genres* were either historically non-specific or else concerned, too, with the 1930s, 1940s and 1950s.[5]

Given the existence of this gap, it is hardly surprising that historians, theorists and and scholars have sought, particularly since the early 1990s, to narrow it. Given the dominance of the studio and transitional eras in accounts of Hollywood and genre alike, it is hardly surprising that they have tended to proceed by means of contrast and comparison, by means of an address to the similarities and differences between the old Hollywood and its genres and the New. This book is no exception. Its contributions are divided into two sections, 'Tradition and Innovation' and 'New Cycles and Trends'. Both contain comparisons and contrasts, but where the former is weighted towards traditional genres and traditional generic categories, paying considerable attention in some cases to old as well as New Hollywood, the latter is weighted towards developments and trends originating in or specifically characterising contemporary Hollywood cinema and its history.

Inflected in varying ways and to varying degrees by recent revisionist work on genre, the contributions to both sections are designed to be exploratory rather than definitive, to open up the topic of genre and contemporary Hollywood from an array of different perspectives rather than provide an overview from a single omniscient position. Genre is itself a multi-faceted phenomenon. Genres can be approached from the point of view of the industry and its infrastructure, from the point of view of their aesthetic traditions, from the point of view of the broader socio-cultural environment upon which they draw and into which they feed, and from the point of view audience understanding and response. Readers will find examples of all these approaches in this book.

The opening contribution to 'Tradition and Innovation' is Sheldon Hall's essay on the blockbuster. Blockbusters are often considered to be one of the defining features of New Hollywood cinema. The placing of Hall's essay in this section and the argument put forward in the essay itself both suggest, though, that blockbusters are by no means a recent phenomenon. Hollywood has produced high-cost, large-scale films since the mid-1910s. During the 1950s and 1960s, when the term 'blockbuster' first came into use, the production of such films was central to the commercial and industrial strategies adopted by major Hollywood companies and mainstream independents alike. However, as Hall points out, there are at least two basic differences between the blockbusters of the studio and transitional periods and the blockbusters of the New Hollywood era. Where the latter are widely and rapidly released in the summer and at Christmas, the former were roadshown – released to select cinemas for long periods at prices and under conditions more akin to the theatre than routine cinema. Thus while an aura of specialness attaches to both, the specialness of the New Hollywood blockbuster is less apparently exclusive. It is also less culturally prestigious. New Hollywood blockbusters, unlike old ones, are principally addressed to the perceived tastes of children, young adults and families. They have therefore drawn heavily on a generic repertoire of science fiction, action and disaster that in the past would have been the province of the B-film, the serial and the programme picture.

A number of the essays that follow in this section focus on genres that have often been central to genre theory. My essay on Westerns and gangster films argues that, while the longstanding traditions of the Western were central, too, to at least one of the principal strands in its re-emergence in the mid-to-late 1980s, the gangster film was much more indebted to *The Godfather* (1972), *Mean Streets* (1973) and other films of the 1970s. Rather than interpret developments in either in accordance with the totalising protocols of traditional genre theory, I attempt to chart the diverse cycles and trends that have marked them both and to pinpoint some of the specific contextual factors that have governed their history since the late 1970s.

J. P. Telotte's essay on musicals and Michael Hammond's essay on war films both look at traditional genres as well. Telotte's essay is specifically concerned with the changes that marked a group of late 1970s and early 1980s musicals – *Saturday Night Fever*

(1977), *The Buddy Holly Story* (1979), *Footloose* (1984) and others. Running alongside more traditionally oriented films such as *Xanadu* (1980) and *Grease* (1978), these 'new musicals' were all marked by their focus on the often circumscribed place – and the often circumscribed expressive or transformative possibilities – of song and dance in the worlds they depict. This focus, he argues, is a mark in turn of their attempt to update the inherently 'escapist' conventions of the musical and render them more pertinent to contemporary society.

Michael Hammond, meanwhile, looks at the intermittent series of films set in Vietnam or during World War II that Hollywood has produced since the late 1970s. Produced in the wake both of the Vietnam War and the advent of 'visceral cinema', these films are often organised, he argues, around traumatic sequences of combat or atrocity the effects of which impact decisively not only on the consciousness and behaviour of the characters, but also on spectators and on the ways in which the films and the wars they depict are 'memorialised'.

One of the most important developments in work on genre in the late 1970s and 1980s was a feminist-led focus on the woman's film. As Karen Hollinger's essay indicates, questions have been raised recently both about the provenance and the institutional existence of the woman's film. In addressing the extent to which the traditional ingredients and approach of the woman's film have their parallels in the 1970s, 1980s and 1990s, Hollinger identifies such cycles and strands as 'the independent woman film', 'the female friendship film' and 'the new maternal melodrama'. Ranging widely across the independent sector as well as Hollywood itself, she also pinpoints 'classic adaptations' as an increasingly important site of and for female writers, directors and audiences. However transformed its ingedients have been, and however diverse its strands have become, it is clear that, although the woman's film disappeared almost entirely in the late 1960s and early 1970s, it has returned in numerous guises since then.

In contrast to the woman's film, the biopic has been somewhat neglected in writing on genre and Hollywood. Taking their cue from George F. Custen's book on the biopics,[6] Carolyn Anderson and Jon Lupo note the extent to which the biopic has remained a staple ingredient in Hollywood's output since the 1970s, the degree to which it has been associated with directors such as Oliver Stone, actors such as Denzel Washington and other genres such as the musical, the Western and sports film, and the degree to which, too, it has for all its fixed formulae sought to accommodate both people of colour as subjects and occasional experiments in form and approach. Like Hollinger, Anderson and Lupo take account of the independent sector. They also pinpoint some of the ways in which biopics have been marketed and note the extent to which they have been commercially successful.

Frank Krutnik and Andrew Tudor look at romantic comedy and horror, respectively, and William Paul at comedy in general. Tudor considers the extent to which 'postmodernism' as a concept can be used to describe or account for the characteristics of horror series and films since the mid-1980s. Pointing out first of all that series, sequels and cycles have characterised horror production since the 1930s (and therefore that 'franchises' as such are nothing new), Tudor goes on to argue that an awareness of 'sequelling' is nevertheless now a major convention. He also notes the degree to which 'comedy-horror' is now ubiquitous and the extent as well to which what he calls 'para-noid horror' remains horror's dominant mode. Sceptical as to the explanatory value of postmodernism, Tudor argues that these and many of the other social, cultural and styl-istics features associated with it are in fact 'products of modernity itself'.

William Paul provides on overview of various strands of comedy in the New Hollywood era. These include 'animal comedy', which he sees as a specific form of slap-stick, the 'comedian comedy' of Bill Murray, Eddie Murphy and Jim Carrey, domestic comedy (a long-neglected area) and romantic comedy, which in an era of change and uncertainty always tends to set romance 'in the quotation marks of self-referentiality or simply be impossible'. Frank Krutnik focuses on romantic comedy in more detail. Following a survey of dominant trends, he considers the various ways in which the films themselves have usually sought to reconcile traditional ideas and ideals of love with con-temporary life and society, contemporary gender politics and contemporary sexual culture. In doing so, he suggests that what marks them is a self-consciousness deploy-ment of generic and romantic conventions on the one hand, and a 'passionate conformism' on the other.

In concluding Section One, Roberta Pearson's essay on Shakespearean cinema dis-cusses films such as *Romeo + Juliet* (1996), *Richard III* (1995) and *Shakespeare in Love* (1998) in terms of a tradition of commercial Shakespearean production and adaptation that stretches back to the 1890s. Looking at such topics as spectacle, language and star-power, and at longstanding debates about commercialism and cultural value, Pearson suggests that what is new about the most recent New Hollywood films is their deploy-ment of 'a dense popular culture intertextuality'. This intertextuality could, of course, be labelled postmodern; however, as is clear from Tudor's, from Krutnik's and from my own contribution, there are times when what has now become the master discourse of postmodernism can confuse rather than clarify the issues at stake.

The developments dealt with in Section Two are of various kinds, but overall the focus here is less on longstanding generic traditions than on specific cycles and trends. The terms 'trend' and 'production trend' have in recent years figured prominently as alterna-tives or additions to 'genre' as means by which to chart the different strands in Hollywood's output. They were first used extensively in *Grand Design*, Tino Balio's con-tribution to Scribner's multi-volume history of the American cinema.[7] Balio here combines the use of these terms with box-office figures and contemporary reviews in order to identify the principal strands in Hollywood's output in the 1990s. Among them he considers 'disaster', 'science fiction', 'horror', 'action' and 'drama'. In these trends, as in others such as 'animation' and 'comedy', he notes that the biggest box-office hits have nearly always been films with an appeal to teenagers, children and families. He underlines as well, in his conclusion, the extent to which Disney as a company and Steven Spielberg as an individual have been consistently successful in this field.

Similar points inform Peter Krämer's essay on children's films and the family audi-ence. His argument is that Disney's family-oriented films and family-oriented ethos were central not just to the films and the figures who helped establish the New Hollywood in the mid-1970s and early 1980s, but also to Hollywood's dominant commercial stategies since then. Following experiments with markedly 'adult' films in wake of the introduction of a ratings system in 1968, Hollywood turned to the family audience and to child-friendly films as its biggest and most stable source of income. In doing so, he suggests, its most successful films now parallel those made under the aegis of the Production Code in the 1930s and 1940s in that they are aimed at or can be enjoyed by an inclusive audience of teenagers, adults and children.

Ratings figure, too, in Kevin Sandler's essay and, teenagers in the essay by Steve Bailey and James Hay. Sandler's starting points are the discussion of 'ratings as genre' in Rick Altman's influential *Film/Genre* and the persistent if numerically minor strand in Hollywood's output since the 1970s which has continued to court adult audiences through the inclusion of erotic or violent themes. As adults-only ratings severely restrict the opportunities for distribution, exhibition and profits, the key for these films and their producers has been to qualify for what Sandler calls an 'Incontestable R', a 'respectable' rating which bars children, but which includes older teenagers. Through a series of case studies, he demonstrates the extent to which this rating has functioned since the late 1970s as a blueprint, a label, a set of representational conventions – and hence as a genre.

Bailey and Hay focus not on adult but on teen films. Rather than look at the transformations in convention or at the fluctuations in output that have marked them since the 1950s, however, they consider the ways in which teenagers and the teen film intersect with one another in terms of a series of spaces or sites (notably the home, the school and the shopping mall) and of a capacity to inhabit and move between them as part of a process of socialisation. Ranging widely across a broad array of films, Bailey and Hay offer a distinctive and thought-provoking perspective not just on teen films, but also on the ways in which cinema and its genres play a part in the organisation of social identity. It is a perspective that might be brought to bear not just on teen films, but also on the 'adult' films that Sandler discusses or the 'children's films' discussed by Kraümer.

It might be brought to bear, too, on the early 1990s 'ghetto action' films discussed by Craig Watkins. Watkins himself notes the degree to which these films identify urban black communities with poverty, with crime, with single-parent families and with aggressively violent male behaviour. He also notes the extent to which they were financed on the basis of their potential appeal to white audiences and on the assumption that the young black film-makers funded to make them would endow them with a racially based 'authenticity'. He argues as well, though, that a number of these film-makers drew on the coming-of-age format and the traditions of the gangster film in order to highlight the oppressive social conditions experienced in particular by black ghetto youth, and thus that the ghetto action cycle as a whole is 'an extremely complex form of cultural discourse ... irreducible to uniform "readings" '.

Keith Bartlett and Peter Stanfield also discuss small groups or cycles of films. Both groups consist of adaptations of the work of popular novelists. Stanfield looks at the cycle of Jim Thompson adaptations that appeared in the early 1990s. He discusses the films, the re-publication of Thompson's novels and the rise of Thompson's reputation within the context of a consideration of 'noir' and of 'neo-noir' both as 'collector's' concepts and as terms with commercial and critical caché. Noting the extent to which the films differ geographically and iconographically from the films of the 'classic' noir canon, and the extent to which, too, they evacuate the historical specificities that mark Thompson's work, he argues that as industrial products they sought to cash in on the aura of transgressive, lowlife 'authenticity' that has always been associated with noir and that would help mark them off from the more overtly 'commercial' products around them.

As one of the best-selling mainstream novelists of all time, John Grisham has by definition lacked Thompson's cult status. However, his commercial success has also ensured that his legal thrillers have been acquired as properties by major Hollywood studios and adapted, one by one, for the screen. Keith Bartlett's essay considers Grisham's novels and their adaptations in terms of both their generic characteristics and their points of popular – indeed populist – appeal. He argues that in displacing the Cold War spy thriller, they deploy standard generic ingredients – conspiracies, investigations, injustices and the like – in such a way as to mount liberal critiques of corporations and legal institutions. He also suggests that, even though the novels, at least, are marked by a growing disenchantment, they secure a place for individuals either as agents of justice or as vehicles for social and moral understanding.

Dan Harries looks at the somewhat neglected topic of parody. While parodies have always been produced in Hollywood, Harries argues that they are now more prevalent in box-office terms than ever before. He also argues that they can be understood not just as instances of intertextuality, nor just as films which feed off other genres, but also as means by which these genres and their rules are subject to 'resuscitation'. Using examples from films such as *Scary Movie* (2000), *Scream* (1996) and *Austin Powers: International Man of Mystery* (1997), he examines the devices parodies use and the ways in which they serve to mark, to violate and to reconstitute the generic conventions at stake in each case. He suggests that in acting as 'guardians of Hollywood's genre-based past', parodies also rely on or encourage 'knowing', intertextually informed spectators and modes of spectatorship.

Spectators and audiences figure centrally in Thomas Austin's concluding contribution, a study of the production, marketing and reception of *Bram Stoker's Dracula* (1992). Taking issue with the orthodoxies of established genre theory, Austin stresses the plural nature of genre and genres, the generically complex nature of *Bram Stoker's Dracula*, the extent to which 'genre headings and hierarchies' are subject to contestation and change in the process of a film's circulation, and the degree to which audiences have an active rather than a passive role to play. While the powers of the various institutions involved in this process are stressed, stressed, too, are the various discursive categories and 'taste maps' that audience members themselves deploy.

In making his case, Austin, like a number of the other contributors to this book, extends as well as draws on new thinking on genre. While exploratory and partial in a number of ways, it is to be hoped that the book as a whole will join the only other collection so far published on genre and recent Hollywood cinema, Wheeler Winston Dixon's *Film Genre 2000*, in stimulating further thinking, in promoting new research on Hollywood and its output since the studio and transitional eras, in adding to our understanding of genre, and in adding, too, to our understanding of Hollywood cinema and its history as a whole.[8] As I hope this book makes clear, genre and Hollywood, for all their familiarity as topics and terms, are far from exhausted as objects of study.

Notes

1. Nick Browne (ed.), *Refiguring American Film Genres: Theory and History* (Berkeley: University of California Press, 1998); Rick Altman, *Film/Genre* (London: BFI, 1999); Steve Neale, *Genre and Hollywood* (London: Routledge, 2000). Published volumes in the Cambridge University Press series include Martin Rubin, *Thrillers* (Cambridge, 1999) and J. P. Telotte, *Science Fiction* (Cambridge, 2001). Published volumes in the Wallflower series include Steven Keane, *Disaster Movies: The Cinema of Catastrophe* (London, 2001); Geoff King and Tanya Krywinska, *Science Fiction Cinema: From Outerspace to Cyberspace* (London, 2000); John Saunders, *The Western Genre: From Lordsburg to Big Whisky* (London, 2001); Paul Wells, *The Horror Genre: From Beelzebub to Blair Witch* (London, 2000).

2. Thomas Schatz, 'The New Hollywood', in Jim Collins, Hilary Radner and Ava Preacher Collins (eds), *Film Theory Goes to the Movies* (New York: Routledge, 1993), pp. 8–36; Jim Hillier, *The New Hollywood* (London: Studio Vista, 1992); David A. Cook, *Lost Illusions: American Cinema in the Shadow of Watergate and Vietnam, 1970–1979* (New York: Scribners, 2000); Stephen Prince, *A New Pot of Gold: Hollywood under the Electronic Rainbow, 1980–1989* (New York: Scribners, 2000); Janet Wasko, *Hollywood in the Information Age* (Cambridge: Polity Press, 1994); Jon Lewis (ed.), *The New American Cinema* (Durham, NC: Duke University Press, 1998); Steve Neale and Murray Smith (eds), *Contemporary Hollywood Cinema* (London: Routledge, 1998).

3. Tino Balio (ed.), *The American Film Industry* (Madison: University of Wisconsin Press, 1985); David Bordwell, Janet Staiger and Kristin Thompson, *The Classical Hollywood Cinema: Film Style and Mode of Production to 1960* (London: RKP, 1985).

4. Edward Buscombe, 'The Idea of Genre in the American Cinema', *Screen*, vol. 11, no. 2 (1970), pp. 33–45; Tom Ryall, 'Teaching through Genre', *Screen Education*, no. 17 (1975/6), pp. 27–33; Andrew Tudor, *Theories of Genre* (London: Secker and Warburg, 1974).

5. Mary Ann Doane, *The Desire to Desire: The Woman's Film of the 1940s* (Bloomington: Indiana University Press, 1987); Christine Gledhill (ed.), *Home Is Where the Heart Is: Studies in Melodrama and the Woman's Film* (London: BFI, 1987); Steve Neale, *Genre* (London: BFI, 1980); Thomas Schatz, *Hollywood Genres: Formulas, Filmmaking, and the Studio System* (New York: Random House, 1981).

6. George F. Custen, *Bio/Pics: How Hollywood Constructed Public History* (New Brunswick, NJ: Rutgers University Press, 1992).

7. Tino Balio, *Grand Design: Hollywood as a Modern Business Enterprise, 1930–1939* (New York: Scribners, 1993).

8. Wheeler Winston Dixon (ed.), *Film Genre 2000: New Critical Essays* (Albany: State University of New York Press, 2000).

SECTION ONE

Genre: Tradition and Innovation

2

Tall Revenue Features:
The Genealogy of the Modern Blockbuster

Sheldon Hall

blockbuster (n. sl.) 1. something of great power or size, esp. an epic film or a book. 2. a huge bomb capable of destroying a whole block of buildings.[1]

In the enthusiastic language of the trade, a blockbuster is, currently, a tall revenue feature. When a picture grosses $10,000,000 or more it's blockbusting.[2]

'Blockbuster' has entered common parlance as a term to describe the kind of cinema most readily associated with the dominant commercial forms of modern, mainstream, 'postclassical' or 'post-studio' Hollywood. It is is typically used to refer to a film which is extraordinarily successful in financial terms. However, the term can also be extended to refer to those films which *need* to be this successful in order to have a chance of returning a profit on their equally extraordinary production costs. It is the possibility of a 'failed blockbuster' which allows the twin dictionary definitions quoted at the head of this chapter to seem complementary rather than contradictory: every blockbuster has the potential to be both an 'epic' of 'great power and size' and a 'bomb' (paradoxically the trade's preferred term for a commercial disaster).

The inbuilt imprecision of the term has led to its colloquial origins (it has only been used to describe films since the early 1950s) becoming obscured and its present meaning fudged. In contemporary public discourse, it is not uncommon to find the words 'Hollywood' and 'blockbuster' considered practically synonymous. While at one time blockbusters were distinguished partly by their exceptionalism, their status as an economic category different from and 'above' the normal run of general releases, it now seems possible to believe that Hollywood makes nothing *but* blockbusters. In seeking to place the blockbuster phenomenon historically, we might begin by considering the extent to which exceptionally successful and exceptionally expensive films have featured in the US industry's annual release schedules and box-office charts.

Throughout the silent period, only sixteen films earned domestic rentals exceeding $2 million, with MGM's *The Big Parade* (1925) earning the highest gross of its era, $5.1 million. No sound-era film earned as much as this until David O. Selznick's *Gone with the Wind* (1939), also released by MGM, took more than $30 million in its first five years. With ticket price inflation, the benchmark for high grosses rose in the 1940s; however, a comparably large gap between the top earners and the majority of successes did not appear until the 1946–7 season, when Selznick's *Duel in the Sun* and Samuel Goldwyn's *The Best Years of Our Lives* (both 1946) each grossed around $10 million, and then again at the end of the decade, when Cecil B. DeMille's *Samson and Delilah* (1949) earned $9 million, nearly twice as much as its nearest competitor. Thereafter, annual box-office charts have always included a few films which have placed well ahead of the rest of the pack, a tendency which was especially pronounced in the 1970s.

Many of these hits were also very high-cost productions. The most expensive silent film, MGM's *Ben-Hur* (1925), cost $4 million and grossed $4.55 million. This was a level of expenditure not matched until *Gone with the Wind*, which cost $4.25 million. Thereafter, new budgetary records were set, in turn, by *Duel in the Sun* ($6.48 million), *Quo Vadis* (1951, $7.1 million) and *The Ten Commandments* (1956, $13.5 million), which challenged and briefly surpassed *Gone with the Wind* as the industry's greatest ever box-office success. In cases like these, exceptional success seemed to depend upon exceptional outlay. It was 'lessons' such as these which led to the spate of blockbuster productions that marked the twenty-year period from the early 1950s to the early 1970s and to the second cycle of high spending which extends from the late 1970s through to the present day.

Heavy investment in production was and is not sufficient alone, however, to guarantee success. Particular marketing and distribution strategies were and are required to maximise the commercial potential of even the most attractively packaged and lavishly produced blockbuster film. Generalising broadly, there have been two distribution patterns typically associated with the release of blockbusters: roadshowing and saturation mass booking.

Roadshows

A roadshow is, or was, a film distributed and exhibited in a manner similar to that of a live stage performance at a legitimate theatre. Such films would open on a limited or exclusive basis in a major metropolitan centre for an extended or indefinite run at 'advanced' (raised) prices. Shows were non-continuous, typically limited to one or two performances a day and seats could be reserved. In the 1950s and 1960s – what I prefer to term the 'roadshow era' – the films might have been projected in some special screen format, such as 70mm or Cinerama, to justify their exhibition under such exceptional circumstances, or they might simply have been especially expensive or prestige-laden productions. Screenings of these films were often preceded by an orchestral overture, usually pre-recorded and played over closed curtains, and the films themselves were usually interrupted by an intermission because of their exceptional length. Souvenir programme brochures might have been offered for purchase in the foyer, and to encourage mass attendance group bookings were sought for the block sale of tickets. Not all of these features needed to be present to attract the roadshow tag in the trade press (raised prices alone could merit such a description, or an exclusive, extended run), but together they constituted the range of possibilities for the industry's elite products.

This was the preferred manner of distribution and exhibition for most would-be blockbusters from the early 1910s to the early 1970s, as it then seemed to offer the best opportunities for a proportionately large return on investment. Particularly successful roadshow engagements could last months, even years, rather than the usual two to eight weeks common for metropolitan first runs. Roadshowing was reserved for a select few releases each year. The near-universal policy for 'general release' was the presentation of films in continuous performances, without breaks between shows, so that patrons could enter the film(s) at any point, a practice carried over from vaudeville. In most cinemas, tickets could not be purchased in advance or seats reserved. These practices accounted for the majority of routine, run-of-the-mill releases and persisted throughout the years of the industry's greatest success. Habitual attendance, whether at 'specials' or 'programmers', seemed guaranteed because of the conditions of the post-Depression 1930s and the wartime and postwar 1940s. To cater for a mass public whose members might visit the cinema several times a week, a rapid turnover of programmes and a flexible admissions policy was more sensible for most houses than extended runs and fixed show times.

The realisation in the wartime boom years that the market could support fewer, more expensive and more ambitious pictures if runs (at the 'pre-release' and first-run stages) were long enough to capitalise fully on audience interest led to a reduction in output and a rise in costs per film. Thereafter, the combination of prosecution under the US anti-trust laws, leading to the divorcement of the studios' theatre chains and a consequent loosening of control over exhibition, along with the postwar decline in attendances such as led to the production of epics *Samson and Delilah* and *Quo Vadis* as essential instruments in the studios' attempt to control the market via distribution.

Encouraged by the astounding success of roadshows such as *The Ten Commandments* and *Around the World in Eighty Days* (1956), the studios were persuaded that the best way to earn large profits was to roadshow their premium product. In the period between 1956 and 1970, roadshowing came into its own as the distribution and exhibition strategy of choice. It was used for an increasing number of big films aimed at attracting back to the cinema that section of the population which no longer attended on a regular basis, but which might be persuaded to go downtown for the kind of special occasion or 'event' which a roadshow offered. Budgets rose, too, to meet the cost of productions conceived and executed on a hitherto unprecedented scale. The production of high-cost, high-prestige blockbusters and their roadshow release was a direct response by the studios to the structural and economic conditions of the 1950s and 1960s. It represented in part the studios' attempt to retain and to extend the established exhibition practices of the studio system following divorcement: it was the first run *par excellence* and represented optimum commercial performance. In addition, roadshow blockbusters offered the kind of prime product needed to entice exhibitors to offer competitive bids against one another, to guarantee extended playing time and to pay advances on box-office receipts. With these films in hand, the studios could remain in control of exhibition even after the formal divestiture of their theatres.

The promise of a blockbuster hit also permitted them, in their role as distributors, to exact a larger than usual proportion of the box-office gross from exhibitors. By the early 1960s in the US, up to 90 per cent of receipts after deduction of the 'house nut' (theatre operating expenses) were to be remitted to the distributor. Although the operating costs of roadshow theatres were greater than for most cinemas, thus creating a larger than usual 'nut' and a lesser portion of the box-office for the distributors, this was doubtless offset by the higher ticket prices and by the payment of advance guarantees. As Tino Balio has explained, although initially reserved only for key theatres in New York and Los Angeles, and for premium roadshow releases, this type of deal became standard for national first-run exhibition of most pictures.[3]

Although roadshowing in its traditional sense has now, in the age of the multiplex, been largely abandoned, certain features associated with it – separate performances, tickets which can be bought in advance, runs limited only by box-office response – have been retained and successfully integrated into regular exhibition practice. The block-buster has also become, once again, the preferred mode of the industry's most characteristic products, though their current forms, and the distribution strategies and marketing techniques associated with them, have all changed significantly. Saturation-booking patterns on the scale of today's were unknown in the studio era, but the principle of 'instant release' – reaching as large an audience as possible as quickly as possible – does also have precedents in the 1940s, 1950s and 1960s, notably in the methods adopted by two independent producer-distributors.

Despite the successful roadshowing of *Gone with the Wind*, David O. Selznick's two other big hits of the 1940s, *Since You Went Away* (1944) and *Duel in the Sun*, were released in a new strategy the producer had devised, which briefly became known as the 'Selznick pattern'. Selznick was concerned that the intensive and expensive advertising necessary to promote a roadshow was not economic when a film was playing in only one theatre, even at advanced prices.[4] His new strategy involved targeting a particular territory which would be blitzed with advertising in advance of a film opening. He opened both the above-named films in several downtown Los Angeles theatres at once, along with concurrent engagements in a larger number of suburban and outlying areas, all playing continuous performances with advanced prices prior to a full general release. Multiple first runs took advantage of the public anticipation built by the advertising by making possible a greater number of admissions in a shorter space of time than with an exclusive roadshow engagement. Play-off was quicker, as were returns on the considerable investments these films represented.

An intensive publicity campaign accompanying saturation release later came to be the policy typically used for exploitation films seeking to tap the curiosity of a gullible public before negative word-of-mouth got around. A case in point is Joseph E. Levine's handling of a number of low-budget, European-made epics, notably *Hercules* (1958) and *Hercules Unchained* (1959). These two films were released through Warner Bros., but Levine himself masterminded their promotional campaigns, spending over $1 million apiece (considerably more than their negative costs) on *national* advertising and publicity, including television slots and full-page newspaper spreads, and circulating some 600 prints of each title simultaneously throughout the country, twice the usual number.

The *Hercules* films and the many other 'peplum' epics of their kind, with their semi-clad, muscle-bound supermen and tongue-in-cheek heroics, aimed primarily at an audience of undiscriminating youngsters, anticipated the action-oriented blockbusters of the 1980s and 1990s. The peplums have more in common with the teenage exploitation pictures produced by American International Pictures from the 1950s on, the spaghetti Westerns which would soon supplant the production of epics in Italy, and the James Bond films which would become the definitive model for future action films in both Europe and America, than with the roadshows, which tended to depend upon an aura of prestige for their relatively up-market appeal. These latter cycles also tended to be released in the rapid mass-booking patterns pioneered by Selznick and Levine.

The adoption by the majors of multiple first runs, via the 'Selznick pattern' and its successor, the 'Premiere Showcase' (developed by United Artists in the early 1960s), was partly meant to mollify the newly built suburban theatres excluded from access to road-shows (which tended to play at the remaining downtown picture palaces) and to enhance the status, as well as speed up the supply, of regular A-movies and general releases. Although the industry, from the silent era onwards, tended to enjoy its most spectacular successes with roadshow 'super-specials', these were, almost by definition, exceptions to the norms of production and release. It is contemporary Hollywood (dating from the mid-1970s) which has become dependent on the regular production of blockbusters as its principal mode of operation. But it is the exploitation-movie release strategy, aiming to book a film on every available screen for as fast a financial return as possible, which has been adopted for them, rather than the roadshow method, which met its demise in the industry crisis of 1969–71.

New patterns of production and consumption

The takeover of the studios by large business conglomerates, at least up to 1969, did not significantly alter the industry's basic assumptions about the rightness of the roadshow policy. The number of roadshows and other blockbuster productions released by Paramount actually increased after its purchase by Gulf + Western in 1966; the same is true of Warners after its 1967 merger with Seven Arts, and United Artists following takeover by Transamerica the same year. It took the convulsion of 1969–71 to convince the studios that the roadshow had outlived its usefulness; however, the industry soon resumed its commitment to blockbusters, albeit distributed in rather different patterns. For explanation of these changes we need to examine the seismic shifts which occurred in the industry in the late 1960s and early 1970s.

Between 1957 and 1964, all the studios had shown a corporate loss in at least one year, and there was no year in which at least one such loss had not been recorded. The years from 1965–8 seemed to suggest a new stability, as box-office receipts began to rise (though not attendances: the rise in income was due mainly to ticket price increases) and most of the corporations showed steady profits. For most of them, both annual revenues and the number of releases per year peaked in 1968, suggesting that Holly-wood was successfully beating both the box-office recession and its own earlier mismanagement. By the end of the following year, however, all was crisis: *Variety* reported the combined annual loss by four of the studios as $110,066,000:

> Factors held responsible are write-downs of story properties not deemed suitable for present audience interest, failure of pictures to register expected box-office, changes in amortization tables to achieve more realistic earning prospects, and higher interest rates on money invested in productions.[5]

As a result of their losses, several of the studios changed corporate ownership or executive management; a number temporarily stopped production; most 'rationalised' their corporate structure, assets and operation; and almost all announced radical new economies and revised production policies.

To read many of the standard accounts of this period, one might think that all Hollywood's troubles were due to the failure of a half-dozen or so big-budget musicals produced to capitalise on the success of *The Sound of Music* (1965). The problems, however, were more fundamental. Several interrelated factors were involved in the virtual abandonment of blockbusters (briefly) and roadshowing (more or less permanently) by the industry and their replacement by other production strategies and marketing methods: first, the high cost of many blockbuster films, set against their often meagre or disappointing returns; second, the excessive number of roadshows in circulation in the late 1960s, many of which were typically aimed at an audience which no longer represented the majority of the moviegoing population, and the consequent saturation of the market; third, general over-production of all categories of release, spreading the revenues available from a declining theatrical market ever more thinly; and fourth, the failure of revenues from ancillary markets to compensate for losses in the theatrical sector: in particular, the drop in sales of broadcast rights to television networks. In addition, the changing demographic composition of audiences in combination with new patterns of theatre construction, including their design and location, led to a rethinking of production, distribution and exhibition policies.[6]

The blockbusters of the later 1960s registered, on a regular basis, production costs which had been highly exceptional in the preceding decade and a half, even by the inflationary standards of the postwar years. Inflation itself only partly accounts for this trend; studio inefficiencies and the over-ambition of film-makers had some responsibility, too. Between 1968 and 1971, at least twenty-four pictures cost over $10 million. Of these, probably only three made a clear profit from the domestic market: *2001: A Space Odyssey* (1968), *Patton* and *Airport* (both 1970). Several of the studios suffering the heaviest losses in this period were those with a number of very high-budget pictures entering release (not all of them on a roadshow basis): Fox, Paramount, United Artists and MGM.

The industry's financial planning generally failed to register the impossibility of making a profitable return on expensive pictures for which, partly due to the roadshow patterns in which many were distributed, receipts were spread over a long period of time, thus increasing the amount of interest which had to be paid on production loans. A further problem was the number of releases bidding for the ever-dwindling consumer dollar.

In 1968, the seven majors collectively released 177 pictures, twenty more than the previous year. But that year also saw the first releases from three new 'mini-majors', ABC/Cinerama, Cinema Center and National General, not to mention those from independents such as Disney, Avco Embassy, Allied Artists and American International, which brought the total number of releases that year to 454.[7] These companies were all competing in the same, mainstream market, which could no longer support such volume of product. Of the ninety films listed by *Variety* as having earned upwards of $1 million in the domestic market for the 1968 season, only twenty-seven earned $4 million or more; of the same number on 1969's chart, only twenty-five earned above $4 million.[8] This left the vast majority of commercial releases fighting over scraps.

The studios' combined annual production expenditure in this period was about $400 million (including independent productions); total potential rental income from the world market was estimated as $600 million, of which little more than a third was available to cover actual production expenses (after deduction of distribution fees and costs). Only the success of a few big-budget pictures disguised the fact that long-term profitability on this continuing basis was impossible. Even if the studios were to handle a reduced number of films, the concomitant reduction in distribution fees – their principal source of profit – would lead to ultimate collective bankruptcy if production costs remained at a constant level.[9]

The complete failure of a large majority of the late 1960s' roadshows can partly be accounted for by changing patterns of audience taste. Many of the major box-office successes at the end of the decade were not purpose-built blockbusters, but relatively low-budget 'sleepers' – surprise hits – such as *The Graduate* (1967, which grossed $44.1 million domestically), *Bonnie and Clyde* (1967, $22.8 million), *Bullitt* (1968, $19 million), *Midnight Cowboy* (1969, $20.5 million), *Easy Rider* (1969, $19.1 million), *M*A*S*H* (1970, $36.7 million) and *Woodstock* (1970, $16.4 million). These films owed their profitability not to the mass family audience at which roadshows were traditionally aimed, but to the up-market adult and college-educated 'youth' audiences, which the studios tried increasingly to cultivate in the early 1970s.

Though many of the 'failed' roadshows were successful enough in terms of audience acceptance – *Hello, Dolly!*, *Paint Your Wagon* (both 1969) and *Tora! Tora! Tora!* (1970) all appeared in the US box-office top tens for their respective years of release – their excessively high production costs (around $20 million each) prevented their making a profit from the theatrical market alone. This fact, in combination with the realisation of the limited revenues possible from the world market, resulted in the capping of budgets by almost all the companies from 1970 and the reduction of output overall. The number of films released by the majors fell from a post-1960 high of 177 in 1968 to an all-time low of seventy-eight in 1977.[10]

Roadshows were not instantly abandoned. Columbia's *Nicholas and Alexandra* (1971) and *Young Winston* (1972), and United Artists' *Fiddler on the Roof* (1971) and *Man of La Mancha* (1972), all among the more expensive pictures of their years, were roadshown in the traditional manner. Only *Fiddler on the Roof* was a success, earning $38.3 million on a negative cost of $9 million. Later in the decade, a few expensive prestige pictures were launched on a limited reserved-seat, advanced-price basis: *The Great Gatsby* (1974), *The Deer Hunter* (1978), *Apocalypse Now* (1979) and *Heaven's Gate* (1980).[11] These, however, were exceptions to the norm.

Roadshows, as has been noted, were conceived primarily for exclusive, pre-release exhibition in metropolitan theatres in downtown situations. Their 'theatrical' aura was geared to this kind of viewing environment, in which the specialness of the occasion partly depended on its differentiation from other film viewing experiences and its similarity to that of the legitimate theatre. This included the scarcity value of the film itself (only one theatre playing it in each territory), as well as the theatre-like surroundings. As the downtown theatre declined, so, too, did the roadshow.

Unlike the British circuits' policy of adapting existing buildings to multi-screen use, the 1960s and 1970s saw a cinema building boom in America, with many new multiplexes being constructed from scratch, often in suburban shopping malls. Eugene Picker, president of the American National Association of Theatre Owners (NATO), explained the economic and cultural logic behind the US 'trend of building smaller theatres, seating between 300 and 500 people ... in the modern shopping centres' as follows:

> These congenial new theatres undoubtedly represent the strong present-day trend of American exhibition, and I look for this pattern to expand in years to come. Construction costs tend to be reasonable in relation to the profit potential of theatres of this kind. They are often built contiguous to each other or within the same overall structure. And with automated booth equipment the theatre operator will have a substantially lower payroll and a better chance to stay on the more profitable side of the ledger.
>
> There is another factor which is perhaps equally basic to the success of these smaller theatres. They have a sociable air and friendly atmosphere that enhances the pleasure of the movie-goer.[12]

According to a 1973 report by the American Film Institute (AFI), 498 new auditoria had been constructed in the previous year (a tenfold increase on 1969), of which 60 per cent had 400 seats or fewer.[13] Thomas Schatz reports that the number of indoor cinema screens in America increased from around 10,000 in 1975 to reach 22,750 by 1990.[14] The pronounced concentration of these new cinemas in suburban and out-of-town shopping malls significantly altered the experience of moviegoing. The combination of the small size of multiplex auditoria, their undistinguished design, the coexistence of ten or more screens within one building and the unprepossessing environment of shopping malls and leisure service complexes hardly conduced to the theatrical pretensions of roadshows.

The new theatres, and the new generation of blockbusters designed for them, also anticipated a different demographic base for the moviegoing population. In the trade's view, most roadshows, with occasional exceptions such as *2001: A Space Odyssey*, appealed 'to family audiences or, less frequently, "serious" adults'.[15] According to research undertaken by the Rank Organisation in Britain, the 'prime family audience' consisted of people in the age ranges twenty-five to forty-four, with children up to the

age of fifteen. Its principal socioeconomic group was ABC 1, or middle-class professionals.[16] Figures published in 1970 showed that this audience accounted for an
average of 7.3 visits per annum. But the bulk of roadshow audiences did not come from
this group:

> The older independent marrieds, we believe, are probably the people who go to see road
> show films most often. The analysis of the audience profile we get with road shows in fact
> confirms this assumption, but they are in the main 45 to 64 ABC 1. I'm talking about the
> musical road-shows, of course.[17]

This audience group accounted for only 4.8 annual visits, the lowest average of all the
segments discussed in the survey; this supports the claim, often made, that roadshows
were made primarily 'for people who don't go to the pictures'.[18]

The most frequent filmgoers were people of all classes aged between sixteen and
twenty-four, who averaged 13.5 visits a year. The AFI's 1973 report showed that seventy-
three per cent of tickets sold in America were bought by people aged between twelve
and twenty-nine. This, of course, was recognised as the prime target audience from the
1970s onwards, and most blockbusters of the past quarter-century have sought to reach
this segment first. Roadshows may have aimed to attract a family audience, but generally targeted adults who, it was hoped, would bring their children along. Today, children
and teenagers are targeted first, and it is their parents and elders who must be persuaded
to accompany them.

Several innovations in exhibition strategies introduced by roadshows were eventually integrated into regular industry practice. Separate performances and bookable
seats are now the norm, and long runs have been made more common by the availability of small auditoria in multiplexes, which routinely play off successful films for
weeks or months on end until their box-office potential has been exhausted. However,
young people are presumed not to be interested in an experience approximating 'live'
theatrical conditions; so multiplexes dispense with presentational frills and operate on
a similar basis to the fast-food concession stands found inside and adjacent to them.
The 'product' is therefore also tailored to match this audience's presumed or demonstrated tastes.

Blockbuster trends in the 'New' Hollywood

Following, and even during, their brief period of thrift in the early 1970s, the studios
once again became committed to blockbuster-oriented production policies. Their hopes
became pinned on the expectation that a small number of hugely successful, and usually
hugely expensive, 'tentpole' pictures would pay not only for themselves, but also for the
studios' overheads and their losses on other releases. After burning its fingers in pursuit
of *Easy Rider*, with the failure of a number of films aimed at the intellectual, college-
educated or drop-out teenage audience, Hollywood returned to mass-market family
entertainment, beginning with the cycle of disaster movies inaugurated by *Airport* and
The Poseidon Adventure (1972). *Love Story* (1970) and *The Godfather* (1972) alerted the

industry to the viability of films made primarily for adult – but not elderly – audiences, a point subsequently confirmed by *The Exorcist* and *The Sting* (both 1973). The success of *Star Wars* (1977), *E.T. – The Extra-Terrestrial* (1982) and other films illustrated the massive profit potential of family films 'sophisticated' enough for adults to enjoy with their children.

The resumption of interest in blockbuster production is not hard to explain. The reasons have been examined at length by historians and industry analysts, and can be summarised briefly here. All the principles of distribution leverage described earlier in relation to roadshows continued to apply for high-profile films exhibited in other patterns. The 'conglomerisation' which characterised all the studio corporations from the 1960s onwards provided not only a safety net for a large investment – losses in theatrical film divisions could be offset by the profitability of other areas – but an incentive as well: the popular success of a blockbuster can be 'spun off' into the various ancillary markets in which the studios also have interests.

The importance of these markets also helps account for the centrality of 'synergy' – the strategic cross-promotion of products in more than one medium, with sales of each helping to spur on those of the other – to recent and contemporary Hollywood. Paramount's manipulation of the novel and film of both *Love Story* and *The Godfather* provide seminal early examples. With the exception of the low-budget 'sleeper' (surprise hit) *American Graffiti* (1973), all the leading box-office hits from 1970–76 were based on, and for promotional purposes tied into, bestselling popular novels.[19]

'New' distribution patterns came to replace the traditional roadshow method. *The Godfather* opened concurrently in five New York theatres and between 350 and 400 theatres nationwide, all of which had paid advance guarantees totalling nearly $14 million. Though advanced prices were charged for seats, the three-hour film was exhibited in continuous performances, without an intermission, and in non-anamorphic 35mm with monaural sound. Screenings ran around the clock, from 9 a.m. to after midnight, and prices on Broadway were raised from $3.50 to $4 after the film's enormous box-office potential had been established with record early attendances.[20] As a result, the film became, briefly, the most successful of all time, grossing more than $80 million domestically. This success led the studios once again to raise their commitment to expensive and heavily publicised 'event' movies: films expressly designed to make an impact on the market.[21]

However, there were other, more surprising successes which also influenced the production and distribution patterns that were to follow. Another of the sleeper hits of the early 1970s was the ecologically aware action movie *Billy Jack* (1971). Released by Warner Bros. to a modest initial gross of $4 million, the film was the subject of a lawsuit brought against the distributor by its director/star Tom Laughlin, which resulted in its being reissued independently in 1973. This re-release was on a large-scale, 'four-wall' basis (i.e. the theatres were hired outright by the producer-distributor for a fixed sum rather than a percentage of the box-office) in mainly rural areas, supported by precisely targeted television advertising: an adaptation of the 'Selznick pattern' previously discussed.[22] The success of this campaign helped the film to an ultimate gross of $32.5

Jurassic Park (1993): released on nearly 3000 prints

million over five years and several further reissues, and to stimulate similar four-wall, regional-saturation releases.

The new blockbuster era is usually dated from the wide simultaneous release of *Jaws* (1975), which cost Universal $12 million to produce, on 464 domestic screens, accompanied by a nationwide print and television advertising campaign.[23] This strategy was no doubt influenced by the extensive use of television advertising for the reissue of *Billy Jack* and by the multiple first-run booking pattern of *The Godfather* (with the precedents of Selznick and Levine further in the background). The success of this strategy has subsequently led to its escalation in each successive year, as each summer seemed to produce at least one film distributed on more prints than the previous year's record-holder, so that in current terms *Jaws*' 'saturation' release qualifies as a limited 'platform' run of the kind now given to films of ostensibly minority interest. A blanket release accompanied by intensive publicity hype involves massive additional costs in prints and advertising, driving up the cost of distribution. Whereas 500–600 prints were once considered sufficient to saturate the US market, and 80–100 for the UK, *Jurassic Park* (1993) was released in the United States on nearly 3000 prints and in Britain on a then-record 434.[24]

Roadshows, which required a tiny number of prints for worldwide use in their early, exclusive release stage, seem highly economical by comparison.[25] Although they seemed to require exceptional advertising budgets to reach the largest possible audience, their actual distribution costs were not significantly higher than for most regular releases and publicity costs were typically shared with exhibitors at local level. The blanket-release strategy is now typically used even for non-blockbusters: few major-studio pictures are now released on fewer than 1500 prints. The corollary and consequence is that a great deal rests on the success of a blockbuster's opening weekend performance, from which a disproportionately large amount of its ultimate theatrical revenue (as much as 50 or 60 per cent) may derive. If a film does not 'open' successfully, prints are very quickly pulled from theatres to make room for the following week's potential blockbuster. Thus, the possibility of a film gradually finding a large audience over a slow, lengthy release period, during which word-of-mouth has time to spread – a process which was the commercial salvation of *Doctor Zhivago* (1965) and *2001: A Space Odyssey* – has been drastically reduced.[26]

The breakeven point on most films is typically in excess of two-and-a-half times their negative cost, which for a full-scale blockbuster may now climb to nine figures. Between 1972 and 1975, only ten Hollywood films cost $10 million or more, and none more than $15 million.[27] One of the most expensive films of this period, *The Towering Inferno* (1974), was backed jointly by two studios, Warner Bros. and Fox, to spread the cost of investment and the risk of failure.

From the late 1970s, as a renewed blockbuster policy took hold, ultra high-budget pictures once again became common: *King Kong* (1976) cost $24 million, *Apocalypse Now* cost $31 million and *Star Trek – The Motion Picture* (1979) cost $42 million, while *Superman* (1978) soared to $55 million, a record which remained for over a decade.[28] A negative cost of $100 million was reached for the first time with *Terminator 2: Judgment Day* (1991) – a figure now regularly hit by special effects-dominated action films – while *Titanic* (1997) topped $200 million in production expenses. The latter also, of course, broke the all-time record for grosses, earning more than $600 million domestically (this figure represents box-office rather than distributor gross, unlike other figures cited in this chapter). The sharing of costs between studios has become increasingly common – *Titanic* was backed jointly by Paramount (which distributed in the domestic market) and Fox (which distributed overseas) – as have co-productions with foreign partners, notably in Germany.

On average, throughout the late 1970s and 1980s, roughly 40 per cent of big-budget films returned their negative costs from domestic theatrical release, and it was thought rare for a flop in this market to break even from foreign theatrical and ancillary markets. However, with the growth of these latter markets throughout the late 1980s and 1990s, a blockbuster may well earn two to three times its domestic gross overseas and recoup theatrical losses through video and TV sales and rentals. Ancillary markets (television, home video and other non-theatrical outlets) now vastly exceed the theatrical sector in the volume of revenue they produce. In 1992, for example, US distributors' income from domestic theatrical exhibition accounted for only 16.9 per cent of total film revenues, with a similar amount coming from foreign theatrical rentals. US home video accounted for 23.4 per cent and foreign video for 19.2 per cent, the remainder being made up from pay and cable TV, hotel and airline syndication and sales to TV networks.[29] Thus a new set of 'runs' has taken the place of the one maintained under the vertically integrated studio system, with the theatrical market *in toto* now effectively occupying the place of first run and the various ancillaries functioning as subsequent runs.

Generic patterns of production have also changed considerably since the 1970s. The roadshows of the 1950s and 1960s mainly drew on classical generic traditions for their material: historical epics, musicals, Westerns, war films and even comedy, all treated on a large scale. The obsolescence of these genres by the 1980s following numerous failures, the influence of exploitation cinema and the need to appeal to young people has determined that the most common genres for recent blockbusters have been fantasy, science fiction and occasionally horror, but most often action-adventure films the collective generic origins of which lie in the matinee serials, B-movies and exploitation movies which once seemed least amenable to blockbuster treatment. Thus, key cycles, series or, in the currently fashionable industry term, 'franchises' of blockbusters have been instituted by the success of, for example, *The Exorcist*, *Jaws*, *Star Wars*, *Superman*, *Star Trek*, *Alien* (1979), *Raiders of the Lost Ark* (1981), *Back to the Future* (1985), *Lethal Weapon* (1987), *Die Hard* (1988), *Batman* (1989), *The Matrix* (1999) and *The Mummy* (1999).

One can even argue that the sequel, once more common among Poverty Row 'programmers' than major-studio A-movies, has itself become definable as a genre in its own right. Repeatable story formulae are certainly a mainstay of blockbuster production with their guaranteed pre-selling of a 'high concept'. Defying past industry wisdom, many blockbuster sequels in the 1980s and 1990s outgrossed their originals by a considerable margin, as for example in the cases of *Rambo: First Blood Part II* (1985), *Lethal Weapon 2* (1989), *Die Hard 2* (1990) and *Terminator 2*. Ancillary media have themselves exerted an influence on the generic forms of blockbusters: MTV and music videos on, for example, *Flashdance* (1983); television series on *The Fugitive* (1993), *The Flintstones* (1994), *Mission: Impossible* (1996) and *Charlie's Angels* (2000); computer games on *Mortal Kombat* (1994) and *Lara Croft: Tomb Raider* (2001); and, of course, theme park rides on *Jurassic Park*.

A very few major-studio films each year achieve industry esteem and commercial success as prestige films as well as blockbusters. Such films as *Dances with Wolves* (1990), *Schindler's List* (1993), *Braveheart* (1995), *The English Patient* (1996), *Titanic*, *Saving Private Ryan* (1998), *The Thin Red Line* (1998) and *Gladiator* (2000), all around three hours in length, would surely once have been roadshown. Several of these films – *Schindler's List*, *The English Patient*, *The Thin Red Line* – were initially presented in relatively exclusive 'platform' releases. This is a distribution strategy typically used for films the commercial potential of which is uncertain or which require the long-term build-up of word-of-mouth, or which are aimed at the art-house and/or up-market middle-class, middlebrow prestige market. Yet even these involved the simultaneous exhibition of several hundred prints, equivalent to the saturation bookings of previous decades, and were followed by more orthodox wide releases.[30]

Six of the films just mentioned won best picture Oscars for their respective years, and the remaining two were nominated in the same category. Yet generally speaking, aside from these and a few other exceptions, blockbusters and prestige films now seem antithetical to one another. For the most part, the synthesis between popularity and prestige which the roadshows attempted to achieve has disappeared. The revival by the above films of the Western, war film, period drama and historical epic is one sign of their aspiration to 'quality' and was presumably instrumental in their earning the approval of the industry. *Gladiator* is a partial remake of *The Fall of the Roman Empire* (1964) and was widely compared, sometimes favourably, with *Ben-Hur* (1959) and *Spartacus* (1960). But *Pearl Harbor* (2001), which re-creates the same historical events previously dramatised in *Tora! Tora! Tora!*, signally failed to achieve critical respectability and, with a negative cost of $140 million and domestic grosses under $200 million, has been seen as a commercial disappointment on a scale little short of its predecessor.

The traditional film musical has largely disappeared, along with the Broadway stage adaptations which characterised the last phase of the genre. Despite the success of *Grease* (1978), it is difficult to recall many screen musicals produced between John Huston's $51.5 million film of *Annie* (1982) and Alan Parker's adaptation of the pop opera *Evita* (1996), both commercial failures.[31] Yet the genre's conventions – and the Broadway show tune – have survived through a merger with those of the feature cartoon. *Beauty and the Beast* (1991) itself become the basis for a West End stage musical, and the London premiere run of each new Disney animation is invariably preceded for a limited period by a live musical prologue. The most recent trend in this genre is for subject matter to be drawn from properties which might once have been – and often have been – the province of live-action drama: for example, Disney's *The Hunchback of Notre Dame* (1996), *Hercules* (1997), *Mulan* (1998) and *Tarzan* (1999), Fox's *Anastasia* (1997) and Warners' *Quest for Camelot* (1998) and *The King and I* (1999). Their computer-assisted animation techniques permit the creation of scenes of spectacle which would be financially prohibitive to stage live, even with the aid of computer-generated images (CGI). The culmination of this development is perhaps DreamWorks' *The Prince of Egypt* (1998), an animated remake of *The Ten Commandments* with songs, and a chariot race clearly indebted to both *Ben-Hur* and *The Fall of the Roman Empire*.[32]

Audiences have apparently not tired of high-concept blockbusters or their saturation-release as they did of roadshows three decades ago. As Chris Hugo noted in 1986, in an observation which can probably still stand for the intervening years:

> In an economic climate where current figures indicate that only one film in ten actually makes a profit, the financial track record of the 'blockbusters' is a good one, even allowing for the odd mistake such as Steven Spielberg's *1941* and the problem of trying to salvage *Heaven's Gate* from expensive obscurity.[33]

Star Wars Episode II: Attack of the Clones (due for release in 2002) is the first major-studio, 'live'-action blockbuster to be filmed entirely on digital equipment. It is likely to provide the model for productions in years to come. With the technological revolution likely to follow from the imminent introduction of digital projection facilities in many of the world's cinemas – a measure which would massively reduce distribution expenses, as theatrical 'prints' could presumably be produced for little more than the cost of pressing a DVD – it seems likely that blockbuster productions and their wide release will only increase in the foreseeable future.

Notes

1. Joyce M. Hawkins and Robert Allen (eds), *The Oxford Encyclopedic English Dictionary* (Oxford: Clarendon Press, 1991), p. 153.

2. Review of '*The Ten Commandments*', *Variety*, 10 October 1956. Unless noted otherwise, figures for 'grosses' throughout this chapter refer to gross rentals: that is, the portion of a film's box-office receipts (usually between 40 and 50 per cent) remitted to the distributor. Unless otherwise specified, they and the production costs cited derive from the annual box-office lists and the occasional lists of big-budget features published in *Variety*.

3. Tino Balio, *United Artists: The Company that Changed the Film Industry* (Madison: University of Wisconsin Press, 1987), p. 208.

4. See David Thomson, *Showman: The Life of David O. Selznick* (London: Andre Deutsch, 1993), pp. 391–403, 448–73.

5. Quoted in 'In Camera', *Films and Filming*, January 1970, p. 24.

6. The best discussion of these problems is to be found in David J. Londoner, 'The Changing Economics of Entertainment', in Tino Balio (ed.), *The American Film Industry* (Madison: University of Wisconsin Press, revised edition, 1985), pp. 606–8, 618–19.

7. Joel Finler, *The Hollywood Story* (London: Octopus, 1988), p. 280.

8. 'Big Rental Films of 1968', *Variety*, 8 January 1969, pp. 15, 18; 'Big Rental Films of 1969', *Variety*, 7 January 1970, p. 24.

9. Michael Pye and Lynda Myles, *The Movie Brats: How the Film Generation Took Over Hollywood* (London: Faber and Faber, 1979), pp. 37–40.

10. Finler, *The Hollywood Story*, p. 280.

11. R. Michael Hayes, 'Roadshow Movies: A Review of Disk Versions of Hard Ticket Features', *Widescreen Review Presents Laser Magic* (1998), p. 193; Michael Coate and William Kallay, 'Presented in 70mm', *Widescreen Review Presents the Ultimate Widescreen DVD Movie Guide*, vol. 1, no. 1, 2000, p. 260.

12. Quoted in 'Product must be right for today's market', *Kine Weekly*, 13 June 1970, p. 13.

13. Chris Hugo, 'American Cinema in the '70s: The Economic Background', *Movie*, no. 27/8 (Winter 1980/Spring 1981), p. 47.

14. Thomas Schatz, 'The New Hollywood', in Jim Collins, Hilary Radner and Ava Preacher Collins (eds), *Film Theory Goes to the Movies* (New York and London: Routledge, 1993), p. 20.

15. Lee Beaupré, 'Clutch of Roadshows in Offing: Detail Par's Marketing Plans for Its Youth-oriented *Romeo & Juliet*', *Variety*, 14 August 1968, p. 5.

16. Terry McGrath, 'The market place changes – so must we', *Kine Weekly*, 29 August 1970, pp. 6–9, 32.

17. Ibid., p. 7.

18. John Gillett, quoted in John Baxter, *Hollywood in the Sixties* (London: Tantivy/Barnes, 1972), p. 152.

19. *Love Story* was written first as a screenplay, then adapted by its author, Erich Segal, into a novel which was published before the release of the film.

20. Peter Cowie, *The Godfather Book* (London: Faber and Faber, 1997), pp. 66–74.

21. See Aljean Harmetz, 'How Do You Pick a Winner in Hollywood? You Don't', *New York Times*, 29 April 1973.

22. For details of *Billy Jack*'s release and the 1970s revival of four-walling, see Justin Wyatt, 'From Roadshowing to Saturation Release: Majors, Independents, and Marketing/ Distribution Innovations', in Jon Lewis (ed.), *The New American Cinema* (Durham, NC: Duke University Press, 1998), pp. 46–86.

23. See Wyatt, ibid., pp. 78–9; Richard Maltby, ' "Nobody Knows Everything": Post-Classical Historiographies and Consolidated Entertainment', in Steve Neale and Murray Smith (eds), *Contemporary Hollywood Cinema* (London: Routledge, 1998), p. 34.

24. *Moving Pictures UK*, 22 July 1993, p. 2.

25. Many US prints intended for the domestic market are redeployed for overseas distribution. It should also be borne in mind that, via interlocked projection in multiplexes, a single print can service more than one screen simultaneously.

26. There are, of course, partial exceptions to this pattern. *Star Wars* opened in the US on only forty-two prints, as, according to some accounts, exhibitors could not initially be convinced of its box-office potential.

27. See the following articles by Lawrence Cohn: ' "Loss of Control" over Film Costs Stressed by *Heaven's Gate* Fiasco', *Variety*, 14 January 1981, pp. 33, 110; 'Domestic Recoup Rare on Mega-Budget Pic Rentals', *Variety*, 12 January 1982, pp. 7, 40; '40% of '87 Big-Budgeters Hit Home', *Variety*, 20 January 1988, pp. 20, 61.

28. It may be significant that a number of the late 1970s' big-budget films were independently produced, by the likes of Dino De Laurentiis, Joseph E. Levine and the Salkinds. Not for the first time, the majors followed the lead of the independents.

29. Figures taken from *Moving Pictures UK*, 29 July 1993, p. 1.

30. 'Roadshowing' is the term now used to describe the staggered release of 'art' films made available in a small number of prints which make their way slowly through the circuit of repertory cinemas.

31. At the time of writing, a film of the Broadway musical *Chicago* is currently in production.

32. Is there a better explanation than coincidence for the fact that all three films Yul Brynner made in 1956 – *The Ten Commandments*, *The King and I* and *Anastasia* – were remade as animated features in the space of two years?

33. Chris Hugo, 'U.S. Film Industry: Economic Background Part Two', *Movie*, no. 31/32 (Winter 1986), p. 86.

3

Westerns and Gangster Films Since the 1970s

Steve Neale

As is well known, Westerns and gangster films have played a major role in discussions of genre and Hollywood. Beginning with Robert Warshow, the roll call of theorists and critics who have focused on the gangster film, the Western or both as paradigmatic Hollywood genres has included André Bazin, John Cawelti, Edward Buscombe, Colin McArthur, Andrew Tudor, Tom Ryall and Thomas Schatz.[1] As I have argued elsewhere, this focus may have helped produce a restrictive definition of genre – a definition geared, for instance, to the unusually central role of iconography in the Western or to the urban setting and the rise-and-fall structure of the so-called 'classical' gangster film.[2] Given the unusual numerical prominence of A-Westerns in particular in the 1940s and 1950s, and given the heterogeneous, discontinuous and intermittent nature of gangster film production not just in the studio era, but in the 1950s and 1960s, too, it may also have helped produce a misleading picture of Hollywood's generic strategies and output from the early 1930s through to the late 1960s. Either way, the fortunes and formulae of Westerns and gangster films have varied a great deal since then. As there as yet exists no overview of the films and the trends that have marked them since the late 1970s, what I aim to do here is to sketch in their features and contours, and to identify some of the contextual factors that help account for the shape they have taken. As we shall see, television production policies, book publishing, legal judgments, demographics, and the nature of the New Hollywood – and the nature of the New Independents that have grown up alongside and interacted with it – have all, at times, been as important as the example set by any of the longstanding generic traditions or 'classic' films to which in varying ways and to varying degrees some – though by no means all – of the post-1970s gangster films and Westerns have alluded. As we shall also see, no single formula and no single cultural or industrial factor can be said to have governed developments in either. To that extent, the generalising tendencies of classical and 'postmodern' genre theory alike are – as we shall see as well – of real but only limited help.

Westerns

By the late 1970s, the production of Westerns in Hollywood had been in decline for over twenty years. As early as 1963, as Edward Buscombe points out, Westerns had already fallen as a proportion of Hollywood's output by as much as 18 per cent.[3] During the

following decade, the Western's numerical decline was either periodically halted or periodically masked by the production of television series such as *The Virginian* and *Bonanza*,
by the impact of the Italian Western and by the visibility, notoriety and critical or financial
success of a number of cycles and films. These included at least two overtly 'revisionist'
cycles, the 'pro-Indian' 'Vietnam Westerns' of the early 1970s such as *Little Big Man*
(1970) and *Soldier Blue* (1970), and the 'modernist or anti-Westerns' of the late 1960s
and early 1970s such as *The Wild Bunch* (1969), *McCabe and Mrs Miller* (1971) and *Jeremiah Johnson* (1972). They also included the 'comic or parodic Westerns' – themselves
often also revisionist – that peppered the mid-1960s to the mid-1970s, and 'traditional
Westerns' such as *True Grit* (1969), *Big Jake* (1971) and *Rooster Cogburn* (1975).[4]

The marked decline in the volume of production in the latter half of the 1970s and
the predominance at this time of parody, comedy and nostalgia (usually marked, as in
Comes a Horseman (1978) and *The Electric Horseman* (1979), by placing Western pro-
tagonists in a contemporary setting) were signs that 'the Western was … in trouble'.[5]
Very few Westerns were released in the early 1980s. They included *Bronco Billy* (1980),
a nostalgic-contemporary Clint Eastwood film; *Windwalker* (1980), an independent
Native American film; *The Ballad of Gregorio Ortez* (1982), a public television-financed,
Latin-oriented outlaw film; *Tom Horn* (1980), *The Long Riders* (1980), *Cattle Annie and
Little Britches* (1980) and *Barbarossa* (1982), revisionist or would-be revisionist outlaw
biopics best viewed as the tail-end of a production trend stretching back to the late
1960s; *The Legend of the Lone Ranger* (1981) and *Zorro the Gay Blade* (1981), both of
them 'comic or juvenile Westerns';[6] and, of course, *Heaven's Gate* (1980), the eventual
but initially unplanned status of which as an epic roadshow production in the tradition
of *Cimarron* (1960) and *How the West Was Won* (1963) seemed anachronistic and out of
keeping with its bleakly revisionist tone in the midst of such up-beat, widely released
summer blockbusters as *Superman* (1979), *Raiders of the Lost Ark* (1981) and *The Empire
Strikes Back* (1980).[7] While the heterogeneity of these films confirmed the flexibility of
the Western as a genre, it also confirmed the absence of what Buscombe calls 'a centre'[8]
and, along with the box-office failure of the films themselves, the trouble the Western
was now clearly in.[9]

Several explanations have been put forward both for the long-term and the short-term
decline in Western production. While the 1950s witnessed an upsurge in the production
of A-, epic and 'adult' Western films and of television series, it also witnessed the demise
of the B- and serial Western, the staple of routine Western ouput since the 1930s.[10]
Postwar suburbanisation and the closure of rural and small-town cinemas helped further
erode a key audience base for Hollywood's traditional Westerns.[11] Meanwhile, with cinema attendances in overall decline, demographic studies and the targeting of audiences
became more and more important. What these studies revealed was the youth of the
industry's audience.[12] What they also revealed was its educated nature.[13] Male teenagers
and children had formed a core audience for B-Westerns and serials in particular during
the 1930s and 1940s.[14] But the nature, culture and tastes of teenagers and children in
the postwar era was rapidly changing. The traditional Westerns that were still produced
in the mid-to-late 1960s and early 1970s catered for a traditional but dwindling adult

audience. They were almost solely reliant on an ageing John Wayne, and Wayne was to make his last Western, *The Shootist*, in 1976. The trends that were to prove especially successful were those with a marked degree of postwar youth appeal: those which appeared to mock, reconfigure or renew the Western's conventions in a cynical, disillusioned or parodically self-conscious way; those which appeared to key in to an increasingly politicised counterculture; and those whose aesthetic characteristics keyed into contemporary, high-school or college-educated notions of art. In other words, Italian Westerns, Vietnam Westerns, modernist Westerns and parodies – revisionist Westerns of all kinds.

Conditioned in particular by the Vietnam War, one of the principal hallmarks of the counterculture and revisionist Westerns alike was a rejection of the imperialism inherent in America's 'frontier mythology' and in its postwar 'victory culture'.[15] While the Western was almost inextricably bound up with both, the very existence of revisionist Westerns was evidence that it could be used to challenge or complicate some of their tenets. However, with the demise of the counterculture in the mid-1970s, with the advent of a new generation of teenagers and with the advent of a New Hollywood geared more than ever to a targeting of the perceived tastes of the under twenty-fives came a series of realignments among and between Hollywood's audiences, cycles and genres.[16] As the 1970s wore on, the under twenty-fives were increasingly addressed in and through science-fiction and action blockbusters. These, it has been argued, acted as vehicles for rehabilitating if ersatz versions of victory culture and frontier mythology and as substitute providers of the Western's action-adventure attractions.[17]

The Western's traditional audience, meanwhile, found itself without an outlet either in the cinema or on television. Prior even to the demise of John Wayne and the John Wayne Western, demographic studies conducted on behalf of the television networks in the early 1970s 'discovered that though Westerns were generally popular, they were much more popular with juveniles and among the rural and less well-off part of the population than with the urban and middle-class audience'. As television:

> needed to sell advertizing time, not programmes, it soon realized that it could do better with shows which appealed to the more affluent. Suddenly, in the 1971–2 season, there was a pitch for what would now be called the 'yuppie' audience; Westerns assumed to be for hicks, were out.[18]

By the end of the decade, there were only three Western series on air. By 1984, there was none at all.[19]

The revival of the western

1984 was also the year in which Westerns were recorded as having a market share of zero in the cinema.[20] However, it was in 1984, too, that a key Western novel was nearing completion and that the first of two cycles of Westerns – one minor – one major, was beginning, in fact, to take shape. The novel was Larry McMurtry's *Lonesome Dove*. The first cycle consisted of three Westerns funded or produced by major Hollywood studios,

Pale Rider, *Silverado* and *Rustler's Rhapsody*, and two independents, *Lust in the Dust* and *Uphill All the Way*. These films were all released during the course of 1985, the year in which *Lonesome Dove*, having been turned down by 'every major television production house', was optioned by Suzanne de Passe, president of the film and television wing of Motown, for $50,000.[21] Whatever their individual merits, *Lust in the Dust*, *Uphill All the Way* and *Rustler's Rhapsody* were largely inconsequential continuations of the parodic, comic or nostalgic trends of the 1970s and early 1980s. However, like *Lonesome Dove*, *Pale Rider* and *Silverado* represented something new and much more significant.

Pale Rider and *Silverado* were both designed and reviewed as attempts by two industrially powerful individuals, Clint Eastwood and Lawrence Kasdan, respectively, to 'revive the Western genre'[22] by blending 'traditional ... elements with some up-to-date attitudes'.[23] The attitudes in question included, in the case of *Silverado*, the paying of lip service to ethnic minorities and the inclusion of a character such as Stella (Linda Hunt), and, in the case of *Pale Rider*, the incorporation of ecological concerns. The traditional elements included a restoration of the role of male heroes as defenders of community and family, and a restoration of a sense of the frontier as an open space – as a space of and for adventure, personal and communal regeneration, and the legitimate exercise of the hero's 'savage' skills. They also included plotlines, situations, lines of dialogue and other 'clichés' which, as Stephen Harvey pointed out at the time, might well have been 'chortled off the screen' a decade earlier.[24] Rather than parody, quote or pastiche them, however, these films mobilised and recycled them with reverent solemnity, in the case of *Pale Rider*, and with enthusiastic exuberance, in the case of *Silverado*. For all these reasons, the term 'neo-traditional' (rather than an alternative such as 'postmodern') seems to me the most appropriate to describe them.

Partly because their box-office fortunes were mixed,[25] partly because of the time it takes to assess the potential of experiments like these, a hiatus ensued in Hollywood and commentators writing a year or so later tended to view these films either as failed experiments or else as the swansong of the Western.[26] However, while there was time lag between this cycle and the next in the cinema, a time lag punctuated only by *Three Amigos!* in 1986, television Westerns underwent the beginnings of a much more sustained revival. 1986 saw the appearance of mini-series such as *Dream West* and *North and South, Book II* and telefilms such as *Houston: The Legend of Texas*, *The Last Days of Frank and Jesse James* and a remake of *Stagecoach*. 1987 saw the appearance of telefilms such as *The Alamo: 13 Days to Glory*, *The Gunfighters*, *The Quick and the Dead* and *Gunsmoke: Return to Dodge*. And 1988 saw the appearance of series such as *Davy Crockett* and *Paradise*, telefilms such *Bonanza: The Next Generation* and remakes of *Once Upon a Texas Train* and *Red River*.

Neo-traditional and new revisionist Westerns

So successful were television Westerns by then that *Variety* reported that a 'mini-trend' was now firmly established and that over twenty television Westerns were now on their way.[27] Among them was a $20 million adaptation of *Lonesome Dove*, which as a novel had won a Pulitzer prize in 1986, which as a miniseries was to top the television ratings in 1989, and which as a franchise was to help sustain both McMurtry and the television Western for over half a decade.[28] *Lonesome Dove*'s traditional ingredients, its mobilisation of frontier mythology, its expansive sense of space and its ambivalent treatment of gender and race have been discussed by Steven Fore, Richard Campbell and Jimmie L. Reeves, and David Thorburn.[29] It can clearly be grouped alongside *Pale Rider* and *Silverado,* and, indeed, most of the television Westerns mentioned above, nearly all of which can be seen as revivals of one kind or another. This revivalism, apparent not just in the remakes, but also in the re-emergence of *Bonanza* and *Gunsmoke*, covered legendary events such as the Battle of the Alamo and legendary figures such as Frank and Jesse James.

By the end of 1988, legendary figures such as Billy the Kid and Wyatt Earp had re-emerged, in addition, in the cinema. *Sunset* paired James Garner as Wyatt Earp with Bruce Willis as Tom Mix in a late 1920s Hollywood setting. *Young Guns* used the story of Billy the Kid to mount a brat-pack production with teen appeal. Both films reinforced rather than revised their protagonists' legendary status. They thus helped cement the neo-traditional trend. The following year, though, while helping to sustain an emerging new cycle, *Glory*, *War Party* and *Powwow Highway* began to complicate the picture, adding new elements to the cycle's mix of formulae, story-types and cultural and ideological characteristics.

Glory is as much a war film as it is a Western, telling as it does the story of the first all-black fighting unit formed by the Union in the American Civil War. It could be criticised, as Robert Burgoyne points out, for 'valorizing war as the defining moment when racial and national self-realization coalesce', for constructing a scenario in which the national identity marked by flag for which the Union soldiers die 'is presumed to dominate and displace the lived identity of race'.[30] It could also be criticised for placing the consciousness of the white Union officer who led the unit at its centre. However, in marking the officer's perceptions as 'limited and subject to error'[31] and in underlining 'the dissonance between white racial identity and the imagined community implied by emancipation' through its insistence on Union racism,[32] *Glory* can also be seen as something different, as perhaps a 'new revisionist' film.

War Party, too, has its contradictions. A modern-day Western in which Native Americans participate in the re-enactment of a frontier massacre which gets out of hand, it has been criticised as 'a straightforward celebration of action-movie clichés' and as a film which ends up installing the stereotype of the doomed plains Indian warrior.[33] However, as Jacquelyn Kilpatrick points out, it can also be seen, particularly from a Native American perspective, as a film which meditates in complex ways on a panoply of Indian stereotypes – drunken Indians, trackers and medicine men, as well as warriors – and their relationship to a plural Native American culture on the one hand and to Anglo-American perceptions and power on the other.[34] It thus neither revises nor endorses familiar Western clichés. Instead, by recontextualising them, it underlines their differential cultural effects and renders them at the same time time contingent and strange.

Powwow Highway also focuses on Native Americans. It, too, has a modern-day setting. Partly road movie, partly comedy, partly Western, the film tells the story of two young

Cheyenne men who journey to Sante Fe to get Bonnie Red Bow (Joanelle Nadine Romero) out of jail. Bonnie has been framed by a mining corporation in order to lure them away from their reservation so that a tribal vote on whether or not to allow it to strip-mine reservation land will go its way. The young men can be seen, as Eric Anderson points out, as comic protagonists, as road movie buddies and, from a traditional Cheyenne point of view, as neophyte warriors.[35] He goes on to underline the extent to which Western and Cheyenne images, formulae and perspectives intersect with one another. Among them are images and formulae from Westerns themselves. At one point Philbert (Gary Farmer) watches William S. Hart in an old silent Western using his horse to pull down a jailhouse. Philbert will later do the same thing 'with his automotive horse' when rescuing Bonnie.[36] In ways such as this, *Powwow Highway* 'tunes in to ... a variety of genres', 'overlays them with each other' and presents 'various Native American points of view while also acknowledging various non-Native ways of seeing'.[37] In ways such as this, it, too, can be considered a new revisionist film.

Whether 'new revisionist' or 'neo-traditional' are useful as terms,[38] what I want to underline here is the plurality of the emerging new cycle and its films. This plurality is evident in its different ideological tendencies, in the heterogeneity of its generic affliations and strands, and in its inclusion of television as well as the cinema. It is also evident in its diverse industrial base. While the television Westerns cited above were nearly all network productions, television itself had undergone a transformation. Cable and satellite, and with them movie and other special-interest channels, were by now providing an outlet for productions of all kinds, including Westerns, as well as an expanding market for recycled classics. As the new cycle took hold, HBO and TNT in particular were to play a more and more important part not just in showing Westerns, but in financing their production as well. And as the patterns of synergy among and between media corporations began to multiply from the mid-1980s on, a number of companies became involved in financing and distributing Westerns not just in these media fields, but in the direct-to-video market as well. Meanwhile, in the cinema, while *Young Guns*, *Sunset* and *Glory* had been financed and distributed by major Hollywood companies (20th Century-Fox in the case of *Young Guns* and TriStar in the case of *Sunset* and *Glory*), *War Party* had been produced through Hemdale, a British company, and released in the United States by Tristar, and *Powwow Highway,* produced independently through another British company, Handmade Films, had been picked up for release by Warner Bros., another Hollywood major.

The Western cycle in the 1990s

Were the new cycle to have ended at this point, its mix might have seemed no different, in its lack of an apparent centre, to the mix that had characterised the early 1980s. However, neo-traditionalism and new revisionism now consolidated themselves as two consistent cyclic threads, as two distinct but sometimes overlapping centres around which the cycle as a whole took shape. Feeding into and out of an equally expanding and equally plural 'New Western' culture, a culture that included novels, paintings, vacations, lifestyles and a revitalised country music scene, as well as a new wave of revisionist academic histories, Westerns were able, in what was now a new post-Cold War world, to reassess as well as reassert a central element in America's national mythology.[39]

During the course of next five years, these threads wove their way in and out of an array of Western films, miniseries, series and documentaries that included *The Young Riders* (1989–92), *Back to the Future III* (1990), *Dances with Wolves* (1990), *Young Guns II* (1990), *The Civil War* (1990), *An American Tale: Fievel Goes West* (1991), *Black Robe* (1991), *Blood River* (1991), *Son of the Morning Star* (1991), *Thousand Pieces of Gold* (1991), *Far and Away* (1992), *The Last of the Mohicans* (1992), *Unforgiven* (1992), *The Ballad of Little Jo* (1993), *Geronimo: An American Legend* (1993), *Geronimo* (1993), *The Broken Chain* (1993), *The Last Outlaw* (1993), *Gettysburg* (1993), *Posse* (1993), *Guns of Honor* (1993), *Tombstone* (1993), *Dr Quinn, Medicine Woman* (1993–8), *Bad Girls* (1994), *Cheyenne Warrior* (1994), *Maverick* (1994), *Squanto: A Warrior's Tale* (1994), *Wagon's East!* (1994), *Wyatt Earp* (1994), *Native Americans* (1994), *Dead Man* (1995), *Pocahontas* (1995), *The Good Old Boys* (1995), *The Quick and the Dead* (1995), *Riders in the Storm* (1995), *Wild Bill* (1995), *Crazy Horse* (1995), *The Way West* (1995) and *How the West was Lost* (1995), as well as the re-release in 1995 of *The Wild Bunch*. Consisting of independent as well as Hollywood productions, the cycle as a whole included teenpics, cross-racial romances, comedies, animated features, and film and television remakes. It also included, sometimes singly, sometimes in combination, female-oriented and feminist Westerns, outlaw Westerns, Westerns about lawmen, Native American Westerns, Civil War Westerns, black Westerns, biopics, Westerns about immigrants, Westerns about settlers, Westerns with a modern-day setting and Westerns set in the eighteenth or nineteenth century.

Academic debate has focused on only a handful of these programmes and films. What is notable is the extent to which it has focused, in turn, on the extent to which they can be considered as revisionist in matters of gender, race and convention – on the extent to which, to use the terms proposed here, they can be considered as new revisionist or as neo-traditional Westerns. (The same is true, incidentally, of *Variety*'s trade reviews, most of which were written by Todd McCarthy.) While *The Ballad of Little Jo* and *Dead Man* have been generally regarded as unequivocal instances of the former,[40] *Dances with Wolves* and *Unforgiven*, and to a lesser extent *Pocahontas, Bad Girls* and *Tombstone*, have been seen either as contradictor, or as projects the revisionist ambitions of which were curtailed during the process of production.[41] Rather than make a series of judgments here, what I would want to emphasise is the extent to which these debates reflect not just the nature of academic priorities, but the nature of the threads that traverse the cycle as well. What I would want to add is that both threads found themselves using or alluding to such fundamental conventions as the shoot-out or battle (a point as true of *The Ballad of Little Jo* as it is of *Unforgiven* and *Tombstone*), and that both threads found themselves using or alluding to the trope of the frontier as a space in which personal or communal realisation is, was or might once have been a possibility (a point as true of the dystopian *Dead Man* and of Westerns with a modern-day setting as it is of *Bad Girls, Wyatt Earp* or *Dances with Wolves*).

Prompted by disappointing box-office returns, especially for *Tombstone, Wyatt Earp* and other later contributions to the cycle,[42] Hollywood stopped making Westerns for theatrical release during the 1995–6 season. Warner Bros. went on to produce *The Wild,*

Wild West in 1999, but principally in order to fulfil a longstanding commitment;[43] Universal released *Ride with the Devil* in 1999, but the film itself was produced independently. The cycle had come to an end in mainstream cinema. It continued, however, on television, and to some extent, too, in the independent sector. *Dr Quinn, Medicine Woman* and *Walker, Texas Ranger* (which had started in 1993) continued as series on televisions, the latter being joined in 1999 by *The Magnificent Seven*. TNT continued to make telefilms such as *Riders of the Purple Sage* (1996), *Buffalo Soldiers* (1997), *Two for Texas* (1998) and *Purgatory* (1999). And the independent sector continued to produce films such as *Lone Star* (1996), *Naturally Native* (1998), *Los Locos* (1998) and *Smoke Signals* (1998), as well as *The Hi-Lo Country* (1999) and the aforementioned *Ride with the Devil*. Two points are worth making here, however, in conclusion. The first is the extent to which TNT's Westerns have been prompted by Ted Turner's personal interests.[44] The second is the extent to which *Smoke Signals* and *Naturally Native*, both of them Native American productions, have relocated to modern-day settings in order to tackle contemporary Native American issues – and in order to avoid the conventions of the Western.[45]

Gangster films

There are a number of parallels between the fortunes of the Western and the gangster film in the 1980s and 1990s. Like the Western, the gangster film was marked by an array of cycles and trends; like the Western, the gangster film underwent a period of decline in the early 1980s and of rejuvenation in the early 1990s, when its numbers increased markedly and when it was fed by a number of new concerns and formulae.[46] As with the Western, these formulae and concerns found articulation both in the mainstream and independent sectors; as with the Western, television played a part as well (although its contributions, governed as they were by different considerations of propriety and by different conceptions of its audience, were restricted to some but by no means all of the genre's trends). However, here the parallels end. For while the box-office failure of *Heaven's Gate* hung over the Western for nearly a decade, putting paid once and for all to 1970s revisionism, the box-office success of *The Godfather* (1972) and *The Godfather, Part II* (1974) and the example set by films such as *Mean Streets* (1973) and *Boulevard Nights* (1979) gave rise to a number of formulae and trends that were to be highly influential in the long term or in the short term, or in both.

The Godfather, the Mafia mystique and the urban retro gangster film

The influence of the *Godfather* films – and of Mario Puzo's 1969 novel – can hardly be overstated. Whether viewed as sophisticated accounts of the parallels between 'legitimate and illegitimate business' within and across the different phases of twentieth-century capitalism,[47] or as something else besides, they cemented a growing public fascination with what Dwight D. Smith has called 'the Mafia mystique'.[48] At the same time, they helped establish a wider 'urban retro' trend, a trend which, like the Mafia mystique itself, centred on bosses and leaders, on historical city-based syndicates and on male codes of fashion and style,[49] and which helped displace the equally retro, equally style-oriented rural-outlaw trend epitomised by *Bonnie and Clyde* (1967).[50] While the putative appeal of these styles was different – *Bonnie and Clyde* was clearly aimed at the young, countercultural market – both helped to detach the gangster film from its traditional, blue-collar audience.[51] A number of additional elements, either singly or in combination, were to have a profound effect, too, not just on the retro gangster biopics that followed in *The Godfather*'s wake – *The Don is Dead* (1973), *Crazy Joe* (1974) and *Lepke* (1975), for instance – but on numerous 1980s and 1990s films, telefilms, miniseries, series and direct-to-video releases as well.

These elements included the emphasis placed on organisational roles and rituals, and on elaborate, ethnically inflected codes of language and conduct; the studied if ironically modified adoption of a 'classical' biographical, rise-and-fall structure;[52] the equally modified adoption of montage sequences and scenes of ritual violence;[53] allusions to actual figures and events; and a 'reinterpretation of the generic conventions of the crime film in the direction of the family melodrama and the epic'[54] through the inclusion of familial and social 'setpieces' on the one hand,[55] and production values and scale on the other. The films, telefilms and television shows included *The Gangster Wars* (1981), *The Gangster Chronicles* (1981–2), *Scarface* (1983), *Once Upon a Time in America* (1984), *Capone's Enforcer* (1985), *The Untouchables* (1987), *Lady Mobster* (1988), *The Revenge of Al Capone* (1989), *The Neon Empire* (1989), *The Godfather, Part III* (1990), *Miller's Crossing* (1990), *Billy Bathgate* (1991), *Mobsters* (1991), *Bugsy* (1991), *Vendetta* (1991), *The Return of Eliot Ness* (1991), *Mobs and Mobsters* (1992), *The Untouchables* (1993–4), *The Funeral* (1995), *Sugartime* (1995), *Hoodlum* (1997), *Bella Mafia* (1997), *The Last Don* (1997) and *The Last Don II* (1998), as well as the numerous releases of various versions of the *Godfather* films on video, the reissue of *The Godfather* itself in 1997, and a series of parodies and comedies – *Johnny Dangerously* (1984), *Prizzi's Honor* (1985), *Married to the Mob* (1988), *Mob Boss* (1990) and *Jane Austen's Mafia!* (a.k.a. *Mafia!*) (1998). They also included a number of miniseries and telefilms drawing on the history of organised crime in New York since the early 1970s, notably *Getting Gotti* (1994), *Gotti* (1996) and *Witness to the Mob* (1998).

There are several points worth making about some of the strands that make up the retro and Mafia trends and about some of the factors that have helped to sustain them. It is notable, for instance, that most of the telefilms and miniseries, unlike most of the films made for initial theatrical release, have tended to emphasise the familial aspects of the *The Godfather* and the Mafia mystique, to become a form of soap opera with a concomitant appeal to women and with a concomitant prominence or focus on female characters. This is especially true of *Lady Mobster*, *Vendetta*, *Sugartime*, *Bella Mafia*, *The Last Don*, *The Last Don II* and *Getting Gotti*. Any epic pretensions there may be tend to be catered for in and through the miniseries format. The only equivalents in the cinema in terms of an emphasis or focus on female characters and female concerns tend to be either one-off productions such as *Gloria* (1980), its 1999 remake and the marginal, heist-oriented *Bound* (1996), or comedies and parodies such as *Johnny Dangerously*, *Prizzi's Honor* and *Married to the Mob*.[56]

One of the variants of the urban retro gangster film, the variant that focuses on law enforcement agents, is also strongly linked to television.[57] It derives, specifically, from

The Untouchables (1959–63) and includes, aside from the 1987 film, *Johnny Ryan* (1990), *The Return of Eliot Ness* and the new 1990s series of *The Untouchables* itself. This variant is virtually the only one to centre on Anglo-American protagonists. The remainder centre almost exclusively on Italian-American and Jewish-American gangsters. (Dutch Schultz, Lucky Luciano and Al Capone appear far more often in the retro films than any other historical gangsters; John Gotti and Paul Castellano feature most frequently in the Mafia films with more recent historical settings.) Although African-American gangsters make occasional appearances in generically marginal retro films such as *The Cotton Club* (1984) and *Kansas City* (1986), *Hoodlum*, which emerged in the wake of a quite separate series black crime, gang and ghetto films, is so far the only retro gangster film to centre on African-Americans. And although they occasionally appear in the margins of other films, *Miller's Crossing*, itself part of an equally separate mini-cycle of Dashiel Hammett adaptations, is so far the only retro gangster film to centre in large part on Irish-Americans. *Scarface*, the settings of which are more up to date and the retro credentials of which – though not its post-*Godfather* epic pretensions – are therefore much more tenuous, is as yet the only film to centre on a (fictional) Cuban gangster.

The urban retro and Mafia trends have both been fed, as gangster films have always been, by novels, biographies, exposés and news. The Mafia trend in particular was augmented in the late 1960s by the publication of *The Valachi Papers* (1968), an insider's account of the Mafia and a major source for the *Godfather* novel and *Godfather* films, and in the 1980s by a series of high-profile government prosecutions brought against a number of Mafia syndicates under the RICO (Racketeer-influenced and Corrupt Organizations) Act.[58] It was further augmented in the late 1980s and early 1990s in three different ways. Ex-FBI agents Joseph F. O'Brien and Andrew Kurins followed the example set by Joseph D. Pistone and published an insiders' account of the ways in which evidence was gathered in one of these cases in *Boss of Bosses: The FBI and Paul Castellano* in 1991. (Pistone published *Donnie Brasco: My Undercover Life in the Mafia* in 1987.) Journalists such as John Cummings and Ernest Volkman in *Goombata: The Improbable Rise and Fall of John Gotti and his Gang* (1990) and John H. Davis in *Mafia Dynasty: The Rise and Fall of the Gambino Crime Family* (1993) began using the evidence produced in these cases to update the Mafia's recent history. And finally, following the example set by Henry Hill in working with Nicholas Pileggi on *Wiseguy: Life in a Mafia Family* (1985),[59] following a Supreme Court decision to overturn the 'Son of Sam' law that had hitherto prevented criminals profiting from accounts of their illegal activities, 'and with the mob buckling under sophisticated racketeering indictments that often produce plea bargaining turncoats', gangsters, too, became involved in publishing their own insiders' accounts.[60]

Some of the books involving ex-FBI officers and gangsters focused on high-ranking mob personnel. But others, such as *Donnie Brasco*, *Wiseguy* and *Mafia Cop* (1993), tended to centre on wiseguys and hit men – on gangsters of lower rank. *Donnie Brasco* was filmed in 1997. It joined an intermittent series of 1990s films in which policemen and FBI agents infiltrated syndicates and gangs, often to find their loyalties tested by the lure of the Mafia mystique, by their ethnic affiliations, by the male friendships they forge, and by the corruption or realpolitik of the legal institutions for which they work.

Donnie Brasco (1997): wise guys and hit men

(Examples include *State of Grace* (1990) and *Deep Cover* (1992), itself also a contribution to the 1990s black crime and gangster cycle.) *Wiseguy* was filmed as *Goodfellas* earlier on, in 1990. Directed by Martin Scorsese and scripted, like Scorsese's later *Casino* (1995), by Nicholas Pileggi, *Goodfellas* helped not only to cement the recent focus on lower-ranking gangsters, but also in doing so to pick up on one of the precedents set in the 1970s by Scorsese's earlier *Mean Streets*.[61]

Wiseguys, hit-men and heists

One of the features of the Mafia and retro trends – as well as of one-off productions such as *King of New York* (1990) – is the focus on gangsters who possess a great deal of wealth and who wield a great deal of power. Their power is never absolute. They struggle with other gangs and other gangsters, as well as with the police and the FBI. They struggle, too, with their own limitations and flaws and with their individual mortality. (It is here, of course, that the often-argued parallels between gangsters and tragic heroes can most frequently be found.)[62] Nevertheless their god-like status, their wealth and their willingness to flout the law all serve to mark their difference from ordinary citizens and are among the principal sources of their glamour and mystique.

In contrast, while they may sometimes exercise power at a local level, and while they may earn their living illegally, the differences between lower-level gangsters and ordinary citizens are much less marked. In consequence, however extraordinary the activities they engage in may be, those activities take place, as Nicole Rafter points out, in a much more down-to-earth, much less controllable 'quotidian' environment, an environment in which, for instance, Henry Hill (Ray Liotta) in *Goodfellas* tries – and fails – to cook 'spaghetti sauce with one hand and ... to move a cocaine shipment with the other'.[63] In this environment, making money is much less a matter of high-level business schemes and much more a matter of everyday work, dreaming less a matter of building Las Vegas (as it is in the retro film *Bugsy*) and much more a matter of joining a car rental business in the Bahamas (as it is in the 1993 film *Carlito's Way*).[64]

Aside from *Carlito's Way*, *Donnie Brasco* and *Goodfellas*, other films in this strand included the earlier *Wise Guys* (1986) and the later *8 Heads in a Duffel Bag* (1997), both of them comedies starring Danny DeVito, as well as *Little Odessa* (1994), an independent film about a Russian Mafia hit man, portions of *Fargo* (1995) and portions, as well, of *Pulp Fiction* (1994). The hit-man theme, which owed its origins to *Pulp Fiction* in particular, continued intermittently throughout the remainder of the 1990s, in films as diverse as *Bulletproof Heart* (1995), *2 Days in the Valley* (1997), *Grosse Point Blank* (1997) and *Ghost Dog: The Way of the Samurai* (1999).[65] In addition, towards the end of the decade, one of the logical consequences of blurring the line between mobsters and ordinary citizens was the advent of a series of films and a TV show in which gangsters, high, low and middling, were depicted as no different, in terms of the emotional, practical or familial problems they faced, from anyone else. The films *Analyze This* (1999), *Gun Shy* (2000) and *The Whole Nine Yards* (2000) were predominantly comic. The TV show, *The Sopranos*, was essentially a drama.

Meanwhile, while one the consequences of *Pulp Fiction*'s success was the casting of John Travolta as an impossibly chic, as opposed to a more typically down-at-heel, Mob soldier in *Get Shorty* (1995),[66] one of the consequences of Quentin Tarantino's earlier *Reservoir Dogs* (1992) was a cycle of heist (or to be more precise heist-gone-wrong) films which tended to centre, if not always on low-level Mafia gangsters, then on amateur or professional criminals drawn from the lower ranks of civil or criminal society. As is well known, *Reservoir Dogs* itself draws on an array of Hollywood and Hong Kong crime films for inspiration.[67] Among the former are such heist films as *The Killing* (1956) and *The Taking of Pelham One, Two, Three* (1974). *Reservoir Dogs* itself focuses on the build-up to a heist that goes wrong and its aftermath, hence on the interactions among and between its all-male cast of characters, rather than on the mechanics of the heist itself.[68] In doing so, emphasis is placed on such typically male themes as competence, incompetence, trust and betrayal. In a film about relatively low-level professional gangsters (and relatively low-level cops), it is also placed on such quotidian elements, to use Rafter's term again,[69] as digressive and mundane conversation.[70]

Reservoir Dogs was an independent production, and it was above all in the upscale independent sector, particularly among male film-school graduates, that its influence was most clearly felt. Bryan Singer's *The Usual Suspects* (1995) is an interesting if slightly marginal example, as, although it focused on a drug deal rather than on a heist, and although it tended (obscenities aside) to lack Tarantinoesque dialogue, it picked up on *Reservoir Dogs*' narrational complexities, on issues of competence and betrayal, and on the lack of power and control of most of its gangster characters. In addition, Todd McCarthy, *Variety*'s reviewer, likened the film to another possible influence on *Reservoir Dogs*, *The Asphalt Jungle* (1950).[71] More straightforward examples include *Killing Zoe* (1994), which was written and directed by Roger Avary (Tarantino's collaborator on the scripts for *True Romance* (1993) and *Pulp Fiction*), *Things to Do in Denver When You're Dead* (1995), *The Underneath* (1995), *Set it Off* (1996), *Albino Alligator* (1997), *City of Industry* (1997), *Blood Guts Bullets and Octane* (1998) and *Hell's Kitchen N.Y.C.* (1999). Others include the charmingly comic *Palookaville* (1997) and *Plump Fiction* (1997), a Tarantino parody. All of them, however, unlike *Reservoir Dogs* itself, depict rather than elide the heists around which they are organised.

Running parallel with these independent films were two more studio heist pictures, neither of which drew its inspiration from *Reservoir Dogs*. One was *Sneakers* (1993), which harked back if anything, albeit in lightly comic mode, to such 1970s conspiracy thrillers as *All the President's Men* (1974) and *3 Days of the Condor* (1975) (both of which, like *Sneakers* itself, starred Robert Redford). The other was *Heat* (1995), in part a follow-up to director Michael Mann's earlier *Thief* (1981), in part a cops-and-robbers film 'about work and its increasing personal costs'.[72] Neither *Sneakers* nor *Heat* focused on low-level gangsters, low-level criminals or low-level social milieux. In addition to the post-Tarantino heist films and to some of the wiseguy pictures, this was the province of the black and Latino street gang and urban ghetto crime films that comprised the other principal strand of gangster films in the 1990s.

Ghetto gangs

Aside from *Knights of the City* (1985), a late low-budget contribution to the trend set by *The Warriors* (1979), and aside from *I'm Gonna Git You Sucka* (1988), the first in an intermittent series of blaxploitation parodies, revivals and comedies that later included *The Return of Superfly* (1990) and *Original Gangstas* (1996), it was not until the arrival of *The Bronx War* in 1990, of *New Jack City*, *Straight Out of Brooklyn* and *Boyz N the Hood* in 1991 and of *American Me*, *Deep Cover*, *South Central* and *Juice* in 1992 that the black and Latino urban ghetto strand was first fully established. One of the hallmarks of this strand was the prominence of black and Latino production personnel, and a number of explanations have been offered both for this and for the general appearance of these films at this time. Some of them are discussed by Craig Watkins elsewhere in this volume. Four essentially industrial reasons (all of which, of course, have ideological implications) are worth stressing here.

The first is the extent to which, as we have seen, there was a general revival of gangster films at this time. The ghetto films received financial backing and distribution from major Hollywood studios as commercially viable contributions to a newly established production cycle. The second is the extent to which the Hollywood majors were at this time also engaged in incorporating independent distributors and independent (or would-be independent) production personnel, including those from ethnic minorities.[73] The third is the extent to which, with regard to the black films, rap music in general and gangsta rap in particular had demonstrated its crossover commercial potential and was thus perceived as a marketable textual and contextual ingredient by an increasingly synergistic industry.[74] And the fourth, finally, is the extent to which demographic research, and a number of the distribution strategies adopted in the light of its findings, indicated or produced a degree of crossover ethnic attendance for the films themselves.[75]

One of the hallmarks of the ghetto films is their diversity. This is especially true of the black films, which were produced in greater numbers and which as a trend interacted with other developments in the gangster film to produce an array of variations and off-shoots. *Deep Cover*, *Hoodlum* and *Set It Off*, for example, contributed, as noted at various points above, to the undercover cop, retro biopic and heist cycles. In addition, while some films, such as *New Jack City*, *Hoodlum* and *Sugar Hill* (1994), focused on emerging or top-level gangsters, others, such as *Boyz N the Hood*, *Juice*, *Menace II Society* (1993) and *Clockers* (1995), focused on teenagers, children and street crime. Both were marked, from time to time, by motifs of redemption or regeneration,[76] while the latter frequently gave rise to a biographical, rites-of-passage structure.[77] This structure was shared by the Latino films, which in addition to *American Me* included *Bound by Honor* (a.k.a. *Blood in Blood out*) (1993) and *Mi Vida Loca* (1994), too. In both groups of films, its educative dimensions included an often militant insistence on the internally divisive effects on black and Latino neighbourhoods of gang rivalries and of the drugs trade in 1980s and 1990s, and on the extent to which they can only benefit the dominant white political order.[78]

In *Mi Vida Loca,* it also included an insistence on the destructive effects of machismo. Machismo, however, is by no means confined to the Latino films. Nor is it confined to the black films, many of which have been criticised for their focus on men, male youths and male children.[79] Male vanity, male codes of honour, male power, male violence and male rage are displayed, and usually indulged, in all of the trends and cycles mentioned above. While not a defining feature of gangster films, the repeated insistence in Mafia films, in retro films, in heist films and in ghetto films alike on rules and the breaking of rules, codes and the breaking of codes, plans and the breakdown of plans and the extent to which they facilitate extravagant displays of machismo would, I am sure, repay further analysis. So, too, would the extent to which what Esther Sonnet has called 'hysterical masculinity', which 'collapses meaningful distinctions between homosocial, homosexual and violent impulses' and which marks 'the endpoint of a longer historical process by which male protagonists have acceded to a profound ... pathologisation' finds persistent articulation in these films.[80] In the meantime, and in conclusion, it is clear that in the 1980s and 1990s at least, such displays, and such hysteria, have been a pervasive feature of gangster films of all kinds.

Notes

1. Robert Warshow, 'The Gangster as Tragic Hero' [1948] and 'The Movie Chronicle: The Westerner' [1954], in *The Immediate Experience: Movies, Comics, Theatre and Other Aspects of Popular Culture* (New York: Atheneum, 1962), pp. 127–33, 135–54; André Bazin, 'The Western, or the American Film Par Excellence' [1953] and 'The Evolution of the Western' [1955], in *What Is Cinema?* (Berkeley: University of California Press, 1971), vol. 2, pp. 140–8, 149–57; John Cawelti, *The Six-Gun Mystique* (Bowling Green, NY: Bowling Green University Press, 1970) and *Adventure, Mystery and Romance: Formula Stories as Art and Popular Culture* (Chicago: University of Chicago Press, 1974), pp. 51–79, 192–259; Edward Buscombe, 'The Idea of Genre in the American Cinema', *Screen*, vol. 11, no. 2

(1970), pp. 33–45; Colin MacArthur, *Underworld USA* (London: Secker and Warburg, 1972); Andrew Tudor, *Theories of Genre* (London: Secker and Warburg, 1974), pp. 131–44; Tom Ryall, 'Teaching through Genre', *Screen Education*, no. 17 (1975/6), pp. 27–33; and Thomas Schatz, *Hollywood Genres: Formulas, Filmmaking and the Studio System* (New York: Random House, 1981), pp. 45–110.

2. Steve Neale, *Genre and Hollywood* (London: Routledge, 2000), pp. 16, 76–82, 133–42.

3. Edward Buscombe, 'The Western: A Short History', in Edward Buscombe (ed.), *The BFI Companion to the Western* (London: Andre Deutsch/BFI, 1988), p. 48.

4. David A. Cook, *Lost Illusions: American Cinema in the Shadow of Watergate and Vietnam, 1970–1979* (New York: Scribners, 2000), pp. 174–82.

5. Buscombe, 'The Western', p. 52.

6. Stephen Prince, *A New Pot of Gold: Hollywood under the Electronic Rainbow, 1980–1989* (New York: Scribners, 2000), p. 312.

7. According to Steven Bach in *Final Cut: Dreams and Disasters in the Making of* Heaven's Gate (London: Jonathan Cape, 1985), p. 130, United Artists, worried about the film's 'outmoded' status as a Western, was initially reluctant to fund the production of what was then entitled *Johnson County War*, even at a modest $7.5 million. It was finally written off for $44 million and was roadshown for only one day before being withdrawn, cut and unsuccessfully re-released on a saturation basis.

8. Buscombe, 'The Western', p. 52.

9. The only film mentioned here to appear in the top fifty in *Variety's* annual box-office listings in the early 1980s was *Bronco Billy*, itself, of course, a marginal Western the success of which was linked to the unique popularity of Eastwood. See 'Big Rental Films of 1980', *Variety*, 14 January 1981, p. 29.

10. Buscombe, 'The Western', pp. 36–41, 48.

11. Ibid., p. 36; Cook, *Lost Illusions*, p. 398; Douglas Gomery, *Shared Pleasures: A History of Movie Presentation in the United States* (London: BFI, 1992), pp. 85–8; Richard Maltby, *Hollywood Cinema* (Oxford: Blackwell, 1995) p. 72.

12. Thomas Doherty, *Teenagers and Teenpics: The Juvenilization of American Movies in the 1950s* (Boston: Unwin Hyman, 1988), pp. 61–6.

13. Jim Hiller, *The New Hollywood* (London: Studio Vista, 1992), p. 14.

14. Jowett, 'Giving Them What They Want: Movie Audience Research before 1950', in Bruce A. Austin (ed.), *Current Research in Film: Audiences, Economics, and Law*, vol. 1 (Norwood, NJ: Ablex, 1985), pp. 23–8.

15. Richard Slotkin, *Gunfighter Nation: The Myth of the Frontier in Twentieth Century America* (New York: Atheneum, 1992); Tom Engelhardt, *The End of Victory Culture: Cold War America and the Disillusion of a Generation* (New York: Basic Books, 1995), pp. 16–53.

16. Thomas Schatz, 'The New Hollywood', in Jim Collins, Hilary Radner and Ava Preacher Collins (eds), *Film Theory Goes to the Movies* (New York: Routledge, 1993), pp. 19–20.

17. John Belton, *American Cinema/American Culture* (New York: McGraw-Hill, 1994), pp. 227–9; Engelhardt, *The End of Victory Culture*, pp. 263–303; John Cawelti, *The Six-Gun Mystique Sequel* (Bowling Green, OH: Bowling Green State University Popular Press, 1999),

p. 119; Geoff King, *Spectacular Narratives: Hollywood in the Age of the Blockbuster* (London: I. B. Tauris, 2000); Slotkin, *Gunfighter Nation*, pp. 635–6. Cawelti, it should be noted, cautions against pushing this thesis too far. 'There are important differences between most science fiction films and the traditional Western,' he writes on page 119 of *The Six-Gun Mystique Sequel*. 'Space adventures portray a mastery of technology requiring both group efforts and an interfacing between man and machine very different from the heroic individualism of the classic Western.'

18. Buscombe, 'The Western', p. 47.
19. Buscombe (ed.), *The BFI Companion to the Western*, p. 428.
20. 'U.S. Market Share by Genre: 1971–84', *Variety*, 22 May 1985, p. 3. It should be noted, though, that a handful of film and television Westerns was released or aired in 1984. They included *Draw!*, *Triumphs of a Man Called Horse*, *The Mystic Warrior*, a television miniseries, and a telefilm, *Calamity Jane*.
21. Steve Fore, 'The Same Old Others: The Western, Lonesome Dove, and the Lingering Difficulty of Difference', *The Velvet Light Trap*, no. 27 (Spring 1991), p. 49.
22. Review of *Silverado*, *Variety*, 3 July 1985, p. 16.
23. Review of *Pale Rider*, *Variety*, 8 May 1985, p. 25. On Kasdan's intentions, see Stephen Harvey, 'Hi-Yo "Silverado"', *Film Comment*, vol. 21, no. 4 (July–August 1985), p. 26; and Richard T. Jameson, 'Pensées: The Sound of One Man Clapping', *Film Comment*, vol. 21, no. 5 (September–October 1985), p. 76. On Eastwood's intentions, see Richard Schickel, *Clint Eastwood* [1996] (London: Arrow Books, 1997), p. 403.
24. Harvey, 'Hi-Yo "Silverado"', p. 25.
25. *Pale Rider* grossed $20.8 million and finished twelfth in *Variety*'s list of 'Big Rental Films of '85', *Variety*, 8 January 1986, p. 22. *Silverado* grossed a respectable $16.6 million. See Joel Finler, *The Hollywood Story* (London: Octopus Books, 1988), p. 75.
26. Jim Hitt, *The American West from Fiction (1823–1976) into Film (1909–1986)* (Jefferson, NC: McFarland, 1990), p. 293; Thomas Schatz, 'The Western', in Wes D. Gehring (ed.), *Handbook of American Film Genres* (New York: Greenwood Press, 1988), p. 36.
27. 'Westerns in Networks' Saddle Again', *Variety*, 2 December 1988, p. 39.
28. The franchise consisted of *Return to Lonesome Dove* (1993), *Lonesome Dove: The Series* (1994 and 1995, retitled as *Lonesome Dove: The Outlaw Years*), *Streets of Laredo* (1995), which was based on McMurtry's 1993 novel, and *Dead Man's Walk* (1996), which was based on McMurtry's novel of 1995. The McMurtry novel and miniseries *Buffalo Girls* (1991 and 1995, respectively), although not part of the *Lonesome Dove* franchise, should probably be mentioned here as well.
29. Fore, 'The Same Old Others'; Richard Campbell and Jimmie L. Reeves, 'Resurrecting the TV Western: The Cowboy, the Frontier, and *Lonesome Dove*', *Television Quarterly*, vol. 24, no. 3 (1990), pp. 33–44; David Thorburn, 'Interpretation and Judgment: A Reading of *Lonesome Dove*', *Critical Studies in Mass Communication*, vol. 10, no. 2 (June 1994), pp. 113–27. Along with most of the other television Westerns mentioned here, *Lonesome Dove* is also discussed in Gary A. Yoggy, *Riding the Video Range: The Rise and Fall of the Western on Television* (Jefferson, NC: McFarland, 1996), pp. 579–88.
30. Robert Burgoyne, *Film Nation: Hollywood Looks at U.S. History* (Minneapolis: University of Minnesota Press, 1997), p. 17.

31. Jude Davies and Carol R. Smith, *Gender, Ethnicity and Sexuality in Contemporary American Film* (Keele: Keele University Press, 1997), p. 74.

32. Burgoyne, *Film Nation*, p. 18.

33. Julian Stringer, quoted in Jacquelyn Kilpatrick, *Celluloid Indians: Native Americans and Film* (Lincoln: University of Nebraska Press, 1999), p. 106.

34. Kilpatrick, *Celluloid Indians*, pp. 106–13.

35. Eric Gary Anderson, 'Driving the Road: *Powwow Highway*', in Peter C. Rollins and John E. O'Connor (eds), *Hollywood's Indian: The Portrayal of the Native American in Film* (Lexington: University of Kentucky Press, 1998), p. 138.

36. Anderson, 'Driving the Road', p. 138.

37. Ibid., p. 139.

38. John Cawelti suggests the term 'post-Western' in *The Six-Gun Mystique Sequel*, pp. 99–126; Lynette Tan the term 'post-revisionist western' in her unpublished PhD thesis 'Gunfighter Gaps: Discourses of the Frontier in Hollywood Movies of the 1930s and 1970s' (Sheffield Hallam University, 1998), pp. 298–305; and Rick Worland and Edward Countryman the term 'new Western' in 'The New Western Historiography and the New American Western', in Edward Buscombe and Roberta Pearson (eds), *Back in the Saddle Again: New Essays on the Western* (London: BFI, 1998), pp. 182–96. The problem with all these all of these terms is that they tend to unify what I regard as a two-pronged plural phenomenon.

39. Neil Campbell, *The Cultures of the American New West* (Edinburgh: Edinburgh University Press, 2000); Michael L. Johnson, *New Westers: The West in Contemporary American Culture* (Lawrence: University Press of Kansas, 1996); Worland and Countryman, 'The New Western Historiography and the New American Western'.

40. On the former, see Jim Kitses, 'An Exemplary Post-Modern Western: *The Ballad of Little Jo*', in Jim Kitses and Gregg Rickman (eds), *The Western Reader* (New York: Limelight, 1998), pp. 367–80; and Tanya Modleski, *Old Wives' Tales: Feminist Re-Visions of Film and Other Fictions* (London: I. B. Tauris, 1999), pp. 149–78. On the latter, see Kilpatrick, *Celluloid Indians*, pp. 169–76; Gregg Rickman 'The Western under Erasure: *Dead Man*', in *The Western Reader*, pp. 381–404; and Jonathan Rosenbaum, *Dead Man* (London: BFI, 2000).

41. See among others, Robert Baird, 'Going Indian: *Dances with Wolves*', in *Hollywood's Indian*, pp. 153–69; Kilpatrick, *Celluloid Indians*, pp. 124–30; Armando José Prats, 'The Image of the Other and the Other *Dances with Wolves*: The Refigured Indian as Textual Supplement', *Journal of Film and Video*, vol. 50, no. 1 (Spring 1998) pp. 3–19; Michael Walker, '*Dances with Wolves*', in Ian Cameron and Douglas Pye (eds), *The Movie Book of the Western* (London: Studio Vista, 1996), pp. 284–93; Leighton Grist, '*Unforgiven*', in *The Movie Book of the Western*, pp. 294–301; Catherine Ingrassia, 'Writing the West: Iconic and Literal Truth in *Unforgiven*', *Literature/Film Quarterly*, vol. 26, no. 1 (1998), pp. 53–9; Carl Plantinga, 'Spectacles of Death: Clint Eastwood and Violence in *Unforgiven*', *Cinema Journal*, vol. 37, no. 2 (Winter 1998), pp. 65–83; Janet Thumim, '"Maybe He's Tough But He Sure Ain't No Carpenter": Masculinity and In/competence in *Unforgiven*' [1993], in *The Western Reader*, pp. 341–54; Gary Edgerton and Kathy Merlock Jackson, 'Redesigning Pocahontas', *Journal of Popular Film and Television*, vol.

24, no. 2 (Summer 1996), pp. 90–8; Kilpatrick, *Celluloid Indians*, pp. 150–54; Pauline Turner Strong, 'Playing Indian in the Nineties: *Pocahontas* and *The Indian in the Cupboard*', in *Hollywood's Indian*, pp. 187–205; Christina Lane, *Feminist Hollywood: From* Born in Flames *to* Point Break (Detroit, MI: Wayne State University Press, 2000), pp. 203–16, on *Bad Girls*; and Allen Barra, *Inventing Wyatt Earp: His Life and Many Legends* (New York: Carroll and Graff, 1998), pp. 365–9, on *Tombstone*.

42. 'Summer's Snaps, Crackles & Flops', *Variety*, 29 August – 4 September 1994, pp. 1, 55.

43. '"The Wild Wild West" May Ride Again', *Variety*, 6 January 1992, p. 30.

44. Review of *Lakota Woman: Seige at Wounded Knee*, *Variety*, 10–16 October 1994, p. 46; 'Beyond "Gettysburg"', *Variety*, 8–14 May 1995, p. 77.

45. Kilpatrick, *Celluloid Indians*, pp. 218–19, 228–32.

46. According to Phil Hardy (ed.), *The Aurum Encyclopedia: Gangsters* (London: Aurum Press, 1998), there were no Hollywood gangster films released in 1982 and only one, *Scarface*, in 1983. In contrast, ten gangster films of one kind or another were released in 1990, seven in 1991 and eleven in 1992.

47. Cook, *Lost Illusions*, p. 185.

48. Dwight D. Smith, *The Mafia Mystique* (New York: Basic Books, 1975). This fascination had been fed in the early 1960s by the Kennedy administration's hearings on organised crime, by the rumoured involvement of the Mafia in John Kennedy's assassination and later, as noted below, by the publication of *The Valachi Papers*. In the cinema and on television it was fed by *The Brotherhood* (1968), *Honor Thy Father* (1971) and *The Valachi Papers* (1972). On the basic features of 'Mafia mythology', see Alessanadro Camon, '*The Godfather* and the Mythology of the Mafia', in Nick Browne (ed.), *Francis Ford Coppola's* The Godfather Trilogy (Cambridge: Cambridge University Press, 2000), pp. 57–75.

49. See Peter Stanfield, '"Good Evening Gentlemen, Can I Check Your Hats Please?": Men's Fashions and the Retro-Gangster Cycles of the 1990s', in Lee Grieveson, Esther Sonnet and Peter Stanfield (eds), *Mob Culture: Essays on the Gangster Film* (forthcoming). Marilyn Yaquinto calls these films 'neo-Prohibition' films in *Pump 'Em Full of Lead: A Look at Gangsters on Film* (London: Twayne, 1998), pp. 202–6.

50. Matthew Bernstein quotes scriptwriter Robert Benton as saying recently that '*Bonnie and Clyde* is about style and people who have style', in 'Perfecting the New Gangster: Writing *Bonnie and Clyde*', *Film Quarterly*, vol. 53, no 4 (Summer 2000), p. 19. The rural-outlaw trend of which *Bonnie and Clyde* was such an important part came to an end, like the revisionist outlaw Western trend, in the early 1970s. Mario Puzo and Michael Cimino's attempt to revive it with *The Sicilian* in 1987 ended in box-office failure. Since then, one or two telefilms and low-budget features such as *Dillinger* (1991) and *Bonnie and Clyde: The True Story* (1992) have, along with *The Newton Boys* (1998), been the only attempts to revive it once more. *Dillinger's* retro ambitions were underlined in *Variety*, 7 January 1991, p. 60. 'The vidpic's texture is sharp,' its reviewer wrote, 'with period cars and fashions . . . right on target.'

51. 'Latest Gang of Mob Pix Arms for Upscale Shootout', *Variety*, 1 October 1990, p. 105. See also Erin A. Smith, *Hard-Boiled: Working-Class Readers and Pulp Magazines* (Philadelphia: Temple University Press, 2000). This detachment may have been specific to the cinema,

which discontinued the production of traditional gangster and B-films in the 1950s, which aimed its low-budget rural gangster films as well as the more expensive ones such as *Bonnie and Clyde* at the countercultural youth market and which, from *The Godfather* on, tended to aim its 'upscale' productions, which included art-house-oriented independents as well as big-budget studio projects, either at demographically mixed audiences of one kind or another or else at upscale spectators. ('Arthouse Purgatory Plagues Season's Upscale Film', *Variety*, 26 November 1990, pp. 74, 78; 'Universal Aims "Mobsters" at Crossover Audiences', *Variety*, 22 July 1991, p. 74;'*Bugsy* Hollers for More TriStar Dollars', *Variety*, 25 November 1991, pp. 1, 61; 'High-Class Heist Pix Steal into H'Wood', *Variety*, 18–24 March, 1996, pp. 11, 16). Some of the low-budget 'B' independents and some gangster films made for cable television and direct-to-video release may, however, have been aimed at blue-collar audiences. *Mad Dog Coll* (1992), for instance, was described by *Variety*'s reviewer as a 'low-rent gloss on the mobster genre' and likened it to a 'solid-'50s programmer in color'. *Variety*, 18 May 1992, p. 18. On 'B' independents and on the action market in general in the early 1990s, see 'They're Alive! The B Movies Refuse to Die', *Variety*, 15 October 1990, pp. M-14, M-132.

52. The entry on *The Godfather* on page 312 of *The Aurum Encyclopedia* calls it a 'rise-and-rise structure'.

53. Ibid., p. 312.

54. Nick Browne, 'Fearful A-Symmetries: Violence as History in the *Godfather* Films', in *Francis Ford Coppola's* The Godfather *Trilogy*, p. 2.

55. Hardy, *The Aurum Encyclopedia*, p. 312.

56. For discussion of the 1980 version of *Gloria* and of the role of women in a number of 1980s and 1990s gangster films, see Esther Sonnet, 'Marked Women: A Short History of Molls and the Gangster Film', in Grieveson, Sonnet and Stanfield (eds), *Mob Culture*.

57. Until the expansion and reconfiguration of television in the 1980s, the television networks were the principal source and outlet for crime films and programmes on US TV. Even in the 1980s, its domestic remit and its programming traditions tended to result in criminals and crime being presented on TV through a focus on the police and other law enforcement agencies. Examples include *Today's FBI* (1981–2), *Wiseguy* (1987–90), *Capone's Enforcer* and *The Revenge of Al Capone*.

58. 'Distribs on a Crime Spree; Mob-Related Pix Fill Slates', *Variety*, 25 February 1991, p. 12; John H. Davis, *Mafia Dynasty: The Rise and Fall of the Gambino Crime Family* [1993] (New York: HarperPaperbacks, 1994), pp. 209–11; James Morton, *Gangland: The International Mafia and Other Mobs* [1998] (London: Warner Books, 1999), p. 164.

59. I would like here to correct the error I made in writing that Nicholas Pileggi and Henry Hill are one and the same person on page 144 of *Genre and Hollywood*. Nicholas Pileggi is a journalist; Henry Hill was a Mafia wiseguy.

60. 'Wiseguys Now Packing Pens, Not Pistols', *Variety*, 9 March 1992, p. 71. This report noted an estimate that over 200 Mafia-oriented titles a year were being published at this time, as well as the extent to which these titles were being optioned by film and TV production companies.

61. Hardy, *The Aurum Encyclopedia*, p. 286.

62. Warshow, 'The Gangster as Tragic Hero'. Just as these parallels were underlined by *Joe MacBeth* (1955) in the 1950s, so they were underlined by another gangster version of *Macbeth*, *Men of Respect* (1991), in the 1990s.

63. Nicole Rafter, *Shots in the Mirror: Crime Films and Society* (Oxford: Oxford University Press, 2000), p. 43. On the specificity and the significance of the wiseguy as a figure in Pileggi's book and Scorsese's film, see Maurizio Viano, '*Goodfellas*', *Film Quarterly*, vol. 44, no. 3 (Spring 1991), p. 44.

64. It is argued on page 442 of *The Aurum Encyclopedia* that, in the 1990s, 'an increasing number of American directors attempted to imbue their gangster films with ... [a] ... reflective, meditative and sometimes elegaic ambience. One clutch of such films bemusedly celebrated the hymn to the dollar that was the creation of modern Las Vegas (for example, *Bugsy*, 1991, *Hoffa*, 1992, and *Casino*, 1995) making dreamers of the gangster protagonists and finding a garish beauty in their creations.' Meanwhile, in films such as *Miller's Crossing*, *Goodfellas*, *Heat* (1995) and *Donnie Brasco*, 'it is the gangsters who dream and are betrayed; amorality is a given but ... the characters retain a real sense of honour'. In other words, both in the retro films and in the films about low-level gangsters, the protagonists' dreams are often presented as decent, innocent, even childlike. As such they are doomed to failure in an essentially unjust and venal world. This element, it might be added, is also central to some of the heist films discussed below, especially *Things To Do in Denver When You're Dead* (1995), *Set It Off* (1996) and the more marginal and hybrid *Dead Presidents* (1995), which culminates in a heist, but which devotes most of its time to the lives of the black characters who become involved in it and to the socio-historical circumstances and events that help to determine their course.

65. Foster Hirsch, *Detours and Lost Highways: A Map of Neo-Noir* (New York: Limelight, 1999), pp. 271–5.

66. The entry on *Get Shorty* on page 491 of *The Aurum Encyclopedia* notes that 'the film accepts criminality as a matter-of-fact way of life for many of its characters, a way of life that in no way segregates them from the rest of humanity among whom they move'. In this world, 'style is the only judgement offered – with the important proviso that no one can match Travolta's wholly engaging mix of charm and latent violence'. Insofar as this is the case, however, the desegregation that is also the hallmark of some of the low-level gangster films and one of the later 1990s trends is somewhat contradicted by a criterion, that of style, imported in large part from the retro and Mafia films.

67. Hardy, *The Aurum Encyclopedia*, p. 463.

68. Ron Wilson, 'The Left-handed Form of Human Endeavor: Crime Films during the 1990s', in Wheeler Winston Dixon (ed.), *Film Genre 2000* (New York: State University of New York Press, 2000), p. 155.

69. Rafter herself characterises *Reservoir Dogs*, along with *Pulp Fiction*, *Fargo* and *Natural Born Killers* (1994) as 'absurdist'. See *Shots in the Mirror*, pp. 41–2.

70. Sarah Kozloff, *Overhearing Film Dialogue* (Berkeley: University of California Press, 2000), p. 231. Kozloff goes on to note the extent to which the dialogue is devoted to storytelling, as well as the extent to which its content and use help to mark the film and its

preccupations as, in a literal sense, 'childish'. Her remarks are part of an extremely interesting chapter on dialogue in gangster films.

71. Review of *The Usual Suspects*, *Variety*, 30 January – 5 February 1995, p. 46.

72. J. A. Lindstrom, '*Heat*: Work and Genre', *Jump Cut*, no. 44 (2000), p. 21.

73. Prince, *A New Pot of Gold*, pp. 158–9; Jesse Algernon Rhines, *Black Film/White Money* (New Brunswick, NJ: Rutgers University Press, 1996), pp. 74–8; Justin Wyatt, 'The Formation of the "Major Independent": Miramax, New Line and the New Hollywood', in Steve Neale and Murray Smith (eds), *Contemporary Hollywood Cinema* (London: Routledge, 1998), pp. 74–105.

74. Yaquinto, *Pump 'Em Full of Lead*, pp. 186–7. The use of rap and hip-hop and the ways in which they can contribute both to the sonic density and to the representational politics of some of these films are briefly discussed in Mark Winokur, 'Marginal Marginalia: The African-American Voice in the Nouvelle Gangster Film', *The Velvet Light Trap*, no. 35 (Spring 1995), p. 27.

75. 'Blacks Taking the Helm', *Variety*, 18 March 1991, pp. 1, 108; 'Latino Pix Have Crossover Dreams', *Variety*, 30 March 1992, pp. 5, 19. See also Hillier, *The New Hollywood*, pp. 147–50.

76. Yaquinto, *Pump 'Em Full of Lead*, pp. 231–2.

77. Manthia Diawara, 'Black American Cinema: The New Realism', in Manthia Diawara (ed.), *Black American Cinema* (New York: Routledge, 1993), pp. 20–25; Yaquinto, *Pump 'Em Full of Lead*, p. 214.

78. Many of these films have been dismissed as collusions with Hollywood, as perpetuating an identification of ethnic minorities with ghettos, crime and hopelessness, and as adopting sensationalist tactics. Ed Guerrero writes in their defence that, whereas violence in the blaxploitation films of the 1970s 'depicted or implied the shaking off of the oppression of "the Man" and, significantly, the movement toward the dream of a liberated future', violence 'in the new black film wave for the most part transcodes the collapse of those very hopes under the assault of the Reagan and Bush years'. That, he continues, 'is their most salient political point'. See 'Black Violence as Cinema: From Cheap Thrills to Historical Agonies', in J. David Slocum (ed.), *Violence and American Cinema* (New York: Routledge, 2001), p. 216. See also Mark A. Reid, 'The Black Gangster Film', in Barry Keith Grant (ed.), *Film Genre Reader II* (Austin: University of Texas Press, 1995), pp. 471–2.

79. For a summary of some of these criticisms, see Sharon Willis, *High Contrast: Race and Gender in Contemporary Hollywood Film* (Durham, NC Duke University Press, 1997), pp. 161–2.

80. Sonnet, 'Marked Women'. A starting point here might be Kevin White's book *The First Sexual Revolution: The Emergence of Heterosexuality in Modern America* (New York: New York University Press, 1993). White argues that a significant source of and for modern regimes of masculinity was the criminal underworld.

4

The New Hollywood Musical:
From *Saturday Night Fever* to *Footloose*

J. P. Telotte

I

While the late 1970s and 1980s saw a marked resurgence of the film musical, only a few of these films followed the path traditionally marked off for the genre. The older musical tradition soldiered on in films such as *Grease* (1978), *Sgt. Pepper's Lonely Hearts Club Band* (1978), *The Wiz* (1978) and *Xanadu* (1980), but a wave of what we might simply term musically oriented films also appeared, far more numerous and in most cases more successful at the box office and with critics than those more conventional works. In them we see a consistent tendency to depict a world whose prime expressive elements – song and dance – are clearly circumscribed. In these films, people no longer suddenly burst into song or go into a dance, for in this era the hills are obviously no longer 'alive with the sound of music'; and, whenever anyone does engage in overtly expressive activities, it is usually within a restricted arena, a limited space the boundaries of which weigh heavily on the moment of song or dance. Michael Wood noted a similar failing in musicals of the late 1950s and suggested that 'what killed off the vivid musical of those years was a growing failure of music in the life outside the movies. By the mid-1950s, it was beginning to seem impossible to break into a general song and dance in America, even metaphorically'.[1] A later revival of the genre might seem to belie Wood's report of its demise, but a closer view shows that the musical probably owes its resurgence to an inherent structural principle which allows it to cope with those cultural limitations that inevitably come with changing times and circumstances. Because of this structure, the 'new' musical tends to generate a more sober though still affirmative feeling, a sense that despite all restrictions, the 'show' – this singing and dancing – can go on.

In outlining an 'aesthetics' of the film musical, Timothy Scheurer describes the 'different mode of reality' through which this genre typically operates; it is one in which 'the inner reality of feelings, emotions and instincts are given metaphoric and symbolic expression through the means of music and dance'. In order to craft a successful musical, as he explains, this 'other' reality must be properly wedded to the normal world from which it derives its existence by means of a 'finely balanced interplay and synthesis of non-musical and musical sequences'.[2] The manner of blending that stylisation of song and dance with a more prosaic reality thus forms a basic structural concern of most musicals.[3] Yet what this principle suggests is that, whether a fully integral part of the exposition or only a momentary digressive or expressive element, the musical number produces a tension within the narrative syntagma between itself and the conventional narrative elements. With this perspective in mind, I want to focus on those expressive features – the song and dance – which usually identify this genre, for the condition of their placement in these later musicals and the tension they evoke open onto the most revealing characteristics of this musical development.

II

Gene Kelly, speaking from his long experience as both an actor and director of some of our most famous musicals, suggested that the genre's expressive elements function most effectively when they arise from one of three filmic sources: first, plot situations; second, character development; or third, incidents that enhance one of these two.[4] He believes, in other words, that song and dance should be natural, expressive extensions of the film narrative, motivated yet not quite invisible components of the conventional classical narrative style. Musicals such as *Grease* and *The Wiz* labour to follow such a formula and tend to integrate the musical components at the expense of a realistic plot. As a result, they seem to deny or denigrate the reality of the world that has given birth to their music. In both cases, this aura of unreality is enhanced by depending on a sense of nostalgia, as in one way or another the films try to evoke our culture's 'good ole days' and what many cannot help but see as the correspondingly 'good ole' movies of a classical Hollywood. However, they seem oblivious to the fact that such an anachronistic stance subtly asks viewers to abdicate from the present, human world. In short, they essentially *compel* escape from our normal lives and force on us the worst sort of effect that critics of the genre have often attributed to it. However, the critical and popular reception accorded the numerous, more sober musical films of later times indicates that we are not completely willing to turn back the pages of our cinematic and cultural history.

The majority of this later generation of musical films take a very different tack, one that pushes Kelly's suggestions to an extreme. While movies such as *Saturday Night Fever* (1977), *The Last Waltz* (1978), *American Hot Wax* (1978), *The Buddy Holly Story* (1978), *The Rose* (1979), *Coal Miner's Daughter* (1980), *Flashdance* (1983), *Purple Rain* (1984), *Footloose* (1984) and *Dirty Dancing* (1985) are pointedly *about* the role of music and dance in our lives, they obviously treat these expressive elements, both the staples of the musical and a primary source of their attraction, with a rather detached attitude. Here the expressive is clearly demarcated from the main narrative, even while realistically arising from it. In fact, any songs and dances these films contain are usually – after a fashion seen in earlier 'backstage musicals' – identified as performances and thus bound by the natural limitations that normally attend such circumscribed events.

Kelly's statements – and no less his performances – indicate that he inherently understood the cause of this treatment of song and dance, that is, the ponderous weight of reality and its tendency to stifle any expressive or fantastic elements. From his own

experience, he notes how much a performance 'loses . . . on film; it loses its third dimension the same way photographed sculpture does. But it loses even more . . . . Lost is the
living, breathing presence and personality of the performer, and gone are the kinetic
forces that make the strongest interplay between audience and dancer.'[5] While the more
conventional musical blithely asserts how easily song and dance can overcome and transform the concrete facts of human existence, then, what I have termed 'new' musicals
demonstrate a compelling sense of the loss Kelly describes and of the limitations involved
in every musical performance today. Instead of denying reality's rule with song and
dance, they construct a realistic frame around those expressive elements, becoming in
the process almost proscenium-oriented. These films masquerade variously as social
commentary, biography and documentary, but they share a common perspective, one
which offers a more sober approach to the expressive role of music in the movies and in
our lives.

Taken together, these two trends might suggest a sort of Jekyll and Hyde character
for the musical genre in recent years, as if once pushed to its extreme in one direction,
it could continue to speak effectively to audiences only by balancing off this effete form,
by acknowledging its inherent limitations with a more realistic context. What has resulted
is, on the one hand, a musical form reminiscent of the large-cast, big-budget musicals of
past years. The most successful of these are obviously *Grease* and *Hair* (1979), films
which create a pleasantly anachronistic world in which we might nostalgically immerse
ourselves, yet worlds whose likeness America has never actually seen before. *Grease*'s
safe and sanitised 1950s and *Hair*'s slight, distanced *angst* of the 1960s and the hippie
movement clearly exist outside reality – and outside, too, of the demands of our
present-day consciousness – so their musical numbers are only minimally bound by its
stifling weight. For nostalgia itself is their concern, their capital, their real appeal. Yet on
the other hand, we have seen the advent of a more realistic counterweight in those musically oriented films described earlier; and they have achieved a great measure of
popularity despite tempering their expressive exuberance and making some demands of
awareness or social consciousness on their viewers. This later form of the musical admits
the restrictions that weigh upon its music, but it seems to do so in order to more directly
address our many modern, extra-musical dilemmas and thus to speak to an audience
unable to put aside those cultural concerns so easily.

While the best musicals have always seemed mindful of the tension between the real
and the expressive, and of the problems involved in trying to wed the two, a sense of
human limitation has hardly been a dominant element in the genre. Even the
Depression-era musicals, such as those choreographed by Busby Berkeley at Warner
Bros., clearly sought both thematically and structurally to counter the impingements of
that external world of joblessness and breadlines, emphasising instead the liberating
power of the musical experience.[6] Human energy – as expressed in song and dance –
was itself celebrated and the basic message was, in the words of Ginger Rogers in *Gold
Diggers of 1933* (1933), 'we've got a lot of what it takes to get along.' Despite all the
physical evidence of the Depression, the Warner Bros. musicals affirmed that some vital
energy simply lay dormant in the American character and had only to be released. When

it was – as in the case of *42nd Street*'s (1933) Peggy Sawyer, who went out 'a youngster' to come back 'a star' – not only was the person changed, but his or her world, too, apparently underwent a dramatic transformation.

Such displays of kinetic energy and its transformative powers were especially the province of those spectacular musical numbers with which the Berkeley movies normally climaxed. Admittedly, the songs and dances were *supposed to be* performances, as according to the narratives they formed key acts in a theatrical production. Yet inevitably Berkeley's numbers were geared to burst beyond the proscenium's confines and to expropriate or create a wholly new sense of space for their action. Musical numbers such as the 'By a Waterfall' sequence of *Footlight Parade* (1933), for instance, with its multiple pools and changing shapes, clearly demolished any notion of spatial limitation. What resulted was a sense of an 'unlimited world within the routine itself'[7] and, more importantly, a feeling that perhaps the real world, too, was not quite as limited and intransigent as the audience had heretofore believed.

In RKO's Fred Astaire – Ginger Rogers musicals, this distinction between the staged performance and the purely expressive activity was often blurred, but the sense of a transforming energy remained constant. In fact, the shift they emphasise, from a stylised performance to purely expressive event, may best demonstrate this power, as it suggests that the human condition is itself open to transformation. More importantly, the Astaire–Rogers films tend to focus on individual human problems, those that have always seemed more susceptible to immediate solutions, rather than the problems facing society at large. Instead of economic or class-related ills, their characters face such timeless issues as thwarted love, mistaken identity and crossed purposes. The mating chase takes centre stage and neither oceans nor continents pose effective barriers to its successful conclusion. When in *Top Hat* (1935), Dale Tremont (Rogers) mistakes Jerry Travers (Astaire) for the new husband of her best friend and flees the country to avoid his advances, Jerry simply charters a plane to pursue her from London to Venice, there to resolve the misunderstanding and woo her. Similarly, in *Shall We Dance?* (1937), Peter P. Peters easily abandons his trendy Parisian dance school to follow Linda Keene across the Atlantic and win her love. Apparently 'Flying Down to Rio' or sailing across the Atlantic is a fairly normal activity in the world Astaire and Rogers inhabit, so they naturally project no awareness of any great barriers to human expression. In their films, as a result, the worlds of fantasy and reality seem to converge, as they inevitably generate a feeling of, as Michael Wood suggests, 'a genuine continuity between ordinary life and music, a sense of the world as filled with pretexts for song and invitations to dance'.[8] When Astaire confesses in *Top Hat* that 'every once in a while I suddenly find myself dancing', he intimates just how natural such activity seems in his environment, as if he inhabited a realm totally ruled by the expressive imagination.

For many musicals of the late 1940s and early 1950s, however, that spontaneity had become forced, that sense of harmony between two people who, the narratives implied, were simply 'made for each other', had dissipated. With the general trend towards more realistic films in this period, the musical, too, felt a similar impulse; however, as Jerome Delamater points out, those 'attempts to achieve a realistic musical . . . often resulted in

conflicts between reality and fantasy.'[9] With ever-increasing international tensions and
the sense of a value crisis in American culture, reality began to seem far less subject to
transformation, even by someone with the grace and skill of Astaire. Fittingly, Gene Kelly,
with his more muscular approach to dance, began to supplement Astaire, becoming
almost his cultural alter ego; as Wood notes, Kelly provided an alternative 'for the more
diffident and superstitious among us, for all of those of us who never can quite believe
in their good fortune, and for whom Astaire's style seems wonderful but inaccessible,
remote in its very unobtrusiveness.'[10] What Kelly offered was something far less remote,
if also less magical, not 'style' so much as a human strength and vitality by which he
seemed to *wrest* some underlying harmony from a recalcitrant world, whether as a sailor
on leave, physically canvassing all of New York in *On the Town* (1949), or as a fantasised
buccaneer, flying through a ship's riggings in *The Pirate* (1948).[11] Kelly's musicals usually
told a tale of this individual struggle, but, at the same time, perhaps as a counterweight,
they frequently included balletic, dream-like sequences, helping to establish this convention for musicals of the era. One consequence is that the expressive elements in these
musicals increasingly came to seem less grounded in the real world. The almost impressionistic finale of *An American in Paris* (1951) and the smoky fantasy sequence of *The
Pirate*, for example, seem conjured from some dream, as if they made no claim to a place
in a world of harsh cultural phenomena.

   And yet, certain harsh realities simply could not be avoided, even by the musical. The
American film industry itself underwent profound changes at a time when the musical
genre, as we have noted, was already struggling with changing cultural attitudes. The
government-mandated break-up of the studio system, a process that would radically
transform the movie-making process by the early 1960s, gradually led to the dispersal
and seeming disappearance of the resources that had produced a golden age of musicals from the 1930s through the 1950s and that had allowed a studio such as MGM
proudly to proclaim itself the 'musical factory'. As the character of the major studios
changed, the stars, writers, musicians and choreographers who had specialised in the
genre, had established a fairly consistent narrative formula and had even helped to define
identifiable studio musical styles left the big studios for small independent production
companies, for the musical theatre and even for that other competing medium, television. In effect, the genre was under assault not only by realistic trends within the
culture, but also by the realities of the industrial process that had engendered it.

III

The musical film of the late 1970s and early 1980s found ways of coping with the problems arising from these different developments, and the very fact that the genre gave
birth to such a variety of subsequent films testifies to a continuing ability to speak to the
desires of a large segment of the movie audience. Yet we might question how, in what
we would like to think of as an even more sophisticated – and probably far more
cynical – age, the musical managed this negotiation with various realistic trends. As I
suggested at the start of this chapter, films such as *The Wiz* and *Grease* look very much
like older, big-budget musicals of the sort produced by MGM in the late 1950s, and they

seem to opt for an escapist world, one that never really existed and that makes little claim of kinship to the world we inhabit. Yet at the same time, musical elements have cropped up in other, more traditionally realistic film types, such as the social exposé and the documentary – types more often associated with independent producers rather than the large studios. As one generic purist laments, though, this class of films seems to lack 'a truly musical style'; at first glance, they appear almost unappreciative of the 'liberating' power of the music with which they deal.[12]

The most successful of these musical films pose a definite puzzle for their audience. On the one hand, they seem to showcase the energy, attractiveness and excitement generated by their musical performances. Few would deny, for instance, that the prime reasons for *Saturday Night Fever*'s great success are John Travolta's dancing and the music of the Bee Gees, just as earlier formulae for success drew on Astaire or Kelly's dance skills and the music of Jerome Kern or the Gershwins. Clearly the expressive continues to hold a very basic attraction, even as its interpretation has undergone major revision. Astaire's almost lyric style has now given way to a controlled frenetic motion, and Kelly's athletic appropriation of space has been brought down to earth, confined to the disco floor. More specifically, we might note that throughout these new musicals expressive activity is consigned to very strict limits. Their performers inhabit a world that bears down upon them, so the stories they tell are usually of that tension between the performers and a realm in which their singing and dancing seem almost out of place. All expressive activity is thus channelled into arenas, stages and enclosed areas and repeatedly defined as 'performance'. In other words, these films seem intent on reminding us that distinct boundaries separate musical activity from the 'real' world, and they do so by acknowledging the very structural tension that musicals long sought to mitigate or deny. While they do admit that there is a 'place' for song and dance in our lives, by underscoring the limited potential of that music, they also affirm that we can no longer withdraw from the real world to immerse ourselves fully in the expressive one.

American Hot Wax, for example, describes a certain poetic energy latent in young Americans of the 1950s and 1960s, an energy which was just beginning to find expression in the rock'n'roll music of the period. It focuses on the disc jockey Alan Freed, who recognized this power and sought to liberate its creative potential by advocating and playing this new form of music. The film closes with a concert that Freed hoped would signal a general acceptance of rock'n'roll, while also celebrating its energetic potential. Instead, the concert is raided by the police and reduced to chaos. The movie ends then with a freeze frame and rolling title, informing us that Freed was subsequently arrested, tried on charges of receiving pay-offs for playing the music and, with his career ruined, soon after died penniless. This ending acknowledges that the cultural forces of conformity and propriety – forces traditionally seen as anti-expressive – have won out, successfully stifling those who refused to compromise, who felt, like Freed, that 'without my music I'm nothing'. This same conflict prevails in movies as seemingly diverse as *The Buddy Holly Story*, *Saturday Night Fever*, *The Last Waltz* and *Footloose* – all films shot by small, independent companies, although released through major distributors. On the one hand, they demonstrate the great power of song and dance, a power which can render our world momentarily more hospitable and our lives more bearable; on the other, they point out the inevitable limitations on that power and admit the overbearing weight of reality.

Of the above-mentioned films, *The Buddy Holly Story* is probably closest to a traditional musical form, that of the musical biography as represented by films such as *The Jolson Story* (1946), *Till the Clouds Roll By* (1946), *Three Little Words* (1950) or even *The Story of Vernon and Irene Castle* (1939). It takes for its focus, however, one of the tragic stories of modern music, the abortive career of Buddy Holly (as played in the film by Gary Busey), who was killed in a plane crash soon after reaching national prominence. The film follows Holly's struggles to express himself musically as he saw fit, even though his style marked something of a revolution in the popular music business. After depicting Holly's struggles for success, for a measure of artistic control over his music, for a chance to reach that young audience which demonstrably yearns for his energetic, driving music, the narrative suddenly ends in the middle of Holly's last concert. A freeze frame, silence on the soundtrack and a rolling title – a common ending for these musical films it seems – inform us of his death and suggest as well the stilling of his music.

The film mainly focuses on Holly's efforts to combat just such a restrictive force throughout his abortive career, especially his culture's efforts to bury his kind of music. In his small Texas hometown, Holly's new musical style clearly failed to fit in with the more conservative ideas of the community, although it obviously appealed to a latent spirit in the young people, as we see in the opening scene at the roller rink when his playing suddenly brings the kids to life. However, that playing also awakens a spirit of repression, as the local radio station is threatened with a loss of sponsorship if it continues to support and play his music. In that same spirit, Buddy's girlfriend and parents repeatedly urge him to abandon his playing for something 'substantial', such as marriage or a college education. And even after he wins a recording contract, he must constantly fight to maintain some control over his music, 'battle the pressure to hurry up and get it over with so he can be turned into more product or to change it into something more mild'.[13] The informing pattern of the film, then, is that of resistance to any restriction or conformity, with the force of this resistance clearly lodged in Holly's music, that which speaks in an immediate way to his young audience of their dreams and feelings heretofore unarticulated. Holly's music thus comes to represent not just the artist's constant desire for creative freedom, but also the normal human opposition to all life-stifling forces, such as the bigotry, greed and pressure in American culture which the film goes on to depict. It is that defiant posture of life itself which Holly voices in his 'Well All Right', a song which might easily serve as a theme for the entire movie:

> Well all right, well all right,
> We will live and love with all our might.

The film presents all of Holly's music – even the above composition that he sings to two neighbouring children – as a kind of performance or rehearsal for performance. Despite the resulting confinement to stage, practice room or recording studio, though, his playing seems to suggest a transforming energy, as if these physically limited arenas were not

actually images of a larger confinement weighing upon his expressive activity. As the
opening musical sequence demonstrates through the spontaneous response of the kids
at the roller rink, Holly's songs have a power to liberate repressed human energy. His
love ballads and ability to easily 'jam' with his friends also point up a more markedly
expressive function for his music; it can serve as an inspiration to others and a celebration
of human harmony. His successful performance at the Apollo Theater – the first white
group ever to play to its all-black audience – demonstrates this capacity, for his music
evokes harmony from a potentially violent situation, uniting whites and blacks in common response and enjoyment at a time when such harmonious relations were scarce
outside the theatre. While the movie thus seems to promise a tale of music's transformative powers, that promise eventually goes unfulfilled, as the film finally undercuts that
vitality which it has so forcefully and repeatedly demonstrated. Instead of suggesting the
continuing relevance of Holly's music, its ability to transcend his death as a sort of living legacy – which, in fact, it has become – *The Buddy Holly Story* closes on an image of
limitation, emphasised by the freeze-frame ending, as his music is abruptly silenced.

IV

While the principal focus is on dance, a similar conception of expressive limitation
infuses *Saturday Night Fever*. Here, too, the film develops a tension between the world
of song and dance – embodied in the disco nightlife to which the film's protagonist, Tony
Manero (John Travolta), rushes every weekend – and the everyday world of human problems. The bright lights, pulsing music and the measure of respect that Tony finds at the
'2001 Odyssey' disco offer him a temporary escape from his dreary, dead-end job in a
paint store and his quarrelsome family life. Yet as Tony gradually comes to realise, that
disco environment is also something of a prison, for it distracts him from the demands
made by that larger, harsher world which remains just outside the portals of '2001'. In
that real world, the film suggests, natural rhythm and dancing ability count for very little.

The film introduces Tony with a close-up of his feet, as he walks down the street, keeping time to the soundtrack music of 'Stayin' Alive'. Manifestly, he is attuned to some
vital rhythm, yet at the same time he is weighed down, constrained from following those
natural impulses – from pursuing a pretty girl he flirts with – by the demands of his job,
in this case, the petty chore of delivering a can of paint. Yet on his own time those dancing feet freely express Tony's attunement; he hurries to the disco to unleash that energy
kept harnessed during working hours. In that world alone, it seems, he finds the respect
he desires, for as he enters, people acknowledge him; as he passes through the disco,
everyone moves aside; and as he steps onto the dance floor, dance itself is transformed.
One of his friends appropriately dubs Tony 'the king' of the disco, and he is clearly a
sovereign who rules by example. In his dancing, he demonstrates that perfect rhythm
and harmony which the other, rather awkward dancers feel and aspire to, but cannot
quite master. Fittingly, then, when Tony comes to the floor, the random dancing couples
gradually form into lines; their actions become patterned after Tony's motions, almost
as if he were leading a chorus in a traditional musical number. And periodically, perhaps
to illustrate why he holds this leader's position, Tony *performs* alone for the group,

clearing the 'stage' of dancing couples and appropriating the entire dance floor for his expressive activity. When he so performs the camera slowly tracks back, creating a sense of expansion, of growth, as if in his unleashing of that frenetic, dancing energy, Tony managed to transform and expand his world, to create a limitless space with the power of his performance. In this respect at least, the '2001 Odyssey' disco becomes just what its name implies, a true 'Space Odyssey'. However, as the film finally emphasises, it is actually a trip into an imaginary space, a temporally limited excursion on the wings of Tony's performance.

Tony himself has an inkling of these restrictions, for he confesses that he would like to get the same 'high' that the disco affords him 'someplace else', too. So far he has been unsuccessful, and his girlfriend Stephanie (Karen Lynn Gorney) warns that 'you're nowhere on your way to no place'. Apparently the constant repetition of the disco experience, gearing his whole life to that small, hermetic world and its values, is slowly and almost unnoticeably stifling Tony. Life itself is becoming simply a series of performances, many of them solo, and his ability to deal with the real world is suffering.

To underscore Tony's increasing sense of confinement within the disco scene and his Bay Ridge neighbourhood, the film repeatedly invokes the image of the Verrazano Bridge, a literal connector between his limited world and the limitless possibilities which the rest of New York seems to hold out. The movie opens on an aerial shot of the bridge that seems to suggest both a means of access to and escape from that dreary Bay Ridge world. The camera's extreme height and its tracking motion, perpendicular to the bridge, however, undercut that latter notion and suggest just how difficult, if not impossible, any flight would be. Still, for Tony, that bridge apparently symbolises his dream of escape, of liberation from the limitations his environment imposes.[14] With Stephanie, whom he has come to associate with that alluring outside world, Tony sits and admires the wonders of the bridge, telling her that 'I know everything about that bridge'. With his friends he clambers over the bridge supports, defying its dangers. And later he helps Stephanie move her belongings to a new apartment on the other side of the bridge. While he can 'know' it, cavort on its rigging and even physically cross over it, though, Tony can find no easy escape, no new life on the other side.

The bridge finally takes on an ironic character, for it proves to be less an access to another world than a reminder of just how confining Tony's situation remains. His friend Bobby (Barry Miller) dies while climbing on its cables, trying to demonstrate his manhood by defying the dangers it poses. And on the other side of the bridge Tony finds that Stephanie has been living with an older man, that her life outside was not the grand thing he had fantasised. Like the disco, then, which itself offers only a temporary escape from the problems of reality, the Verrazano Bridge promises what it can never deliver. It is a hopeful but ironic image, its promise of escape distracting Tony from awareness of his larger confinement. The bridge thus works to underscore the concentric circles within which Tony lives his life – the disco, his Bay Ridge neighbourhood, all of New York – just different levels of repression that will continue to govern his various 'performances'.

These limitations to the physical movement implied in the opening camera shot, in the incessant dancing and in the image of the bridge are well summed up with the freeze

Saturday Night Fever (1977)

frame that closes the film. In Stephanie's bare and dark apartment, she and Tony are framed together, looking through a background window – another frame confining them – at the light outside. This frame-within-a-frame composition once more underscores their ongoing limitations, locks them into a circumscribed world, but also points our attention to a glimmering hope, that background light on which their eyes focus. While they obviously have not escaped from anything, they have gained some new understanding of themselves and their situation; and whatever measure of hope remains is plainly lodged less in any notion of escape – or the expressiveness of dance – than in their new-found relationship.

Recalling how numbers function in traditional musicals, the key musical scene in the film, the '2001' dance contest, summarises this theme. With Tony and Stephanie matched against the best disco dancers from nearby areas, the narrative emphasises a black and a Hispanic couple, both obviously outsiders and, as even Tony notes, clearly superior dancers. The ensuing dances are emphatically performances geared to a limited arena – the dance floor cordoned off by onlookers, judges and other participants. During their turn on the floor, however, Tony and Stephanie abandon their carefully choreographed and rigorously rehearsed routine for a spontaneous embrace and kiss. As this *true* expression of feeling supersedes the *staged*, even the camera becomes a dancer, twirling about the couple and involving us in their sudden discovery of what they mean to each other. And this transformation of staged expressiveness into sincere expression marks a major shift in Tony's life. Never again will he be able to rely upon the dance to supply the vital impulse in his life. In fact, when Tony sees that the contest has been rigged in favour of the local contestant (himself), when he recognises that, despite his friends' assurances otherwise, he is clearly not 'the greatest', he realises, as Greg Keeler points out, 'that even the dance is vulnerable to the inconsistencies that have been over-shadowing the rest of his life'.[15] The disco floor proves no haven from real world problems, only a gaudy disguise for them. With this expressive awakening, Tony can reject the first place award and come to some terms with his limitations. Being dethroned is no shame, especially as what he desires cannot be found in the disco world. That for-malised expression of dance, he now sees, is only a meagre substitute for the real thing.

Even with its disco trappings, then, *Saturday Night Fever* accomplishes an impressive feat. On the one hand, it acknowledges in its story-line, as well as with its tremendous commercial success, just how important the expressive activity of song and dance remains in the lives of many Americans. Specifically, it graphically demonstrates the importance of particular industrial forces on film. For in its symbiosis between film and the music industry – one wherein the soundtrack of songs by the Bee Gees helped to sell the film, just as the film allowed for the release of what would eventually become one of the top-selling record albums – *Saturday Night Fever* helped to establish the importance of the record 'deal' and soundtrack to the musical film. On the other hand, this film also clearly demonstrates the limitations on expressive activities, showing a need to transcend performance. Just as his brother Frank (Martin Shakar) must leave the priesthood – itself an occupation locked into ritualistic performance – to fulfil his human needs, so, too, must Tony emerge from the confined space of the '2001' to live his life. And even if that life will only be subject to further restrictions, at least he has learned of his limits, of his real needs and of the problems of those around him, and with this knowl-edge he can go on from there. As in many traditional musicals, the music has brought a level of awakening, but the next and most important step is part of no dance. He and Stephanie must together find the terms under which they can survive in a world so little bound to the expressive.

V

A sense of persistence in the musical spirit shows especially strongly in such later films as *Dirty Dancing* and *Footloose*. The latter, particularly, is worth considering in this con-text for the ways in which it repeats some of the same imagery we have already noted and foregrounds the key themes of what I have termed the 'new musical'. For example, just as *Saturday Night Fever* opens with a close-up of Tony's feet, keeping time to the film's theme music, *Footloose* starts with a montage of feet dancing in time to its theme song, 'Footloose'. Those 'loose' feet – physically separated from their bodies by the fram-ing – suggest a vital energy that propels this narrative, even as they point towards the central conflict of the film, the town's efforts to proscribe by law all dance, along with drugs, alcohol and rock'n'roll music, while its teenagers seek a natural outlet for their energies. The subsequent cut, first to a bleak Midwestern landscape, then to the interior of a church where we see the bodies to which those feet belong, completes the sense of disjunction from which the narrative springs. In the church, the Reverend Shaw Moore harangues the teenagers and other townsfolk of Bomont, warning them that God 'is test-ing us . . . every day our Lord is testing us' through 'the demon rock'n'roll music' and its attendant 'easy sexuality and relaxed morality'. With this immediate juxtaposition, the 'words' of one of the town's most powerful institutions have not only replaced the lyrics of the title song and stilled those 'loose' feet, but they have also determined what sort of music and even what sort of company are permissible here, as the scene ends with the injunction to sing hymn 397, 'What a Friend We Have in Jesus'.

While the central figure of this film, Ren McCormack (Kevin Bacon), is no insider like Tony Manero, but rather a recent import from the big city of Chicago, he faces a situation very similar to that of *Saturday Night Fever*'s protagonist. This small Midwestern town seems a dead-end, where teenagers look forward to working in the local mill, as Ren already does after school, farming like his friend Willard, or escaping like Reverend Moore's daughter Ariel (Lori Singer) to some college far away. Even Reverend Moore relates to a group of his parishioners how his colleagues wonder why he lives in such a tiny community – one where dancing is against the law, where the high school English teacher has been fired for teaching controversial material and where books are banned for their potentially subversive content. While there is here, as in *Saturday Night Fever*, an icon of escape – a bridge leading away, across the county line – it seems to signal danger, rather than a possible way out. Thus, Willard confesses that the bridge 'gives me the creeps'; we hear the story of how Ariel's brother, along with several other teens, died on it; and we repeatedly see in the background a 'One Way Bridge' sign, suggesting that, while it might allow people to enter the town, it offers no escape. The forces of restriction – the church, town council, its various prohibitions and even the geography – are obviously in ascendance and forecast little more expressive possibility for this world than Tony Manero faces in his New York neighbourhood.

Yet precisely because he is an outsider from a big city – a situation of which he is repeatedly reminded – Ren is far more aware of his limited situation than Tony and treats it as a challenge. He readily accepts, in a scene lifted from *Rebel without a Cause* (1955), a 'chicken-run' on tractors, he pursues Ariel despite her father's objections, and he determines to push for a senior prom, regardless of the ban on dances. More significantly, his resistance is, in the best musical tradition, in the form of music and dance. When Reverend Moore appears at the local teen hang-out, a drive-in restaurant, he makes his presence immediately felt by turning off a radio playing rock music, in the process seemingly shutting down all the lively activity we have seen there. In counterpoint, when Ren arrives at the high school the next day, he drives up with that same music blaring from his car stereo, effectively announcing his oppositional status. After making a friend of the farmboy Willard, Ren proceeds to teach him to move to rhythm and ultimately to dance (in the final dance scene, Willard even strikes a Tony Manero pose). When he feels frustrated by the closed-minded small town, he retreats to an old factory where he dances out his feelings. Later, when he must fight off the school bully Chuck, Ren does so with dance kicks. And ultimately he crusades for the idea of a school dance, fights the town council to lift its ban and, when it does not, locates a venue just beyond the city line in the mill where he works. The conversion of the mill – an icon of the community's dead-end job prospects – into a privileged arena of music and dance, and of expressive spirit, recalls *The Last Waltz*'s final musical scenes in a warehouse and attests to Ren's own transformative power, a power pointedly lodged in his musical spirit and demonstrated when he, again like Tony Manero, leads the others in dancing, providing them with a model that they all then follow, as if members of his chorus line.

If *Footloose*, particularly in its final dance scene, seems to offer a greater affirmation of the expressive spirit than the other films discussed here, we should recall that it, too, adds a sober dimension to its celebration. Ren's mother, after all, has lost her job because the locals have branded her son as a 'trouble-maker'. The repressive attitude of the townsfolk literally flares up just prior to the dance, as we see a group bringing books out of the library and burning them. And the town council, despite Ren's argument that draws on the Bible for support, has held to its opinion that a dance is 'an enterprise fraught with ... genuine peril', so the ban against such activity remains firmly in place – at least within the city limits. What the film suggests, though, is that while such repressions remain in force, they ultimately cannot stop that spirit. Although a popular English teacher can be fired and books banned, the students come to the abandoned factory and there write their thoughts out freely as graffiti – poems, song lyrics, musings – all part of what they term 'our yearbook'. Despite the ever-watchful eye of her father, Ariel announces that she is 'not a virgin' and comes to recognise that, when he preaches, 'I see the stage; I see costumes. It's show business, isn't it?' And even the Reverend Moore, prodded by his wife and by Ariel's recriminations, recognises the legitimate nature of that expressive spirit and cannot resist going to the site of the dance, looking in and recalling how he and his wife once felt those same emotional stirrings. More than simply a celebration of youthful exuberance, *Footloose* reaches for such recollection, for a sense of how much of that expressive spirit, despite our culture's various repressions, remains in us all.

VI

Certainly, all of the films discussed here seem far removed from the traditional Hollywood musical. But then the 'all talking, all singing, all dancing' movie ill fits the needs of the postmodern era. Yet they also clearly signal the continuing attraction which song and dance hold for us, and, with their industrial extensions in the recording industry, their soundtrack albums, they clearly provide a measure of the power of their music. Furthermore, all of these movies also underscore the fact that the function of music and dancing has radically changed, in film narratives as in the larger culture. While the energy and poetry embodied in the expressive hint at a continuing creative, life-affirming potential that we still seem able to tap, those elements (and hence their power) are pointedly circumscribed in the world these films depict. Therefore, any transformation which song and dance might work on our existence, they suggest, might be seen as a fleeting protest against a general loss of vitality afflicting modern society.

And yet that moment apparently remains worth reaching for, as the existence and box-office success of these films and the sales of their soundtracks attest. Faced with a world where song and dance seem ever out of place with an environment either prosaic or threatening, we go to these movies, or more recent works such as *The Doors* (1991), *Evita* (1996) or *Moulin Rouge* (2001), as one of the few arenas where such expressive activity appears somewhat appropriate and where life can still, for a time, seem harmonious. In this sense, we assist in creating, even finding some pleasure in that very structural tension noted earlier. By reducing them to such spatially and temporally limited screen performances, we help to circumscribe that musical impulse, yet we do so as a form of self-renewal.

Notes

1. Michael Wood, *America in the Movies* (New York: Basic Books, 1975), p. 153.
2. Timothy Scheurer, 'The Aesthetics of Form and Convention in the Movie Musical', *Journal of Popular Film*, vol. 3, no. 3 (Autumn 1974), p. 308.
3. On page 71 of *Beyond Formula: American Film Genres* (New York: Harcourt Brace, 1976), Stanley Solomon also points out that the most common analytical device applied to musicals is the 'distinction between films that integrate the musical numbers and dramatic intervals into a consistent story line and films that make little or no attempt at such integration'.
4. Gene Kelly, 'Some Notes for Young Dancers', in Richard Koszarski (ed.), *Hollywood Directors, 1941–1976* (New York: Oxford University Press, 1977), p. 356.
5. Ibid., p. 356.
6. As the original Warner's advertisement for *42nd Street* claimed, it was supposed to inaugurate 'A New Deal in Entertainment'. See Tony Thomas and Jim Terry, *The Busby Berkeley Book* (New York: A & W Visual Library, 1973), p. 50.
7. Jerome Delameter, 'The Musical', in Stuart Kaminsky, *American Film Genres* (New York: Dell, 1974), p. 162.
8. Wood, *America in the Movies*, p. 147.
9. Delameter, 'The Musical', p. 174.
10. Wood, *America in the Movies*, pp. 163–4.
11. Kelly was often questioned about the numerous dance sequences in his films which 'are so physical they look dangerous'. While acknowledging the dangers as quite real, he holds that the risks helped to achieve a properly realistic effect, as any audience, he said, could 'tell a dancer's body from a stuntman's' and 'the minute you see that it's somebody else in the middle of a dance, the phoniness ruins it'. A sense of the tension between the realistic and the expressive, therefore, implicitly guided Kelly in working out some of the American cinema's most celebrated musical numbers. A failure adequately to address that tension might be seen as a key weakness in *Flashdance*, which assumes that its audience could not 'tell a dancer's body from a stuntman's' – or an actress's. See Kelly's comments in 'Dialogue on Film: Gene Kelly', *American Film*, vol. 4, no. 4 (February 1979), p. 40.
12. Dave Marsh, 'Schlock around the Clock', *Film Comment*, vol. 14, no. 4 (July–August 1978), p. 7.
13. Ibid., p. 9.
14. Greg Keeler in '*Saturday Night Fever*: Crossing the Verrazano Bridge', *Journal of Popular Film and Television*, vol. 7, no. 3 (Fall 1979), p. 158, describes the bridge as 'the main symbol' of the movie, an image both of 'permanence and traditional values' and 'of transition into the future'. I would only add that the bridge is a bit more ambiguous than Keeler makes it out to be, for at times it almost seems to mock Tony with its promise of 'transition'.
15. Ibid., pp. 165–6.

5

Some Smothering Dreams: The Combat Film in Contemporary Hollywood

Michael Hammond

In William Friedkin's recent hit film *Rules of Engagement* (1999), there is a Vietnam sequence which is, in the director's own words, central to the film's narrative. Its purpose is twofold: to show that the character Colonel Terry Childers (Samuel L. Jackson) '... will stop at nothing to save the lives of his marines' and Hays Hodges (Tommy Lee Jones) owes Childers '... a debt for the rest of his life'.[1] In both cases, the debt owed by the film and the characters to the American war in Vietnam is emblematic of the 'debt' that contemporary Hollywood war films owe to that war's narrative inconclusiveness, its blurring of boundaries between good and evil, right and wrong, left and right. This article explores the importance of this 'debt' in considering the continuing evolution of the combat film in contemporary Hollywood.

Rules of Engagement relates a fictitious event at the US embassy in Yemen, where a US marine rapid deployment force, after rescuing the ambassador and his family, opens fire on a crowd of Yemeni demonstrators, killing sixty-three, wounding a hundred others and creating an international incident which threatens to destabilise the whole of the Middle East. The leader of the marines is Colonel Childers, who has, in the Vietnam sequence that opens the film, shown his ability to act ruthlessly by executing a North Vietnamese radio operator to persuade their commander, Colonel Cao (Baoan Coleman), to pull off the men who have ambushed his friend's squad and are annihilating his force. Colonel Cao does so only when Childers puts the gun to his head. This is presented as a memory for Hodges on the night of his retirement party thirty years later. After the event at the US embassy, Childers is put on trial for murdering civilians and is defended by Hodges, his friend. The trial is effectively an exposition of the moral dilemma entailed in fighting a guerilla force that is making strategic use of innocent civilians.

William Friedkin states in his commentary on the DVD that he worked very hard to bring ambiguity to the film so that the audience becomes the jury. However, he states that the 'ultimate jury' was the audience in the test screenings. 'I personally don't believe what he did was right – I too am caught up in the need to vindicate this man ... I believe the jury would have found him guilty on all three accounts ...' However, Friedkin reports that the test screenings revealed a 'movie transformation' enacted by

Rules of Engagement (1999): haunted by the iconography and imagery of Vietnam

the audience. 'What mitigates against his terrible behaviour is the fact that Sam Jackson is playing the part.' The audience did not want to convict Jackson. Friedkin also commented that: 'If I had made this film in the '70s I might have been able to end the film on a more ambigous note ... I would not have offered them as much closure ...' The film ends with credits which state what happened to the main players after the film's end. Friedkin stated, 'I didn't want to but which I had to do [*sic*] – because that's what the audience demanded.'

The story of the film and its reception in the test screenings and the comments of the director expose the main points I wish to make about the combat film in contemporary Hollywood. Friedkin's comments and the narrative of *Rules of Engagement* help to contextualise the shifts and changes that the combat film has undergone since the early 1970s. The first point lies in Friedkin's suggestion that the 1970s was a time when audiences would tolerate, and film-makers could make, films with ambiguous endings. To what extent have things changed since then? Second, *Rules of Engagement* mixes actual history with fictional and speculative 'history'. It possesses a sombre undertone in its evocation of the Vietnam combat experience. Related to this are expectations of realism provoked by the war film generally and the combat film specifically. From its beginnings in the late nineteenth century, cinema has created expectations of the possibility of accurately visualising war, warfare and combat. The depiction of violence in contemporary Hollywood, from *The Wild Bunch* (1969) to *Saving Private Ryan* (1998), is part of an aesthetic history in which the war film has often been involved. Sophisticated special effects and in particular the use of squibs, slow motion and sound have played an important part in the drive to depict the physical impact of bullets, shrapnel and explosions on the human body and thus in contemporary American cinema more generally. Third, the use in *Rules of Engagement* of the characters' memories of an ambush in Vietnam to establish character motivation is just one example of the extent to which the trauma of the memory of the Vietnam War has impacted on Hollywood film texts more generally during the course of the past thirty years. By realistically depicting the horror of a fire-fight, it is considered possible to put the audience through a traumatic experience in ways which clarify the motivations of the characters. Chris (Charlie Sheen) in *Platoon* (1986) and Captain Miller (Tom Hanks) in *Saving Private Ryan* behave the way they do because of the violence they have undergone along with the audience. Meanwhile, the intensity of the bond that links Colonel Childers and Colonel Hodges central to the narrative of *Rules of Engagement* depends upon the depiction of the horror and confusion of the combat situation they undergo together. With a few notable exceptions, if one thing characterises combat films in the New Hollywood however, it is, not only the memory of the issues it raised, but also the belief (on the part of some film-makers) and expectation (on the part of some critics) that these films are somehow able to resolve those issues and/or somehow redeem the nation. Friedkin's statement that the salute between Childers and the North Vietnamese Lieutenant Colonel Cao 'was our attempt to bring some sort of closure to the Vietnam War'[2] is only a recent example in a long line of war films that have tried to do this.

Double coding in the 1970s

Discussion of the influence of the war in Vietnam on the war film in the 1970s should probably begin, as many critics do, with John Wayne's *The Green Berets* (1968). However, *The Dirty Dozen* (1967) should certainly be mentioned as well. Both were financial successes and both attracted criticism. The Robert Aldrich film is notable for its violence and brutality at the moment when the new ratings system replaced the old Production Code. The film acts as an important precursor to *Bonnie and Clyde* (1967), and later *The Wild Bunch*, of the new, violent tone the new system would foster. *The Green Berets*, on the other hand, was a fairly traditional war film set in Vietnam and called attention to the limits of the genre, and indeed the dated nature of the Production Code guidelines in the late 1960s, as much as it outraged most contemporary film critics. It thus exemplified and presaged divisions in critical and generic expectations of the war film in the Vietnam era. There were concerns on the one hand with violence (underpinned by the representations of the war on television news programmes: to what extent could or should war films be 'realistic'?). On the other hand, political divisions were brought into focus by the virulent anti-Communist rhetoric of *The Green Berets*.[3]

The crisis generated by the war, together with changes undergone by Hollywood itself, meant, as is well known, that Vietnam War films were few and far between during most of the 1970s. However, its influence was felt on films as diverse as *M*A*S*H* (1970) and *American Graffitti* (1973), and, as Thomas Elsaesser has argued, on a whole series of contemplative, even downbeat, movies that managed to avoid what he calls the 'affirmative-consequential model' of the traditional Hollywood film.[4] In this context, *The Boys in Company C* (1977), *Go Tell the Spartans* (1978), *The Deer Hunter* (1978) and *Apocalypse Now* (1979) can all be viewed as films which, at the end of the decade, were on the one hand to retain a sceptical attitude to the model and to the war, while on the other seeking to find new ways of representing the war and the issues it raised.

The Deer Hunter sought to provide absolution through the depiction of the sacrifice of a local community. *Apocalypse Now* sought aesthetic solutions which spun off from the narrative openness of the war itself and from the madness of US political and military strategy. In doing so, it provided the Vietnam War, and many subsequent Vietnam War films, with a visual and aural aesthetic; helicopters, napalm and the popular music soundtrack. Moreover, both films contain atrocity scenes which were to become central to Vietnam War films in the mid-1980s. The scene of the massacre of the Vietnamese family on the boat clearly resonates with most of the later films. In its depiction of the Russian roulette games, the atrocity in *The Deer Hunter* is represented obliquely (although it should be borne in mind that as a metaphor for random death, Russian roulette is repeatedly used by soldier-authors in the steady flow of novels and autobiographical accounts of the war that began in the late 1970s).[5] Central to its ideological work is the fact that these games (and the atrocities that they represent) are perpetrated by the Vietnamese. Meanwhile, as Nicky (Christopher Walken) stays in South Vietnam after the war and rejects the possibility of ever coming home, issues of redemption and survivor guilt, issues dealt with also in later films, are clearly raised. These films utilised and reworked the generic conventions of the combat films of the late 1940s and 1950s. However, they did so with significant modifications and crucially acknowledged, at least tacitly, the defeat in Vietnam, using it as the setting for meditiations on futility, duty and sacrifice.

Celluloid redemption

While Michael Cimino's film garnered academy awards and enjoyed popular success as well, *Apocalypse Now* received mixed reviews and smaller domestic rental figures than were initially hoped by United Artists. Both films also indicated that the Vietnam War film brought with it a weight of audience and critical expectation that was insurmountable. What was expected was no less than the redemptive resolution of a war that had undermined the certainties of the classical Hollywood war film and American exceptionalism generally. These dreams of redemption were however, played out in the revenge fantasy 'Missing in Action' (MIA) films, such as *Uncommon Valor* (1983), *Rambo: First Blood Part II* (1985) and the Chuck Norris *Missing in Action* series. Along with *Red Dawn* (1984), *Top Gun* (1986), *Heartbreak Ridge* (1986) and others, these films are characterised by Stephen Prince as 'New Cold War Films'.[6] As such they are distinct from 'Rebellion and Rebel' films such as *Salvador* (1986), but also from the Vietnam War cycle that emerged in the wake of *Platoon* and that included *Hamburger Hill* (1987), *Full Metal Jacket* (1987) and *84 Charlie Mopic* (1989).

Rambo, as Yvonne Tasker points out, 'has been repeatedly used to define the quality of other Vietnam movies, broadly along the lines of opposition between realism and comic-book fantasy . . .'[7] However fantastic their resolution of the traumas of Vietnam, the MIA cycle of films were able to attract audiences around two issues: the first was the well-publicised attempts to determine the existence and return of soldiers missing in action, but still held by the Vietnamese; the second was the adoption by the films' protagonists of the type of guerilla tactics that had been used so effectively against the US forces. The MIA films were able to utilise the uncontentious issue of the return of US soldiers from overseas to construct melodramatic enemies and action spectacles. *First*

Blood, the first film to feature the Rambo character, was pivotal in the sense that it depicted a character who used the tactics of the North Vietnamese. In adopting these tactics in a small US town, he was literally bringing the war home.[8] However, the Rambo of *First Blood* can perhaps also be seen as an important precursor to the later Vietnam combat cycle in that he 'does to' the local sheriffs what the realist aesthetic, so crucial not just to the Vietnam combat cycle but also to later films such as *Saving Private Ryan*, seeks to do to the audience.

First Blood, like *Platoon* and to a lesser extent *Hamburger Hill,* depicts the guerilla warfare that the Vietnam veterans had fought. This included the setting out of ambushes, the danger of being ambushed by a resilient and determined, often unseen, enemy and the feelings of frustration that resulted in the killing of unarmed men, women and children. Tim O'Brien's description of the effect of this type of war on the foot soldier could also describe the desired affect of the realist aesthetic in these films:

> You hallucinate. You look ahead a few paces and wonder what your legs will resemble if there is more to the earth in that spot than silicates and nitrogen. Will the pain be unbearable? Will you scream or fall silent? Will you be afraid to look at your own body, afraid of the sight of your own red flesh and white bone? You wonder if your friends will weep.[9]

Thomas Elsaesser has linked this aesthetic not to realism, but to the horror film:

> ... the jungle becomes the epitome of the horrible not because reluctant G.I. conscripts face a determined and ruthless enemy. Instead, it is because the films draw on the familiar horror trope of the 'monster in the swamp – nowhere to be seen but when heard, effective action comes too late – that they succeed so well in 'rendering' the bodily sensations of danger in the face of the Vietcong.[10]

Either way, *Platoon*'s effectiveness in terms of its contemporary reception had to do with the cinematic construction of the soldier's point of view and with the affect of fear described by Tim O'Brien. David Halberstam remembered his first viewing of *Platoon* by describing the affect of the initial ambush scene in similar, visceral terms:

> There is an eerie truth to the scene: the terrain itself is lush and therefore terrifying, the NVA soldiers move with a lethal professionalism on soil far more familiar to them than to Americans. The Americans seem utterly immobilised even as the North Vietnamese are right on top of them. It is the moment that anyone who ever went to Vietnam feared the most, and it seems unlikely that anyone will get out of this moment alive, including, because of the power of Stone's direction, those of us in the theater.[11]

In addition to being a part of the general stylistic trend of visceral cinema, this has a narrative function that is also reminiscent of the horror film in that it builds towards the moment of revenge. The narrative function of constructing a terrifying unseen enemy in *Platoon*, and in other Vietnam films, is to build towards a scene of atrocity. In this way

Platoon confronts the audience with an impossible choice. Alexander Walker's review of the film seems to illustrate this:

> Simply as a study of battlefield behaviourism, it's vivid and awesome and awful. A body that's just had both arms blown off staggers around on its remaining limbs in unimaginable agony; a Vietnam village nearly goes crazy with panic as an American platoon works itself up to massacre fever.[12]

The accumulation of stomach-wrenching fear leads to the atrocity scene in the village. Walker's description does not emphasise the atrocity itself, but the film clearly calls up the memory of the My Lai massacre. This memory informs and reinforces the narrative energy provoked by the hallucinatory realism of the ambush scene and the booby-trap scene that Walker refers to. What may make this film emblematic of the combat film in contemporary Hollywood is precisely this invocation of a doubly inscribed memory: that of veterans remembering real events on the one hand (David Halberstam recalls that the audience he watched it with in New York City were mainly middle-aged males, recognisably veterans),[13] on the other that of any spectator remembering traumatic scenes of combat depicted earlier in the narrative.

Platoon was released in December 1986. Important literary antecedents included Tim O'Brien's *If I Should Die in a Combat Zone* (1973), Phillip Caputo's *A Rumor of War* (1977) and Larry Heineman's *Close Quarters* (1977), all of which contain atrocity stories. Along with these novels, PBS broadcast *Vietnam: A Television History* in 1983. The combination of the novels and the televisual images have confirmed Paul Fussell's observation regarding '. . . the virtual disappearance during the sixties and seventies of the concept of prohibitive obscenity, a concept which has acted as a censor on earlier memories of 'war'.[14] The double coding trend in the New Hollywood acts in a similar way to 'authentic realistic' war films in the past.[15] They are, more or less, educational, intended to inform an ignorant (innocent?) audience about the crucible of war, an experience that has rendered the participants silent, but which is 'spoken' on their behalf by the films. Kevin Bowen, a veteran, encapsulates this in his summation of *Platoon*: 'The crushing emotional weight of the film attempts to diminish the distance between the veteran and the non-veteran for a time. This is the greatest strength of *Platoon* but also a potential limitation.'[16] The limitation is that 'there is more to know'. For Bowen, who writes about *Platoon*'s ability to evoke the visceral emotions associated with the combat experience in Vietnam, the film's affect is a beginning: '. . . the evocation of the conflicting emotions that surround the trauma of loss must move forward toward other articulations'.[17] These include the social inequities implied by the film's representation of social relations of class and ethnicity; 'Stone's film frees us from Vietnam for the first time so that we may speak of what truly ails us . . .' Bowen's hope for cinema, and the emotionally authentic combat film, as a means of social enlightenment and emotional therapy may be misplaced. The resilience of the tropes of the Vietnam veteran and the memory of Vietnam as a national, social and psychological trauma are more redolent, perhaps, of the hysteria of repetition than they are of effective therapy.

There are parallels in this hope for the cinema implicit in the criticisms of *Platoon*. These often revolved around Chris's words: 'We were at war with ourselves.' Vincent Canby wrote of this as the weakest part of the film: 'Chris is idealised but without sentimentality. Part of him remains unknown and private, at least until the final minutes of the film, when Mr. Stone unfortunately feels called upon to have Chris say what has been far more effectively left unsaid.'[18] Such criticisms reveal the weight of expectation attached to the war film in the 1980s and 1990s. Meanwhile, *Platoon* itself was able to achieve two things: first, to render the experience of the war in a manner endorsed by veterans and to use it to generate empathy and revulsion in its atrocity scene; second, to place the issues, or the memory of the issues, of the war back on the agenda of public discussion. The first evinced a catharsis which rendered the final monologue in the film necessary, perhaps, after all; the second brought the old issues into focus as a consensus rallying point in a factionalised cultural landscape in which the dichotomies of the 1960s and 1970s – liberalism and conservatism, doves and hawks – had given way to single-interest groups and the rise of an activist radical right. In this sense, the traditional generic convention that the ethnic and class heterogeneity of the combat unit represents the melting pot of America bonded together in conflict acted not so much as an assimilation structure, but as a nostalgic, if painful, distraction.

'Immersion Cinema': baptisms of fire in the 1990s

> Seeing warfare as theatre provides a psychic escape for the participant: with a sufficient sense of theatre, he can perform his duties without implicating his real self and without impairing his innermost conviction that the world is still a rational place.[19]

Paul Fussell is trying here to convey the sense of unreality, the performative impulse, to which soldiers resort in order to endure the experience of combat. Writing about the nature of heroism in contemporary Hollywood, William Goldman uses the eyewitness accounts of military experts to make the point that '... what is genuinely heroic in life may not work for film'. He points out that often heroics in real life are either unimpressive on film or they are '... what Sylvester Stallone does in an action picture before the credits start to roll':

> In *Adventures in the Screen Trade* I wrote about trying to translate to film what many military experts feel was the single most heroic action of the entire war [World War II]. It involved a river crossing. ... what the experts were talking about as incredibly brave was not the soldiers who made the first crossing – the normal group glorified in a movie – it was the next wave of soldiers, the ones who saw the first group get slaughtered, who knew they were mostly going to die, and who made the second crossing anyway.[20]

Fussell and Goldman are talking about two seemingly different phenomenon: one an internal psychic protective mechanism and the other an event which violently compromised that mechanism. However, both position the soldiers as an audience or spectators.

Fussell's soldier in real combat composes a theatrical frame, an important de-realisation process which allows the soldier to suspend belief. The military experts provide Goldman with an audience of soldiers, the second wave, which they describe as the bravest because they witnessed the 'theatre' in which they would soon 'perform'. These experts are calling attention to the bravery of this second wave insofar as their suspension of belief has been severely tested. They have seen what awaits them and have gone ahead. Goldman's purpose is to explain modern cinema audience expectations to the budding scriptwriter. Hence the second wave of soldiers are in the same position as the audience for the combat film. The intention and expectation are that the audience will be encouraged, through visual and aural effects, to adopt the same position as the second wave and thereby adopt to a greater or lesser degree the protective psychic mechanism that Fussell describes.

This is a significant development in the cycle of combat films during the late 1990s. It is represented most distinctly by *Saving Private Ryan* and *The Thin Red Line* (1998). If *Platoon*'s rhetorical structure depended upon the cinematic construction of the experience of combat by drawing on the techniques of the horror film, the hit combat film of the 1990s, *Saving Private Ryan*, depends on state-of-the-art technologies, filmic and pro-filmic, developed by the likes of Industrial Light and Magic, and Skywalker Sound. These played a significant part in the high-impact, visceral cinema that has been such a hallmark of recent Hollywood cinema. In her analysis of *Jurassic Park* (1993), Constance Balides describes this cinema as a 'cinema of immersion', a form of cinema in which, through the '... framing strategies and point-of-view shots used in some of the film's movie-ride scenes, spectators are invited to experience ephemeral effects as if they were inside diegetic events'.[21]

Balides notes the extent to which *Jurassic Park* addresses its spectators as 'economic subjects'. She notes that its project is in this sense 'hypervisible, not hidden – its own economics out there, on the surface and celebrating commercial success'.[22] She points to numerous instances where consumerism is displayed, celebrated and critiqued. She argues that, while the critiques of consumerism are bound up in the investigative narrative, this narrative ultimately resolves the ethical, political and ecological problems through conservative notions of a reconstituted family.[23]

If *Jurassic Park* addresses an audience of 'worker/consumers' invested in the 'lustre of capital', *Saving Private Ryan* addresses its audience as 'survivors/consumers' plunged into the carnage of history – albeit with the caveat that the images are double coded in the narrative, as well as in the faded colours of the image, as a memory and as memorial. In that sense it, too, is explicit in this address to both the generation who lived through the war and to their children and grandchildren. (The film ends and begins with the older Ryan [Harrison Young] visiting the Normandy cemetery with his wife, children and grandchildren.) Its project is explicit: it is a celluloid memorial. Insofar as this is the case, Spielberg confronts the ideological function of traditional war memorials by exposing the carnage, confusion and tragedy of combat, normally subsumed under the iconography of remembrance and sacrifice through his commitment to a cinema of immersion.

So effective were the battle sequences that critics consistently referred to the film as having two parts, the gut-wrenching D-Day landing sequence (which is often erroneously referred to as the opening of the film) and the 'conventional' war melodrama of the rest of the film.[24] Balides' observations about *Jurassic Park* are appropriate to *Saving Private Ryan* and, of course, *Schindler's List* (1993), in that these films' simulation gave rise to a highly visible, public 'locus of debate'. *Saving Private Ryan*'s reception was marked by the comments of veterans who testified to the veracity of the war sequences. Historian Stephen Ambrose endorsed the film and Spielberg himself recounts his meeting with veterans while preparing the production. They asked him if he were finally going to tell the story of 'their war' and not Hollywood's war.[25]

Times Literary Supplement critic Ben Shephard highlighted the legacy of the war in Vietnam with its reconsideration of the soldier's individual experience and the ironies implicit in being caught up in a directionless conflict at the mercy of an indifferent and dishonest leadership. 'In this new climate, the memories of Second World War soldiers – especially front-line infantrymen – take on an almost priestly authority.'[26] While this can be seen as sidestepping the continuing public history trauma represented by Vietnam, it may also be seen as a means of attempting to establish an equivalence between the veterans of World War II and those of the Vietnam War as part of the memory-work of recuperating and recording their experience.

The impact of the Vietnam experience on the contemporary war film generally, and *Saving Private Ryan* specifically, can be noted in the lack of emphasis placed on the enemy as the agent responsible for the conflict. The middle section of the Spielberg film may be construed as not only a B-movie plot in its deployment of all of the conventions of the 1950s combat film, but also as a Vietnam platoon film the mission of which does not make sense to those involved on the ground. FUBAR (Fucked Up Beyond All Recognition) is a World War II term that is held in place (in war films, if not in war literature) by the ultimate righteousness of the fight against fascism. However, in Willard's search for Kurtz in *Apocalypse Now*, where the background setting is Vietnam, this becomes 'the horror'. Spielberg himself has commented on the legacy of Vietnam for contemporary Hollywood audiences and, by association, the combat film: 'Without Vietnam I never could have made *Ryan* as honestly as I did because Vietnam sort of showed everybody, and sort of prepared audiences to accept war for what it was, not war as an excuse to romanticise an event.'[27]

Early in James Jones's novel *The Thin Red Line*, the soldiers witness from the shore the bombing of their transport ship. As they witness the dead and wounded being brought ashore, the narrator comments as follows:

> They [the wounded] had been initiated into a strange, insane, twilight fraternity where explanation would be forever impossible. Everybody understood this; as did they themselves, dimly. It did not need to be mentioned. Everyone was sorry, and so were they themselves. But there was nothing to be done about it. Tenderness was all that could be given and, like most self-labelled human emotions, it meant nothing when put alongside the intensity of their experience.[28]

This experience and its sense of these men having 'crossed a line' articulates the kind of experiential distance that exists between the cinema audience and the events on the screen. This gap is the subject of both *Saving Private Ryan* and *The Thin Red Line*, but the film-makers address it from opposite directions. Spielberg brings his considerable skill as an action film-maker to bear on the battle scenes in seeking to bridge the gap, to encourage the audience to empathise *with* the soldiers. He does this by not allowing the audience to turn from the screen, creating a kind of 'cinema of unpleasure'. On the other hand, Terrence Malick's film works always to turn away and thereby to evoke sympathy *for* the characters. It does this on a number of levels and in a number of different ways: in its refusal to focus on a single figure, with the camera consistently moving between a number of different soldiers, it articulates the structures of power under which they labour; in working through voice-overs and point-of-view flashbacks it constructs their interiority in such a way as to move between reality, fantasy and memory. He privileges only two characters with memories; Private Bell (Ben Chaplin), whose mind, particularly in situations of stress, runs back to moments with his wife Marty (Miranda Otto), and Private Witt (James Caviezel), who first remembers his mother's death, then recalls the Malanese village where he had been AWOL at the beginning of the film. Two other significant characters, Captain Staros (Elias Koteas) and Colonel Tall (Nick Nolte) are granted voice-overs, but more importantly they act out a power struggle across the chain of military command. On the eve of the battle Staros prays that he does not betray his men. The result of this shifting emphasis seems a polar opposite to Spielberg's concern with identifying, and creating empathy with, Miller and Ryan (Matt Damon). *The Thin Red Line* seems to drift towards the character of Witt, who has found a kind of absolution in the juxtaposition of his memories, his sense of duty, and the carnage and the natural beauty that surrounds him. He responds with a look of serenity and wonder when Sergeant Welsh (Sean Penn) says to him, 'What difference can one man make in all this madness?'

Witt's characterisation echoes the narration of the film itself as it alternates between the lush flora and fauna of the island and its destruction by the intrusion of warring modern armies. This alternation calls up the kind of ironic juxtapositions incorporated by the Great War poets and the observations that Paul Fussell has made: 'It signals a constant reaching out towards traditional significance ... [and] reveals an attempt to make sense of the war in relation to inherited tradition.'[29] Malick is reported to have worked with his actors in such a way which suggests similar appeals to literary tradition: 'Malick relies on associations when directing actors. He shows them paintings, old photographs, plays them music (he ran the soundtrack to *Where Eagles Dare* at the first reading). He talks in metaphors, makes literary references.'[30]

In both cases, these epic war films draw explicitly on pre-existing traditions to frame the depiction of combat. Where Malick draws on literary tradition and metaphor, Spielberg draws on the tradition of the Hollywood war film. Both, however, are working towards a meditation on the experience of combat through mythical sense-making which contrasts sharply with the laconic denial of meaning implicit in not only the poetry and literature of World War II and the Vietnam War, but also the films of the early 1970s such as *M*A*S*H* and *Catch 22* (1970) and, particularly, the combat films of Sam Fuller such as *The Steel Helmet* (1951) and *The Big Red One* (1980). Like Fuller, they redirect the narrative focus from the national narrative to the individual, yet Fuller's films depict characters which are cynical and are born of the extreme circumstances in which they find themselves. As they both appear out of the fog, one cannot imagine the life of Zack in *Steel Helmet* or the Sergeant in *The Big Red One* outside the war. In contrast, the characters in both *The Thin Red Line* and *Saving Private Ryan* are constantly referring to their lives outside the war. Spielberg references Fuller in two ways, first by depicting the horror of war in a way Fuller refused to do and, second, by depicting his characters' responses to those extreme circumstances.[31] In an interview in 1963, Fuller talked of his plans for a book which ultimately became *The Big Red One*: 'I'm going to tell a story of war without too much action, with a lot of humour, feeling and a total exposé of the deceit which I think exists in war-time.'[32] This exposure did not, however, entail or include scenes of explicit carnage. On the other hand, Spielberg places his story of the salvation of Miller within a scenario that could be from a Fuller film. In their search for Ryan, they come across a machine-gun nest which they could either pass by or attack. Miller, as perhaps Zack in *The Steel Helmet* or the Sergeant in *The Big Red One* would, decides that they have no choice but to attack it and this results in the death of their medic. The bitterness and rage of the men is vented on the one German, Steamboat Willie, whom they have captured alive. The predominant theme of Fuller's film is the border between killing and murder. (The film opens with the killing of a German soldier after the armistice has been signed and ends with the Sergeant, having stabbed his German counterpart after the surrender, working frantically to save his life to achieve a kind of redemption.) Spielberg and Malick both dare to show the killing of prisoners, a dilemma which Fuller avoids. Crucially, Captain Miller lets the prisoner go and stops the ensuing argument between the men by calling attention to a pool they have running on who can guess what Miller did before he was called up. This direct link between the characters' lives at home and war lies at the centre of the absolution that Ryan seeks and that Witt represents.

Conclusion: smothering dreams

Both *The Thin Red Line* and *Saving Private Ryan* are special cases. They are prestige projects the green light for which was made possible only through the reputation of the film-makers themselves. There are few, if any, combat films in the 1990s which have the underlying melancholy that they possess. More often in the 1990s, combat films embody the principles of what Justin Wyatt has called 'high concept'.[33] *Three Kings* (1999) is a heist film which takes place during the Gulf War. *Courage under Fire* (1995), another Gulf War film, spins its narrative around the issues of women in the military and instances of 'friendly fire'. Yet these, like *Rules of Engagement*, are haunted by the iconography and imagery of the American war in Vietnam. Archie Gates (George Clooney) leads the heist, but undergoes a transformation from mercenary intent to altruism. The film culminates at the moment at which he decides to help the Iraqi people. This is sparked by the murder of the mother of a little girl. The Iraqi soldier shoots her in the side of the head and the imagery is a direct quote from the television footage of the murder of a Vietcong suspect by a South Vietnamese colonel at the height of the Tet offensive. This is the moment, the plot point, at which Gates decides to rescue the people of the village rather than leave them behind. This image is only one of many that are part of director David O. Russell's idea of layering 'textures' into his film. His aim, as he put it, was to 'take a basic action/adventure motor and put layers and layers of texture on top of it'.[34] He researched the Gulf War and tried to achieve the look of it by bleaching the film stock so that it looked like the 'colour photos in the *LA Times*'. He also used special effects to show the damage caused by a bullet as it enters the human body. Other textures include the rapid-fire ironies of patriotism (the Lee Greenwood song 'Proud To Be an American' sung by drunk American soldiers), the conflation of consumer culture and contemporary warfare (cell phones, computers and televisions are stacked in the bunkers alongside the gold bullion), and the moral relativism of the news media (the lament by presenter Nora Dunn (Adriana Cruz) veers between pathos and irony when she sees the ecological damage, cries and then says 'This story has been so done.'). These touches Russell attributes to 'Steve Ross tradition at Warners ... [which] gives talent a lot of room.' He also adds that the coda of the lives of the main characters was put in not simply to show that their 'lives were now worth living', but also, like the coda in *Rules of Engagement*, in order 'to reach the audience'.

Courage under Fire utilises a similar structure to *Rules of Engagement* in that it is an investigative narrative dependent upon the memory of witnesses in terms of exonerating or condemning the characters' behaviour. In both cases, crucially, the normally all-seeing technologies of the media and the military are rendered useless. The character Nathaniel Serling (Denzel Washington) has, through mistaken identification, fired on his best friend's tank and killed him. Haunted by this, he is asked to authenticate the action of Karen Walden (Meg Ryan) in order for her to be posthumously awarded the Medal of Honor. Prevented from telling the truth about his own action, he becomes obsessed with finding out the truth about hers. Serling's investigation is hounded by a journalist (Scott Glenn) who is on the verge of uncovering the friendly fire incident and is also a Vietnam veteran. Serling pieces together Karen Walden's story from the differing accounts of the men who were under her and finally uncovers the truth from the medic, Ilario (Matt Damon). Surrounded by stories, the ones he hears and the ones he has to tell, Serling finally absolves the guilt of the crew members who had crumbled under the stress of the situation and covered up for the fact that one of them had accidentally shot her and that they were all responsible for leaving her behind. At the same time, he is absolved when a tape recording reveals that, after the initial mistake of killing his friend, he had recovered and given the order which saved the lives of the rest of his command. As in *Rules,* the investigation ultimately lies in the witness of the chaos of combat and what can be termed a 'primary scene'. The project of the narrative is to have the characters bear witness to this scene, thereby providing access for the audience.

These narratives, which revolve around the crucible of combat as originary moment, are of course open to analyses which highlight the centrality of patriarchal discourse. Much of the work on the combat film in contemporary Hollywood has taken this approach. However, the tendency towards an emphasis on spectacular visceral affect has, as I have argued, played an important part in the development of the generic conventions of the combat film, which demands more attention. What seems to happen in the serious combat film in contemporary Hollywood is that a series of intertextual associations are produced that slip out of the purview of the confines of the narrative and reveal a 'political unconscious'. This is more or less explicit in the scripts and the intentions of the industry, whether it is Spielberg's stated intention of memorialising 'what they did for us'[35] or Friedkin's attempt to bring 'closure' to the Vietnam War. Central to this tendency towards affect is its place in a melodramatic representational and narrative paradigm centred on catharsis. In that sense, the contemporary Hollywood cinema continues in the longer search for the realistic depiction of combat, an industrial and social 'dream' which holds that such depictions are necessary and desirable. These dreams of un-pleasure recall the 'smothering dream' Wilfred Owen wished upon his readers, hoping for a catharsis so that they '. . . would not tell with such high zest to children ardent for some desperate glory'.[36] It is an old dream and an old hope.

Notes

I am grateful to Steve Neale, Peter Stanfield and Mark Kermode for their advice and comments while researching this article.

1. This is taken from the director's commentary on the DVD version of the film.
2. Ibid.
3. David Cook, 'Ballistic Balletics: Styles of Violent Representation in the *Wild Bunch* and After', in Stephen Prince (ed.), *Sam Peckinpah's* The Wild Bunch (Cambridge: Cambridge University Press, 1999), pp. 130–54. Cook cites Jack Valenti's comment that 'When so many movie critics complain about violence on film, I don't think they realize the impact of thirty minutes on the Huntley-Brinkley newscast – and that's real violence.'
4. Thomas Elsaesser, 'The Pathos of Failure: American Films in the 1970s – Notes on the Unmotivated Hero', *Monogram*, 6 (1975).
5. Toby Herzog, *Vietnam War Stories: Innocence Lost* (London: Routledge, 1992). Herzog notes that James Webb, the soldier-author of *Fields of Fire* (Ingelwood Cliffs, NJ: Prentice Hall, 1978), uses the metaphor in a passage: 'I get the feeling this is kind of like Russian roulette . . . just as senseless.' Webb also wrote the original script for *Rules of Engagement*, another film upon which the ultimate fate of the soldiers depends on a game of chance . . . the flip of a coin.
6. Stephen Prince, *A New Pot of Gold: Hollywood under the Electronic Rainbow, 1980–1989* (New York: Scribners, 2000), p. 316.
7. Yvonne Tasker, *Spectacular Bodies: Gender, Genre and the Action Picture* (London: Routledge, 1993) pp. 93–4.
8. Prince, *A New Pot of Gold*, p. 332.
9. Tim O'Brien, *If I Die in a Combat Zone* (1973, reprint London: Flamingo, 1995) p. 126.
10. Thomas Elsaesser, 'Francis Ford Coppola and *Bram Stoker's Dracula*', in Steve Neale and Murray Smith (eds), *Contemporary Hollywood Cinema* (London: Routledge, 1998). See also

Thomas Elsaesser and Michael Weden, 'The Hollow Heart of Hollywood: Sound Space in *Apocalypse Now*', in Gene Moore (ed.), *Conrad on Film* (Oxford: Oxford University Press, 1997).

11. David Halberstam, '*Platoon*', in Robert Brent Toplin (ed.), *Oliver Stone's USA: Film, History, and Controversy* (Lawrence: University of Kansas Press, 2000), p. 111.

12. Alexander Walker, 'Overwrought and Over Here', *Daily Mail*, 23 April 1987, p. 28.

13. Halberstam, '*Platoon*', p. 110.

14. Paul Fussell, *The Great War and Modern Memory* (New York: Oxford University Press, 1975).

15. I am thinking here of the double intention of war films to educate and to entertain such as *The Longest Day* (1962) and *Midway* (1976), but also the propaganda films of World War I and World War II.

16. Kevin Bowen, 'Strange Hells: Hollywood in Search of America's Lost War', in Linda Dittmar and Gene Michaud (eds), *From Hanoi to Hollywood: The Vietnam War in American Film* (New York: Rutgers University Press, 1990), p. 234.

17. Ibid.

18. Alexander Walker, 'Over Wrought and Over Here', p. 28.

19. Fussell, *The Great War and Modern Memory*, p. 192.

20. William Goldman, *Which Lie Did I Tell?: More Adventures in the Screen Trade* (London: Bloomsbury, 2000) p. 83.

21. Constance Balides, 'Jurassic Post-Fordism: Tall Tales of Economics in the Theme Park', *Screen*, vol. 41, no. 2, Summer 2000, p. 153.

22. Ibid., p. 160.

23. Ibid., p. 157.

24. To mention only one Samuel Hynes, soldier and historian compared the film to Terence Malick's *The Thin Red Line*: 'My vote, if I had one would go to Malick … In my view *Private Ryan* is 25 minutes of virtual D-Day and the invasion of Europe followed by a conventional special-unit story, a war movie made out of war movies with only high-tech spectacles at the beginning and end to distinguish it.' '*The Thin Red Line*', *The New Statesman*, 26 February 1999, p. 42.

25. *War Stories: Mark Cousins Talks to Steven Spielberg*, BBC2 documentary, broadcast 13 September 1998.

26. Ben Shephard, '"The Doughboy" D-Day: Steven Spielberg, Saving Private Ryan', *Times Literary Supplement*, 18 April 1998, p. 23.

27. *War Stories*, BBC2.

28. James Jones, *The Thin Red Line* (1962, reprint London: Hodder and Stoughton, 1998) p. 46.

29. Fussell, *The Great War and Modern Memory*, p. 57.

30. Jerry Glover, 'All Guns Blazing', *Inside Film* (London: A & R Publishing, 1999), no. 3, pp. 18–19.

31. According to an interview with Tim Robbins before Fuller's death, Fuller claimed that audiences would be repelled by an accurate depiction of the slaughter of battle. Colin McCabe refers to this interview in his review of *The Thin Red Line* in *Sight and Sound*, February 1999, vol. 9, no. 2, p. 13.

32. 'Interview: Samuel Fuller Talking to Jean Louis Noames', *Samuel Fuller* (Edinburgh: Edinburgh Film Festival 69, 1969), p. 97.

33. Justin Wyatt, *High Concept: Movies and Marketing in Hollywood* (Austin: University of Texas Press, 1994).

34. From the director's commentary on the UK DVD of *Three Kings*.

35. *War Stories*, BBC2.

36. 'Dulce Et Decorum Est', Dominic Hibberd (ed.), *Wilfred Owen: War Poems and Others* (London: Chatto and Windus, 1973).

6

From Female Friends to Literary Ladies: The Contemporary Woman's Film

Karen Hollinger

At this time in the history of film studies, it is difficult to write about the woman's film because its very existence is being called into question. Steve Neale, for instance, points out that although the types of films traditionally considered woman's films are still being made, the term itself has fallen out of fashion.[1] The fact that the woman's film is actually composed of so many diverse subcategories and does not really exhibit a distinctive visual style also renders it a problematic generic entity. Conventionally, it has been associated with melodrama, but this connection seems dubious in light of melodrama's position as the dominant mode of all Hollywood film-making. As Linda Williams points out, to characterise woman's films as inherently more melodramatic, meaning more fraught with heightened emotion, than other film genres identifies melodrama inaccurately with the notion of female sentimentality and ignores its connections with what have been considered traditionally male action-oriented generic forms, such as Westerns, war films and action-adventure dramas.[2]

Another problem is the lack of a definitive history of the woman's film. Most work on the genre focuses on what can be characterised as its golden age in the 1930s and 1940s. Molly Haskell, Mary Anne Doane, Janine Basinger, Christine Gledhill and Linda Williams, among others, have debated the contours and concerns of the genre in those halcyon days of its existence, but its inception in the silent period has hardly been examined.[3] Clearly, D.W. Griffith's woman-centred melodramas, such as *True Heart Susie* (1919), *Broken Blossoms* (1919) and *Way Down East* (1920), represent distinct silent predecessors of the woman's film.[4] But Steve Neale has pointed out that the same can be said of the 'serial queen' series, such as *The Woman Who Dared* (1910), *The Exploits of Elaine* (1914–15), *The American Girl* (1917) and *Ruth of the Rockies* (1920).[5] These films indicate that the woman's film's origins are not so solidly attached to the sphere of domesticity and romance as has often been suggested and that at least some of its representatives also fall into the category of the woman's adventure film.

This problem of which films actually do represent the major categories of the woman's film also troubles discussions of the genre. Certainly, the woman's film has traditionally been associated with domesticity, femininity and sentiment; nevertheless, when critics attempt to define it, they point to other general characteristics. Both Doane and Basinger suggest that the genre is defined by the centrality of its female protagonist, its attempt to deal with issues deemed important to women and its address to a female audience. This definition indeed encompasses a wide range of films branching out from the central stalwarts of the genre in the 1940s that Doane examines: the maternal melodrama (focusing on a mother's joys and tribulations), the love story (concentrating on the vicissitudes of heterosexual romance), the medical discourse film (with its focus on a physically or mentally ill woman) and the paranoid gothic thriller (centred on a wife's fear of her husband's possibly murderous designs on her). Also to be considered as perhaps more peripherally within the genre are career woman comedies, female biopics and adaptations of woman's novels.

Because of its wide-ranging generic composition, Rick Altman has even proposed that the woman's film is largely a critic-created entity, a 'phantom genre' not even recognised by the films' producers and really representing 'a succession of already existing genres' brought together as a way to study films addressed to a female audience.[6] Altman even suggests that the term has come 'to take on a life of its own, drawing to its corpus virtually any film apparently addressed to women', and not just films, but television soap operas and gothic romance novels as well. For Altman, the term represents nothing more than a 'multimedia banner' for feminist critical analysis, useful to feminists perhaps, but unrelated to the realities of film production and consumption.[7]

In spite of these objections, I believe it is important to study the woman's film and that this study has foregrounded issues of importance to film scholarship. For example, analyses of 1930s and 1940s woman's films have been especially important in highlighting issues of audience address. As Neale points out, feminist scholars have closely focused in on:

> the extent to which these [women's] genres and forms allow for the articulation of a female
> point of view, and on the extent to which that point of view – and the fate of female
> protagonists – may be channeled, distorted, recuperated or dictated by patriarchal contexts
> of production, circulation and reception.[8]

An issue only tangentially addressed, but one that warrants much fuller study, is the relationship of these 1930s and 1940s woman's films to their contemporary successors. Christine Gledhill and Tania Modleski have made strides in this area in their attempts to tie the woman's film to soap operas and other forms of woman's fiction,[9] but the historical connection between earlier woman's films and their recent descendants remains largely untheorised.

The fate of the woman's picture after the 1940s has, in fact, proved to be a rather thorny question. Certainly, the genre seems to have fallen off in the 1950s. With the return of the absent GIs following World War II, films seem to have concentrated on extending their address to male, as well as female, viewers. Thus, the period is marked by the popularity of family or dynastic melodramas such as *Written on the Wind* (1957) and *Giant* (1956), yet films that are primarily aimed at a female audience are certainly not absent from this decade, a point to which the Doris Day/Rock Hudson romances and Douglas Sirk's remake of *Imitation of Life* (1959) certainly testify. But there does seem to be a clear decline in the woman's film in the 1950s, which after all is the time when the term 'woman's film' began to lose its currency.

If the 1950s and 1960s represent the dark ages of the woman's film, the 1970s can be characterised as a renaissance with the rise of what critics termed the 'New Woman's Film'. This group of films falls largely into two categories: the independent woman film and the female friendship film, both of which were unquestionably popular cultural by-products of the 1960s women's movement. The independent woman film, represented most notably by *An Unmarried Woman* (1979) and *Alice Doesn't Live Here Anymore* (1974), was a rather short-lived cycle focusing on the tribulations of a traditional wife and mother as she struggles to establish her independence and make it on her own after a divorce or the death of her spouse. Following a brief period of popularity in the 1970s, the independent woman film quickly began to fade and was replaced in the 1980s and 1990s by a resurgence of maternal melodramas, such as *Terms of Endearment* (1983), *The Good Mother* (1988) and *Stella* (1990; the Bette Midler remake of the 1937 *Stella Dallas*). These new maternal melodramas tended to incorporate into their traditional tales of long-suffering mothers some characteristics of the independent woman film, forming what might be categorised as the independent mother film. This development served to modify the most patriarchally challenging aspects of the subgenre by prob-lematising rather than championing female independence. The independent mother film, represented most recently by *Tumbleweeds* (1999) and *Anywhere But Here* (1999), modifies its female protagonist's sense of independence by combining it with or pitting it against her devotion to motherhood, a much more traditionally feminine trait.

Whereas the independent woman film rather quickly faded away, the female friend-ship film flourished from the late 1970s through the 1990s. Stimulated by the women's movement's emphasis on the importance of relationships among women, the female friendship film, with its focus on the intimate bonds among two or more female friends, developed numerous cycles, heightening its wide appeal to different types of female viewers. For instance, sentimental female friendship films, with their focus on close, emo-tionally effusive ties among women and on the nurturing and psychologically enriching qualities of these relationships, offer women's friendship largely as a means of integrat-ing women into patriarchal society. The dominance of this category of female friendship films places an essentially conservative message of social integration at the forefront of the genre. Except for early representatives of the category, such as *Julia* (1977) and *Girlfriends* (1978), both of which focus on an emotionally intense portrayal of dyadic female bonding, the sentimental female friendship film consistently demonstrated a tendency to move beyond the friends' personal psychological growth and present female friendship as a means of women's integration into the existing social order.

Increasingly, as the subgenre developed, the sentimental female friendship film became a vehicle for the propagation of a conservative social message of female accom-modation to a reformed patriarchy. Women's relationships came to represent a nurturing tie that not only binds women to each other, but also leads them back from a state of alienation to renewed social involvement. This socially conforming message represents the most prominent feature of 1990s female friendship films, and group female friendship portrayals came to provide the privileged format for its expression. The mid-1990s wave of sentimental group female friendship films, such as *Moonlight and Valentino*, *How to Make an American Quilt* and *Boys on the Side* (all 1995), all show one or more alienated young woman aided in her return to societal accommodation by the advice and consolation of a group of female friends. The sentimental female friendship film's movement into the realm of group female friendship did not in any way diminish its sentimental qualities or the emotionally intense response it sought to provoke in its spectator. Over the period, the movement to group female friendship films was accompanied by a parallel progression to a heightened sentimentality that reached its peak in the late 1980s with the release of *Beaches* (1988) and *Steel Magnolias* (1989), but is also represented in 1990s films such as *Moonlight and Valentino* and *Boys on the Side*. In these films, a heightened emotional effect is produced not so much by the increased sentimentality of the female friendship portrayal as by its amalgamation with earlier 1930s and 1940s woman's film plot formulae associated with maternal melodramas and medical discourse films. By opening up female subject positions in regard to the texts that are antithetical to progressive readings, these older woman's film forms facilitated the sentimental female friendship film's propagation of an increasingly conservative message.

In contrast to the sentimental female friendship film, which came to dominate the subgenre and at the same time to contain its most regressive qualities, female friendship films that focus on women's maturation and psychological development offer more progressive possibilities. Their strong association with feminist theories of female psychological development lead them to concentrate, in ways that sentimental female friendship films do not, on women's need for both relatedness and autonomy in their formation of a sense of identity. Unfortunately, these maturational female friendship films have difficulties envisioning exactly where the female quest for autonomy might lead. *Desperately Seeking Susan* (1985), *Housekeeping* (1987), *Mystic Pizza* (1988), *Now and Then* (1995) and *The Babysitters' Club* (1995) leave their female audience with the image of women's autonomous self-determination, but with few practical suggestions for where this autonomy might fruitfully find expression.

While the sentimental female friendship film quickly established itself as the dominant branch of the subgenre, the less emotionally intense but more patriarchally challenging political female friendship film all but disappeared as the subgenre developed in the 1990s. The rarity of mainstream political female friendship portrayals that focus on social ills affecting women clearly demonstrates how limited the radical potential of the Hollywood woman's film really is. In fact, *Thelma & Louise* (1991) stands alone as the only contemporary female friendship film that can be read as unrecuperatedly political. Even *Thelma & Louise*, this most politically 'radical' of popular female friendship films, does not provide an incisive political analysis of women's issues, but rather represents a popular cultural attempt at political critique contained within a comedic female buddy road movie formula that undercuts the film's socially critical message.

If *Thelma & Louise* represents the high point in the development of the political female friendship film, it also seems to have initiated the demise of this branch of the subgenre. Before *Thelma & Louise*, political female friendship films, such as *9 to 5* (1980) and *Outrageous Fortune* (1987), presented cartoonish representations of female revenge scenarios and culminated in fantasy happy endings. As long as it continued to maintain this formula throughout the 1980s, the political female friendship film continued to find limited representation. Once it became associated in the early 1990s with female violence presented in a more serious context, as it is in *Thelma & Louise* and *Mortal Thoughts* (1991), a movement that suggests a heightened level of women's political desperation, the political female friendship film seems to have become too politically challenging for mainstream cinematic representation. As a result, by the mid-1990s political female friendship portrayals all but completely disappeared and no longer really could be considered a prominent branch of the subgenre.

This does not mean that female friendship films with political implications completely disappeared after the early 1990s. These politically challenging films were, however, largely confined to the independent sector, outside mainstream Hollywood production. Independently made lesbian films and female friendship films that deal with race and ethnicity, such as *Go Fish* (1994) and *Mi Vida Loca* (1994), continued to develop politically challenging thematic possibilities. For instance, in the 1990s, independent lesbian films moved in the direction of lesbian-authored, lesbian-directed and lesbian-affirmative films made for lesbian audiences. Films such as *Go Fish* not only originated within the lesbian community itself, but also tried to portray the diversity of lesbian lifestyles with greater verisimilitude. Independent lesbian representations throughout the period of the 1980s and 1990s also demonstrated a movement from an earlier tradition of sombre coming-out stories, such as *Lianna* (1983), that focus on a woman's painful coming to terms with her lesbianism, to lighter-toned portrayals of lesbian romance within the lesbian community, such as *Go Fish*, *Bar Girls* (1994) and *The Incredibly True Adventures of Two Girls in Love* (1995). These films reject earlier notions of doomed lesbian love and document instead the formation of lesbian relationships that end happily.

Optimism about the progress of lesbian portrayals must be tempered, however, by a recognition of the confinement of this development to the sector of independent production. While progressive changes in lesbian representation became more visible to mainstream audiences because of the movement of independent films into mainstream theatrical distribution, these changes did not trigger reciprocal developments in Hollywood lesbian representation. Hollywood films, such as *Fried Green Tomatoes* (1991), for example, kept their characters' lesbianism closeted in ambiguity. A rare openly lesbian portrayal, such as Whoopi Goldberg's character in *Boys on the Side*, is very problematic in terms of its representation both of sexual preference and race. Although Goldberg's character is presented as openly gay, she remains throughout the film decidedly asexual. She is allowed to engage only in an ambiguously lesbian romance with a dying AIDS victim, who proclaims herself resolutely heterosexual until she is on the brink of death. Only then does she declare her love, which is never specified as either sexual or platonic, for Goldberg's character. Thus, while presenting an openly lesbian character with some sympathy, Hollywood still seems determined to avoid constructing an unambiguously positive representation of a lesbian relationship. As *Boys on the Side* demonstrates, lesbians in Hollywood films, even in the mid-1990s, were still being presented as unhappy or dying, albeit now in sympathetic contexts, and their relationships were shown to be plagued by ambiguity and doomed to failure.

If lesbian portrayals, at least in the independent sector, made significant advances throughout the 1990s, female friendship films dealing with issues of race and ethnicity unfortunately made very little progress. Hollywood films representing relationships among women of colour or between them and white women are both rare and highly problematic in their attempts to deal with minority issues. The rarity and inadequacy of these representations reflect not only the paucity of women of colour involved in the film industry, but also Hollywood film-makers' reluctance to take their films openly into the political realm that a discussion of race and ethnicity necessitates. Regrettably, the segregated nature of the industry and its apolitical tendencies have prevented female friendship films from even laying a foundation for a serious consideration of these very important issues.

One of the most popular contemporary female friendship films to deal with racial issues is without question *The Color Purple* (1985), Steven Spielberg's extremely flawed bowdlerisation of Alice Walker's important novel that nevertheless found remarkable success with female audiences. On the other hand, the independently produced *Mi Vida Loca*, a serious attempt by female film-maker Alison Anders to portray chicana gang culture, refused to pander to Hollywood-created viewer expectations and was never able to attract a mainstream audience. The female friendship film's portrayal of women of colour did experience a landmark development with the 1995 release of *Waiting to Exhale*, the first Hollywood film to focus on a group of black female friends. Directed by an African-American director, Forest Whitaker, the film was also co-written by an African-American screenwriter, the book's female author, Terry McMillan.

Based on McMillan's bestselling novel, *Waiting to Exhale* found a wide, primarily black, female audience and attained almost immediate cult status with African-American women viewers. Its box-office success did not, however, precipitate the production of more mainstream intraracial female friendship portrayals, and the political implications of its narrative content were, in fact, extremely limited. The film is preoccupied with its female characters' troubled heterosexual romances and seems primarily concerned with expressing black women's frustrations with their relationships with black men. The female friendship component is all but lost in the process and in any case is presented in the sentimental, rather than the political, female friendship film tradition. Female friendship in *Waiting to Exhale*, following the conventions established by other sentimental female friendship films, serves as a place of refuge for African-American women from their problematic romantic entanglements with what are presented as insensitive and irresponsible black men.

Surprisingly, in the conservative 1980s and 1990s, manipulative or anti-female friendship films were a rarity in the female friendship film subgenre. Given the dominance of group sentimental female friendship portrayals that thematically support women's acclimatisation to the status quo, this lack of overt attacks on female friendship is easily explained. Anti-female friendship films, such as *The Hand That Rocks the Cradle* and *Single White Female* (both 1992), represent a short-lived response to the politically challenging association of female friendship with violence found in films such as *Thelma & Louise* and *Mortal Thoughts*. As long as female friendship films affirmed sentimental, rather than political, female friendship, there was no need for anti-female friendship films. In fact, they represent a very problematic division of the female friendship film sub-genre. Their overt attacks on female friendship risk alienating a substantial segment of the female audience, and, within a genre that attempts to achieve a wide address to different types of women viewers, this quality is particularly damaging. Group sentimental female friendship films work much more subtly and effectively than overt anti-female friendship portrayals to subvert the radical potential inherent in representations of female bonding, yet they can still remain female-affirmative on a personal level. Given this situation, the anti-female friendship film is rendered superfluous. At the same time, however, the female friendship film's concentration on the socially ameliorating group female friendship plot at the expense of other plot possibilities that would take the genre into the realm of the social problem film has precipitated a current decline in the sub-genre's popularity. As the female friendship film seems to have exhausted its range of plot possibilities, it has been replaced by a new cycle of literary adaptations that are directed primarily towards a female audience.

Timothy Corrigan has identified more generally a current wave of film adaptations that he has dubbed a 'return of the classics' movement. He believes it reflects 'a therapeutic turn from cultural complexity', 'an increasing concern with manner over matter' and a conservative reaction against postmodernist film-making trends that diminish traditional plot and character.[10] What Corrigan fails to recognise is that a significant segment of this movement, which he seems too eager to paint in an unfavourable light, involves substantial input from female film-makers and to a large extent is directed towards a female audience. Many current classic adaptations represent attempts by female screenwriters, directors and production executives to recapture for a contemporary female audience the distinctive voices of prominent women of the past, either real or fictional. Films such as *Little Women* (1994), *Sense and Sensibility* (1995), *Clueless* (1995), *The Portrait of a Lady* (1996), *Mrs Dalloway* (1997) and *Washington Square* (1997) are all adapted by female screenwriters, and often female directors and producers as well, from novels written by female authors or focusing on female protagonists, or both. If these films are nostalgic attempts to escape from current 'cultural complexity' by returning to an idyllic past, as Corrigan maintains, this past is one dominated by female figures who are reshaped in images framed by a contemporary female sensibility for a contemporary female audience.

As Neale points out, woman's films have always benefited from a certain amount of female input.[11] Until quite recently, this input came primarily from female novelists (whose works were used as source material), screenwriters and stars, whose ideas were then filtered through the hands of male directors and production executives. This is not only true of 1930s and 1940s woman's films – even contemporary female friendship films are overwhelmingly the work of male producers and directors. The 1990s, however, witnessed a significant rise in women's involvement in the film industry as producers and directors, as well as an increase in the clout of female stars, who became more involved in production than they had been in the past. These developments changed the contours of woman's films, and one of the first changes they brought about is this turn to classic woman's literature as a source of female-centred plots and characters. This new women's 'return to the classics' movement relies heavily upon female film-makers not only to push to get the films into production, but also for a refashioning of their nineteenth-century heroines in accord with twentieth-century feminist ideas.

The case of *Little Women* is exemplary. Through their combined efforts, screenwriter Robin Swicord, producer Denise Di Novi, director Gillian Armstrong and star Winona Ryder transformed Louisa May Alcott's dated children's classic into a box-office hit with a contemporary feminist edge. The film's press book explains *Little Women*'s genesis:[12] in 1980, Swicord, a largely unknown young Hollywood screenwriter, discussed with Amy Pascal, an equally young development executive at Columbia Pictures, the idea of adapting Alcott's novel to the screen. Although Pascal could do nothing to bring the project to fruition at that time, twelve years later when Pascal became a vice-president at Columbia, Swicord was able to resume discussions. Pascal then put Swicord in contact with producer Denise Di Novi, who in turn began conversations with the actress Winona Ryder. Ryder, who would become one of the film's major female stars and was also instrumental in casting the other young actresses to play her sisters, had seen an earlier film by Australian director Gillian Armstrong. Impressed by the strong female characters in Armstrong's work, Ryder recommended her to Di Novi to direct. Armstrong, who had previously directed *My Brilliant Career* (1978), *Mrs. Soffel* (1985) and *The Last Days of Chez Nous* (1992), all feminist-inflected films, says that she was drawn to the project by the theme of 'sisterly love in particular'.[13] Although Armstrong claims a reluctance to use the word 'feminist' because of what she sees as its negative connotations, she nevertheless proposes that when she first read the *Little Women* screenplay, she became determined not to make 'a cute little movie for girls',[14] but to create, instead, as the film's press book suggests, a new, admittedly feminist version of the 'time-honored story of a young rebellious woman's dream of freedom'.[15] Similarly, producer Di Novi, who says she wanted the film to achieve a balance between, as she puts it, the 'too serious message movie and pure fluff',[16] suggests that she felt the film needed to be grounded in 'an evolved kind of feminism ... a more humanist and inclusive feminism that's able to embrace men and motherhood in a way '60s feminism couldn't'.[17]

With the support of her director and producer, screenwriter Swicord wrote a screenplay that created a *Little Women* that deviated substantially from Alcott's original text. Swicord admits to having adapted the novel not as Alcott wrote it, but as Swicord believed Alcott would have written it today. In an interview with the *Village Voice*, Swicord explicitly states that while she wanted 'to do a true adaptation', she also hoped her script would express 'what was important today, ... to say what was not being said, particularly to young women and about young women'. Because some of the things that Swicord apparently wanted to say were not explicit themes in Alcott's text, she turned to historical sources outside the novel to discover a history of nineteenth-century

Little Women (1996): collaboration among female creative talent

women's progressivism, focusing on educational reform, abolition and women's suffrage. In order to show women's 'politics of the times', Swicord confesses to having drawn much of her material directly from this historical reading, rather than from *Little Women* itself.[18] With the support of her producer, director and star, Swicord rewrote Alcott's novel, undertaking a transformation so extensive that it shows Alcott's major female characters to be not only little women, but also early feminists.[19] This revisionist *Little Women*, released at Christmas 1994, was a resounding box-office success, especially with female viewers, in spite of the fact that Swicord claims Columbia Pictures, cautious about the marketability of a 'movie about a bunch of girls', as she describes their attitude, refused to give it an adequate budget or marketing campaign.[20]

There are obvious differences, yet underlying similarities, between the efforts of the female production team involved in the creation of *Little Women* and writer-director Amy Heckerling's tireless determination in the face of limited studio interest to bring *Clueless* to the screen in the summer of 1995. *Clueless* is a female-centred teen comedy that re-envisions Jane Austen's novel *Emma* through the lens of contemporary Beverley Hills youth culture. Whereas *Little Women*'s press material played up the film's prestigious literary source, the press book for Heckerling's *Clueless* never even mentions its inspiration in Austen's novel. Heckerling, a writer-director with a background in light comedies, such as *Fast Times at Ridgemont High* (1982), *National Lampoon's European Vacation* (1985), *Look Who's Talking* (1989) and *Look Who's Talking Too* (1990), says that the *Clueless* screenplay originated in her desire to make a film with a teenage female protagonist who for once was both attractive and intelligent. Asked originally by Fox Entertainment to create a teen-oriented television pilot that was about 'cool' teenagers, not 'losers', Heckerling set out with feminist designs to shape a female character who, as Heckerling puts it, 'knows she is beautiful' and is 'really an optimistic character', but is not a typical teenage female airhead.[21] Whereas other adaptations of nineteenth-century women's novels aimed for a mature female audience, *Clueless* was specifically directed at eight-to twenty-year-olds. The film's star, Alicia Silverstone, was even cast for her teen appeal after Heckerling saw her in one of the rock group Aerosmith's videos, and promotional items for the film included tie-ins to *Clueless* dolls manufactured by Mattel, as well as *Clueless* T-shirts and music videos.[22]

Heckerling, who maintains that she is not even a Jane Austen fan, decided to use the plot of Austen's novel only after she had already begun to develop the *Clueless* project (originally entitled *I Was a Teenage Teenager* and *No Worries*).[23] She saw Austin's story-line as a way to create in her words a 'timeless' 'comedy of manners'.[24] Like Swicord in adapting *Little Women*, Heckerling wanted to create a film that spoke to young women today. She approached Austen's characters as 'wealthy and privileged people [of another era] who,' as Heckerling puts it, 'rode around in carriages and made calls on each other', much as the wealthy residents of Beverly Hills drive around in their expensive cars today.[25] Heckerling, in fact, seems to have been much more concerned with creating characters and situations true to the life of affluent Beverly Hills teenagers than with rendering a faithful version of Austen's novel. According to the film's press materials, Heckerling's primary research comprised 'hanging out' with high school students and studying their language, style, customs, feelings and music, rather than investigating the mores of Austen's time.[26]

In spite of these differences, there are also definite similarities between *Clueless*'s production history and *Little Women*'s. Like Swicord's script for *Little Women*, Heckerling's feminist-inflected screenplay did not find immediate studio acceptance. After originally contracting Heckerling to write a teleplay, then a screenplay, Fox dropped the project as too female-oriented. Heckerling has spoken in interviews of the pressure she experienced at Fox 'to create more of a life for the boys in the film, to create more of an ensemble piece, which,' she says, 'didn't make sense to [her] at all'.[27] After Fox dropped its option on the film, it was picked up in turnaround by Paramount, where again, as with *Little Women*, a female studio executive became involved. Sherry Lansing, chairwoman at Paramount, took Heckerling's project under her wing and shepherded it through production. After its release in July 1995, it went on to become a major summer box-office success.

Also released in 1995, Columbia's *Sense and Sensibility* was the result of the combined efforts of a female star-turned-screenwriter, Emma Thompson; a female producer, Lindsay Doran; and a male director, Ang Lee. Although the director is generally given credit as the artist who leaves his or her creative imprint on a film, the case seems to be very different in regard to *Sense and Sensibility*. Doran describes the project as 'the fulfillment of a long cherished dream'.[28] She says she first read Jane Austen's novel in the year she graduated from college and decided then that it would make a perfect film adaptation. It took her twenty-five years to make this dream a reality. Her problem, she says, was, first of all, to find the right screenwriter who would not render the text to the screen in a way that was in Doran's words 'too polite, or too melodramatic, or too modern, or too arcane'. According to Doran, every screenwriter she approached turned out to be a disappointment: 'The funny ones weren't romantic and the romantic ones weren't funny.'[29] Then Doran met Emma Thompson and Kenneth Branagh when she was producing Branagh's *Dead Again* (1991), in which Branagh and his then wife Thompson also starred. Doran clearly thought she had found the prefect screenwriting and directing team in the husband and wife. She had seen skits written by Thompson for her British television comedy series, entitled *Thompson*, and was attracted by her ability to write comedy in period settings.[30] The fact that Thompson was attached to Branagh, who had directed a very popular film adaptation of Shakespeare's *Henry V* (1989), also undoubtedly helped to stimulate Doran's interest.

Thompson, however, was a first-time screenwriter who describes herself as totally at sea when it came to composing a screenplay. She began, as she tells it, by dramatising every scene from the novel, which resulted in a 300-page hand-written manuscript.[31] According to Thompson, it took her four years, endless drafts and the constant collaboration and support of Doran to construct a viable screenplay. As she describes it:

> The novel is so complex and there are so many stories in it that bashing out a structure was the biggest labor. I would write a version, Lindsay would read it and send me notes. Or, if we happened to be in the same city, we would sit down together and talk out the problems. Then I would cry for a while and then go back to work. And that's how it was for three years.[32]

Even when Thompson had finished the screenplay, she wanted to have it interpreted by actors, so she set up a full-scale read-through at a London theatre with many of the actors who later would be cast in the film, including one of its major male leads, Hugh Grant.[33]

In the meantime, Doran set out to sell the film to a studio. She says she shopped it around as early as 1990 to Paramount, Universal, Disney and Fox, and 'all said no'.[34] When she was on the point of giving up, Columbia/TriStar finally expressed interest. By this time, however, Thompson and Branagh were in the middle of a divorce, and a new director had to be found. Doran chose the male director Ang Lee, but Thompson and Doran never seemed to allow him into the inner sanctum of their female creative collaboration. In the film's press book, Doran is said to have been attracted to Ang because she saw him as 'an inquisitive outsider with a sense of humor', and an outsider he seems to have remained.[35] Ang himself describes his input largely in terms of visually re-creating the historical period of the early 1800s and working with the actors to enhance their performances. He says that, even in regard to casting, Thompson read at all of the call-backs and offered her opinions in regard to casting choices, although she did leave the final decisions to him.[36]

While Ang obviously had some input, the project was clearly dominated by Thompson and Doran. Most likely because her participation would help assure that the studio would take the film seriously and give it an adequate budget, Thompson even agreed somewhat belatedly to star in a role that she transformed from one written for a much younger actress into a portrayal of a mature, self-possessed and fiercely intelligent feminist heroine. Ang, in fact, admits that he was initially attracted to the project by Thompson's presence.[37] Even with Thompson attached, the film was budgeted rather modestly for a major studio release at $16 million.[38] It was, however, given a prime release date during the Christmas season in what Doran admits was a blatant attempt to replicate *Little Women*'s success.[39] Indeed, *Sense and Sensibility* became a resounding box-office hit, grossing $42.7 million in the United States, very close to *Little Women*'s $50 million.

This recent women's 'return of the classics' movement represents a major new swerve in the woman's film's development. In distinct contrast to earlier representatives of the genre, female influence within the industry has succeeded both in stimulating and bringing to fruition feminist-imbued adaptations of classic women's novels. The creation of films within this new cycle of women's literary adaptations often involves the tireless efforts of a coterie of female screenwriters, directors, stars and production executives. This close collaboration among female creative talent represents a substantial deviation from the production of earlier woman's films, which may have benefited from some female input, but were nevertheless substantially the work of male creative talent. In the production of the new woman's literary adaptation, we see the formation of networks of talented women who band together in their determination to bring their contemporary vision of a classic women's novel to film, even in opposition to studio directives. This creative bond seems to be formed through the mediation of a nineteenth-century heroine whose story is rendered with a decidedly feminist slant, even if this slant is not always explicitly named as such. It seems also to have resulted in a new, or at least newly prominent, subgenre of the woman's film, one that places a genre that has long been dominated by male influence, especially in terms of production and direction, finally and firmly in the creative hands of women.

Notes

I would like to thank Judy Dubus for her help in locating sources the exact whereabouts of which eluded me.

1. Steve Neale, *Genre and Hollywood* (London: Routledge, 2000), p. 4.

2. Linda Williams, 'Melodrama Revisited', in Nick Browne (ed.), *Refiguring American Film Genres: Theory and History* (Berkeley: University of California Press, 1998), p. 59.

3. Molly Haskell, *From Reverence to Rape: The Treatment of Women in the Movies* (New York: Holt, Rinehart and Winston, 1974); Mary Ann Doane, *The Desire to Desire: The Woman's Film of the 1940s* (Bloomington: Indiana University Press, 1987); Jeanine Basinger, *A Woman's View: How Hollywood Spoke to Women, 1930–1960* (New York: Knopf, 1993); Christine Gledhill, *Home Is Where the Heart Is: Studies in Melodrama and the Woman's Film* (London: BFI, 1987); Linda Williams, '"Something Else Besides a Mother": *Stella Dallas* and the Maternal Melodrama', *Cinema Journal*, vol. 24, no. 2 (Winter 1984), pp. 2–27.

4. Scott Simmon, 'The Origins of the Woman's Film at Biograph', in *The Films of D. W. Griffith* (Cambridge: Cambridge University Press, 1993), pp. 68–103.

5. Neale, *Genre and Hollywood*, p. 191.

6. Rick Altman, *Film/Genre* (London: BFI, 1999), p. 72.

7. Altman, *Film/Genre*, p. 77.

8. Neale, *Genre and Hollywood*, p. 184.

9. Christine Gledhill, 'The Melodramatic Field: An Investigation', in Gledhill (ed.), *Home Is Where the Heart Is*, pp.5–39; Tania Modleski, *Loving with a Vengeance: Mass-produced Fantasies for Women* (New York: Methuen, 1982).

10. Timothy Corrigan, *Film and Literature: An Introduction and Reader* (Upper Saddle River, NJ: Prentice Hall, 1999), p. 72.

11. Neale, *Genre and Hollywood*, p. 192.

12. The Press Books for all of the adaptations discussed in this essay are housed in the Margaret Herrick Library of the Academy of Motion Picture Arts and Sciences, Beverly Hills, California.

13. *Little Women* Press Book, p. 2.

14. Kristine McKenna, 'Not So "Little Women"', *Los Angeles Times*, 27 December 1994, p. F14.

15. *Little Women* Press Book, p. 4.

16. Ibid., p. 2.

17. McKenna, 'Not So "Little Women"', p. F14.

18. Manohla Dargis, 'Reworking Women', *Village Voice*, 3 January 1992, p. 71.

19. For a detailed analysis of Swicord's transformation of Alcott's novel, see Karen Hollinger and Teresa Winterhalter, 'A Feminist Romance: Adapting *Little Women* to the Screen', *Tulsa Studies in Women's Literature,* vol. 18, no. 2 (Autumn 1999), pp. 173–92.

20. *Buzz*, December/January 1995. Article contained in *Little Women* clippings file at the Margaret Herrick Library of the Academy of Motion Picture Arts and Sciences, Beverly Hills, California. All clippings files for the films discussed in the essay are housed in this collection.

21. Bernard Weinraub, 'A Surprise Film Hit about Rich Teen-age Girls', *New York Times*, 25 July 1995, p. C10.

22. *Clueless* Press Book, no pagination.

23. Ibid.

24. Quoted in Weinraub, 'A Surprise Film Hit about Rich Teen-age Girls', p. C10.

25. Ibid.

26. *Clueless* Press Book, no pagination.

27. Quoted in Weinraub, 'A Surprise Film Hit about Rich Teen-age Girls', p. C10.

28. *Sense and Sensibility* Press Book, p. 6.

29. Ibid.

30. Ibid.

31. Ibid., p. 7.

32. Ibid.

33. Ibid.

34. Dalya Alberge, 'Film Nonsense and Insensibility Almost Stopped Austen Epic', *The Times* (London), 22 February 1996, p. A5.

35. *Sense and Sensibility* Press Book, p. 8.

36. Bruce Feld, 'Director Ang Lee Believes *S&S* May Be His Best Film to Date', *Drama-Logue*, 21 December – 3 January 1996, p. 8.

37. Michael Tunison, 'A Sense of Balance', *Entertainment Today*, 14–21 December 1995, p. 6.

38. Leonard Klady, 'Cents and Sensibility', *Variety*, 26 December 1995, p. 8.

39. Oscar Moore, *'Sense and Sensibility'*, *Screen International*, 7 July 1995, p. 18.

7

Hollywood Lives: The State of the Biopic at the Turn of the Century

Carolyn Anderson and Jon Lupo

Introduction

In a 1986 interview, film scholar, genre critic, screenwriter and director Paul Schrader declared that the biopic was 'now in the provinces of television' and cautioned prospective film-makers that 'you have to have an original approach if you try to do a cinematic biography'.[1] Several years later, in the first scholarly book devoted exclusively to the genre, George Custen declared the biopic theatrically dead, claiming the genre had gravitated to television.[2] In the 1980s and 1990s, television was saturated with biographical offerings, with made-for-television biopic docudramas broadcast commercially and documentary biographies regularly broadcast on public television; biographical profiles on the History Channel and celebrity bios on the Biography Channel were ubiquitous. Nevertheless, Hollywood biopic production in the 1980s actually increased. Steve Neale found the genre accounting for 5.3 per cent of Hollywood output of the decade, 'its highest ever point'.[3] And the theatrically released biopic's vigour has not diminished in the past decade. Why is this so?

Genres are notoriously flexible constructs; consequently, genre history is a story of evolution and mutation, rather than extinction. In hindsight, it is clear that what had reasonably appeared to thoughtful scholars as a dead end was only a fork in the road. Theorist Rick Altman has offered the term 'genrification' to capture Hollywood's response to changing audience interests.[4] Neale has been especially attentive to how changing industry demands shift generic expectations. Beginning with the assumption that genres are pliable, with edges subject to an ongoing process of cultural negotiation, we offer a description of the shape of the Hollywood biopic at the turn of the century and speculate on the genre's continued liveliness.

'Biopic' is a term more often used by film critics and historians than in marketing campaigns, among moviegoers or as a shelving device at rental stores.[5] Still, the literary construct biography is understood so widely that the term biopic is easily recognisable.[6] As with all category systems, the biopic has contestable boundaries, as it shares borders with historical drama, docudrama and social issue drama; its subsets overlap with other genres to create gangster biopics, musical biopics, sports biopics, African-American biopics and so forth.[7] Using the common genre definition of a biopic as a film that takes a life story of an actual person as its central narrative, we considered sixty-one biopics produced and nationally released in the United States from 1990 through 2000. Films in our sample range from Hollywood epics such as *Anna and the King* (1999) – which 20th Century-Fox produced for $75 million and opened on 2132 US screens – to low-budget independent projects such as *Before Night Falls* (2000) – which Fine Line opened in only eight theatres. To create a genre profile of the decade, we compared our sample to earlier biopics as described by Carolyn Anderson, Custen and Neale. This comparison revealed patterns which we will first summarise, then discuss more fully.

Studio biopic production remained stable, with an increase of low-budget activity and independently produced projects. A group of notable directors became associated with biopic production, but across funding sources. The genre continued to be risky financially, with historical projects and big-budget tonal experiments losing the most money.

Our sample continued the genre's emphasis on the lives of men, with only eight films concentrating on a single female subject.[8] Artists, defined broadly as including performing artists, constituted the most common profession depicted. Multiple productions on the same biographical subject were fairly common. An emphasis on contemporary North American subjects intensified. The most significant change in subject profile was a marked increase in attention to the lives of people of colour. Biopics continued to function as star-vehicles, with a concomitant persistence of acting honours. Performances based on historical characters produced at least one nominee, and often several, for acting Oscars between 1990 and 2000.

Biopics continued to depend heavily on sentimentality. An ironic approach to the biographical enterprise or the biographical subject was rare and, even then, incomplete; however, more attention (proportionally) was directed towards conflicted, eccentric or irascible subjects. Overall, 1990s biopics continued a psychological approach to story-telling, with personal struggle as the nodal dramatic action which incorporated a presumption of the US (and often the world) as a meritocracy. The full life story approach decreased, frequently replaced by a focus on a pivotal childhood experience, followed by a narrative of peak adult incidents, not always presented chronologically.[9]

In contrast to the exploitation of conglomerate ownership patterns by many 1990s genres, the biopic rarely offered product 'tie-ins', with the exception of published biographies and an occasional movie soundtrack. The genre had minimal participation in the decade's embrace of special effects, except for the digital manipulation of images presented as archival footage. The most popular manipulations occurred in the *faux* biopic *Forrest Gump* (1994); the most controversial in *JFK* (1991). The intensity and breadth of responses to *JFK* demonstrated abiding generic expectations of historical and biographical 'accuracy' – or at least accountability – by critics and general audiences.

Heroic lives of people of colour: old formulae revisited

A striking change in Hollywood biopic production in the 1990s was the significant increase in biopics about people of colour. Custen found 'the corpus of famous people ... overwhelmingly white (91 per cent post-studio versus 95 per cent studio era)';[10] another sample of over 200 theatrical biopics released between 1929 and 1986 showed 2 per cent African-American subjects.[11] In contract, our corpus was only 76 per cent white.[12] Why has such a startling change occurred? The commercial imperatives of Hollywood certainly have not changed. This shift in focus in biopic production responds to generic demands, movie industry personnel, national demographics and ideological trends.

Although the Hollywood biopic has traditionally taken a psychological approach to explain its protagonist's life, focusing on a person of colour creates a structural given of historical racism in the US, thus adding a rich social context which requires little evidence to establish dramatic tension. Placing individual and institutional racism in the past, which must be the setting for at least part of every biopic, appeals to Hollywood. A narrative can easily be constructed that denounces (past) racism while celebrating the protagonist's personal triumph over such racism and entry into what is presented as a contemporary American meritocracy.

Biopics operate as star-vehicles and thus provide an attractive site for actors of colour with crossover appeal, such as Denzel Washington (see below); Angela Bassett in *What's Love Got To Do with It* (1993); Jason Scott Lee in *Dragon: The Bruce Lee Story* (1993); Wes Studi in *Geronimo: An American Legend* (1993); Jennifer Lopez in *Selena* (1997); Cuba Gooding Jr in *Men of Honor* (2000) and Will Smith in *Ali* (2001). For the first time in Hollywood history, a small number of African-American writers, producers and directors, most notably Spike Lee, are perceived as commercially viable industry players and celebrities in their own right.

As the 2000 census made clear, racial and ethnic demographics in the US changed drastically in the 1990s. Niche marketing accelerated throughout this period, with Hollywood intent on diversifying its products and their markets. A cluster of low-budget comedies and 'hood movies with predominately African-American casts were marketed successfully to teen audiences, especially teens of colour. The biopic is typically considered a genre with adult (or educational) appeal yet, because many biopics avoid graphic sexuality and violence, they often provide the sentimental (and conservative) gratifications of family melodrama. Biopics of people of colour simultaneously offer an opportunity to market what studio distributors consider progressive political ideology. These films have not participated in the 'revisionist *pathography* that would characterize *all* biographical musings in the post-Watergate world';[13] rather, these revisions celebrate biographical subjects either misrepresented or neglected by previous historical narratives. By moving people of colour into central roles as admirable, and often heroic, biographical subjects, Hollywood has managed to revisit conventional audience-pleasing formulae and expand notions of whose lives are worth considering.

In his discussion of studio-era production, Thomas Schatz introduced the phase 'star-genre formulations' to describe the joining of a concept like star-vehicle to the realities of story popularity and studio facilities for maximum commercial gain.[14] Although contemporary production conditions are far more fluid, a version of the 'star-genre formulation' continues; for example, star of colour + biopic = Denzel Washington. Yet, as Rick Altman has noted, publicity systematically stresses proprietary characteristics (star, director) over shared determinants such as genre.[15] Both admirers and detractors have described Denzel Washington as his generation's Sidney Poitier, a handsome leading man who signifies intelligence, dignity and a sense of controlled power, and who has demonstrated wide audience appeal. Between 1987 and 2000, Washington played more biopic roles than any other star, bringing a heroic dimension and often a sense of justified rage to each part. Washington's first biopic performance was the martyred South African leader Steve Biko in *Cry Freedom* (1987); two years later, he gained international attention and a supporting actor Oscar for a searing portrayal of a noble former slave and Union soldier in the docudrama *Glory* (1989).

Before his film career, Washington had played Malcolm X in the play *When the Chickens Come Home to Roost*. A decade later, Washington was everyone's choice for the challenging biopic role. His exceptional performance in *Malcolm X* was followed by another intense portrayal, as boxer Rubin 'Hurricane' Carter in *The Hurricane* (1999). Washington received numerous awards for these two virtuoso performances of defiant African-American men, but, although nominated, he was twice denied the Academy Award for best actor. In 2000, Washington played Herman Boone, a legendary football coach at a newly integrated Virginia high school. Boone's authoritarianism is presented as admirable; he forms a team out of suspicious individuals, leading the young men to racial understanding and athletic success in the popular family film *Remember the Titans*. Washington continued with the genre in a new capacity when he directed (and played a supporting role in) *Finding Fish* (in production), a biopic of a troubled life based on an autobiographical screenplay by African-American ex-convict Antwone Fisher.

Denzel Washington's preparation for and commitment to his portrayal of Malcolm X was unprecedented in a career marked by dedication and success. In addition to extensive research on the black leader, Washington conducted a personal *hajj*, fasting, abstaining from alcohol and reading the Koran during the long production period. Director Spike Lee filmed the script chronologically because Washington's hair had to grow back from the 'conk job' required when the actor played the young Malcolm Little, a Boston numbers runner attracted to street fashion. Even more importantly, shooting in sequence allowed Lee and Washington to incorporate manifestations of the actor's spiritual pilgrimage. The resulting performance achieves a palpable transcendence. Although magnificent performances can and do result from great writing, directing and acting – and much of the thrill of performance for both actors and audience flows from the magic when characters 'come alive' – there is a material authenticity of referent, a potential embodiment in biographical performance that cannot exist in the creation of a fictional character, no matter how fully and imaginatively developed. Biopic audiences hope, even expect, to witness and enjoy such embodiments. It is a central appeal of the genre.

Malcolm X (1992) was a generic landmark. Not only was it the first studio-financed biographical film of truly epic proportions artistically controlled by an African-American cast and crew, but also it presents as heroic a historical figure whose political and religious views were and remain, if not threatening, at least off-putting to many mainstream white Americans. The film covers four decades (from 1925–65), includes over 200 speaking parts, employed over 400 crew members, used tens of thousands of extras and

Malcolm X (1992): a generic landmark

was filmed on three continents. It was Spike Lee's first union film and his first – and last – with Warner Bros. The director has not hidden his contempt for what he labels 'the plantation'. When the studio, and the bonding company associated with it, refused to extend Lee's budget to film in South Africa, Lee appealed directly to wealthy African-Americans for monetary gifts to assure completion as he wished. This appeal was unprecedented. Its success speaks not only to Lee's persuasiveness, but to the importance of this project to other African-Americans as well.

More explicitly than any other biopic in our sample, *Malcolm X* marked its historical moment of production through a provocative prologue and epilogue. Lee had screened the rough cut of *Malcolm X* for Warner executives the day after the verdict in the Rodney King case, when Los Angeles was burning. In the final cut, Lee opened the film with the infamous home video footage of the King beating by members of the Los Angeles Police Department, followed by an American flag which burns into an 'X'. The film's epilogue features ex-political prisoner President Nelson Mandela, talking with a group of black South African school children, who urge a diasporic reading of the film through their repetition of the phrase, 'I am Malcolm X.' To Lee's critics, these framing devices are self-indulgent, even incendiary, gestures; to his admirers, they demonstrate the political viability and social utility of the biopic.

Biopic film-makers as auteurs

In the post-studio era, a variation of the studio-generated genre film has developed in the personal careers of successful film-makers despite the realities of single-production financing. Recent biopic examples include directors Milos Forman (*Amadeus* [1984], *The*

People vs. Larry Flynt [1997], and *Man on the Moon* [1999]); Phillip Kaufman (*The Right Stuff* [1983], *Henry and June* [1990] and *Quills* [2000]); Martin Scorsese (*Raging Bull* [1980], *Goodfellas* [1990] and *Kundun* [1997]); and screenwriters Scott Alexander and Larry Karaszewski (*Ed Wood* [1994], *The People vs. Larry Flynt* and *Man on the Moon*), self-described as 'the crazy biopic guys'.[16]

Although Oliver Stone and Julian Schnabel have both directed biopics of people of colour – Stone based *Heaven and Earth* (1993) on the autobiographical writings of a Vietnamese woman Le Ly Hayslip; in *Basquiat* (1996), Schnabel profiled the life of black street artist Jean-Michel Basquiat and, in *Before Night Falls,* Schnabel told the story of Cuban writer Reinaldo Arenas – discussions of these films have centred less on the race/ ethnicity, or even the lives, of their protagonists than on the politics and personal styles of their high-profile directors.

When Julian Schnabel entered film-making in the 1990s he was already known as a talented painter, a flamboyant personality and a self-promoter. In a pair of visually rich, independently produced biopics released within a four-year period, Schnabel told the tragic life stories of two contemporary artists who died unrecognised by a mass audience. In both films, Schnabel utilised the talents of magnetic actors (then) largely unknown in the US in leading parts – Jeffrey Wright and Benicio del Toro in *Basquiat*; Javier Bardem and Oliver Martinez in *Before Night Falls* – along with cameos by famous performers known for their alternative work – David Bowie, Dennis Hopper and Gary Oldman in *Basquiat*; Johnny Depp and Sean Penn in *Before Night Falls*. However dictated by prac- tical exigencies, this strategy resulted in compelling (and award-winning) performances, but biopics whose major press attention, especially in New York City, focused on Schnabel himself.

As co-writer and director of *Basquiat*, Schnabel recreated the frenzy of the 1980s New York art world in which both he and Jean-Michel Basquiat had flourished. Legal and economic realities pulled Schnabel deep into the project: the director painted the art that represented Basquiat's work in the film (as the graffiti artist's estate would not allow the appearance of any original work) and used his own West Village (New York City) studio as a major set. With *Before Night Falls*, which Schnabel also co-wrote, the personal links were less solid (although Schnabel cast his wife and co-executive producer, Olatz Lopez Garmendia, as the mother of Arenas and their son as Arenas as a child).

Perhaps as much in response to Julian Schnabel's reputation as a neo-expressionist painter and sculptor as to the film, many mainstream critics considered *Before Night Falls* experimental. The biopic's narrative is episodic, interweaving recreations of key inci- dents in Arenas's life with archival footage of the Cuban revolution and the 1980 Mariel Harbor boat lift; the sound design ranges from Laurie Anderson and Lou Reed to the effective use of (subjective) silence; and striking imagery re-creates the terrors and plea- sures of Arenas's life and his erotic dreams (some based on Arenas's writing). Still, the film's innovative status is partly a consequence of its membership in a deeply conserva- tive genre. That conservatism expresses itself in structural and aesthetic choices, in uses of source material and also in the larger question of what constitutes greatness. Custen, citing the influence of tabloid television, charts a shift in biopic subjects in the 1980s towards celebrity and sensationalism, and a resulting reconfiguration of 'our notions of fame itself'; he sees the chain of influence folding back as the biopic 'continues to play a significant part in determining how our culture constitutes its notions of fame, and what it takes to be a celebrated figure'.[17] Basquiat, who died of a drug overdose, and Arenas, a gay man suffering from AIDS who committed suicide, led aggressively non-conventional lives and died sensational deaths. The lament of the tortured artist is a biopic trope with particular appeal to film-makers who are, or fancy themselves, artists. Hollywood biopics of artists made in earlier decades implied, if not so clearly pictured, lives that ranged from alternative to deviant, often with as much sensationalism as official or unofficial codes allowed. In these indie biopics, Schnabel has introduced two unique artists and their particular worlds to new (although still small) audiences. In addition, *Basquiat* interrogates the manufacturing of celebrity and its consequences; *Before Night Falls* recognises the sometimes terrible price of artistic and personal freedom through the life of an irrepressible writer. Just as biopics of show business greats made during the studio era functioned as 'Hollywood's song to itself', contemporary biopics about artists on the fringe are the iconoclasts' song to themselves.[18]

Oliver Stone operates on a much larger, more popular, but no less extravagant canvas than Schnabel. Although Stone writes, directs and produces big-budget, studio-backed productions and his biopics usually centre on well-known North Americans, the controversial auteur considers himself a Hollywood outsider politically.[19] He has been outspoken and often contentious in his insistence on a film-maker's right to artistic licence in the creation of biopics. Approaching history as the biographies of great men (and a rare woman), Stone has expressed his fascination with the most violent decade in recent American history through a series of biopics that reach their narrative climaxes in the late 1960s or early 1970s. In an unparalleled seven years of biopic activity, Stone co-wrote and directed *Born on the 4th of July* (1989), about paralysed Vietnam veteran and anti-war activist Ron Kovic, and *The Doors* (1991), about rock star Jim Morrison; Stone wrote, produced and directed *JFK*, *Heaven and Earth* and *Nixon* (1995). In addition, Stone wrote the screenplay for *Evita* (1996) and produced *The People vs. Larry Flynt*.

Stone's concentration on the recent American past, his characteristic thematic and ideological concerns, his signature visual and editing styles (partly due to his ten-film collaboration with cinematographer Robert Richardson), his willingness to grant extensive and provocative interviews, his claim that his films challenge what he considers 'official history' and the popularity and critical acclaim of many of his films all combine to confirm his auteur status and to make his work controversial.

Stone's most recent biopic, *Nixon*, begins with a qualification ('This film is a dramatic interpretation of events and characters based on public sources and an incomplete historical record. Some scenes and events are presented as composites or have been hypothesized or condensed.'), followed by a biblical quotation ('Matthew: What shall it profit a man if he shall gain a whole world and lose his own soul?'), then hurtles into an audacious opening scene in which a group of seven men sit in a darkened room, watching a training film on 'really selling yourself' produced by the

United States Department of Labor.[20] Superimposed on an image of the projection light source is the title and the auteur credit 'An Oliver Stone Film'. A date and setting are flashed on screen: June 17, 1972; Watergate Hotel. That information is enough for an audience to follow the generally cryptic conversation among the men whose faces are shown in shadowed close-ups. Some comments are direct, such as 'We're going to do McGovern's office later tonight' and, most provocatively, in response to directions on procedures if 'anything goes wrong', one man (Howard Hunt, played by Ed Harris) says, 'Personally I'll be calling the President of the United States.' While the scene plays, credits appear. The training film ends with a direct-address caution: 'Always look 'em in the eye. Nothing sells like sincerity.' The men leave the room, crossing in front of the blank screen. Cut to a series of rapidly edited images, which include the exterior of the Watergate Hotel and mug shots (of the actors, identified by the historical parts they play) accompanied by an audio news report of the Watergate break-in.

This bold opening triptych is vintage Stone in its declaration of artistic licence; its thematic and metaphoric telegraphing; its dramatic staging and provocative use of invented dialogue; its confident display of technical virtuosity and shock tactics, both ideological and material. The quintessential event in Nixon's life will be the Watergate break-in; the man's goal, success based on studied sincerity. The typical Stone protagonist is a man who struggles with self-doubt in a male-dominated, often ruthless world as he attempts to prove his worthiness, especially to a disapproving or emotionally absent father. *Nixon* turns on that struggle as Stone constructs a historical narrative of the politician's actions and their national and international consequences.

Although Stone's character study of Nixon is more sympathetic to the disgraced president than anticipated, many American historians and political journalists had rehearsed their quarrels with the director over *JFK* and repeated essentially the same complaints regarding the liberties of Stone's interpretations and insinuations. Still, the outrage was diminished. In an ironic parallel to the competition between the two politicians that continually frustrated Nixon, critics and moviegoers worldwide were far less interested in *Nixon* than they had been in *JFK*.

Double lives, duelling biopics

Although repetition is the essence of all genres, topic duplication is most obvious in biopics. These pairs of duelling biopics were in production simultaneously, then released within a year of each other: *Christopher Columbus: The Discovery* and *1492: Conquest of Paradise* (both 1992); *Tombstone* (1993) and *Wyatt Earp* (1994); *Prefontaine* (1997) and *Without Limits* (1998); *The King and I* and *Anna and the King* (both 1999); and, to a lesser degree, *JFK* and *Ruby* (1992), and *Kundun* and *Seven Years in Tibet* (1997).

Some of these overlapping films can be explained by their proximity to contemporaneous events (the 500th anniversary of Columbus's voyage) or to each other (the success of *JFK* enabled *Ruby*). The adjective 'duelling' most appropriately fits two biopics on runner Steve Prefontaine. Their production histories involve overlapping geneses, conflicting rights and threatened lawsuits. These projects highlight the pitfalls of constructing a recent life and demonstrate how much biographical construction is fuelled by film-makers' resumes, production budgets, star-power and Hollywood hubris.

Prefontaine was released by Hollywood Pictures (a division of Disney) in the spring of 1997; it starred television actor Jared Leto (*My So-Called Life*) and was the fiction-film debut of Steve James, who directed the acclaimed sports documentary *Hoop Dreams* (1994). *Without Limits* (originally titled *Pre*) was released in spring 1998. Produced by Tom Cruise – who had intended to star – and Warner Bros., the film was directed by Robert Towne, a Hollywood veteran who wrote the screenplay with Kenny Moore, a *Sports Illustrated* writer and friend of Prefontaine. Up-and-coming actor Billy Crudup portrayed the runner.

In 1977, Moore contacted Towne for some screenwriting consulting for a TV movie on the recently deceased track star. The project never happened, but the two continued to discuss a film about Prefontaine. In 1994, TV producers John Lutz and Mark Doonan purchased the rights to Prefontaine's story from his family. The pair intended to produce a documentary and then a feature film about the runner. They accomplished the former when Nike (which Prefontaine's coach Bill Bowerman co-founded) assisted in a 1995 CBS special, *Fire on the Track* – which Moore co-wrote. When Lutz and Doonan began preparing for a film, Moore became involved, as did Towne and Tom Cruise. Agreements broke down among the quintet; Lutz and Doonan made a deal with Disney, who in turn brought in Steve James, who quickly co-wrote the script, and filming began on 1 July 1996 with a budget of $8 million. One month later, with the backing of Warner Bros. and just over triple the budget of Disney's film, Towne and Cruise's version started shooting.[21]

This game of biopic chicken caused friction among the competing producers, who were battling not only for the rights to filmed footage of Prefontaine's races, but also among key figures close to the runner. Disney had the ABC sports rights to the Munich Olympics, while Warner Bros. had to make do with the BBC film of the events. Also, Warner Bros. secured the use of Prefontaine's alma mater, the University of Oregon, and booked it for four months, leaving Disney either to wait and endanger their early release date or to film elsewhere. Director James chose the latter and shot the college track scenes at the University of Puget Sound in Seattle. At the script stage, fellow runner Don Kardong objected to attitudes ascribed to him in *Without Limits*, while Prefontaine's coach Bill Bowerman considered filing a lawsuit against *Prefontaine* as he felt James and Corr's script 'turned Pre into a sex maniac'.[22] In both cases, the individuals' concerns were addressed and the scripts modified.

As the Disney producers paid for the Prefontaine family's rights, family members are more prominent in *Prefontaine*. Perhaps in deference to the family, some facts of Prefontaine's fatal accident (concerning his elevated blood alcohol level) are obscured. In contrast, Warner Bros. owned the rights to Bill Bowerman's story and hired the coach as a consultant. Disney in turn secured assistant coach Bill Dellinger. Consequently, in *Prefontaine*, Dellinger (Ed O'Neil) delivers the news to the runner in Munich that the Israeli hostages have been killed, whereas in *Without Limits* the messenger is Bowerman.

Yet in *Prefontaine,* neither Dellinger nor Bowerman (R. Lee Ermey) is depicted with as much gravity and reverence as Bowerman in *Without Limits*. Performed with a hushed intensity by Donald Sutherland, Coach Bowerman, in familiar sports movie theatrics, teaches Prefontaine about life off the track as much as on. *Without Limits* hinges on the Bowerman–Prefontaine relationship, presented in father–son terms, made even more pronounced as Prefontaine's father is not depicted at all. In both films, the Bowerman figure has the last word: at Prefontaine's funeral, Ermey's Bowerman delivers a subdued eulogy, while Sutherland's speech is more nakedly emotional and is followed by Prefontaine taking a slow-motion victory lap, superimposed over a freeze half-frame shot of Bowerman. Each film's conception of Bowerman is summarised in its respective 'update' crawls. While both films list the positive Congressional effect of Prefontaine's efforts at securing more athletes' rights in the Amateur Athletic Union (AAU), *Prefontaine* provides information on Prefontaine's still-unbroken records and on the contemporary careers of fellow runners and friends Mac Wilkins and Pat Tyson before offering this note on Bowerman: '[He was the] co-founder of Nike [who] co-authored *Jogging*, universally recognized as the book that launched the jogging craze.' In *Without Limits*, after asserting Prefontaine's efforts to reform the AAU, the film offers a 1978 update on Bowerman's founding of Nike and then a 1998 note that he 'continues to advise Nike, be advised by Barbara [his wife] and in his spare time breed small but occasionally feisty Dexter cattle on the banks of the McKenzie River'.

More importantly, the films differ in their overall conceptions of Prefontaine's life, differences which partly reflect the directors' résumés. Stylistically, James's *Prefontaine* employs a semi-documentary style, consistent with his previous work, featuring familiar documentary techniques, including the use of the 'talking head' interview. In *Prefontaine,* the interviews, with characters in old-age make-up reminiscing about the runner, frame the central narrative; the obviousness of the sentiments expressed actually works to expose them as contrived. *Prefontaine* features news and Olympic footage of the actual Prefontaine, which strengthens the 'authenticity' of its semi-documentary approach. However, this reliance on ABC archives, combined with a cast best known for TV work and a modest production budget, results in a production that resembles a made-for-TV movie more than a theatrical release.

Robert Towne's approach is more elaborate and mythic. The large production budget is obvious, most notably in the re-creations of large-scale events. Stylistically, the mythic quality appears in visceral running sequences that alternate with elegiac vistas (shot by Conrad Hall). While *Prefontaine* argues that the runner was important for breaking records and the AAU's hold on amateur athletes, *Without Limits* presents a more universalised portrait of the runner (approaches evident in their titles). The narrative of *Without Limits* pivots on 'believing in oneself', with Prefontaine's successes portrayed as the result of self-determination. After his mid-film defeat at the Munich Olympics, the third act turns on Prefontaine's recovering his self-confidence. He returns to train with Bowerman, then runs in a fundraising event for University of Oregon against his American contemporaries and former teammates.

In *Prefontaine*, the drive to return to competing comes from Prefontaine's desire to restage the Munich race with arch-rival Lasse Viren and to challenge the AAU's stronghold on where amateur athletes compete. He wins the latter battle, but not the former, as Viren declines. In *Prefontaine,* the runner is as much humbled as emboldened by this race and, at a party later that night, says as much, while his parents, coaches, girlfriend *and* teammates look on adoringly. The film then cuts to Prefontaine driving alone on a winding road (an insert shot of the speedometer shows thirty miles per hour). He swerves to avoid an oncoming car and flips over. In *Without Limits,* a different race is presented as the pivotal 'return to form' for Prefontaine and an alternative celebration is portrayed less as a familial canonisation of the runner than as a typical college party. Driving ailing fellow runner Frank Shorter home, Prefontaine confides that he has a new time to break before the next Olympics. The accident (set to Elton John's 'Rocket Man' heard on the car's radio) happens on the way back to the party while Prefontaine narrates his assured win at this future race. These differing senses of how Prefontaine's life ended (and what he was feeling at the time of the accident) are emblematic of the films' differing hypotheses of what made the runner 'tick'.

Production and exhibition in the 1990s

Despite lavish budgets, acclaimed directors and some of Hollywood's biggest stars, the biopic was inconsistently successful in the 1990s. Perhaps the most important factor affecting the genre's success involved the rapid sophistication of technology and special effects which fuelled an ever-vigilant pursuit of the 'event' blockbuster and thus created an environment in which the biopic rarely fitted. This disconnect was intensified with the teen-dominated audiences of the 1980s and 1990s. Furthermore, the biopic does not lend itself to sequels or the possibility of becoming a long-range or integrated franchise.

Only four among the sixty-one biopics we surveyed reached the $100 million domestic box-office mark and 'blockbuster' status: *Schindler's List* (1993); *Patch Adams* (1998); *Remember the Titans*; and *Erin Brockovich* (2000). These biopics are all glossy star-vehicles, amenable to cross-genre marketing. While ads for *Patch Adams* and *Remember the Titans* do not entirely ignore their biopic lineage, generic references are nevertheless displaced under the less constrictive 'based on a true story' rubric, combined with other story elements. *Patch Adams* was showcased less as a doctor's biography and more as a tale of how star Robin Williams's ingratiating persona clashes with an uncaring medical establishment. *Remember the Titans'* ads downplayed the specific struggle of coach Herman Boone (Denzel Washington) in favour of emphasising an inspirational race-relations story marketed to families.[23] *Schindler's List*, although based on the life of Oskar Schindler, was sold as an educational film, a historical drama, a Holocaust film, a World War II drama and a Steven Spielberg production. Multiple marketing approaches are not necessarily misrepresentations, nor is a multi-genre approach new to the biopic; rather, marketing techniques have become more sophisticated in emphasising sometimes disparate but more usually interdependent elements to different segments of the audience. These techniques are not limited to the biopic, but are especially vital to ensuring the genre's success.[24]

The biggest 1990s blockbuster biopic, *Erin Brockovich*, demonstrates this multi-faceted approach, in marketing and in its cross-generic construction. Julia Roberts plays a working-class single mother who uses her street-smarts to great effect while investigating pollution by a local utility company. She is instrumental in the damage suit's success, achieves financial security and proves wrong everyone who underestimated her. *Erin Brockovich* was promoted through its star and the landmark salary of $20 million Roberts received for the role. Its release continued Roberts's streak of hits after a mid-1990s slump of ill-received dramatic roles.

Despite some financial successes, the vast majority of major studio-produced biopics in the 1990s were flops – and conspicuously expensive ones. Stars Jack Nicholson (*Hoffa,* 1992), Bette Midler (*Isn't She Great,* 2000), Kevin Costner (*Wyatt Earp*) and Brad Pitt (*Seven Years in Tibet*) did not draw moviegoers. Established directors such as Ridley Scott (*1492: Conquest of Paradise*), Tim Burton (*Ed Wood*), Oliver Stone and Martin Scorsese could not assure profits. Whether played by a popular actor or directed by a critically acclaimed auteur, many of these flops centre on 'unpopular' or previously marginalised figures or are ironic or revisionist in tone or form.

Although independent production attracted hopeful (and even fawning) press attention, indie biopics and their protagonists were not necessarily radically different from their Hollywood counterparts. While films such as *Swoon* (1992), *Naked Lunch* (1991), *Before Night Falls* and the *faux* biopic *Velvet Goldmine* (1998) featured stylish imagery and dabbled in semi-baroque narrative techniques, none was as visually dense as Stone's work in *JFK* and *Nixon,* nor did any of the indie biopics disturb the genre's conventions to any great extent. Indie biopics did feature such offbeat figures as would-be assassin Valerie Solanas (*I Shot Andy Warhol,* 1996), beat poet Neal Cassady (*The Last Time I Committed Suicide,* 1997) and 1960s activist Abbie Hoffman (*Steal This Movie,* 2000), but the major studios produced biopics (and more of them) on such eccentric or controversial figures as B-movie director Ed Wood, 'shock jock' Howard Stern, romance novelist Jacqueline Susann, repellent baseball player Ty Cobb and pornography publisher Larry Flynt.

While it is too facile to claim the only differences between studio and indie biopics were differences in budget, the blurring of distinctions as to where Hollywood ends and independent cinema begins was intensified as conglomerates such as Disney and Time-Warner acquired previously independent companies such as New Line and Miramax. In addition, major studios further co-opted the indie film movement by instigating internal independent divisions which acquired or developed films previously relegated to the independent market. *Boys Don't Cry*, for instance, was one of the biggest independent successes of 1999 and was subsequently acquired by Fox Searchlight Pictures. It earned six times its $2 million budget, a host of critics' awards, a best actress Oscar for Hilary Swank, and a supporting nomination for Chloe Sevigny. *Boys Don't Cry* – which told the story of Teena Brandon, a young Midwestern woman who was raped and murdered after the revelation that she had been posing as a man called Brandon Teena – was justly praised for its unflinching portrait of the youth's plight.

Despite their uneven financial track record, the appeals of the biopic endure. But producers and studios must now, it seems, look beyond these appeals in order to ensure sufficiently large audiences and profits. These demands are evident in the production of *Ali*, the biopic of the legendary boxer released in late 2001. Budgeted at $109 million, it is the most expensive biopic to date and stars Will Smith, arguably the most versatile performer of his generation. Despite the presence of Smith (who has worldwide appeal),

Sony, the film's producer and distributor, threatened to cancel the picture unless Smith and director Michael Mann assumed some of the accountability for any budget over-runs. Co-star Ron Silver has said that Mann uses 'Ali's life to probe the complexities of race in America'; the director sees the project as a portrait of 1960s rebellion and a personal parable as Mann 'identifies with Ali's fight to carve his own fresh path in the culture'.[25] Sony Chairman Amy Pascal predictably plays the 'Producer's Game', conceived as the process whereby producers emphasise elements employed in recently successful films in order to reproduce that success.[26] Acknowledging that the most (financially) successful recent biopics have been either low-budget sleepers or glossy, conventional star-vehicles, Pascal optimistically stresses the universal appeal of Ali's life: 'It's a great underdog story ... And if you look at the movies that have worked, they're often about an underdog who fights the system and wins. People identify with that – they want to see a hero who wins. And that's Ali. He's a hero to the whole world.'[27] It remains to be seen whether or not these words prove prophetic.

Notes

1. Karen Jaehne, 'Schrader's *Mishima*: An Interview', *Film Quarterly*, vol. 39, no. 3 (Spring 1986), p. 13. Schrader's radically structured screenplay for *Gershwin* has not as yet secured funding. His more conventional screenplay for *Dino*, the life story of Dean Martin, is, however, now in production.

2. George F. Custen, *Bio/Pics: How Hollywood Constructed Public History* (New Brunswick, NJ: Rutgers University Press, 1992). In 'The Mechanical Life in the Age of Human Reproduction: American Biopics, 1961–1980', *Biography*, vol. 23, no. 1 (2000), pp.127–57, Custen qualifies his earlier prediction, yet still claims that more recent Hollywood biopics reflect the influence of tabloid television, with 'ridicule and envy replace(ing) reverence', ibid., p. 156. For a survey of biographical film that includes documentary production, see Carolyn Anderson, 'Biographical Film', in Wes D. Gehring (ed.), *Handbook of Film Genres* (Westport, CT: Greenwood Press, 1988), pp. 331–51.

3. Steve Neale, *Genre and Hollywood* (London: Routledge, 2000), note 10, p. 144.

4. Rick Altman, *Film/Genre* (London: BFI, 1999).

5. See Altman, ibid., for an original and convincing account of biopic genre formation in the early 1930s studio system.

6. Altman, ibid., p. 177, argues that 'most viewers ... accept the biopic pattern as a shared schema'.

7. See Thomas Cripps, *Black Films as Genre* (Bloomington: Indiana University Press, 1978).

8. Additional women's lives were represented in three dual biographies, one group biography and one story of a transgendered subject. Earlier studies show the biopic as overwhelmingly male, but by differing degrees. Anderson, in 'Biographical Film', p. 336, charts 28 per cent female subjects in her 1929–86 sample; Custen's figures, in *Bio/Pics*, p. 144, are 35 per cent female for the studio era and 39 per cent female for the post-studio era.

9. Dramatising an entire life has always slowed the rhythm of the biopic and presented difficult casting challenges. In addition to participating in a cross-genre move to ever faster tempos, the theatrical biopic has good reasons to distinguish its narrative design from the output of

the Biography Channel on TV, which faithfully subscribes to a full-life documentary formula. *Erin Brockovich* (2000) ingeniously responded to expository demands without slowing its pace: a pre-credit scene places Brockovich in a job interview in which she spills out her life story to a prospective employer.

10. Custen, *Bio/Pics*, p. 145.
11. Anderson, 'Biographical Film', p. 336.
12. Recent biopics are more chauvinistic than ever: 78 per cent of single-person biopics in our sample were US citizens, compared to Custen's figures of 42 per cent in the 1970s, 46 per cent in the 1960s and 66 per cent in the studio era.
13. Custen, *Bio/Pics*, p. 134.
14. Thomas Schatz, *The Genius of the System: Hollywood Filmmaking in the Studio Era* (New York: Pantheon, 1988).
15. Altman, *Film/Genre*, p. 117.
16. Scott Alexander and Larry Karaszewski, Man on the Moon: *The Shooting Script* (New York: Newmarket Press, 1999), p. vii.
17. Custen, *Bio/Pics*, pp. 154–5.
18. Ibid., p. 153.
19. Confirming Stone's status as a commercially viable auteur, Warners has released a ten-movie 'Oliver Stone Collection' on DVD. This set includes a 52-minute documentary grandly entitled *Oliver Stone's America* and a four-hour 'director's cut' of *Nixon*.
20. Although this opening scene seemed a ludicrous invention to many, Howard Hunt did in fact, according to a screenplay note, rent this 16mm training film and screen it to the burglars on the night of the break-in attempt. See Eric Hamburg (ed.), Nixon: *An Oliver Stone Film* (New York: Continuum, 2000), p. 84.
21. Dave Kuehls, 'Pre-viewed', *Runner's World* (February 1997), pp. 48–56; Merrell Noden, 'A Mad Dash: Two Films about Prefontaine Go Neck and Neck', *Entertainment Weekly*, 7 February 1997, pp. 21–2.
22. Kuehl's, 'Pre-viewed', p. 56.
23. The overseas marketing for *Remember the Titans* completely elided the biopic angle as the studio was concerned with overcoming 'the usual barriers surrounding American sports or black-themed pictures' by highlighting the 'inspirational leader element'. See Don Groves, 'It's a Whole New Ballgame', *Variety*, 1 January 2001, p. 17.
24. For example, print ads for *Before Night Falls* presented at least three marketing approaches: the critically acclaimed art film, the critically acclaimed art film about a gay man and a historical-political drama about Cuba. The first two approaches featured a barrage of quotes from critics surrounding a central image of Javier Bardem. In the gay press, Bardem was pictured sunbathing next to another man. After Bardem's Academy Award nomination, smaller ads dropped the raves, headlined the nomination and presented a ragged image of Bardem next to copy referencing the 1980 Cuban exodus.
25. Patrick Goldstein, 'A Couple of Real Fighters', *Los Angeles Times*, 12 June 2001, Calendar.
26. See Altman, *Film/Genre*, pp. 38–43.
27. Pascal, quoted in Goldstein, 'A Couple of Real Fighters'.

8

From Paranoia to Postmodernism?
The Horror Movie in Late Modern Society

Andrew Tudor

Even the most eager advocates of the claim that we live in 'postmodern' times would have to concede that the currency of the term itself has become somewhat devalued over the past couple of decades. What may have seemed a reasonably concise expression in, say, Lyotard's early use of it[1] has been spread ever more thinly across a wider and wider range of social and cultural circumstances. This is as true in film studies as elsewhere, where it has become almost *de rigueur* to invoke postmodernity in seeking to characterise the state of the cinema at the turn of the century. Quite what the term suggests about contemporary film (or, indeed, about contemporary society) is far from agreed, and I shall try to clarify some its range of meanings later in this discussion. For the moment, however, I want to look at the term 'postmodern' as it is invoked in application to contemporary horror movies.

It is not clear quite when critical discussion began to talk of late-century horror as somehow 'postmodern'. Certainly by 1986 Tania Modleski felt able to make a case linking current developments in the horror movie and postmodern theory.[2] In 1989, almost as an afterthought to my study *Monsters and Mad Scientists*, I suggested that certain aspects of modern horror related to at least some of the social and cultural changes that had been characterised as postmodern.[3] A year later, Noël Carroll made a similar although rather more subtle point, arguing that 'the contemporary horror genre is the exoteric expression of the same feelings that are expressed in the esoteric discussions of the intelligentsia with respect to postmodernism'.[4] Neither Carroll nor I was overly enthusiastic about using the term itself, about so-called 'postmodern theory', or about the desire to diagnose our times as a social condition of postmodernity, but the parallels were too obvious to resist and the cultural resonance too rich to ignore. Since then there has been a proliferation in use of the expression 'postmodern horror' as an apparently unproblematic descriptive term and rather fewer attempts to examine the proposition that there is indeed something about the modern horror movie which merits the designation. A good instance of the latter, and one to which I shall return, is Pinedo's 1997 volume.[5] But for the most part, recent horror movies have been dubbed 'postmodern' with little or no discussion of what that involves or implies.

In this chapter I want to explore the implications of that tendency by pursuing two related lines of argument. First, I shall examine late twentieth-century horror movies with a view to establishing their distinctive characteristics. In this I shall build upon the account of horror movie history laid out in *Monsters and Mad Scientists*, seeking to extend that analysis from 1985 to the century's end. Note, however, that I have not attempted to replicate the kind of detailed statistical analysis found in the original study. The increasing tendency to distribute horror direct to video limits the representativeness of such figures when based solely on theatrical distribution. Instead, I have been more concerned to see if the horror discourse that I called 'paranoid horror' in the original study has mutated into some more distinctively 'postmodern' form or if, as Pinedo suggests, my 'paranoid horror' simply equates to what she calls 'postmodern horror'.[6] Having examined the recent history of the horror movie, my second line of argument then goes on to ask what, if anything, is to be gained by describing contemporary horror as 'postmodern' and how that relates – if at all – to the larger social context of the so-called postmodern world.

The horror film since 1985

What, then, has happened to the horror movie since 1985? If one were to advance a naive description, that is to say one without the benefit of detailed historical comparison, several features would be immediately apparent. Perhaps most obvious would be the growing dependence of the genre on clearly defined cycles in which one sequel follows hot on the heels of another. The *Friday the 13th* franchise – the term seems appropriate in a consumerist culture – which had already reached its alleged 'final chapter' with the fourth film in 1984, was revived in 1985 in *Friday the 13th Part V: A New Beginning* and ran through three more sequels before reaching an apparent apotheosis in 1993 with *Jason Goes to Hell: The Final Friday*. Needless to say, there is now a *Jason X* (2001), in which he is revived in the future. The enormous success of *A Nightmare on Elm Street* (1984) meant that it was speedily followed in 1985 by Part 2 and then generated another four sequels, five if you include the elegantly reflexive *Wes Craven's New Nightmare* (1994). Scattered among the rest, and now choosing examples almost at random, we find three sequels to *Alien* (1979); *House* (1986) and *House II: The Second Story* (1987); *Psycho III* (1986) and an almost shot-by-shot remake of *Psycho* (1998); a couple of *Fright Night*s; three each in the *Hellraiser* and *Child's Play* cycles; a couple of *Candyman*s; no less than *Halloween 8* (2001); and a string of one-off sequels and remakes. And, in addition, there are those films that follow both directly and indirectly in the wake of the hugely influential *Scream* (1996), of which more later.

In a historical perspective, of course, one might wonder whether any of this is really new? There is a sense in which I think that it might be. While it is true that the horror movie has always worked with clearly marked cycles (consider, most obviously, the Frankenstein, Dracula, werewolf and mummy cycles which have recurred throughout the genre's history), the recent reliance on rapid sequences of sequels which, in their marketing, are offered as precisely that, does appear to be a genuinely distinctive feature of 1980s and 1990s horror. It is as if the concept of a 'sequel' – or, if you like, the process of 'sequelling' – has itself become a major convention of the genre, a phenomenon fully understood and, more important, expected and embraced by a generically competent horror audience. As a character observes in *Scream*, 'these days you've got to have a sequel' – the quality of which phenomenon, appropriately enough, then turns up as a topic for classroom discussion early in *Scream 2* (1997).

A second aspect of contemporary horror which would be as immediately apparent to the naive viewer as to the sophisticate is the prominence of comedy. Around thirty or so of the films I viewed for consideration here would merit the description 'comedy-horror', while a substantially larger group regularly introduce comic elements into what are otherwise 'serious' narratives. Again, historically this is not new. There has always been a thread of comedy running through the genre, especially at the low-budget end, but the ubiquity of comic elements in recent horror is striking, as is the character of the comedy itself. Two features of that stand out. One is the linking of comedy to 'splatter'. In 1980s films such as *Re-Animator* (1985), *Brain Damage* (1987) and *Evil Dead II* (1987), much of the comic fun to be had derives from the excess of gory detail. The other aspect, in this case more a development characteristic of the 1990s than the 1980s, is the tendency to reflexively generate humour by openly appealing to a knowing audience's familiarity with the genre conventions. There are some quite subtle variations on this – the delightful *Tremors* (1989), for example, has half an eye on 1950s horror – but the real *locus classicus* is *Scream*, succeeded by its own two sequels as well as by the likes of *The Faculty* (1998), *Scary Movie* (2000) and *Cherry Falls* (2000). It is such films as these that have so often attracted the designation 'postmodern', if only superficially, because of their studied self-consciousness and their use of pastiche.

Apart from sequelling and comedy, an account of late-century horror would have little else to add that had not been already apparent by the 1980s. A continuation of the trend towards the youth market, seen in the constant use of American high school and college environments as a setting and source of typical characters. A further extension of highly skilled, gory special effects, with a concomitant emphasis on the spectacle of splatter and on 'body-horror'. The familiar return of classical horror stories in the form of big-budget films from 'respectable' directors, such as Coppola's *Dracula* (1992) or Branagh's *Mary Shelley's Frankenstein* (1994). Proof, if proof were needed, that it is still possible for the occasional low-budget horror film such as *The Blair Witch Project* (1999) to make the jump from the genre ghetto into more general commercial success, in this case made interesting because of the role played by the World Wide Web in selling the project direct to the public. And, sadly, precious few films with the power to disturb found in, say, *Night of the Living Dead* (1968), *The Last House on the Left* (1972), *The Texas Chainsaw Massacre* (1974), or *Shivers* (1975); perhaps only *Henry, Portrait of a Serial Killer* (1986), *Man Bites Dog* (1992), or, in a rather different mode, *Tetsuo: The Iron Man* (1991), even aspires to that kind of assault on horror movie sensibilities.

None of these features – apart from the role of the Internet in selling *The Blair Witch Project* – is significantly new. To appreciate what might be genuinely innovative or unusual, it is necessary to frame the historical context a little more systematically. To do so I shall return to the central ideas of *Monsters and Mad Scientists* and look again at my characterisation of modern (i.e. post-1960s) 'paranoid' horror as being qualitatively different to the 'secure' horror discourse that preceded it.[7] This contrast can usefully be introduced in the schematic form of a table summarising the main contrasting components of the two discourses:

Secure Horror	Paranoid Horror
successful human intervention	failed human intervention
effective expertise	ineffective expertise
authorities as legitimate	authorities as unreliable
sustainable order	escalating disorder
'external' threats	'internal' threats
centre-periphery organisation	victim groups organisation
defined boundaries	diffuse boundaries
closed narratives	open narratives

Table 8.1   **The Discourses of Secure and Paranoid Horror**

Essentially my claim is that the dominant discourse of film horror prior to the 1960s presupposed an ultimately secure world in which the monstrous threat was finally defeated and order restored. Established authorities were broadly reliable, the boundaries between known and unknown were clearly marked, and protagonists were able to intervene with some realistic hope of success. In marked contrast, horror movie discourse from the 1970s onwards presumes a world in which the monstrous threat is increasingly beyond control and order is therefore unlikely to be restored at narrative end. Experts can no longer provide credible protection, the threat from the unknown pervades the everyday world, and there always remains potential for escalating disorder. Individually the difference is perhaps best seen in the contrast between a classic 'mad scientist' narrative such as *Frankenstein* (1931) and a terrorising psychotic narrative such as *Halloween* (1978). In the former, the narrative's central threat is a consequence of human volition, is 'external' to the human body and mind, is clearly distinguished from 'normality', and is finally defeated. Human expertise is effective; authorities are broadly legitimate. In the latter, the threat is unexplained, it is 'internal' in the sense that it emerges from the psyche and is located in an ordinary everyday world, and the boundary between 'normality' and 'abnormality' is not clearly marked. The monster survives, and 'experts' are unable to deal with it. At every turn, the world of *Halloween* and its many successors is thoroughly unreliable and insecure.

Key to the development of such psycho-movies as *the* most prominent feature of post-1960s horror is the distinction between internal and external threats. Even where no explanation is offered for their behaviour, the rampaging psychotics who follow in the wake of, first, *Psycho* (1960) and *Peeping Tom* (1960), then *Halloween*, are constituted as monstrous threats by virtue of some characteristic presumed to be internal to their being. This was a major change of emphasis in as much as most horror movie threats prior to the emergence of the psycho-killer were externally derived: they came from space, for example, or supernature, or were created by virtue of scientific interference

in the proper order of things. Internality also finds expression in the growing use of contemporary and prosaic everyday settings such as small towns, suburbs, ordinary houses,
family groups, and the like. This renders the characteristic threats of paranoid horror
'internal' in the sense of belonging within our familiar physical and social world, not distanced from us as they are in the Gothic *elsewhen* of an imaginary Transylvania or among
the exotic equipment of a fanciful laboratory. 'Internal', then, suggests internality in both
a mental and a social sense. In the course of the 1980s and 1990s, furthermore, it also
developed an associated physical dimension with the further growth of 'body-horror', its
ferocious and graphic destruction of victims' bodies a very direct and visceral expression
of the turn to internality.

Parallel to this growing emphasis we find a change in the tacit social structure of the
typical horror movie world. In secure horror, where constituted authorities (e.g. scientists, military, the police, etc.) are generally seen as legitimate, those authorities are
central to narrative resolution and essential if the larger population of potential victims
are to be saved. The tacit social model is one of centre and periphery, authority and
dependence. In paranoid horror, where constituted authorities are no longer seen as
legitimate and are no longer effective in combating the monstrous threat, the social structure of the horror movie is reduced to an assembly of potential victims. Resistance, if it
can be mounted at all, is based upon loose alliances between those victims, rather than
on authoritative expertise or the variously coercive arms of the state. The old centre-
periphery model of social life, which largely characterised secure horror, gives way to a
victim-oriented world in which embattled individuals and groups struggle for survival.

Does this characterisation of paranoid horror still hold as an adequate description of
the dominant horror movie discourse of the late twentieth century? Broadly I believe
that it does. Most of its major features are still in place, even if their frequency varies
and their narrative articulation has altered. It may be, for example, that the balance
between open and closed narratives has shifted slightly back towards the former since
the 1980s, or that the psycho-killer is no longer quite as prominent a figure, but seen
against the background of secure horror, recent horror movies remain 'paranoid' through
and through. This does not mean, of course, that there are not some broadly traditional
films to be found in this as in any other period. *Haunted* (1995), as befits a film from a
director as long established as Lewis Gilbert, has many attributes of the classic ghost
story, while, as always, films directed at the mainstream market, such as *The Sixth Sense*
(1999) and *What Lies Beneath* (2000), routinely compromise on the more excessive
demands of the paranoid discourse. But the general 'shape' of the world presumed by
late modern horror remains that mapped out in the secure/paranoid model.

Within that broad pattern, however, it is still possible that the character of the paranoid discourse has been modified significantly by the seemingly new elements in 1990s
horror: most notably, generically self-conscious comedy and the accelerating incidence
of sequelling. The significance of these two features is that they interact to add a further
level of reflexivity to the relation between audience and film, inviting the moviegoer to
participate in the construction of the horror experience via modes of response which are
increasingly self-aware. That gives rise to a number of obvious but important questions.

Does such self-awareness undermine the 'seriousness' of the paranoid vision of the world? Do these characteristics of modern horror distance spectators from the emotional intensity of the experience? Does the affectionate mockery implicit in their pastiche of generic conventions also apply to the underlying assumptions which make the discourse meaningful? Or, is the effectivity of the basic discourse untouched by these essentially superficial changes? For if the paranoid assumptions of modern horror work for their audiences because they resonate metaphorically with features of everyday social experience – and that claim is central to my analysis – then humourous or not, self-conscious or not, the basic structures of meaning implicit in the genre remain constant. Let us examine some of these issues a little more closely in relation to what has arguably been the most successful 'reflexive' horror movie of the 1990s: *Scream*.

Scream

Scream did not introduce self-consciousness about genre conventions into horror – some degree of awareness has always been a key element in the genre audience's response in as much as generic competence is routinely textually played upon and audiences have usually been willing to rise to that bait. What *Scream* has done is find a highly commercial (and therefore influential) form for expression of the kind of knowing reflexivity that its director, Wes Craven, achieved with rather less commercial success in *Wes Craven's New Nightmare*. In that film, the conceit was that both actors and director from *A Nightmare on Elm Street* (the first and best of the cycle, and the only one directed by Craven) find themselves under threat from the original film's monster, Freddy Krueger, who has, as it were, escaped the confines of cinema into the 'real' world of the *New Nightmare*. The slipperiness of the boundary between reality and dreamworld which drives the *Elm Street* narratives is thus turned back on itself, and the shift of levels generates a kind of meta-film in which the actors (and Craven) play meta-versions of themselves. This relativising of the film's reality frame raises complex issues of involvement and verisimilitude, and in consequence the film was perhaps too knowing for its own commercial good. *Scream*, in some contrast, keeps its reflexivity and self-consciousness firmly within the confines of the diagesis, its characters explicitly articulating genre conventions (in both dialogue and action) in such a way as to ensure that their self-consciousness remains a verisimilitudinous component of the narrative and does not therefore question the 'reality' of the film's world. As Randy (*Scream*'s horror movie expert) observes in the course of explaining horror conventions: 'You get too complicated, you lose your target audience.' Just so with *Wes Craven's New Nightmare*, but not with *Scream*.

Unlike *New Nightmare*, *Scream* declines to blur the line between film and film-makers (although the briefly appearing janitor, named as Fred and wearing a Freddy Krueger striped top, is surely Craven himself). Its self-consciousness is contained: an occasion for humour and joyous audience involvement, but not a mechanism for questioning the workings of the horror movie as such. Indeed, *Scream*'s distinctive quality lies in its skilful balancing of knowing humour with well-crafted, tension-filled sequences. Consider, for example, the film's famous opening in which Casey, the generically archetypal, alone-at-home, androgynously named teenage girl played by Drew Barrymore, is terrorised by telephone and finally murdered by the masked killer. This sequence never sacrifices the tension to the gags or to the genre references. Instead the insertion of allusions to horror films actually adds to the mounting sense of pursuit. 'Do you like scary movies?' asks the telephone voice early in the scene, its slightly strange tonal quality belying the apparently jocular character of the question and of the interchanges thus far. By the time the now angry voice insists that 'You should never say "Who's there?". Don't you watch scary movies? It's a death wish,' the genre references are actively contributing to the rising tension. We watch scary movies and we know exactly what this means. And the series of questions that follow – 'name the killer in *Halloween*' … 'name the killer in *Friday the 13th*' … 'what door am I at?' – pushes that yet further even where (as I witnessed more than once on the film's first release) audiences are shouting out the correct answer when a panicking Casey wrongly names Jason in response to the second question.

Similarly with the long party sequence which climaxes the film, as the killer terrorises one victim after another. This meticulously constructed 40 minutes of rising anxiety moves effortlessly between the Casey/Billy relationship, tension-building, humorous asides, the jokey Deputy Dewey/Gile Weathers subplot, and increasingly graphic violence, without allowing any of the elements to undermine progress towards the grand climax. So, for example, in the set-piece scene in which Tatum is trapped in the garage – with its carefully cued echoes of *Halloween* which is even then playing on the VCR in the house – tension, humour and violence combine. Having ensured that we are aware of the mechanised garage door by having her accidentally raise and lower it as she enters from the house (and thus having also ensured that as a cinematically competent audience we now expect it to play a significant part in what follows), Tatum is then treated in the classic genre fashion of those who blithely enter cellars, attics, garages and the like. After the business with the garage door, she walks out of shot, leaving us uneasily contemplating the open door to the main house. We see the reverse shot of her heading towards the fridge, then the reverse from within the fridge as she takes the beer bottles. Then a close shot of the house door as, predictably, it slowly (and creakily) closes, followed by a rising low chord on the music track as the camera rapidly closes in behind her. Tension builds, there is a sudden noise, and a precipitate series of cuts to garden tools falling over, to Tatum jumping with fright and to the cat fleeing through the cat flap. Tension is released and our expectations are fulfilled in the familiar manner of the 'suspense-shock cycle', in which growing tension is punctured by a shock (or, indeed, by humour, or by both) and then rebuilt.[8] Throughout this manipulation we, as genre filmgoers, know exactly what is happening; we are both willing victims of the technique and simultaneously self-aware parties to its construction.

Having captured us in this way, the process now begins again. Tatum returns to the closed house door only to find that it is locked. Suddenly the lights go out and the music once more begins to build. She sets the garage door to rising, but before she can escape, it stops and starts to close. Tatum turns, and the reverse shot reveals the masked killer, hand on the door switch. The 'dialogue' that follows is constructed almost entirely from movie references. 'Is that you, Randy?' she asks. The masked figure slowly shakes its head. 'What movie is this from?' as she walks towards him, 'I spit on your garage?' He

Scream (1996): knowing humour, crafted tension, reflexive horror

blocks her exit. 'Oh, you wanna play psycho-killer.' The camera angle is down into her face as she stands below him. 'Can I be the helpless victim?' The mask nods, and the camera again reverses to the downward-angled close-up. 'OK, let's see,' and, in an affected, high-pitched voice, 'No, please don't kill me Mr Ghostface; I wanna be in the sequel.' He still prevents her leaving, and losing patience she tries to push past: 'Cut, Caspar,' she says, 'that's a wrap.' They struggle, he produces the knife and very deliberately slashes her arm.

I have described this scene at such length because its evident self-consciousness and the comedy contained in the dialogue do nothing to undermine the growing tension and our expectation of nastiness to come. We may well be amused by the references to *I Spit on your Grave* (1978), to psycho-movies, to sequelling, and even to *Caspar* (1995), but we also remain fully involved in the scene's dramatic dynamics. Unlike Tatum, we know that 'ghostface' is for real, and the simultaneous deferral and suggestion of imminent violence achieved in the self-conscious movie references actually stretches out the tension. When the violence does come (after a pitched battle, Tatum is killed when, jammed in the cat flap as the garage door rises, she is crushed against the door's frame), it serves as both temporary tension release and a further turn of the overall screw.

This balance between self-consciousness, humour, tension and horror is maintained right through the rest of *Scream*'s climactic sequence, with the genre allusions multiplying as rapidly as the gore. However, it should be said that not all recently successful horror movies manage this balance as well as *Scream*. *Scary Movie*, for instance, resorts to slapstick, and is mostly a none too subtle replicative parody of *Scream* with some good jokes, but little or no tension. Similarly with *Cherry Falls,* the comedy largely displaces the horror. This is perhaps unsurprising given a story-line in which a rampaging killer (who, inverse to slasher conventions, is attacking only virgins) precipitates a mass deflowering among the population of college kids. The typical character of this humour is more than apparent in the pun of the film's title or in the admittedly rather splendidly tasteless line: 'we are talking hymen holocaust here'. Nor are these lesser copies of *Scream* exceptions. When the record is examined, few films actually aspire to *Scream*'s carefully judged balance between self-consciousness and tension, let alone achieve it. In fact, the modern horror movie has hardly been overwhelmed or even dominated by such reflexivity and pastiche, and there still remains an enthusiastic audience for relatively straightforward 'stalk-and-slash' such as *I Know What You Did Last Summer* (1997) – written by Kevin Williamson, who also wrote *Scream* – which is well crafted and remains largely non-reflexive. While *Scream* has indeed played a key role in turning modern horror in a more reflexive direction, it would be a mistake to characterise the whole genre in terms of this 'postmodern' shift.

Postmodernism and contemporary horror

Where, then, does this leave the common claim that we live in a period characterised by 'postmodern horror'? There are, I think, three broad ways in which this claim can be understood and assessed, and I shall examine them in ascending order of generality. At its least ambitious, the diagnosis of recent horror as distinctively postmodern is simply a claim about stylistic attributes of texts: particular styles or techniques may conveniently be labelled 'postmodern'. At the second, broader level of generality, the designation encompasses these stylistic features, but in addition sees them as symptomatic of a larger pattern of cultural and moral change – postmodern*ism* as a world view, a doctrine, an ideology, perhaps even a philosophy. At the third level, the argument is as much about postmodernity as postmodernism. Yes, it claims, there are aesthetic attributes properly to be considered as postmodern; yes, there is an emergent pattern of postmodern cultural and moral change; however, all this must be seen as part of the historical social transition from modernity to postmodernity. To this extent postmodernity is indeed 'post'; markedly different to what has gone before.

At each of these three rungs on the ladder of generality, successive claims are more difficult to sustain in the sense that the weight of evidence required to make them plausible becomes ever more demanding. On the first and lowest level, the case is easy enough to make. Films such as *Scream*, its sequels, successors and imitators, are considered postmodern by virtue of their overt resort to a number of distinctive textual features. The use of pastiche and humour is seen as inviting the audience to be complicit and self-aware, to participate in what Paul Wells describes as 'knowing deconstructions of the subgenre'.[9] For Wells and similarly disposed commentators, the postmodern horror movie is concerned above all openly to articulate the rules of the game and play them out as exactly that: a game. In so doing, or so it is claimed by some, they lose their potential for subversion or critique, and are able to 'speak only limitedly about the culture that produces them'.[10] Wells regrets this alleged diminution of the horror movie's power and sees it as a logical outcome of the '*McDonaldisation* of horror', but others are more positively disposed to this kind of 'postmodern' cinema. Just as postmodernism in architecture – arguably the main context from which the term entered common parlance – was aesthetically celebrated for pastiche and self-consciousness, for freeing design from the (alleged) strictures of modernism, so, too, the postmodern horror movie can be positively valued for its aesthetic reflexivity. Use of the term in this sense, then, is not inappropriate, perhaps even useful, in as much as it draws our attention to specific artistic features of (some) recent horror movies. However, given the additional social and cultural baggage that the ascription 'postmodern' routinely now carries, its invitation to presume more general claims may mean that its analytic disadvantages outweigh its advantages.

In any case, it is now rare for analysts of the postmodern, in film or elsewhere, to limit application of the term simply to the descriptive and aesthetic. They tend rapidly to escalate to the second level of generality, where to speak of postmodern horror is also to invoke a whole series of assumptions about the distinctive nature of the cultural and moral context in which such horror thrives. Fragmentation, the rejection of traditional forms as inappropriate to contemporary life, the denial of orthodox narrative conventions, the decline of fixed identity, the rise of relativism and 'nihilism' are all ideas now commonly associated with postmodern forms. The characteristic cultures of the late twentieth century are said to embody these features, with horror no exception. A well-known difficulty with such views, however, is not that they do not speak to some of the evident characteristics of the age, for they clearly do, but that they have done so throughout the twentieth century. So, for example, the transition in literature and art from nineteenth-century realism to twentieth-century modernism has often been described in just these terms: fragmentation, narrative innovation, relativism, variable identity, and the rest. What then of specifically *postmodern* horror? Is it no more than the delayed application of modernist precepts in the hitherto largely traditional world of popular culture? And if so, does it merit the distinctive qualities attributed to it by those determined to see postmodernism in culture as a reflection of profound changes?

Pinedo provides a stimulating example of an analysis pitched at this second level of generality. The postmodern horror movie, she suggests, 'transgresses the rules of the classically oriented horror genre', increasingly deals in 'hybrids' with other genres and constructs an audience for whom overturning conventions itself becomes a new convention.[11] She further proposes five key characteristics of this postmodern genre: unremitting violence in everyday life; blurred boundaries and endemic danger; rationality questioned and authority undermined; rejection of narrative closure; extreme violence which 'attests to the need to express rage and terror in the midst of postmodern social upheaval'.[12] Yet for all the care with which she addresses these features, it is significant that Pinedo has difficulty in precisely demarcating what is actually postmodern about contemporary horror. As she says herself, four of the five main features with which she is concerned are characteristics of horror more generally, but have been treated with greater intensity or elaboration in postmodern horror. None of them is qualitatively new. Indeed, among Pinedo's criteria it seems to me that only open transgression of genre rules, possibly hybridity (although I am not convinced that there is any more hybridity in the late twentieth-century genre than there was in, say, the 1950s or the 1970s) and an audience both aware of and expecting the overturning of genre conventions genuinely distinguish late-century horror from earlier forms of the paranoid discourse. Essentially, that is, an extension of reflexivity on the part of both the genre audience and the texts themselves. But is that enough to locate contemporary horror as part and parcel of a larger postmodern culture? Or is there, as Neale persuasively suggests, a tendency to overstate the significance of allusion, pastiche, hybridity, 'sequelitis' and the like in New Hollywood's genres?[13]

One way of dealing with such questions, of course, is to shift levels yet again and mount a case about the radical character of late twentieth-century social change. This kind of account suggests that a state of postmodernity exists in late modern society and that postmodern horror is no more (or less) than a popular cultural articulation of that state. Pinedo formulates a version of this argument when she sums up the 'postmodern world' in the following terms:

> For my purposes, the postmodern world is an unstable one in which traditional
> (dichotomous) categories break down, boundaries blur, institutions fall into question,
> Enlightenment narratives collapse, the inevitability of progress crumbles, and the master
> status of the universal (read male, white, monied, heterosexual) subject deteriorates.
> Consensus in the possibility of mastery is lost, universalizing grand theory is discredited, and
> the stable, unified, coherent self acquires the status of fiction.[14]

Whether that state of affairs should properly be called 'postmodern' is, of course, a matter for some debate, and many have argued that the social changes of the late twentieth century represent recognisable extensions of earlier social patterns – 'late modernity', if you will – rather than radical dislocations. For those holding this view, such as Anthony Giddens, what we are witnessing is a process of 'modernity coming to understand itself' through a growing capacity for individual and institutional reflexivity.[15] The potential for reflexive awareness, for doubting the credibility of experts and the knowledge systems upon which they rely, for relativising subjectivity and the self, for experiencing a generalised anxiety, are all implicit in modernity itself. There is no need to postulate an epochal transition to make sense of these features of modern life, and to do so is to misunderstand the character of late modern society and its culture.

Faced with this escalation to the grander reaches of social theory, there is a temptation to think that in the end it may all reduce to a question of semantics. My 'paranoid horror' is much the same as Pinedo's (and others') 'postmodern horror', and perhaps it matters little which term is used. In as much as we agree on the central features of horror in the latter part of the twentieth century, and they correspond to features of recent culture that are afforded the label, then 'postmodern' is as good a term as any. Where such pragmatism falls down, however, is that specific theoretical and historical assumptions are now irreducibly incorporated into the usage. To employ the term 'postmodern' is to make claims about both the causes and consequences of the cinema (or cultural trait) thus described. There is no doubt that the modern horror movie, like all popular culture, tells us something about the society in which we live. That it is a society in which we have become more aware of risks; a society in which we are less convinced by the systems of expertise that surround us and the institutions that seek to regulate our lives; a society in which our concept of the self is unreliable; and a society in which anxiety and fear have become ubiquitous. But to attribute this to postmodernism or postmodernity is to evade a crucial truth: that the social, cultural and environmental crises of the late modern era are manifestly products of modernity itself and of those capitalist forms of economic and social organisation in which it found consummate expression. We are not yet postmodern, nor shall we be until we have overcome the awesome consequences of that history.

Notes

1. Jean-François Lyotard, *The Postmodern Condition: A Report on Knowledge* [1979] (Manchester: Manchester University Press, 1986).

2. Tania Modleski, 'The Terror of Pleasure: The Contemporary Horror Film and Postmodern Theory', in Tania Modleski (ed.), *Studies in Entertainment: Critical Approaches to Mass Culture* (Bloomington: Illinois University Press, 1986), pp. 155–66.

3. Andrew Tudor, *Monsters and Mad Scientists: A Cultural History of the Horror Movie* (Oxford: Blackwell, 1989).

4. Noël Carroll, *The Philosophy of Horror, or Paradoxes of the Heart* (New York: Routledge, 1990), p. 210.

5. Isabel Cristina Pinedo, *Recreational Terror: Women and the Pleasures of Horror Film Viewing* (New York: State University of New York Press, 1997).

6. Ibid., p. 10.

7. Tudor, *Monsters and Mad Scientists*, pp. 102–4, 211–14; Andrew Tudor 'Unruly Bodies, Unquiet Minds', *Body & Society*, vol. 1, no. 1 (1995), pp. 34–7.

8. Tudor, *Monsters and Mad Scientists*, pp. 108–11.

9. Paul Wells, *The Horror Genre: From Beelzebub to Blair Witch* (London: Wallflower, 2000), p. 97.

10. Ibid. See also Kim Newman, *Nightmare Movies: A Critical Guide to Contemporary Horror Films* (London: Bloomsbury, 1988), pp. 211–15.

11. Pinedo, *Recreational Terror*, p. 14.

12. Ibid., pp. 14, 17–50.

13. Steve Neale, *Genre and Hollywood* (London: Routledge, 2000), pp. 245–51.

14. Pinedo, *Recreational Terror*, p. 11.

15. Anthony Giddens, *The Consequences of Modernity* (Cambridge: Polity Press, 1990), p. 48. See also Anthony Giddens, *Modernity and Self-Identity: Self and Society in the Late Modern Age* (Cambridge: Polity Press, 1991); and Ulrick Beck, Anthony Giddens and Scott Lash, *Reflexive Modernization: Politics, Tradition and Aesthetics in the Modern Order* (Cambridge: Polity Press, 1994).

9

The Impossibility of Romance: Hollywood Comedy, 1978–1999

William Paul

The rise of Animal Comedy

Hollywood comedy in the last quarter of the twentieth century witnessed a radical reorientation, in part in response to newer freedoms granted by the rating system, in part because of changes in the culture at large. Following the enormous popular success of *National Lampoon's Animal House* (1978) there arose a series of comedies defined by their raunchiness and an apparent desire to push beyond acceptable bounds of good tast.[1] While the films had enough in common to constitute a distinct comic genre, their power at the box office established them as the dominant comic form for American audiences in the early to mid-1980s. For the previous sixty years or so, romantic comedy was *the* comedy in Hollywood. While it did not become as dead as the Western in the 1980s, it certainly went into decline.[2] The new style that precipitated the decline I have dubbed 'Animal Comedy' in honour of its primary progenitors, *Animal House* (1978) and *Porky's* (1981). Animals are never very far from these films, at least metaphorically, occasionally literally, and, often enough, presented in strikingly similar ways.

The insistent emphasis on animality points to physicality as a key attribute of these films. As a consequence, physical comedy generally receives pride of place over verbal. Physical comedy of a fairly broad sort is hardly a new thing in American movies, but in the sound period at least it had generally been either limited to moments within a romantic comedy plotline or, if spread throughout the film, relegated to the lower-class realm of B-movies and shorts featuring the likes of the Bowery Boys and the Three Stooges. Animal Comedy represented a return to slapstick on a fairly grand and insistent scale. Its origins lie, I would argue, in the 1960s.

In the mid-1960s, a couple of films starring The Beatles and directed by Richard Lester appeared and instantly prompted comparisons to the Marx Brothers. While invocations of the Marx Brothers comedies were apt, the Beatles films actually appeared under the guises of different genres. *A Hard Day's Night* (1964) presented itself as a kind of documentary, one however given to flights of fancy, while *Help!* (1965) parodied the spy genre suddenly made popular by the James Bond films. In neither case could the films be regarded as romantic comedy, but in order to escape the dominant comic mode of the time, both films had to invoke other genres, as if there were no formal precedent for what they were attempting. Even the Marx Brothers, having almost managed to escape romantic comedy plots in their Paramount period, found themselves saddled with and occasionally subservient to romantic comedy plots and the likes of Kitty Carlisle and Alan Jones when they moved to MGM and classier films in the mid-1930s.

Silent comedy, but most especially silent comedy *shorts*, were more and more evoked throughout this period, most notably by Blake Edwards with *The Great Race* (1965), dedicated to 'Mr Laurel and Mr Hardy', and *The Party* (1968), the first film very freely structured, the second apparently plotless. Other Edwards films of the mid-1960s, *The Pink Panther, A Shot in the Dark* (both 1964) and *What Did You Do in the War, Daddy?* (1966), invoke other genres (mystery-suspense and war films), but, like *Help!*, they are comedies that rely on other genres to provide a sense of form for very loose structures.

What all these films have in common are ambling narratives, more episodic than dramatic, and an emphasis on *groups* of people brought together by some common activity or location. In all of the films I have mentioned, as in the later comedies, it is often the activity or location that provides the film's coherence rather than tightly structured plots or complexly defined characters. There are possibilities for romance in these films, as there are possibilities for romance almost everywhere in the movies; however, at best, romantic interest always remains secondary. If the focus in romantic comedy is generally on two gloriously glamorous individuals, the focus of Animal Comedy and its precursors is finally more social.

A similar movement from the individual to the social with a complementary undermining of the notion of the lone hero takes place around this time in the rise of the buddy films. The presence of the two stellar actors Paul Newman and Robert Redford makes *Butch Cassidy and the Sundance Kid* (1969) something different from the hero-and-his-sidekick formula of earlier action films because the eye-catching equality of the stars undermines the recognisable hierarchy of importance routinely designated by casting in earlier films. In the screen-stealing aura of Newman and Redford, Katharine Ross must emerge, like romance itself, as a distinctly secondary concern. Or, perhaps, it has been transmuted into something else. Implicitly locating this new formula in romantic comedy, Molly Haskell smartly observed, Newman and Redford were 'on their way to becoming the Myrna Loy – William Powell of the seventies'.[3] This was also a period that saw a sharp decline in major female stars, something that would only begin to reverse itself with the return of romantic comedy in the late 1980s.

The doubling up on the men points to a comic style ultimately different from romantic comedy as it simultaneously increases both aggression and regression. Writing in the early 1980s, Dave Kehr attributed the phenomenal success of *Animal House*, 'the highest grossing comedy ever made', to 'an unusual emotional subtext: the tight and cozy bonds of an all-male, post-adolescent pack'.[4] As I have tried to indicate by invoking the buddy films, this 'subtext' was not in fact unusual for the period. What struck the observant eye of this contemporary critic as unusual was its location in comedy, normally the domain of male–female relations. And it proved to be a good deal more common subsequently. From *Animal House* on, many of the comedies influenced by it have a male duo, occasionally a trio, at the centre of the group.

The heterogeneous groups where individuals register as distinct types suggest a comic reworking of the World War II combat genre.[5] With its levelling impulses and complementary attacks on the forces of authority, Animal Comedy also uses its groups as a way of honouring democratic ideals. My specific purpose in invoking combat films here lies in the singular importance of *M*A*S*H* (1970) for the later comedies. In addition to the ambling quality of the narrative, *M*A*S*H* has three key elements that proved to be central for Animal Comedy: a caustic sense of humour, a paradoxically exclusionary attitude towards those not considered fit for the heterogeneous group and a buddy relationship holding the centre together.

M*A*S*H and *American Graffiti* (1973), in which the combat group is in effect reconstituted among suburban high school students, are the two clearest progenitors of the later Animal Comedies. Many of the later films display a conscious awareness of these two films which might be seen variously as imitation, parody or homage. Whatever you make of it, reference to these earlier works, often of a very specific nature, occurs frequently: for example, the PA announcement, complete with low-angle shots of speaker horn, used to give some sense of coherence to the episodic plot in *M*A*S*H*, turns up in *Car Wash* (1975) and *Meatballs* (1979), while the what-happened-to-them-after epilogue in *American Graffiti* turns up again in *Animal House*, *Stripes* (1981), *Fast Times at Ridgemont High* (1982) and *Heaven Help Us* (1985), among others.

After inevitable repeated attempts to capitalise on the success of *Animal House*, the key features of Animal Comedy began to emerge as follows:

- Characters in Animal Comedy are defined chiefly in terms of their sexual desires. It is probably inescapable that guys attending a bachelor party should think of sex, but in these films high school and college students think chiefly of sex, summer campers think chiefly of sex, workers and members at a country club think chiefly of sex, soldiers think chiefly of sex, police trainees think chiefly of sex, even kibutzniks think chiefly of sex.

- Character typology concomitantly moves along lines of sexual interest. Because animality in the films is regarded as a freedom from inhibition, characters are defined negatively or positively by the extent to which they have embraced their animal natures, ranging from the anally repressed to the genitally aggressive, from tight-assed to cock of the walk.

- There is an element of the grotesque in all these films that derives in part from the insistent animality of the characters, although the general tone and feel of individual films may differ. In this instance, the grotesque is generally celebratory.

- A more derisory use of the grotesque is made for figures of authority and power. They are usually the most overtly stylised in presentation, even in films such as *Fast Times at Ridgemont High* and *Heaven Help Us*, where character is given a more realistic definition than is common in the genre.

- As a complement to the insistent sexual dimension, character definition is often extended to a generalised desire for liberation. This might act in some of the softer core films as a substitute for specifically sexual desire.
- Characters are generally aligned to an institution, which may be construed as loosely as a country club or even a bachelor party, but is most often seen as high schools (with summer camp a seasonable variation), prep schools, college, a police academy, a driving school or the armed forces.
- The alignment of characters with an institution keeps the focus of the films more on groups of people, rather than individuals. Individuals may stand out from the group, but they are nonetheless identified by their participation in the group.
- The group is generally defined in the mode of the World War II combat film by a variety of types. As a consequence, there is an underlying and occasionally explicit concern with defining a pluralistic society as a desired goal, although the pluralism does not encompass figures of authority.[6]
- The structure of the narrative reflects the focus on a social group by being episodic, contingent, always retaining the possibility of veering off with a character who might have previously seemed minor.
- A revenge motif is present in at least one plot strand, the resolution of which, marked by the triumph of the group of animals, signals the end of the plot for the entire film.
- The plot moves through a series of random or interconnected contests, generally marking victories for the various protagonists along the way. These little contests culminate in a final contest, the most fully elaborated and usually involving the entire cast, either in the form of a sporting event (derived from the football game in *M*A*S*H* and the drag race in *American Graffiti*) or an elaborate prank that is usually motivated by the revenge plot (*Animal House* and *Porky's*).[7]
- An us-versus-them mentality pervades all these films, providing the only real forward dynamic in the loose plot structure. The central group generally defines itself by values inimical to its opponents, who are often the ruling power structure.

This list is not exhaustive. Nor does it claim to account for the most notable elements of individual films. By it, I have merely tried to establish a community drawn together from some of the most popular comedies from the late 1970s to the mid-to late 1980s, something like a linguistic community which provides a discourse that each film utilises for its own particular enunciation.[8] Not every element will appear in every film, and some that are foregrounded in one film may well move into the background in another. And not every element is exclusive to Animal Comedy. Finally, there is a potential for paradox in Animal Comedy to the extent that it values libidinal drives of the individual at the same time as it valorises its central group. Tensions that might exist between the two are rarely touched openly by these films, although the best of them derive part of their value from how they play with this tension.

Comedian comedy: from Bill Murray to Eddie Murphy and Jim Carrey

A look at some of the most popular comedians from the 1970s through the 1990s shows a development that parallels transformation of comedy in this period. Bill Murray was the most popular comic actor of the late 1970s and early 1980s, and his screen persona gave full expression to the paradoxes of Animal Comedy. As an actor whose screen persona is balanced between proletarian slob and egalitarian snob, he became something of an icon of the genre. Murray's first big success came when he succeeded Chevy Chase in the second year of broadcast on *Saturday Night Live* after Chase left to make feature films. When Murray himself moved into feature films a year later with *Meatballs*, a *Time* reviewer complained that the film demanded John Belushi-type antics from Murray while Murray was really more suited to a romantic comedy like *Foul Play*, Chevy Chase's first film.[9] At about the same time, a *Rolling Stone* reporter, in an extended profile on Murray, attacked Chevy Chase for thinking comedy was nothing but sex.[10] Murray was above this, and, although the article does not say it explicitly, the style implies that Murray was better than Chase because he focused on power rather than sex. It is a fair indication of the contradictions in Murray's persona that he could be compared to both Belushi and Chase. This should be enough explanation for why he has had difficulty in playing romantic comedy, but it also explains why he was a major comic star for a period in which romantic comedy was in retreat.

In a minor part, as in *Caddyshack* (1980), Murray can be purely an anarchic spirit, operating in a world of his own that is constantly threatening to destroy the real world. But for all the aggression he projects, Murray is not really a comic anarchist. In fact, in his first film role, in *Meatballs*, he heads a summer camp and does the job effectively enough to turn a shy and weak boy with whom he sentimentally identifies into a gregarious and successful athlete. As always with Murray, there is an unresolved confusion between strength and weakness, sadism and masochism. Murray is a bully who allies himself with weaklings. As a consequence, in starring roles, Murray's character is inevitably fleshed out in contradictory ways.

Murray has some affinities with comic American anarchists of the past, but he also differs from them in that he inevitably and unironically moves into the power position in his movies, much as the animals in *Animal House* move into the power structure of the dominant society in the epilogue. The revels of *Animal House* invoke childish irresponsibility, especially as they are opposed to the parent-authority figures of the administration and the Wasp fraternity, but they are also preparation for taking over the reins of authority. Sowing wild oats turns out good power figures, while the repressiveness of the Wasp fraternity turns out staff members for the Nixon White House and Watergate shenanigans. Murray is often akin to the animals of *Animal House* in that he always aims towards taking over power.

The most insistent plot pattern of Murray's films throughout the 1980s has him transform the rest of the world into an image designed to confirm a sense of self that must perversely always remain uncertain to itself. Murray's screen persona seems to have become increasingly trapped in this kind of plot pattern, which made it difficult to conform in leading roles to new trends in comedy. A rare and charming attempt to do a

Caddyshack (1980)

romantic comedy crossed with a caper film, *Quick Change* (1990), failed commercially. His comeback film, *What About Bob?* (1991), restores the plot pattern with a vengeance so that it explicitly defines a genuine pathology. *Groundhog Day* (1993) remains Murray's only real success in a romantic comedy, although the romantic plot is arguably of secondary importance to the fantasy conceit of a man who must relive the same day over and over again. The effectiveness of this film may lie in the way the fantasy plays on the sadomasochistic aspects of Murray's persona I have outlined here: he is both helpless in his inability to escape the ever-repeating day and at the same time given extraordinary power over events by that very repetition. Generally, Murray has never been comfortable in the world of romantic comedy.

Eddie Murphy and Jim Carrey, who would take over from Murray in the late 1980s and 1990s as Kings of Comedy, often appeared in films that did draw on conventions of romantic comedy. By the late 1990s, *Variety* would nominate Jim Carrey 'Showman of the Year' and declare him the 'Comic pix icon of the '90s'.[11] Like Murray, Carrey had begun in stand-up comedy and achieved national attention through a ground-breaking comedy sketch show, in Carrey's case, as the one white male cast member of *In Living Color*. Carrey's comedy, like Murray's, is often described as anarchic. Finally, Carrey's carefully planned move into feature film starring roles had his managers 'poring over all the leftover Bill Murray projects in development ...'[12] The resulting film, *Ace Ventura: Pet Detective* (1994), was not a Murray project, but Carrey's fifth starring film, *The Cable Guy* (1996), can be seen as a darker version of *What About Bob?*

The differences between the two films are instructive. In *What About Bob?*, extremely needy and isolated Bill Murray attaches himself to psychiatrist (Richard Dreyfuss) to the point that he becomes a virtual member of Dreyfuss's family. By the end of the film, a near brush with death perversely gives Murray a new confidence in his self and moves him into a position of power as Dreyfuss declines into catatonia; at the end, he becomes the successful, bestselling psychiatrist-author that Dreyfuss had sought to be. In *The Cable Guy*, Jim Carrey attaches himself to Matthew Broderick to the point of becoming a virtual member of Broderick's family. The film ends with Carrey unchanged even though he has had a near brush with death: after Broderick has succeeded in breaking the attachment, Carrey moves to forge an attachment to another man.

In the course of the film, Carrey appears more out of control than Murray in two ways. He is given to sudden expressions of violence and he is more overtly libidinal, so that the attachment to Broderick achieves an overtly homoerotic expression completely absent in the Murray film. There are, in fact, many jokes about homosexuality in Carrey's films, although the character is always heterosexual. This seems to derive from the kind of anarchy that sets Carrey apart from Murray and even masters of anarchy such as Groucho Marx. If Carrey is anarchic, he never really threatens power structures like Marx, nor does he move into positions of power like Murray. He might declare at the end of *The Cable Guy* that 'Someone has to kill the babysitter', television, but he hardly poses a threat to the increasingly powerful media conglomerates which the film suggests shape our lives. Rather, his attempt to destroy the babysitter is actually coupled with a suicide attempt, suggesting a self-destructive quality to Carrey's anarchy. His anarchic spirit is so freewheeling and uncontrolled that it can either turn on Carrey himself or lead him into areas he apparently wants to stay away from.

Carrey is a character that is divided against himself. Where Murray's masochism always seems at the service of his sadism, Carrey has more trouble integrating conflicting impulses. Of his ten starring roles, three (*The Mask* [1994], *Liar Liar* [1997] and *Me, Myself & Irene* [2000]) feature split personalities, one actually clinical, the other two released by fantasy conceits; while two (*The Truman Show* [1998] and *Man on the Moon* [1999], both regarded as venturesome forays into more dramatic films) suggest the possibility of an underlying personality at odds with what we see. In *The Truman Show*, Carrey's performance keeps directing the audience towards the manic energy they are already familiar with under the apparently placid surface because he pursues normality with such feverish dedication. In *Man on the Moon*, a split personality is made apparent by the radically different characters that Andy Kaufman creates and seems to inhabit completely.

If Murray has his two opposing halves, the masochistic and the sadistic, working in concert to bolster the ego, Carrey is more divided, with conflict expressed in a face that has more spastic moves than Jerry Lewis's body. If Murray achieves integration by assuming positions of power, it is only the conventions of romantic comedy that finally allow Carrey integration, either through dedication to a woman or, in the case of *Liar Liar*, dedication to the family. This renewed sense of the power of romantic love and value of family that became features of 1990s comedy is evident in the other most prominent comic actor of the late 1980s and 1990s, Eddie Murphy.

Murphy's professional background is similar to Murray's and Carrey's: he began in stand-up comedy, moved onto *Saturday Night Live*, then went into feature films. But the move into features was different in a number of ways: two of his first three films (*48 Hrs* [1982] and *Beverly Hills Cop* [1984]) were actually action films with strong comic elements, as if Hollywood were not quite as certain what to do with a *black* comedian, while the first two (*48 Hrs* and *Trading Places* [1983]) paired him up with a white male co-star. *Trading Places* makes the underlying political strategies of *Animal House*, also directed by John Landis, explicit by tying them to a racial issue. In this later film, the two characters on the outs, Dan Aykroyd and Eddie Murphy, also end up becoming like their oppressors, Ralph Bellamy and Don Ameche. *Trading Places* might present Eddie Murphy in a starring role that in effect raises him to the top of a social heap, but it still has a kind of double standard in the way it treats him. A romantic plot is presented in great detail for white co-star Aykroyd, but Murphy goes it alone for most of the film, even though he is a performer with far greater sexual presence on screen that Aykroyd. Much the same thing happens even in *Beverly Hills Cop*, Murphy's breakthrough hit where he does not have to share billing with a white male co-star as he did in both *48 Hrs* and *Trading Places*. In *Beverly Hills Cop,* Murphy does have a white female co-star in Lisa Eilbacher, but he retains a chastely platonic friendship with her throughout. Eilbacher's position in the film is quite oddly defined, as if she should be a romantic lead, but never becomes one.

Operating within the white worlds of his first three films, Murphy could potentially be a disruptive if not fully anarchic force; he is, after all, a policeman in *Beverly Hills Cop*. By the end of the decade, a different side of Murphy had begun to appear that surfaced, oddly enough, first in a concert film, *Eddie Murphy Raw* (1987). Although the film received complaints for its apparent misogyny and levels of anger, it actually began, sweetly, with a dramatised memory of seven-year-old Eddie startling his family with a gross joke. Much as the rawness of the joke could set Murphy apart from his family, in a sense, the introduction to the 'raw' Eddie within the context of family points to an important aspect of Murphy's screen persona: even at his most outrageous, he remains the little kid indulged in by a loving family. If Jim Carrey's physically manic performances could call Jerry Lewis to mind, it was Murphy who actually remade a Lewis film, focusing more on the child-like aspects of Lewis. Eddie Murphy is always fully available to us most apparently in the most inviting comic smile since Harold Lloyd.[13] It is hard to imagine Murphy's comic impulses taking him towards the malignance that Murray achieves in *Mad Dog and Glory* (1993) or the invocation of horror monster with Carrey in *The Cable Guy*.

By the late 1980s, when Murphy began to take control of his career and move into straight comedies, the resulting films were often romantic comedies. Murphy himself would become fully domestic, often defined by his position within a family (*Coming to America* [1988], *The Nutty Professor* [1996], and *Dr Dolittle* [1998], as well as sequels to the last two). Murphy can contain multitudes within himself as the multiple roles in both *Coming to America* and *The Nutty Professor* suggest, but these are reflections of an expansive ego that is itself a source of pleasure, much like Bottom in *A Midsummer Night's Dream*, who imagines he can act every part in the play. Securely ensconced within his various screen families, he might play a multitude, but he is never as divided as either

Murray or Carrey. Jim Carrey had gained some initial fame in stand-up comedy for his impressions of other actors, the satirical impulse placing a distance between performer and subject. But Murphy's impressions are more playful than ridiculing; in effect, they all become expansions and variations on Eddie himself, which is why it makes sense for him to play all the members of his family in *The Nutty Professor*. He is the most domestic of raucous comedians.

Comedy on the home front

Murphy's move into domestic realms reflected a return to family comedies in the late 1980s to early 1990s. Woody Allen's most mainstream comedy of the period, *Hannah and Her Sisters*, both popular and a big award winner, as well as Blake Edwards's *That's Life!*, critically well received but not as popular, were both released in 1986, and both demonstrated family values in their production by using actual residences and relations of their respective film-makers. This led to rediscovering the joys of family life in *Baby Boom* (1987), *Moonstruck* (1987), *Three Men and a Baby* (1987) and its 1990 sequel, *Look Who's Talking* (1989) and its 1990 sequel, *Parenthood* (1989), *Uncle Buck* (1989), *Honey, I Shrunk the Kids* (1989) and its 1992 sequel, *Hook* (1991), *Mrs Doubtfire* (1993), *The Santa Clause* (1994) and even a remake of *The Father of the Bride* (1991) and its 1995 sequel.

In *Big* (1988), the central character finally renounces the adult world of romantic comedy for the security of a snug childhood place within the family. But domestic comedy need not be opposed to romantic comedy. *Moonstruck*, as I will discuss below, was a key film in the revival of romantic comedy as the dominant form of comedy, but in the context of the period, it is particularly striking that it achieved this with a celebration of the family that vies with the celebration of the couple traditional in romantic comedy. The final lines of *Moonstruck* are: 'A la famiglia! To family! A la famiglia! Salute!' And, for all his disruptive energy, even Jim Carrey could move into the worlds of both domestic and romantic comedy with *Liar Liar*, something that would have been unthinkable with Bill Murray.

In a sense, this shift might seem a redirection of the emphasis on the group in Animal Comedy, a redirection that found descendants in two forms: not just comedies centred on the family, but also comedies centred on the workplace.[14] The workplace comedies would figure in the return of romantic comedy, although elements of romantic comedy could certainly be found in family comedies. The family comedies of the late 1980s and early 1990s, with their strong emphasis on parenthood, were a very different stripe from the earlier Animal Comedies which seemed to deny the existence of parents in order to keep the focus squarely on adolescent animals aggressively breaking restraints. A comparison of *American Pie* (1999) to *Porky's*, the film that the film-makers acknowledge as their primary inspiration, offers the clearest evidence of a sea change. In *Porky's*, parents are virtually non-existent, although school officials and the evil Porky himself might be taken as metaphorical stand-ins. In *American Pie*, the leading character's father is an important character in his own right, and the relationship between the two is central to the film's narrative.

The chief work of these new family comedies was to cover over the fissures in family relations that had been opened by Animal Comedy. In 1990, John Hughes, responsible for a number of rebellious teen comedies in the previous decade, wrote and produced *Home Alone*, which went on to become the top-grossing film of the year. It told the tale of a child whose parents inadvertently leave him behind when they take a trip to Paris. This would appear to be a film about an unwanted child, but the film works very hard to cover this over, raising an issue that it insistently seeks to deny through the rest of its narrative. And although the film has a great deal of slapstick that could bring it close to the world of Animal Comedy, it is slapstick in the service of keeping the home inviolate. *Home Alone* begins with a shot of clouds breaking apart to reveal a full moon, accompanied by mysterioso soundtrack music; this shot reappears to introduce a series of events that will explain the inexplicable. How could loving parents possibly forget their child? They cannot unless they are deeply ambivalent or downright hostile about the child in the first place, but the magic of the moon assures us that they are not. In similar fashion, *Honey, I Shrunk the Kids* displaces parental ambivalence through the magic of fantasy, which allows for the striking image of a father throwing his newly miniaturised kids out with the garbage.

The return of romance as quotation or impossibility

The three comedians I have discussed above are all male, which very much follows past Hollywood traditions of the feature film, although television often developed major female comedians in situation comedy. The feature films of the 1990s nevertheless marked a change in the status of women stars within the industry that speaks to a larger change in comic form. Where the buddy films of previous decades usurped the role of women as romantic partners, women stars rarely achieved power at the box office in this period. The 1990s saw the return of big female stars who could 'open' a movie. And these women were often specifically identified with romantic comedy: Julia Roberts, Meg Ryan, Sandra Bullock, Cameron Diaz. As a complement, a number of male stars who rose to prominence in the 1980s and 1990s became strongly associated with romantic comedy: Tom Hanks in particular, but also Matthew Broderick, Ben Stiller and Nicolas Cage.

The watershed year for the revival of romantic comedy as the dominant Hollywood comic form was 1987. As gross-out comedy declined in popularity and production, two films of that year enjoyed a critical and commercial success: *Moonstruck* and *Broadcast News*. The two films established two contrasting models for subsequent romantic comedies. *Moonstruck*, the more commercially successful of the two, set romance in quotation marks, with self-conscious reference to the romanticism of Italian opera and the notion that the seemingly supernatural properties of the moon, as in *Home Alone*, were needed to make the impossible possible and authorise the magic of the heterosexual couple. The magic of nature would subsequently be given elaborate expression through special effects in *Forces of Nature* (1999). In a period that became increasingly obsessed with movie magic, love itself could become something of a special effect, apparently real, but ultimately not really there. On the other hand, *Broadcast News*, operating within the context of a workplace setting, presented romance as a longed-for impossibility: Holly Hunter shares sensibility and sympathies with co-worker Albert Brooks, but is erotically attracted to another co-worker, William Hurt. In the end, all three give up romantic longing for professional satisfaction. In both *Moonstruck* and *Broadcast News*, romance could seem, implicitly in the former and explicitly in the latter, an unrealisable ideal.

Julia Roberts starred in two of the most commercially successful romantic comedies of the 1990s: *Pretty Woman* (1990) and *My Best Friend's Wedding* (1997). Both evidenced a shrewd manipulation of new conventions: *Pretty Woman* followed in the self-conscious mode of *Moonstruck*, while *My Best Friend's Wedding* expanded on the notion of the romantic impossibility of *Broadcast News*. In line with the direction set out by *Moonstruck*, the pedigree of *Pretty Woman*'s tradition is foregrounded, with explicit reference to fairy tales and, as in *Moonstruck*, Italian opera. At the end, when Richard Gere's prince effectively climbs a tower to rescue the princess, a street person, one of the black savants that seemed to become important in films of the 1990s, pronounces the film's final words: 'This is Hollywood, land of dreams. Some dreams come true. Some don't. But keep on dreaming. This is Hollywood. Always time to dream. So keep on dreaming.'

My Best Friend's Wedding begins with Julia Roberts at work: she is a food critic attended by a bevy of anxious men waiting for her pronouncement on a culinary preparation. She is partnered at the meal by a gay male friend (Rupert Everett), who, as the film contrives it, will be the only real male partner for her. Following the pattern established by *Broadcast News*, professional commitment for women stands in the way of romance: her profession provides the greatest sensual pleasure via the food she eats. *My Best Friend's Wedding* dramatises the dilemma of the dedicated professional woman in the central contest between Julia Roberts and Cameron Diaz for control of Dermot Mulroney. Diaz presents herself as a woman who is willing to give up college and independence for the sake of her husband and marriage, but Roberts sees through this and eventually forces Diaz to acknowledge that she in fact has no intention of giving up those things that would establish her as a separate individual.

In *There's Something about Mary* (1998), Cameron Diaz as Mary not only has a profession, but is stunningly successful at it as well. She is also beautiful, loves sports and demonstrates maternal instincts in caring for a retarded brother. In other words, she is a male fantasy, given insouciant charm in Diaz's bouncy performance. The film engineers a reversal of sexual roles by having the four men lusting after her abandon their professions and expose increasingly disturbed personalities as the film progresses. As one of the helpless males seeking a supremely accomplished female, Ben Stiller appears as eternally infantilised because he is eternally fixated on the originating moment when he caught his genitalia in a zipper. The film does force a happy end of uniting the deranged Stiller to the maternal Diaz, with the promise that romance can work by her taking care of him. But the happy end can only be achieved at the cost of the film's actually killing off its narrator – certainly the most overt acknowledgment of any of the 1990s romantic comedies of the impossibility of its own conventions.

Superwomen and helpless males figure prominently in *Being John Malkovich* (1999) as well. Possibly the quirkiest romantic comedy of this period, the film achieves its quirky status by extending and making overt what was implied in other comedies. It repeatedly inverts sexual roles by repeatedly impregnating John Malkovich with other people. And it definitively collapses the contrast between professional and homebound women by having the two earth mother women of Catherine Keener and Cameron Diaz leave behind their inferior male mate and, through the magic of the central fantasy conceit, create a child together: the only perfect marriage in this world is one centred on two women who have taken over conventional male and female roles for themselves. They can realise a romance of perfectly matched personalities as long as it does not involve a man.

One of the most powerful conventions of romantic comedy in the past is the sense of spiritual grace in romance: the coupling of romance offers a form of redemption for the individual lovers.[15] The sexual rawness of Animal Comedy could not make room for this spirituality, and, even with the revival of romantic comedy, it was difficult for films to return to the *status quo ante*. The ways that the new romantic comedies might work around this can be seen in the clever manipulation of old and new conventions in *Pretty Woman*, utilising the new levels of explicitness, but then renewing a sense of romance by the prostitute's interdiction against kissing on lips: contact with her lovers must all be lower body, in the manner of Animal Comedy. When the kiss finally does come, then, it has a meaning for the couple that moves the relationship into the spiritual realm more often associated with romantic comedy.

The value of romance in the films of the 1990s is never an easy matter. In *Pretty Woman*, Julia Roberts says to Richard Gere about their developing involvement, 'The bad stuff is easier to believe. You ever notice that?' It is as if the film is self-consciously dealing with the will to believe in the Hollywood trope of love as spiritual redemption; belief can only be arrived at by an awareness of belief itself as a convention. Much as the street hawker in *Pretty Woman* exhorts the audience to keep on dreaming, romantic comedies can implicitly or explicitly make us question what finally shapes those dreams. The repeated foregrounding of convention *as* convention in these films suggests that the need to believe in belief derives from a contemporary uncertainty about what we once thought were eternal verities. The new romantic comedy replaces the aggressively masculinist quality of Animal Comedy not with a feminist or feminine sensibility so much as confusion and uncertainty.

As *There's Something about Mary* and *Being John Malkovich* make explicit, the specific eternal verity of sex roles is most fully in flux in these films. In *Dumb and Dumber*, Jim Carrey, who has spent much of the film trying to find his love object, Lauren Holly, finally has the chance to declare his love. He rehearses the following lines: 'I feel like a schoolboy again. A schoolboy who desperately wants to make sweet, sweet love to you.' But when he actually sees her, he takes hold of her and declares, 'Mary, I desperately want to make love to a schoolboy.' Trying to straighten this out, he comes up with, 'What do you think the chances are of a guy like you and a girl like me ending up together?' Set this against the moment in *The Awful Truth* (1937) when Irene Dunne asks Cary Grant if he remembers the toast he made on the occasion of their engagement. Grant says he does not remember, to which Dunne replies, 'Well, being a woman, I do.' Comedy of the sexes, whether sex farce or romantic comedy, perhaps depends on such a clear sense of what it means to be a man and what it means to be a woman, even in periods such as the Depression when the social order may seem in disarray. Without this certainty, romance must be set in the quotation marks of self-referentiality or simply be impossible.

Notes

1. A key defining aspect of this comedy is summed up in the title of Tony Hendra's *Going Too Far*, a history of comedy in the 1960s and 1970s that concentrates chiefly on stand-up

comedy, the *National Lampoon* and *Saturday Night Live*, all important precursors of Animal Comedy. Hendra, *Going Too Far* (New York: Doubleday, 1987).

2. Even in some of the most commercial comedies that might have been treated as romantic comedy in the past, the romantic half of the generic name became a secondary element. The difference between *Some Like It Hot* (1959) and *Tootsie* (1982) makes clear how different this situation is from the past. *Some Like It Hot* is romantic comedy, but, in *Tootsie,* the romance is relegated to a subplot as both Jessica Lange and Teri Garr subordinate themselves to the star turn of Dustin Hoffman, who is listed twice, as his own co-star in the end credits, ahead of both Lange and Garr. And in 1984, *Splash* emerged as a romantic comedy reworking of *E.T.* (1982), but with the fantasy given greater play than the romance.

3. Molly Haskell, *From Reverence to Rape* (New York: Holt, Rinehart and Winston, 1974), p. 187.

4. Dave Kehr, 'Funny Peculiar', *Film Comment*, July 1982, p. 13.

5. See Jeanine Basinger, *The World War II Combat Film* (New York: Columbia University Press, 1986) for an analysis of the distinctive identity group in World War II films.

6. Ibid., p. 37.

7. In an article that explores the cultural significance of the James Bond films in the late 1960s and 1970s, Lee Drummond, drawing on an analysis of William Arens, notes the ascendancy of professional football in this period which he ties to 'an emergent corporate culture in the postwar United States'. I do not want to push the possible analogies to Animal Comedy too far, but they at least come to mind because of the final football game in *M*A*S*H*, and they at least suggest some of the ambivalences at the heart of Animal Comedy: the group in the comedies are dedicated to the indulgence of individual desire, yet the primacy of the group also suggests that individual desire must, as in a football game, be to some degree made subordinate to the demands of the group. Drummond, 'The Story of Bond', in Hervé Varenne (ed.), *Symbolizing America* (Lincoln: University of Nebraska Press, 1986), pp. 82–5.

8. Thomas Schatz draws a comparable analogy between genre and language as structures that facilitate communication through expectation. Schatz, *Hollywood Genres* (New York: Random House, 1971), pp. 18–22.

9. *Time*, 16 July 1979, p. 60.

10. John Swenson, 'Bill Murray: Maniac for All Seasons', *Rolling Stone*, 20 April 1978.

11. Steve Gaydism, 'The Man and the Plan', and Beth Laski, 'Movie Icon', in '93rd Anniversary Supplement', *Variety*, 24–30 August, 1998, pp. 3, 6.

12. Laski, 'Movie Icon', p. 6.

13. James Agee's description of Lloyd's 'thesaurus of smiles' would be an apt phrase for Murphy as well. See 'Comedy's Greatest Era', in *Agee on Film*, vol. 2 (London: Owen, 1967), p. 12.

14. In choosing family or workplace as the central locus, feature films were in fact following the pattern that had been set out by situation comedies of the previous decade. James L. Brooks, who created *Taxi* and *The Mary Tyler Moore Show*, would be responsible for the prototypical workplace comedy of this period, *Broadcast News*.

15. For a rumination on the spiritual meaning of the perfectly matched couple in Hollywood comedy of the 1930s–1950s, see Stanley Cavell, *Pursuits of Happiness: The Hollywood Comedy of Remarriage* (Cambridge, MA: Harvard University Press, 1981).

10

Conforming Passions?:
Contemporary Romantic Comedy

Frank Krutnik

> Romance lives by repetition, and repetition converts an appetite into an art.
>
> Oscar Wilde

> When one is in love, one always begins by deceiving one's self, and one always ends by deceiving others. That is what the world calls a romance.
>
> Oscar Wilde[1]

This chapter examines the repositioning of romantic comedy in the 1980s and 1990s. The first section will suggest some of the 'external' transformations the genre has experienced since the early 1980s – for example, how it has been remodelled for (and reappropriated by) niche audiences defined by ethnicity, sexual orientation or age. My findings in this section are based on a survey conducted during July 2001 of romantic comedies produced and/or released in the US across the preceding two decades.[2] Every one of the 500 or so films included in my final inventory has been described as a romantic comedy by at least two of these sources, but there is no necessary agreement across all of them that each and every film qualifies as such.[3] My aim was to produce a rough overview of the range of films that have been marketed or understood as romantic comedy, identifying some of the dominant trends within their production and reception. This work should thus be seen as diagnostic rather than definitive, exploratory rather than systematic.

The second section presents a more 'internal' approach to the new romance that explores the distinctive uses to which these films put the genre's familiar conventions.[4] The various historical cycles of Hollywood romantic comedy are all driven by a process of negotiation between traditionalist conceptions of heterosexual monogamy and an intimate culture that is constantly in flux. For example, the cycle of sexual comedies that Cecil B. DeMille initiated after World War I – with such films as *Old Wives For New* (1918), *Don't Change Your Husband* (1919) and *Why Change Your Wife?* (1920) – sought to reconcile the Victorian ethos of dutiful marriage with the sensuous pleasures of Jazz Age consumerism. These films achieve this compromise, Sumiko Higashi argues, by 'the sanctioning of consumer behaviour through appeals to Victorian moralism'.[5] Later cycles reveal a similar dialogue between the inherited voices of heterosexual monogamy and the transformed horizons of amorous possibility. I will indicate, however, that the new romances are more than usually self-conscious about the forms and modalities of such mediation.

New romantic frontiers

Surveying the script purchasing policies of the major Hollywood studios during 1998, the InHollywood website noted that:

> If even half the projects picked up this year actually get the greenlight, the first decade of the next millennium may be known as 'the Romantic Comedy Decade'. Sales totals for the genre surged ahead of former rivals Action-Adventure and Science Fiction, landing squarely in the coveted fourth spot [below Comedy, Drama and Thriller].[6]

1998 saw a 50 per cent increase over the previous year in the number of romantic comedy scripts bought by the studios, a factor attributable to such recent hits as *Four Weddings and a Funeral* (UK; 1994), *While You Were Sleeping* (1995), *Jerry Maguire* (1996), *My Best Friend's Wedding* (1997), *There's Something About Mary* (1998), *As Good as It Gets* (1997), *The Wedding Singer* (1998) and *Shakespeare in Love* (UK/US, 1998). However, the contemporary resurgence of this most emphatically traditional genre had actually been under way since 1984. Where a mere handful of romantic comedies were produced each year from 1981–3, seventeen appeared in 1984 alone. The following chart shows that, with the exception of comparative lulls in 1985 and 1993, the trend in most years is towards a much higher volume of production – with especially sustained activity from 1997–9.

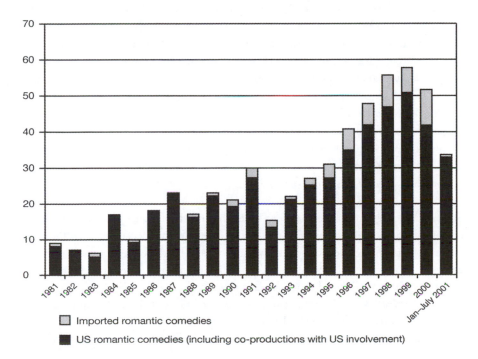

Imported romantic comedies

US romantic comedies (including co-productions with US involvement)

The chart also highlights the increased profile of romantic comedy imports in the US marketplace from the mid-1990s, spearheaded in particular by the international success of *Four Weddings and a Funeral* and the Australian comedies *Strictly Ballroom* (1993) and *Muriel's Wedding* (1995).[7] *Four Weddings* and its sequel *Notting Hill* (1999) both paired Hugh Grant with American actresses – respectively, Andie MacDowell and Julia Roberts – who were already known for their work in Hollywood romantic comedies. Like the Australian–French co-production *Green Card* (1990), another commercial hit starring MacDowell, the two Grant films were clearly devised to tap into the proven international market for English-language romantic comedies.[8] The remarkable success of these films encouraged Hollywood involvement in such co-productions as *Sliding Doors* (UK/US, 1998) and *Bridget Jones's Diary* (France/UK/US, 2001), which similarly capitalised upon the exotic appeal of British cultural and scenic milieus. Most of the US–British partnership ventures, however, are adaptations of prestige literary or dramatic properties targeted at international audiences – including *Much Ado about Nothing* (UK/US; 1993), *Sense and Sensibility* (UK/US; 1995), *Emma* (UK/US; 1996), *An Ideal Husband* (UK/US; 1999) and *Love's Labour's Lost* (France/UK/US; 2000). Although not based on a specific prior text, *Shakespeare in Love* likewise operates within the 'heritage' paradigm of cultural distinctiveness.[9]

Any attempt at a close analysis of romantic comedy faces the problem of defining its generic boundaries. Brian Henderson has argued that the prevalence of romance and comedy across the spectrum of Hollywood production makes it difficult to isolate romantic comedy as a self-contained genre:

> Romantic comedy: a genre, a family of genres (marriage, manners, screwball), a category of production and marketing, a category of analysis, a realm of specialities (Ernst Lubitsch, Gregory La Cava), a notion. Definition, even delimitation, is difficult or impossible because all Hollywood films (except some war films) have romance and all have comedy. We might specify 'comic *about* the romance' but nearly always at least some of the comedy concerns some of the romance. A workable subset 'romantic comedy' might refer to those films in which romance and comedy are the primary components or to those without other such components as crime, detection of crime, Western adventure, war, etc. But what is 'primary' in a given case is difficult to determine where romance and comedy are pervasive. Moreover, even if crime, westerns, war, etc. films are eliminated, the remainder is vast and its modes of conjoining romance and comedy myriad.[10]

Such critical doubts are shared neither by the Hollywood companies that have continued to pour forth so many romantic comedies over the past two decades nor by the audiences that has, lapped them up so readily. Indeed, as a brand identity, the term 'romantic comedy' carries such commercial potency that distributors and reviewers routinely apply it to films with only minimal or tangential romantic plotlines – such as *The Money Pit*, *Corrina, Corrina* (both 1994), the gay exposé comedy *In & Out* (1997) and the crime comedy *Miss Congeniality* (2000). The term 'romantic comedy' thus serves not only to identify a particular type of story centred upon two lovers that is told in a particular manner, but, as Henderson suggests, it also circulates as something of a free-floating signifier that can designate a bewildering array of possible combinations of sex and comedy. The term can be applied to an offbeat independent comedy of sexual mores such as *The Opposite of Sex* (1998), which blatantly spurns the romantic idealism of a film such as *You've Got Mail*, released the same year.[11] The term also encompasses films that oscillate between dramatic and comic registers in their treatments of romantic relationships, such as *Heartburn* (1986), *Once Around* (1991), *Home for the Holidays* (1995), *Afterglow* (1997), *Twice Upon a Yesterday* (1998), *The Other Sister* (1999), *Bounce* (2000) and *The Anniversary Party* (2001).

In *Writing the Romantic Comedy: the Art and Craft of Writing Screenplays that Sell*, a manual based on screenplay classes conducted as part of the UCLA Extension Writers' Program, Billy Mernit endeavours to narrow down the field by prioritising the genre's structural logic. Mernit describes a romantic comedy as, reasonably enough, 'a comedy whose central plot is embodied in a romantic relationship'.[12] Not only does the dominant plot (or 'A Story') focus on the relationship between the amorously involved protagonists, but the subplot (or 'B Story') is *also* dependent upon it as well. Thus Mernit regards *Shakespeare in Love* as a romantic comedy because the story-line of young Will Shakespeare's search for artistic inspiration is integrally bound up with the story of his relationship with muse and lover Viola (Gwyneth Paltrow). By contrast, *Analyze This* (1999) makes the relationship between Ben (Billy Crystal) and his fiancée Laura (Lisa Kudrow) secondary to the ambivalent intimacy he shares with mobster Paul Vitti (Robert De Niro). Mernit suggests that: 'If you were to remove Billy Crystal's relationship with Lisa Kudrow from *Analyze* and plug in another conflict, you'd still have very much the same movie.'[13] By contrast, in a romantic comedy:

> We may be identifying with one protagonist more than the other, and their union may
> ultimately prove more metaphorical than that found in traditional happy endings (e.g., the
> close of *Shakespeare in Love*), but our stakes and involvement in the story are focused on the
> 'coupling' problem.[14]

Despite his insistence on a structural template organised around the 'coupling' problem, Mernit ascribes the continuing success of romantic comedy since the 1980s to its ability to crossbreed with other genres.[15] 'For romantic comedy to stay alive,' he claims, 'it's had to hybridise and what used to be perceived as classic romantic comedies doesn't pull in an audience anymore.'[16] Mernit somewhat overstates his case here. First, hybridity is by no means a new development within Hollywood genre films, and it is certainly no stranger to romantic comedy. *Ball of Fire* (1941), for example, combines a romantic comedy plot with elements of the gangster film; *The Thin Man* (1934), its sequels and imitators yoke together romantic comedy and detective story; *Test Pilot* and *Too Hot to Handle* (both 1938) blend romantic comedy with aviation adventure (a prominent cycle in the 1930s); *I Married a Witch* (1942) merges romantic comedy and supernatural fantasy; and *It Happened One Night* (1934), *Red Salute* (1935) and *It's a Wonderful World* (1939) are all hybrids of romantic comedy and road movie.

The second problem with Mernit's account of generic crossbreeding is that he marginalises the numerous romantic comedies that have resisted this process:

> Though there are many exceptions that prove the rule (e.g., the thoroughly old-fashioned *Pretty Woman*), contemporary mainstream audiences seem amenable to movies that mix it up. And this is true of your buyers (the studios); a romantic comedy that promises crossover potential is more likely to pique their interest than a straight-up traditional one.[17]

The surprising and sustained commercial success of *Pretty Woman* was perceived to mark a return to the female-centred and female-oriented romantic comedy tradition of Hollywood's past.[18] However, the film was by no means the only new romance to wring variations from *within* the traditional generic paradigm instead of 'mixing it up' with other genres. Other relatively 'pure' romantic comedies include *Murphy's Romance* (1986), *Overboard* (1987), *Switching Channels* (1988), *When Harry Met Sally . . .* (1989), *Green Card, L.A. Story* (1991), *Housesitter* (1992), *Speechless* (1994), *While You Were Sleeping* (1995), *One Fine Day* (1996), *You've Got Mail, The Runaway Bride* (1999), *Notting Hill* and *The Wedding Planner* (2001).

Nevertheless, there is no denying the profusion of romantic comedy hybrids in the past two decades. Unlike the postmodern critics who prize (generic) hybridisation as a challenge to established master narratives, Mernit is more concerned with the economic rationale of genre mixing. Where 'straight' romantic comedy is known for its appeal to women, the cross-genre film can attract a broader audience base. Thus *Romancing the Stone* (1984) was a fusion of adventure film and romantic comedy whose 'huge profit far exceeded the chick-flick and date-crowd numbers that a studio would normally expect from our genre. *Stone*'s canny structure so welds its A and B plots at the hip that they become one central story.'[19] Subsequent films attempting a similar merger of adventure and romantic comedy include *Romancing the Stone*'s 1985 sequel *Jewel of the Nile, Joe Versus the Volcano* (1990), *Excess Baggage* (1997) and *Six Days, Seven Nights* (1998). As Mernit remarks, the adventure hybrid 'features action set-pieces, and it's a good genre [*sic*] for getting protagonists involved superquickly – thrust together in big jeopardy that forces intimacy upon them'.[20]

Another entrenched generic hybrid that can work in a similar fashion is the fusion of romantic comedy and crime thriller, represented by such films as *American Dreamer* (1984), *Desperately Seeking Susan* (1985), *Something Wild* (1986), *Forever, Lulu* (1987), *Her Alibi* (1989), *Bird on a Wire* (1990), *Undercover Blues* (1993), *I Love Trouble* (1994), *Heartbreakers* and *Sugar and Spice* (both 2001). Several other hybrids likewise combine romantic comedy with subject areas presumed to appeal more directly to male audiences, a strategy that boosts their chances as 'date movies'. Like *Ball of Fire* and *Some Like it Hot* (1959), romantic comedy is juxtaposed with elements of the gangster film in *Prizzi's Honor* (1985), *Married to the Mob* (1988), *Honeymoon in Vegas* (1992), *Grosse Point Blank* (1997), *Mickey Blue Eyes* (1999), *Friends and Family* (2000), *The Whole Nine Yards* (2000) and *The Mexican* (2001). A handful of new romances have also made use of sporting backgrounds, in particular *Bull Durham* (1988), *The Cutting Edge* (1992), *Tin Cup*

(1996) and *Jerry Maguire*. In a similar manner, *Dave* (1992), *The American President* (1995) and *Bulworth* (1998) situate a comic romance both within and in opposition to the macho arena of US politics.

Mernit claims that the most commercially successful romantic comedies of the past two decades have incorporated aspects of high-concept situation comedy.[21] In particular, a large number of films are propelled by such outlandish fantasy conceits as ghosts, angels, aliens, witches, mermaids, androids, reincarnation, body swapping, time travel, alternate realities and the like. Among these fantasy/romantic comedy hybrids are:

1983	*Two of a Kind*
1984	*Splash*
1985	*The Purple Rose of Cairo*
1986	*Peggy Sue Got Married*
1987	*Making Mr. Right, Made in Heaven, Mannequin*
1988	*Big, My Stepmother Is an Alien*
1989	*Chances Are, Dream a Little Dream*
1991	*Love Potion Number 9, L.A. Story, Switch*
1992	*Prelude to a Kiss*
1993	*My Boyfriend's Back, Groundhog Day*
1996	*Michael*
1998	*Practical Magic, Sliding Doors* (UK/US)
1999	*Blast from the Past, The Mating Habits of the Earthbound Human*
2000	*What Planet Are You from?, Happy Accidents*

The high-concept hook provides an especially prominent means of repackaging the attractions of romantic comedy for a broad-based mainstream audience. Another significant development within the past two decades has been the targeting of niche audiences – or, at least, the incorporation within romantic comedies of cultural groups previously marginalised within or excluded from mainstream cinema's amorous fictions. A significant cohort of romantic comedies has centred upon African-American characters, including:

1986	*She's Gotta Have It*
1988	*Coming to America*
1991	*Strictly Business*
1992	*Boomerang*
1996	*The Preacher's Wife*
1997	*Love Jones, Hav Plenty, Sprung, Booty Call, How I Spent My Summer Vacation*
1998	*Woo*
1999	*The Best Man, The Wood*
2000	*Love and Basketball*
2001	*Two Can Play That Game, The Brothers*

While some of these films are showcases for such established mainstream stars as Eddie Murphy and Whitney Houston, others seem to be geared more specifically to African-American constituencies. Since the mid-1990s, there has also been an increasing number of romantic comedies with Hispanic protagonists, undoubtedly stimulated by the large Latin populations in certain US cities. These small-scale independent films include *I Like It Like That* (1994), *The Perez Family* (1995), *Rum and Coke* (1999), *Tortilla Soup* (2001), *Blue Diner/La Fonda Azul* (2001) and *Desi's Looking for a New Girl* (2000). The glamorous Hispanic performers Salma Hayek, Jennifer Lopez and Antonio Banderas have also been profiled in more mainstream cross-ethnic romances (respectively, *Fools Rush In* [1997)] *The Wedding Planner* and *Two Much* [1996]).[22]

A further major innovation in the genre since the early 1990s has been the extension of the romantic comedy process to gay relationships. Numerous independent films, many targeted predominantly at gay audiences, have explored intimate same sex relationships.[23] These include:

1993   *Three of Hearts, The Wedding Banquet* (Taiwan/US)
1994   *Go Fish, Bar Girls*
1995   *The Incredibly True Adventure of 2 Girls in Love, Jeffrey*
1996   *Everything Relative, Late Bloomers, Beautiful Thing* (UK), *Indian Summer/Alive and Kicking* (UK)
1997   *Kiss Me Guido, Love! Valor! Compassion, Butch Camp, Broadway Damage, I Think I Do*
1998   *Billy Hollywood's Screen Kiss, Leather Jacket Love Story, It's in the Water, Edge of Seventeen, Relax . . . It's Just Sex, Bedrooms and Hallways* (UK), *Get Real* (UK)
1999   *Trick, Broken Hearts Club – A Romantic Comedy, Just One More Time, Gypsy Boys, Better than Chocolate* (Canada)
2000   *Big Eden, Desi's Looking for a New Girl, In the Boom Boom Room, Friends and Family*
2001   *All Over the Guy, A Family Affair*

During the same period, gay characters and scenarios have also been incorporated within comedies directed at wider audiences, such as *Frankie and Johnny* (1991), *Clueless* (1995), *As Good as It Gets* and *Chasing Amy* (both 1997), *In & Out* and *Dream for an Insomniac* (1998) and *Three to Tango* (1999). *My Best Friend's Wedding, The Object of My Affection* (1998) and *The Next Best Thing* (2000) represent a particular interesting subset of romantic comedy that seeks to redefine the conventional heterosexual order by focusing on close relationships between a woman and a gay man. In flight from dissatisfying experiences with heterosexual men, the heroines of these films – played by Julia Roberts, Madonna and Jennifer Aniston, respectively – all enjoy intimate but non-sexual affiliations with gay men that provide 'all the benefits of a relationship with none of the detriments'.[24]

Contemporary romantic comedy has been reconfigured for audiences on the basis of age as well as ethnicity and sexual preference. A small number of films deal with relationships between mature individuals or with cross-generational romances between an older and younger partner. These include *Murphy's Romance, Cin Cin/A Fine Romance* (1991), *Used People* (1992), *Grumpy Old Men* (1993), *Grumpier Old Men* (1995), *First Wives' Club* (1996), *As Good as It Gets, The Out-of-Towners* (1999), *Town and Country* (2001), *Never Again* (2001), *Fast Food, Fast Women* (2001) and *Queenie in Love* (2001). Far more prominent are films that focus upon the amorous escapades of teenagers or young adults – hardly surprising given the continuing importance of this generational cohort to the mainstream Hollywood box office.[25] There are two broad waves of youth-oriented romantic comedy over the past two decades. The first runs from the mid- to late 1980s and includes:

1984	*Where the Boys Are '84, Sixteen Candles*
1985	*The Sure Thing, Secret Admirer*
1986	*Pretty in Pink, Seven Minutes to Heaven, One Crazy Summer, My Man Adam*
1987	*Can't Buy Me Love, Some Kind of Wonderful*
1988	*You Can't Hurry Love, It Takes Two*
1989	*Say Anything, Shag*

The second run of teen-oriented romantic comedies arises in the mid-1990s and continues to the present. Among these films are:

1995	*Clueless*
1998	*Can't Hardly Wait*
1999	*10 Things I Hate about You, Drive Me Crazy, Never Been Kissed, She's All That*
2000	*Boys and Girls, Down to You, Loser, Whatever It Takes, But I'm a Cheerleader*
2001	*Get Over It, Summer Catch*

Also worth noting in regard to the issue of generational specification are films that approach heterosexual coupling as part of a broader network of family relations – or, in some cases, of surrogate familial relations. The films I am thinking of here include *Baby Boom* (1987), *Three Men and a Baby* (1987) and its 1990 sequel, *Look Who's Talking* (1989) and its sequels (1990, 1993), *Mermaids* (1990), *Father of the Bride* (1991) and its 1995 sequel, *Bye Bye Love* (1995), *Home for the Holidays, Stepmom* (1998), *Meet the Parents* (2000) and *The Family Man* (2000). Robert C. Allen points out that the growing importance of home video as a site for consuming films, as well as protests about R-rated product, encouraged Hollywood to cultivate the cross-generational family audience as a crucial market in the late 1980s and early 1990s.[26] Romance in the family films functions as but part of the complex ensemble of 'parental, sexual, filial, domestic and kinship relations' that define both real and culturally idealised families.[27] Besides the films just noted that actively engage with issues of familial definition, other family-oriented Hollywood fare has also drawn upon the conventions of romantic comedy, including such pre-teen romances as *Willy/Milly* (1986), *My Girl* (1991), *My Girl 2* (1994) and the animated Disney features *The Little Mermaid* (1989) and *Beauty and the Beast* (1991).

Wring out the old, ring in the new

> In romantic comedies, the real subject is the power of love. Love is not merely the catalyst
> for action in a romantic comedy, it's the shaper of the story arc. Although many romantic
> comedies seem to initially set up their protagonist's eventual mate as their antagonist, in
> most cases love itself is the antagonist. It's the force that the story's characters have to
> reckon with; they either succumb to love's power or reject it. Wrestling with love can force a
> character to grow or to resist growth, but either way, love's effect on the central character is
> what drives the story.
>
> Billy Mernit[28]

But what, Cole Porter once asked, is this thing called love? Never simply a personal or
interpersonal affair, romance is a multifaceted cultural formation that comes to us
through a bewildering array of texts, voices and discourses. The struggle against love
involves wrestling not just with the poetics of individual attraction, but also with the complex inheritance of received opinion that defines amorous relations. Hollywood itself has
played a crucial role as part of the apparatus of intimate culture, its widely disseminated
fictions translating affairs of the heart into accessible conceptual and emotional forms.
Negotiating between the private and the public, the past and the present, Hollywood
romantic comedy seeks to shape coherent perspectives on love from the contradictory
utterances that compose it. Conceptualisations of love may constantly be in flux – along
with the broader configurations of romance, sexuality, gender identity and marriage –
but the genre routinely celebrates it as an immutable, almost mystical force that guides
two individuals who are 'made for each other' into one another's arms. Love is shown
triumphing over all manner of obstructions, over all kinds of differences in social status,
cultural background and personality.

The comedies that have flourished since 1984 aim to revive the mythic potency of
romance for the post-liberationist era.[29] Where the ethic of sexual liberation discredited
monogamy and romantic idealism in favour of self-fulfilling erotic pleasure, the new
romances seek to reconcile old-fashioned romance with the erotic openness that is a legacy of the 1960s. Witness, for example, the performative brio with which they flaunt
scenes of erotic daring such as Meg Ryan's simulated orgasm in *When Harry Met
Sally . . .* or the telephone masturbation of Ben Chaplin and Janeane Garofalo in *The
Truth about Cats and Dogs* (1996). Moments such as this proclaim the extent to which
contemporary romantic comedy, while maintaining allegiance to romantic idealism, has
unshackled itself from the decorous displacements of earlier representations.

The nervous romances of the late 1970s and early 1980s had also wrestled with
the problem of love, but found it a slippery opponent.[30] As they detail the difficulties of trying to initiate or sustain attachments in a context that has stripped credibility
from heteroromantic monogamy, these stories of neurotically conflicted amour set up
a tentative dialogue between romantic tradition and the contending discourses of contemporary intimate culture. Mourning the lost certainties of (hetero)sexual
engagement, the nervous romances blame the insurgency of 'sexual revolution' and

feminist liberation for shattering the foundations of intimate discourse. Nervous romancers such as Alvy Singer (Woody Allen) in *Annie Hall* (1977) yearn for old-fashioned romance, but are unable to maintain confidence in its language, conventions and values. Alvy abstains from the hoary old romantic clichés because he fears that their very exhaustion threatens the integrity of self-expression and opens him to potential humiliation or rejection.

The new romance, by contrast, replaces such agonised self-questioning with an ardent yet ironic embrace of romantic possibility. In an earlier discussion, I compared the logic of the post-liberationist new romances to an amorous scenario devised by Umberto Eco to illustrate the forms of communication required in a postmodern culture that is haunted by the 'already said'.[31] Eco suggests that users can productively reanimate a discredited legacy of expression such as romantic discourse in a manner that both addresses and transcends its redundancy:

> ... the past, since it cannot really be destroyed, because its destruction leads to silence, must be revisited: but with irony, not innocently. I think of the postmodern attitude as that of a man who loves a very cultivated woman and knows he cannot say to her 'I love you madly', because he knows that she knows (and that she knows that he knows) that these words have already been written by Barbara Cartland. Still, there is a solution. He can say, 'As Barbara Cartland would put it, "I love you madly"'. At this point, having avoided false innocence, he will nonetheless have said what he wanted to say to the woman: that he loves her, but he loves her in an age of lost innocence. If the woman goes along with this, she will have received a declaration of love all the same. Neither of the two speakers will feel innocent, both will have accepted the challenge of the past, of the already said, which cannot be eliminated; both will consciously and with pleasure play the game of irony ... But both will have succeeded, once again, in speaking of love.[32]

Because submission to the clichés of romantic discourse threatens to jeopardise integrity and sincerity, lovers must tread very carefully in opening their hearts to one another. Unlike the nervous romance, however, the new romances refuse to abandon the degraded language of love, but subject it instead to a process of creative resignification that enables the films both to speak through yet to set themselves apart from convention. Problems in identifying and utilising the established codes of amorous communication are hardly novel in romantic comedy, but the negotiation of the 'already said' emerges as a particularly delicate issue in the contemporary films because they must salvage romance from the emotional debris of the 1960s and 1970s. Whereas the sex comedy cycle of the 1950s and 1960s directly remade numerous screwball films as a means of holding in place transformations within postwar cinema and intimate culture,[33] there are very few remakes among the new romances.[34]

Even so, the current cycle persistently remobilises the signifiers of old-fashioned romance, with many comedies invoking keynote romantic texts of the past. Thus the discourse of love in *Never Been Kissed* (1999) explicitly draws upon Shakespeare's *As You Like It*, while *You've Got Mail* uses Jane Austen's *Pride and Prejudice* in similar fashion.

Sleepless in Seattle (1993) riffs off the Cary Grant – Deborah Kerr romance *An Affair to Remember* (1957), while the eponymous romancers of *When Harry Met Sally …* continually debate the fictional love between Rick (Humphrey Bogart) and Ilsa (Ingrid Bergman) in *Casablanca* (1942). *The Runaway Bride* uses Miles Davis's 1959 album *Kind of Blue* and the celebrated romantic casualty W. B. Yeats to encode romantic sensibility, while *The Object Of My Affection* makes comparable use of the 'You Were Meant for Me' number from *Singin' in the Rain* (1952). Countless other films build a romantic atmosphere with the aid of recycled love songs, especially from the heyday of Tin Pan Alley.[35]

This dialogue with the past takes on almost obsessive proportions as the films seek to bridge the gap between then and now, identifying love as something from a long-lost era that needs to be rediscovered in the modern world. By using such evocations of amorous tradition to validate their ideal of romantic intimacy, the new romances insinuate that rather than being something that simply happens between people, love is essentially the product of aesthetic fabrication. The screwball films define love as a kind of creative gamesmanship, with lovers engaging in duels of wit to secure the terms of compatibility. Teasing, testing and also teaching one another, the screwball protagonists reveal their ability to love on an elevated plane by avoiding the banalities of sentimental love-speak to communicate through indirection. In opposing the familiar rituals and protocols of romance, these exceptionally sophisticated lovers discover a liberatory capacity for self-transcendent creative gamesmanship, both within themselves and within one another.[36] Where the screwball lovers take pains to steer clear of the 'already said', the new romancers embrace it with the kind of have-your-cake-and-eat-it logic Eco describes. Although the contemporary romances continue to value love as a source of creative inspiration, their aesthetic emphasis shifts from the internal interpersonal dialectic of the film to the ludic relationship the film builds with its audience. The credibility of the relationship is often sustained not by the couple themselves so much as by a highly self-conscious mode of amorous signification that blatantly manipulates conventions and discourses to generate an expressly stylised rendition of the mating game.

The fabrication of romance in the contemporary films is further signalled by their reliance upon deception scenarios. While these are not rare in the genre as a whole, scenarios of fabricated identity do seem to have increased prominence in the new romances – and appear to be especially symptomatic of their aesthetic and ideological priorities. By their nature, deception scenarios raise questions about the authenticity of both self and desire. Although Brian Henderson blamed the intrusion of 'false presences' into the sexual dialectic for killing off the genre in the late 1970s,[37] romantic comedy has always exploited the tension between false and true identities in the game of love. The genre may insist repeatedly on the principle of 'to thine own self be true',[38] but the fact that authenticity rests upon a foundation of simulation suggests a more complexly mediated grounding for the construction of romance. Being true to oneself really comes down to a question of being true to *one* self, whereas the beauty of the deception narrative is that it allows for the exploration of two selves in one. Unshackled from day-to-day limitations, the dissimulators of romantic comedy can escape their 'real' selves to investigate alternative possibilities for self-imagining. And by opening themselves to the joys of spontaneous invention, they are able to retain control of the romantic adventure, an adventure of fabricolage.

A few examples will suggest why these deception scenarios are so useful to the new romance. *Green Card* deals with the relationship between an earthy French chef (Gérard Depardieu) and a prim American botanist (Andie MacDowell) who engage in a marriage of convenience to realise self-seeking goals: he wants to remain in the US, and she wants a New York apartment with a magnificent garden. Subjected to the scrutiny of the US immigration officials, the pretend lovers get to know about one another 'for real' – and fall in love. Where *Green Card* centres upon a mutual deception that unites the lovers against the world, other films involve more one-sided masquerades.

In *While You Were Sleeping* (1995), Lucy Moderatz (Sandra Bullock) fantasises about high-flying lawyer Peter Callaghan (Peter Gallagher), who is a regular customer at the Chicago subway booth she works in. After Peter is violently assaulted by muggers, Lucy attempts to gain access to the object of her desire by posing as his fiancée. With Peter in a coma, and thus unable to deny her masquerade, she is welcomed into his family. The subterfuge enables Lucy to enjoy satisfactions that would not otherwise be available, allowing her to forsake the loneliness of day-to-day life for the warm affections of an ideal family. Like the calculating fantasists of *Green Card*, Lucy Moderatz must ultimately renounce her initially self-seeking desires when the amnesiac Peter wakens from his coma to believe she actually is his fiancée. Standing in the registry office, her romantic dream about to be realised, Lucy confesses the truth. Despite her deception, Lucy is nevertheless permitted to join her beloved Callaghan family, but as the bride of Peter's artistic and sincere brother Jack (Bill Pullman). The film thus gratifies her wish for a family, while disentangling it from the one-sided romantic fantasy that impels the subterfuge.

The Truth about Cats and Dogs similarly concerns a woman who constructs a masquerade to realise her wishes. Veterinary surgeon Abby Barnes (Janeane Garofalo) hosts a radio phone-in show on which she offers advice to callers about problems they have with their pets. She strikes an instant rapport with one of the callers, handsome English photographer Brian (Ben Chaplin), and they arrange to meet. Insecure about her appearance, Abby portrays herself to Brian over the telephone as her direct antithesis – a tall, slim blonde. She then convinces her gorgeous but vacuous neighbour Noelle (Uma Thurman), the inspiration for Abby's duplicitous self-representation, to impersonate her in a meeting with Brian. In this female-oriented replay of *Cyrano de Bergerac*, a romance subsequently develops between Brian and the composite 'perfect woman' that Abby has contrived. She herself attracts him with her voice and intelligence, while Noelle engages him with her supermodel looks.

This deception scenario permits a complexly nuanced take on the pleasures of romance. Although the subterfuge is inspired by Abby's lack of self-esteem, it also enables her to reign supreme as the mistress of fabrication. Proffering Noelle as an idealised self-embodiment, Abby remains the controlling player in a strangely perverse game of identity and seduction. In a daring scene that flamboyantly exhibits the phantasmic nature of desire, Abby and Brian conduct a highly charged erotic conversation over the telephone that climaxes with their synchronised orgasms. Brian is enticed by Abby's aural

Housesitter (1992): upwardly mobile and passionately conformist

promise, yet he masturbates by visualising her as the alluring Noelle. The contradictory things men want from women, the film suggests, cannot be found in any one woman. Abby knows this and manipulates the fact to her own erotic advantage. As in *While You Were Sleeping*, the woman's scheme of deception permits access to forms of emotional and imaginative empowerment that run counter to conventional romantic expression and which cannot wholly be dispelled by the generic happy ending. As in many other new romances, the man–woman story seems to operate as an alibi for other, less orthodox satisfactions – suggesting that quite diverse projects may actually be working in the name of love. Although real relationships are posited as growing out of pretend ones, the deception narrative explicitly frames romance as the construction of a representation. This issue is explicitly addressed in the 1992 comedy *Housesitter*, which is similarly propelled by a duplicitous scheme initiated by a woman.

Housesitter is an exemplary new romance in the way it communicates a vision of romance by reactivating a past representation. The template for the film is provided by Howard Hawks's famously delirious comedy *Bringing up Baby* (1938), in which an eccentric woman sets the orderly routine of a man's existence in turmoil ... and makes him all the better for it. In a bid to evoke the freewheeling screwball spirit, *Housesitter* unites two of the most seasoned comic performers in contemporary Hollywood. Goldie Hawn plays Gwen, a protean cyclone who continually reorders the world in accordance with her fantasies – and forces architect Newton Davis (Steve Martin) to play along. After sleeping with Gwen, Davis sneaks away in the morning because he cannot relinquish his attachment to Becky Metcalf (Dana Delany), who jilted him months earlier. On one of her many flights of fancy, Gwen decides to follow Davis to his idyllic New England hometown, Dobbs Mill. Once there, she installs herself in the unoccupied house he built as a testimonial to his love for Becky. Posing as Davis's new bride, Gwen ingratiates herself with his friends and family, who warm to her off-the-wall charm.[39]

When Davis returns to Dobbs Mill, his shock at Gwen's subterfuge recedes when he realises that he can exploit her scheme to his own advantage. He colludes with Gwen's fabricated marital scenario in the hope that his pose as a dutiful husband who is tied to an unsuitable woman will entice Becky back. However, like David (Cary Grant) in *Bringing up Baby,* Davis eventually comes to recognise that he loves the liberating spontaneity the eccentric woman brings to his life. He proposes marriage to Gwen by improvising an awesome monologue of lies that rivals her own considerable achievements in the field (Davis tags her 'the Ernest Hemingway of bullshit'). As with Susan (Katharine Hepburn) in the Hawks film, the woman's invasion of the man's world is both an assault and a rescue. His obsessional fixation on Becky illustrates that Davis is an imaginative man who is stuck in a rut. Gwen frees him from a life of stifling rigidity by forcing him through a dizzying succession of imaginative fabrications, to which he must respond spontaneously and creatively. The film's high points are the scenes in which Gwen and Davis try to outdo one another in vertiginous contests of dissembling, as they compete to see who can wrest control of the process of fantasy scripting. But while it pays homage to *Bringing up Baby*'s anarchic take on the representation of heterosexual desire, *Housesitter* ultimately contains and domesticates the wildness of screwball love. *Bringing up Baby* ends with Susan provoking the collapse of the dinosaur that symbolises the paleontologist-hero's life and work.[40] *Housesitter*, though, proffers a far more cautious resolution.

Where Davis has never strayed far beyond the bounds of Dobbs Mills and Boston, Gwen is an urban nomad who adapts her identity to suit her shifting circumstances as she moves from job to job, from city to city, from improvisation to improvisation. Ultimately, however, the film codifies Gwen's emancipation from conformist regimes of identity as a sign of lack. Suggesting that her compulsive self-reconstruction is a defence mechanism, the film declares that all Gwen 'really wants' is the home and family that life has denied her. She is saved from rootlessness by the reward of a lovingly constructed house and an accommodating husband, together with the readymade family and community she has always craved. In exchange, Gwen enables Davis to surmount his self-limiting attachment to the overly pragmatic Becky. He can also enjoy a playful wife, a job promotion and reconciliation with his family.

When Davis proposes, he promises: 'I love you Gwen and I want to marry you … I can change, Gwen. I can live in a make-believe world. Hell, I already was. Half the things we tell ourselves are fiction. The only thing I know that's real is that I love you.' Towards the end of their pretend relationship, Gwen comes to believe that the fictional marriage she has constructed is for real. Just as Davis adapts to her capacity for fluidity, Gwen's spontaneity gives way to fixity, attachment, accommodation. The film concludes with the couple sharing the house that Davis built as an expression of his creativity and romantic idealism, the house Becky spurns in the film's opening scene because Davis is too staid for her. As they bounce off to the bedroom for a marital romp, Gwen confides that her real name is Jessica. This announcement may be but one of Gwen's many surprises, but it also amounts to a final surrender. She hands over her ultimate secret, swapping her past for a new identity as the legitimate occupant of the house, Mrs Newton Davis.

Housesitter thus recodifies the vivacious and risky screwball desire of *Bringing up Baby* within a reinvigorated bourgeois order. As Michael Slagrow observed in his review of *Housesitter* for *New Yorker* magazine, the film 'isn't anarchically egalitarian, like the great screwball comedies; it's upwardly mobile'.[41] Assuring Davis and Gwen of a glowingly comfortable lifestyle in the white middle-class haven of Dobbs Mill – a Capraesque idyll of self-protective neighbourliness – the film reaffirms edifices rather than dismantling them. As such, it can be regarded as emblematic of the passionate conformism that rules the new romance.

Notes

1. The first quotation derives from a speech Lord Henry makes to the Duchess of Monmouth in Chapter 17 of Wilde's *The Picture of Dorian Gray* (1891). The second derives from advice Lord Henry proffers to Dorian in Chapter 4 of the novel (which is redeployed by Lord Illingworth in Act 3 of Wilde's 1893 play *A Woman of No Importance*).

2. The entertainment trade journal *Variety* provided the starting point for this project as it provides explicit or implicit generic descriptors in its reviews of contemporary releases. I subsequently consulted numerous other sources that categorise films generically (such as the Internet Movie Database and online video/DVD catalogues), which were useful in expanding and qualifying my initial list.

3. In this regard, the first section is concerned not with an 'exclusive' approach to the romantic comedy genre that concentrates on a handful of select canonical texts, but with a more broad-based 'inclusive' approach that maps the genre's contours through the diverse articulations of everyday discourse and industrial categorisation. For further discussion of these contrasting approaches to genre, see Rick Altman, 'A Semantic/Syntactic Approach to Film Genre', in Barry K. Grant (ed.), *Film Genre Reader* (Austin: University of Texas Press, 1986), p. 27; and Tom Ryall, 'Genre and Hollywood', in John Hill and Pamela Church Gibson (eds), *The Oxford Guide to Film Studies* (Oxford: Oxford University Press, 1998), pp. 334–5.

4. Steve Neale applied the term 'new romance' to contemporary romantic comedy in his article 'The *Big* Romance or *Something Wild?*: Romantic Comedy Today', *Screen*, vol. 33, no. 3 (Autumn 1992), pp. 284–99.

5. Sumiko Higashi, *Cecil B. DeMille and American Culture: The Silent Era* (Berkeley: University of California Press, 1994), p. 144.

6. Jason A, 'The Literary Report – 1998 Year in Review', InHollywood Website, http://www.inhollywood.com/ih/trends/literary/literary 1998review.htm.

7. The chart amalgamates international co-productions that have US involvement within the annual total for US films proper, even though this occasionally produces bizarre results – such as categorising *Shirley Valentine* as a US rather than a British film.

8. MacDowell subsequently appeared in the British romantic comedy *Crush* (2001). A few years earlier, American star Jeff Goldblum had been cast in the British romantic comedy *The*

Tall Guy (1989), based on a script by Richard Curtis (who later wrote *Four Weddings and a Funeral* and *Notting Hill*).

9. Several films have also updated classic texts, including *Roxanne* (1987; based on *Cyrano de Bergerac*), *Love's Labours Lost* and the teen romantic comedies *Clueless* (1995; based on Jane Austen's *Emma*) and *10 Things I Hate About You* (1999; based on Shakespeare's *The Taming of the Shrew*). These films have coincided with a series of non-comic modernisations of period literary and dramatic texts, including *Great Expectations* (1998), *Cruel Intentions* (1999; based on *Les Liasons Dangereuses*) and *William Shakespeare's Romeo + Juliet* (1996).

10. Brian Henderson, 'Romantic Comedy Today: Semi-Tough or Impossible?', *Film Quarterly*, vol. 31, no. 4 (Summer 1978), p. 12.

11. Other comedies that deal with sexual mores without following a romantic courtship format, or doing so in orthodox manner, include *Two Girls and a Guy*, *Dog Park* (both 1998), *Sleep with Me*, *Threesome* (both 1994) and *Chasing Amy* (1997).

12. Billy Mernit, *Writing the Romantic Comedy: The Art and Craft of Writing Screenplays that Sell* (New York: HarperResource, 2000), p. 12. Mernit has worked as a playwright, screenwriter and songwriter, and was a script consultant and story analyst for TriStar, Castle Rock, Universal, Sony and Paramount.

13. Ibid.

14. Ibid., p. 13.

15. Mernit (*Writing the Romantic Comedy Screenplay*, pp. 13–15) follows conventional wisdom among Hollywood screenwriting instructors by insisting that the narrative should follow a three-act structural formula, which in romantic comedy consists of: *Meet* (girl and boy have significant encounters); *Lose* (girl and boy are separated); and *Get* (girl and boy reunite). For an explication and critique of the three-act model, see Kristin Thompson, *Storytelling in the New Hollywood: Understanding Classical Narrative Technique* (Cambridge, MA/London: Harvard, 1999), pp. 22–44.

16. *P.O.V. Hollywood*, 'Writing Romantic Comedy: Interview with Billy Mernit – Part One' (1998), http://hollywoodnet.com/pov/pov11.html.

17. Mernit, *Writing the Romantic Comedy Screenplay*, p. 21.

18. Peter Krämer, 'A Powerful Cinema-going Force?. Hollywood and Female Audiences since the 1960s', in Melvyn Stokes and Richard Maltby (eds), *Identifying Hollywood's Audiences: Cultural Identity and the Movies* (London: BFI, 1999), pp. 99–102.

19. Mernit, *Writing the Romantic Comedy Screenplay*, p. 21.

20. Ibid., p. 22.

21. *P.O.V. Hollywood*, 'Writing Romantic Comedy: Interview with Billy Mernit – Part One'.

22. By contrast, the blonde Hispanic star Cameron Diaz appeared in several romantic comedies – *My Best Friend's Wedding*, *A Life Less Ordinary* (1997) and *There's Something about Mary* – in Anglo roles.

23. In a review of *Relax . . . It's Just Sex* (1998) for the *Mr. Showbiz* website, Ken Maynard noted that 'queer lifestyles seem to be indie film du jour', http://mrshowbiz.go.com/movies/reviews/RelaxItsJustSex 1999/review.html.

24. Baz Dreisinger, 'The Queen in Shining Armor: Safe Eroticism and the Gay Friend', *Journal of Popular Film and Television*, vol. 28, no. 1 (Spring 2000), p. 6.

25. Where the thirteen to twenty-one age group had represented 55 per cent of all US cinema admissions in 1983, it was responsible for only 38 per cent of ticket purchases in 1992 – a decline that was in line with broader demographic shifts in population (Robert C. Allen, 'Home Alone Together: Hollywood and the "Family Film" ', in Melvyn Stokes and Richard Maltby (eds), *Identifying Hollywood's Audiences: Cultural Identity and the Movies* (London: BFI, 1999), p. 117). Nevertheless, teenagers and young adults still constitute a sizable segment not just of the cinema market, but also of the broader industries of popular culture serviced by Hollywood.

26. Ibid., pp. 113–16.

27. Ibid., pp. 114.

28. Mernit, *Writing the Romantic Comedy Screenplay*, p. 17.

29. For discussion of the rise of counter-liberationist ideologies, see Steve Seidman, *Embattled Eros: Sexual Politics and Ethics in Contemporary America* (New York: Routledge 1992), pp. 58 ff.; and John D. D'Emilio and Estelle B. Freedman, *Intimate Matters: A History of Sexuality in America*, 2nd edn (Chicago: University of Chicago Press, 1997), pp. 326–77.

30. For further discussion of the nervous romances, see Frank Krutnik, 'The Faint Aroma of Performing Seals: The "Nervous" Romance and the Comedy of the Sexes', *The Velvet Light Trap*, no. 26 (Autumn 1990).

31. Frank Krutnik, 'Love Lies: Romantic Fabrication in Contemporary Romantic Comedy', in Peter William Evans and Celestino Deleyto (eds), *Terms of Endearment: Hollywood Romantic Comedy of the 1980s and 1990s* (Edinburgh: Edinburgh University Press, 1998), pp. 28–9.

32. Umberto Eco, 'Postmodernism, Irony, the Enjoyable', in Peter Brooker (ed.) [1992], *Modernism/Postmodernism* (London: Longman, 1992) [originally 1985], p. 227.

33. Frank Krutnik, 'Too Many Boarders in the House of Love: Remaking Romance in *The More the Merrier* and *Walk, Don't Run*' (forthcoming 2002).

34. The most notable new romantic remakes are: *Switching Channels* (1988), based on *His Girl Friday* (1940), itself a heterosexual variant of buddy comedy *The Front Page* (1931); *Born Yesterday* (1993), based on 1950 original; *Love Affair* (1994), based on 1939 original that was also remade as *An Affair to Remember* (1957); *Sabrina* (1995), based on 1954 original; *The Preacher's Wife*, based on *The Bishop's Wife* (1947); and *You've Got Mail*, based on *The Shop around the Corner* (1940).

35. For a discussion of the various roles played by romantic song standards in contemporary romantic comedy, see Ian Garwood, 'Must You Remember This? Orchestrating the 'Standard' Pop Song in *Sleepless in Seattle*', *Screen,* vol. 41, no. 3 (Autumn 2000), pp. 282–98; and Neale, 'The Big Romance or *Something Wild?*', p. 293.

36 The screwball comedies depict men and women establishing compatibility through a shared quirkiness or intelligence that pits them against dullness and routine (these qualities personified exquisitely by Ralph Bellamy's iconic wrongful partner in *The Awful Truth* and *His Girl Friday* [1940]).

37. Henderson, 'Romantic Comedy Today', p. 19.

38. The most literal articulation of this principle can be found in *Once upon a Honeymoon* (1942), when Cary Grant's reporter remonstrates with Ginger Rogers's Brooklyn slummy for

adopting the airs of an Austrian duchess. For a particularly convoluted and self-contradictory handling of the issue of authenticity in a new romance, see *The Runaway Bride*.

39. As is also the case in *While You Were Sleeping* and *The Truth about Cats and Dogs*, *Housesitter* takes pains to purify the woman's lies of the taint of maliciousness. Gwen's fabrications are always invited by others: for example, when Davis meets her in the restaurant and assumes she is Hungarian, she merely responds to his cue. Nevertheless, several reviewers noted similarities between *Housesitter*'s narrative premise of a woman invading a man's space after a night of sex and that of *Fatal Attraction* (1987). Alexander Walker, for example, described Gwen as 'a mythomaniac, a fantasist compelled to re-invent herself', '*Housesitter*' (review), *Evening Standard*, 10 September 1992, p. 14. See also Sheila Johnston, '*Housesitter*' (review), *The Independent*, 11 September 1992, p. 18.

40. For further discussion of the ending of *Bringing up Baby*, see Celestino Deleyto, 'Narrative Closure and the Comic Spirit: The Inconclusive Ending of *Bringing up Baby*', in Celestino Deleyto (ed.), *Flashback: Re-Reading the Classical Hollywood Cinema* (Zaragoza: Servicio de Publicaciones, 1992), pp. 161–84.

41. Michael Slagrow, '*Housesitter*' (review), *The New Yorker*, 26 June 1992, p. 73.

11

Pleasing the Million:
Shakespearean Cinema of the 1990s

Roberta E. Pearson

> I heard thee speak me a speech once, but it was
> never acted; or, if it was, not above once; for the
> play, I remember, pleased not the million; 'twas
> caviare to the general.

Hamlet, Act 2, Scene 2

Most scholars who have written about Shakespearean cinema, knowing rather more about Shakespeare than they do about cinema, are primarily concerned with the plays, their adaptations and their adapters. Knowing rather more about cinema than I do about Shakespeare, I am more interested in Shakespearean cinema as a distinctive genre of film-making within a particular historical context. The majority of the books and articles written from the Shakespeare scholar perspective adopt either the originary text principle – for example, the Olivier and/or Branagh version of *Henry V* – or the auteur principle – for example, the Shakespearean films of Olivier and Branagh.[1] To my knowledge, only Jack Jorgens has formulated a grand unifying theory, constructing a typology of Shakespearean cinematic genres. Jorgens distinguishes among the theatrical mode, in which the film simply records performances; the realist mode, which takes advantage of the 'camera's unique ability to show us *things*'; and the filmic mode, 'the mode of the film poet' who uses 'a great variety of angles and distances, camera movement'.[2] In keeping with much genre theory of the 1970s, Jorgens's formulation tends to the essentialist, ignoring specific historical conditions of production and reception, in a book that ranges from Reinhardt in Hollywood, to Olivier in London to Kurosawa in Tokyo. By contrast, this essay focuses on the common characteristics of 'popular' English-language Shakespeare films made primarily for commercial purposes, that is, putting millions of bums in seats and the money in the cashbox. 'Popular' is a relative term where Shakespearean cinema is concerned, but the term does omit the more experimental, avowedly non-commercial work of directors such as Peter Greenaway and Derek Jarman.

From the first to the penultimate decade of the twentieth century, 'popular'

Shakespeare films, many of which originated in Hollywood, maintained strong continu-
ities with the radical text-cutting, spectacle, realism, star casting and high culture
intertextual references of the Victorian stage. In the last decade of the century, however,
such films as *Richard III* (1995), *William Shakespeare's Romeo + Juliet* (1996), *Titus*
(1999), *Hamlet* (1996) and *Shakespeare in Love* (1998) signalled a shift in producers' conceptions of a commercially viable Shakespeare, adding a dense popular culture
intertextuality to the Victorian's radical text-cutting, etc. As at the time of writing neither
Titus nor *Hamlet* is available on video in the United Kingdom, this essay establishes con-
tinuities/discontinuities with the Victorian tradition through analysis of four films: the
previously mentioned *Richard III*, *Romeo + Juliet* and *Shakespeare in Love*, together with
William Shakespeare's A Midsummer Night's Dream (1999). The most commercially successful of these films was *Shakespeare in Love*: made for $25 million, it grossed $100
million in the United States, playing, at its widest distribution, on 2030 screens. Second
was *Romeo + Juliet*, which was made for $17 million and took $46 million in the US,
playing on 1963 screens. Next came *A Midsummer Night's Dream*, which grossed a rather
disappointing $16 million in the US, playing on 1099 screens. Most disappointing of all
was *Richard III*, which, produced for $10 million, grossed just $2.7 million in the US.[3]

Some of these films were relative commercial successes and some relative failures;
however, despite the fact that three of the titles include the word 'Shakespeare', a reluctance to invoke the Bard united the films' publicists. Consider the films' previews. Here
are some excerpts from the voice-over narration:

Midsummer Night's Dream: From the greatest storyteller of all time comes the romantic
comedy that proves that true love never did run smooth. Love makes fools of us all.

Richard III: For centuries he's been called the greatest villain of all time. Now a motion
picture tells his story as it's never been told before.

Romeo + Juliet: From age to age one classic story.

The producers may think that Shakespeare is a saleable commodity, but apparently they
do not trust the audience to respond to his poetry. The *Midsummer Night's Dream* trailer
contains a paraphrase of 'the course of true love never did run smooth', the faux Shakespearean 'love makes fools of us all', and a few snatches of dialogue in the excerpted
scenes. The *Romeo + Juliet* trailer does include one line of dialogue, the suggestive and
easily (mis)understood 'Juliet, I will lie with thee tonight.'[4] The *Richard III* trailer
includes no dialogue. The trailers seem to imply, 'Shakespeare may be the greatest storyteller of all time, may have created the greatest villain of all time and may have written
the classic story of *Romeo and Juliet*, but we mustn't let on that the language can be difficult.' Rather, as Russell Jackson has already said about trailers for Shakespeare films,
'The identity of the principal actors and the scale of the production are usually the main
selling points. Love interest (or sex) and action may be emphasised . . .'[5]

The 'spoonful of sugar makes the Shakespeare go down' strategy evident in these trailers has shaped producers' attitudes to popular Shakespeare since at least the 1890s. The drama critic Max Beerbohm, half-brother of Sir Herbert Beerbohm-Tree, one of the leading actor-managers of the Victorian stage, explained the economic exigencies which motivated Tree's lavishly mounted Shakespearean productions. Beerbohm pointed out that his brother:

> having to fill the vast auditorium of His Majesty's [Theatre], was bound to consider the tastes, not of sections, but of the public at large. He always insisted on this fact. 'I have to find something which will be agreeable to stalls, upper circle, pit, gallery – all at once.' And directly we think of the many-headed public who keep theatres going, and the difficulty there is in finding a common focus for their ardent, unsophisticated enthusiasm and their uncritical approval, we shall begin to recognize the burden laid on theatrical entrepreneurs ...[6]

Continuities with Victorian Shakespeare

For the past century, Shakespearean film producers have been employing the same tactics as Sir Herbert to placate the many-headed public.[7] First among these is catering for those who might find Shakespeare's language difficult. Tree's production of *Henry VIII*, for example, famously cut over 47 per cent of the text and still managed to provide over four and a half hours of costumed pageantry through including scenes that the Bard only suggested. One critic said of Tree's similarly staged *Merchant of Venice*, 'The Bard's story drags itself through a long succession of scene-shiftings and interpolated business. When the action halts that revellers may romp across the stage and small mobs begin miniature pogroms before our eyes the play itself grows weary.'[8] Modern audiences, and perhaps more importantly, modern exhibitors, have little tolerance for four-and-a-half-hour films; producers of Shakespearean cinema must cut the text as radically as Sir Herbert.[9] The official website for *Richard III* says: 'On stage, RICHARD III ... has some forty-five subsidiary characters and can run for well over three hours! To pare the text down to a hundred minutes, simplification and clarification were in order.'[10] Following in Sir Herbert's footsteps, Loncraine and McKellan not only pared the text, but added their own equivalents of small mobs and miniature pogroms, the first ten minutes of the film including not a line of Shakespeare's text and departing significantly from the backstory established in *Henry VI*.[11] Set in a fascistic Britain of the 1930s, the film opens with an explanatory title followed by scenes of King Henry and Prince Edward in the Lancastrian headquarters. A tank crashes through the walls and a gas-masked figure emerges, kills both the Lancasters and takes off his mask to reveal Ian McKellen/Richard III. Following this sequence, the main protagonists prepare for and travel to a coronation ball at the royal palace. After several shots of the characters at the ball, Richard takes the bandleader's microphone to declare, 'Now is the winter of our discontent ...'

Both the battle and ball sequences typify the spectacle and visual pleasure common to popular Shakespeare since Tree's time, perhaps the *locus classicus* in Shakespearean cinema being Olivier's seventeen-minute battle of Agincourt in *Henry V*. Producers' discourse often links spectacle and visual pleasure to authenticity, whether of location, *mise en scène* or historical details. Noting that *A Midsummer Night's Dream* was shot in Italy, the *San Francisco Chronicle*'s critic said, 'From its setting in the romantic, glowing Tuscan countryside that shifts to the grand dream sequence in a magic forest of deep shadows and strange goings-on, this film is a visual tour de force to brighten eyes.'[12] Just as Sir Herbert notoriously included real fauna (rabbits) in his *Dream*, the producers of this film version included real flora. An Internet critic comments, 'The garden was created using all real plants and flowers – not a plastic branch in the bunch. This is astounding when you first see the giant acorn love bed of Titania.'[13] Locations made much of in the official website included Montepulciano, the Villa d'Este and the Palazzo Farnesi in Caparolla. In *Richard III*, Loncraine and McKellen opted for the historical authenticity of their 1930s setting. 'It's a wonderful period visually – the clothes, the cars, the architecture are marvellous,' said Loncraine. During pre-production, costume designers and location scouts sought out the proper period clothes and locations, rifling the 'vintage clothing stores of London and Paris for thirties originals' and identifying such lavish sets as 'the Holbein room at historic Strawberry Hill House' and 'the Senate House, the chancellery of London University, with its large expanses of marble'.[14] Even the very hip *Romeo and Juliet* appealed to the spectator's visual pleasure, successfully so judging by comments on the Internet Movie Database. 'I have to give kudos for the Oscar-nominated art direction/set design. It is eye candy from the first shot to the last.'

Some less than kind critics suggested that Sir Herbert resorted to his spectacular productions not to lure the many-headed public, but to disguise his own histrionic inadequacies. 'In the sixteenth century an actor who could neither speak nor walk would have been an impossibility. Such a one has triumphed in our time, because his imperfections are easily obscured in a welter of the false picturesque.'[15] Sir Herbert may not have been a great actor, but he was manifestly a star whose star power undoubtedly contributed to the popularity of his Shakespeare productions. Stardom (particularly American stardom) rather than acting ability in general or Shakespearean experience in particular often shapes the casting of Shakespeare films. *Romeo + Juliet* featured two young actors who were not yet stars, but who had appeared in previous teen-oriented productions: Leonardo diCaprio in *What's Eating Gilbert Grape* (1993) and *Basketball Diaries* (1995) and Claire Danes in American television's *My So-called Life. Shakespeare in Love* featured the very popular American star Gwyneth Paltrow, together with Ben Affleck and Geoffrey Rush who had recently attained stardom on the basis of *Good Will Hunting* (1997) and *Shine* (1996), respectively. *A Midsummer Night's Dream* had a mix of actors familiar to the public from cinema and television: Kevin Kline, Michelle Pfeiffer and Rupert Everett from the former and Stanley Tucci (*Murder One*) and Calista Flockhart (*Ally McBeal*) from the latter.

Star casting can noticeably influence the interpretation of the play. For example, Bottom, together with the other rude mechanicals, lacks the emotional depth that Shakespeare provided his more aristocratic characters, but not so in this latest cinematic version. Director Michael Hoffman said:

What if Bottom, as the king of amateur dramatics, has delusions of grandeur about himself
as an actor because he doesn't have any love in his life? So I started to build a story for
him – a frustrating life and an unhappy marriage.[16]

The wife's on-screen appearances, together with the privileging accorded by editing and
close-ups, give Kevin Kline's Bottom an interiority that purists might see as distorting
the original text in order to provide the star a juicier role. Purists might be less offended
by the star casting of *Richard III*, in which American actors Annette Bening and Robert
Downey Jr play Queen Elizabeth and her brother, Earl Rivers. Having an American play
the Queen to the King of a fascist 1930s Britain conjures up a possible alternative history in which Edward VIII remained on the throne after marrying Wallis Simpson and
put his fascist sympathies into action. The casting and the setting resonate with the original text's portrayal of the Woodville family as interlopers. But the critics still complained.
The *San Francisco Examiner* observes:

I have one hesitation about the movie. Annette Bening and Robert Downey Jr. do not seem
so much people from another town as from another, non-literate, planet ... When Bening
(who was trained to speak verse) and Downey (who was not) attempt the lines, in
comparison [to McKellen and Maggie Smith], they seem sadly inept.'[17]

Critics responded similarly to the lovers in *Romeo + Juliet*. According to Roger Ebert,
'Leonardo DiCaprio and Claire Danes are talented and appealing young actors, but
they're in over their heads here. There is a way to speak Shakespeare's language so that
it can be heard and understood, and they have not mastered it.' But, continued Ebert,
Pete Postlethwaite and Miriam Margolyes have mastered it.'They know the words and
the rhythm, the meaning and the music, and when they say something, we know what
they've said.'[17]

The fact that Ebert lauded the only Brits in the cast, Postlethwaite and Margolyes, for
mastering the verse points to a contradiction at the heart of popular Shakespeare with
which Sir Herbert was all too familiar: pleasing the million does not necessarily mean pleasing the literary experts. Catering for the many-headed American public necessitates the
casting of well-known Americans, but this often offends the critics, who expect
Shakespeare to come trailing clouds of high culture. In a country that still suffers from a
colonialist cultural cringe, the casting of classically trained British actors alongside the familiar American faces ensures the requisite cultural connotations. The same critic who
complained that Bening and Downey could not handle Shakespeare's language continued,
'Few English actors can speak verse with the rhythmic ease and assurance of McKellen
and Maggie Smith. The scene between them is one of the movie's high points simply
because the language is spoken so magnificently.'[19] Or as *The Washington Post* remarked,
'What's best about *Richard III* is what's best about most British Shakespeare productions.
You can sit back and listen to performers who have been raised on Shakespeare.'[20]

As the issue of casting illustrates, producers of Shakespearean cinema must have one
eye on the box office and the other on critical reviews and similar indices of cultural

acceptance. By the turn of the twentieth century, producers of theatrical Shakespeare had no worries about respectability. The transformation to a disciplined, middle-class entertainment that the stage had undergone in the second half of the previous century, coupled by the favourable contrast with the vulgar newcomers of cinema and television, had placed the live theatre firmly at the top of the cultural pinnacle, so firmly indeed that, at the more rarefied heights such as Shakespeare, the medium in the United Kingdom has become dependent upon a combination of state and corporate funding rather than box-office success. But producers venturing into the new, vulgar media may sacrifice their respectability, as Sir Herbert was aware when undertaking in 1916 to make *Macbeth* for Triangle Pictures. 'Our purpose in making this picture ... was educational as well as financial. I believe it will be a great benefit to children to see picturizations similar to this one before studying Shakespeare's plays.'[21] Sir Herbert's strategy of appealing to children, or rather their teachers, had been pioneered as early as 1910 when the General Film Company, the distribution arm of the American film trust, the Motion Picture Patent Company, established an educational unit with a catalogue that included many Shakespearean films.

Ninety years later, producers still seek approval from the educational establishment. The official website for *A Midsummer Night's Dream* includes a 'viewer's study guide' prepared by Youth Media International in co-operation with Fox Searchlight Pictures and Regency Enterprises. The guide contains suggested activities to follow up a class-room viewing of the film and is intended to 'help students appreciate the universality of Shakespeare's characters and the poetic richness of his language'. The guide declares that 'Shakespeare's genius is evident in *A Midsummer Night's Dream* in the way he intro-duces what seems at first a bewildering variety of characters and plots and then proceeds to manipulate them deftly to convey coherent themes.' Aimed at the young viewers rather than their teachers, *Romeo + Juliet*'s official website takes a less didactic stance. 'This is not a scholarly report – just a few pertinent biographical notes on the immortal Bard we thought you might find interesting.' Among these biographical notes is the fol-lowing: 'Incontrovertible historical evidence strongly suggests actors of Shakespeare's times would regularly trash inns, drink heavily, chase locals and generally wreak havoc.' After a few more such notes: 'For the kind of detail and scholarship worthy of Shakespeare we suggest enrolment in Oxford University for a few decades.'[22] Postmodern irony as an appeal to young viewers' sensibilities or genuine belief in the Bard's transcendent genius? Hard to tell, but the critics reviewing *A Midsummer Night's Dream* certainly did not heed Ben Jonson's injunction to admire Shakespeare 'but this side of idolatry'. Roger Ebert went so far as to approvingly reference the conservative Shakespearean scholar, Harold Bloom.

> Why is Shakespeare so popular with filmmakers when he contains so few car chases and explosions? Because he is the measuring stick by which actors and directors test themselves. His insights into human nature are so true that he has, as Bloom argues in his book, actually created our modern idea of the human personality. Even in a comedy like 'Midsummer,' there are quick flashes of brilliance that help us see ourselves.[23]

William Shakespeare's Romeo & Juliet (1996) played on 1963 US screens – 'eye candy from the first shot to the last'

Heather Clisby, of the Internet *Movie Magazine International*, exhibited an even more severe case of Bardolatry. Calling the film a 'testament to the world's greatest playwright', she concludes, 'Leaving the theatre, I was impressed with not only the filmmakers but the movie-goers as well – the computer generation still claps for Shakespeare. There is some hope for the human race after all.'[24] Clisby, by vesting her hope for humanity in an appreciation of Shakespeare, echoes Bloom even if she does not reference him. Shakespeare, for Bloom, Clisby, Ebert, the writers of the *Midsummer Night's Dream* study guide and perhaps even those of the *Romeo + Juliet* website is *the* great writer who holds a central position in Western individual humanism. As it has done since 1908, popular Shakespearean cinema pays obeisance to this ideological centrality in a bid for cultural bona fides, while simultaneously cutting the texts, inserting spectacle and casting stars in a bid for economic profits.

Discontinuities with Victorian Shakespeare

Reviewing *Shakespeare in Love*, critic Rex Read called it 'a sprawling, sumptuous film that instructs, engages the eye, and entertains simultaneously'.[25] Any Shakespeare film that hopes to appease both the many-headed public and the critics must instruct, engage and entertain as has popular Shakespeare since at least Sir Herbert's day. But as I said at the outset, *Richard III*, *Romeo + Juliet* and *Shakespeare in Love* add to the Victorian tradition a dense popular culture intertextuality. Popular Shakespeare has always been as eager to include high cultural references in its bid for respectability as it has been to include spectacle and visual pleasure in its bid for profits. In Sir Herbert's much abridged *Henry VIII*, the actor appeared in an exact copy of the costume worn by the king in the famous Holbein portrait. In this as in so much else, the recent *A Midsummer Night's Dream* conforms to the Victorian tradition. The official website tells us that:

> For the fairy world hidden within the forest, Hoffman and Arrighi [the production designer] drew on traditions that identify fairies with pre-Christian deities. 'We decided they were Pagans and should inhabit the temples and other places of a former civilization,' says Arrighi, 'specifically the Etruscan civilization that preceded Roman culture on this part of the Italian peninsula.' Titania's world, inspired in part by pre-Raphaelite paintings, is more feminine.

Viewers who spot Etruscan temples or pre-Raphaelite paintings might also notice resemblances to the heritage genre, particularly as embodied in the films of Merchant/Ivory. *A Midsummer Night's Dream* has the lush Italian settings and gorgeous nineteenth-century costumes (right down to Bottom's white linen suit) of films such as *A Room with a View* (1986) and *Portrait of a Lady* (1996). Any Shakespearean film will inevitably partake of the cinematic styles and genres of its time. For example, Harry Keyishian draws parallels between three cinematic Hamlets and different cinematic genres. Olivier's *Hamlet* (1948) shares many characteristics with film noir: 'extensive tracking shots through Elsinore, inventive dramatisations of subjectivity (including the voice-overs . . .), the wonderful use of shadows and deep focus to express the isolation that affects the protagonist'. The Zeffirelli/Gibson *Hamlet* (1990) is 'a Hollywood action movie, a natural format for a star like Mel Gibson because it provides the occasion for enjoyable violence'. The Branagh *Hamlet* (1996) 'in terms of pacing, settings and scope' resembles epic pictures such as *Ben-Hur* (1959) and *The Ten Commandments* (1956).[26]

An intertextuality consisting of high-culture allusions and resemblances to a single cinematic genre has characterised popular cinematic Shakespeare for at least several decades, but Shakespearean films of the twentieth century's last decade revel in dense, multiple and diverse intertextual and generic references. *Shakespeare in Love*'s intertextual density successfully appealed to several niche markets, the reason for its inclusion in this analysis despite the fact that it is not strictly a Shakespearean adaptation like the other films under discussion. Here is the voice-over from the trailer:

> Young Will Shakespeare is having a bad year. His last two shows flopped, his theatre is about to go bankrupt and the gangsters are moving in. The last thing that he needs right now is a nasty case of writer's block. Enter his very own Juliet. A truly romantic comedy of errors. Academy Award winner Geoffrey Rush. Academy Award nominee Judi Dench.

This Will Shakespeare is a struggling young playwright, suffering from writer's block at a crucial point in his career, not the world's greatest writer. The trailer casts Will as the hero of several genres: gangster, romance and a 'let's put on a show' comedy. The references to two of Shakespeare's plays, *Romeo and Juliet* and *A Comedy of Errors*, reassure the Shakespeare fans, or the 'Bardies' as my friend Henry Jenkins has dubbed them. The inclusion of Rush and Dench guarantees viewers familiar faces and histrionic quality. The accompanying images show sex and violence, the historically 'accurate' sixteenth-century sets and costumes and the radiantly beautiful Gwyneth Paltrow. The end credits mention highly respected British playwright Tom Stoppard, known among other things for the semi-Shakespearean *Rosencrantz and Guildernstern Are Dead*.

The trailer compressed into a minute or two the multifaceted appeals of a film that aspired to have something for everyone. Potential viewers may have appreciated the full gamut of intertextual references or attended to those that most directly addressed their particular interests. On the film's release, critics recognised and responded positively to the dense intertextuality the producers had foregrounded in their publicity. The *Montreal Gazette* described the film's Shakespeare as 'playwright-as-rock star', continuing, the 'script . . . has it all: humour, romance, sex, swordplay, intrigue, in-jokes, bosomy Elizabethan costumes, tavern ribaldry, classic tragedy and many of the most beautiful words ever written in the English language'.[27] The *San Francisco Examiner* recognised the producers' deft blend of high and popular culture.

> The opening sequence is a Monty Python-style goof on Elizabethan times, and some later
> jokes bring to mind the daffy old 'Black Adder' [sic] series. Other material aims considerably
> higher; for instance, the picture toys with gender-bending Elizabethan theater traditions in
> ways that might tickle a graduate student nimbly balancing the pratfalls with the
> Shakespearean in-jokes ('Twelfth Night' references, appearances by the macabre playwright-
> to-be John Webster as a strange boy, etc.).[28]

The film's $100 million US gross, as compared to the next most successful *Romeo + Juliet*'s $46 million US gross, no doubt stemmed partially from the producers' pleasing both the Bardolators and the sceptics by simultaneously paying homage to Shakespeare as humanist icon and sending him up as a bit of a bumbler.[29] The film portrays Shakespeare both as an inspired genius capable of winning a woman with his words and as a hustling, ambitious man of the theatre who has to include 'a bit with a dog' to appease the groundlings. The film references both the highbrow and the lowbrow: the cross-dressing conventions of the Elizabethan theatre and the low humour of *Monty Python* and *Blackadder* at their most vulgar. The film assumes both extremely knowledgeable and utterly clueless viewers. The former get the young John Webster, Will Kemp (the famous clown in the company) asking Shakespeare to write him a tragedy and Will appearing like Banquo's ghost to Colin Firth's stunned Wessex. The latter get internal *York/Cliff Notes* in the form of Will's explaining the plot of *Romeo and Juliet* to the players. The film is simultaneously historically correct, with its re-created Globe and muddy London streets, and parodically anachronistic with its shot of the Stratford souvenir mug in Will's lodgings, Antony Sher's astrologer shrink and cheeky London boatmen (cabbies). The film may be *Shakespeare in Love*, but Shakespeare inhabits a densely crowded intertextual frame, jostled by the vulgar, the anachronistic and several cinematic genres. Previous popular Shakespeare played down the Bard in its publicity and sugarcoated him with spectacle, visual pleasure and star casting, but Shakespeare remained the dominant element in the intertextual references of the actual films.

Shakespeare in Love is a biopic not an adaptation, but even adaptations of the plays do not necessarily give the Bard pride of place amidst the crowd of competing intertexts.

Numerous critics, both journalistic and academic, noted the extraordinarily complex intertextual frame of the Loncraine/McKellen *Richard III*, some complaining that the numerous and diverse references overshadowed Shakespeare and others celebrating the vitality stemming from such a rich range of associations. Barbara Freedman said in her fairly negative assessment of the film that, 'Shakespearean verse is undercut by the film's intensely visual language, including visual quoting of other films ... Verbal referentiality is here undercut by visual intertextuality ...'[30] H. R. Coursen, disliking the film even more than Freedman, said 'it seemed a parody of Hollywood films, at times mildly amusing, most of the time simply grotesque ...' Most offensive to Coursen seem the numerous borrowings from other films, such as *The Godfather* (1972) (Clarence's death resembles the 'enforced suicide of the old capo' scene and Rivers's death 'a hood and his moll are tommy-gunned in bed while the christening is going on' scene) and 'a thousand old films' upon which the final chase sequence draws 'How many detectives and courageous cops have pursued their culprits upwards into the scaffolding?'[31] As Coursen and others have remarked, Richard's suicidal leap from that scaffolding into the metaphoric flames of hell that open before him directly references gangster Cody Jarrett's (James Cagney) fiery end on top of a petroleum tank in *White Heat* (1948). *The Washington Post*'s Hal Hinson, who also disliked the film, compared it with an American talk show ('[the] murder, rude seduction and gory domestic violence ... would peel the paint off the walls of 'Geraldo's' studio'), a rock opera and 'Nazi chic'.[32] As noted by James Loehlin, the film's fascist world recalls *Triumph of the Will* (1935), especially in a scene deliberately invoking Riefenstahl's infamous masterpiece, in which Richard appears at the podium on a raised dais against a background of huge red, black and white banners. Those favourably disposed to the film included *Time Magazine*'s Richard Corliss, who invoked a dizzying range of references in his review: 'the orgasmic affinity of love and death ... devised by Eszterhas for *Basic Instinct*', 'a Tupac Shakur lyric sung in Westminster Abbey', 'Hitler as Scarface' and 'the killer-comedy genre' of *Kind Hearts and Coronets* (1949) and *Dr. Strangelove* (1966).[33] Loehlin points to the film's quotations from several popular genres ranging from the slasher film (Rivers's death) to the Western (Richard firing a truck-mounted machine gun like William Holden in *The Wild Bunch* [1969]), but argues that the film draws mainly upon the gangster film and the heritage film. Kenneth Rothwell agrees that some aspects of the film are 'heritage', but says that it also quotes from:

> the John Woo action movie, documentary newsreels, traces of the gangster movie, tropes from Dennis Potter's television scripts, and in some sequences, a destabilising mix of realism and surrealism reminiscent of a Luis Buñuel movie like *The Discreet Charm of the Bourgeoisie* (1972).[34]

The critics may have loved or hated *Richard III*, may have characterised it as a gangster film, a slasher film or a Dennis Potter television programme, but all felt obliged to review it in terms of its multiple referentiality, indicating that Shakespeare, as in *Shakespeare in Love*, figures as simply one element among others in the intertextual frame.

Reviewers criticised *William Shakespeare's Romeo + Juliet* for drowning the Bard in a sea of intertextuality. Desson Howe of *The Washington Post* asked, 'How far do you take such license before losing relevance to the play?':

> Luhrmann ... pays homage to everything he has loved in the movies and on television. 'Romeo & Juliet' is an explosion of appreciative nods to Hollywood musicals, detective TV shows, the films of Federico Fellini and Jean-Luc Godard, Australian cult pictures (this movie could have been called 'Montague, Road Warrior'), Hong Kong gangster flicks and the gangland settings of several thousand rap music videos.[35]

USA Today headlined its review of the film 'Wherefore Art Thou, Shakespeare?'; the critic observed:

> We might as well be watching William Shakespeare's The Cable Guy. Savorers of 70s cinema are likely to think Ken Russell has passed the directorial torch ... The barrage of stylized violence, gymnastic camera shots and other visual effects overpowers the verbal poetry – which used to be the most important aspect of a Shakespeare play.[35]

The *San Francisco Chronicle*'s reviewer also objected to the (mis)treatment of Shakespeare's language. 'Modern songs with modern lyrics underscore most scenes, making the Elizabethan dialogue sound jarring.'[37] More sympathetic to the film's blending of the Shakespearean and the ultra-modern, academic Rothwell commented, 'The verbal runs against the grain of the visual semiotics ... But once the ear adjusts it becomes a probable improbability.' Rothwell spots intertextual references ranging from 'John Woo's Hong Kong action movies and the hiphop and gangsta rap of MTV' to 'the set for a sci-fi movie' and applauds the film's innovative intermediality.[38]

In a reflexive gesture, Kenneth Branagh filmed *Henry V*'s chorus on a soundstage, but Luhrmann, yet more intermedially aware, has *Romeo and Juliet*'s prologue read by a black anchorwoman on the Verona Beach evening news programme. The film begins with a long shot of a static-filled television set against a black background. The camera zooms in as the news presenter delivers the start of the prologue in television news cadences against a chromo-keyed 'star-crossed lovers' graphic. A male voice-over picks up the prologue over a dizzyingly edited sequence introducing Verona Beach (complete with buildings topped with giant Montague and Capulet billboards) and the characters. Phrases from the prologue – 'ancient grudge', 'new mutiny', 'civil blood makes civil hands unclean' – appear as headlines in *The Verona Beach Herald*. Television, print journalism and advertising continue to play a significant role in the film's semiotic system. Romeo learns of the recent affray between the Montagues and the Capulets from a news report on a portable television and about the Capulet ball from another news report on a television in his parent's home. 'Dave' Paris appears on the cover of *Time Magazine*. A security guard observes the Capulet mansion on his closed-circuit television. The anchorwoman reads the play's last lines (usually spoken by the Prince). Neon signs and billboards advertise the Globe Theatre, the Merchant of Verona Beach, Rosencrantzky's hamburger stand, and the Bound of Flesh and Mistress Quickly strip clubs. The back cover of the security guard's magazine reads 'such stuff as dreams are made on – Prospero', the phrase later echoed on a billboard.

Some of these visual in-jokes flash by so quickly that they can be fully appreciated only with the VCR's rewind function and even then probably only by the Shakespearean cognoscenti attuned to them. Further gestures to the Shakespeareans include cleverly updated visual embodiments of verbal references: the swords and long swords become the brand names of pistols and assault rifles; the grove of sycamores in which Romeo wanders becomes Sycamore Grove, a seedy seaside amusement park. Other references are aimed at an entirely different audience. Rothwell tells us that the soundtrack includes a 'melange of pop singers and bands' including 'Garbage, Everclear, One Inch Punch, Butthole Surfers, The Wannadies'. A post to the Internet Movie Database comes from one member of the intended audience for this aspect of the film. 'The sound track is amazing. I used to have it but my brother broke it in half but if you have a chance to hear it listen to it. Especially the theme song by Des'ree.' But the film's score also features music by Mozart and Wagner, indicating that, like *Shakespeare in Love*, the film targets several different audiences simultaneously: in-jokes and the classics for the Shakespeareans; rock music, Leo DiCaprio and stylised violence for the kids.

Shakespeare for the million, Shakespeare for the few

The dense intertextuality of *Shakespeare in Love*, *Richard III* and *Romeo + Juliet* distinguishes them from the more conventional *Midsummer Night's Dream*, which contents itself with the radical text-cutting, visual splendour and star casting of the Victorian stage. Nonetheless, all four films still aim to give the viewer the spoonful of sugar that will make the Shakespeare go down, as the popular Shakespearean cinema must continue to do if it intends to please the million. Purists, however, might wish to look elsewhere for their Shakespeare, as, as in Sir Herbert's time, there remains a strong distinction between popular, commercially driven Shakespeare and non-commercial Shakespeare aimed at minority audiences. In the spring of 1916, the tercentenary of Shakespeare's death, two vastly different Shakespearean productions ran opposite each other in New York City. Sir Herbert presented a *Merchant of Venice* at the New Amsterdam Theatre. At the same time, the amateur Drama Society of New York offered a two-week run of *The Tempest* at the Century Theatre, the Society performing the play in accordance with their understanding of the customs of Elizabethan stagecraft. New York's critics, who only a few years earlier had praised Tree's spectacular productions, now claimed that the Drama Society's *Tempest* approached much more closely the true spirit of Shakespeare than Tree's visually excessive *Merchant*. *Vogue*'s critic said:

> The production prepared by the Drama Society affords the poet an unimpeded appeal to the imaginations of the public, whereas the production provided by Sir Herbert Tree inhibits the enjoyment of imagination by a sedulous insistence on superfluous details of actuality ... We have learned that the only way to be fair to the greatest of Elizabethan dramatists is to

produce his plays with a reasonable approximation to the conditions and conventions of the Elizabethan stage.[39]

By 1916, directors such as William Poel, Edward Gordon Craig and Harley Granville-Barker had rejected the spectacular tradition in favour of a less representational staging that shifted the emphasis back to Shakespeare and his texts.[40] At the same time, cinema had taken over the Victorian tradition, as indicated by several films released that year: Sir Herbert's own *Macbeth*, mentioned above; two versions of *Romeo and Juliet*, one produced by the William Fox Company and starring Theda Bara and the other produced by Metro and starring Francis X. Bushman; and *King Lear*, produced by the Thanhouser Company and starring Frederick Warde. Over the next decades, the cinema replaced the theatre as the mass medium, firmly establishing the dichotomy between popular cinematic Shakespeare and minority theatrical Shakespeare. At the beginning of the twenty-first century, purists can still turn to the theatre for a non-sugarcoated Shakespeare, but strangely enough they can also occasionally turn, at least in Britain, to the dominant medium of the second half of the twentieth century, television. This has not to do with any essential, transhistorical conception of the different capacities of theatre, cinema and television, but rather with the shifting relationships among the media and the producers' conception of their audiences. In Britain, BBC 2 and Channel Four, somewhat free of commercial pressures, can appeal to minority tastes, among which is unadulterated Shakespeare.

Notes

1. The several recent books on Shakespearean cinema include Richard Shaughnessy (ed.), *Shakespeare on Film* (London: MacMillan, 1998); Russell Jackson (ed.), *The Cambridge Companion to Shakespeare on Film* (Cambridge: Cambridge University Press, 2000); Lynda E. Boose and Richard Burt (eds), *Shakespeare, the Movies: Popularising the Plays on Film, TV and Video* (London: Routledge, 1997); Anthony Davies and Stanley Wells (eds), *Shakespeare and the Moving Image* (Cambridge: Cambridge University Press, 1994); Kenneth S. Rothwell, *A History of Shakespeare on Screen* (Cambridge: Cambridge University Press, 2001); and Douglas Brode, *Shakespeare in the Movies* (Oxford: Oxford University Press, 2000).
2. Jack Jorgens, 'Realising Shakespeare on Film', in Shaughnessy, pp. 18–20.
3. Even more disappointing were *Titus*, which grossed just $1.9 million in the US, playing on only thirty-five screens, and *Hamlet*, which grossed an even smaller $1.5 million in the US despite playing on almost twice as many screens, sixty-four. To put all these figures in perspective with regard to Shakespeare's relative popularity, the blockbuster *X-Men*, produced for $75 million, opened on 3025 screens in the US on 14 July 2000 and by 19 November 2000 had a domestic gross of $157.3 million. These figures are taken from the Internet Movie Database and Boxoffice Guru.com.
4. Romeo is saying that he will lie dead next to the dead Juliet that night.
5. Russell Jackson, 'Introduction', in Jackson, *The Cambridge Companion to Shakespeare on Film*, p. 8. Michael Bristol also comments on Shakespeare's omission from advertisements

for Shakespearean cinema. 'Oddly, one area where Shakespeare's name is conspicuous by its absence is in promotional material for filmed versions of his plays. Reviews, advertising and even the film credits themselves speak of Zeffirelli's *Hamlet* and Kenneth Branagh's *Henry V*.' (*Big-Time Shakespeare* (London: Routledge, 1996), p. ix).

6. Max Beerbohm, *Herbert Beerbohm-Tree* (New York: E. P. Dutton and Company, n.d.), pp. 264–5.

7. For more on pre-Hollywood American Shakespearean cinema, see William Uricchio and Roberta E. Pearson, *Reframing Culture: The Case of the Vitagraph Quality Films* (Princeton: Princeton University Press, 1993). For more on Sir Herbert Beerbohm-Tree's Shakespeare, see Roberta E. Pearson and William Uricchio, ' "Shriekings from below the Gratings": Sir Herbert Beerbohm-Tree's *Macbeth* and His Critics', in A. J. Hoenselaars (ed.), *Reclamations of Shakespeare* (Amsterdam and Atlanta, GA: Rodopi, 1994), pp. 249–71.

8. *Evening Globe and Commercial Advertiser*, 9 May 1916.

9. The exception is Kenneth Branagh's uncut *Hamlet*, which ran for over four hours, but was also released in a much-cut print.

10. http://www.mgm.com/richard/production.html.

11. In Part III, the York brothers, Edward, George and Richard, slay Edward, Prince of Wales, after the Battle of Tewkesbury. Richard then leaves for London to kill Henry VI in the Tower.

12. Peter Stack, 'Dream Interpretation', *San Francisco Chronicle*, 14 May 1999, http://www.sfgate.com.

13. Heather Clisby, *Movie Magazine International*, http://www.shoestring.org/mmi_revs/midsummer99.html.

14. http://www.mgm.com/richard/production.html.

15. 'The Limits of Stage Illusion', *The Living Age*, 3 December 1910, p. 588.

16. Official site.

17. Barbara Shulgasser, 'McKellen Masterful as Evil Richard III', *San Francisco Examiner*, 19 January 1996, http://www.sfgate.com/cgi-bin/article.cgi?f=/examiner/archive/1996/01/19/WEEKEND2880.dtl.

18. http://www.suntimes.com/ebert/ebert_reviews/1996/11/110104.html.

19. Shulgasser, 'McKellen Masterful as Evil Richard III'.

20. Desson Howe, 'A Rich Richard III Rules', *The Washington Post*, 19 January 1996, http://www.washingtonpost.com/wp-srv/style/longterm/movies/videos/richardiii.htm.

21. 'Sir Herbert Tree Sees His Macbeth Shown on Screen', *The New York Herald*, 3 June 1916.

22. http://www.romeoandjuliet.com/.

23. http://www.suntimes.com/ebert/ebert_reviews/1999/05/051404.html.

24. Clisby, *Movie Magazine International*.

25. www.miramax1998.com/shakespeareinlov.

26. Harry Keyishian, 'Shakespeare and movie genre: the case of *Hamlet*', in Jackson (ed.), *The Cambridge Companion to Shakespeare on Film*, pp. 72–81.

27. John Griffin, 'Vibrant script does Shakespeare proud', *Montreal Gazette*, http://www.southam.com/montrealgazette/cgi/efiles.pl?section=movies&subsection=reviews&file=Shakespeare+in+Love&article=review1&record=1.

28. Walter Addiego, 'The Bard would approve', *San Francisco Examiner*, 25 December 1998, http://www.sfgate.com/cgi-bin/article.cgi?file=/examiner/archive/1998/12/25/WEEKEND10910.dtl.

29. Although I am arguing that the film breaks in some respects with the traditions of popular Shakespeare, it should be noted that this simultaneous upholding/debunking of Shakespeare is a strategy that dates back to Shakespearean parodies of the silent cinema. For example, *Old Bill through the Ages* (UK; 1926) acknowledges Shakespeare's importance to current construction of national identity, but also includes a scene in which the 'great' man performs for Queen Elizabeth and is first mocked by Old Bill (a cockney Tommy) and then blown up by a Mills bomb.

30. Barbara Freedman, 'Critical Junctures in Shakespeare screen history: the case of *Richard III*,' in Jackson, *The Cambridge Companion to Shakespeare on Film*, p. 65.

31. H. R. Coursen, 'Three Films of Richard III', in Jackson, *The Cambridge Companion to Shakespeare on Film*, pp. 102–3. For a more positive academic assessment of the film's dense intertextuality, see James N. Loehlin, ' "Top of the World, Ma": *Richard III* and Cinematic Convention', in Boose and Burt, *Shakespeare, the Movies*, pp. 67–79.

32. http://www.washingtonpost.com/wp-srv/style/longterm/movies/videos/richardiii.htm.

33. http://www.time.com/time/magazine/archive/1996/dom/960115/cinema.shakespeare.html.

34. Rothwell, *A History of Shakespeare on Screen*, p. 231.

35. Desson Howe, 'This "Romeo" Is Bleeding', *The Washington Post*, 1 November 1996, http://www.washingtonpost.com/wp-srv/style/longterm/movies/review97/romeoandjuliethowe.htm.

36. http://www.usatoday.com/life/enter/movies/lef445.htm.

37. Mick Lasalle, 'This "Romeo" Is a True Tragedy', *San Francisco Chronicle*, 1 November 1996, http://www.sfgate.com/cgi-bin/article.cgi?file=//chronicle/archive/1996/11/01/DD15503.DTL.

38. Rothwell, *A History of Shakespeare on Screen*, p. 241.

39. 'The Merchant of Venice', *Vogue*, 15 June 1916.

40. For a brief history of theatrical Shakespearean staging, see Richard Eyre and Nicholas Wright, *Changing Stages: A View of British Theatre in the Twentieth Century* (London: Bloomsbury, 2000).

SECTION TWO

New Cycles and Trends

12

Hollywood Production Trends in the Era of Globalisation, 1990–99

Tino Balio

Introduction

The merger movement that began in the 1980s in response to the growing demand for motion picture entertainment worldwide continued unabated in the 1990s and led to the globalisation of Hollywood. After the mergers ran their course, the same names dominated the business, but motion pictures no longer dominated the balance sheets of the new media conglomerates such as AOL Time Warner, Viacom, News Corp and Disney; filmed entertainment became one of many profit centres and today contributes around a third of the total proceeds of its respective parent companies.[1]

The majors released close to thirty features a year at the start of the 1990s and about half that on average at the end. (Subsidiaries such as Miramax and New Line released a comparable number of low-budget films each year.) The goal of every studio was to gross $1 billion worldwide each year to offset overhead expenses and to feed cable, video and satellite platforms, domestic and foreign. To hit this target, studios relied mainly on high-concept blockbusters and star-vehicles for the mainstream theatrical market. However, no studio had the financial means to produce blockbusters exclusively. Annual rosters regularly contained a few mid-range entries and an occasional niche picture budgeted at around $10 million or less. Studios were motivated to look kindly on low-budget projects when a fluke such as Fox Searchlight's *The Full Monty* (1997) scored big. But only a handful of limited releases crossed over to the mainstream market to gross more than $5 million.[2] For this reason, niche pictures were relegated pretty much to studios' specialised production arms.

In constructing their annual release schedules, studios evaluated new projects on their potential to reach a specific segment of the audience. The 'teen and pre-teen bubble' constituted the core audience. Consisting of avid filmgoers aged between ten and twenty-four, this segment comprised around a quarter of the audience, but regularly generated the largest share of the box office. Young males in this segment, with 'tons of leisure time, plenty of spending money and a burning desire to be first in line for the hot new pop sensation' were a driving force in the market.[3] 'Boomers with kids', consisting of children, parents and grandparents in the eight-to-eighty demographic, had almost as much box-office clout when the right family film came around. According to *Variety*:

> Visions of limitless synergistic possibilities danced in the heads of studio/theme park conglomerates such as Disney and Universal, who envisioned this year's family film hit as next year's amusement ride, live ice-skating show or maybe even a Broadway musical.[4]

'Geezers', people over fifty, attended the movies infrequently and were largely ignored by the studios.

This analysis of Hollywood production trends is based on *Variety*'s 'Top All-Time Grossers', a chart listing pictures that generated $80 million or more at the US box office. As *Variety* points out, an $80 million threshold does not automatically indicate that a film earned a profit, as the chart does not factor in production costs, distribution fees and marketing expenses; nevertheless, the films on the chart received a stamp of approval from filmgoers and can be regarded as bellwether movies. A total of nearly 300 pictures made it to the chart, approximately half of which were released in the 1990s and are the objects of this study.

To classify the films by production trends, I consulted reviews and articles about the films in *Variety* (the leading trade publication), in the *Los Angeles Times* (the leading company town newspaper) and in the *New York Times* (the leading US national newspaper). The exercise resulted in a classification of the films themselves into eight broad trends – disaster, science fiction, horror, animation, family, action, comedy and drama. The trends overlap and certain hybrid films are perforce classified arbitrarily. The ordering of the trends corresponds to the relative performance of the top twenty films of the 1990s (see Table 1). Limiting the sample to twenty might also seem arbitrary, but it is large enough to reveal patterns. (Because *Variety*'s All-Time Grossers chart is easily accessible at the company's website, <www.variety.com>, I have opted not to quote the box-office tallies of the films under consideration to streamline the discussion.) This article examines 1990s production trends from a 'top-down' perspective; excluded are many interesting and critically acclaimed pictures below the $80 million threshold that would have enriched this overview of the decade.

Disaster

'The biggest roll of the dice in film history', *Titanic* (1997), paid off handsomely to become the biggest commercial success of the decade. Paramount and Fox together put up the $200 million to co-finance the three-hour film, which was written and directed by James Cameron. A 'spectacular marriage of technology and passion, special effects and romance', *Titanic* framed the celebrated sinking of the liner within a modern-day prologue and epilogue, and injected a central love story 'as effective as it is corny . . . between a brash lad from steerage (Leonardo DiCaprio) and an upper-class young lady bursting to escape her gilded cage (Kate Winslet)'. *Titanic* differed from other high-concept disaster films of the 1990s by appealing to a predominantly female audience of all ages.[5] It was also the first film to cross the ultimate worldwide box-office threshold of $1 billion.

Table 12.1 **Variety's 20 Top-grossing Films of the 1990s**

Title	Director/Producer	Distributor	Trend	Box-office domestic ($000s)
1. Titanic (97)	J. Cameron; J. Cameron/J. Landau	Paramount	Disaster	600,788
2. Star Wars Episode 1, The Phantom Menace (99)	G. Lucas; G. Kurtz	Fox	Sci-Fi	431,088
3. Jurassic Park (93)	S. Spielberg; K. Kennedy/G. Molen	Universal	Horror	357,068
4. Forrest Gump (94)	R. Zemeckis; W. Fineman/S. Tisch/S. Starkey	Paramount	Drama	329,694
5. The Lion King (94)	R. Allens, R. Minkoff; D. Hahn	Buena Vista	Animation	312,856
6. Independence Day (96)	R. Emmerich; D. Devlin	Fox	Sci-Fi	306,169
7. The Sixth Sense (99)	M. N. Shyamalan; K. Kennedy/F. Marshall/B. Mendel/S. Mercer	Buena Vista	Horror	293,506
8. Home Alone (90)	C. Columbus; J. Hughes	Fox	Family	285,761
9. Men in Black (97)	B. Sonnenfeld; W. Parkes/L. MacDonald	Sony	Sci-Fi	250,016
10. Toy Story 2 (99)	A. Brannon/J. Lasseter; S. McArthur/H. Plotkin/ K. R. Jackson	Buena Vista	Animation	245,852
11. Twister (96)	J. De Bont; K. Kennedy/I. Bryce/M. Crichton	Warner Bros.	Disaster	241,722
12. The Lost World: Jurassic Park (97)	S. Spielberg; G. Molen/C. Wilson	Universal	Horror	229,086
13. Mrs. Doubtfire (93)	C. Columbus; M. Williams/R. Williams/M.Radcliffe	Fox	Family	219,195
14. Ghost (90)	J. Zucker; L. Weinstein	Paramount	Comedy	217,631
15. Aladdin (92)	J. Musker/R. Clements	Buena Vista	Animation	217,350
16. Saving Private Ryan (98)	S. Spielberg; S. Spielberg/I. Bruce; M. Gordon/G. Levinsohn	DreamWorks	Action	216,335
17. Austin Powers: The Spy Who Shagged Me (99)	J. Roach; S. Todd/D. Moore/M. Myers/J. Lyons/E. McLeod	New Line	Comedy	206,040
18. Terminator 2: Judgment Day (91)	J. Cameron; J. Cameron/G. A. Hurd/M. Kassar	TriStar	Sci-Fi	204,843
19. Armageddon (98)	M. Bay; J. Bruckheimer	Buena Vista	Sci-Fi	201,578
20. Toy Story (95)	J. Lasseter; R. Guggenheim/B. Arnold	Buena Vista	Animation	192,800

Unlike *Titanic*, other disaster films depicted 'natural' catastrophes. Only one such film, *Twister* (1996), came close to *Titanic*'s box-office performance. In *Twister*, a team of fun-loving 'storm chasing' scientists working out of the National Severe Storms Laboratory in Oklahoma, led by Helen Hunt and Bill Paxton, provide the excuse for presenting tornado footage with 'ominous and angry funnels of wind capable of making cows fly (not to mention tanker trucks and even houses).'[6] Two other 'natural' disaster films are worth mentioning: Universal's *Dante's Peak* and Fox's *Volcano* (both 1997); both contained volcanic eruptions, both cost around $100 million to make and both were rushed to the market in a race to pre-empt *Titanic*. *Dante's Peak* arrived first and contained an eruption that took place in a bucolic town located in the Pacific Northwest; the eruption in *Volcano* occurred in an urban setting – to be more precise at the La Brea Tar Pits in Los Angeles.

Science fiction

Popular throughout the decade and released mostly as summertime event films, the science-fiction trend accounted for five titles in the top twenty. Like the disaster trend, sci-fi contained a mixed bag of elements and relied heavily on technical wizardry and special effects. George Lucas's epic *Star Wars Episode I: The Phantom Menace* (1999) led the pack. 'Wildly anticipated and heavily hyped', its arrival was 'trumpeted ... on the cover of just about every magazine except the *New England Journal of Medicine*', said the *Los Angeles Times*.[7] A Fox release with a $115 million price tag, *The Phantom Menace* was the first instalment of George Lucas's proposed three-part prequel to the original *Star Wars* trilogy and reached the screen sixteen years after the conclusion of the series. Taking special effects cinematography to new heights, the film used almost 2000 effects shots that took up sixty minutes of screen time.[8] Lucas reportedly aimed his picture at a new crop of children who were familiar with the series via video, rather than the original audience, which was now in its thirties.

Fox's *Independence Day* (1995) and Buena Vista's *Armageddon* (1998) are sci-fi versions of disaster films. Unlike the 'natural' catastrophes that occurred in conventional disaster pictures, sci-fi disasters are caused by invading aliens or by collisions with comets. Containing marauding Martians who have 'absolutely no interest in making nice with the earthlings', *Independence Day* was a throwback to the 'Keep watching the skies' films of the 1950s such as *The War of the Worlds* (1953), *The Day the Earth Stood Still* (1951) and *Invaders from Mars* (1953) that were inspired by H. G. Wells's *The War of the Worlds*.[9] A Jerry Bruckheimer – Michael Bay action film, *Armageddon* starred Bruce Willis, as an oil wildcatter who saves the world from a collision with a deadly asteroid with the help of a team of *Dirty Dozen*-type roughnecks.

A 'cop partners cum alien creatures' movie, Sony's *Men in Black* (1997) teamed rap star Will Smith and veteran actor Tommy Lee Jones, who play elite agents responsible for policing alien activity on Earth for a super-secret government agency known as the Men in Black. Much of the comedy in the movie comes from a running gag that almost anyone could be an alien. A summer blockbuster from Steven Spielberg's Amblin Entertainment, *Men in Black* opened on 5400 screens nationwide to become the 1997 box-office champ and the most successful picture ever released by Columbia Pictures.[10]

TriStar's *Terminator 2: Judgment Day* (1991) differed from the 1984 original by presenting 'a kinder, gentler Terminator'. Schwarzenegger, now an outmoded but still canny T-800 automaton, is 'reprogrammed to look kindly on humans and returns to give them a hand' at averting a nuclear disaster. 'Watching Schwarzenegger's Terminator cope with these new ethical guidelines is one of this sequel's more delicious conceits,' wrote Kenneth Turan.[11]

Other notable sci-fi efforts include TriStar's *Total Recall* (1990) starring Arnold Schwarzenegger, which injected the element of psychological terror into the sci-fi trend, and two very different entries from Warner Bros., *Contact* (1997) and *The Matrix* (1999). Stylistically at the opposite extreme from the special effects extravaganzas, *Contact* is based on Carl Sagan's 1985 bestseller that 'explores how contemporary society might react to the detection of verifiable signals from another world'.[12] *The Matrix*, a film by writer-directors Andy and Larry Wachowski, starred Keanu Reeves, who plays 'a late-20th-century computer hacker whose terminal begins telling him one fateful day that he may have some sort of messianic function in deciding the fate of the world'. The film wielded 'in spades . . . a smorgasbord of effects [for example, morphing and super-human martial arts] that in some cases goes beyond what the sensation-seeking sci-fi audience has ever seen before,' according to *Variety*.[13]

Serving as a bookend to the *Star Wars* franchise is the *Star Trek* series. Paramount's long-running series grew by three instalments beginning in 1991. *Star Trek: First Contact* (1996), the third and most successful instalment, contained no actor from the original 1960s TV series (a first for the franchise). Starring Patrick Stewart, *First Contact* revolves 'around the initial encounter between humankind and extraterrestrials'. No speculative film this. As described by *Variety*, *First Contact*:

> introduces horror-film elements to a traditional *Star Trek* plot . . . The Borg drones and Borg-ified humans, like their counterparts in the original TV episode, look a lot like malevolent bit players from the *Hellraiser* movies. Purists who recall Gene Roddenberry's original vision of a less blood-soaked *Star Trek* universe may be put off by the rough stuff. But mainstream audiences will be more approving of the greater emphasis on high-voltage shocks and action-movie heroics.[14]

Horror

'Horror is the most cyclic of genres,' observed a Fox executive. 'It goes through peaks and valleys every decade and just when it reaches low ebb, something comes along to perk it up.'[15] That 'something' in the 1990s just happened to be *Jurassic Park* (1993), Steven Spielberg's eagerly anticipated horror-thriller about a 'catastrophe in a theme park stocked with flesh-and-blood dinosaurs from the Jurassic Period'. Based on Michael Crichton's 1990 bestseller, the film had affinities with the Hollywood B-film of the 1930s, but 'delivered where it counts, in excitement, suspense and the stupendous realization of giant prehistoric reptiles'.[16] Close to ten million people paid 'a record-devouring $48.5 million the first weekend of its release to unleash a wave of dinosaur mania across the United States'.[17] *Variety* observed that 'Universal tour attractions and sequels will extend the profits enormously'.[18] *The Lost World: Jurassic Park*

(1997) later brought in just shy of $100 million its opening weekend from 5000 screens nationwide – 'a phenomenon by any standard in movie history' – but did not surpass *Jurassic Park*'s final tally.[19] *Jurassic Park* inspired only a few noteworthy monster movies, among them Sony's *Anaconda* (1997) and TriStar's *Godzilla* (1998).

Pursuing a different course, the prestige horror film injected an element of class into the trend and utilised the talents of some of Hollywood's best actors. One type of prestige film was based on 'horror-lit' classics, such as Columbia's *Bram Stoker's Dracula* (1992), Francis Ford Coppola's adaptation of the 1897 Gothic novel starring Winona Ryder and Anthony Hopkins, and Warner Bros.' *Interview with the Vampire* (1994), Neil Jordan's version of the Anne Rice novel starring Tom Cruise and Brad Pitt. Another type was based on Universal horror classics from the 1930s, for example, DreamWorks' *The Haunting* (1999), Jan De Bont's version of James Whale's *The Old Dark House* and Universal's *The Mummy* (1999), Stephen Sommers's remake of the 1932 Boris Karloff film. Prestige films were costly, high-profile projects from major studios that reconceptualised their sources to appeal to contemporary sensibilities. Of the group, *The Mummy* generated the most interest at the box office.

After several years of conspicuous quiescence, the low-budget horror film made a comeback with *Scream* (1996), a slasher film parody released by Dimension Films, Miramax's genre arm. Produced for less than $15 million, *Scream* attracted teenagers in huge numbers to become the most successful Dimension release up to that time.[20] Dimension brought out *Scream 2* (1997) the following year. The summer of 1999 saw a renaissance of the trend. Two back-to-back successes, *The Blair Witch Project* (1999) and *The Sixth Sense* (1999), demonstrated the enduring durability of the psychological horror film and 'the triumph of basic storytelling values over flashy special effects'.[21] The indie sleeper of the year, *The Blair Witch Project* purported to be a documentary consisting of footage left behind by three young film-makers who mysteriously disappeared in a forest while searching for Maryland's legendary Blair Witch. The film debuted at the 1999 Sundance Film Festival and turned the no-name writer-directors Daniel Myrick and Eduardo Sanchez into stars. Picked up by Artisan Entertainment for over $1 million, this raw, low-budget thriller, which cost only $35,000 to produce, grossed over $140 million, 'making it probably the most successful film from a cost versus box-office standpoint that anyone's ever made'.[22] Trumpeted on simultaneous covers of *Time* and *Newsweek*, *The Blair Witch Project* owed its success partly to a savvy Internet marketing campaign that blurred the line between fiction and documentary (the site was viewed more than 30 million times) and partly to its appeal to the same young viewers who made paranormal programmes such as *The X-Files* major television hits.[23]

Although *The Sixth Sense* was a $40 million Buena Vista release starring Bruce Willis, it, too, was a sleeper. A ghost story written and directed by M. Night Shyamalan, a 29-year-old NYU film school graduate, *The Sixth Sense* purports to tell the story of how Bruce Willis, a respected child psychologist, comes to the aid of Haley Joel Osment, 'a kid with oversized glasses and the posture of a beaten puppy, who suffers from a possible mood disorder'.[24] But the ending changes the perspective of the movie. Few could have predicted that this clever ghost story would have exploded at the box office.

The Sixth Sense received several Oscar nominations, including the best supporting actor for Haley Joel Osment, a first for a child actor. Although *The Sixth Sense* lost out to *American Beauty* (1999) in the Best Picture category, it more than doubled *American Beauty*'s box-office take.

Animation

The Lion King (1994), a Disney animated musical about Simba, a cub who endures certain rites of passage before becoming the ruler of his kingdom, was the number-one box-office hit of 1994 and sold more than $1 billion worth of licensed merchandise, including Disney's first number-one soundtrack since *Mary Poppins* (1964). The first of thirty-two animated Disney features not to be based on outside source material, *The Lion King*'s otherwise serious narrative was leavened by the voices of Nathan Lane, Whoopi Goldberg and Matthew Broderick. *The Lion King* sold $100 million in tickets in only eleven days. *Jurassic Park* reached that plateau in nine, but, considering that easily half the tickets sold for *The Lion King* were at children's prices, the $100 million milestone was all the more impressive.[25]

The animation boom of the 1990s began with *The Little Mermaid* (1989), which launched a string of record-breaking hits from Disney that included *Beauty and the Beast* (1991) and *Aladdin* (1992). *The Little Mermaid* marked Disney's first open attempt to court baby-boomers and their children. Janet Maslin noted that 'in combining live-action directorial techniques with animation, devising a story that reflects adult attitudes and recalling baby boomers' fond memories of the traditional Broadway score, Disney has made its target audience clear'. *Beauty and the Beast* developed this strategy further by 'combining the latest computer animation techniques with the best of Broadway. Here, in the guise of furthering a children's fable, is the brand of witty, soaring musical score that is now virtually extinct on the stage.'[26] *Aladdin* expanded the appeal of mainstream animation by adding extravagant humour, courtesy of Robin Williams who was the voice of the Genie.

After *The Lion King*, Disney continued producing cutting-edge entertainment with *Toy Story* (1995), a Pixar film that made computer animation a commercial and artistic force. *Toy Story*'s computer-animated characters were admired for having the same facial mobility as hand-drawn characters of cel animation. It was also admired for its provocative and appealing story about a group of toys that included Woody, a cowboy marionette, and Buzz Lightyear, a galactic superhero with an arsenal of flashy gadgets. (They were voiced by Tom Hanks and Tim Allen, respectively.) Bolstered by the massive success of their 1995 blockbuster, which grossed $362 million worldwide, Pixar and Disney produced *Toy Story 2* (1999), a rare sequel that outperformed the original.

The success of Disney's animated films attracted other studios to the trend. DreamWorks Pictures, for example, produced *Antz* (1998), the second computer-animated feature to be released after *Toy Story*, and Paramount produced *The Rugrats Movie* (1998), which was based on the wildly popular Nickelodeon children's cartoon. Produced at a modest cost of $20 million, *The Rugrats Movie* was the first non-Disney animated feature to earn over $100 million at the box office.

Animated feature production increased yearly. The *Los Angeles Times* calculated that the output in 1999 would be 'roughly equal to the number of features produced in America during the 13 years between *Snow White and the Seven Dwarfs* in 1937 and *Cinderella* in 1950'.[27] Not only did the number increase, but also the varieties of animation including traditional cel, computer-generated, stop motion and claymation. The Academy of Motion Picture Arts and Sciences responded to this surge in output by deciding to hand out its first competitive award for feature animation in 2001. As *Variety* commented, 'This development might not appease those who felt *Pinocchio* or *The Lion King* should have been in the running for best picture in their respective years, but it will make it easier for animated features to finally share the spoils of Oscar glory.'[28]

Family

Disney's success in creating 'palatable entertainment for the whole family' extended to live action, but as a group Disney's live-action films underperformed the animated line both critically and financially. Disney's most successful live-action effort, *The Santa Clause* (1994), grossed $145 million, about equal to the studio's eighth-ranking animated feature. In *The Santa Clause,* Tim Allen of TV's *Home Improvement* is a hapless toy-company executive who is pressed into service as a substitute St Nick.

Disney used a number of techniques to protect its position. Inspired by the sports film – particularly *The Bad News Bears* (1976), which starred Walter Matthau as the hard-drinking Coach Buttermaker who takes a team of Little League losers almost to the top – Disney made *The Mighty Ducks* (1992) about 'a disgraced boozer in need of redemption [Emilio Estevez as Gordo Bombay] and the hapless bad-mouthed hockey dorks he coaches as a community service'.[29] An Avnet/Kerner production, *The Mighty Ducks* spawned a National Hockey League franchise and two sequels. Disney also re-cycled past hits. *101 Dalmations* (1996), for example, a remake of the popular 1961 animated feature, starred Glenn Close as the arch villainess, Cruella De Vil, 'whose most passionate desire is to make a unique fur coat out of the too-precious puppies'.[30] And *Flubber* (1997) was a remake of the 1961 live-action hit *The Absent-minded Professor* that starred Robin Williams as 'an easily distracted college professor' who 'quite by accident … invents Flubber – "flying rubber" – a greenish translucent goo with a mischievous personality all its own'.[31]

Disney had the animation field pretty much to itself until late in the decade; not so with live-action family fare. In 1990, New Line released *Teenage Mutant Ninja Turtles*, a $12 million production from Golden Harvest in Hong Kong containing human-size, animatronic Turtles. Popularised in comic books and a syndicated animated series, the live-action version of the Turtles was created by Jim Henson's Creature Shop. *Ninja Turtles* opened to startling business, eventually grossing $136 million in the US alone to become the top-grossing independent release in film history. Licensing spin-offs from the film generated an estimated $1 billion the first year and two sequels.[32]

The *Turtles* phenomenon was unexpected and unusual. It took Fox's *Home Alone* (1990) to convince other studios 'to enter into the battle for the family crowd'. A modestly budgeted film directed by Chris Columbus that starred a nine-year-old Macaulay

Culkin, *Home Alone* is commercially the most successful comedy in film history. Audiences loved Macaulay Culkin and identified, *Variety* argued, with the 'anguish of two parents who accidentally leave their child behind in the mad rush to the airport for their Christmas vacation is Paris'.[33] Fox wasted no time producing *Home Alone 2: Lost in New York* (1992). Trying to wring extra mileage from the *Home Alone* formula, Fox engaged Columbus to produce *Mrs. Doubtfire* (1993) and *Jingle All the Way* (1996). *Mrs. Doubtfire* 'shrewdly brings together many of the same selling points as . . . the *Home Alone* movies, mixing broad comedic strokes with heavy-handed messages about the magical power of family,' said *Variety*. An unemployed actor who 'botches his son's birthday party and ends up getting tossed out by his wife [Sally Field]', Robin Williams and his brother (Harvey Fierstein), 'a gay make-up artist, hatch the plan of having Williams masquerade as a matronly nanny – the better to steal precious hours with his three adorable moppets'.[34] An Arnold Schwarzenegger vehicle, *Jingle All the Way* lays 'the same guilt on parents for neglecting their children as did *Home Alone*' by reversing 'the 1990 blockbuster's p.o.v. Instead of focusing on the children . . . the tale centers on the desperate efforts of a workaholic father to get his son his desired Christmas gift.'[35] *Mrs. Doubtfire* performed the better of the two and made it to the top twenty.

Universal tried to reach the kiddie audience by producing 'Steven Spielberg's favorite TV shows as a kid'.[36] Spielberg's company, Amblin Entertainment, made two big family hits for the studio, *The Flintstones* (1994) and *Casper* (1995). Both displayed synergistic potential. According to *Variety*, watching *The Flintstones:*

> is akin to taking a quick spin on the Universal Studios tour with a detour through the City Walk attraction, so loaded is it with technical gizmos, showbiz in-jokes and product plugs. In a day when popular movies have more in common with theme parks than old-school artistic traditions, this one fits right in.[37]

As for *Caspar*, the studio 'seems to be thinking along the lines of the next Universal Studios attraction, down to a roller-coaster set in the movie that's probably being drawn up for the tour right now'.[38]

Universal had high hopes for *Babe* (1995), an Australian film produced by George Miller and directed by Chris Noonan about 'a piglet who becomes a championship sheep dog'. This 'dazzling family entertainment with enormous charm . . . utilizing breathtaking technical innovation' drew from a wide demographic and was nominated for an Academy Award as best picture, the only film of its kind to receive such recognition.[39] Universal naturally ordered up a sequel and spent $90 million to produce *Babe: Pig in the City* (1998) under the direction of George Miller. The sequel received generally positive reviews, but was crowded out of the market in the summer of its release and came nowhere near recouping its investment.[40]

The other studios contributed only marginally to the trend. Columbia/TriStar's principal effort consisted of *Hook* (1991), Stephen Spielberg's modern reworking of *Peter Pan*, the J. M. Barrie play about 'The Boy Who Wouldn't Grow up'. Warner Bros. primary effort consisted of *Free Willy* (1993), a film about a friendship between a troubled young boy (Jason James Richter) and a sad whale in the local oceanarium he befriends and which turns the boy's life around in the process. The picture did well enough at the box office to spin off two sequels.

Action

Whether mixed with fantasy, adventure, comedy or suspense, action films followed the same basic formula. As one film executive described it, 'You need antagonists, the bigger the better. Also, most of our films are about one lone underdog triumphing over a system of some kind. And so you need as easily identifiable a system as possible.' The end of the Cold War meant that film-makers turned away from using Soviets as villains and substituted 'the world's seemingly endless supply of rabid nationalists, religious fanatics and all-round troublemakers'.[41]

Several franchises anchored the trend, among them *James Bond*, *Batman*, *Lethal Weapon* and *Die Hard*. All had pre-1990s origins. Of the group, *James Bond* was the ultimate sequel success story. After *Licence to Kill* (1989), starring Timothy Dalton as 007, which grossed a mere $33 million in the US, producers Barbara Broccoli and Michael Wilson rescued the series from possible extinction by casting Pierce Brosnan as the new 007, by commissioning scripts with 'clashing '90s attitudes' and by developing stronger female characters to counter 'Bond's unrepentant sexism and brutality'.[42] From 1995, the series was back on track. Like clockwork, MGM/UA brought out three new entries, *Goldeneye* (1995), *Tomorrow Never Dies* (1997) and *The World Is Not Enough* (1999), raising the total to nineteen films and creating the longest-running franchise in film history.

As always, action films were constructed as vehicles for the most bankable male stars. Arnold Schwarzenegger, Sean Connery and Sylvester Stallone held the limelight at first with films such as *Last Action Hero* (1993), *The Hunt for Red October* (1990) and *Cliffhanger* (1993), respectively, but were soon eclipsed by a new breed of action hero – the likes of Tom Hanks, Tom Cruise, Harrison Ford and Mel Gibson.

Tom Hanks's films include Steven Spielberg's *Saving Private Ryan* (1998) and Ron Howard's *Apollo 13* (1995). *Saving Private Ryan* gained its notoriety from the 24-minute sequence near the beginning that re-created the first wave of American soldiers hitting the beach 'from the grunt's p.o.v. as it is fought inch by inch, bullet by bullet, in all its arbitrariness and surreality'.[43] *Apollo 13*, a Universal release, is a straightforward account of the *Apollo 13* space flight to the moon in 1970, during which 'three astronauts barely avoided becoming the first Americans to die in outer space – the story of three brave explorers who manage to find a way home in the face of hazardous obstacles and heavy odds'.[44] Tom Hanks played Jim Lovell, the flight leader of the space mission. As Kenneth Turan observed:

> This is a quintessential guy movie, filled with tough talk, cigarette smoke and no end of significant man-to-man looks. What it resembles most is a war movie without a human enemy, a kind of 'combat lite' where heroism and camaraderie can be displayed without the messiness of blowing anybody away.[45]

Harrison Ford and Tom Cruise catered to baby-boomer nostalgia by making a pair of thrillers inspired by vintage television series. In Warner Bros.' *The Fugitive* (1993), Ford reprised the familiar role of televisions Dr Richard Kimble, who after being unjustly accused of fatally beating his wife stops running from the law and exposes the real murderer. Paramount's *Mission: Impossible* (1996), starring Tom Cruise, resurrected enough signature traits of the spy series also to rekindle fond memories. Cruise is a hotshot member of an elite, unnamed US intelligence team, the 'mission [of which] is to interrupt a former Russian spy who is planning the theft of a computer disk containing the true identities of the world's top undercover agents'.[46] Although *The Fugitive* and *Mission: Impossible* succeeded at the box office, Harrison Ford made a greater impact on the action trend in two adaptations of Tom Clancy bestsellers, Paramount's *Patriot Games* (1992) and *Clear and Present Danger* (1994).

Finally, in addition to the *Lethal Weapon* films, Mel Gibson made *Braveheart* (1995), a swashbuckler, and a series of suspense films including Touchstone's *Ransom* (1996), Warner Bros.' *Conspiracy Theory* (1997) and Paramount's *Payback* (1999). Part of a costume film cycle that included Kevin Costner's *Robin Hood: Prince of Thieves* (1991), Michael Mann's *The Last of the Mohicans* (1992) and Michael Caton-Jones's *Rob Roy* (1995), *Braveheart* won an Oscar for best picture, for Mel Gibson's direction and for make-up, sound effects editing and cinematography.

Comedy

Whoopi Goldberg, Robin Williams and Steve Martin entertained audiences throughout the decade doing their regular routines. Remakes of popular old TV shows (Paramount's *The Addams Family* [1991], *The Brady Bunch Movie* [1995] and Fox's *The Beverly Hillbillies* [1993]) and a slew of sports comedies (Columbia's *A League of Their Own* [1992], Fox's *White Men Can't Jump* (1992) and Warner Bros.' *Tin Cup* [1996]) also attracted customers.

The defining comedy type of the 1990s was the 'dumb-and-dumber' film. The dumb-and-dumber cycle consisted, according to the *Los Angeles Times*, of a:

> string of raucous films devoted to the celebration of stupidity [that] has transformed youth comedies into a carnival of jokes about spit, vomit, farts, dildos, diarrhoea, premature ejaculation, talking turds, semen in your hair, semen in your beer – let's just say that no bodily part, fluid or excretion is off limits.[47]

The cycle owed a debt to the 1981 film *Porky's*, but gained momentum in 1994 when the back-to-back successes of *Ace Ventura: Pet Detective* and *Dumb and Dumber* made Jim Carrey an overnight star. A Warner Bros. release, *Ace Ventura: Pet Detective* was a slapstick vehicle designed to capitalise on Carrey's popularity as a writer and performer on the Fox TV comedy sketch show *In Living Color*. In *Ace Ventura*, Carrey is 'a goofball private gumshoe whose speciality is finding missing pets' – in this case, a kidnapped dolphin mascot of a pro football team in time for the Super Bowl.[48] *Ace Ventura* grossed $100 million worldwide and launched Carrey's film career.

Dumb and Dumber marked the directorial debut of Peter and Bobby Farrelly, who wrote for TV's *Seinfeld*. *Variety* described this New Line release as 'a flat-out celebration of stupidity, bodily functions and pratfalls'. The film co-stars Jeff Daniels, 'a rather inept dog groomer who has transformed his van exterior to resemble a sheep dog' and Jim Carrey, 'a limo driver with higher aspirations – he's saving to open a worm supply warehouse he's imaginatively dubbed "I Got Worms"'.[49] *Dumb and Dumber* earned more than $340 million globally and started a trend. Warner Bros. was quick to exploit the trend by releasing *Ace Ventura: When Nature Calls* (1995), which sent the intrepid animal investigator to Africa. The sequel surpassed the original's worldwide take in the domestic market alone.

Mike Myers made the transition from TV to films with *Wayne's World* (1992). A Paramount release based on a skit Myers wrote for *Saturday Night Live*, *Wayne's World* is a talk-show parody from the American heartland; Wayne Campbell (Mike Myers) and Garth Algar (Diana Carvey), 'a cheery pair of high school headbangers', host a cable access show on which 'they play music badly and expound – they believe – on deep subjects'.[50] *Wayne's World 2* (1993) inevitably followed. Myers went on to make the most commercially potent film of the cycle, New Line's *Austin Powers: The Spy Who Shagged Me* (1999). As Austin Powers, Myers is a 'psychedelic superagent' *à la* James Bond who is 'transported lock, stock and barrel from the [Carnaby Street of the] '60s to the '90s, where he is a sexist anachronism'.[51] Outperforming the original *Austin Powers: International Man of Mystery* (1997), this sequel opened in a record 3312 theatres and generated $54.7 million in the first three days of its run, the biggest comedy opening ever.[52] Adam Sandler, meanwhile, served a four-year stint on *Saturday Night Live* in the 1990s creating a collection of characters that included Opera Man, Shaky-lipped Guy, Canteen Boy, Cajun Boy and Herlihy Boy, all with their own distinctive quirks. His first big hit film, Disney's *The Waterboy* (1998), was based on his *SNL* routine about a slow-witted Cajun who becomes the star linebacker for a second-rate Louisiana college. Sandler's other big hit along this line was Sony's *Big Daddy* (1999).

The dumb-and-dumber trend continued on this trajectory, with film-makers pushing the envelope as far as possible. For example, *Variety* described Universal's *American Pie* (1999) as having 'but a single ambition – to be the king of gross-out comedy – and will happily wear that crown until another film sets out to steal it, say, around this time next year'.[53] *There's Something about Mary* (1998) was the exception. Produced and directed by the Farrelly brothers, this Fox release starring Cameron Diaz, Ben Stiller and Matt Dillon contains the usual teen gross-out elements. But the film distinguished itself from the pack by marrying these elements to romantic comedy. As *Variety* observed:

> In *Mary*, rude humor is put to the service of workable ideas. Viewers laughed so hard throughout they almost forgot the movie was not about sex but about love, about the fantasy of reliving adolescent amorous obsessions, of reuniting with high school sweethearts.[54]

There's Something about Mary demonstrated one way to successfully adapt romantic comedy to the 1990s. Film-makers interested in romantic comedy had to confront the problems of how to adhere effectively to the traditional conventions of the trend in an era of AIDS, of increased sexual frankness on the screen, of spiralling divorce rates and widespread confusion over gender roles in courtship.[55] Ten romantic comedies made it to the All-Time Grossers chart. Paramount's *Ghost* (1990), the biggest hit of the group, was the first solo directing effort of Jerry Zucker, a former member of the three-man directing team responsible for comedies such as *Airplane!* (1980) and *Ruthless People* (1986). *Ghost* is a hybrid about:

> a New York banker (Patrick Swayze) who is killed by a mugger but remains on Earth as a
> ghost. Watching over his grieving lover (Demi Moore), he soon realizes she is in mortal
> danger. In desperation, he manages to communicate with her through a fake psychic
> (Whoopi Goldberg) who is astounded to discover that her powers are real.[56]

Goldberg won an Oscar for best supporting actress for her efforts. Miramax's *Shakespeare in Love* (1998), the most honoured romantic comedy, upset DreamWorks' *Saving Private Ryan* by winning the best picture Oscar and six others, including best actress, supporting actress and original screenplay.

In the years between the release of *Ghost* and *Shakespeare in Love*, romantic comedy revolved around the talents of a star, Julia Roberts; a writer-director, Nora Ephron; and a producer-writer, James L. Brooks. Julia Roberts became a major star in Buena Vista's *Pretty Woman* (1990). In this Pygmalion tale for the 1990s, Julia Roberts is a hooker with a heart of gold who strikes up a business relationship with a lovelorn corporate raider (Richard Gere) for a $3000 fee. Spending a week with him on a shopping spree, she is transformed from 'gum-smacking, stiletto-heeled tart to femme d'elegance' who can fill the void in his lonely life.[57] Roberts went on to make *My Best Friend's Wedding* (1997), a Sony release about a 'successful young writer of culinary guides, who decides she's in love with a great pal only when he announces he's marrying someone else',[58] and *Notting Hill* (1999), a Polygram release from Britain that teamed Roberts with Hugh Grant in 'a modern fairytale about a shy London bookseller who falls for a Hollywood megastar (and vice versa)'.[59] In *Runaway Bride* (1999), Roberts reunited with *Pretty Woman*'s co-star Richard Gere to make a screwball comedy about a small-town woman who 'becomes a media celebrity by continually jilting her fiancés at the 11th hour'.

Having achieved her greatest writing success with Rob Reiner's wildly popular *When Harry Met Sally . . .* (1989), Nora Ephron followed up with *Sleepless in Seattle* (1993), a TriStar release starring Meg Ryan and Tom Hanks, which she co-wrote and directed. In the earlier film, Ephron delayed the romance by making the couple (Meg Ryan and Billy Crystal) bickering friends; in *Sleepless*, Ephron varied the formula by creating a long-distance relationship that literally kept the lovers separated by a continent until the ending of the movie. After directing New Line's *Michael* (1996), a romantic fable starring John Travolta as a 'heaven-sent angel who brings joy, love and redemption to a team of cynical and frustrated tabloid journalists', William Hurt and Andie MacDowell, Ephron teamed up again with Tom Hanks and Meg Ryan to make *You've Got Mail* (1998) for Warner Bros.[60] An updated version of Ernst Lubitsch's 1940 classic *The Shop around the*

Corner, You've Got Mail is a story of anonymous, affectionate e-mail pen pals who dislike each other in person. Unlike the Lubitsch film, Ephron's version provides a very good reason for the friction between the two lead characters – Hanks is part of a huge, family-owned bookstore chain that threatens to swallow Meg Ryan's small children's bookstore.

James L. Brooks, the multiple Oscar winner for *Terms of Endearment* (1983) and nominee for *Broadcast News* (1987), co-produced two romantic comedies for Sony designed to appeal equally to males and females, *Jerry Maguire* (1996) and *As Good as It Gets* (1997). In both films, a maverick falls for a warm-hearted single working mum with a young son and become humanised in the process. In *Jerry Maguire*, written and directed by Cameron Crowe, Tom Cruise is a slick pro sports agent who suffers a momentary pang of conscience about the business and is fired from his firm for expressing it. The romance element links Cruise with Renee Zellweger, who has quit her job as a drone in the sports agency to join Maguire in his 'Quixotic effort to be true to himself and stay in the game at the same time, this despite her being a single mother to 6-year-old Jonathan Lipnicki'.[61] In *As Good as It Gets*, which was written and directed by Brooks, Jack Nicholson is a 'homophobic, racist, anti-Semitic and all-around misanthropic author of 62 top-selling romance novels . . . whose idea of a good turn is tossing a neighbor's pesky insect dog down the garbage chute of their Manhattan apartment house'.[62] He eventually falls in love with Helen Hunt, an earthy waitress at the neighbourhood restaurant where he has his daily breakfast, who has a seven-year-old son who 'suffers from pervasive allergies that unhinge his life'.[63]

In a niche by themselves are three acclaimed comedies that are vastly different from mainstream Hollywood fare – Miramax's *Pulp Fiction* (1994), DreamWorks *American Beauty* (1999) and Gramercy's *Fargo* (1996). Commonly labelled black comedies, these hybrids mix comedy and drama, and play with conventional narrative form. They were made by independent producers to appeal to filmgoers who were as equally at home in an art-house as a mall theatre. Of the three, *American Beauty* represented a larger production cycle; it culminated a cycle critical of American family life that included Todd Solondz's *Welcome to the Dollhouse* (1996), Ang Lee's *The Ice Storm* (1997), Gary Ross's *Pleasantville* (1998), Paul Schrader's *Affliction* (1997) and Victor Nunez's *Ulee's Gold* (1997). Starring Kevin Spacey and Annette Bening, *American Beauty* won five Oscars for best picture, actor, director, original screenplay and cinematography.

Drama

'Drama' is a term of convenience that I have used to encompass a range of production trends, among them the Western, thriller, courtroom, social problem, romance and woman's film. Only one drama, and a hybrid at that, made it to the elite top twenty – *Forrest Gump* (1994) – and about thirty dramas of all stripes to the All-Time Top Grossers chart. Approximately fifteen of the group consist of thrillers and courtroom dramas that involve serial killers, predatory women, contract murderers and revenge killings.

A Robert Zemeckis film, Paramount's *Forrest Gump* is 'a picaresque story of a simpleton's charmed odyssey through 30 years of tumultuous American history'. Like

Zemeckis's *Back to the Future* (1985) and *Who Framed Roger Rabbit?* (1988), *Forrest Gump* relied heavily on computerised visual legerdemain for comic effect, in particular from placing Forrest next to US presidents and leading figures in newsreel and television footage.[64] Tom Hanks won an Oscar for his title role, his second such award in two years. (He received the first Oscar for his portrayal of an attorney dying of AIDS in *Philadelphia* [1993]). Although *Forrest Gump* won the best picture Oscar and numerous other awards, it did not spawn imitators.

Orion Pictures' *Dances with Wolves* (1990), which ranked second behind *Forrest Gump,* was more influential. A three-hour Western epic directed by Kevin Costner, *Dances with Wolves* starred Costner as an idealistic cavalry officer whose life is transformed when he encounters members of a Lakota Sioux tribe. Like the classic Western of the 1940s and 1950s, *Dances with Wolves* contains traditional set-pieces and, like the revisionist Westerns of the 1960s, *Dances* is respectful of Indians and their culture. *Dances with Wolves* prepared the way for another Western hit, Clint Eastwood's *Unforgiven* (1992). Like *Dances with Wolves*, this Warner Bros. release attracted a more mature audience while still attracting younger customers to become both a commercial and critical success. And like its predecessor, *Unforgiven* won an Oscar for best picture and direction. Within a year, some sixty Westerns were placed in production or development.[65]

But the bread-and-butter film was the thriller. The cycle consisted of three strands: courtroom/law; serial killer; and predatory female. Paramount set the pace with *The Firm* (1993), an adaptation of John Grisham's bestseller. Commenting on the formulaic quality of the film, Roger Ebert wrote that:

> Watching *The Firm*, I realized that law firms have replaced Army platoons as Hollywood's favorite microcosm. The new law thrillers have the same ingredients as those dependable old World War II action films: various ethnic and personality types who fight with each other when they're not fighting the enemy. The law movies have one considerable advantage: the female characters participate fully in all the action, instead of just staying home and writing letters to the front.[66]

Warner Bros. took over the Grisham franchise by producing *The Pelican Brief* (1993), a thriller about a law student (Julia Roberts) who discovers the murderer of two Supreme Court justices, in addition to *The Client* (1994) and *A Time to Kill* (1996).

The courtroom drama is best represented by Columbia's *A Few Good Men* (1992). Adapted by Aaron Sorkin from his hit Broadway play, *A Few Good Men* investigates a hazing incident at Guantanamo Bay that resulted in the death of a marine private. Jack Nicholson, the commander of the base, is a 'tough, bigoted Vietnam veteran, a career officer shaped by decades of cold-war politics'.[67] Tom Cruise and Demi Moore play young naval lawyers assigned to defend the enlisted men charged with the crime.

The serial killer film is best represented by Jonathan Demme's *The Silence of the Lambs* (1991). Based on the Thomas Harris novel, *The Silence of the Lambs* pits Clarice Starling (Jodie Foster), a promising FBI trainee, against Dr Hannibal Lecter (Anthony

Hopkins), a brilliant psychiatrist-turned-cannibal. A critically acclaimed film as well as a huge box-office success, *Silence of the Lambs* did a sweep of the Oscars at the 1992 Academy Awards. Only two other pictures – *It Happened One Night* (1934) and *One Flew over the Cuckoo's Nest* (1975) – had won in the top five categories of best actor, actress, director, screenplay and picture. *Silence of the Lambs* grossed over $130 million and started a trend; however, it could not save Orion Pictures, a mini-major than won best picture Oscars two years in a row for *Dances with Wolves* and *Silence*, from bankruptcy.

The predatory female thriller is best exemplified in TriStar's *Basic Instinct* (1992) and Warner Bros.' *Disclosure* (1994), the second and third instalments of a 'rough-trade trip-tych' Michael Douglas began in 1987 with *Fatal Attraction*. In *Basic Instinct*, Douglas is a tough cop who falls for a sultry murder suspect, played by Sharon Stone. In *Disclosure*, Douglas plays a mid-level computer-company executive, the victim of phony sex harass-ment charges brought against him by his former lover and competitor for a coveted job (Demi Moore). It was adapted from the Michael Crichton novel, which Warner acquired for $3.5 million.

Serious dramas dealing with social problems, politics or humanistic concerns were few and far between, and only four made it to the All-Time Top Grossers chart. The most prestigious of the group was *Schindler's List* (1993), Steven Spielberg's 'historical and biographical drama about a Nazi industrialist who saved some 1,100 Jews from certain death in the concentration camps'. A departure from the Spielberg canon, this Universal release also departed from standard studio practice – the film was shot in black and white to give it a documentary look, contained no major stars and lasted three hours and fifteen minutes. Spielberg's effort to create 'as indelible a picture of the Holocaust as fiction film allows' won him numerous awards, including Oscars for best picture and direction.[68] The biggest money earner of the group of Miramax's *Good Will Hunting* (1997), an inspirational film directed by Gus Van Sant about 'a brilliant working-class youngster who's forced to come to terms with his creative genius and true feelings'. It starred Matt Damon as a '20-year-old lad who works as a janitor at MIT and spends most of his time with his coarse friends at the neighborhood bar' and Robin Williams as a community college therapist who tries to save him from self-destruction.[69]

The woman's film was ushered in by *Driving Miss Daisy* (1989), a best picture Oscar winner about an enduring friendship of an old Jewish woman (Jessica Tandy) and her African-American chauffeur (Morgan Freeman) in the American South. Universal's *Fried Green Tomatoes* (1991), a low-key drama directed by Jon Avnet, followed in its wake and described the friendship of Idgie Threadgoode (Mary Stuart Masterson) and her intimate friend Ruth (Mary-Louise Parker), who together run the Whistle Stop Café in Alabama where such dishes as fried chicken, berry pies and fried green tomatoes are served.[70] *Fried Green Tomatoes* opened on only five screens nationally and to mixed reviews, but strong word-of-mouth, especially in smaller towns, ignited interest in the film. Over seven weeks, Universal Pictures systematically expanded the release to include 1229 screens. Produced at a cost of $11 million, *Fried Green Tomatoes* eventu-ally grossed $82 million at the box office and helped to demonstrate the bigger-than-expected market for woman's films.[71]

The Flintstones (1994): Steven Spielberg's 1990s hits present a microcosm of 1990s production trends

What the small audience received was another matter. Paramount's *Indecent Proposal* (1993) is an example of the 'Woman as Door Prize' film. *Indecent Proposal*'s title refers to an offer of a 'cool million' by billionaire Robert Redford to 'down-on-their-luck married couple Woody Harrelson and Demi Moore' in exchange for spending a night with the latter.[72] Miramax's *The English Patient* (1996), an adaptation of Michael Ondaatje's Booker Prize-winning novel set in pre-war North Africa, was ostensibly about 'loyalty, personal betrayal, healing and unexpected passion', but in essence was a conventional adulterous melodrama.[73] And Sony's *Stepmom* (1998), a modern feel-good tragic melodrama starring Julia Roberts and Susan Sarandon, returned the woman's films to its 'soap opera' heritage.

Conclusion

The globalisation of Hollywood kept production tightly focused on the two main segments of the theatrical market, the 'teen and pre-teen bubble' and the 'boomers with kids'. Satisfying these segments meant that studios devoted their resources to high-concept projects that could easily be pitched in national marketing campaigns and released simultaneously in thousands of mall theatres. This is just another way of saying that nothing much changed in Hollywood in the 1990s. Familiar formulae in familiar production trends aided by increasingly sophisticated computer-generated imagery and attuned to changing pop-culture trends kept audiences entertained. As always, an elite coterie of stars attracted the crowds and an elite group of mass-market bestsellers generated the buzz. Disney was the most profitable company in the business and captured the largest market share five times.[74] But not even Disney, whose name was synonymous with the animated/family film, had a lock on the production trend. No longer a déclassé source of story ideas and talent for 'tentpole' studio projects, television, or at least those parts of the medium admired by the 'teen and pre-teen bubble', provided fodder for potential remakes, a source of fresh comic stars and a benchmark to measure changing audience tastes. Seen against this backdrop, the achievements of superstar director Steven Spielberg are all the more impressive. Hollywood's answer to Bill Gates, Spielberg had 'the unprecedented distinction' of being associated with a string of $100 million-plus blockbusters year after year either as director and/or (sometimes uncredited) executive producer.[75] Spielberg's 1990s' hits, which include *Jurassic Park*, *Schindler's List*, *The Flintstones*, *Twister*, *Men in Black*, *Antz*, *Saving Private Ryan* and *American Beauty*, are a microcosm of 1990s production trends. Spielberg's commercial success can be attributed in part to a combination of a childlike sense of wonder and an ability to expertly manipulate the medium's most evocative techniques. These qualities also characterise some of the best that the 1990s had to offer. Regardless, Hollywood carried out the mandate of its corporate parents to keep the distribution pipelines in all markets full.

Notes

1. Bernard Weinraub and Geraldine Fabricant, 'The Revenge of the Bean Counters', *New York Times*, 13 June 1999, p. C1.
2. Limited releases are defined as regular-format films showing on 350 or fewer screens at their widest point of release. Andrew Hindes, 'Arthouses Face Empty Seats', *Variety*, 13–19 July 1998, p. 7.
3. Patrick Goldstein, 'Hollywood Stoops to Conquer', *Los Angeles Times*, 11 July 1999, Calendar, p. 8.
4. Richard Natale, 'Family Films Abound, but Successes Don't', *Los Angeles Times*, 25 August 1994, Calendar, p. 1.
5. Leonard Klady, 'Epics "Titanic", "Wind" Crush Formulas', *Variety*, 2–8 March 1998, p. 105.
6. Kenneth Turan, *Twister*, *Los Angeles Times*, 10 May 1996, Calendar, p. 1.
7. Kenneth Turan, 'The Prequel has Landed', *Los Angeles Times*, 18 May 1999, Calendar, p. 1.
8. Eric Harrison, 'F/X of Time Are Inevitable', *Los Angeles Times*, 21 June 1999, Calendar, p. 1.
9. Kenneth Turan, '*Independence Day*', *Los Angeles Times*, 2 July 1996, Calendar, p. 1.
10. Leonard Klady, 'Amblin's Double Play', *Daily Variety*, 1 August 1997, p. 1.
11. Kenneth Turan, '*Terminator 2: Judgment Day*', *Los Angeles Times*, 3 July 1991, p. F1.
12. Todd McCarthy, '*Contact*', *Variety*, 14–20 July 1997, p. 43.
13. Todd McCarthy, '*The Matrix*', *Variety*, 29 March–4 April 1999, p. 6.
14. Joe Leydon, '*Star Trek: First Contact*', *Variety*, 18–24 November 1996, p. 59.
15. Leonard Klady, 'Scary Future for horror pix', *Variety*, 11–17 April 1994, p. 13.
16. Todd McCarthy, '*Jurassic Park*', *Daily Variety*, 7 June 1993.
17. David J. Fox, ' "Jurassic Park" Gobbles up $48 Million in Opening', *Los Angeles Times*, 14 June 1993, Calendar, p. 1.
18. McCarthy, '*Jurassic Park*'.

19. Judy Brennan, ' "Lost World: Jurassic Park" Stomps Record for Openings', *Los Angeles Times*, 26 May 1997, Calendar, p. 1.

20. Monica Roman, 'Genre Pix Give Miramax an Added Dimension', *Variety*, 20–26 January 1997, p. 7.

21. Eric Harrison, 'Horror in the Things Unseen', *Los Angeles Times*, 14 August 1999, Calendar, p. 1.

22. Kenneth Turan, 'Witch's Brew Bad for Studios', *Los Angeles Times*, 16 August 1999, Calendar, p. 1.

23. Ibid.

24. Todd McCarthy, *'The Sixth Sense'*, *Variety*, 2–8 August 1999, p. 33.

25. David J. Fox, 'It's Still Clear Which Movie Is the "King" ', *Los Angeles Times*, 5 July 1994, Calendar, p. 1.

26. Janet Maslin, 'Target: Boomers and Their Babies', *The New York Times*, 24 November 1991, p. B2.

27. Charles Solomon, 'Animated Heroines Finally Get in Step with the Times', *Los Angeles Times*, 26 June 1998, Calendar, p. 18.

28. Richard Natale, 'New Animation Category', *Variety*, 11–17 December 2000, p. 10.

29. Michael Wilmington *'The Mighty Ducks'*, *Los Angeles Times*, 2 October 1992, Calendar, p. 14.

30. Todd McCarthy, *'101 Dalmations'*, *Daily Variety*, 25 November 1996.

31. Joe Leydon, *'Flubber'*, *Variety*, 24–30 November 1997, p. 63.

32. Pat Broeske, ' "Turtles" Wax the Opposition at Box Office', *Los Angeles Times*, 3 April 1990, Calendar, p. 1.

33. William Grimes, *'Home Alone 2: Lost in New York'*, *New York Times*, 15 November 1992, p. B15.

34. Brian Lowry, *'Mrs. Doubtfire'*, *Daily Variety*, 22 November 1993.

35. Emanuel Levy, *'Jingle All the Way'*, *Variety*, 25 November – 1 December 1996, p. 71.

36. Richard Natale, 'Family Films Ready for the Heat of Battle', *Los Angeles Times*, 6 November 1998, Calendar, p. 2.

37. Todd McCarthy, *'The Flintstones'*, *Variety*, 23–29 May 1994, p. 51.

38. Brian Lowry, *'Caspar'*, *Variety*, 22–28 May 1995, p. 92.

39. Leonard Klady, *'Babe'*, *Variety*, 24–30 July 1995, p. 70.

40. Robert W. Welkos, ' "Bug's Life" Is Walking off with the Turkey', *Los Angeles Times*, 28 November 1998, Calendar, p. 1.

41. John Clark, 'Hollywood's Patriotic Games', *Los Angeles Times*, 4 July 1998, Calendar, p. 1.

42. Steven Smith, 'In Search of Hollywood's Holy Grail', *Los Angeles Times*, 22 August 1997, Calendar, p. 1.

43. Todd McCarthy, *'Saving Private Ryan'*, *Variety*, 20–26 July 1998, p. 45.

44. Todd McCarthy, *'Apollo 13'*, *Variety*, 26 June–9 July 1995, p. 78.

45. Kenneth Turan, *'Apollo 13'*, *Los Angeles Times*, 30 June 1995, Calendar, p. 1.

46. Greg Evans, *'Mission: Impossible'*, *Variety*, 20–26 May 1996, p. 29.

47. Patrick Goldstein, 'Hollywood Stoops to Conquer', *Los Angeles Times*, 11 July 1999, Calendar, p. 8.

48. Steve Gaydos, '*Ace Ventura: Pet Detective*', *Variety*, 7 February 1994, p. 40.

49. Leonard Klady, '*Dumb and Dumber*', *Daily Variety*, 15 December 1994.

50. Kenneth Turan, '*Wayne's World*', *Los Angeles Times*, 14 February 1992, Calendar, p. 1.

51. Dennis Harvey, '*Austin Powers: The Spy Who Shagged Me*', *Variety*, 14–20 June 1999, p. 32.

52. Richard Natale, 'Feelin' Pretty Groovy', *Los Angeles Times*, 14 June 1999, Calendar, p. 1.

53. Todd McCarthy, '*American Pie*', *Variety*, 28 June–11 July 1999, p. 69.

54. Emanuel Levy, 'Rude, crude, with a heart of gold', *Daily Variety*, 8 March 1999, p. A26.

55. David Kronke, 'What Happened to Adorable?', *Los Angeles Times*, 12 February 1995, Calendar, p. 8.

56. Kirk Honeycutt, 'Name: Jerry Zucker', *Los Angeles Times*, 13 July 1990, Calendar, p. 12.

57. Sheila Benson, '*Pretty Woman*', *Los Angeles Times*, 23 March 1990, Calendar, p. 14.

58. Kenneth Turan, '*My Best Friend's Wedding*', *Los Angeles Times*, 20 June 1997, Calendar, p. 1.

59. Derek Elley, '*Notting Hill*', *Variety*, 3–9 May 1999, p. 83.

60. Jack Matthews, 'Hollywood's Feel-Good Fantasies', *Los Angeles Times*, 5 August 1990, Calendar, p. 4

61. Todd McCarthy, '*Jerry Maguire*', *Variety*, 9–15 December 1996, p. 101.

62. Kenneth Turan, '*As Good as It Gets*', *Los Angeles Times*, 23 December 1997, Calendar, p. 1.

63. Todd McCarthy, '*As Good as It Gets*', *Daily Variety*, 10 December 1997.

64. Todd McCarthy, '*Forrest Gump*', *Variety*, 11–17 July 1994, p. 41.

65. Leonard Klady, 'Westerns Roam the H'wood Range Again', *Daily Variety*, 8 April 1993, p. 21.

66. Roger Ebert, '*The Firm*', *Chicago Sun-Times*, 30 June 1993.

67. Vincent Canby, '*A Few Good Men*', *New York Times*, 11 December 1992, p. C20.

68. Todd McCarthy, '*Schindler's List*', *Daily Variety*, 6 December 1993.

69. Emmanuel Levy, '*Good Will Hunting*', *Variety*, 1–7 December 1997, p. 73.

70. David J. Fox, 'Green Tomatoes: Why a Little Film Bloomed', *Los Angeles Times*, 10 February 1992, Calendar, p. 1.

71. Ibid, p. 1.

72. Patrick Goldstein, 'A Flurry of Women-as-Barter Films', *Los Angeles Times*, 18 April 1993, Calendar, p. 8.

73. Todd McCarthy, '*The English Patient*', *Variety*, 11–17 November 1996, p. 57.

74. Dade Hayes, 'Box Office: Reel Fine in 1999', *Variety*, 10–16 January 2000, p. 9.

75. Leonard Klady and John Voland, 'Amblin amassin' ample coin for Spielberg's kitty', *Variety*, 4–10 August 1997, p. 4.

13

'The Best Disney Film Disney Never Made': Children's Films and the Family Audience in American Cinema since the 1960s[1]

Peter Krämer

When it comes to research on American cinema, children's films are very low on the academic agenda, at least in film studies.[2] There is, for example, not a single index entry for the term 'children's films', nor for the related term 'family films', in Barry Keith Grant's 1986 collection *Film Genre Reader* (as compared, for example, to three entries for 'women's films').[3] The recent fundamental revisions to genre studies proposed by Nick Browne, Rick Altman and Steve Neale also fail to mention children's or family films.[4] Browne's collection, *Refiguring American Film Genres*, contains plenty of material on 'family melodrama' and 'women's films', as does Altman's *Film/Genre*, yet there is no generic label in the indices for films addressed primarily to children (and their parents). Altman's genre index moves from 'chick flick' to 'college comedy' and from 'exploitation' to 'fantastic'. Similarly, there is a blank spot in Neale's index between 'chase film' and 'chiller'. However, in his survey of *Variety* reviews from the mid-1980s, Neale did come across the labels 'family film' and 'family pic' (the latter being applied to *The Muppets Take Manhattan* (1984)).[5] This begins to acknowledge the common-sense assumption that the labels 'children's film' and 'family film' are used both by the film industry and by film audiences, even if they do not feature in genre studies. Confirmation of this assumption, if such is needed, comes from the classification system of video stores, which tend to have a children's section, and from audience surveys. When, in 1982, 1000 Americans aged eighteen and over were asked about their cinemagoing habits and movie preferences, one of the nine types of film offered to them was 'children's': 19.2 per cent said they had recently seen a children's film, and 30.2 per cent said they were interested in viewing children's films in the coming year; not surprisingly, many of these respondents were women aged twenty-five to fifty-four, most likely mothers.[6] Also, not surprisingly, in respondents' ranking of favourite movie types, children's films came last (only 2.6 per cent said it was their favourite), while comedy, drama and science fiction came first; these were also the types of films respondents had seen most often recently and most wanted to see in the future.

It seems, then, that children's and family films are viable categories in the marketing and reception of contemporary Hollywood films, but at first sight they appear to be quite marginal for the majority of the non-child audience and for the film industry. A simple working definition would be that children's films are films made specifically for children. (Children are here understood as those aged twelve and younger; thirteen- to nineteen-year-olds are specifically targeted with teen films, a much more prominent category in film studies.) Similarly, family films can be defined as those films aimed at both children and their parents. Of course, there is considerable overlap between the two categories because the producers of children's films, just as those of children's literature, will often attempt also to appeal to parents who, after all, have to pay for their children's entertainment and often join them in it.[7] An important practical reason for the neglect of children's and family films in film studies is their sheer diversity: they range from comedies to adventure stories, from fairy tales to science fiction, and, apart from the frequent presence of child or animal protagonists and slapstick humour as well as magical spectacle, they do not have much in common and therefore resist the systematic analysis of iconography, narrative patterns and thematic concerns underpinning much of genre studies.

However, it would appear that another reason for the academic neglect of children's and family films is a set of prejudices, namely that by and large they are cheaply made and simply not very good and not even very important commercially. But what if these assumptions are misleading with respect to contemporary Hollywood? What if many of the most cherished and most successful (and not always very cheap) American films in recent decades can be understood as children's or family films?

E.T., Steven Spielberg and George Lucas, 1977–84

Let us begin with another look at the September 1982 audience survey referred to above. Comedy was by far respondents' preferred type of film: 33.5 per cent declared it to be their favourite, whereas 17.8 per cent said drama and 12.4 per cent science fiction; 80.1 per cent of respondents expressed an interest in seeing comedies in the coming year, 59 per cent drama and 43.3 per cent science fiction. However, when it came to the types of film that they had recently seen, science fiction was well ahead of drama and almost tied with comedy (at around 50 per cent). The reason for this was the enormous popularity of a single film, namely Steven Spielberg's *E.T. – The Extra-Terrestrial* (released in June 1982), which had been seen by about 50 per cent of all respondents.[8] The impact of *E.T.* on the survey's respondents does not come as a big surprise when one considers the fact that, in September 1982, *E.T.* was about to surpass the box-office take of *Star Wars* (1977) and become the top-grossing film of all time in the US. By the end of the year, *E.T.* had a domestic gross of $367.7 million, which was more than 10 per cent of the film industry's total American box-office revenues in 1982 of $3452.7 million.[9] Thus, more than ten out of every one hundred cinema tickets bought in the US in 1982 were purchased for *E.T.*

Respondents in the audience survey on the whole classified *E.T.* as science fiction, yet they could just as easily have classified it as a children's film, taking their lead from many of the film's enthusiastic reviewers. The *Christian Science Monitor*, for example, declared that 'children are the natural audience for *E.T.*' because Spielberg 'understands what makes kids tick'.[10] The *New York Times* predicted that it 'may become a children's classic of the space age' because it was 'full of the timeless longings expressed in children's literature of all eras'.[11] *Variety* wrote that *E.T.* 'may be the best film Disney never made' and 'is certain to capture the imagination of the world's youth in the manner of most of his (Spielberg's) earlier pics, as well as those of George Lucas'.[12] The Disney reference makes it clear that with 'youth' *Variety* was first and foremost thinking about children and that therefore many of Spielberg's and Lucas' earlier films could also be subsumed under the category of children's films. Indeed, *Variety*'s reviews of *Star Wars*, *The Empire Strikes Back* (1980) and *Raiders of the Lost Ark* (1981) had compared these films to classic children's entertainment; according to *Variety*, *Star Wars* 'equals the genius of Walt Disney', watching the opening of the sequel is 'like walking through the front gate of Disneyland' and *Raiders* is 'the stuff that raucous Saturday matinees at the local Bijou once were made of'.[13] It is important to note, however, that *Variety*'s reviewer had been reluctant to use the label 'children's film' because of 'all the derogatory overtones that go with that description' – presumably the prejudice that children's films on the whole were cheap, badly made and *only* suitable for children.[14]

Instead of using this problematic label, *Variety* reviews of Spielberg's and Lucas's blockbusters had emphasised their 'all-age appeal' (*Star Wars*) and the fact that they were designed 'to reach a very broad blockbuster-type mass audience' (*Close Encounters of the Third Kind* (1977)) or 'broad-based summer audiences' (*Raiders*), which emphatically included children, but which strongly signalled that teenagers and adults were by no means excluded.[15] This rhetorical strategy is also in evidence with the two megahits that followed *E.T.*: *Variety*'s review of *Return of the Jedi* (1983) highlighted the Ewoks, 'a tribe of fuzzy, sweet little creatures that continually cause ahhs among the audience (and will doubtlessly sell thousands of dolls)';[16] and its review of *Indiana Jones and the Temple of Doom* (1984), while never using the label children's film, contained a whole paragraph about child audiences: 'Kids 10–12 upwards will eat it all up, of course', but the film 'might prove extraordinarily frightening to younger children, who, indeed, are being catered to ... by the presence of the adorable 12-year-old Ke Huy Quan'.[17] Thus *Variety* indicated, albeit somewhat indirectly, that an important audience segment for Spielberg's and Lucas's megahits from *Star Wars* onwards were children aged twelve and younger. The fact that by 1983 *E.T.*, the *Star Wars* trilogy and the first Indiana Jones film occupied five of the six top places on the list of all-time American Top Grossers (the other film was *Jaws* (1975)), and that in 1984 the second Indiana Jones film also made it into the all-time top ten,[18] clearly establishes the central importance of the child audience and of films addressed, at least partially, to children during the years 1977–84. Is this an exceptional period or is it representative of American cinema since the 1960s? In order to answer this question, let us first of all take a look at the 1960s and 1970s and, in particular, at the operations of the Disney company, which, as we have seen, was one of the main reference points for critics commenting on the special appeal of Lucas's and Spielberg's films.

Disney after Walt and the changing status of family entertainment, 1966–84

From the 1920s onwards, the Disney label was associated with children's and family entertainment to such an extent that the company managed the rare feat of having its brand name become largely synonymous with the product categories to which its output belonged. Just as 'Kleenex' could be used as a synonym for paper handkerchiefs, 'Disney' stood in for all manner of children's and family fare. By the 1950s, the Disney brand was prominent, if not dominant, in each of the following arenas: animated features, theme parks, nature films, cartoon shorts, children's television and children's merchandise. It is often assumed that Walt Disney's death in 1966 brought an end to the company's glory days, initiating an eighteen-year period – until the arrival of Michael Eisner as chief executive in 1984 – of corporate instability and commercial crisis, especially with respect to Disney's animated and live-action features. However a look at Disney's financial statistics and at box-office hit lists reveals a more complicated picture.

The late 1960s and 1970s were a period of explosive growth for the Disney company. Profits rose from $12.4 million in 1965, the year before Walt Disney's death, to $21.8 million in 1970 and $61.7 million in 1975, climaxing with $135.1 million in 1980 (more than ten times the figure for 1965), before they declined again.[19] The value of the company's assets almost doubled between 1970 and 1971 (from $275.2 million to $505.2 million), mainly due to the opening of Walt Disney World in October 1971, and, unlike the profits, asset value never stopped rising: between 1965 and 1980, it increased almost fifteenfold (from $90.8 million to $1347.4 million), and between 1980 and 1983 it almost doubled again (to $2381.1 million).[20] Revenues also grew healthily in the late 1960s and throughout the 1970s, from $109.9 million in 1965 to $167.1 million in 1970, $520 million in 1975 and $914.5 million in 1980. After virtually zero growth between 1980 and 1981, revenues rose again dramatically in subsequent years.[21] This overview suggests that Disney's much talked about crisis came in the early 1980s and not in the years immediately following Walt Disney's death.

What about the performance of Disney's feature films (as distinct from its theme parks and merchandising)? Even Janet Wasko, Disney's most knowledgeable analyst, describes the 1970s as a period of crisis for Disney's feature film division.[22] Yet the evidence is ambiguous. It is certainly the case that the theme parks and the consumer products division easily outperformed the division concerned with the release of theatrical features. In 1975, for example, Disneyland generated revenues of $109.1 million and Walt Disney World $225.3 million. Together the two parks made up the Entertainment and Recreational Activities division, which had an operating income of $64.1 million.[23] For consumer products (including merchandising, educational media, records and publications), revenues were $70.4 million and operating income was $21.7 million.[24] With $112.5 million, the Motion Picture and Television Distribution division generated far less revenue than the theme parks, yet more than the Consumer Products division. Its operating income of $56.6 million was much higher than the figure for Consumer Products and came close to the figure for the theme parks. Thus, while the theme parks clearly dominated Disney's operations in 1975 (and, indeed, in the 1970s as a whole), the Motion Picture and Television Distribution division performed reasonably well, though its relative importance was clearly in decline. Domestic film rentals rose from $35.5 million in 1971 to $61.2 million in 1975 and to $65 million in 1978.[25] Foreign rentals grew more rapidly, from $21.6 million in 1971 to $37.6 million in 1975 and $58 million in 1978. The overall revenues of the Motion Picture and Television Distribution division (including a relatively small amount for TV) increased from $65.1 million in 1971 to $161.4 million in 1980.[26] But the increase was less than threefold, compared to the sixfold increase in company revenues as a whole across the decade. Furthermore, the division's operating income (and thus its profitability) was shrinking; the figure for 1980 was $48.7 million, which was less than the 1975 figure and also less than the 1980 operating income for Consumer Products ($55.1 million).[27] In 1981, the operating income for film and television had further shrunk by more than a third. Thus, by the early 1980s, Disney's film and television division was indeed in definite crisis.

What about the box-office performance of individual Disney releases in the 1970s? It is often assumed that after *The Jungle Book* (1967) Disney failed to produce big hits and instead generated its theatrical income from cheaply produced and only moderately successful films (and of course from highly profitable re-releases). A look at *Variety*'s annual hit lists for the US market shows that the situation was in fact by no means clear cut.[28] It is true that, compared to some of the high points in the company's past (three of the top four hits of 1961 were Disney releases; when it was first released in 1964, *Mary Poppins* became one of the top-grossing films of all time), Disney's feature films of the late 1960s and 1970s underperformed. However, it should also be noted that *Variety* listed the live-action film *The Love Bug* as the top hit of 1969.[29] *The Love Bug* was followed by two successful sequels, *Herbie Rides Again* (released in 1974, and ranked number 5 in *Variety*'s hit list for the year) and *Herbie Goes to Monte Carlo* (1977, number twenty). Other top hits included *The Happiest Millionaire* (1967, number twenty in 1968), *The Island at the Top of the World* and *Escape to Witch Mountain* (both released in 1974, yet listed as numbers fourteen and twenty, respectively, for 1975), as well as *The Apple Dumpling Gang* (1975, number eleven), the animated *The Aristocats* (1970, number six in 1971), *Robin Hood* (1973, number eighteen in 1974) and *The Rescuers* (1977, number fifteen); and the animation/live-action hybrids *Bedknobs and Broomsticks* (1971, number eleven in 1972) and *Pete's Dragon* (1977, number sixteen in 1978). With rentals of $10–20 million, Disney's hits performed well below the blockbuster business of *The Godfather* (1972, $86.3 million), *The Exorcist* (1973, $82.2 million) and *Jaws* $121.3 million). Yet it is important to note that the studio consistently managed to produce new hits.

Thus the movie charts of the 1970s were by no means devoid of Disney films (one or, more often, two top twenty hits per year up to 1978). Furthermore, as noted earlier on, Disney was a rapidly growing multimedia corporation with even greater strengths in the equally child and family-oriented theme park business and in the selling or licensing of a wide range of children's products. It is understandable, then, that Disney was a common reference point for reviewers when they tried to make sense of Lucas's and Spielberg's child-friendly blockbusters. However, in the light of the lacklustre performance of Disney's film division in the 1970s (when compared to the performance of Disney's other divisions and to the blockbusters released by other studios), it is also understandable that film-makers such as Lucas and Spielberg did not want to be associated too closely either with Disney's films or with children's films in general.

The early publicity for the production of *Star Wars* described it as a science-fiction adventure for teenagers, rather than children. Privately, Lucas came to realise, however, that he was in fact making a children's film, and he himself invoked the name of Disney: '[T]hat's what we're going for, eight- and nine-year-olds. This is a Disney movie.'[30] He was uncertain about the value of this comparison. After a disastrous screening of *Star Wars* for friends and colleagues early in 1977, Lucas felt the film would reach '[o]nly kids – I've made a Walt Disney movie ... It's gonna do maybe eight, ten million.'[31] Similarly, Spielberg developed *Close Encounters* in the 1970s with reference to two key cinematic childhood memories, the 'Night on Bald Mountain' sequence in Disney's *Fantasia* (1940) and the performance of the song 'When You Wish upon a Star' in Disney's *Pinocchio* (1940): 'I pretty much hung my story on the mood the song created, the way it affected me emotionally.'[32] At the same time, Spielberg did not want *Close Encounters* to be associated too closely with Disney, and after a test screening he removed 'When You Wish upon a Star' from the end of the movie: '[T]his song seemed to belie some of the authenticity and to bespeak fantasy and fairy tale. And I didn't want *Close Encounters* to end just as a dream.'[33] For film-makers as well as reviewers, then, references to Disney and to children's films were double-edged. They linked new releases to one of the undisputed masters of American cinema and signalled their address of basic human desires and emotions, yet they also indicated that the films in question might be unsuitable for teenagers and adults, and therefore of only limited commercial appeal. What Lucas and Spielberg tried to achieve from 1977 onwards – and what the largely positive reviews of their films duly noted – was a return to old-fashioned family entertainment which was suitable for children not because it exclusively or even primarily was addressed to them, but because it was accessible to everyone.

Not coincidentally, the Disney company was aiming to do the same thing from the mid-1970s. As early as 1973, after *The Godfather* (1972) had raised the stakes in the blockbuster game, the cultural and commercial limitations of Disney's film output, and of children's films in general, became a topic of public debate. Richard Schickel argued in *Time* magazine that Disney's recent successes were a result of the fact that the company:

> carefully – and exclusively – addresses itself to the most common problem of the entertainment consumer: 'Where can we take the kids?' In order to do so, the corporation has sacrificed creative vitality, cultural relevance and its former, justifiable pretensions to genuine, if inevitably industrialized, artistry.[34]

Schickel explained this development with reference to the lack of competition in, and critical attention to, the field of family entertainment, and to the narrowing definition of acceptable 'family fare' among 'the general audience': 'cuddly animals, bland costume pictures enlivened by painfully obvious song-and-dance numbers and not much else'.

Whether one agrees with Schickel's condemnation of Disney's output in the early 1970s or not, he pinpoints a number of crucial developments in American cinema during this period. Until its modification in 1966, the film industry's Production Code had been designed to make Hollywood's films suitable for audiences of all ages; most importantly, the removal of bad language, explicit sex and graphic violence was meant to ensure that parents would not have to worry about taking their children to the movies. Thus, notwithstanding age-related taste differences at a basic level, all of Hollywood's releases were intended for the whole family. By the early 1960s, however, various commentators noted that the increasingly 'adult' subject matter of many Hollywood films had undermined this ideal. They called for an increase in the production of 'family movies', which they began to see as a separate category, rather than as the underlying ideal of Hollywood's overall output.[35] Predictably, the Disney company was identified as the most important producer of family films, and, while these commentators upheld the ideal of family entertainment and celebrated Disney's output, they also pointed out the negative connotations that were beginning to accrue to them: 'Too often we tend to classify as family film that which is harmless, flavourless, empty and insipid.'[36]

The modification of the Production Code in 1966 and its replacement by a ratings system in 1968 consolidated the identification of family films as a separate and, in many ways, rather negative category within Hollywood's output. The original ratings were G ('Suggested for general audiences'), M ('Suggested for mature audiences'), R ('Restricted – Persons under 16 not admitted, unless accompanied by parent or adult guardian') and X ('Persons under 16 not admitted').[37] They were intended to ensure that children and young teenagers would not be allowed to see certain (X-rated) films, films which went beyond mainstream taste and morality in their 'treatment of sex, violence, crime or profanity'. As far as all other films were concerned, they were intended to enable parents to make an informed decision about which films they wanted their children to see.

Early reports in November 1968 seemed to indicate that G would be the most frequently used rating (44 per cent of all films) and therefore that Hollywood's traditional conception of its audience would survive the abandonment of the Production Code: Hollywood's G-rated pictures 'will serve the motion picture wants of youngsters of 6 to 12, their parents and those in-between'.[38] However, in November 1969, it became clear that G-rated films were a clear minority (32 per cent).[39] Furthermore, there were indications that the G rating would take on a more specific meaning than originally envisioned: rather than indicating a film's suitability for children as part of a general audience, it began to be understood as a label for films 'that are unfit for adults'.[40] Specific reference was made to Disney's *Mary Poppins* (1964) and to what was at this point the highest-grossing film in Hollywood history, *The Sound of Music* (1965).[41] Thus the very films that had represented Hollywood's ideal and defined its mainstream were increasingly considered as a separate, indeed marginal, category. Not surprisingly, apart from the Disney films discussed above, very few G-rated movies made it into *Variety*'s annual top twenty in the late 1960s and early 1970s, and, of these, most were big-budget musicals such as *Oliver!* (1968, number eight in 1969), *Hello Dolly!* (1969, number six in 1970) and *Fiddler on the Roof* (1971, number two in 1972). These were probably the films Schickel had in mind when referring to 'bland costume pictures enlivened by painfully obvious song-and-dance numbers'. Within a couple of years, the big-budget family-oriented musicals had disappeared from the annual charts, and the only non-Disney hits with G ratings were now lower-budget films, mostly slapstick comedies such as the Pink Panther films, animal films such as *Benji* (1974) and nature films such as *The Wilderness Family* (1975).[42] By 1978, the G-rating had not only become associated with comparatively cheap children's films, it had also become virtually synonymous with Disney, and Disney, in turn, with blandness: 'Makers of non-Disney family films … have lamented the tendency of audiences to prejudge G pictures as scrubbed and bland'.[43]

At this point, Disney was well into the production of its most expensive film ever, *The Black Hole* (1979), its first non-G-rated film. *The Black Hole* (then entitled *Space Station*), had been announced in 1975 as Disney's 'most ambitious live-action feature to date'.[44] It was thus initially not so much a response to *Star Wars* (and *Close Encounters*) as a parallel development. Like Lucas and Spielberg, Disney in the mid-1970s sought to overcome the commercial limitations of children's films by returning to an older conception of family entertainment, one which embraced all age groups and in particular the cinema's core audience of teenagers and young adults. Disney's decision to make a science-fiction film was perhaps influenced by the success the company had had with its special-effects-driven big-budget production of Jules Verne's *20,000 Leagues under the Sea* (1954, number three in *Variety*'s hit list for 1955). (*The Black Hole* would feature another 'mad scientist' autocratically ruling his little empire until disturbed and eventually destroyed by a group of unwelcome visitors.) But in any case, the success of *Star Wars* had raised the stakes. The budget for *The Black Hole* shot up from around $10 million to $18 million, and Disney's initial resistance to the PG rating gave way to the company's wholehearted embrace of this rating as a sign of new-found (or rediscovered) maturity. When the film was finally released at Christmas in 1979, studio president Ron Miller was quoted as saying:

> When a studio gets a reputation for making a certain kind of movie and that movie is considered kiddie stuff, you lose your entire audience when it turns 15. Those people don't come back until they have kiddies of their own.

He was confident that with *The Black Hole* Disney would:

> win back that slightly older crowd – the audience we used to have back in the 1950s with films like *20,000 Leagues under the Sea* … Ideally, this is the film that will take Disney to that all-important 15- to-30 year old group. The people who have seen *Star Wars* or *Close Encounters* two or three times.[45]

As it turned out, with rentals of $25.4 million, *The Black Hole* became Disney's biggest hit since *Mary Poppins*, though it fell well short of the blockbuster business of Lucas's and Spielberg's megahits and, because of the size of its budget, was less profitable than Disney's other hits in the 1970s.[46] Disney's big-budget productions of the early 1980s – *Popeye* (1980) and *Dragonslayer* (1981), both co-produced with Paramount, and *Tron*

(1981) – at best achieved the level of success of *The Black Hole* (*Popeye*'s rentals were $24.6 million) and at worst were commercial disasters.[47] Thus the Disney company failed to break out of the children's ghetto, despite its clearly stated objective that 'we must attract more teenagers and young adults' and its claims that the 'elements synonymous with our company's reputation' were 'fantasy, escape, adventure and the potential for innovative special effects'.[48] In fact, instead of moving Disney back into the highly profitable cinematic mainstream, increased production costs meant, as we have seen, that the profits of the film and TV division were in decline in the early 1980s. It is somewhat ironic that, at the very same time, Lucas and Spielberg were breaking box-office records with their Disney-influenced family films, that most of their megahits generated huge income through what had previously been almost exclusively a Disney speciality – namely, movie-related merchandising – and that family entertainment moved back to the centre of Hollywood's operations between 1977 and 1984. What has happened to children's films and family entertainment since then?

Kids rule: children's films and family entertainment since 1984

The most successful films in contemporary Hollywood are what I have elsewhere called 'family-adventure movies', films which depict the spectacular adventures of familial groups and which are addressed to children and their parents as well as to the cinema's core audience of teenagers and young adults.[49] These films derive, on the one hand, from Lucas's and Spielberg's hugely successful attempt between 1977 and 1984 to broaden the appeal of big-budget action-adventure and science-fiction films to reach children and their parents, and, on the other hand, from Disney's initially unsuccessful attempt to upgrade traditional children's fare with bigger budgets, more spectacle and more mature themes so as to reach teenagers and young adults. Since 1984, almost every year has seen one or two films of this kind become megahits, leaving the competition far behind by achieving a market share of around 5 per cent of total US box-office revenues, as well as doing exceptionally well in foreign markets, video sales and rentals, on TV and in terms of merchandising, sequels and spin-offs. Examples include *Ghostbusters* (1984) and *Back to the Future* (1985), as well as the more recent *The Phantom Menace* (1999) and *Toy Story 2* (1999). As a look at the Internet Movie Database's list of all-time top-grossing movies at the US box office reveals, the main producers of such megahits are Spielberg, Lucas and Disney.[50] With the exception of Disney's animated features, none of these megahits is G-rated; indeed, their PG or PG-13 rating signals their dual address to both children and parents.

What can we say about the status of films primarily, and sometime exclusively, addressed to children? Here we need to look at G-rated films and animation. The relative decline in the number of G-rated films has continued into the 1990s: whereas in 1968–69 about a third of all films were rated G, between 1993 and 1997 it was only 4.4 per cent.[51] With their declining share of Hollywood's output, G-rated films have become ever more closely identified with children's entertainment. Interestingly, their share of box-office revenues was much higher (6.1 per cent) than their share of films on the market[52] because, on average, they performed better than films with other ratings, earning $45.3 million per film in the domestic market as compared to $32 million for PG-rated films, $42.1 million for those rated PG-13 and $29.2 million for those rated R.[53] As G-rated films also tended to be cheaper than films in other categories, they were more profitable – costing less and earning more.

The most successful G-rated films were animated features, most importantly those released by Disney. While animated features are generally understood first and foremost as children's films, they can do blockbuster business by reaching other age groups. To increase their chances with teenage and adult audiences and to differentiate themselves from Disney products, most other producers of animated features (in particular DreamWorks with, for example, *The Prince of Egypt* [1998], *Antz* [1998], and *The Road to El Dorado* [2000]) have gone for PG ratings, mostly without success.[54] Nevertheless, overall output and market share have increased in recent yeasrs.[55] Between 1994 and 1997, the number of major animated releases was steady with around five films a year, but since 1997 the number has doubled.[56] Disney has the bulk of the animation market share (over 50 per cent), but Warner Bros., Sony, Paramount and especially DreamWorks are also significant players. From 1994–7, total American box-office revenues for animated features were mostly between $300 million and $400 million, yet since 1998 there has been a dramatic increase (in line with the increased output), with 1999 marking an all-time high with almost $750 million, which was 10 per cent of total domestic box-office revenues in that year.[57] When it comes to calculating children's share of total cinema admissions, there are, unfortunately, no reliable statistics, as the industry's audience surveys only include persons aged twelve and older. Estimates for ticket sales to children aged twelve and younger (attending children's films as well as others) range from an unrealistic low of 6 per cent to up to 20 per cent of total ticket sales.[58]

However, the real importance of children and children's films for contemporary Hollywood only becomes really apparent when we examine video sales, which are the single most important source of income for the major studios.[59] The list of all-time top-selling videos in the US as of June 1998 (that is, before the video release of *Titanic* (1974) and Disney hits such as *Toy Story 2*, which have no doubt made it into the top ten by now) was headed by Disney's *The Lion King* (1994), which sold 28.8 million wholesale units (that is, videos sold to retailers and video stores for sell-through or rental purposes), generating $427 million in wholesale revenues (that is, money paid by retailers and rental stores to Disney; the money paid by customers buying or renting the videos is, of course, much more).[60] To put wholesale video revenues in perspective, let us compare them to the film's box-office rentals, that is, the money paid by cinemas to Disney (usually about half of the overall box-office gross paid by audiences to cinemas). By the end of 1998, *The Lion King* was number eight in *Variety*'s list of all-time rental champions in the US with $173.1 million, that is less than half the wholesale video revenues.[61] The video sales list continues as follows:

- *Snow White and the Seven Dwarfs* (1937, Disney), 25.1 million units generating $372 million in wholesale video revenues (as compared to $81 million in box-office rentals)

Shrek (2001): another non-Disney blockbuster

- *Aladdin* (1992, Disney), 22.4 million units/$352.7 million ($112 million box-office rentals)
- *Beauty and the Beast* (1991, Disney), 20.2 million units/$318 million ($69 million box-office rentals)
- *Toy Story* (1995, Disney), 19.5 million units/$290 million ($103 million box-office rentals)
- *Jurassic Park* (1993, Universal), 20 million units/$275 million ($213 million box-office rentals)
- *Independence Day* (1996, Fox), 20.4 million units/$258 million ($177 million box-office rentals)
- *Men in Black* (1997, Columbia), 16.9 million units/$232 million ($118 million box-office rentals)
- *Pocahontas* (1995, Disney), 17.1 million units/$216 million ($68 million box-office rentals)
- *Fantasia* (1940, Disney), 13.3 million units/$209 million ($42 million box-office rentals)

The fact that seven of the top ten films are Disney animated features, and that the other three belong into the category of family-adventure movies, is, as common-sense and industry analysts tell us, 'thanks to the voracious repeat-viewing demands of children'.[62] It is also the demands of children which drive the huge market in movie merchandising (most of it tied in with children's or family films), from which the major studios earn licensing fees of around 6–7 per cent of the wholesale price, and the growing theme park market, in which several of the major studios have a stake.[63]

Conclusion

Children's and family films are at the very heart of today's media conglomerates and indeed today's popular culture, because the majority of the most popular and most profitable films and multimedia franchises are primarily (but not exclusively) 'kids' stuff'.[64] After Hollywood's marginalisation of family entertainment in the late 1960s and early 1970s, it was the combined efforts of Disney on the one hand and Spielberg and Lucas on the other that moved children (and their parents) back to the centre of the cinema and related media markets. This trend is not abating. Quite the contrary, DreamWorks' *Shrek* (2001) proved that blockbuster success in the animation field is no longer limited to Disney.[65] *Dr Seuss' How the Grinch Stole Christmas* (the top grossing movie in the US in 2000) showed that there is a lot of classic children's fiction just waiting to be adapted for the big screen. And the excitement about Chris Columbus's Harry Potter adaptation sent all of Hollywood into what *Variety* called 'Pottermania'.[66] It is time, then, for the study of film genres to take note of children's films.

Notes

1. Research for this essay in American archives was made possible by a Small Grant from the Arts and Humanities Research Board.
2. The situation is different in folklore studies and the study of children's fiction (within the disciplines of literary or educational studies). Here, there is a steady output of publications on fairy-tale and children's films.
3. Barry Keith Grant, *Film Genre Reader* (Austin: University of Texas Press, 1986). This situation has not changed in the book's updated second edition *Film Genre Reader II* (Austin: University of Texas Press, 1995).
4. Nick Browne (ed.), *Refiguring American Film Genres: Theory and History* (Berkeley: University of California Press, 1998); Rick Altman, *Film/Genre* (London: BFI, 1999); Steve Neale, *Genre and Hollywood* (London: BFI, 2000).
5. Neale, *Genre and Hollywood*, pp. 245–6.
6. 'Movie Omnibus – September 1982', report contained in the 'Audiences' clippings file, Film Study Centre, Museum of Modern Art, New York. Similar findings are reported in Jim Robbins, 'Survey Says Public Likes Sci-Fi But Really Loves Comedy', *Variety*, 22 September 1982, p. 22.
7. See Cary Bazalgette and Terry Staples, 'Unshrinking the Kids: Children's Cinema and the Family Film', in Cary Bazalgette and David Buckingham (eds), *In Front of the Children: Screen Entertainment and Young Audiences* (London: BFI, 1995), pp. 92, 95; and Heather Addison, Children's Films in the 1990s', in Wheeler Winston Dixon (ed.), *Film Genre 2000: Critical Essays* (Albany: State University of New York Press, 2000), p. 177. For other work on children's and family films, see Marsha Kinder, *Playing with Power in Movies, Television and Video Games: From Muppet Babies to the Teenage Mutant Ninja Turtles* (Berkeley: University of California Press, 1991); and Peter Krämer, 'Would You Take Your Child To See

This Film?: The Cultural and Social Work of the Family-Adventure Movie', in Steve Neale and Murray Smith (eds), *Contemporary Hollywood Cinema* (London: Routledge, 1998), pp. 294–311.

8. 'Movie Omnibus – September 1982' and Robbins, Survey Says 'Public Likes Sci-Fi But Really Loves Comedy'.

9. 'The 1980s: A Reference Guide to Motion Pictures, Television, VCR, and Cable', *The Velvet Light Trap*, no. 27 (Spring 1991), pp. 78, 82.

10. David Sterritt, review, *Christian Science Monitor*, 17 June 1982, p. 18.

11. Vincent Canby, review, *New York Times*, 11 June 1982, p. C14.

12. Review, *Variety*, 26 May 1982, reprinted in George Perry, *Steven Spielberg: The Making of His Movies* (London: Orion, 1998), pp. 114–16.

13. *Variety*'s reviews of these films are reprinted in Chris Salewicz, *George Lucas: The Making of His Movies* (London: Orion, 1998), pp. 123–5, 128–32.

14. A. D. Murphy, *Star Wars* review, *Variety*, 25 May 1977, reprinted in Salewicz, *George Lucas*, p. 124.

15. The reviews of *Star Wars* and *Raiders of the Lost Ark* are reprinted in Salewicz, *George Lucas*, pp. 123–5, 130–2, and of *Close Encounters of the Third Kind* in Perry, *Steven Spielberg*, pp. 108–9.

16. *Variety*, 18 May 1983, reprinted in Salewicz, *George Lucas,* p. 133.

17. *Variety*, 16 May 1984, reprinted in Salewicz, *George Lucas*, p. 136.

18. Other child-friendly hits of 1984 were *Ghostbusters*, *Gremlins* and *The Karate Kid*, all joining *Indiana Jones and the Temple of Doom* in the top five for the year.

19. Walt Disney Productions Annual Report 1975, contained in 'Walt Disney Productions' clippings file, Performing Arts Research Center (PARC), New York Public Library; Janet Wasko, *Understanding Disney: The Manufacture of Fantasy* (London: Polity Press, 2001), p. 31.

20. Walt Disney Productions Annual Report 1975; Wasko, *Understanding Disney*, p. 31.

21. Walt Disney Productions Annual Report 1975; Wasko, *Understanding Disney*, p. 31.

22. Ibid., p. 30.

23. Walt Disney Productions Annual Report 1975.

24. Operating income is calculated by subtracting the costs generated by the division in question from its revenues. It is only after the further deduction of general corporate expenses and income tax that the figure for net income, or profits, is arrived at.

25. Walt Disney Productions Annual Report 1975; 'New Disney World High', *Variety*, 18 October 1978, p. 4.

26. Walt Disney Productions Annual Report 1975; 'New Disney World High', p. 4; Walt Disney Productions Annual Report 1981, contained in file MFL+n.c.2,331 No. 20, PARC.

27. Ibid.

28. For hit lists and rental figures, see Cobbett Steinberg, *Film Facts* (New York: Facts on File, 1980), pp. 3–8, 24–8.

29. Of all films released in 1969, only *Butch Cassidy and the Sundance Kid* would eventually earn more.

30. Peter Biskind, *Easy Riders, Raging Bulls: How the Sex-Drugs-and-Rock 'n' Roll Generation Saved Hollywood* (New York: Simon and Schuster, 1998), p. 328.

31. Ibid., p. 334.

32. Sarah McBride, *Steven Spielberg: A Biography* (London: Faber and Faber, 1997), p. 262.

33. Lester D. Friedman and Brent Notbohm (eds), *Steven Spielberg: Interviews* (Jackson: University Press of Mississippi, 2000), p. 97.

34. Richard Schickel, 'The Films: No Longer for the Jung at Heart', *Time*, 30 July 1973, p. 65.

35. 'A Family Movie', *Christian Science Monitor*, 19 September 1962, unpaginated clipping, 'Cinema-Audiences' clippings file, PARC; Rose Pelswick, 'Needed: Family Films', *New York Journal-American*, 13 July 1964, 'Children as Audiences – Cinema' clippings file, PARC.

36. 'A Family Movie'.

37. 'The Revised MPAA Code of Self-Regulation', *Variety*, 8 October 1968, pp. 6–7. In the following years, the ratings were changed: the age limit was raised from sixteen to seventeen, and M became first GP and then PG ('Parental guidance suggested'). See Jack Valenti, 'The Voluntary Movie Rating System', in Jason E. Squire (ed.), *The Movie Business Book, Second Edition* (New York: Fireside, 1992), pp. 396–406.

38. Ben Shlyen, 'A Hopeful Sign', *Boxoffice*, 18 November 1968, unpaginated clipping, 'Ratings, Jan–Sep 68' clippings file, Academy Center for Motion Picture Study, Academy of Motion Picture Arts and Sciences (AMPAS), Beverly Hills.

39. Joe Broady, 'In lst Year of MPAA Ratings Only 6 Per Cent of Films Branded X', *Daily Variety*, 5 November 1969, unpaginated clipping, 'Ratings 1969' clippings file, AMPAS. In this survey of 441 films, 39 per cent were rated M and 23 per cent R. By the end of the following year, the R rating was dominant with 37 per cent and its share continued to grow throughout the early 1970s, stabilising around 50 per cent in the mid-1970s. See Justin Wyatt, 'The Stigma of X: Adult Cinema and Institution of the MPAA Ratings System', in Matthew Bernstein (ed.), *Controlling Hollywood: Censorship and Regulation in the Studio Era* (London: Athlone, 2000), p. 244.

40. William Zinsser, 'Let's Have a Symbol To Protect Pop', *Life*, 7 February 1969, unpaginated clipping, 'Ratings 1969' clippings file, AMPAS.

41. When these films were re-released in the 1970s they received G ratings. This also applies to most of the other superhits of the 1950s and 1960s such as *Cleopatra* (1963) and *Ben-Hur* (1959). Information on ratings can be obtained from http://www.mpaaorg/movieratingsearch/content.asp.

42. In addition to these big hits listed in *Variety*'s annual list of top-grossing movies, there also was, as Brian Rose has pointed out, a substantial market in the first half of the 1970s for the limited distribution of 'family-oriented wilderness films, particularly in small towns and rural regions'. Small companies such as American National employed 'four-walling' (a practice wherein the distributor rented movie theatres, rather than movie theatres renting films) specifically to service the needs of those audiences largely neglected by the major studios – small-town or rural folk, working-class people, families. In the mid-1970s, the majors picked up on this strategy by re-releasing films such as *Jeremiah Johnson* (1972, rated GP) in this fashion and turning them into major hits. In newly promoting these films, the studios organised 'enormous advertising strategies emphasizing the family/adventure elements of their product'. See Brian Rose, 'From the Outdoors to Outer Space: The Motion Picture Industry in the 1970s', in Michael T. Marsden, John G. Nachbar and Sam L. Grogg Jr (eds),

Movies as Artifacts: Cultural Criticism of Popular Film (Chicago: Nelson-Hall, 1982), pp. 53–5.

43. David Sterritt, 'Disney aims to attract adults, too', *Christian Science Monitor*, 11 November 1978, p. 2.

44. Walt Disney Productions Annual Report 1975.

45. Ed Naha, 'Disney: On the brink of the PG void', *New York Daily News*, 16 December 1979, Leisure section, pp. 7, 14. See also, Charles Schreger, 'Production at Disney', *Variety*, 7 December 1977, p. 7.

46. Joel W. Finler, *The Hollywood Story* (London: Octopus, 1988), p. 278.

47. One problem appeared to be that cinemagoers attached very specific expectations to the Disney label and were easily disappointed when Disney tried something new. This problem was later solved through the Disney company's creation of separate labels for non-children's films – Touchstone in 1984 and Hollywood Pictures in 1989. Touchstone's first release – a major hit – was *Splash* (1984), an adult romantic comedy version of the fairy tale *The Little Mermaid*.

48. Disney chief executive Card Walker and Ron Miller writing in the company's 1981 annual report (contained in file MFL+n.c.2,331, No. 20, PARC) and quoted in Andrew Neff, 'Disney Takes Plunge in Co-Production', *Variety*, 5 December 1979, p. 7.

49. Krämer, 'Would You Take Your Child To See This Film?' For another account of the centrality of family-oriented films in contemporary Hollywood, see Robert Allen, 'Home Alone Together: Hollywood and the "Family Film"', in Melvyn Stokes and Richard Maltby (eds), *Identifying Hollywood's Audiences: Cultural Identity and the Movies* (London: BFI, 1999), pp. 109–31.

50. The close links between Spielberg and Lucas on the one hand and Disney on the other are again in evidence when we look at the fate of Disney's animation division. In the wake of the disappointing box-office performance of *The Black Cauldron* (1985), there were rumours that the new management might close down the animated feature division. However, despite another box-office disappointment the following year with *The Great Mouse Detective*, Disney continued and even increased its commitment to feature animation. This decision was encouraged by the impressive box-office performance of the Steven Spielberg production *An American Tail* (1986), which Spielberg followed with the equally successful *The Land before Time* (1988, co-produced by George Lucas) and the blockbuster success of the animation/live-action hybrid *Who Framed Roger Rabbit?* (1988, co-produced by Touchstone and Amblin). See Kim Masters, *The Keys to the Kingdom: How Michael Eisner Lost His Grip* (New York: William Morrow, 2000), pp. 212–27; and Leonard Maltin, *The Disney Films, Third Edition* (New York: Hyperion, 1995), pp. 286–9.

51. 'EDI Box Office News', *Variety*, 20 October 1997, p. 18. These statistics relate only to wide releases (in at least 600 cinemas). Across the period 1968–2000, 7 per cent of all films submitted to the MPAA were rated G. MPAA, '2000 US Economic Review', p. 13, http://www.mpaa.org/useconomicreview/2000Economic.

52. For the period 1995–9, the figures were: 4 per cent of film supply and 6 per cent of box-office for G-rated films. 'Box Office News', *Variety*, 21 June 1999, p. 20.

53. 'EDI Box Office News', *Variety*, 20 October 1997, p. 18. It has to be noted, however, that the figures for G-rated movies are somewhat inflated by the exceptional box-office

performance of *The Lion King* (1994); without this film, the average box-office gross for G-rated films is $36.4 million for this period.

54. Other PG-rated animated features include Fox's *Titan A.E.* (2000) and Warner's *The Iron Giant* (1999). For *Small Soldiers* (1998), DreamWorks went for a PG-13, and even more adult-oriented animation – which was quite prominent in the 1970s with, for example, *Fritz the Cat* (1972) – making a comeback, most notably with *South Park: Bigger, Louder, Uncut* (1999), which is rated R and has a story-line revolving precisely around child audiences and movie ratings.

55. For discussions of the recent trends in animation, see Denis Seguin, 'Quest for gold', *Screen International*, 26 May 1995, pp. 14–15; Dade Hayes, 'H'w'd sings new toon tune', *Variety*, 31 January 2000, pp. 1, 49; Dade Hayes, 'Cel-mates suffer toon traumas', *Variety*, 7 August 2000, pp. 1, 41.

56. 'Box Office News', *Variety*, 7 August 2000, p. 37.

57. A somewhat double-edged recognition of the importance of animated features is the introduction of a new category for Best Animated Feature at the Academy Awards for the year 2001. While highlighting the achievements of animators, the new Oscar also marginalises them insofar as the Academy assumes that animated features cannot compete in the Best Picture category. Indeed, only one animated feature (Disney's *Beauty and the Beast*) has ever been nominated for best picture. See Richard Natale, 'New animation category raises the ante for creators and studios', *Variety*, 11 December 2000, pp. 1, 12.

58. 'ShoWesters play the numbers', *Variety*, 10 March 1997, p. 15; Leonard Klady, 'Studios flog family values', *Variety*, 1 July 1996, p. 10.

59. See Allen, 'Home Alone Together', pp. 111–13, 116.

60. Nik Jamgocyan, 'Big boat, small screen', *Screen International*, 26 June 1998, p. 9; Adam Sandler, 'Biz Ponders Oscar's Effect on Gump Vid', *Variety*, 24 April 1995, p. 7.

61. The editors of *Variety*, *The Variety Insider* (New York: Perigee, 1999), p. 52.

62. Jamgocyan, 'Big boat, small screen', p. 9.

63. Allen, 'Home Alone Together', pp. 118–21. See also Janet Wasko, *Hollywood in the Information Age* (London: Polity Press, 1994).

64. For a study of the centrality of a single film to the operations of a major media company, see Peter Krämer, 'Entering the Magic Kingdom: The Walt Disney Company, *The Lion King* and the Limitations of Criticism', *Film Studies*, no. 2 (Spring 2000), pp. 44–50.

65. At the beginning of August 2001, *Shrek* was at number fifteen in the Internet Movie Database's list of All-Time American Top Grossers, with revenues of $255 million, http://us.imdb.com/Charts/usatopmovies.

66. Jonathan Bing, 'Harry-ed Hollywood hunting kid fodder', *Variety*, 29 January 2001, pp. 1, 10.

14

Movie Ratings as Genre: The Incontestable R

Kevin S. Sandler

> What we call genre is in fact something quite different from what has always been supposed.
>
> Rick Altman[1]

In his ground-breaking approach to thinking about Hollywood cinema, Rick Altman in *Film/Genre* suggests that genre theorists have shared a litany of unexamined assumptions in their work. One assumption, contends Altman, is that 'genre theorists have generally sought to describe and define what they believe to be already existing genres rather than create their own interpretive categories'.[2] The Western, the musical and the horror film have often received the most attention by theorists because they have pre-existing patterns clearly identified by the industry and recognised by the public as genre. The semantic and syntactical consistency of each genre have thus led theorists and spectators to primarily think of genre in terms of a 'corpus of films'.[3] And it is the textual determinacy of these films that have constituted the nature of genre study.

Altman himself reinforced this 'corpus of films' tradition in his earlier work *The American Film Musical*. However, in *Film/Genre*, he extends his definition of genre to address the phenomenon as a site of perpetual struggle among different users, rather than a unified and transparent entity.

> Far from simply replicating industry categorization, pre-viewing notions of a film's generic identity depend on multiple (often contradictory) sources: studio discourse (which, because it targets multiple audiences, usually offers conflicting genre cues), claims made by critics (who do not necessarily deploy generic discourse for the same reasons or in the same manner as other sectors of the film industry), and several networks of genre viewers (with no guarantee of alignment among home, office, church, and bar evaluations).[4]

In proposing a discursive dimension to all textual configuration and generic claims, Altman locates the nature of genre in language. Genres are thus by-products of discursive activity by real speakers, deployed within and between various interpretative communities, all with diverse interests, desires and goals.[5] Instead of focusing solely on the question of how texts are organised or what films belong to which genre, Altman suggests that we should always ask: 'Who speaks this generic vocabulary? To whom? And for what purpose?'[6]

Even though the active constitution of genres occurs in discourse, the generic terminology shared by audiences, critics and readers, for the most part, argues Altman, derives heavily from the discursive orientation of the production companies and the exhibitors, two institutions that actively labour to establish the definition of genre in the United States.[7] The industry's attempt to anchor and solidify generic affiliation can be explained by the economic and commercial dimensions of the Hollywood film-making enterprise. Genres, like stars, can guarantee a certain style, a predictable structure and a particular atmosphere to audiences.[8] Striving for a uniformity in perception enables Hollywood to produce and market their film for profit.

If generic communication occasionally does exist between producers, marketers and consumers, Altman demonstrates its sustenance as an anomaly. In actuality, he argues, the durable Western and musical genres are atypical cases of generic stability and not representative of the actualities of genre usage. Hollywood studios during the studio system era usually avoided identifying films with a single generic label and promoted multiple genre identification. Industry practice leant more towards 'genre mixing' in order to maximise the audience potential for a given film. As Altman puts it, the goal was to 'attract those who recognize and appreciate signs of a particular genre, while avoiding repulsion of those who dislike the genre'.[9]

Weaving many genres into a single film was an easy and profitable task for Hollywood during vertical integration. Such stability and affluence ended in the 1950s and 1960s, as industrial, legal and cultural change swept over American cinema and society. The Paramount Consent Decree, civil rights, free speech protection, competition from television and the emerging youth culture made it difficult, if not impossible, for Hollywood to provide for and maintain a mass audience on the level it did before. Race, class, age, ethnicity, education and other demographic categories replaced an accepted homogeneity to become determining factors of audience identity.

To reconstruct its products for broad-based consumption, the Motion Picture Association of America (MPAA), the trade organisation of the industry, replaced the single-seal-for-all-films approach of the Production Code Administration (PCA) with the four-tiered rating system of the Code and Ratings Administration (CARA) in November 1968.[10] Separating films into age categories of G, M, R and X[11] inevitably altered the characteristics of genre mixing in contemporary Hollywood as the industry now could market different films to different and diverse audiences.[12] Various plots, themes and tones that before had to be contained within a single orthodoxy could now be treated across a spectrum of rating designations, from all ages to adults only. Such classifications, argues Altman, did have a 'genre-like effect on producers, exhibitors, and audiences',[13] and it this contention which guides the arguments of this chapter.

While Altman only briefly considers 'rating as genre' in *Film/Genre*, claiming that rating designations 'hardly constitute genre distinctions',[14] I intend to apply his discursive approach to genre to the MPAA rating system. Indisputably, producers, critics and audiences use the vocabulary of the present G, PG, PG-13, R and NC-17 categories to describe, label and define films. *The Little Mermaid* (1989) was developed, marketed and recognised as a G movie, *Star Wars* (1977) a PG, *Armageddon* (1988) a PG-13, *The Cell* an R, and so on.

The NC-17, however, is rarely put into use by the members of the MPAA: Sony, MGM, Paramount, 20th Century-Fox, Walt Disney, Warner Bros. and Universal.[15] Since 1976, the major Hollywood distributors have widely released only two non-foreign films in the adults-only category – Universal with *Henry and June* (1990) and MGM with *Showgirls* (1995).[16] While profit certainly does play an important role in the elimination of this product line by the MPAA studios – the X/NC-17 prohibits the lucrative teen audience from attending the film – the pornographic stigmatisation and MPAA-wide abandonment of the rating has in fact ensured an unusual industrial stability under the mediating regulatory practices of CARA for over thirty years. The disappearance of X/NC-17 pictures in effect created what I call the 'Incontestable R' category or genre. The Incontestable R – in theory a 'restricted' category, but in fact a category permitting all-age consumption – enabled Hollywood to successfully portray itself once again as a producer of universal entertainment for an undifferentiated audience.

In examining the Incontestable R as a genre, I will apply Altman's semantic/syntactic/pragmatic approach to generic discursivity. For Altman, content (semantic) and structure (syntax) alone cannot fully explain genre because both depend directly on changes in the discursive situation. His approach thus treats genres not as deterministic textual structures, but as complex systems of meanings processed among studios, filmmakers, exhibitors, critics, moral reformers, spectators and other generic users. Altman defines 'genre' as follows:

> Genre as *blueprint*, as a formula that precedes, programmes and patterns industry production;
> Genre as *structure*, as the formal framework on which individual films are founded;
> Genre as *label*, as the name of a category central to the decision and communication of distributors and exhibitors;
> Genre as *contract*, as the viewing position required by each genre film of its audience.[17]

I believe that the Incontestable R genre functions in a manner similar to the Western or the musical: as a blueprint, structure, label and contract for multiple users. The genre's definition may be fairly coherent and bounded at any given time or period, but its stability and meaning is always in flux, operating differently in another institutional, historical or cultural context.[18] Generic communication of the R rating is often a site of struggle between authors and consumers who seek to naturalise their own discursive claims of the category. While the production, distribution and exhibition of the Incontestable R is a collusive and vertically integrated strategy practised by the major distributors and exhibitors, consumption of the film text itself can never be regulated. The category is continually remapped by its many spokespersons, each with a different agenda and purpose. The Incontestable R genre is not just a political clash over individual texts; it is a discursive battle over the nature of Hollywood entertainment, one that the industry has been shown to easily manipulate and manage.

Incontestable R as blueprint, structure and contract

As a formula that guides contemporary Hollywood praxis, the blueprint for the Incontestable R descended from the industry's abandonment of the X in the late 1960s and its subsequent and similar renunciation of the NC-17 from 1990 onwards. Responsible for the renunciation of the X are the MPAA distributors and the National Association of Theater Owners (NATO),[19] partners in the ratings system, although CARA is managed by the MPAA. The MPAA and NATO originally formed this alliance in 1968 to help revitalise the beleaguered motion picture business; today, it still remains an vital business strategy for both industrial organisations.

Prior to the creation of CARA, Hollywood had seen a two-decade-long decline in box-office revenue. According to Jon Lewis in *Hollywood v. Hardcore*, this slide partly resulted from the studios and theatre-owners discarding longstanding codes of industry conduct for short-term industry gain after the Paramount Consent Decree.[20] This bygone, shared commitment was a business arrangement that guaranteed the appearance of what Richard Maltby has called 'harmless entertainment': movies detached from political significance that were as inoffensive as possible, appealing to the lowest common denominator of public taste.[21] The standards and practices of the industry's centralised system, the PCA, itself governed by a set of narrative and representational conventions, endowed Hollywood entertainment with an affirmative cultural function that maximised profit in the studio system.

However, a series of events after World War II shook the industry's economic structure. The absence of vertical integration, free speech protection of films, the fragmenting of the mass audience, the targeting of specific demographic markets by American International Pictures and foreign film distributors, and dwindling attendances affected Hollywood's system of self-regulation. As a result, the PCA could no longer guarantee the 'harmlessness' of Hollywood entertainment, as its system became non-functional and anachronistic, unable to adapt to changing audience compositions and tastes.

When Jack Valenti was named the president of the MPAA in 1966, he saw the creation of a rating system as a way for the industry to regain control and authority over the marketplace. It was a means for the studios to update their product lines without changing their business model: what Maltby has identified as maximum pleasure for the maximum number for the maximum profit.[22] The one drawback to the rating system was the existence of the X rating, a category off-limits to children and limitless in terms of content. The development of the Incontestable R, while never identified by this name or any other name, enabled the studios to manage their films much like the Production Code: as generic blueprints for mass entertainment.

The mechanisms of Hollywood self-regulation have always served the ends of mass entertainment: to minimise any potential miscommunication, unpredictablity or offence brought on by Hollywood product while simultaneously maximising the industry's earnings. As Lewis has suggested, the policing of images 'derives from concerns about the box office, about how to make a product that won't have *problems* in the marketplace'.[23] These so-called 'problems' are those adults or groups likely to condemn Hollywood's products as unrepresentative or inappropriately representative of American society and culture. During the Production Code era, the Catholic Legion of Decency was an institution that made known its positions on which depictions of morality and nation they considered 'harmful and incorrect'. The American Family Association, the Religious Right and opportunistic congressmen are currently those crusaders most likely to attack Hollywood entertainment as harmful and antithetical to appropriate American values.

The initial task of the industry was to develop a formula – what I call the Incontestable R – to guide production, to ensure profitability and to stave off criticism. I have argued in an earlier essay that the term 'respectable entertainment', rather than 'harmless entertainment', best describes the model of entertainment that CARA is committed to categorise, as rating thresholds, for the most part, no longer reflect a proscribed notion of morality.[24] The term 'respectable' embraces the nature of Hollywood film as a commercial commodity – and helps to explain the appearance and formula of the Incontestable R genre. By virtually abandoning X/NC-17 production and sequestering potentially controversial films into less stigmatised, Incontestable R ratings, Hollywood, by way of CARA, can be seen by moral watchdogs as enforcing a responsible code of production, distribution and exhibition for its films. Curbing free expression is a small price to pay in order for such reformers to classify Hollywood's products as respectable entertainment for them and their supporters.

Initially, however, the blueprint for the Incontestable R was not a label that all MPAA distributors and NATO exhibitors would follow or practise. This prevarication was by no means actively embraced or encouraged by Valenti. From the onset of the rating system, Valenti understood that in order for the industry to re-establish its commercial efficiency, the studios, in the words of Lewis, had to stay out of the 'dirty movie business'.[25] Hollywood had no choice but to appear respectable in the wake of two 1968 Supreme Court decisions that strongly implied that unrestricted and unenforced exhibition could not continue. *Interstate Circuit versus Dallas* concerned the possibility of state-by-state obscenity regulations, and *Ginsberg versus New York* upheld the constitutional power of states and cities to deny children access to films that could be viewed by adults. The integrity of the system was dependent on the containment of cinematic expression and the control of the box office. Although the rating system liberalised the Production Code by allowing its administrators to permit handling of any and all subjects, it also permitted the studios to avoid the tasteless or amoral handling of any and all subjects.

The MPAA was much quicker in adopting the generic practice of the Incontestable R than NATO. Some studio films did carry the X rating in the early days of the rating system: legitimate ones such as *The Killing of Sister George* (1968), *Midnight Cowboy* (1969), *A Clockwork Orange* (1971) or soft-core features such as *Beyond the Valley of the Dolls* (1970). However, the MPAA's brief if minimal zeal for distributing X pictures shortly gave way to the rating's economic limitations and legal liabilities.[26] An X, as opposed to an R, decreased a film's audience base, limited its marketing opportunities in newspapers and on television, and meant that it played poorly outside the major cities. Partly responsible for this disaffection was the industry itself, whose failure to copyright the X rating immediately led to its appropriation by independent soft- and hard-core exploiteers. The stigmatisation of the X with pornography made it almost impossible for serious films to carry the rating and for MPAA distributors to widely distribute those films.

The social stigma of the X thus gave way to the respectability of the R and the development of the Incontestable R. Described by *Variety* as the year of the 'wandering X',[27] 1970 saw CARA raising the R age limit from sixteen to seventeen in order to absorb previous X-rated content into the R category. R-rated films, once 20 per cent of CARA's categorisations, now made up 37 per cent of its rating; four years later, that figure would rise to 48 per cent, a plateau, states Lewis, more or less maintained until the present.[28] Mirroring the rise of the R was a drop in X categorization, as CARA awarded sixteen Xs in the 1968–9 fiscal year to its MPAA members, with a drop in the subsequent three-year period from twelve, to three, to one certificate. And a reduction in X output and increase in R production paralleled a gain in box office, as domestic theatre admissions finally rose in 1972, halting a seven-year slide, and progressing ever since. As the X became synonomous with 'harmful entertainment', the R solidified itself as a marker of 'respectable entertainment' in the New Hollywood. *Variety*, in its annual overview of CARA in 1972, noted that Hollywood's sudden shift away from X-rated material helped to reduce public criticism of its standards for other categories.[29] The long-term stability of the industry must be partly attributed to the MPAA abandoning the contestability of the X for the incontestability of the R.

While the generic practice of the Incontestable R still continues to guide industry production and CARA categorisation, the discursive ossification of the category is also dependent upon its widespread adoption and enforcement by NATO exhibitors.[30] Communication and support between NATO, the MPAA and CARA are vital to the existence of the Incontestable R label because the burden of enforcing voluntary self-regulation in a rating system falls on the box office. At the dawn of the rating system in 1968, the MPAA believed that with NATO representing 85 per cent of the nation's theatres and 95 per cent of the domestic box office, the presence of a CARA rating at their box-office could work once again like the Code seal before the Paramount Consent Decree: a box-office guarantee for MPAA-distributed films. If all MPAA films were rated R or lower, the industry, in practice, would only be distributing and exhibiting Incontestable R entertainment, while, in theory, it would be committed to unfettered artistic expression contained within the X rating.

However, generic communication between the MPAA and NATO in the early days of CARA was incomplete at best, despite NATO president Julian Rifkin's assurance of his members' compliance a month before the inauguration of the rating system. He wrote: 'Theater owners across the nation have agreed to support the rating system, not only in theory, but at the box office where they will enforce the age restrictions which accompany certain ratings.'[31] Enforcement would include checking IDs for X-rated films, policing children who jumped theatres, refraining from playing an R- or X-rated trailer to a G or M audience, being aware that the severest rating prevailed on a double feature, and running the rating trailer before each film.

Some of the criticism of the rating system in its first few years can be attributed to NATO's failure to implement these obligations carefully. Many newspapers reported that neighbourhood theatres neglected to police the box office. For example, in 1969, the *New York Sunday News* conducted a study that found underage children being admitted to X-rated films.[32] In other instances, inattentive exhibitors showed X-rated trailers with G-rated films. In July of that year, Charlie Poorman of the *Motion Picture Herald* warned exhibitors to forgo X-rated features altogether. 'While it is true that a powerful segment of the populace will patronize the maximum in perversion, there is no industrial future in this.'[33] Opining that the X rating 'doesn't represent our best cinematic efforts', Poorman suggested that theatre-owners replay older films in lieu of 'unsuitable' ones.[34]

It appears that many theatre-owners took his advice, as a survey conducted by NATO on 30 September 1969 reported that 47 per cent of its members – who accounted for 89 per cent of the nation's 13,000 theatres – automatically excluded X-rated films from potential engagements for their theatres.[35] These policies corresponded with the growing number of newspapers which refused to accept advertising for X films. While the newspaper chains in major cities (New York, Philadelphia, Chicago, Los Angeles and San Francisco) did not turn away advertisements, dailies in smaller cities (Chattanooga, Miami, Wichita, San Diego) censored X-rated ads to conform to the standards of their respective communities.[36] Banning X films from their leases certainly helped exhibitors to avoid community pressure, especially if they could not properly promote an X film in the local newspaper. Refusing X films also avoided the expense of modifying prints and trailers for local censor boards, the costs of which, partially, if not entirely, would fall on the individual theatres.

Nevertheless, some major circuits – Loews, RKO, Brandt – departed from their tacit agreement with the MPAA and the rating system. While the major studios abandoned the X product line by expanding the parameters of the R rating, there still remained plenty of independently distributed, self-applied, X-rated exploitation films available for exhibition. Such films appealed to many NATO exhibitors at that time, argues Lewis, because they made more money on a screen-by-screen basis than some very big MPAA releases.[37] These choices threatened to have industry-wide ramifications. In an unprecedented chastising of a major exhibitor, Valenti blasted Loews for eroding faith in the rating system for its booking of the Danish sex film *Without a Stitch* in State I and Cine, two Manhattan first-run theatres, in 1970. For the first time, he made it clear to the industry that they could not simultaneously be both sex voyeur and a responsible community enterprise:

I told the chief executive of [Loews] that if other large, responsible theater operators decide to play this kind of film, then we are going to be witness to the death of quality exhibition in this country. The theater cannot have it both ways. The theater cannot be half quality and half smut ... If there is a proliferation of the quasi-porn film playing in first-class houses to the exclusion of product of wider appeal, we are in trouble.[38]

Valenti's words spell out Hollywood's commercial strategy in the age of classification: only G-, GP- and R-rated films (later G, PG, PG-13 and R) should play in NATO theatres. At the same time, he isolates and penalises the X, demanding that NATO boycott all X films not produced or distributed by MPAA members – which rarely would happen. This wedge driven between 'quality' adult films and pornography would forever distort the rating, as the stigma attached to this outer category would always imply a violation of the industry's responsibility to the 'standards of the larger society'.

Following Valenti's tirade about keeping exploitative sex out of key flagship theatres, NATO exhibitors would soon screen only films with an MPAA seal. A $30-million damage suit against the MPAA filed by Tonlyn Productions, Inc., the distributor of *Without a Stitch*, claimed that Paramount told Loews that it would withhold its products from the chain if they continued to book X films from non-MPAA members.[39] Also responsible for the demise of soft- and hard-core features at NATO theatres were local efforts to censor X-rated films found obscene, a statutory power given to local communities after *Miller versus California* in 1973. Threat of bans, taxation, or legal proceedings proved too risky for theatre-owners who found loyalty to the rating system and responsible entertainment a much safer, if less immediately profitable, business arrangement.[40]

By abandoning adults-only film distribution and expressing a commitment to protecting children from harmful elements on the screen, the MPAA and NATO signed a contract with its viewing audiences. The Incontestable R rating guaranteed the system's legal and political detractors the promise of respectable mass entertainment and averted the creation of state and local classification boards. But the assurance that all CARA-certified and NATO-exhibited films would carry an R rating also helped to protect the MPAA from the independent distributors and exhibitors who were significantly left out of the ratings agreement in the first place. The alliance between the MPAA and NATO, contends Lewis, forced the independents to accept the industry's classifications if they wanted their films to be booked at NATO theatres.[41] Independent film companies could adopt the non-copywritten X rating, but, given its abandonment by the majors, its appropriation by pornographers and denial of exhibition by most theatre-owners, these companies would forever have problems marketing and exhibiting films with the adults-only rating. Such industrial collusion gave the MPAA control over entry into the entertainment marketplace, setting a national censorship standard of respectable (films with MPAA ratings of R or lower) versus non-respectable entertainment (films without MPAA ratings). That is the burden of the Incontestable R; respectable entertainment could and would only be played at the first-run movie houses.

The Incontestable R as structure

On one hand, the Incontestable R is the blueprint and label of film-making and exhibition practised by the MPAA and NATO. The genre is inextricably linked to both distributors and theatre-owners deferring to CARA: the MPAA allowing CARA to regulate its product and NATO abiding by and solely exhibiting films with CARA's ratings. However, for a genre to be a contract, that is, for the Incontestable R to be recognised by viewers as respectable mass entertainment, the films that inhabit that category must have a formal framework indicating the genre is at work. The MPAA and NATO must continually deliver on this contract, providing respectable R movies that cannot be mistaken for a disrespectable X/NC-17 by those likely to condemn Hollywood's products as unrepresentative or inappropriately representative of American society and culture. As harmfulness or obscenity is a historically situated understanding, the Incontestable R genre must be a historically stable but always transitory category that can withstand or, better yet, stave off prosecution of MPAA films by local communities and criticism from moral reformers. The primary mission of CARA, in this regard, is to find the formal line that enables the industry to conduct its business profitably and unheeded, and never cross it. Determining the boundary between the R and NC-17 categories, or, more specifically, identifying those representations that cross the line between 'tastefulness' and 'offensiveness', between 'entertainment' and 'pornography', make's CARA's function no different than the PCA. Both regimes kept Hollywood's adult detractors at bay by arranging its products into a respectable package.

Two actions are crucial to the process of shaping the features of the Incontestable R genre at any given historical moment: first, film-makers must sign a contract agreeing to deliver an R picture if they want mass distribution of their films by an MPAA member, and, second, studios must not deliberately bankroll or choose to distribute potentially controversial projects containing contractual R ratings. An MPAA member's decision to usurp the industry's commitment to the Incontestable R places CARA in a bind because, unlike the PCA, CARA does not really have the industrial or public support for arranging films into a single category. They do not perceive themselves as censors of free expression or guardians of morality like the PCA, but rather as a service that makes educated judgments as to which rating most American parents would find appropriate for a film. As CARA, for the most part, only regulates films after their completion, the rating board sometimes is forced into a position to arrange potentially 'non-respectable' X-rated product into 'respectable' R-rated films. In such cases, an R film may become 'contestable' once it has been released in theatres.

If, says Altman, 'genres require shared perceptions in order to be perceived as genres',[42] the survival of the Incontestable R is certainly dependent upon a synergy between the MPAA, NATO and CARA. This is no more apparent than in the case of *Cruising* (1980), a film directed by William Friedkin and starring Al Pacino as a cop tracking down a murderer in the New York homosexual S & M underworld. While United Artists may have felt that the Gerald Walker novel contained market exploitation value for itself and NATO that fell within the boundaries of the Incontestable R, practically all other users of the genre disagreed. The chairperson of CARA at the time, Richard Heffner, admitted that 'no picture has given us so much anguish as *Cruising*', as the film was resubmitted to CARA five or six times to soften the violence and sodomy sequences to an R rating.[43] *Variety* wrote in its review that 'if [*Cruising*] is an R, then the only X left is hardcore',[44] a point made by many film critics who unanimously found the film's 'disrespectable' and 'unpleasant' subject matter, theme and tone inappropriate for an R rating. The ramification of United Artists failing to provide CARA with a sufficiently respectable product that CARA could arrange into an Incontestable R film was many

NATO exhibitors abandoning their compliance with the rating system. For example, General Cinema Theatres, the largest cinema chain at the time, cancelled all their engagements in fear of community backlash, issuing a statement that read: 'General Cinema Corporation's policy is to refuse to play X rated pictures or pictures which in our judgment should be X rated.'[45] In addition, United Artists Theatres took it upon itself to re-rate *Cruising* with an X, further damaging the integrity of the rating system and the incontestability of the R rating.[46]

Fortunately for Hollywood, *Cruising* is an isolated case, revealing the importance of exhibition in anchoring the Incontestable R; no other MPAA-distributed or NATO-exhibited film since, not even *Natural Born Killers* (1994), has dramatically undermined the industry's system of self-regulation and commitment to respectable entertainment. Nevertheless, the assumptions made about *Cruising* that an R film can clearly be distinguished from an X film testifies to a formal structure inherent to the Incontestable R.

In most cases, CARA's negotiations with a producer or distributor on an acceptable R cut are done secretly and unaccompanied by media fanfare. CARA itself is a private trade organisation whose internal documents of rating decisions are never made available to the public. As such, it becomes quite difficult to pinpoint the formal arrangments by which CARA ensures that MPAA films conform to an externally generated definition of respectable entertainment. The task becomes harder as the Incontestable R, like all genres, is a process, supported, twisted and reformed by discursive forces. Generic communication is rarely shared, understood or left unquestioned among multiple users; exhibitors, parents, moral reformers and politicians use Hollywood and the Incontestable R to satisfy their own needs and desires. The upper boundaries for an R rating are surely different today than they were in 1990, as the perceptions that shaped the category are historically contingent and continually in flux.

Even though genres are permanently contested sites, argues Altman, sometimes a generic system may appear perfectly balanced and at rest by a 'momentary equilibrium of countervening concerns'.[47] With *Cruising*, this was not the case, but in most other instances, CARA must have a set of criteria that satisfies the requirements of the Incontestable R genre which, in turn, satisfy those who carefully monitor Hollywood's commitment to respectable entertainment. The existence of a set of standards separating the R and X/NC-17 ratings suggests that the industry still abides by a production code that distinguishes between 'presentability' and 'indecency'. By abandoning production of X/NC-17 films, these representations serve to delimit the boundaries of Hollywood filmmaking and define, at a given time, Hollywood's conception of respectable entertainment.

While CARA has never followed a particular idelogical agenda like the PCA, editing films down from an X/NC-17 to an R came to be used in a parallel fashion to filter out those images, words, themes and tone that certain adults may find objectionable or inappropriate for Hollywood. This argument is best supported by the accusations perennially made by critics and film-makers about CARA's more lenient approach to violence in comparison to sexual matters. Film critic Arthur Knight, writing in 1969, noticed that 'incest, regicide, and self-mutilation', in the G-rated *Oedipus the King*, 'are apparently "acceptable for all audiences, without consideration of age" – so long as they

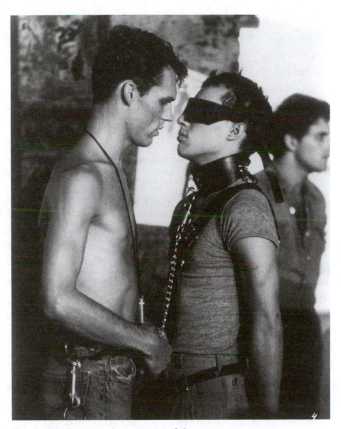

Cruising (1980) was a challenge to the integrity of the ratings system

take place off screen and there are no nude scenes'.[48] Two decades later, the same cry was heard from critic Sam Frank: 'The [B]oard's double standards are blatant. Explicit acts of nonstop murder are acceptable in an R movie but explicit sex acts are not.'[49] Director Phillip Noyce concurs, believing that the Board is 'far more lenient about acts that end life than those that engender it.'[50] And Jean-Jacques Annaud, the director of *The Lover* (1992), claims: 'There is too much violence – heads are chopped off and it's still an R. But to take the girl you love to bed is wrong. Why the hypocrisy?'[51]

What is surprising is that Valenti does not disagree with these insinuations. He publicly admits that CARA indeed treats violence less severely than sexuality, partly because violence is more difficult to classify and qualify than sex, and partly because Americans are more offended by sex than violence.

> What is too much violence? Is John Wayne at Iwo Jima killing a thousand Japanese more violent than the Boston Strangler?
>
> But with sex – there's nudity and you know what it is. There is also a deeply ingrained Puritan ethic in this country, and people who are uptight about these things tend to be more uptight about sex than violence, although violence is very much monitored by the rating system.[52]

Given the subjectivity of the rating process and the fact that sex, not violence, is open to charges of obscenity, the dividing line between what is 'all right' and what Valenti calls 'too much' is inevitably controversial. Yet, it is this sometimes hit-or-miss measurement that determines whether an R is incontestable or not to exhibitors, critics, politicians, moral reformers and other users.

Paul Verhoeven understands that cutting a film down to an R rating is a condition of working in Hollywood, where one always has to balance artistic aspiration with industrial economics: 'If you want to be in this business, you have to realize that people, companies, are investing money and are dependent on the success of the movie in order to survive.' Consider *Basic Instinct* (1992), he says. 'The movie cost $45 million, so you cannot say "Fuck you all." '[53]

Basic Instinct came out two years after the NC-17 replaced the X, and this period provides a better opportunity to analyse the boundaries of the Incontestable R than the 1970s and 1980s. Both unrated or director's cut (i.e. NC-17) of films and their respective Incontestable R versions are primarily available for films released in the 1990s. Supplementing these videos, laser-discs and DVDs are interviews, trailers and commentary tracks, which, used in conjunction with written reports, allow one to reconstruct the semantic difference between an R and unrated/NC-17 film. While it is impossible to determine how CARA responds to wider social forces in addressing troublesome material, and it is beyond the scope of this essay to discuss the parameters involved in editing syntax, the following taxonomy does demonstrate that CARA's standards of operation for the Incontestable R category have pretty much remained uniform from 1992–6.

Six criteria (theme, language, violence, nudity, sex, drug use) appear on the 'green' ballot completed by CARA examiners in the rating process; rating battles over the R/NC-17 boundary made public in the 1990s almost exclusively dealt with two of these criteria: sex and nudity. These films are *Basic Instinct*, *Body of Evidence* (1992), *Damage* (1992), *Bad Lieutenant* (1992), *Wide Sargasso Sea* (1992), *Sliver* (1993), *Boxing Helena* (1993), *Dangerous Game* (1993), *Color of Night* (1994), *Showgirls* (1995), *Delta of Venus* (1995), *Crash* (1996), *Kama Sutra: A Tale of Love* (1996) and *Broken English* (1996). Comparing two versions of a film in terms of camera distance, camera angle, time length of shot and shot selection reveals an overwhelmingly consistent formal structure for the Incontestable R.

First, a double standard does not exist for male and female frontal nudity. The penis, vagina and pubic hair are allowed in R-rated films. Second, shots of vaginal entry and the close proximity of an actor's face to another actor's pubic hair or genitals in the same frame are not permitted. Third, masturbation and oral sex movements are allowable off-camera and in certain cases involving long shots, darkened scenes or obscure camera angles, but the actors must always be clothed. Fourth, sexual grinding below the waist can last only two to three seconds and pubic hair cannot be shown in this shot. Exceptions include darkened long shots and scenes with clothed actors. Fifth, shots of naked lovers in a missionary or female dominant position are permitted without any movement.

Together, these criteria show that the management of the Incontestable R is often an easily definable and observable process revolving around sex and nudity. Yet, it is one deliberately camouflaged by CARA due to its discursive commitment to self-regulation, not censorship. Discrepancies can sometimes occur – as in the case of MGM's *The Lover* – when the Rating Appeals Board (RAB), an industry organisation predominantly comprised of MPAA and NATO members, overturns a CARA rating. Lengthy shots of sexual grinding suggest arbitrariness not on the part of CARA, but of the RAB, raising serious questions about the political and economic rationales influencing RAB decisions. That *The Lover* never served as a precedent for the outer limit of sexual imagery in future Incontestable R applications is remarkable. This two-tiered set-up, nevertheless, breeds inconsistency, confusion and hostility for the rating system, a discursivity that CARA occasionally needs to repair in order to maintain the Incontestable R genre.

The future of the Incontestable R

Altman states that 'genres are not only formal arrangements of textual characteristics; they are also social devices that use semantics and syntax to assure simultaneous satisfaction on the part of multiple users with apparently contradictory purposes'.[54] *Cruising* reveals that its R rating, despite its arrangement into respectable entertainment by CARA, was contestable and non-satisfactory, put to many different discursive uses by exhibitors, critics and viewers. *Basic Instinct*, on the other hand, which had similar protests from gay rights groups, proved to be incontestable and satisfactory for the R rating. Such incongruity demonstrates the discursive status of all genre claims as studio pronouncements may not always match audience positions; in other words, the generic contract, at any time, can be severed.

The MPAA and CARA certainly realise that the Incontestable R contract, like all genre, is continually in process, subject to reconfiguration and reformulation. The semantics of the Incontestable R have periodically been adjusted to adapt to changing mores in society, and the syntax of respectable entertainment has remained the same since the auteur renaissance fizzled in the early 1970s. Yet, it is the MPAA's discursive claims to respectable entertainment that repeatedly are under attack by users and therefore repeatedly under revision by CARA.

However, the MPAA's response to these attacks explains the dominance of the Incontestable R genre for over thirty years: its revisions are always token cosmetic alterations that fail to address CARA's systematic abandonment of the X/NC-17 and its discrimation against independent film-making practices. Examples include: the creation of the red-banded trailer and green-banded trailer in 1971, the former warning the projectionist that a trailer could only be attached to an R or X feature; the changing of the C in CARA's name from 'Code' to 'Classification' in 1977; the alteration of the composition of its rating board in 1978, from industry farmhands to parents; the replacement of the X with the copy-written NC-17 in 1990; and the provision of brief explanations in 1996 that described the reasons behind an R rating.

For the most part, opponents of the Incontestable R – general audiences, parents, critics, exhibitors, politicians, moral reformers – have never been truly been unified over one cause. The genre, even during periods of contestation – has always been capable of benefiting multiple, if not all, users at one particular time or another. As Altman has observed, 'for a genre to exist, a large number of texts must be produced, broadly distributed, exhibited to an extensive audience and received in a rather homogeneous manner'.[55] However this homogeneity appears to be in danger, as most genre users have heavily criticised the semantics and syntax of the Incontestable R in the wake of the myriad school shootings in the United States.

Extreme and amoral violence, once acceptable under the auspices of the R rating, now appears for many users to be antithetical to respectable Hollywood entertainment. After Columbine, exhibitors have cracked down on allowing underage or unaccompanied children to purchase tickets for R-rated features or to purchase tickets for PG or PG-13 features and sneak into an R-rated screening. Additionally, in April 2001, Senator Joseph Lieberman unveiled legislation called the Media Marketing Accountability Act that would outlaw advertising of adult-rated movies to minors. This legislation followed the Marketing Violence to Children hearings in the US Senate in September 2000, which revealed that the MPAA studios routinely target minors in advertising for R-rated films and use minors in focus groups for test screenings of R-rated films such as *Judge Dredd* (1995). While all of these industry practices have been in place since the dawn of the rating system, and despite the fact that R-rated pictures do not actually prohibit minors from atttending them, the Incontestable R is discursively under attack by exhibitors and democrats, two groups traditionally supportive of industry self-regulation.

A June 2001 report from MarketCast, a show business research firm, suggests that these discourses have adversely affected studio profit. Movies such as *Tomcats* (2001) and *Freddy Got Fingered* (2001), both MPAA R-rated films with teenage appeal, lost 30 to 40 per cent of potential weekend earnings by not being PG-13. Surveys done by MarketCast found that increased pressure from parents' groups and politicians strengthened enforcement at NATO theatres, accounting for the box-office loss.

Such news may spell doom for the Incontestable R. The increased permissiveness of sex, violence and intensity in the genre over the past two decades may have finally run its course. Might the studios attempt to reach adults with the NC-17 rating now that the R rating may economically and politically be a bad investment? Could the PG-13 rating become the incontestable category for respectable entertainment? Whatever keeps making the studios money is the answer.

Notes

1. Rick Altman, *Film/Genre* (London: BFI, 1999), p. 214.
2. Ibid., p. 11.
3. Ibid., p. 24.
4. Ibid., p. 144.
5. Ibid., p. 120.
6. Ibid., p. 108.
7. Ibid., pp. 91–3

8. Ibid., pp. 24–5.

9. Ibid., p. 128.

10. CARA changed its name to Classification and Ratings Administration in 1977.

11. The initial design of the rating system was: G (for general audiences, all ages admitted), M (for mature audiences, parental guidance suggested, but all ages admitted), R (for restricted audiences, children under sixteen should not be admitted without an accompanying parent or adult guardian) and X (for no one under sixteen). The age limit for the X was raised to seventeen in 1969. GP replaced the M in 1970, then became PG in 1972. The upper age limit for R was raised to seventeen in 1970. The PG-13 was added between the PG and R in 1984 and the NC-17 replaced the X in 1990.

12. To target a fragmented array of spectators in the New Hollywood, Altman argues that the industry did not abandon the practice of genre mixing, but developed new techniques for its usage. In a close analysis of the R-rated *Cocktail* (1988), he reveals that stylistic developments in contemporary Hollywood directly tied to audience demographic research have led to a greater dependency on genre mixing. See Altman, *Film/Genre*, pp. 132–9.

13. Ibid. p. 93.

14. Ibid., pp. 93–5, 110–11.

15. While DreamWorks is not an official member of the MPAA, it does abide by the same policies as the other distributors.

16. United Artists Classics released Pier Paolo Pasolini's *Arabian Nights* with an X rating in 1979.

17. Altman, *Film/Genre*, p. 14.

18. As both an active process and stable formation, the Incontestable R can work as a 'discursive cluster', constituted not only by the text itself, but by the contextual practices that locate a text within a given genre as well. This approach to genre analysis, theorised by Jason Mittel, provides an account of how genre categories evolve and redefine themselves through discursive shifts and rearticulations. See 'A Cultural Approach to Television Genre Theory', *Cinema Journal,* vol. 40, no. 3 (2001), pp. 3–24.

19. NATO, the result of a merger between Allied States and Theater Owners of America in the mid-1960s, comprised 10,000 of the nation's 13,000 theatres. The IFIDA (International Film Importers and Distributors of America), a less powerful trade organisation, was also a partner in CARA.

20. See chapter 4 of Jon Lewis, *Hollywood v. Hardcore: How the Struggle over Censorship Saved the Modern Film Industry* (New York: New York University Press, 2000).

21. Richard Maltby, *Harmless Entertainment: Hollywood and the Ideology of Consensus* (Metuchen, NJ, and London: Scarecrow, 1983), 53–6.

22. Richard Maltby, *Hollywood Cinema* (Oxford: Blackwell, 1995), p. 6.

23. Lewis, *Hollywood v. Hardcore*, p. 7. Italics in original.

24. See Kevin S. Sandler, 'The Naked Truth: *Showgirls* and the Fate of the X/NC-17', *Cinema Journal,* vol. 40, no. 3 (2001), pp. 69–93.

25. Lewis, *Hollywood v. Hardcore*, p. 153.

26. See pp. 71–5 of 'The Naked Truth: *Showgirls* and the Fate of the X/NC-17', for a more in-depth discussion of these two issues.

27. A. D. Murphy, '$-Sign over MPAA Alphabet, Distribs Wanna Shun Risky "R" ', *Variety*, 25 November 1970, p. 5.

28. Lewis, *Hollywood v. Hardcore*, p. 188.

29. A. D. Murphy, 'Code in Perspective over 4 Yrs.: Measure Indie Production Flood; U.S. Makers Seek G and PG Ratings', *Variety*, 8 November 1972, p. 19. The trade paper also added that the possibility of a new adult rating to cover 'quality' films had been severely undermined after Stanley Kubrick pulled *A Clockwork Orange* out of release in August for sixty days in order to qualify for a lower rating after cutting two scenes.

30. In *Film/Genre*, Altman claims that exhibition is too often underestimated by scholars in anchoring generic affiliation, p. 92.

31. 'Rifkin on Rating System', *NATO News*, October 1968, p. 1.

32. In New York, the X rating barred anyone under sixteen, not seventeen.

33. Charlie Poorman, 'Survival Booking . . . in the Days of G, M, R, and X', *Motion Picture Herald*, 16 July 1969, p. 7.

34. Poorman, 'Survival Booking', p. 8.

35. Vincent Canby, 'Will They Censor the Teenybopper?', *New York Times*, 22 March 1970.

36. 'Protecting "Public" vs. "Censorship" ', *Variety*, 25 February 1970, p. 7.

37. Lewis, *Hollywood v. Hardcore*, p. 168.

38. Quoted in Gene Arneel, 'Valenti Raps Loew's "Stitch" Booking: Can't Be Voyeur & Respectable Biz', *Variety*, 28 January 1970, p. 4.

39. 'Harris Sues MPAA, TOA, Par Alleging Conspiracy and "Trade Libel" vs. "Stitch" ', *Variety*, 11 February 1970, p. 4.

40. Lewis, *Hollywood v. Hardcore*, p. 170.

41. Ibid., p. 150.

42. Altman, *Film/Genre*, p. 157.

43. Aljean Harmetz, 'How "Cruising" Received Its "R" Rating', *New York Times*, 16 February 1980.

44. Review of *Cruising*, *Variety*, 12 February 1980.

45. Quoted in Harmetz, 'How "Cruising" Received Its "R" Rating'. General Cinema Corp. viewed the picture a second time after announcing the cancellation, but stood by its previously revealed decision. See '2nd Look Nix by GCC: "Cruising" an X Pic', *Variety*, 13 February 1980, pp. 5, 219.

46. 'UATC Posts Warning at Windows: "Cruising" is X Film in R Clothing', *Variety*, 20 February 1980. UATC similarly notified its patrons with the showing of Columbia's *Hardcore* in 1979.

47. Altman, *Film/Genre*, p. 195.

48. Arthur Knight, ' "G" as in Good Entertainment', *Saturday Review*, 1 March 1969, p. 40.

49. Sam Frank, 'Counterpunch: Ratings Boards an Affront to First Amendment', *Los Angeles Times*, 31 May 1993, Calendar.

50. Quoted in Bruce Feld, ' "Sliver" Deliverer Phillip [*sic*] Noyce', *Drama-Logue*, 27 May – 2 June 1993.

51. Quoted in Stephen Schaefer, 'Director Annaud Hates Rating Game', *USA Today*, 17 November 1992, p. 10D.

52. Quoted in R. M. Townsend, 'An Interview with Movie Boss Jack Valenti', *Mainliner*, February 1974, p. 24.

53. Quoted in Laurent Bouzereau, *The Cutting Room Floor* (New York: Citadel Press, 1994), p. 207.

54. Altman, *Film/Genre*, p. 195.

55. Ibid., p. 84.

15

Cinema and the Premises of Youth: 'Teen Films' and Their Sites in the 1980s and 1990s

Steve Bailey and James Hay

In this article, we are interested neither in establishing a definition of the teen film nor in relating its manifestations in the 1980s and 1990s to its putative origins in the 1950s. Instead we are interested in questions that genre analysis (at least in its most widely accepted practice) has been incapable of addressing. What has genre to do with cinema's link to particular spaces, particular sites? How have these sites – the movie theatre or the classroom, for instance – mattered for youth? And how have the sites in which youth and cinema intersect become spaces for organising and governing behaviour? Pursuing these questions involves a different consideration of cinema's relation to social forma- tion and a different understanding of power than is typical of genre criticism in general and criticism of the 'teen film' in particular. Addressing them within the context of a book on 'New' Hollywood cinema means that we are not interested in explaining how the New Hollywood has developed out of the old nor in exploring how this may or may not have involved changes in the generic make-up of the teen film (at least as tradition- ally understood). Instead we are interested in asking what the new-ness of Hollywood cinema has to do with the changing paths, the changing mobility and the changing spa- tial attachments of youth. With this in mind, we offer here a 'map' of recent intersections of the practices of youth and cinema. Within this map, we pay particular attention to three critical sites: the home, the school and the shopping mall. These sites, we argue, are neither simply iconographic (a matter of recently recurrent generic settings) nor simply contextual spaces (places in which young people encounter films). Rather they are spaces in which the social identities of youth find articulation.

Thus as a locale for film viewing, the household has served as a space in which 'music television', whose increasingly diverse programming addresses youth as a taste culture and as what might be termed a 'lifestyle cluster', has taken its place alongside a new relation to video as a *personal* (rather than a communal or familial) space. The VCR has also made the home an important site of teen viewing practices – the very premise, for example, of the hit film *Scream* (1996) – while the school has become an important location for both a new generation of educational films and, more recently, for the incur- sion of the paradigmatically domestic practice of television viewing. The shopping mall and the freestanding multiplex, meanwhile, have extended the terrain of teen cinema, as well as providing an increasingly crucial narrative setting for teen films themselves.

The use of spaces such as these as settings for narrative action, and the representation of a capacity to move between them and to cultivate knowledge and practices appropriate to each, becomes, we argue, a critical element in the depiction of the teenage experience. Here, the articulation of the teenager as a 'mobile' subject becomes linked to a sense of the teen as a kind of well-rounded individual, occupying the place of a family member, a citizen-in-training and a consumer, and developing the ability to shift between all three subject positions as circumstances demand. Adding an additional level of symbolic complexity is the tendency in many films to treat all three locations with a fundamental ambivalence, posing each as the site both of possibility and of restriction, of an increasing personal autonomy and of a simultaneous conformity to social norms. Along with these sites comes an emphasis on the automobile as a means of mobility and, consequently, of potential liberation from an excessively narrow material and symbolic milieu. The continual tension between practices of freedom and practices of discipline works as a kind of technology for youth and as a means for the cultivation of a 'teen subject' who is both mobile and self-disciplined. Particularly interesting in the light of these issues is a number of popular films which feature a protagonist who is initially a stranger to the world of contemporary teens, thus providing a kind of 'ethnographic' perspective on the spaces of youth and making the development of space-specific knowledge and the resultant emergence of a suitable 'teen self' an explicit narrative theme.

Domestication and liberty: the ambivalent suburban home

The tendency for many films to utilise distinctly affluent suburban settings, evident in popular 1980s comedies such as *Risky Business* (1983), *Ferris Bueller's Day Off* (1986) and *Fast Times at Ridgemont High* (1982), as well as the more recent *Clueless* (1995), *Drive Me Crazy* (1999) and *American Pie* (1999), certainly supports this ambivalence by playing off a conventional understanding of upper middle-class suburban life as one of both material comfort and stultifying conformity. In this milieu, the dynamic of liberty and restriction is amplified, both for comic effect and as an extension of the tendencies of mobile privatisation discussed above. This is compounded, of course, by the natural liminality of adolescent home life, one in which the individual is both materially and emotionally dependent upon parents, but also resentful of the restrictions that accompany such dependence. It is important to note that such restrictions often include access to media; the recent debates regarding the Internet and filtering software provide a good example of the attempt to maintain control over domestic technology.

As Bernstein and Pratt note in their analysis of *Risky Business*, much of the comedy in the film revolves around the relationship of protagonist Joel Goodson (Tom Cruise) to the trappings of affluence which surround him, particularly his father's Porsche and elaborate stereo system; as Bernstein and Pratt argue in regard to Joel, 'none of the toys he plays with are his'.[1] Here, the barriers enacted by the parents to bar access to domestic technology become the initial motivation for practices of liberation, referenced in Joel's famous underwear dancing (while playing forbidden music on the father's stereo) and subsequent escape to the city. In *Ferris Bueller's Day Off*, Ferris (Matthew Broderick) uses the resources provided by his privileged background to enable an escape from sub-urban boredom through an urban adventure – rigging his (as opposed to his parents') array of stereo equipment to fake an illness. Clever Ferris, though, is balanced by the neurotic Cameron (Alan Ruck), who is emotionally stunted by the bland, unloving mate-rialism of his parents, represented, significantly, in the prohibition on his use of the father's automobiles. *Clueless* features a broader comic variation on this scenario, in which apparently vacuous but actually quite savvy Cher (Alicia Silverstone) deals with a gruffly protective father, self-righteous stepbrother and absent mother while operating within a broader milieu of fantastic affluence and preternatural sophistication.

In *American Pie*, the ambivalence is explicitly sexualised, as Jim's hapless father attempts to explain sex with the help of pornographic magazines while Jim (Jason Biggs) and his friends discuss a 'mom I'd like to fuck' and broadcast sexual adventures from their bedrooms via the Internet. In the latter case, the film directly references the kinds of illicit practices of spectatorship that are of course connected to the act of viewing films such as *American Pie* – available in an 'NC-17' version only on videocassette or laser-disc – within the family home. Here, the Internet – the source of much hysteria involving youth and potentially dangerous information[2] – becomes the means for teens to reclaim and sexualise the domestic sphere.[3] In all of the aforementioned films, suburban home life, and especially affluence, is understood as the location of a struggle to assert one's self in material, social and sexual terms – in the face of authority and restriction as well as the undeniable (and in this case significant) comforts of home. These practices of self-assertion, of course, are linked to the same technologies – electronic equipment, computer networks and automobiles – that are absolutely essential in allowing teenagers to access the kinds of representations that are provided within films themselves.

While the films noted above present an acutely ambivalent take on home life, other films point to a troubled domestic sphere as the origin of a kind of adolescent moral crisis. *River's Edge* (1986) and *Less than Zero* (1987) are exemplary in this regard, pre-senting the home as emotionally and morally empty. In the former (based on an actual event in Milpitas, California), Matt (Keanu Reeves) struggles with his decision to inform on a murderous friend; his home is a near caricature of dysfunctionality with an over-worked, pot-smoking mother living with a boyfriend whose contribution to the household is purely financial and a violent, completely amoral younger brother, who threatens to kill him for 'narking'. John (Daniel Roebuck), the murderer in the film, lacks even a dysfunctional family, living alone with his disabled aunt and driven into a homi-cidal rage by a girlfriend's comments about his dead mother. *Less than Zero* offers a similarly bleak view of domesticity, with the film's hyper-affluent milieu adding an air of decandence to a more generalised amorality. This is particularly evident in the opulent and heavily staged Christmas celebration of protagonist Clay's (Andrew McCarthy) fam-ily, which is contrasted with the debauchery of a youthful and similarly staged 'Fuck Christmas' party. In these films, the domestic sphere has become hopelessly corrupted and subjective development is only possible in spite of the home. In both, the protag-onists seek an escape; Matt to a park where he has sex with Clarissa (Ione Skye) – one of the few other sympathetic characters in the film – and Clay through his return to col-

Sexualising the domestic sphere: *American Pie* (1999)

lege in New England. The gloomier scenario posed by these films, as well as by the more recent *Kids* (1995), *The Craft* (1996) and *Wild Things* (1998), extends some of the negative implications of family life as depicted in the comedies noted above, thus providing a kind of 'worst case' model of the domestic sphere. The kind of excessive dysfunctionality referenced in all of these films is echoed in the moral panic surrounding school shootings, infanticide and other exemplars of 'nihilistic' youth corrupted by a degenerate popular culture. In this sense, the films work as a mechanism of discipline, offering an emphasis on the need for appropriate methods of restriction (on both youth and adults) and also offering a sort of moralistic mirror-image to the tentative explorations of liberty in films such as *Risky Business* and *Ferris Bueller's Day Off*. The need for self-regulation, particularly in cases where external regulation – from parents, schools or the state – is absent becomes a crucial aspect of the formation of teenage subjects, an aspect common to the films mentioned above and to the wider cultural demand for 'responsible children'. The ungovernable teen, this discourse suggests, is as much a failure of liberal society as the quasi-fascist conformist; both lack the depth, in terms of ethical development and cultural sophistication, to operate successfully within the challenging terrain of contemporary youth.

In this light, it is worth noting that several films, including such diverse examples as *Over the Edge* (1979), *Foxes* (1980), *Sixteen Candles* (1984) and *Can't Hardly Wait* (1998), as well as *Risky Business*, use the physical imperilling of the family home as an important narrative device. The out-of-control party, a staple of many youth-oriented films, often involves a domestic sphere which is freed from parental control and becomes the site of a social and sexual freedom. The tentative reclamation of the family space for youth is

extended here into an out-of-control assault on the physical space of the family resi-
dence. *Can't Hardly Wait*, for example, uses a wild graduation party as the setting for the
vast majority of its narrative, complete with a nervous, stereotypically bourgeois teen
hostess – an over-disciplined subject – who tries desperately but fruitlessly to protect the
house from any damage. The sense of the domestic sphere as an inevitably temporary
space of personal autonomy, with a restrictive but reassuring return to parental control,
provides a grounding, quite literally, for the youthful subject. In the more serious cinematic variations on the endangered home – *Foxes* and *Over the Edge*, for example – the
sort of teen nihilism noted above threatens to permanently wreck the space and unbal-
ance the careful weighting of restriction and liberty. Thus, in regard to the domestic
sphere, the pleasures and strictures of suburban affluence, the more dangerous threat
of dysfunctionality and the pliability of the physical space of the home work together to
ground a sense of teenage home life as ambiguous terrain, setting a pattern which is further reflected in the more conventionally social spaces discussed below.

Teen citizens and unofficial knowledge: the suburban school

Even more ubiquitous than the family home as a setting for films, the school, and the
culture that goes along with it, provides a complementary and equally ambiguous space
within the genre. Naturally enough, it is a site for the transmission of knowledge, though
the emphasis is usually on forms of unofficial knowledge rather than the official lessons
offered by the institution. Of course, one of the means, much discussed and often under-
standably reviled, for the transmission of official forms of knowledge within the schools
has been through the use of commercial television broadcasting in the classroom, most
notably the Channel One project. In these cases, youth viewing practices associated with
the domestic sphere are imported into the schools as a means of converting the 'wasted'
energies associated with television viewing into the dissemination of lessons regarding
current events. The common liberal critique of such schemes as 'privatising' public
schools reflects precisely the concern that such mingling of the spaces – the home has
already been surrendered to commercial interests – will inevitably deform the citizen-
building function of such institutions, although this may overlook the less obvious
intersection of interests inherent in the task of producing citizens. What the critics and
supporters of commercial television in the schools share, often, is a commitment to maintaining the subject-forming and conduct-developing powers of the school site. Despite
this debate, though, schools continue to function as the site for the transmission of less
official youth knowledge as well, an aspect of teen life continually referenced in 1980s
and 1990s cinema.

For example, in *Fast Times at Ridgemont High,* a notable comedic scene involves
pseudo-worldly Linda (Phoebe Cates) demonstrating oral sex techniques with the aid of
a carrot in the school cafeteria for novice Stacy (Jennifer Jason Leigh). In *Clueless*, Cher
offers a more extensive set of lessons regarding fashion, dating and other aspects of teen
life to Tai (Brittany Murphy), a newcomer from 'the hood' who becomes a 'project' for
Cher and her wealthy friends. In a less comedic vein, John Hughes's influential *The
Breakfast Club* (1985) depicts Saturday detention as a kind of informal psychotherapy,

in which a collection of stereotypes – jock, weirdo, prom queen, bookworm and delin-
quent – exchange confessional narratives, recognise a common humanity and find love.
In all three films, and in a number of other teen films, the teachers are often comically
irrelevant figures, blustering pointlessly in the face of indifferent students or, as in
Clueless, being secretly manipulated by them. The emphasis on the development of
modes of conduct and personal comportment appropriate to a given social situation, and
the relative insignificance of the official knowledge offered by the school itself, thus
complements the similar conception of the home as a space to be claimed from familial
authority. It also works to balance the use of the school as a mechanism for the more
'enlightened' viewing practices posed by educational authorities.

As with the dysfunctional family films noted above, a number of films present the high
school as a more monolithically oppressive environment. This appears comically in
Ferris Bueller's Day Off, in which Ferris is pursued by an inept principal intent on uncovering the ruse of his phony 'sick day'; the film also features a droning, hyperbolically
tedious history teacher facing a class of utterly indifferent students. *Permanent Record*
(1988), a more serious film about teen suicide, depicts the school principal as a heart-
less authoritarian, obsessed with rules but oblivious to the troubled youth around him.
The Faculty (1998), an example of the popular teen horror film (including *Scream*, *I
Know What You Did Last Summer* (1997), and their respective sequels), satirises the
oppressive character of school authority by transforming the school faculty into vessels
for an alien invasion. The teachers are ultimately defeated by a *Breakfast Club*-esque
assortment of teen social types – drug dealer, fashion snob, punk rocker and nerd. The
film is particularly interesting as it makes a winking reference to an earlier cult favourite,
1983's *Pink Floyd: The Wall* (based on the hit album of the same name), which features
a similarly oppressive portrait of school life. The latter was a hugely popular midnight
feature and reflected a re-articulation of rock'n'roll (of a particularly intellectual variety)
and cinema; the reference, within *The Faculty*, to *The Wall* as an important way of understanding school-based oppression thus works to re-emphasise its own status as a kind
of 'educational film'.

Other popular films focus on the school as the site of intrastudent power dynamics,
as opposed to the more conventional authority of the faculty and administration. For
example, Richard Linklater's comedy *Dazed and Confused* (1994), which straddles 'indie'
film culture and teen cinema, focuses on hazing practices in a 1970s Texas high school
in which male students are paddled by a gang of jockish bullies and female students must
face the wrath of Darla (Parker Posey), a particularly cruel senior. *Heathers* (1989), an
even darker comedy, depicts a high school ruled by an elite clique of wealthy and attractive girls – 'Heathers' – and brutish jocks; in this case, opposition comes from Veronica
(Winona Ryder), a rebellious 'Heather', and her murderous boyfriend Jason (Christian
Slater). A more sincere examination of high school snobbery, *Pretty in Pink* (1986), takes
class distinctions as its primary focus, with 'richie' Blane (Andrew McCarthy) struggling
to overcome the opposition of his wealthy parents and elitist friends – epitomised by his
cartoonishly decadent, relentlessly snobbish friend Steff (James Spader) – and build a
romance with poor but good-hearted Andie (Molly Ringwald); this scenario is repeated

nearly verbatim, albeit with a gender switch, in *Some Kind of Wonderful* (1987), also by writer John Hughes and director Howard Deutch.

The latter two films are interesting in that they also reflect the sense of school as a kind of sociological microcosm of a wider society, one in which the more monolithic character of the domestic sphere (and especially upper middle-class suburbia) is mitigated by the necessary commingling of a broader array of social types. Certainly this is the case for recent films such as *Disturbing Behavior* (1998), *Never Been Kissed* (1999) and *She's All That* (1999), in addition to any number of 1980s films. Here, the school acts as a space in which power dynamics evident in larger social formations – which usually involve bullying, snobbery, humiliation and other forms of social domination – are played out on a more modest scale. If the home and the domestic sphere work within teen cinema as the site of a gradually increasing autonomy and individuation (whether this is from overprotective, authoritarian parents or from nihilistic dysfunctionality), the school acts as the place of socialisation that is posed against the more uniform structures of the family. The type of knowledge which becomes most important in this environment, 'unofficial' and closely tied to membership in a subgroup within the larger school, provides a kind of ironic counterpoint to the putative function of the school – preparing students for citizenship and participation in the adult world. A kind of 'teen citizenship' is implied here, but it is vastly different from the model offered by a naive adult world; this is an important narrative element in these films, but also an effective means of producing teen subjects.

The status of such films as the source of a kind of unofficial knowledge and a form of non-institutional training for teens is evident in a 1987 essay from the pedagogically minded *English Journal* by Harold Foster titled 'Film in the Classroom: Coping with "Teenpics"', which outlines five tasks for English teachers in dealing with these films, including 'transforming students into discriminating viewers who can distinguish good from bad, exploitation from communication', 'educating them so they can understand films visually and thematically, so they can analyse and critique films they see' and 'developing critical awareness so students would occasionally pass up the worst of these films and stay home and read a book'.[4] The essay then recommends five films – including the aforementioned *Risky Business, Sixteen Candles* and *The Breakfast Club* – which are 'well-made and powerful to young people', though the author also mentions that 'I warn you that the values these films teach teenagers are not always positive'.[5] 'Locking these films out of our schools, hiding from their influence, can only serve ignorance,' Foster argues; resituating the films in the classroom and within a wholly different framework of knowledge production, the essay implies, can redirect the genre into a weapon against 'the subconscious absorption of messages which leads to the subconscious acceptance'. Resituating these films within the school – the space posed as both the source of unofficial knowledge and social oppression in the same films – thus redirects the genre towards the purposes of state-sanctioned knowledge and a set of critical faculties which serve this institution. The shift from educational films to films-as-education thus works to transform the school into a 'socially responsible' multiplex in much the same manner as a strategy such as Channel One attempts to transform the same space into a benevolent 'TV room', redirecting the dangerous and/or wasteful energies of youth viewing practices into mechanisms for building productive, critical citizens.

Shopping for a self: the shopping mall and teen cinema

The third significant cinematic space for youth reflects a completion of the functions performed by the first two. If the home serves as the space of individuation and the school of socialisation, then the shopping mall works within contemporary films as the location of an integration within the world of consumption and also within a semi-public sphere. Unlike the school, the space is devoid both of an official, state-mandated purpose and of the obvious authority invested in the former sites in parents and teachers, respectively. The shopping mall serves as the space of possibility, both as an individual and as a consumer, as much as these two roles are separable in contemporary culture. Much as the home became an important site for viewing practices in the 1980s with the proliferation of VCR technology, the shopping mall enjoyed a slightly earlier rise as an important site for cinematic consumption. The decline of town centre cinema and the subsequent decline of drive-in cinemas in the 1960s and 1970s were accompanied by the explosion of multiplex cinemas, which were often built within or adjacent to shopping centres. The connection of cinematic spectatorship with other activities – shopping, eating and socialisation – critical to teenage life thus produces an integration of practices which had been at least partially separated. In this sense, the shopping mall, and later the freestanding multiplex which is normally attached to a strip mall, acts as a kind of 'drive-to' which replaces the earlier 'drive-in' as a critical site for both cinematic spectatorship and a wider array of youth practices. As 'drive-to' indicates, the automobile remains an important element in the access to cinema by youth – the shopping mall and the multiplex are rarely destinations that can be easily accessed on foot or even by public transportation, particularly in the suburbs. At the same time, they work to immobilise individuals by providing a compact array of practices that are important to youth.

It is interesting, then, that 'the mall' carries so many connotations of conformity and mindless consumerism which are at least partly at odds with its status as the space for the realisation of a kind of personal freedom and mobility. The former quality is nicely illustrated by the presentation of the shopping mall in George A. Romero's *Dawn of the Dead* (1979), a film which was a popular midnight feature – and thus youth attraction – but which pre-dates the 1980s 'golden age' of teen films. In the film, the shopping mall becomes the refuge for a group of surviving humans fleeing from flesh-eating zombies and outlaw bikers – not unlike the school-based scenario of the aforementioned *The Faculty*. The film makes numerous mocking references to the shopping mall; we are told, for example, that the zombies have headed to the mall out of instinctive response, as it was 'an important place in their lives'. This is compounded by numerous visual gags that feature the living dead riding escalators and staring vacantly into shop windows. Here the shopping mall is the space of pure social entropy, the logical destination for those operating without a brain.

In Kevin Smith's *Mall Rats* (1995), an affectionately mocking pastiche of 1980s youth films, the shopping mall is similarly lampooned as the space of mindlessness, with characters dazedly wandering through the film with little purpose other than aimless amusement and thoughtless consumption. They are only marginally more alive than *Dawn of the Dead*'s zombies, and the titular 'rats' refers at least partly to the Skinnerian reflexivity of their wanders through the mall. A milder version of this critique of the shopping mall appears in Martha Coolidge's *Valley Girl* (1983), in which the Sherman Oaks Galleria in the San Fernando Valley near Los Angeles stands as an emblem of the phony, snobbish culture of upper middle-class suburbia against the punk rock authenticity of Hollywood, personified in the film by the archetypal sensitive rebel Randy, played by a young Nicolas Cage. The use of rock and especially New Wave music in the film can usefully be contrasted with the mall muzak which is used for comic effect in *Dawn of the Dead*; in that film, the soundtrack points to the distance of the shopping mall from the energy of youth culture, while in *Valley Girl* a similar point is made through the situation of rock within the anti-mall of Hollywood. Here, a neo-liberal critique of consumption and conformity provides, like the dysfunctional home and mind-controlling school, a kind of worst-case version of a popular youth cultural site, an understanding which lurks behind the sunnier depiction of mall culture in other films.

The presentation of the shopping mall and its place in youth culture in more conventional films is a bit more complex than Romero's witty but ultimately banal countercultural parody or the less vituperative but still critical views of Smith and Coolidge. For example, in *Fast Times at Ridgemont High*, the same Sherman Oaks Galleria serves as a space for the operation of a social world that, while still rife with aimless consumerism, is also the venue for the cultivation of independent practices and the exploration of an approaching adulthood. Several major characters work in the shopping mall at such typical teenage workplaces as fast food outlets and movie theatres, and much of the courtship and romance in the film occurs in the same space, with protagonist Stacy dating both an 'audio consultant' from the stereo store and Mark (Brian Backer), the heroically mild-mannered movie theatre usher. The mall is also the site of both official and illicit commerce, as it serves as a retail location for the ticket-scalping lowlife Damone (Robert Romanus). In *Fast Times at Ridgemont High*, then, the shopping mall provides a counterspace to the school and the home, the most autonomous and most complex locale for teenage life, and a critical one in the development of an identity and the preparation for participation in the adult world of working, shopping and sex. Here, the linkage of critical youth practices achieves a peculiar reflexivity in a film which itself acts as a ritual for mall visitors – viewing the film itself – and in its status as a model of youthful behaviour.

In *Clueless*, the shopping mall assumes a more explicitly positive function, albeit comically, serving as the space of possibility for the realisation of a personal identity and as a place to 'gather my thoughts and gain strength', as Cher ironically explains before a shopping trip. The film itself is largely a fantasy about consumption, with frequent references to shopping and allusions to the feminine quality of the activity; it is taken as evidence of his homosexuality that Christian (Justin Walker), one of Cher's potential boyfriends, enjoys shopping. Similarly, the selection of sexual partners is equated with shopping when Cher explains that she is waiting for the right person to lose her virginity to by telling Tai, 'You know how picky I am about shoes and I only put my feet in them.' Here, shopping assumes an almost mythical status, standing for an entire range of human pursuits. Of course, with the re-situation of the cinemas into the mall, the multiple-screen venue became a standard arrangement, so the choice of a film itself became an act of shopping – both integrated into the mall physically and thus epistemologically, as an act of consumer choice. No longer is the mall simply a physical site that is central to teenage lives as the space of socialisation, shopping (as a paradigmatic and identity-determining practice) and spectatorship, but it is also the metaphorical location for the assumption of a mature lifestyle. In this sense, the shopping mall reflects a shift from the earlier town centre cinemas and drive-ins, as it reflects a recognition that shopping – for meals in the food court, for films in the multiplex, for a 'lifestyle' and an identity in the larger space of the mall – is an absolutely critical task in human development. Liberty no longer stands in opposition to consumption, as in both Romero's critique and a wider progressive (and, by the 1980s, apparently obsolete) notion of civil society, but becomes bound up with a variety of practices all united around the organising structure of shopping.

'Where do you think you are?': the city as unmappable

If the home, school and shopping mall serve as critical territory for youth and contemporary teen cinema, 'the city' serves as a kind of radical 'other' to these spaces, which are often experienced as explicitly suburban. The city is the site of both liberation from the binding norms of suburban order and a real threat to the comfort and safety provided by the same; in this sense, then, the treatment of the city mirrors the afore-mentioned ambivalence regarding the more conventional suburban milieu of cinema teens. It is variously rhapsodised and demonised, but in both cases the city offers a con-trast to the social order epitomised by the world of the bourgeois home, the cliquish school and the sanitised shopping mall. Particularly important is the fact that, unlike the subur-ban spaces noted above, the city seems to exist as a kind of unmappable space, one which is truly 'other' in that it cannot easily be placed within the normal grid of teen cinema.

The romantic view of the city is evident, as noted, in *Valley Girl*, where its gutsy authenticity stands in stark contrast to the phony world of the Valley; this is referenced most notably in a long sequence in which the major characters – a mix of Valley dwellers and urbanites – cruise down the Sunset Strip at night, encountering a world that is por-trayed as far livelier than the boring, homogeneous vision of the Valley earlier in the film. In *Ferris Bueller's Day Off* it becomes the site of a flight from the mundane. Interestingly, the Chicago that Ferris and his friends visit is a version of the city one would associate with tourists rather than locals: the Art Institute, a Chicago Cubs game, a downtown parade and an expensive restaurant are the major stops on the surburbanites' unofficial field trip. Here, the vision is less one of untamed street life and authentic culture than one of unfettered recreation, of the city as playground for the affluent.[6] The map of city life offered by the latter film is essentially a suburban version, with the city charted as a set of pleasure destinations for visitors.

Chicago appears again in *Adventures in Babysitting* (1987), another John Hughes pro-duction (this one directed by Chris Columbus), but in this film it is the site of a perilous encounter with the criminal world. In the film, suburban babysitter Chris (Elisabeth

Shue) must drive into the city with two children she is supervising to rescue a friend who is stranded at the bus station, a location portrayed as a home for degenerates and the mentally ill; as a vagrant tells Chris's friend, 'You're in my home.' On the way, the car breaks down and this event begins an ordeal that involves Chris and the children witnessing a crime and subsequently being pursued by criminals and journeying through a variety of rough neighbourhoods, including a brief encounter with a teenage prostitute. In a particularly telling sequence, Chris must sing 'the blues' to an entirely black audience at a nightclub (once again, music serves as a badge of urban cultural authenticity); she whips the crowd into a frenzy and is thus able to escape her pursuers. Here the film utilises a particularly crude caricature of African-American 'soulfulness' as an emblem of a world alien to the white suburbanite protagonist. When they ask to be dropped at a shopping mall, a helpful and streetwise African-American who has given them a ride jokingly responds, 'A mall ... Where do you think we are?' elucidating both the distance of this urban environment from the suburbs and the utter lack of comprehension of this environment by the visitors. Here the city is presented as cartographically incomprehensible to the teenage protagonists – its spaces cannot be understood within the set of co-ordinates offered by the suburban life.

Judgment Night (1993) uses a similar premise, though in this case it structures an action film rather than a comedy. The protagonists are four young men, not explicitly posited as suburban, but clearly alien to the city, who become lost attempting a short cut to a sporting event and end up witnessing a crime and being chased through a nightmarish urban wasteland. The major characters are initially portrayed as arrogantly macho, but they are quickly rendered helpless by the dark streets and ruthless gang members they must face. As the title suggests, the urban space becomes a kind of proving ground for even the toughest interloper, a theme supported through the noirish cinematography and particularly intense hip-hop and heavy metal soundtrack. The sense of the urban space, and especially 'the ghetto', as a kind of hell – this is 'judgment night', after all – thus provides a nearly precise opposite to the sunnier (literally) vista provided by *Ferris Bueller's Day Off*. Whereas the latter places the urban space within a framework of suburban leisure, *Judgment Night* offers an impressionistic but ultimately uncharitable urban space, one which can never be mastered, but only fled.

Both poles of the imaginary urban continuum are evident in *Risky Business*, a film in which the city, once again Chicago, serves as a space of both liberation and menace. There is a chase sequence involving 'Guido the killer pimp' (Joe Pantoliano), who serves as the film's emblem of the urban criminal class, one quite similar to the chases in both *Adventures in Babysitting* and *Judgment Night*. However, the city also becomes the site of Joel's sexual awakening and his first real steps away from the comforts and limits of his suburban life, epitomised in the film's most memorable visual passage, in which Joel and Lana (Rebecca DeMornay) make love on an elevated train, an event presented in a luminous slow-motion sequence. The equation to sexuality with both mobility and urban space is important here, as it concretises the link between forms of adult knowledge and movement into a new territory, a theme which appears across a number of films and which is a critical part of the way that youth becomes conceived as a set of meaningful spaces in these films. There is a kind of symptomatic switch here from the sexual awakening in the back seat of an automobile – which, by the 1980s, was rather clichéd – to carnal knowledge in public transport, a more forbidden and mysterious (and even frightening) space to the suburbanite.

'Dude, where's my car?': the persistence of automobilia

The automobile is perhaps the most important element in the attention to mobility in recent films, though the car, of course, has a long history as a potent symbol in films about youth. This is continued in recent films, with the car serving as an emblem of the kind of freedom and escape which is at the thematic centre of a number of films, including several mentioned above. What is particularly important, though, is the way driving emerges as a particular form of knowledge, as a technology for self-development and for the cultivation of appropriate adult practices. In *Ferris Bueller* and *Risky Business*, as well as films such as *Moving Violations* (1985) and the Corey Feldman/Corey Haim comedy *License to Drive* (1988) which take driving as the major narrative focus, mastering the automobile serves as a mode of escape and an initial step towards adulthood. In the former two films, the action centres upon the use of a forbidden vehicle, in both cases the father's luxury sports car. In the latter two, the focus is on the legal impediments – the attainment and maintenance of a license – that limit the ability to drive, although *License to Drive* also includes a plotline involving the illicit borrowing of a grandparent's car. In addition to the linkage of the automobile with freedom and the adult world, driving is more directly construed as a form of knowledge in a number of films, including the aforementioned *Clueless* and *Valley Girl*. In the former, there is considerable attention to Cher's quest to attain a driver's licence (she already has her own car), which is posed quite directly, along with shopping and sex, as a fundamental pursuit for teenagers, and, like the others, it requires a body of crucial knowledge. This is reinforced in a scene in which Dionne (Stacey Dash), Cher's best friend, accidentally enters the freeway while learning to drive and nearly crashes the car in her frantic and hapless inability to cope with the overwhelming, menacing traffic. Her feminine hysteria is presented as comic evidence of the premature nature of her attempt to master this skill and explore a mobility that she is not equipped to negotiate. Likewise, in *Valley Girl*, there is an early scene involving a disastrous driving lesson, which provides an effective contrast with the latter, aforementioned scenes involving a cruise through Hollywood. In this film, driving is positioned as a mechanism of escape from the Valley and the inability to drive, embodied in the pompous, mewling figure of the driving instructor, as yet another restriction imposed by the adult world on the movement of teenagers.

The destruction of a parental automobile, like the destruction of the family home noted above, becomes the specific focus of critical scenes in three popular films – *Road Trip* (2000), *Risky Business* and *Ferris Bueller's Day Off*. In *Ferris Bueller*, Cameron attacks his father's beloved Ferrari and accidentally pushes it out the window of his museum-like garage and into an adjacent gorge, while in *Risky Business*, Joel's farther's Porsche rolls into Lake Michigan during a trip into downtown Chicago with Lana. In *Road Trip*, a car supplied by the bullying father of Kyle (D. J. Qualls), a socially and sexually inept nerd, is destroyed in a freak accident on the titular journey. In all three scenes, the destruction works symbolically as both a renunciation of parental authority – in each case the vehicle is borrowed or used illicitly – and a simultaneous marking of adulthood, of independence from the social and material resources of the parents. The surrounding events are telling in this regard, as the destruction scenes are correlated with other assertions of autonomy and maturity. The destruction of the Goodson Porsche in *Risky Business* leads to Joel's business partnership and his 'sharp lessons in enterprise capitalism', as Bernstein and Pratt put it, which signal his mastery of crucial adult skills.[7] Cameron's destructive rage follows a psychological epiphany in which he realises the emptiness of his life and of his parent's loveless marriage. In *Road Trip*, the car is destroyed in a journey that also includes Kyle's comic sexual initiation and a final confrontation with his father in which he is finally able to demand paternal respect. The achievement of a personal mobility separated from the equipment provided by the father becomes the centrepiece of the articulation of a broader and timeless theme of the teenager's 'coming of age'. Technologies supplied by the adult (and especially parental) world are useful in the initiation of practices of self-development, but become barriers in the longer term and are then renounced. Mobility is ultimately a matter of self-discipline and self-realisation, one that cannot be achieved if one is still tied to the home – with the automobile serving as a kind of extension (given its tight restriction) of the stifling suburban home.

Self-discipline and the 'ethnographic' voice

While the automobile and the sense of maturity as an issue of an increased and independent personal movement is an important aspect of the way in which space is a crucial theme in recent cinema, this issue is also reflected in what might be described as the 'ethnographic' mode of some recent films. Here, the linkage between particular spaces and forms of knowledge critical to the world of teenagers is thematised through the use of a protagonist who is initially exterior to this world and thus must cultivate a better understanding of the territory. Of course, in a general sense, this theme is present in the wide range of films which take the outsider or 'new kid' as their focus; for example, films as diverse as *My Bodyguard* (1980), *Footloose* (1984), *Tuff Turf* (1985) and *Billy Madison* (1994) reflect a variation on this strategy, ranging from the struggles of city boy Ren (Kevin Bacon) in a conservative small-town high school in *Footloose* to the comic tribulations of *Billy Madison*'s obnoxious title figure, played by teen favourite Adam Sandler, who must return to school to secure his inheritance.

However, in *Hiding out* (1987) and *Never Been Kissed*, the struggle to adapt is foregrounded through the use of characters who are completely removed, initially, from the milieu of youth. The plot of *Hiding Out* involves a young stockbroker-turned-informant, Andrew (Jon Cryer), who hides from the Mafia by posing as a high school student, while *Never Been Kissed* involves a novice newspaper reporter, Josie (Drew Barrymore), who returns to high school to write an exposé of contemporary teenage life. Interestingly, the latter is essentially a fictionalised version of the real story behind the creation of *Fast Times at Ridgemont High*, which was based on a book by *Rolling Stone* writer (and future film director) Cameron Crowe in which Crowe, in his early twenties at the time, enrolled in a California high school. Here, practices of creative production – posing as a teenager to uncover the specific knowledge associated with their world in order to create a more compelling creative work – become the subject of a film which in turn works as a form of knowledge for teen viewers.

The world of high school, as construed in both films, is remarkably similar, with a focus on the routine humiliations of everyday teenage life, the social stratification into distinct and heavily marked cliques, and the gradual mastery of a complex set of codes regarding social and sexual conduct. The twist here is that this knowledge and the practices it engenders are explicitly thematised through the use of a figure from the 'outside world' (as a teenager describes Andrew in *Hiding Out*) and, in the case of *Never Been Kissed*, one specifically charged with uncovering the mores of youth for an uncomprehending adult world. The alien quality of the protagonists of both films is established through the depiction of an initial situation that is drastically removed from their subsequent re-immersion in high school. Both live in urban environments – Boston and Chicago – and work in professional jobs before returning to non-urban schools. This distance is registered culturally as well: *Hiding Out*'s Andrew is portrayed as a prototypical yuppie who drives a Ferrari, drinks scotch and chain smokes, while *Never Been Kissed*'s Josie is a mild-mannered frump who lives alone with her cats – fantasy and nightmare visions of adulthood, respectively. As the narratives of both films develop, though, these characters achieve a remarkable degree of success in their new surroundings; Andrew (who has assumed the pseudonym 'Max Hauser') is elected class president and Josie becomes a member of the school's most exclusive clique, overcoming her actual high school past as 'Josie Grossy', the quintessential geek. This success, both films reveal, is the result of a careful mastery of the critical knowledge associated with youth culture: navigating the social structure of the high school, appropriate taste in music, clothing and cars, and dealing with adult authorities – 'Max' wins the respect of his classmates by standing up to a bullying right-wing history teacher while Josie falls in love with and ultimately seduces her hip English teacher. In the end, both characters return to the adult world with a new sense of the often brutal character of the adolescent world, particularly in terms of its social pecking order, and, in the case of *Never Been Kissed*, with the knowledge that had been lacking in an initial adolescence.

These 'ethnographic' films, along with the broader subgenre of 'new kid' films, thus provide a particularly intense version of the larger representation of critical spaces and technologies of youth. By de-familiarising this territory through the deployment of the outsider as narrative protagonist, the films present these spaces – across both films, there are representations of the home, the shopping mall and the school – as requiring the cultivation of a very specific knowledge and, consequently, developing appropriate modes of conduct. In this sense, they also flatter the teenage audience by representing the autonomy of their milieu and providing a sense of distinction and separation from the adult world. The eventual triumph of both protagonists is a result of their instruction by savvy 'native informants', a process which reverses the standard model of knowledge – and especially 'life lessons' – by placing the adult in the position of the student. Mobility in this case becomes a question of reacquaintance with the teenage culture rather than a gradual mastery of 'adult' space, thus acknowledging a specificity to this 'moral universe' that is critical to the status of teen cinema as a genre in the spatial materialist as well as formalist sense.

The ethnographic mode would thus seem an appropriate place to end this discussion of 1980s and 1990s cinema, as it poses, cinematically, the heart of a broader generic issue: the ways in which the critical sites associated with youth – and the ability to move between these sites – serve as mechanisms for developing forms of conduct for youth. In this regard, such films might be understood as a relocation of the 'educational film' from the classroom to the cinema, a move that complements the importation, endorsed by Foster, of the Hollywood film into the classroom. Traversing the home, the school and the shopping mall – the cinematic premises of youth in recent years both diegetically and in terms of spectatorship – the new teen subject faces a set of directives regarding proper conduct which produce a rather different map of the adolescent world.

In historical terms, one might consider the new map of teen cinema as illustrative of a shift from an unstable relationship with mass culture, evident in the awkward attempts to use jazz records and other popular cultural forms for educational purposes in films such as *Blackboard Jungle* (1955), to an acceptance of the mass culture-saturated character of social life. In more recent films, and in the broader array of practices which constitute 'teen cinema', there is a post-liberal acceptance of the absolute primacy of the commodity system and that practices of self-development and self-discipline cannot be separated from this logic. Second, the path from the home to the school to the shopping mall traces a gradually diffused system of discipline, from the stark binary of home as stifling but comfortable to the more fluid implications of the mall space. The increasing distance from direct forms of authority – although these are present in the enforced entropy of the mall, particularly as construed in the zombie/rat model of mall action – suggests a move towards a kind of self-governing subject in the new understanding of teen cinema. No longer is the struggle simply to contain youth practices – though this remains, particularly in its more hysterical manifestations (for example, the fears over a teenage nihilism springing from a corrupt popular culture) – but also to evade this need through an appropriately self-disciplined teen.

An afterthought about fun: placing cinema and youth within new regimes of mobility

In *Back to the Future* (1985), the path to engineering the accomplished, self-confident and fully realised family occurs through time travel, in a modified Delorean, back to the 1950s and literally to the threshold of mass suburbanisation. If 'home' is a place that can only be realised by going somewhere else, then cinema becomes an important site in the 1980s for fashioning a relationship between baby boomers and their children, for *re*-embodying youth; being so hyper-mobile (notwithstanding the technical glitches that the film ascribes to time–space compression) requires new portable accoutrements, such as the protagonist's Walkman and camcorder, as well as new lessons about youth at the steering wheel of retrofitted cultural technologies such as the car, school, home, prom and rock music. As an ethnographic narrative, *Back to the Future*'s young protagonist is considerably more mature, sober and responsible than the 1950s youth that he encounters (or than the adults, introduced at the film's beginning, which the 1950s seems to have produced).[8] The pre-suburban California town to which the film's young protagonist returns – a model of life around a town square that in 1984 was just a gleam in the eyes of the architects of Disney's Celebration – is constructed of chronotypes from 1950s TV and the classroom film. Quite literally, the passage between the past and the present is through the strip mall parking lot and the movie theatre, whose place in a post-suburban arrangement is marked by the passage from a pristine marquee advertising a 1950s Reagan film to a dilapidated marquee advertising a contemporary porn film – the ultimate *degradation* of the town centre movie theatre in an era of the Meese Commission report and other neo-conservative panics about youth's access to 'adult' material from the home. In this respect, the film is a gesture towards securing a future, post-suburban environment wherein social authority derives more from embodiments of youth as a category of advanced temporal-spatial mobility than from the disciplinary enclosures such as the school, the theatre or the house. Furthermore, the mobility requires and produces active, *entrepreneurial* (self-actualising and self-governing) youth, embodied both by the protagonist (Michael J. Fox, who for years had played the hyper-earnest neo-conservative Alex on TV's *Family Ties*) and by the 'youthful' parents cum entrepreneurs that his time travel produces. If self-realisation is a key to and an effect of self-discipline for advanced (or neo-) liberal governance, then societies committed to governing that way require technologies (in this case fashioned out of cinema) that represent the relation of youth to its own advanced/mature freedoms – beyond home, school and earlier sites of self-realisation.

Our account has attempted to underscore that genre and youth are neither entirely fixed nor entirely free social bodies and categories, but rather that, as bodies/categories, they have become attached to particular places through regimes of mobility – that their freedom and governance occurs through, indeed depends upon, their attachments to these places and through a society's ways of regulating mobility. We have discussed cinema and youth (and their intersection) in this way so as to counter the notion, particularly common in film criticism, that they are merely or primarily ideological constructions. Films and youth circulate individually and as aggregations, but the freedom of their circulation (their mobility) has been governed through their relation to places that have been deemed and made acceptable, receptive and useful for their separate objectives. The domestic sphere, the school and the theatre/shopping mall have all been sites that have been made appropriate for youth and cinema as spaces where the potential unruliness of youth could be managed. Yet the potential desires and unruliness of youth, as individuals and social aggregations, has also been a matter of youth's mobility among these places and its claim upon these places. The question that we have attempted to address, therefore, is less 'Where has youth gone to escape adult supervision?', than 'How are the pleasures and desires of youth a matter of their relative mobility across social spaces and of their relative access/attachments to particular places, and second, how are their access and attachment to particular places a matter of their freedom *and* governance?' Governing the pleasures of youth at school or at home is different than at the theatre or the mall, or in the car, but only in that these latter sites involve different mechanisms for governing youth through their freedom. We thus would agree with Grossberg that youth have constructed their own places in the space of transition between institutions of domesticity, schooling and consumption – in the space that 'the dominant society assumed to be no place at all – merely a transition'. We would add, however, that this space of mobility and the locations of congregating and of fun, such as the theatre/shopping mall, have been places where youth are always subject to being governed *in their freedom*, in their mobility.

To link the governance of youth, as social bodies, to their relative social mobility (i.e. their mobility across social spaces) and to their attachment to particular places also entails recognising that these sites relied upon one another and that their interdependence was not fixed. During the 1950s, the theatre mattered to youth as a site for fun precisely in youth, film and the theatre's relation to home and school. The theatre also was made available as a site for fun as part of a socio-spatial *arrangement* – a social distribution and contract about places for fun. The theatre, as a place where cinema and youth intersected, was subject to an *established* set of expectations about theatres and an *emerging* set of uses that involved the mobility of youth. As such, its relevance to youth and to cinema became part of a broad socio-spatial *re*arrangement and a new regime of mobility that were shaping the circulation of youth and cinema. We emphasise this point in part to counter the tendency in genre criticism to explain social change through the conventions, negotiations and counterconventions of film narrative as 'cultural logics'. We do so also to emphasise (after Henri Lefebvre) that societies are organised spatially, that 'the production of social space' refers to instantiations that are both representational and material, and that social space, in these terms, is a condition for social transformation, for making history. While we thus would agree with genre criticism that genres are regulatory mechanisms (that they have a capacity to regulate in their regularity), we are decidedly more interested in their capacity to regulate the access and mobility of cinema and youth to places and to regulate (through) the production of social space. In this sense, the suburban mall and multiplex cinema developed out of a social arrangement that instrumentalised the school, home and indoor/outdoor theatre in their relation to one another. The cinematic, the value of which within this arrangement was predicated upon its dispersal across these sites during the 1950s was thus semantically and spatially redefined in the 1980s through these sites and through their changing relation to one another. Although our account of this development is partial and selective (emphasising the trends in white, middle-class enclaves), a more elaborated and micrological analysis would consider particular zones where emerging and residual formations of the movie theatre were redefining the spatial distribution/paths of classes of youth, for example, the showing of blaxploitation and martial arts films at downtown movie theatres in Austin, Texas, that drew together – briefly during the 1970s – African-American youth from the city's east side and white students from the nearby university.[9]

The changing place of cinema is not merely an ontological issue – what *is* cinema any longer in the age of DVD and video streaming? – but also a matter of regulating the conduct of social bodies (such as youth) at particular places and *in* their relative mobility. In this respect, the question of how youth is embodied and mobilised is deeply a question of where youth is located through technologies of embodiment and mobilisation such as movie theatres, the household or the school. In that respect, the relation of youth to particular sites that has occurred since the 1950s panics and responses to films such as *Blackboard Jungle* needs to be seen as interdependent with changing modalities of progressive education and liberal governance in a nation so committed to articulating freedom and youth and to governing youth through their 'immaturity', through the paths made available for becoming fully responsible citizens, social bodies and revellers.

Notes

1. Matthew Bernstein and David Pratt, 'Comic Ambivalence in *Risky Business*', *Film Criticism*, vol. 9, no. 3 (1985), p. 35.
2. See Jon Katz, *Virtuous Reality* (New York: Random House, 1997), p. 174.
3. Interestingly, the much earlier *Pretty in Pink* (1986) had featured a much more innocent variation on the use of information technology in a gentle computer-mediated seduction scene in a school library.
4. Harold Foster, 'Film in the Classroom: Coping with "Teenpics"', *English Journal*, vol. 76 (March 1987), p. 87.
5. Ibid., p. 88.
6. Interestingly, the release of *Ferris Bueller's Day Off* roughly coincides with the attempt in Chicago to create a kind of 'urban mall' in the city's downtown and Michigan Avenue districts, thus effectively suburbanising the urban space.
7. Bernstein and Pratt, 'Comic Ambivalence in *Risky Business*', p. 35.
8. *Back to the Future* is one of several films, including *Forrest Gump* (1994) and *Pleasantville* (1998), wherein passages back to the 1950s frame narratives about the enlightenment of youth from the 1980s and 1990s.
9. Based on Hay's experience at that theatre. See also Dan Streible, 'The Harlem Theater: Black Film Exhibition in Austin, Texas, 1920–1973', in Manthia Diawara (ed.), *Black American Cinema: Aesthetics and Spectatorship* (New York: Routledge, 1993).

16

Ghetto Reelness: Hollywood Film Production, Black Popular Culture and the Ghetto Action Film Cycle

S. Craig Watkins

Introduction

In 1996, New Line Cinema, a studio specialising in niche-themed films, released *Don't Be a Menace to South Central While Drinking Your Juice in the Hood*. In truth, the comedy was crude, dull and only marginally humorous. More a pastiche or parody than a story, *Don't Be a Menace* spoofed some of the more memorable scenes and lines from a group of movies – *Boyz N the Hood* (1991), *Juice* (1993), *Menace II Society* (1993), *South Central* (1993) – that provided the inspiration for its own title and narrative. Like most Hollywood parodies, the film signalled both the popularity and waning appeal of one the most intriguing film production trends of the 1990s, the ghetto action film cycle. More specifically, it suggested that the narrative strategies, conventions and formulae that made up the cycle had become predictable, worn and clichéd. Ironically, *Don't Be a Menace* simultaneously critiqued and complied with a cultural imagination and a production logic that had invested enormous resources – economic, marketing and emotional – in a flurry of popular culture products that made ghetto dislocation the defining experience of late twentieth-century black American life and a fountainhead of commercial cultural production.

Many of the films that critics and commentators variously referred to as ''hood narratives' and 'homeboy cinema' proved to be extremely competitive at the box office in the 1990s, generating enormous sums of money for major and independent film distributors. The breakthrough success of *New Jack City* (1991) and *Boyz N the Hood* fuelled an imitative cycle that eventually produced over twenty similarly packaged feature-length films between 1991 and 1996. The backstory to Matty Rich's film *Straight Out of Brooklyn* (1991) is especially revealing. Prior to making *Straight Out of Brooklyn*, Rich had no directorial or screenwriting experience. But as the wave of ghetto-themed narratives in music, film and video began to grow, the eighteen-year-old Rich saw film as a therapeutic exercise, an opportunity to deal creatively with the personal frustration and pain of growing up in the impoverished Red Hook housing projects in Brooklyn, New York. After a series of personal solicitations over a popular radio station in New York, Rich raised enough money to shoot the film. The success of the film at the Sundance

Film Festival generated enough publicity and notoriety to win a distributor, Samuel Goldwyn. Though alternative media such as music video and independent cinema were and are creating non-conventional routes to feature film-making opportunities, Rich's breakthrough remains eye-opening and illustrates the lengths to which some film distributors travelled in order to release ghetto-themed films.

The emergence of the ghetto action cycle illustrates the degree to which production trends in Hollywood are shaped by social and political as well as industrial and economic factors. In addition, a close examination of the cycle reveals how the racial hierarchies in Hollywood have not dissolved, but rather shifted and reformed. In the context of an industry that has historically excluded blacks from its production networks and practices, its ascendancy highlights, too, some of the changes that remapped the terrain of popular media culture in the 1990s. Though elements of the cycle continue to exist, the production of ghetto-themed narratives came to a virtual halt by the end of the decade due mainly to a backlash against the film industry and the young, creative community that was largely responsible for its rise.

Though specific factors facilitated the making of ghetto-themed films, the ghetto action cycle also reflected some of the general changes that have marked the production of Hollywood films specifically and popular media culture more generally since the 1970s. The first part of this essay examines the social and industrial contexts that drove Hollywood's interests in ghettocentric narratives. The repetitious production of ghetto-themed action films in the 1990s was a swift response by the commercial film industry to the perversely prominent rise of the post-industrial ghetto in the American popular and political imagination, a reconfigured popular culture economy and youth marketplace, and the commercial vitality of hip-hop culture in general and the popularisation of gangsta rap music specifically. The second part turns to the representational politics, narrative strategies and ideological worldviews that informed the cycle as the films themselves engaged with some of the most ideologically charged issues of late twentieth-century American life: ghetto dislocation, poverty, juvenile crime and racial inequality.

Made in America: the ghetto action cycle

Any serious contemplation as to why ghettocentric pictures became a popular trend in the 1990s should not limit itself to the internal operations and economics of Hollywood. The industry's sudden interest in and exploitative turn to films about ghetto life was a swift response to new market opportunities and popular appetites made possible by the currents of social change. The association of the term 'exploitation' with African-Americans conjures up ideas of unfair, even racist, treatment. In the case of film, for example, the expression 'blaxploitation' was added to our critical cultural vocabulary to refer to the wave of commercial films produced in the early to mid-1970s that targeted black urban moviegoers. My association of the term 'exploitation' with the 1990s film cycle, then, should be carefully delineated. Exploitation films are neither recent nor new to Hollywood. As far back as the early twentieth century, exploitation films have been immensely popular with moviegoers.[1] Over the years, exploitation films have come in many genre forms, appealed to different segments of the moviegoing population and capitalised on a mixture of topics and social trends. The ghetto action cycle is in this specific sense part of a tradition.

The evolution of the ghetto action cycle is consistent with the recent social and economic history of film production in the United States and is therefore not especially unique. It represented the film industry's efforts to manage, once again, shifts in the cultural and political landscape. It amassed much of its popular and commercial appeal as a result of two contradictory developments: the central position of the post-industrial ghetto in the US political imagination and the growing influence of black youth on the pop-culture landscape. Throughout the 1980s and 1990s, the symbolic efficacy of the ghetto developed sharp contradictions. For instance, public concern about crime, welfare and decaying moral values in the US invariably invoked the ghetto as a source of moral panic and political antagonism. At the same time, the language, fashions, commodities and cultural practices associated with ghetto youth achieved a high degree of cultural cache and influence on the larger popular culture scene.[2] It is within the context of this historically specific moment that the film cycle developed its most revealing and exploitative features.

The ghetto action film cycle was both timely and sensational. The cycle's most poignant, popular and problematic themes were shaped by the social and economic dislocations of poor inner-city youth. Its films were premised on a production strategy designed to serve an audience already titillated with and primed for action-oriented narratives about the deterioration of America's inner cities. The ideas that define 'authentic' urban ghetto life conform neatly with two elements that commonly arouse popular appetites: sex and violence. Young African-American men 'strapped' (armed with guns), 'gangbanging' (killing each other) and 'slingin'' (dealing drugs) became staple images in the ghetto film cycle. In addition, young 'unwed' (read immoral), 'welfare-dependent' African-American mothers were obligatory components in representations of life in the 'hood. The cycle's iconography, then, drew heavily from the nation's collective lexicon of common-sense ideas about black culture. The menacing spectre of ghetto youth culture became *the* exploitative hook that made the production of this particular film cycle timely, sensational and, oddly enough, more easily marketable.

In addition to the rise of ghetto imagery in American culture, the repetitious production of ghetto-themed action movies reflected the flexible priorities of Hollywood film production in the face of a changing popular culture landscape. The currents of social change that nourished the cycle also represented the industry's ongoing effort to remain relevant to young consumers and trendsetters. The film industry, like all popular culture industries, invests enormous resources in servicing specialised markets and young consumers in particular. The targeting of youth by Hollywood dates back to the mid-1950s, when, according to Thomas Doherty, Hollywood realised that youth could sustain impressive box-office revenue alone and to the exclusion of adults.[3] However, while youth audiences continue to occupy a crucial position in the industry's production logic, the process by which this translates into genres, trends and films is neither predictable nor static. The film industry is constantly modifying its production strategies and product offerings in order to remain popular with successive generations of youth.

In the 1990s, it would be the popular cultures of black American youth that the culture industries would seek to appropriate and profit from most. More specifically, the ghetto action film cycle was Hollywood's attempt to exploit the growing popularity of hip-hop culture. The evolution and vitality of hip-hop demonstrate, at one and the same time, the unpredictability of popular cultural formations and the ways in which they can generate change by enabling the formation of new identities and emergent regimes of cultural production. Rap music is the most prominent symbol of hip-hop culture. As with most emergent cultural trends, the major media companies did not immediately appreciate or understand its commercial potential. Thus the culture industry's response to the earliest signs of rap's commercial potential in 1979 was slow at best. By the mid-1980s, however, the crossover potential of rap had come to fruition.

Historically, black music genres that find a larger audience achieve greater commercial credibility and wider circulation because of the potentially lucrative sums of money white and middle-class patronage can generate. The growth and popular appeal of rap groups facilitated an important link between the sensibilities reconfiguring black youth expressive cultures and the larger popular culture scene. Moreover, in a media landscape driven increasingly by corporate media synergy, the rising popularity of rap performers gave powerful credence to the idea that hip-hop culture could be variously packaged and successfully marketed to white youth. The ability of rap to cross over into a broader sphere of youth consumption was crucial to its eventual absorption into other arenas of popular cultural production. Moreover, the incorporation of rap into mainstream commercial culture shaped and was shaped by the rapid commodification of black popular culture in general in the 1980s.[4] Whereas the media industries – television, film, advertising – once excluded blacks, the growing currency of black youth popular culture necessitated new production strategies and new commercial tactics. Hip-hop not only changed the terms in which black popular culture circulated, but also refigured the terrain of youth culture more generally.[5] This shift was especially evident in youth-oriented expressive cultures, commodities and media industries such as MTV, fashion, advertising and sports apparel.

The widespread appropriation of black youth expressive cultures in the late 1980s enhanced the cultural capital and power of black youth. More importantly, mainstream commodification broadened the market for the cultural forms, styles and practices of black youth by projecting them into the pleasure spaces – suburban homes, dorm rooms, dance clubs, cars – inhabited by white youth. As rap began to grow in popularity and develop a broader youth constituency, the vocabulary of the music also acquired additional accents, styles and narrative innovations. New York City had initially been the epicentre of rap music production. But by the late 1980s it had expanded to the West Coast. With the emergence in addition of hardcore or 'gangsta' rap, rap's landscape had dramatically changed.

Gansta rap evolved as a distinct style in the 1980s and is associated most closely with the California hip-hop community.[6] It was intimately related to the rhythms of post-industrial change that shaped the social and economic structure of segregated black working-class communities such as east Oakland and south-central Los Angeles. In the context of disintegrating black urban life, poverty, a burgeoning illegal drug economy and America's war on the poor, gangsta rappers purported to give voice to the alienation and rage experienced by many young, dislocated black males. During its early days, it thrived in the underground music cultures and entrepreneurial ghettos of poor and working-class black and Latino youth. As it began to surface from its underground roots in the late 1980s, it was at first considered too explicit and as a result not amenable to merchandising. However, gangsta eventually supplanted other rap subgenres – message, Afrocentric, pop – as the most commercially viable hip-hop product in the early 1990s, its breakthrough reflecting some of the changes under way in the repertoire of youth culture, style and rebellion.[7]

The popular music industry is especially volatile, primarily because its core audience consists of young teenagers whose tastes can and do often change. The film and music industries are especially sensitive to trend shifts in youth culture. The identification of many teenagers with the sensibilities of the hardcore style stimulated the creation of products designed to exploit this particular moment in the ongoing formation of youth culture. Gangsta rap sales grew rapidly and impressively, even though it was virtually excluded from radio airplay.[8] Despite the numerous barriers which confronted it, and much to the discontent of the larger society, gangsta rap successfully penetrated the mainstream music market and redefined how youth culture in general and black youth culture specifically would be packaged for global consumption. Much to the surprise of music industry analysts and music chainstore-managers (and probably even the producers of hardcore), the lofty sales of gangsta rap were driven mainly by white youth purchasing CDs and cassette tapes from suburban shopping centres.

It was, then, the successful merchandising of hardcore and the ensuing expansion of rap's consumer market that built the foundation for the rise of tie-in commodities and other cross-promotional uses.[9] Although the expansion of rap's appeal did not signal the erasure of the racial, class and gender boundaries that structure the youth marketplace, it did, nevertheless, produce significant shifts. In particular, young white males, a chief target of the major media industries, were emerging as major consumers of black popular cultural products. It was this reconfigured youth marketplace that the film industry inevitably noticed.

The ghetto action film cycle emerged as the film industry's swift response to a rapidly changing youth culture and marketplace. This response was not unprecedented to the extent that it was a direct attempt to appeal to the film industry's most stable market – young moviegoers – even if it was based on social currents that were clearly not of the industry's making. In this instance, the job of film industry executives was to select scripts that translated the popular appeal of hip-hop, and especially hardcore, into saleable film product. In a high-stakes industry faced with market uncertainty, escalating costs, a volatile youth demographic and intense competition, the production of ghetto-themed films was a low-risk venture. Industry executives embraced film projects that could be directly marketed to a cross-section of youth by appropriating the language, style and sensibilities of hip-hop culture, and especially the allure of hardcore.

The relationship between black popular music and black cinema has a long history, ranging from the highly staged studio musicals of the 1940s to the blaxploitation pictures of the early 1970s. The success of music soundtracks in the marketing of blaxploitation films had demonstrated how heavy radio airplay and album promotion could build and sustain a market for black-themed films. In the case of the ghetto action cycle, it was the heightened visibility of rap music throughout American culture that convinced industry executives that the synergy opportunities were essentially established and therefore more easily exploitable. The link between rap and the ghetto action film cycle was further strengthened by the rising influence of music videos in youth culture, consumption and identity formation. Starting with the success of *Flashdance* in 1983, the release of films targeting young moviegoers has been customarily accompanied by a music video promoting the soundtrack and film simultaneously. The expanding market for rap music and video influenced the texture and types of black-themed films produced in Hollywood. In fact, young film-makers such as the Hughes brothers used the shooting of music videos to hone their skills, build a body of work and acquire experience they could translate into feature film-making.

One additional factor drove the making of the ghetto action film cycle: low production costs. As the special effects, big-event star-vehicles continue to raise production and marketing costs in Hollywood, the industry has also turned to smaller scale, low-budget features.[10] Niche market films – black films, cult films, teen films – enable the industry to continue production output while also significantly curtailing costs. The average cost of the ghetto action film cycle's three most commercially successful films (*New Jack City*, $6 million; *Boyz N the Hood*, $6 million; and *Menace II Society,* $3 million) was $5 million, a figure well below average for Hollywood films in the 1990s. Furthermore, the average US domestic box-office receipts collected from these same three films, $44 million (*New Jack City*, $48 million; *Boyz N the Hood*, $56 million; and *Menace II Society*, $27 million), far exceeded what the film industry considered a successful return on investment.

The production of the 1990s ghetto action films followed a typical pattern in which the film studios enforced extremely low budgets, moderate to moderately wide distribution, and inexpensive marketing campaigns that relied heavily on rap music's appeal in radio airplay, soundtracks and music video.[11] This production formula indicated that while the industry was eager to appropriate the most popular elements of black popular culture it would do so in terms that prescribed extraordinarily low capital investments, thus making production relatively risk-free and even a limited theatrical run a money-making endeavour. At the same time, the emergence of the cycle marked a decisive change in the production, distribution and consumption of black popular culture. In an industry that operates on the basis of precedent, the box-office appeal of hip-hop-influenced films such as *House Party* (1990), *New Jack City* and *Boyz N the Hood* to young white moviegoers inspired a new ethos that placed the feature films of African-American film-makers on a decidedly different course. Black American cinema, in this context, could be packaged not only for black consumption and pleasure, but, more important, for white consumption and pleasure as well.

Boyz N the Hood (1991): 'homeboy cinema' breaks through

However, to comprehend the ghetto action film simply as a product rigidly governed by the commercial film industry, market trends and demographics is to simplify its significance. Though these factors were crucial, the cycle was also shaped by developments in black youth culture and politics. Its discourse engages in a vigorous way with an historically specific experience – the social and economic dislocation of black youth. Consequently the thematic ideas, cinematic techniques and stylistic conventions that define it as a form of African-American film-making possess complex ideological dimensions.

Hollywood film genres, cycles and the ghettocentric imagination

While studio executives saw the ghetto action cycle as an efficient means of exploiting the growing market for rap-related commodities and hip-hop celebrity culture, the vitality of ghetto-themed narratives was also driven by the inventive ways in which black youth turned to the sphere of popular culture to articulate their views and ideas about the social world in which they lived. It is within the context of an historically specific dialogue about race, youth and urban poverty that the cycle generates its most poignant and problematic discursive features.

Despite the presence of themes and images that seem to comply with popular notions of youth villainy, many of the films in the cycle mobilise complicated meanings about the lived experiences of youth in poor ghetto communities. Moreover, this particular film-making practice is structured by a historically specific *ghettocentric imagination*, that is, a loosely organised world view that cultivates varying ways of interpreting, representing and understanding the changing social, economic and political contours of ghetto dislocation. While the cinematic elaboration of this historically specific youth discourse gave rise to charges of excessive violence, misogyny and youth corruption, the ideological contours of the cycle were far more complex than many critics were willing or even able to acknowledge. Moreover, the films comprising the cycle not only circulated alongside each other, they circulated, too, alongside television programmes, news journalism, literature and even political discourses, each of which struggled to render post-industrial ghetto life and, as a result, racial inequality, juvenile delinquency and poverty more comprehensible.

The ghetto action film cycle therefore represents an extremely complex form of cultural discourse and is irreducible to uniform 'readings', generic or otherwise. In a cultural milieu marked by pastiche, ambiguity and boundary-crossing, genre lines are often blurred, disrupted and/or recombined, thus making 'genre' a difficult term to sustain analytically. The films within the ghetto action film cycle differed from one another in a number of ways and cut across a wide terrain of established Hollywood formulae and genres. Thus while *Menace II Society*, for instance, is a self-consciously styled gangster film, *Boyz N the Hood* is a classic coming-of-age tale.

Nevertheless a combination of film-related elements – setting, characters, themes and plots – and external factors – studio publicity, target audience, music and marketing – inevitably bound these films and their creators together. Nearly all the films in the cycle focus almost exclusively on the perilous relationship between young, disadvantaged black males and an economically impoverished and segregated ghetto landscape. More generally, the films wrestled with some of the most prominent issues – poverty, drugs, homicidal violence, idleness and alienation – associated with the changing state of poor youth and the communities they inhabited. Moreover, many of the film-makers who contributed to the cycle saw the films as a way to engage, if not reshape, popular debates about the lived experiences of ghetto youth.

Take, for example, Allen and Albert Hughes's *Menace II Society*, one of the more aesthetically and ideologically provocative entries in the cycle. The Hughes brothers immerse the spectator in the fictional world of young teenagers who rely on street crime to negotiate the hostile environment and circumstances of ghetto dislocation. Rather than romanticise youth criminality, however, the Hughes brothers aim to create a cinematic world that constructs a compelling framework for understanding why some poor teenagers turn to crime and violence. The film's representational strategies are profoundly political. Its most enduring thematic attribute is its relentless critique of a social and political system that continues to reproduce young 'menaces to society'. As a result, the film is an elaborately arranged set of characters, sequences and dialogue that attempts to think critically about black youth alienation.

The Hughes brothers, like many of the film-makers who contributed to the cycle, were quite literate in the techniques and history of cinema. They drew and expanded on a vast system of conventions, genres and stylistic choices. *Menace*'s aesthetic and representational forms are influenced by classical Hollywood and European art cinema, as well as by music video. Most crucially, though, the film is indebted to the continuing appeal of the gangster film. For much of its history, the urban gangster/crime film has exploited the perceived chaos of America's ethnically and racially diverse cities.[12] Despite the enduring presence of the gangster genre in

American popular film culture, its deployment must be understood in historically and culturally specific terms. As a genre, the gangster/crime film has been shaped by numerous factors: public fascination with real-life gangsters, censorship and techno-logical innovations in film production, especially sound.[13] Jack Shadoian argues, however, that the basic structure of the genre is 'ready made for certain kinds of con-cerns', particularly those that reflect the tensions between America as the land of opportunity and corporate hegemony. According to him, the gangster film is 'a way of gaining perspective on society by creating worlds and figures that are outside it'.[14] The setting and central characters in *Menace* are precisely constructed as worlds and fig-ures positioned outside the social mainstream.

Despite the persistence of strong genre markers, the vocabulary of the gangster film is often revised as different film-makers accent the genre in various ways. The critical and commercial success of *Menace II Society* clearly points to the durability of the genre and its ability to adapt to, engage with and remain relevant to the shifting contours of American social life. While the Hughes brothers rigorously studied the gangster films of Brian DePalma and Martin Scorsese, their particular elaboration of the genre subjects a historically specific societal conflict – the hyper-segregated status of ghetto communities and the impoverishment of black youth – to cinematic exploration.

Menace unabashedly participates in one of the nation's politically charged debates in the US during the 1980s and 1990s: the state of black American youth, ghetto poverty and criminality. The film's central characters animate the collective experiences of black youth who must live daily with the humiliation and alienation brought on by the trans-formations of post-industrial ghetto life. But whereas poor black youth are seldom, if ever, accorded a public voice, *Menace* seeks to privilege their point of view. A promi-nent feature of the ghettocentric imagination is its ability to foreground the views of black youth. In *Menace,* the Hughes brothers use voice-over, for example, to commu-nicate directly to the spectator the film's central character's thoughts on poverty, the surveillance of black youth and the lack of meaningful economic opportunities for the poor. Rather than exclusively address other characters in the film, this character, Caine (Tyrin Turner), also addresses the spectator and the various circuits of authority that shape popular definitions of youth dislocation. This is a strategy that clearly invites the spectator to make sense of ghetto poverty and youth delinquency from Caine's point of view.

Caine's disdainful disposition towards society and the ghettocentric world view in gen-eral are emblematic of the ways in which the lived experiences of black youth and their cultural practices have evolved. One of the recurrent ideological features of the ghetto-centric imagination is its critique of the practices and institutions that produce and reproduce poor black communities. In *Menace II Society*, the Hughes brothers' strategic rewrite of the gangster film genre suggests that black youth are growing increasingly hos-tile towards a society that essentially makes menial labour and a restricted opportunity structure a humiliating way of life. It is, then, precisely because access to the formal economy and meaningful employment is so limited that the underground sector, an anni-hilative alternative, strikes youth such as Caine as a viable option.

Caine's refusal to participate in the legal economy and comply with the arrangements of social subordination is complicated. The Hughes brothers' representation of youth dislocation brings to the arena of popular film entertainment a provocative discourse that animates the changing world and world views of poor black youth. Ultimately, Caine's refusal to 'slave' in the formal economy and his decision to 'hustle' in the informal economy hint that black youth are not necessarily against capitalism; rather they are against the subordinate positions and economic disadvantages to which capitalism restricts them. The creators of the film suggest that to the extent that capitalism is unable adequately to incorporate poor youth it will continue to produce young 'menaces to society'. Finally, and from this point of view, the audience is invited to contemplate the ways in which society and hyper-ghettoisation rather than pathology and deviance are implicated in youth criminality.

Reimagining and recoding the urban ghetto

By endowing black youth with a more public voice, the ghetto action film cycle forged open the space to produce a number of counter-ideological themes. One of the most persistent themes of these is the representation of poor black communities as sites of repression and entrapment. This motif suggests that the status differential between the black urban poor and more affluent social groups is reflected in certain types of spatial arrangements that sustain prevailing class and racial boundaries. This interpretation of space permeates the cinematic elaboration of the ghettocentric imagination and serves as one of the main circuits of ideological critique.

In the cinema, film-makers can employ both visual and auditory cues to imagine and construct notions of space. In *Boyz N the Hood*, director John Singleton explores the entrapment theme and the ways in which urban space structures the everyday milieux of ghetto life. Thus while *Boyz* takes shape along the lines of Hollywood's familiar 'coming-of-age' tale, Singleton uses this device to comment on the obstacles facing poor and working-class boys. The film explores how sports, the lack of meaningful employment and the illegal drug economy produce an acute sense of entrapment and anxiety about future prospects for social mobility.

The idea that the post-industrial ghetto suffocates the lives and opportunities of poor African-American youths also reverberates throughout Matty Rich's *Straight Out of Brooklyn*. This interpretation of space is evoked in almost every frame, shot and sequence. Unlike Singleton or Spike Lee, both graduates of prestigious film schools, Rich's screenwriting and directorial style are markedly rough and unpolished by Hollywood standards. But the apparently 'amateurish' look of the film complements Rich's intention to represent ghetto life as confining, imprisoning and grim. Rich encodes urban ghetto life as a condition of social, economic and physical imprisonment. The main characters in the film work in the most menial sectors of the service economy. The interior shots that situate life inside the housing project employ frames that are tight and enclosed. The proxemic patterns between characters also accentuate the idea that life in the projects is tenaciously confining. The narrative is a powerful coding of urban ghetto life and explores the combination of despair, humiliation, deprivation and anger that poor African-Americans must constantly negotiate.

Many of the films in the cycle depict the urban ghetto as a theatre for state-sanctioned coercion. The critique of post-industrial ghetto life is in this instance a direct reference to the surveillance operations that deploy coercive technologies against ghetto communities as a means of exercising greater social control. This theme is, of course, dialogically related to the 'law-and-order' discourses typically employed by elected officials and police forces as a means to discipline black youth perceived to be wildly terrorising the streets. Singleton, for example, incorporates this theme through the skilful use of offscreen sound. Auditory cues, like visual cues, can be instrumental in solidifying the spatial context in which narration takes place. As is the case with the arrangements of visual weights, the film-maker's selection of details in arranging acoustic materials, while generally less obvious, is an important element of film-making that creates a (sound) perspective that gives the film additional layers of meaning. In *Boyz N the Hood,* a dominant motif structuring the representation of space is the deployment of offscreen sounds associated with the coercive technologies of the state – police sirens, helicopters and other surveillance mechanisms. This use of offscreen sound complements Singleton's interpretation of the post-industrial ghetto by allowing him to manipulate sound perspective spatially. The constant intrusion of forceful and threatening sounds from police surveillance suggests that black communities are targets of military-style operations. Throughout the film, this use of space is accompanied by shots of blacks engaged in non-threatening acts, suggesting that entire black neighbourhoods are wrongfully criminalised.

A core narrative strategy in the ghetto action film cycle is the representation of the state coercive apparatus as an illegitimate means of social control that violates black bodies and communal life. The police are figured as hostile agents who routinely step outside the legal boundaries of law enforcement to assert control over black communities. An important imaginative function is executed in this discursive ploy: the state rather than black youth is criminalised. In the years immediately following the rise and fall of the ghetto action film cycle, corruption scandals involving the United States' largest police departments in Los Angeles and New York added weight to this critique and to the concerns it raised about race and the criminal justice system.

Gendering the ghetto action film cycle

Any discussion of the narrative strategies that shaped the ideological contours of the ghetto action film cycle must address the gender politics of the films. While there were some exceptions – *Poetic Justice* (1993) and *Not Just Another Girl on the IRT* (1994) – the films from the ghetto action film cycle privileged the experiences, narratives and voices of young black males. As a result, the collective body of films from the cycle, like the ghettocentric imagination more generally, obscured the experiences, narratives and voices of young black girls. Thus even as the creators of the ghetto action film cycle sought to mobilise counter-representations of urban ghetto life, they also produced intensely gendered narratives and representations.

The gendering of the cycle, to be sure, did not occur in a vacuum. Ghettocentric narratives were influenced by the larger shifts that transformed the production and consumption of black popular culture in the 1990s. Because the cycle was so heavily influenced by the growing commercial appeal and cultural politics of hip-hop culture, it was shaped by many of the gender fault-lines that structured the youth movement. Most notably, as the commercial prospects of black popular culture grew in unprecedented fashion throughout the 1990s, the most marketable, visible and popular forms also tended to assume and to celebrate the privileges of patriarchy.

In addition to matters of race and place then, gender, too, was a central theme around which these films were organised. Most of the films relegated female characters to secondary roles. Moreover, many of the narratives were premised on a set of values that positioned male authority and privilege as normal. Consistent with most of the films produced in Hollywood, the women who populated the filmic worlds of 1990s ghetto action pictures were restricted to familiar and extremely limited character roles: they tended either to play support roles to the male hero or to function as objects of heterosexual desire.

The hyper-masculinist tendencies of the cycle symbolised the degree to which the values and practices of male pleasure and the subjugation of women have come to occupy a decisive role in the most visible and commercial forms of black popular culture. Though young black women have always been central figurers in the formation of black popular culture, it is usually the styles, performances and productions of their male counterparts that receive the greatest rewards, notoriety and commercial sponsorship. At the same time, the political implications of the cycle were particularly stark for black women. Though ghettocentric narratives proposed to address the lived experiences of the black urban poor, in truth this particular discourse spoke primarily to the problems associated with the plight of alienated black males.

In many ways, then, the issues that were central to women living in poor ghetto communities were made marginal. Moreover, the representations of women in the ghetto action film cycle failed to challenge what feminist critic Patricia Hill Collins refers to as the 'controlling images' of black womanhood. Collins maintains that representational figures such as the mammy, welfare mother and jezebel reflect how the intersections of race, gender and class work to oppress black women.[15] Many of the 'controlling images' discussed by Collins populate the world of the ghetto action film cycle. Thus although black film-makers often positioned themselves as critical commentators, their representational politics and, more specifically, the ways in which they imagined black familial life and women reinforced popular ideas about the role of social pathology in the making of the black urban poor.

Conclusion: ghetto reelness

In spite of its overwhelming and obvious entertainment function in a vast popular culture marketplace, the ghetto action films were and are typically viewed by critics, the news media and filmgoers as an authentic portrayal of ghetto life. Indeed, one of the most fascinating developments of the cycle's reception is the notion that this group of popular movies represent official transcriptions of the lived experiences of poor black youth. African-Americans working on films in the cycle were and are typically viewed as documentarists capturing the grim realities of post-industrial ghetto life rather than professional film-makers who deploy the conventions of popular film.

This widespread view that African-American–directed feature films are more 'realistic' can in part be attributed to studio marketing strategies and news media reports that stressed the allegedly true-to-life qualities of the ghetto films. The films were often promoted by studios and defined by the news media as realistic rather than interpretive portrayals of urban ghetto life. Take, for example, New Line Cinema's promotional campaign for *Menace II Society*. After a successful initial box-office performance, the film studio developed a second promotional campaign that included the following tagline: 'This is the Truth. This is what's Real.' Throughout this period, black American film-makers became 'hot copy'. In fact, numerous national news media outlets began touting how the cycle's films portrayed the purportedly nihilistic lifestyles of black youth with candid precision. Both the print and television news devoted large amounts of space and time to the commercial film industry's revitalised interest in the film projects developed by African-Americans. One of the persistent themes that emerged from this coverage was that black films provided a unique look into black American life.

The common belief that African-Americans are *naturally* able to produce 'realistic' representations of ghetto life is informed by the peculiarities of an inherently flawed racial logic. Cultural critic bell hooks maintains that this viewpoint tends to ignore the class positionality of African-American film-makers and the peculiar whims of a cultural economy that derives immense pleasure from ghetto misery. Hooks urges critical analysis 'of a cultural marketplace wherein blackness is commodified in such a way that fictive accounts of underclass black life in whatever setting may be more lauded, more marketable, than other visions because mainstream conservative audiences desire these images'.[16] This assertion is noteworthy because it suggests that certain types of representations of blackness are more likely to be merchandised not because they are more authentic, but rather because they fit neatly with the prevailing common-sense characterisations of black life.

By the late 1990s, a wave of harsh and calculated criticism began to question the film industry's investment in the ghetto action film cycle. For many critics, the cycle represented the continuation of a media industry logic and a mode of production that simply exploited the vigour of the expressive culture of black youth. Although the cycle certainly illustrated the racial hierarchies that structure the culture industry, it was influenced by a complex set of factors. It was patterned, for example, by crucial shifts in the youth culture industry and the changing demeanour and commercial status of black youth popular culture. By the 1990s, for better or worse, the popular cultures of black American youth exercised an enormous amount of influence over the cultural representations of African-Americans. While the transformation of hip-hop culture into a multi-billion industry enlarged the creative and commercial terrains in which black youth could mobilise its own entrepreneurial ambitions and cultural productions, it also worked to obscure other forms of culture and representation in the African-American community. Ironically, then, the ghetto action film cycle represented what is so intriguing about the widespread popularisation and commodification of black youth expressive cultures. While forging open a space in an industry that historically has excluded black Americans, it also represented the formation of new barriers that still limit the scope and complexity of black American cultural production.

Notes

1. See the special issue of *Film History*, vol. 6, no. 3 (Autumn 1994).

2. Two of the most successful forms of commercial culture since the mid-1980s have both been associated with the urban ghetto: basketball and hip-hop culture. (See Todd Boyd, *Am I Black Enough for You?: Popular Culture from the 'Hood and Beyond* (Bloomington: Indiana University Press, 1997). In addition, both have developed global appeal. George Lipsitz, in *Dangerous Crossroads: Popular Music, Postmodernism, and the Poetics of Place* (New York: Verso, 1994), and Nina Cornyetz, in 'Fetishized Blackness: Hip Hop and Racial Desire in Contemporary Japan', *Social Text*, vol. 41 (Winter 1994), pp. 113–39, both discuss the global appeal of rap. Meanwhile, it should be noted that the selection of professional basketball players to represent the United States in Olympic competition has been in part a strategic response to the fact that basketball has now become so popular worldwide that many European countries are developing internationally competitive styles, skills and teams.

3. Thomas Doherty, *Teenagers and Teenpics: The Juvenilization of American Movies in the 1950s* (Boston: Unwin and Hyman, 1988).

4. See Herman Gray, *Watching Blackness: Television and the Struggle for 'Blackness'* (Minneapolis: University of Minnesota Press, 1995) for a discussion of the competing discourses and claims on blackness in the 1980s.

5. Tricia Rose, *Black Noise: Rap Music and Black Culture in Contemporary America* (Hanover: Wesleyan University Press, 1994).

6. For an excellent discussion of the history and evolution of the hardcore style in hip-hop, see Robin D. G. Kelley, *Race Rebels: Culture, Politics, and the Black Working Class* (New York: The Free Press, 1994). Kelley maintains that the gangsta style was part of the general hip-hop scene from its origins in the South Bronx in the mid-1970s. In fact, two of the earliest gangsta-style recordings were by Schooly D ('Smoke Some Kill'), a Philadelphia rapper, and the Bronx-based rapper KRS-1 and producer Scott La Rock ('Criminal Minded').

7. Rap music is a multi-layered expressive culture that combines a broad range of discourses. Nationalist rap groups such as Public Enemy tended to develop a performance aesthetic that focused much of its symbolic energies on reappropriating, for example, black nationalist traditions such as 'black power'. See Jeffrey Decker, 'The State of Rap', in Andrew Ross and Tricia Rose (eds), *Microphone Friends* (New York: Routledge, 1994), pp. 00. Michael Eric Dyson defines 'pop' rap as an 'exploration of common territory between races and classes, usually devoid of social messages', *Reflecting Black: African American Cultural Criticism* (Minneapolis: University of Minnesota Press, 1993), p. 8. Conversely, he defines hardcore rap as marked by social consciousness and racial pride.

8. Janice McAdams, 'Low "Priority": N.W.A.'s Chart Topping Album – Violence, Misogyny Mar Un-Eazy-E "Efil4zaggijn" ', *Billboard*, 26 July 1991, p. 23.

9. The creation of *Vibe* magazine is an example of a tie-in rap commodity. The creators of *Vibe* acknowledge that rap has given rise to the same kind of pervasive culture that rock 'n'roll did a generation ago. (See Deirdre Carmody, 'Hip Hop Dances to the Newstands', *New York Times*, 14 September 1992, pp. C6, D8.) The magazine is packaged in a similar way to *Rolling Stone* and targets eighteen-to 34-year-olds. Some 200,000 copies of the introductory issue were distributed in major metropolitan areas. The editor in chief admits that the

creators of *Vibe*, which was initially bankrolled by Time-Warner, anticipated a multi-ethnic readership.

10. Thomas Schatz, 'Show Me the Money: In Search of Hits, the Industry May Go Broke', *The Nation*, 5 April 1999, p. 00.

11. For details on production costs and earnings, see Craig S. Watkins, *Representing: Hip Hop Culture and the Production of Black American Cinema* (Chicago: University of Chicago Press, 1998), pp. 188–95.

12. Ibid., pp. 00.

13. Todd Boyd, in *Am I Black Enough For You?*, contends that films such as *Colors* (1987), *Warriors* (1986), *New Jack City* and *American Me* (1991) address the figure of the gangster in specifically racialised terms.

14. Jack Shadoian, *Dreams and Dead Ends: The American Gangster/Crime Film* (Cambridge, MA: MIT Press, 1977), p. 3.

15. Patricia Hill Collins, *Black Feminist Thought: Knowledge, Consciousness, and the Politics of Empowerment* (New York: Routledge, 1991), pp. 67–90.

16. bell hooks, *Outlaw Culture: Resisting Representations* (New York: Routledge, 1994), p. 152.

17

'Film Noir Like You've Never Seen': Jim Thompson Adaptations and Cycles of Neo-noir

Peter Stanfield

Three adaptations of Jim Thompson's 1950s pulp novels were given cinema releases during the 1990–91 season – *The Kill Off*, *After Dark, My Sweet* and *The Grifters* – while three others were reported to be in preproduction.[1] Not even Stephen King could match that kind of action.[2] The *Los Angeles Times* announced that Thompson was 'the hottest writer in Hollywood',[3] and beneath the headline 'Thompson Mania', *Variety* reported that Hollywood's 'obsession with nihilist novelist Jim Thompson is a classic case of publishing meeting showbiz "synergy"'.[4] Not that any of this had an effect on Thompson – he had died thirteen years earlier, with a virtually nonexistent public profile and none of his books in print in Britain or America. Yet such was the hype that, as film critic Richard Corliss noted, Thompson was 'suddenly in danger of becoming that most fashionable of renovation projects, the overrated underrated writer'.[5] How, then, did this forgotten writer of crime novels gain such critical and cinematic currency that most of his stories would be optioned by film-makers and he would eventually be proclaimed as a master of the genre alongside Hammett, Chandler and Cain?[6]

The trajectory that leads Thompson from obscurity to hyper-visibility can be traced through the journalistic and scholarly reception that accompanied the re-presentation of his oeuvre in the specialised book markets aimed at fans of hard-boiled pulp fiction. *Time*, *Newsweek*, *Vanity Fair*, *New York Review of Books*, *Film Comment*, *The New York Times Book Review*, *The New Republic*, *Rolling Stone*, *The Nation* and *American Film* all published reviews and articles on Thompson in the 1980s, and all showed a remarkable willingness to participate in his lionisation.[7] Thompson had garnered some limited support among the intelligentsia prior to his death. Critic and author Anthony Boucher regularly reviewed his novels for *The New York Review of Books*, and, as Thompson's biographer Robert Polito notes, he did so in terms that often 'anticipate the critical reclamation of his work'.[8] Before the 1980s, academic criticism was confined to an essay by R. V. Cassell in a collection on hard-boiled writers, but it, too, anticipated critics and scholars who were eager to develop the idea of Thompson as an 'American Original'.[9] If what the critics had to say about Thompson in the 1980s lacked originality, the depth and breadth of the coverage given to Thompson in this period was something altogether new.

More crucial to Thompson's critical exhumation, however, was the publication in 1981 of Geoffrey O'Brien's *Hardboiled America: The Lurid Years of Paperbacks*.[10] This study offered connoisseurs of noir the knowledge necessary to build a personal library that extended way beyond the then over-familiar figures of Hammett, Chandler and Cain. O'Brien's book not only acted as a guide to pulp fiction for fans of film noir, but also aided enterprising publishers in their bid to exploit this fan market. In a surprisingly short space of time, publishers, predominantly small independents, reissued many of the titles that had been critically validated by O'Brien. Works by previously obscure or all but forgotten authors such as W. R. Burnett, David Goodis, Horace McCoy, Cornell Woolrich, Charles Willeford and, most significantly, Jim Thompson were by 1983 readily available in bookstores on both sides of the Atlantic.[11]

Though he devotes fewer than 500 words to Thompson, O'Brien's description of his oeuvre had the effect of promoting him above and beyond all other pulp authors:

> Thompson could certainly not be accused of offering much by the way of public enlightenment. It is probably the persistent nastiness of his books that accounts for his status as Most Neglected Hardboiled Writer . . . Thompson's preferred subject is not the righteous bully but rather the cool, calm, and collected psychopath who is the most charming fellow in the world until he decides it would be appropriate to kill you.[12]

It was not, however, simply Thompson's 'persistent nastiness' that appealed to his new readers (*that* could be found in abundance elsewhere) so much as the view that his novels bridged the gap between lowbrow popular fiction and highbrow avant-garde literature. Reviewing *Savage Night* in the 1950s, Boucher wrote, 'Written with vigor and bite, but sheering off from realism into a peculiar surrealist ending of sheer Guignol horror. Odd that a mass-consumption paperback should contain the most experimental writing I've seen in a suspense novel of late.'[13] As Polito suggests, Thompson did not seek to transcend the hard-boiled tradition as an 'important writer might be expected to do'. Rather, he 'detonated the clichés' of the tradition he inherited, and this is partly why Thompson, rather than, say, the more formulaic Woolrich, became singled out by film-makers and critics. It was also because Thompson putatively managed at least one act of transcendence (albeit one empowered by critics writing in the 1980s and 1990s) and that was to move beyond the cultural and social context in which his novels were produced. Polito writes:

> The nods to hard-boiled conventions do not so much toughen Thompson's novels as humanize them – they're all we have to hang on to in the downdraft. Everything else is a wasted, sucking nihilism that's as unsparing as the most lacerating rock 'n' roll – the Velvet Underground's 'Sister Ray,' say, or the Sex Pistols' 'Bodies' – and as final as a snuff film.[14]

Polito's analogy with the Velvet Underground and the Sex Pistols is revealing because Thompson's fictions appealed primarily to a new hip readership weaned on the negationist rhetoric of punk.[15] Summed up in the following extract from an unfinished novel, Thompson foreshadows punk's rotten view on life:

'Things're not as they seem.'
'Nothing? Nothing is ever as it seems?'
'Only – hic! – only if it stinks. If it stinks then that's the way it is. Livin' proof of it . . .'[16]

According to the terms of the analogy between Thompson and punk, Woolrich, Goodis et al. seemed hopelessly tied to the past. Polito's location of Thompson within a popular negationist tradition connects the writer to those cultural movements that have (thus far) been exempted from critiques of commercial co-option. The artist operating outside capitalist imperatives is imbued with an aura of authenticity that is, as we shall see, crucial to the reception of the novels of Jim Thompson.

O'Brien concluded his short appraisal of Thompson by calling for an 'enterprising publisher . . . to resurrect some of his prolific output'.[17] In addition to the compendium of four of his novels published in the Black Box Thriller series by the British company Zomba Books (1983), from 1984 the US company Black Lizard/Creative Arts published another thirteen of Thompson's twenty-nine novels. Mystery Press (an independent publisher acquired by Time-Warner in 1989) added a further seven titles in 1988, including a new collection of short stories.[18] With the backing of Time-Warner, Mystery Press had the clout to ensure that Thompson's books received even wider and more penetrating distribution. From 1988, Corgi books gave his work an equivalent profile in Britain, publishing eight titles in all. Coinciding with the vogue for film adaptations of his novels, Vintage Books, a division of Random House, bought Black Lizard and the rights to Thompson's work in 1990. It would eventually republish most of his work.

This highly visible publishing activity precipitated Hollywood's cycle of Thompson adaptations and testifies to a more widespread reclamation by Hollywood of pulp writers for what it explicitly marketed as 'neo-noir' productions. Behind the simple neo-noir classification, however, lies a complex history of the consumption of pulp novels, the critical status of pulp writers and their relationship to discourses of film categorisation. The explicit conjunction of film noir and pulp fiction in the marketing and consumption of neo-noir forms the first part of this history.

The republication of Thompson's novels was part of a growing public recognition of film noir. In 1977, the year of his death, noir had been as obscure a film category as Thompson was a crime writer. The critical reception and validation of Thompson's novels runs parallel with, and is at times intimately linked to, the popularisation of film noir. Since the mid-1980s, Thompson has increasingly been used to represent a noir sensibility. In a typical review of *The Hot Spot* (1990), an adaptation of Charles Williams's 1950s pulp novel *Hell Hath No Fury* directed by Dennis Hopper, the film is described as a 'rock hard film noir . . . This is a sweaty, really dirty movie. There's a Jim Thompson pulp tinge to the script.'[19] In academic circles, the concept of noir is still open to debate and, as late as 2000, Steve Neale was arguing that as a 'single phenomenon, *noir* never existed' and as such is an incoherent critical object.[20] Yet, in the realm of the

popular, as the review of *The Hot Spot* suggests, there was something akin to a consensus on the meaning of noir and Thompson's relationship to that category in the early
1990s. To a degree, this was a kinship that had been formed by collectors of pulp fiction and film noir. The French film scholar Marc Vernet writes: 'As an object or corpus
of films, *film noir* does not belong to the history of cinema … *Film noir* is a *collector's
idea* that, for the moment, can only be found in books [my emphasis].'[21] The critical
and commercial association of Thompson and film noir developed out of a fan base
(which included scholars) whose acts of consumption were defined in large part by a
collector's sensibility – the apparently endless retrieval and cataloguing of film and book
titles. 'Who,' Vernet asks, 'has seen and studied all the films listed by Silver & Ward?'
in their encyclopaedia of film noir.[22] In *Somewhere in the Night*, Nicholas Christopher
answers in the affirmative and confirms Vernet's observation that 'there is always an
unknown film to be added to the list'.[23] 'I have viewed all 317 titles in the *Film Noir
Encyclopedia* published in 1988,' writes Christopher, 'as well as about fifty other films
I would classify as films noirs which are not included in that compendium.'[24] Mystery
writer Arthur Lyons has fashioned a whole book based on this concept, *Death on the
Cheap: The Lost B Movies of Film Noir*, adding over a hundred new titles to the canon.
Academics such as James Naremore are equally guilty of playing this game: 'I also nominate neglected titles as film noirs, or at least question their absence in previous
writings.'[25] As a game, film noir is open to anyone with an interest in what Vernet has
called Hollywood's 'middling productions'.[26] 'This is the scenario,' writes Paul Duncan
in his pocket guide to film noir, 'You are sitting down with a copy of the TV listings,
trying to work out whether or not to record a film on video. Is it, or is it not a Film
Noir? A decision has to be made.'[27] Indeed.

As a 'collector's idea', noir is not just found *in* books, but is also manifest in the acqui-
sition *of* books.[28] The desire to collect together films under the rubric 'film noir', however
defined, is carried over to the films' source novels. With the establishment of something
like an agreed corpus of *films noir*, the process of cataloguing and republishing books
either connected to that corpus through adaptation or by some other loose understanding of generic resemblance began in earnest.

As Neale has noted, using even the most inclusive list of *films noir*, the number of
films so identified represents a little less than 5 per cent of Hollywood's output between
1941 and 1958.[29] So despite the ever-growing number of films listed as noir, the category is also marked in terms of the relative scarcity of examples. 'For the collection or
hoard,' as folklorist and cultural critic Robert Cantwell has written, is 'at once treasury,
armory, sanctum, and shrine' which has as 'its own context an absence or vacuum; the
hoard is an index of scarcity, vulnerability, exile, and isolation'.[30] Like Duncan's noir fan
searching through the TV listings, O'Brien perfectly displays this collector's sensibility
in his preface to *Hardboiled America*, where he notes that the devotee of America's lowbrow literary past had actively to search out elusive titles: 'Naturally, the lack of
availability made them all the more tantalising.'[31]

The vulnerability of film noir as a category and the anxiety on the part of the collec-
tor/critic when his or her 'treasury' or 'sanctum' comes under attack is manifest in Alain

Silver's symptomatic rebuke to Vernet's accusation that the Emperor Noir has no clothes. Vernet writes:

> Complacent repetition is more or less general, rare being those who venture to say that *film noir* has no clothes, [who] have the courage to cry out in the desert that the classical list of criteria defining *film noir* is totally heterogeneous and without any foundation but a rhetorical one.[32]

Silver counterclaimed that 'Vernet's revisionism is like any of the neo-Freudian, semiological, historical, structural, socio-cultural, and/or auteurist assaults of the past.' Vernet's work is like none of these things. Silver's anxiety in the face of academic criticism is to defend his middlebrow position on the basis of 'evidence' provided by the films themselves: 'In order to see the subject of *film noir* as it is, one need look no further than the films.'[33] To which Vernet might answer, 'Did you read my essay?' because Silver's solipsistic return to the films as primary evidence of noir's existence is precisely what, according to Vernet, occludes a fundamental understanding of noir as a critical construct. For Vernet, Silver's noir collection is empty of meaning except as it is defined by the collector whose critical turn is inevitably towards a definition based only on the films themselves.

Is film noir, then, little more than the fulfilment of critics' wishes and imaginings – a subject in search of an object? And, if film noir is a rhetorical construct that does not identify a genre, style, narrative or even a production cycle, to what does 'neo-noir' refer? Neale writes:

> However, and somewhat ironically, if in [Elizabeth] Cowie's words *noir* is a 'fantasy', or if an attachment to the term can in Naremore's words mark 'a nostalgia for something that never existed', the phenomenon of neo-*noir* – itself vehicle for this fantasy – is much more real, not only as a phenomenon but also as a genre.[34]

As an idea, neo-noir followed in the wake of widespread acceptance among consumers (critics, academics, film-makers and filmgoers) of film noir as a form of categorisation, but which, as Naremore noted, is at the same time a 'kind of mythology':

> noir is almost entirely a creation of post-modern culture – a belated reading of classic Hollywood that was popularised by cinéastes of the French New Wave, appropriated by reviewers, academics, and filmmakers, and then recycled on television.[35]

The process of disseminating the idea of film noir began in the early 1970s and reached maturity around the time of the publication of Silver and Ward's encyclopaedia *Film Noir* (1979).[36] Noir's critical maturation was signalled, as Rick Altman suggests, by the shift from 'full noun-plus-adjective expression' (film noir) to the 'neologistic use of "noir"', which he witnessed occurring between the completion of Thomas Schatz's dissertation on Hollywood genres and its publication as a book in 1981.[37]

However, most critical accounts of post-1950s noir offer retrospective categorisa-tions that permit chosen films to be incorporated within the traditions of the 'classic' period. This has direct bearing on assessing the emergence of 'neo-noir' as a produc-tion cycle. As with the beginning and end of 'classical' film noir, there is no consensus regarding the first occurrence of post-classical noir as a distinct cycle of film produc-tion. Was it as early as the first years of the 1960s and, more specifically, immediately following the assassination of President Kennedy, a suitably dark phase in America's history, as Nicholas Christopher suggests?[38] Leighton Grist considers it to have begun slightly later with *Harper* (1966), which he argues is the 'most generally accepted start-ing point for modern *film noir*'.[39] However, Edward Gallafent argues that the starting point was in the mid-1970s, when films such as *Chinatown* (1974), *The Long Good-bye* (1973), *Farewell, My Lovely* (1975) and *Marlowe* (1969) 'explicitly signalled themselves to their audience as contemporary *films noirs*'.[40] But it might also have begun following the publication of such widely disseminated texts as E. Ann Kaplan's *Women in Film Noir* (1978), Silver and Ward's encyclopaedia and Foster Hirsch's *Dark Side of the Screen* (1981), which were followed by the early 1980s film cycle that included *Body Heat* (1981), *Hammett* (1982), *Dead Men Don't Wear Plaid* (1982), *The Postman Always Rings Twice* (1981) and *Union City* (1980). Hirsch, though, contends, that noir did not conclude its project in 1958 with the release of *Touch of Evil*, but continued to linger in the margins, a 'shadowy presence in the negative space sur-rounding genres of the moment; and that from 1959 to 1966, there were some choice thrillers that began the work of reinventing noir for the "post-noir" era'.[41] Not until 1990, however, were films such as *The Hot Spot* being explicitly marketed as 'film noir', or, to be more accurate, as 'FILM NOIR LIKE YOU'VE NEVER SEEN'.

The Hot Spot was part of a much remarked upon cycle of films exhibited during the 1990–91 season that focused on the trio of movies adapted from Jim Thompson work alongside adaptations of a number of other crime novels (Chester Himes's *A Rage in Harlem*, Charles Willeford's *Miami Blues*, Barry Gifford's *Wild at Heart*, David Goodis's *Street of No Return*), related films based on original screenplays, such as the *Chinatown* sequel *The Two Jakes*, and remakes of such 1950s noirs as *Narrow Margin* (1952) and *Desperate Hours* (1955).[42] The mid-1970s cycle was defined in large part by adaptations of Raymond Chandler's novels and the figure of the private eye, which offered a link back to classic 1940s noir. The early 1980s cycle continued this process of adapting novels filmed during the 1940s, but the emphasis shifted away from the private eye to adaptations of James M. Cain's novels and character-types derived from his work. This is significant because the neo-noirs produced during the 1990s, as exem-plified by John Dahl's films (*Kill Me Again* [1989], *The Last Seduction* [1994], *Red Rock West* [1992]), do not revisit the mean streets patrolled by detectives Spade and Mar-lowe, but rather concern themselves with the Cain-like topoi of 'desire and transgression'. 'Cain's tales', as Frank Krutnik suggests, 'replay the scenario of men who invest all in the gamble of sex, in pursuit of the thrill of transgression'.[43] They are character-types for whom it appears, as Joyce Carol Oates writes, that 'the world extends no further than the radius of one's desire':[44]

> Cain's parable, which is perhaps America's parable, may be something like this . . . Giving oneself to anyone, even temporarily, will result in entrapment and death; the violence lovers do to one another is no more than a reflection of the proposed violence society holds back to keep the individual passions in check.[45]

This would work equally well as a description of the male protagonist in *The Hot Spot*, whom Hopper characterised as 'an amoral drifter led around by his sex',[46] or any of the male leads in the Thompson adaptations. Krutnik's and Oates's concise definitions of Cain's work can be effortlessly and transparently used to elucidate the concerns of the neo-noirs that followed the early 1980s cycle. But this would be to obscure the fact that Cain's currency had diminished, primarily because his work too strongly signified its historical context of the 1930s and was therefore less amenable for contemporary adaptation. Certainly, Jim Thompson has superseded Cain as an eminently marketable property. Only Cain's 'Hollywood trilogy' – *The Postman Always Rings Twice*, *Double Indemnity* and *Mildred Pierce* – is presently in print, while nearly all of Thompson's twenty-nine novels are widely available. Yet when the first revival of interest in Cain's work occurred in the late 1970s and early 1980s (evident from the film and television adaptations of his stories, in the publication of a monumental biography, scholarly studies and the republication of six of his novels by Vintage Books in 1978–9), Thompson's work was virtually invisible. Indeed he had had nothing in print since 1972, when Sam Peckinpah's adaptation of his novel *The Getaway* gave occasion for its republication alongside two other titles in the UK, at least.

What, then, fed into the retrieval of Jim Thompson from the trash can of history?[47] In a 1987 commentary on 1950s pulp fiction, V. Vale and Andrea Juno noted that:

> America is rediscovering, on a massive scale, the cynical, hard-boiled novels (Jim Thompson, David Goodis, Charles Willeford, and others) that were a product of the fifties/early sixties – the last transitional decade before television saturated language. At a time when millions of ordinary folk still *read* . . . In contrast to the bland, homogenized speech and entertainment purveyed by today's mass media, this fiction was strong and colorful, etching vivid pictures in the reader's mind. The power of this language yet survives to speak to new generations of readers dissatisfied with the superficial, predictable quality of experience commonly accepted as adult entertainment.[48]

The references to literate 'ordinary folk' and the attack on homogenised entertainment in this introduction to two early Charles Willeford novels suggest that the work of Thompson and his cohorts should be read, against its actual existence as mass-market fiction, as 'authentic'. After dismissing the claim for Thompson as simply a writer of 'hard-boiled' fiction, David Thomson, in a 1985 edition of *The New Republic*, restates Cassell's seminal 1968 argument by suggesting that it would be better to think of him as 'one of the finest American writers and the most frightening, the one on best terms with the devil'.[49] Cassell claimed that, rather than hinder his ascension to the ranks of America's great literati, the paperback/pulp fiction status of Thompson's novels actually helped: 'what I would like to declare is that in Thompson's hands, the mode of the paperback original, husks and all, turns out to be excellently suited to the objectives of the novel of ideas'.[50] To which the mass-produced pulp novel is more appropriate than the elitist hardback for echoing the voice of the democratic American Everyman or the lowlives that Thompson documents, in particular, the production of something distinctly American. As Lawrence Block writes, 'Thompson's characters are holdup men and small-time grifters, corrupt lawmen, punch drunk fighters, escaped lunatics. They lead horrible lives …'[51] Finding in Thompson's characters the raw material of a modernist dramaturgy, Cassell equated them to those of Conrad and Sartre. Similarly, David Thomson evoked the ghosts of Nabokov and Faulkner, while Luc Sante wrote:

> In literary-historical terms he is something of a missing link, the strand that ties together Celine and Dostoyevsky and Faulkner and James M. Cain and George Bataille and Edward Anderson (*Thieves Like Us*). If he never existed, someone, maybe the French, would have to invent him.[52]

Critical discussions of Thompson's work most commonly reference Dostoyevsky. In the Black Lizard editions of Thompson's novels, Geoffrey O'Brien's afterword carries the title 'Jim Thompson – Dimestore Dostoyevsky', a reworking perhaps of film-maker Lewis Milestone's description (following the publication of *The Postman Always Rings Twice* in 1934) of James M. Cain as an 'American Dostoyevsky'.[53] The references to the most celebrated European chronicler of lowlife, as with the name checking of high modernists, claims cultural capital for Thompson that his status as a writer of paperbacks originally precluded. Thompson is thus celebrated for his distinctly low American origin while simultaneously elevated to the rank of 'Artist'.

This process is not dissimilar to that which helped form the idea of film noir, a concept that James Naremore traces with great success across four decades of critical work. In summary, he writes: 'Film noir occupies a liminal space somewhere between Europe and America, between high modernism and the "blood melodrama," and between low-budget crime movies and art cinema.'[54] In his analysis of the critical reception of *Kiss Me Deadly* (1955), Richard Maltby makes a similar observation about the hybrid cultural status of film noir when he notes that the film:

> Occupied a position of double privilege: itself located at a pivotal moment in *noir*'s becoming and thus part of a critically-created American art cinema, it also came to be understood as itself enacting the postmodern critical turn by transforming commodified trash into vanguardist art through critique.[55]

But, as Maltby concludes, the critical validation of *Kiss Me Deadly*, and by implication other canonical films noir, 'was a neat trick if one several times removed from the circumstances of its own production'. Thompson's work has undergone a similar meta-morphosis: what was once little more than commodified literature for a mass readership has now been become, by the act of critical interpretation, a modernist intervention in the realm of the popular. American critics' elevation of Thompson's work to the status of 'Art' was made easier by a pre-existing critical celebration of his novels in France. Thompson's work may have been out of print in the US at the time of his death, but it remained available in translation as part of the estimable *Série Noire* imprint. Adaptations of *A Hell of a Woman*, filmed as *Série Noire* (Alain Corneau, 1979), and *Pop. 1280*, filmed as *Coup de Torchon* (*Clean Slate*; Bertrand Tavernier, 1981), also helped to seal his reputation as something other than hack writer. As Luc Sante notes, however, validation by the French does not necessarily ordain a similar recognition in the US:

> There is a peculiar purgatory of esteem reserved for those American artists who have been lionized in Europe while enduring neglect at home. The obligatory jokes about Jerry Lewis aside, the history of this ambiguity stretches back to Poe and forward to such disparate figures as Nicholas Ray, David Goodis, Sidney Bechet, Samuel Fuller, Memphis Slim, Jim Thompson, Joseph Losey, and the Art Ensemble of Chicago. These writers, musicians, and filmmakers failed to be prophets in their own country, were recognised too late or too little, in part because they worked the side of the street deemed 'popular' (although not sufficiently popular), ever a focus of American cultural insecurities.[56]

In figurative or literal exile in Europe, Thompson and his compatriots offered a view of America that Europeans found particularly beguiling. In his introduction to the British compendium of Thompson's novels published in 1983, Nick Kimberley takes particular pleasure in the vernacular American aspects of Thompson's work, which are characterised as low, gaudy and brutal, but, then, like so many others since, he justifies his pleasure by a critical sleight of hand that recalls 'the Surrealists' delight in the "maudit" aspects of American culture' and that allows him to recast Thompson as a primitive artist. This is similar to Polito's designation of Thompson's work as 'savage art', which in turn recalls Manny Farber's classification of film director Samuel Fuller's *art brut* styling. Farber celebrated Fuller's work against the critical consensus of the time (1960s) because it rejected the 'realm of celebrity and affluence' and instead embraced, or rather, 'burrowed' like a 'termite' into, the 'nether world of privacy'. Fuller's films lacked the pretension to great art, but instead engaged in the horizontal, which is to say democratic, mobility of both 'observing and being in the world'.[57] In forsaking any pretension to great art, like his friend and contemporary Sam Fuller, Thompson can be reclaimed by later generations as unbesmirched by corrupt middlebrow or highbrow values and instead celebrated as a cipher for an authentic American culture.

In the 1997 expanded edition of *Hardboiled America* Geoffrey O'Brien reflected on the change of fortune accorded to Thompson's estate since the publication of the first edition in 1981:

What would once have been inconceivable was that Jim Thompson should seem, if not exactly a voice of reason, then at least a reassuring voice from down home, a both-feet-on-the-ground messenger from a time and place where things looked just as cheap as they were. In the faux Roman atriums of the mega-malls, amid the shrink wrapped luxuries of microchip art, any reminder of the drab and sullen world of Thompson's bellhops and roughnecks carried the pungent force of real blood, real oil stains.[58]

The 'real' that Thompson represented was seized upon in the media buzz around the 1990 adaptations: 'Part of the resurgence of the Film Noir tradition', *The Kill Off* is 'down beat and down right depressing, it sweeps the dirt right back from under the carpet of sanitised America'.[59] *The Kill Off*'s director Maggie Greenwald considered that the interest in Thompson's writing grew out of a dissatisfaction with the unreality of early 1980s soap operas such as *Dynasty* and other forms of *bourgeois divertissements* which she called 'white telephone' films and arts:

> People are willing to look again at the ugliness, and at the sadness, and at the tragedies of life, and not to brush them under the carpet. Part of that is to be willing to look at characters who are evil, who are cruel, who are violent, and let their stories be told.[60]

The conceptual link between authenticity and pulp fiction is always relative to that which is deemed inauthentic – the character types that populate soap operas, romantic comedies, action-adventure blockbusters, and so on. Rather than the formulaic character-types and cartoon plotting of primetime television and mainstream cinema, the Thompson adaptations offered a more individuated view of character, setting and story. The Thompson adaptations and their like suggest that their characters exist in a recognisable world of work, sex and dirt: '*After Dark, My Sweet* segues from a thriller to a profound psychosexual tragedy.'[61] 'I don't think anybody will be thinking this [*The Hot Spot*] is a typical Hollywood film,' Hopper says. 'I hope it's a commercial film, and I hope it will have all the gloss and look of one, but it's not going to be your run-of-the-mill Hollywood movie. That's because of the locations, because of the characters.'[62] A tawdry *déclassé* world which is matched by relatively low production budgets: 'It was a cheap novel,' says Stephen Frears the director of *The Grifters*, 'You have to humor the spirit of the cheapness; the idea of making a vast production out of it didn't seem right. To spend $20 million turning it into something polished ... it seemed vulgar somehow.'[63]

The temporal distance from the books' original publishing and consumption contexts is sufficiently great to obscure counterclaims that their inescapable status as themselves products of a capitalist mediated consumerist culture must ultimately discount avowals of authenticity. Such historical amnesia is also registered in the fact that 1990s access to Thompson's 'pulp authentic' is significantly eased by the lack in his stories of what we would commonly recognise as the dominant signifiers of the 1950s: rock'n'roll, tail fins, the Cold War, conspicuous consumption, juvenile delinquents, and so on.[64] For the adapter of Thompson's work, it is precisely the

Frears' *The Grifters* (1990): the virtue of having low aspirations

indeterminacy of any temporal signposts in his stories that makes them particularly use-ful in the construction of an imaginary yet authentic American pulp storyscape. Maitland McDonagh notes that 'Frears didn't want to do a period piece, and he did-n't have to. *The Grifters* unfolds in a world in aspic: racetracks, down-at-the-heels hotels, gloomy bars, and low slung apartment complexes.'[65]

The adaptations of Thompson's stories as well as films such as *The Hot Spot* arouse associations with films produced in the decade following the end of World War II, but shy clear of unambiguously setting their stories either in the present or the past. This produces a set of temporal conjunctions where imagined fragments of the 1930s, 1940s, 1950s and 1990s clash. The temporal ambivalence of the films' settings was noted by contemporary reviewers: 'a story that seems to take place in a film noir echo chamber',[66] 'a torrid film noir',[67] 'Like the best '40s B movies', 'Jason Patric, has the John Garfield quirks for the part',[68] 'James Foley has shifted Thompson's tale from the 1950s to the present. And, unlike most Thompson adaptors, he resisted the impulse to stylise the material.'[69] 'Set in the contemporary Southwest [*The Grifters*], it's full of racetracks, motels, leased-by-the-week offices and people who feel at home in them. It's a movie about the virtue of having low aspirations.'[70] In *The Grifters*, critic William Johnson notes, the 'sets and clothing do not assert any particular time period, so that they could belong almost as easily to Thompson's 1950s as to the present'.[71]

The ambivalent temporal settings are thus a defining feature of neo-noir. They are compounded by the displacement of the iconographic spatial setting of the dark city of classical noir to the arid, sun-bleached settings of southwestern desert towns, the small cities of southern California or the isolated small town of Nowhere America. Though it can be argued that the settings echo a group of films that have only lately been admitted into the core canon of classic film noir – *The Devil Thumbs a Ride* (1947), *Road House* (1948), *The Hitch-Hiker* (1953), *Jeopardy* (1953) – this says more about the needs of 1980s/1990s culture than about generic tradition.[72] The transient antiheroes of 1930s and 1940s fictions and films were economic exiles from the American dream of plenitude. Their 'outsider' status is marked against a coercive cultural consensus formed around material acquisitiveness, moral conformity, political and sexual conservatism. As Polito suggests, Thompson's drifters are alienated from political structures, but their characterisations are nonetheless political:

> Thompson's crime novels of the 1950s and 1960s, with their shadowy Depression settings and anachronistic anti-heroes (grifters, roughnecks, travelling salesmen), reanimate this 1930s marginal man, but without the typical 1930s suggestion that his terrible circumstances are remediable.[73]

The drifters in neo-noirs, however, are cultural migrants fleeing a contemporary landscape defined by the 1990s negatives of post-1960s, postfeminist, postcolonial, post-industrial America. In this sense, the neo-noir outsiders are appropriating the authenticity of the drifter figure, wresting it from the social, political and sexual context that had made it a potent emblem of dissent.

Discussing a similar process in the production of seemingly authentic American folkways, Cantwell writes:

> diverse fragments of authentic cultures already fixed unawares in the imagination by half-forgotten popular arts – the movies, perhaps, or the magazine ads of a generation ago, always capable of arousing an association but never of articulating it – call out like impounded dogs to the bewildered consumer.[74]

Locating these associations and giving them meaning occupies much contemporary critical energy. Critical acts of reclamation still the 'progressive' flow of culture and rework the canonical distinctions of the past, elevating the lowbrow to the status of the high.

Between the production and reception of 1990–91 cycle of films, the authenticity that the film-makers sought and which critics such as O'Brien found in the pulp novels of the 1950s had dissipated. As Mike Newirth has written, Thompson's writing, like that of his pulp peers, was often overshadowed by the fetishisation of the books' original jackets and covers: 'Reproduced in glossy postcard books and endlessly rehashed in film and advertising and rock band imagery, it is these unambiguous images that have resonated most powerfully for American consumers of the Eighties and Nineties.'[75] This fetishisation of the surface imagery of pulp fiction is similarly displayed in the self-reflexive performances of the actors in neo-noir films. Corliss argued:

> What lingers about the high-polished *After Dark, My Sweet* and *The Grifters* is the spectacle, entertaining but way off the point, of actors acting. They come close to fusing with their

characters; instead they keep busy by commenting on them, playing up their desperate tawdriness. I wouldn't cede a moment of my pleasure watching Rachel Ward in *After Dark* or Annette Bening in *The Grifters* (or Virginia Madsen in *The Hot Spot*, another softcore essay in the hardboiled genre) – they all execute their cartoon strokes with, say, Ronald Searle's acid finesse. But still. These actresses are straining to slum. The quotation marks of backdated irony hang from their performances like rummage-sale earrings worn for their new value as trash chic.[76]

As a relic of an authentic America brought into view via the mass media industries of publishing, film and television, Thompson, like the book jackets and slumming actors, became just another momentary distraction in the loop of a once illegitimate culture reworked as 'hip'. As cultural critic Thomas Frank notes, hip consumption depends upon staying 'one step ahead' of the crowd through fostering an image of illegitimacy such as that which constitutes the apparently 'endless cycles of rebellion and transgression that make up so much of our mass culture'.[77] The reclamation of Thompson's work from the forgotten margins of America's publishing history gave it the necessary air of illegitimacy, but on his elevation to exploitable box-office commodity his outlaw status diminished – he has become mainstream, as has noir.

Discussing the relative success of *L.A. Confidential* – 'a hit but no box office bonanza' – *Newsweek* reported on the continued fascination with noir, quoting Chris Paula who had charge of marketing the film at Warner Bros.: 'the bulk of the audience who enjoys film noir are directors, film students, critics and the most ardent, generally upscale film enthusiast'. 'But in blockbuster-hungry Hollywood of 1997, nostalgia-driven noir is a no-no. Teenagers aren't interested in the '40s and '50s. If *Chinatown* were pitched today, it would be turned down,' says one studio marketer. 'Everybody avoids the moniker of "film noir" because it's so hard to sell a period piece.'[78]

Placed against the contemporary cycle of retro gangster movies that sought to exploit the success of *The Untouchables* (1987) – *Miller's Crossing* (1990), *Bugsy* (1991), *Havana* (1990), *Dick Tracy* (1990), *Billy Bathgate* (1991) and *Mobsters* (1991), among others – the 1990 cycle of neo-noirs was not period pieces. However, the 1998 adaptation of Thompson's posthumously published novella *This World, Then the Fireworks* shows how the hold on the contemporary was at best tenuous. The only temporal signifier in the original story is a reference to a wish to drop the Bomb on Moscow. Yet the adaptation is sunk in a world of cars with white-walled tyres, fedora hats, 1950s lingerie, cigarettes and nickel-plated pistols, bathed in blue and red lighting for night scenes and yellow and brown for daytime. The soundtrack is dominated by Chet Baker-style muted trumpets, saxophones and bongo drums, and the visuals and dialogue are a bunch of hard-boiled clichés. In their quest for period verisimilitude, the film-makers lose what no doubt drew them to the project in the first place: Thompson's unique vision of the human condition. But then this is no different from earlier adaptations that also fail to find a cinematic means to reveal the fragmentation of character subjectivity that is central to Thompson's best work.[79]

In *Savage Night*, the tubercular Charles Bigger is literally and figuratively wasting away from the opening page to the last where he has been sliced into pieces: 'You can do that, split yourself up into two parts. It's easier than you'd think. Where it gets tough is when you try to get the parts back together again.' This is told from beyond the grave. *A Hell of a Woman* ends with the narrator split into two, with alternate lines of text given over to the competing subjectivities. After several brutal murders, *The Killer Inside Me* ends with the subject diagnosing himself as suffering from 'dementia praecox. Schizophrenia, paranoid type. Acute, recurrent, advanced.' The final chapter of *The Getaway* – the part that both film versions avoid – turns the book from a formulaic tale of a heist into a view of life as a living Hell. This Dantesque turn is actually a fairly penetrating critique of capitalism that Thompson equates with cannibalism. With this, as in so many of his novels, Thompson reveals his political sympathies formed through the Depression years and in his association with the Popular Front. Like his modernist experiments with form and character subjectivity, however, his novels' proletarian roots remain untouched by Hollywood adaptations.

Notes

Acknowledgment for help received while drafting this essay to Esther Sonnet (my co-conspirator and collaborator), Frank Krutnik (noir's King Ink) and Richard Maltby.

1. Maitland McDonagh, 'Straight to Hell', *Film Comment*, vol. 26, no. 6 (November–December 1990), p. 31.

2. Richard Corliss, 'By the Book', *Film Comment*, vol. 27, no. 2 (March–April 1991), p. 42.

3. Cited in Michael J. McCauley, *Jim Thompson: Sleep with the Devil* (New York: Mysterious Press, 1991), p. 302.

4. William Stevenson, 'Jim Thompson Mania', *Variety*, 22 August 1990, p. 91.

5. Richard Corliss, 'By the Book', p. 42.

6. 'For better or worse, a scholarly industry, including incomprehensible structural analysis of Cain's work and the movies derived from it, was one of *Double Indemnity*'s unintended consequences. For better or worse, we are now required to take Jim Thompson – and Elmore Leonard – more seriously than we probably should in part because of the train of events Wilder set in motion in 1943. And that says nothing about enduring the *film noir* pastiches a couple of generations of impressionable film school graduates insist on turning out for us now.' Richard Schickel, *Double Indemnity* (London: BFI, 1992), p. 21.

7. Those not cited elsewhere in the text are: Terry Curtis Fox et al., 'City Knights', *Film Comment*, vol. 20, no. 5 (October–November 1984); Luc Sante, 'The Gentrification of Crime', *New York Review of Books*, 28 March 1985; Peter Prescott, 'The Cirrhosis of the Soul', *Newsweek*, 17 November 1986, p. 90; and Malcolm Jones Jr, 'Furtive Pleasures from a Pulp Master', *Time*, 4 February 1991.

8. Robert Polito, *Savage Art: A Biography of Jim Thompson* (New York: Knopf, 1996), pp. 338–9.

9. R. V. Cassell, 'The Killer Inside Me: Fear, Purgation, and the Sophoclean Light', in David Madden (ed.), *Tough Guy Writers of the Thirties* (Carbondale: Southern Illinois University Press, 1968), pp. 230–38.

10. Geoffrey O'Brien, *Hardboiled America: The Lurid Years of Paperbacks* (New York: Van Nostrand Reinhold Company, 1981).

11. Other than those discussed in the text, important reissue series of hard-boiled writers included Ballantine reprints of Cornell Woolrich edited by Francis M. Nevins Jr (eleven volumes, 1982–4), the Blue Murder series which focused on source novels of noir and crime films, initially published by Simon and Schuster (thirteen volumes, 1988–9) and subsequently by Xanadu Books (eleven volumes, 1990) and edited by Maxim Jakubowski, who was responsible for the Zomba Black Box Thrillers series (nine volumes, 1983–4) and No Exit Press Vintage Crime that republished crime writers of the 1920s and 1930s (eleven volumes, 1987–8).

12. O'Brien, *Hardboiled America*, p. 121.

13. Polito, *Savage Art*, p. 339.

14. Ibid., pp. 9–10.

15. I am thinking in particular of Nick Cave, who was an early champion of Thompson in the British music press and who posed for publicity pictures alongside copies of Thompson reprints, but also Green on Red who named their 1987 album after *The Killer Inside Me* and dedicated it to the memory of Thompson. See also Greil Marcus's linking of Thompson with Dadaist cut-ups in the context of his history of punk, *Lipstick Traces: A Secret History of the Twentieth Century* (London: Secker and Warburg, 1989), p. 206. Thompson continues to have a hold on a post-rock imagination.

16. From the unfinished novel *The Horse in the Baby's Bathtub*, cited in Polito, *Savage Art*, p. 295.

17. O'Brien, *Hardboiled America*, p. 123.

18. Karen Angel, 'Independent-Bookstore Presses Keep Alternative Voices Alive', *Publishers Weekly*, 21 April 1997, p. 24.

19. R. J. Smith, 'Star Complex', *Film Comment*, vol. 26, no. 1 (January–February 1990), pp. 4–6.

20. Steve Neale, *Genre and Hollywood* (London: Routledge, 2000), p. 173.

21. Marc Vernet, '*Film Noir* on the Edge of Doom', in Joan Copjec (ed.), *Shades of Noir: A Reader* (London: Verso, 1993), p. 26.

22. Vernet, '*Film Noir* on the Edge of Doom', p. 2.

23. Ibid., p. 1.

24. Nicholas Christopher, *Somewhere in the Night: Film Noir and the American City* (New York: Owl Books, 1998), p. xii.

25. James Naremore, *More than Night: Film Noir in Its Contexts* (Berkeley: University of California Press), p. 4.

26. Vernet, '*Film Noir* on the Edge of Doom', p. 26.

27. Paul Duncan, *Film Noir: Films of Trust & Betrayal* (Harpenden: Pocket Essentials, 2000), p. 41. As a domestic appliance, the videotape recorder was first marketed in large numbers during the early 1980s, paralleling the popular recognition of film noir as a category of film and making it possible for the consumer to amass a large private collection.

28. As well as in the programming of repertory cinema or television seasons and the recording and cataloguing of private videotape libraries.

29. Neale, *Genre and Hollywood*, p. 156.

30. Robert Cantwell, *Ethnomimesis: Folklife and the Representation of Culture* (Chapel Hill: University of North Carolina Press, 1993), p. 79.

31. O'Brien, *Hardboiled America*, p. 4.

32. Vernet, '*Film Noir* on the Edge of Doom', p. 2.

33. Alain Silver and James Ursini (eds), *Film Noir Reader* (New York: Limelight Editions, 1996), p. 6.

34. Neale, *Genre and Hollywood*, pp. 173–4.

35. James Naremore, *More than Night* pp. 2, 10.

36. Alain Silver and Elizabeth Ward (eds), *Film Noir* (London: Secker and Warburg, 1979).

37. Rick Altman, *Film/Genre* (London: BFI, 1999), p. 61.

38. Christopher, *Somewhere in the Night*, p. 232.

39. Leighton Grist, 'Moving Targets and Black Widows: Film Noir in Modern Hollywood', in Ian Cameron (ed.), *The Movie Book of Film Noir* (London: Studio Vista, 1992), p. 267.

40. Edward Gallafent, '*Echo Park* Film Noir in the 'Seventies', in Cameron (ed.), *The Movie Book of Film Noir*, p. 254.

41. Foster Hirsch, *Detours and Lost Highways: A Map of Neo-Noir* (New York: Limelight Editions, 1999), p. 15.

42. That these films formed part of a cycle was noted in contemporary reviews and in the programming of film festivals. See, for instance, Brian D. Johnson, 'The Reel Thing: Toronto's Film Festival Unwraps a Party Pack of Big Stars and a Treasure Trove of Good Movies', *Maclean's*, 24 September 1990, p. 56; and Richard Corliss, 'By the Book'. Paul Duncan, *Film Noir*, pp. 86–8, lists thirty neo-noir titles for 1990, sixteen for 1989 and twenty-one for 1992. Though Chester Himes shares pulp paperback original status with Thompson and Willeford, he shares nothing else with them, yet the similar forum for their work has been responsible for a surprising amount of critical activity with rather forced points of connection, for example: Woody Haut, *Pulp Culture: Hardboiled Fiction and the Cold War* (London: Serpent's Tail, 1995); James Sallis, *Difficult Lives: Jim Thompson, David Goodis, Chester Himes* (New York: Gryphon Books, 1993); David Cochran, *America Noir: Underground Writers and Filmmakers of the Postwar Era* (Washington DC: Smithsonian Institution Press, 2000).

43. Frank Krutnik, 'Desire, Transgression and James M. Cain', *Screen*, vol. 23, no. 1 (May–June, 1981).

44. Joyce Carol Oates, 'Man under Sentence of Death: The Novels of James M. Cain', in Madden, *Tough Guy Writers of the Thirties*, p. 111.

45. Oates, 'Man under Sentence of Death', pp. 127–8.

46. Steve Dougherty, 'With a New Wife, Son and Movie . . .', *People Weekly*, 19 November 1990, p. 119.

47. Since his death, a monetary indicator of the value placed on Thompson's work can be found in the records of auction houses – one sold a copy of his first novel in 1998 for $6325. See *Biblio*, May 1998, p. 62.

48. V. Vale and Andrea Juno (eds), Afterword to Charles Willeford, *Wild Wives/High Priest of California* (1956 and 1953; San Francisco: Re/Search Publications, 1987).

49. David Thomson, 'The Whole Hell Catalog – Reconsideration: Jim Thompson', *New Republic*, 15 April 1985, p. 37.

50. Cassell, 'The Killer Inside Me', p. 233.

51. Lawrence Block, 'A Tale of Pulp and Passion: The Jim Thompson Revival', *The New York Times Book Review*, 14 October 1990, pp. 37–8.

52. Luc Sante, review of 'Savage Art: A Biography of Jim Thompson', *New Republic*, 25 December 1995, p. 34.

53. Roy Hoopes, *The Biography of James M. Cain* (Carbondale: Southern Illinois University Press, 1982), p. 246.

54. Naremore, *More than Night*, p. 220. Dennis Hopper described *The Hot Spot* in similar terms: 'It's more like *Last Tango in Taylor* than *Gigi Goes to the Beach*', cited in Smith, 'Star Complex', p. 6.

55. Richard Maltby, '"The Problem of Interpretation . . .": Authorial and Institutional Intentions in and around *Kiss Me Deadly*', *Screening the Past* http://www.latrobe.edu.au/www/screengthepast/firstrelease/fr0600/rmfr10e: htm.

56. Luc Sante, 'An American Abroad', *New York Review of Books* (16 January 1992), p. 8. Maggie Greenwald, the director/screenwriter of *The Kill Off*, aligned herself with the tradition of the American exile in an interview to promote the film: 'I like my situation now, being in New York with one hand reaching out to England and the other across America to Hollywood. Yes,' she muses, 'I kind of like that.' Quoted in Lizzie Francke, 'The Pay Off', *Producer*, vol. 10 (Winter 1989), p. 10.

57. Manny Farber, *Negative Space* (New York: Da Capo, 1998), pp. 3–11.

58. Geoffrey O'Brien, *Hardboiled America: Lurid Paperbacks and the Masters of Noir* (expanded edition; New York: Da Capo Press, 1997), pp. 173–4. The new subtitle reflects noir's rising market value in book publishing.

59. Francke, 'The Pay Off', p. 10.

60. Interview, 'Jim Thompson', *Media Show*, Channel Four (Broadcast, 11 February 1990).

61. Robert Seidenberg, '*After Dark, My Sweet*; James Foley Translates Jim Thompson's Cynicism to Cinema', *American Film*, vol. 15, no. 10 (July 1990), pp. 48–9.

62. Smith, 'Star Complex', p. 6.

63. McDonagh, 'Straight to Hell', pp. 30–31.

64. Cochran, *American Noir*, pp. 19–38, bases his thesis on the notion that Thompson's work is rooted in Cold War culture, yet he provides only two very tentative pieces of evidence to support his argument.

65. McDonagh, 'Straight to Hell', pp. 30–31.

66. Stanley Kauffman, review of *The Grifters*, *The New Republic*, 17 December 1990, p. 26.

67. Dougherty, 'With a New Wife, Son and Movie . . .', p. 119.

68. Ralph Novak, review of *After Dark, My Sweet*, *People Weekly*, 24 September 1990, p. 11.

69. Brian D. Johnson, review of *After Dark, My Sweet*, *Mclean's*, 8 October 1990, p. 73.

70. Stuart Klawans, review of *The Grifters*, *The Nation*, 7 January 1991, pp. 23–4.

71. William Johnson, review of *The Grifters*, *Film Quarterly*, vol. 45, no. 1 (Autumn 1991), p. 35.

72. As an example, see Barry Gifford's collection of plot summaries, *The Devil Thumbs a Ride and Other Unforgettable Films* (1988), republished in an expanded edition as *Out of the Past: Adventures in Film Noir* (Jackson: University of Mississippi Press, 2001).

73. Polito, *Savage Art*, p. 270.

74. Cantwell, *Ethnomimesis*, p. 44.

75. Mike Newirth, 'The Prole Inside Me', *The Baffler*, no. 12 (1999), p. 95. See Piet Schreuder, *The Book of Paperbacks* (London: Virgin, 1981); and Lee Server, *Over My Dead Body: The Sensational Age of the American Paperback, 1945–1955* (San Francisco: Chronicle, 1994).

76. Corliss, 'By the Book', p. 42.

77. Thomas Frank, *The Conquest of Cool: Business Culture, Counterculture, and the Rise of Hip Consumerism* (Chicago: University of Chicago Press, 1997), p. 31.

78. David Ansen, 'The neo-noir '90s: *L.A. Confidential* is one sign that this is a decade of danger, at least in our fantasies. It's stylish to be sultry and shady', *Newsweek*, 27 October 1997, p. 68.

79. Apart from those mentioned in the text, other Thompson adaptations are Burt Kennedy's *The Killer Inside Me* (1976) and Roger Donaldson's 1994 remake of Walter Hill's script for Peckinpah's *The Getaway*. Steven Shainberg's terminally dull *Hit Me* (1996) was based on the 1954 novel *A Swell Looking Babe*. Thompson's short story 'The Frightening Frammis' was part of the Showtime televison series *Fallen Angels: Six Noir Tales for Television* (1993) which was reprinted alongside the other stories and their screenplays in an anthology with a preface by James Ellroy (New York: Grove Press, 1993). A further eight episodes were subsequently commissioned.

18

Grisham Adaptations and the Legal Thriller

Keith Bartlett

Between 1993 and 1997, John Grisham's first six novels – *A Time to Kill* (1989), *The Firm* (1991), *The Pelican Brief* (1992), *The Client* (1994), *The Chamber* (1994) and *The Rainmaker* (1995) – were adapted for the screen. These adaptations all featured rising or established stars working with talented directors; they were all produced by major studios and enjoyed a degree of success at the box office.[1] How and where can these films be located generically? How can the Grisham cycle be positioned in relation to recent work on the law, film and American politics? What are the cycle's defining characteristics? These are some of the questions that I intend to tackle in this chapter.

Legal thrillers, conspiracies and American politics

American legal fiction has a history which encompasses the turn-of-the-century work of Melville Davisson Poste, Earle Stanley Gardner's Perry Mason novels of the 1930s, Harper Lee's *To Kill a Mockingbird* (1960) and Tom Wolfe's *The Bonfire of the Vanities* (1988). Like their cinematic counterparts, these novels are not easily reducible to a single genre. But they share lawyer protagonists who confront moral or political dilemmas and who become embroiled in narratives which are vehicles for commentary about the US legal system. Like detectives or private eyes, these lawyers become investigators searching not just for knowledge, but also for solutions to the moral or political dilemmas which the mysteries they investigate tend to involve.[2]

During the 1990s, a particular form of legal fiction, the legal thriller,[3] attained huge popularity in the hands of a number of writers, the most significant being John Grisham and Scott Turow, themselves qualified lawyers.[4] The popularity and success of Grisham's work in particular can be attributed to various factors, not least his mastery of a formula which has kept his readership not only growing, but also returning for more every time a new novel hits the bookstalls. It has been argued that the legal thriller has, as a genre, replaced the spy novel, the demise of which in the 1990s was prefigured by the break-up of the Soviet Union and the end of the Cold War. In the legal thriller, as in the spy novel, 'There is the same relentless insistence . . . on the process of discovery, the same murky subterfuge, the same sense of divided loyalties, of fundamental allegiances gone awry, of being caught in a world where black and white have given way to shades of gray.'[5]

In different ways, both Grisham and Turow have used narratives about law and legal processes to highlight the moral and political state of contemporary America. The popularity of their work has been paralleled by the success of TV series such as *LA Law*, *Murder One* and, most recently, *Ally McBeal*. Turow uses the legal system as a backdrop and context for the lives, experiences and relationships of his protagonists. His prose, often written in the first person, explores the impact of events both large and small on his characters and is used to create a strong impression of the transience of life and the tensions between right and wrong in moral and legal realms. Grisham employs a prose style which is plainer and more journalistic, a style which clearly appeals to his huge international audience. The simple fact of his popularity as one of the world's biggest-selling novelists has given him a central place in the development of the legal thriller during the 1990s. It makes his work fertile ground for exploring the relationships between law, politics and ideology in contemporary America.

The legacy of American politics and the rise of America's conspiracy culture since the mid-1970s provide a rich context for the legal thriller in the 1990s. Under Presidents Reagan and Bush, the Cold War came to an end and, with it, as has already been noted, the popularity of the spy novel. However, Iraqgate and Iran-Contra reawakened fears of conspiracy; events in Waco and Oklahoma fermented a sense that all was not well with American values; and scandals such as Savings and Loan threw a spotlight on corruption and incompetence in big business. The Clinton era, the first Democratic presidency since Carter, began with hope but descended into something less than this as the Whitewater and Lewinsky narratives unfolded. Once again, the presidency was beleaguered by doubt, conspiracy and suspicions of criminality.

In parallel with these developments, the American legal profession has witnessed the decline of what Anthony T. Kronman has called 'the ideal of the lawyer-statesman'.[6] 'This crisis,' Kronman writes, 'has been brought about by the demise of an older set of values … [at the centre of which] was the belief that the outstanding lawyer … is not simply an accomplished technician but a person of prudence or practical wisdom as well.'[7] This can be seen in the Grisham cycle, the lawyers of which endeavour to live up to a 'prudent sense of where the balance between principle and expediency must be struck'.[8] To a lesser or greater extent, all of the protagonists in the cycle act out of a sense of civic and moral duty and see the law as a socially useful practice. Even Mitch McDeere in *The Firm* eventually sides with the FBI to bring down the Mob's exploitation of his law firm, although along the way he is not above tapping into the financial rewards of the Mob's activities for his own benefit. Rudy Baylor in *The Rainmaker* takes on a case which promises much in terms of personal and professional fulfilment, but, like Darby Shaw in *The Pelican Brief*, the outcome makes him decide to give up the practice of the law. The dual populism and cynicism of the cycle allows Grisham to nail his colours firmly to Kronman's mast while also highlighting the weakness and corruptibility of the legal system itself.

During the 1990s, legal thrillers, including those in the Grisham cycle, brought conspiracy narratives into the realms of the everyday. They centred their attentions on 'ordinary' lawyers and their clients and blended these with 'big' American issues, thereby connecting the personal to the political and the local to the national or federal.

The Firm (1993): Grisham's hallmark mix of populism and cynicism

These conspiracies mark the Grisham cycle not only as a variant of the thriller, but also as a mirror for the growth of America's conspiracy culture and its threat to the status quo. While these works feature lawyers who are trying to do what is right, they also highlight a distrust of authority as represented by the legal system and by law enforcement agencies alike. At the same time, the issues which the lawyers in the Grisham cycle confront (racism, the power of the Mob, corporate and political conspiracy, the death penalty) are political. American political films can thus be seen to embrace the legal thriller, while the legal thriller can be seen to be imbued with conspiracy and politics. If American political films explore the impact of key issues and events on politicians, the legal thriller can be said to explore their impact on ordinary citizens.

Martin Rubin has argued that the conspiracy thriller cycle of the 1970s, which included such films as the *The Conversation* and *The Parallax View* (both 1974) 'reflected the [1970s] tendency to turn the focus of political paranoia strongly inward, towards America's own fundamental institutions, rather than towards external threats (such as communism or gangsterism) to those institutions'.[9] If so, the legal thriller of the 1990s represents something new. For in the Grisham cycle, the threat to America's legal and political institutions comes from internal *and* from external sources – from the weak and corruptible elements *within* those institutions and also from the criminal and corrupt forces (racists, the Mob, conservative businessmen) that conspire against them from outside.

Grisham, law and film

David A. Black has set out a theoretical framework for the critical appraisal of law in film, in particular the extent to which films either endorse or critique the legal status quo.

He makes a case for three concepts: 'automatic reflexivity', 'elective reflexivity' and 'refraction'. 'Reflexivity,' he argues, 'will serve us centrally as a common and connecting property of films about law, a theoretical "home base" from which other ways of looking at films-about-law may be examined.'[10] He suggests that any film which represents law or the legal process possesses automatic reflexivity because both films and the law are engaged in storytelling: 'films about law are stories about the process of storytelling ... *narratives about narrative.*'[11] Elective reflexivity he defines as:

> the reflexivity of films that dwell in the courtroom; whose plots actually hinge on legal issues; that put acts of legal storytelling at the centre of dramatic crises; that engage the historical surrounds of their representations; and that bring to the surface the linkages and frictions among legal, cinematic, and representational problems attending the several institutions in question.[12]

(This argument can, I think, be pushed further to include films – and novels – which feature lawyer protagonists, but which do not dwell only in courtrooms. Much time in these texts is spent in associated legal spaces such as law offices, police stations and prisons, as well as in private homes, cars and bars. The key point is that even when the action takes place away from the courtroom itself, legal storytelling still continues.)[13] 'Refraction', finally, refers to 'the *significance* of reflexivity in any particular case'.[14] It means, in particular 'taking a position, or offering a point of view that involves some kind of real critique of, or dissent from' the ideological status quo.[15]

Are the Grisham novels and adaptations reflective or refractive? To a greater or lesser extent, each work in the cycle reveals the exploitation of law for good or ill, highlighting opportunities for the corrupt and unscrupulous. Each work also emphasises the impact of law on ordinary lives, the disenchantment that results for some of Grisham's lawyer-protagonists, and the social commitment that others are led to. They thus question the values of individualism and legalism on which the US legal system is founded. The many sleazy lawyers who act as secondary characters or bit-players are indicative of the cynicism with which lawyers and the legal system are viewed in spite of – or because of – America's culture of litigation. The cases fought by Grisham's protagonists are not only corporate or political, but also moral (Jake Brigance's defence of a man who is guilty of premeditated murder in *A Time to Kill*, Adam Hall's opposition to the gas chamber in *The Chamber*, and so on). Grisham does not propose solutions to these moral dilemmas, nor does he offer a developed view of the under-representation of women or ethnic groups in the legal profession. However, I would argue that the creeping disenchantment of Grisham's protagonists, and the increasingly cynical tone of the texts themselves, nevertheless help to define them as refractive.

Formula and refraction in the Grisham cycle

Each of the texts in the Grisham cycle is set either in Mississippi or in neighbouring Southern states, and each one features lawyers as primary or secondary protagonists. In two of the texts the central protagonists are female (*The Pelican Brief* and *The Client*), while a third, *A Time To Kill*, incorporates a female law student as a secondary character. Each of Grisham's lawyer-protagonists initially subscribes to the values of individualism and legalism. However the extent to which their faith holds good by the end of the narrative tends to vary from text to text. Each protagonist is, in his or her own way, an idealist, and each displays a keen independence of spirit. They are clearly drawn by Grisham and tend to view the world in black-and-white terms. However, they undergo emotional and in some cases physical trauma. The narratives in which they figure are complex, at times improbable or predictable, and they centre on conspiracy and corruption. All of them pitch a 'David' versus a corporate, criminal or political 'Goliath'. In each text can be found a host of minor lawyers who contrast with the protagonist. The protagonists themselves come through in the end, either by winning the legal case which has structured the narrative or through redemption gained from some new moral understanding. The narratives expose weaknesses in the legal system, and the corruption of many of its players leads most of the protagonists to disenchantment or cynicism, with some of them actually leaving the legal profession. The issues on which the novels and films centre – and which they refract – tend to have a strong contemporary American significance: racism in *A Time To Kill* and *The Chamber*, the power of the Mob in *The Firm* and *The Client*, corporate and political conspiracy in *The Firm*, *The Pelican Brief* and *The Rainmaker*, the death penalty in *The Chamber*, and law as revenge in *A Time To Kill*, *The Chamber* and *The Rainmaker*. These all tend to be dealt with in what might be called liberal populist terms.

Peter Robson has suggested that the Grisham cycle can be divided into 'chase' texts (*The Firm*, *The Pelican Brief* and *The Client*) and 'issues' texts (*A Time to Kill*, *The Chamber* and *The Rainmaker*).[16] The issues texts tend to display their thriller pedigree less vociferously than the chase ones. However, suspense and conspiracy are present in them all, the former created by the sense that time is always running out for the lawyer-protagonists and their clients. Conspiracies, meanwhile, are by definition illegal. However, it can be argued that while Grisham's protagonists are ensnared in conspiracies of others` making, their own efforts to expose and resolve them constitute something like their legal equivalent. For example in *A Time to Kill* (an 'issues' text), Jake Brigance uses his legal expertise and acumen to outsmart the DA who wants Carl Lee to be given the death penalty. What else do his meetings with his associates show us if they do not show him conspiring to win the case? Similarly in *The Pelican Brief* (a 'chase' text), Darby Shaw and Gray Grantham have to use their skills as law student and investigative journalist, respectively, in order to keep Darby alive and expose a conspiracy that reaches all the way to the White House. Like Grisham's other protagonists, they have to outsmart the opposition. Their furtive plans and actions are conspiratorial in nature, albeit with just – or 'legal' – aims.

The following discussion explores the narrative and thematic concerns of the two subgroups identified by Robson. It highlights ways in which the texts bring conspiracy narratives into the realms of the everyday, linking the everyday with both the legal and the political, and, to use Black's term, refracting aspects of Grisham's dissent from the legal status quo.

Issues texts

A Time To Kill concerns itself with the efforts of its lawyer-protagonist, Jake Brigance, to defend Carl Lee Hailey, a black man who has shot dead two young rednecks who, at the outset of the novel and film, have viciously raped his ten-year-old daughter. Jake's commitment and his sympathy for Carl Lee are sharpened by the fact that he, too, has a ten-year-old daughter, and both novel and film heighten the sense of good doing battle with a Goliath by pitching Jake against a judge who is a drunkard and a pompous district attorney seeking to use the case for political advantage. The conspiracy narrative (Carl Lee conspires to take revenge, and both the state and the Ku Klux Klan then conspire to take revenge on *him*) and the struggle between Jake and the DA are heightened by the suspense of the legal narrative and of various subplots. Ultimately, Jake saves Carl Lee. Both the novel and the film, in different ways, end with the two men united. In allowing Carl Lee his freedom, Grisham, through the character of Jake, asserts a position which is at variance with the reliance on the death penalty in the American legal system. He is thus, to quote Black again, 'taking a position ... offering a point of view that involves some kind of real critique of, or dissent from' the 'ideological status quo ...'

The outcome of *A Time to Kill* is not repeated in *The Chamber*, Grisham's other novel about the death penalty. *The Chamber* centres on the efforts of Adam Hall, a newly qualified Chicago lawyer, to prevent his grandfather, Sam Cayhall, from going to the gas chamber for a racist double-murder committed thirty years earlier. Sam has conspired in racist terrorism and now the state is 'conspiring' to avenge the deaths for which he was (partly) responsible. *The Chamber* marked a departure for Grisham, surprising 'readers expecting Grisham's usual chase-'em-and-catch-'em tale' by offering instead 'a thoughtful investigation into capital punishment, a novel that explores from multiple points of view the state's taking of human life.'[17] As in some of the other texts in the cycle, there are differences between the novel and the film. For example, in the novel Sam's accomplice Rollie Wedge 'lurks around corners ... yet never jumps out to really scare anyone',[18] whereas in the film he and Adam confront each other. However, these are outweighed by similarities between the novel and the film, and between *The Chamber* and Grisham's other work.

Like Mitch McDeere in *The Firm* and Rudy Baylor in *The Rainmaker*, Adam Hall is newly qualified and idealistic. Like other Grisham protagonists, Adam is deeply affected by the chain of events and by the impact of the law both on his own life and on the lives of those of his family. At the end of the novel he resolves, like *The Client*'s Reggie Love, to concentrate on a particular area of socially committed legal practice. He has realised the complexities of Sam's case and has also reached the conclusion, rightly or wrongly, that it is impossible to blame him for his deeds because Sam is the product of the values and attitudes of a specific historical time and milieu. Adam's commitment to death penalty litigation, like that of Reggie Love to the protection of children in *The Client*, once again reflects Grisham's interest in the law as a force for good. Yet the moral issues here are made more complex by the issue of the death penalty, which is central to the narrative and which itself represents the ultimate exploitation of law for the purposes of revenge.

Grisham's cynicism about law and the legal system reaches its peak in *The Rainmaker*. Here Grisham's attention is turned to the collusion of law firms in corporate conspiracy. The only novel of the six to be written in the first person, *The Rainmaker* concerns a case brought by Dot Black, the mother of a dying victim of leukaemia, against Great Benefit, the insurance company which has refused to pay the cost of her son's medical treatment. Written from the perspective of the central protagonist, Rudy Baylor, the novel also incorporates a number of subplots, including Rudy's developing relationship with a young woman hospitalised after repeated savage beatings by her husband. The sombre tone of both novel and film is tempered by moments of humour, a good example from the film being the scene in which Rudy meets with defence attorney Leo F. Drummond to discuss a potential out-of-court settlement.

Fresh out of law school, Rudy has been reduced to ambulance chasing to pay off his debts. In both the novel and the film, Rudy provides the reader with a running commentary on the legal system, the place of the lawyer in American culture and society, and Rudy's attitudes towards these, which encompass idealism, cynicism and, eventually, resignation. Other commentary is provided by characters such as Bruiser Stone, the shady lawyer who gives Rudy his first 'break'. Bruiser is damning about legal processes and the operating practices of powerful corporate law firms such as Tinley Britt, who represent Great Benefit. He may be the lowest of the pile in terms of legal ethics (and by implication could drag Rudy down to the same level), but his down-to-earth street savvy together with his sharp opinions about the underhand tactics that Tinley Britt choose to employ, and the firm's relationship with the first of the appointed judges, ring truer than the more idealistic musings which pepper the novel and film. In Bruiser's view, justice is ultimately determined by money, class and influence.

Rudy wins the case. But justice cannot prevail because Great Benefit are bankrupted and, as a consequence, Dot Black cannot get the $50 million settlement which Rudy has won for her. This finally drives home, again, both Rudy's and Grisham's cynicism about the vagaries of the law. In yet another way, the law has taken revenge, but this time on the family who dared to challenge the corporate edifice. Rudy's victory is a hollow one. The law has not been able to save Donny Ray Black, whose leukaemia has claimed him well before the conclusion of the case. It has thus had little if any impact on his life, and, while Rudy is victorious, the law's impact on the life of Donny Ray's mother is neutered by Great Benefit's bankruptcy. Rudy's decision to leave the practice of the law at the end of the narrative speaks volumes about the law's role in his disenchantment. It also contrasts with the decision of Adam Hall (*The Chamber*) to concentrate on one aspect of legal practice in the hope of effecting change. In so doing, *The Rainmaker* represents Grisham's bleakest critique of the legal status quo.

Chase texts

Like *The Rainmaker,* the three 'chase' texts centre their critiques of the legal status quo on the exploitation of corporate law; the difference between them and *The Rainmaker* is that their narratives occupy the dark territory in which criminals conspire with corrupt lawyers and politicians. All three connect 'local' scenarios to larger, national and political contexts, with the Mafia looming large in two of them.

By the time it was published in 1991, the film rights to *The Firm* had already been bought by Hollywood. The film version was eventually released in 1993. In *The Firm*, 'good' law triumphs over 'evil' law, but without the sense of personal fulfilment experienced by Jake Brigance at the end of *A Time To Kill*. *The Firm*'s protagonist, Mitch McDeere, is young and idealistic, and chooses his first job with care, only to find himself sucked into a Mafia-controlled conspiracy. Both the novel and film centre on the role played by Mitch and his wife Abby, at the insistence of the FBI, in exposing the conspiracy, although the film version introduces a number of plot changes. Key among these, as one reviewer noted, is that the conclusion of the film allows Mitch 'to come away from his ordeal almost unscathed'.[19] At the end of the film, Mitch promises the Morolto crime family that he will use attorney-client privilege to protect them as long as he and Abby remain safe and the law firm is destroyed. He and Abby leave Memphis to return to Boston. In contrast, by the end of the novel, the mobsters and crooked lawyers have been brought down and Mitch and Abby have fled the US to escape possible mob retribution. Disillusioned by his experiences, Mitch's short legal career is at an end. The only saving grace is that he and Abby are safe and have been reunited with his brother Ray, whose early release from jail Mitch has secured in return for co-operation with the FBI. In itself, this subplot involving Ray is a neat take on Grisham's theme of law as revenge, for the lawyer, Mitch, leans on the FBI, law-*enforcers*, to spring Ray from the punishment (or revenge) which has been meted out to him by the law-enforcement system.

The aforementioned reviewer also notes that the novel's ending is 'truer to the inflexible come-uppance of the Faustian pact: Mitch is allowed no way back into "normal" society but has to become a permanent fugitive from the mob, cruising the Caribbean on a never-ending limbo holiday ...'[20] However, irrespective of the comparative weakness of the film's conclusion, both it and the novel refract disillusionment and cynicism about corporate law. Both texts use the Mafia to represent the law as bad and corruptible. Additionally, they depict the FBI as pushy and inefficient, hardly the good guys. Caught between them are Mitch and Abby, who display a youthful naiveté, a wish to do good (Abby as a teacher, Mitch as a lawyer) and a desire for affluence. But their shared dream of materialism and domesticity is only allowed to come true as a fruit of the conspiracy in which Mitch has become ensnared. The power of the Mob is seen not only in its ability to use the practice of the law as a front for conspiracy, but also in the impact of this on the lives of the innocents in the narrative. Mitch helps to end the conspiracy and learns something in the process; near the end of the film, he tells FBI agent Wayne Tarrance that his experiences have helped him to rediscover the law after three years of not thinking about it, meaning that he has woken up to the folly of his blind commitment to corporate law (as opposed to criminal or civil law or even *pro bono* work). In other words, he has rediscovered the idea of law as a force for good.

At the conclusion of *The Pelican Brief*, the protagonist, Darby Shaw, also departs the world of law for a different life. While female characters occupy key roles in the Grisham cycle, Darby is one of only two female central protagonists. She is also unusual in that she is not yet qualified, although like Mitch in *The Firm* she is a high-flier and rated number two in her class. The brief of the title, authored by Darby, centres on her argument that oilman Victor Monteith (Mattiece in the film) has sanctioned the assassinations of two Supreme Court Justices as part of a conspiracy to gain control of the oil beneath an ecologically significant area of marshland. Also involved are the US president, the White House chief of staff, the director of the FBI, and corrupt law firms acting on Monteith's behalf. Darby's law professor and lover Thomas Callahan is killed by a bomb intended for Darby, who subsequently goes on the run. She makes contact with investigative journalist Gray Grantham who eventually helps her to publish her story in the *Washington Herald*. Both novel and film thus enable Grisham to play out the themes of corporate and political conspiracy, the exploitation of law for both good and bad ends, and its impact on the lives of Darby and Callahan. Towards the end of the novel, Darby reveals to Grantham her growing disdain for the greed of the legal profession, and the reader is reminded of the materialism which, at the outset of *The Firm*, has driven Mitch McDeere.

Reggie Love, the divorced, ex-alcoholic lawyer who is one of two central protagonists in *The Client*, is the other female lawyer-protagonist in the Grisham cycle. Like Jake Brigance and Darby Shaw, she is driven by a social commitment, in this case the protection of abused and neglected children. Other similarities between *The Pelican Brief* and *The Client* are that their narratives are stimulated by ecological issues and both demonstrate the corrupting influence of political power. In *The Pelican Brief*, this reaches all the way to the White House; in *The Client*, politics is represented by New Orleans District Attorney, Roy Foltrigg, who happily uses underhand methods to get his way.

Reggie is only introduced in chapter 8, just under a quarter of the way into the novel, when she is approached by eleven-year-old Mark Sway. Mark is desperately seeking protection for himself, his mother and his younger brother after the two boys have witnessed the suicide of Jerome Clifford, a Mafia lawyer. Before killing himself, the lawyer has revealed to Mark the location of the body of a US senator killed for opposing a Mafia-owned toxic dump. Mark is torn between telling the truth about the location of the body and remaining silent. The latter will clearly bring down on Mark the wrath of the FBI and the courts, separating him from his mother and brother. At the same time, whether he speaks out or remains silent, the chances are that both he and his family will be killed by the Mafia. The conspiracy narrative reverberates with the tensions thus created, heightened by the growing bond between Reggie, who specialises in the care of disturbed children, and Mark, whose mother has escaped from a violent and abusive marriage. Ultimately the location of the senator's grave is revealed and Mark and his family are flown away into the government's Witness Security Programme.

As with other examples, there are differences between the novel and the film. In the novel Foltrigg's final appearance has him resolving to bust Reggie for helping Mark to escape; however, unknown to Foltrigg, he is himself to be subpoenaed by a Memphis judge. Conversely, at the end of the film, Reggie does a deal with Foltrigg under which, in return for helping Mark and his family to escape, she will let him take credit for the case. In common with *The Firm* and *The Pelican Brief*, *The Client* highlights the effect of the law on an individual's life. Mark and his family are thrown into turmoil by his witnessing of Jerome Clifford's suicide and the ensuing legal action by Roy Foltrigg and his team. The new life they are flown to at the end of both the novel and the film will, like that of the McDeeres and Darby Shaw, be one of uncertainty, although it will at least be an improvement in material terms. Greed is once again present as a motivating force, represented this time both by the Mafia and by the figure of Roy Foltrigg, who is hungry for personal and political glory. Foltrigg prioritises this over the safety of Mark and his family, and both he and Jerome Clifford form a link between the themes of greed and the exploitation or manipulation of the law for questionable ends. Mark is even taunted by none other than an FBI agent who is eager to puncture the young boy's delusion that lawyers can somehow help.

Conclusion

The texts in the Grisham cycle can be seen as variations on the suspense thriller. They feature a hero or heroine embroiled with a villain (individual and/or organisational and/or institutional), a conspiracy narrative in which personal and/or social and/or institutional values are under threat, and an investigative structure. One way of concluding this piece would be to compare them to the subtypes proposed by Charles Derry. Derry defines the suspense thriller as 'a crime work which presents a generally murderous antagonism in which the protagonist becomes either an innocent victim or a nonprofessional criminal within a structure that is significantly unmediated by a traditional figure of detection'.[21] Of the six subtypes Derry goes on to identify, at least four are applicable to the Grisham cycle. *The Firm*, *The Pelican Brief*, *A Time To Kill* and *The Rainmaker* each incorporate variations on the 'political thriller', with its 'revelation of the essential conspiratorial nature of governments and their crimes against the people'[22] and its dramatisation of 'the acts of assassins, conspirators, or criminal governments, as well as the oppositional acts of victim-societies, countercultures, or martyrs'.[23] They also share aspects of the 'thriller of moral confrontation', with its 'confrontation between a character representing good or innocence and a character representing evil'.[24] *The Chamber* provides a variation both on this and on the 'psychotraumatic thriller'[25] insofar as Adam represents 'good', Sam represents 'evil' and Adam's decision to represent Sam hinges on the former's 'traumatic' discovery of their family ties. And both *The Client*, *The Pelican Brief* and *The Firm* share aspects of the 'innocent-on-the-run thriller', which is 'organised around an innocent victim's coincidental entry into the midst of global intrigue' and in which 'the victim often finds himself running from both the villains as well as the police'.[26] However, what I would like to emphasise here is the extent to which the texts in the Grisham cycle (and thrillers more generally) tend to centre on the powers and limitations of individuals on the one hand and legal and illegal institutions on the other. It seems to me that where some thrillers insist on the powerlessness of individuals (the thrillers of Alfred Hitchcock and of Fritz Lang would be good examples), in the Grisham texts, individuals, however disillusioned, can and do make a difference. Whether or not this is linked to their status as lawyers, as middle-class professionals with 'insider knowledge', is perhaps a matter for further debate.

Notes

1. *The Firm* (1993) starred Tom Cruise and Gene Hackman and was directed for Paramount by Sydney Pollack. Its US opening weekend gross was $32,476,785. *The Pelican Brief* (1993) starred Julia Roberts and Denzel Washington and was directed for Warner Bros. by Alan J. Pakula. Its US opening weekend gross was $16,864,404. *The Client* (1994) starred Susan Sarandon and Tommy Lee Jones and was directed for Warner Bros. by Joel Schumacher. Its US opening weekend gross was $17,174,262. *A Time To Kill* (1996) starred Sandra Bullock, Samuel L. Jackson and Matthew McConaughey and was directed for Warner Bros. by Joel Schumacher. Its US opening weekend gross was $14,823,159. *The Chamber* (1996) starred Chris O'Donnell and Gene Hackman and was directed for Universal by James Foley. Its US opening weekend gross was $5,612,095. *The Rainmaker* (1997) starred Matt Damon, Danny DeVito, Jon Voight and Mickey Rourke and was directed for Paramount by Francis Ford Coppola. Its US opening weekend gross was $10,626,507. Box-office comparisons are not straightforward. However, the US opening weekend grosses of the following films help place the Grisham adaptations in some kind of context: *Jurassic Park* (1993): $50,159,460 *Mrs. Doubtfire* (1993): $20,468,847; *Forrest Gump* (1994): $24,450,602; *Pulp Fiction* (1994): $9,311,882; *The Nutty Professor* (1996): $25,411,725; *Men in Black* (1997): $51,068,455; and *L.A. Confidential* (1997): $5,211,198. (The source for all the figures cited here is the *Alltime A.C. Nielsen database – Domestic Box Office Totals to 01.01.01*).

2. Michael Eaton, *Chinatown* (London: BFI, 1997), pp. 16, 40.

3. Aside from David A. Black's *Law in Film: Resonance and Representation* (Urbana: University of Illinois Press, 1999), the literature on legal thrillers and law and lawyers in film is sparse. In film studies, little has been written outside the generic confines of the courtroom drama; see, for instance, Carol J. Clover, '"God Bless Juries!"', in Nick Browne (ed.), *Refiguring American Film Genres: Theory and History* (Berkeley: University of California Press), pp. 255–77.) There is a growing body of material by legal scholars; see, for instance, Paul Bergman and Michael Asimov (eds), *Reel Justice: The Courtroom Goes to the Movies* (Kansas City: Andrews and McMeel, 1996); John Denvir (ed.), *Legal Reelism: Movies as Legal Texts* (Urbana: University of Chicago Press, 1996); and Stephan Machura and Peter Robson (eds), *Law in Film: Representing Law in Movies* (Oxford: Blackwell, 2001).

4. Aside from those cited above, Grisham's novels are: *The Runaway Jury* (1996), *The Partner* (1997), *The Street Lawyer* (1998), *The Testament* (1999), *The Brethren* (2000), *A Painted House* (2001), *Skipping Christmas* (2001) and *The Summons* (2002). Scott Turow's novels are *Presumed Innocent* (1987), *The Burden of Proof* (1990), *Pleading Guilty* (1993), *The Laws of Our Fathers* (1996) and *Personal Injuries* (1999). *Presumed Innocent* was adapted for the cinema in 1990 and *The Burden of Proof* for television in 1992.

5. Verlyn Klinkenborg, 'Law's Labors Lost', *The New Republic*, 14 March 1994, p. 36. See also Nick Heffernan, 'Law Crimes: The Legal Fictions of John Grisham and Scott Turow', in Peter Messent (ed.), *Criminal Proceedings: The Contemporary American Crime Novel* (London: Pluto Press, 1997), pp. 190–1.

6. Anthony T. Kronman, *The Lost Lawyer: Falling Ideals in the Legal Profession* (Cambridge, MA: Harvard University Press), p. 3.

7. Ibid., p. 2.

8. Ibid., p. 3.

9. Martin Rubin, *Thrillers* (Cambridge: Cambridge University Press, 1999), p. 149.

10. Black, *Law in Film*, pp. 55–6.

11. Ibid., p. 55.

12. Ibid., p. 70.

13. Clover, '"God Bless Juries!"', p. 261.

14. Black, *Law in Film*, p. 71.

15. Ibid., pp. 73.

16. Peter Robson, 'Images of Law in the Fiction of John Grisham', in John Morison and Christine Bell (eds), *Tall Stories?: Reading Law and Literature* (Aldershot: Dartmouth Press, 1996), p. 206; and 'Adapting the Modern Law Novel: Filming John Grisham', in Machura and Robson, *Law in Film*, p. 151.

17. Mary Beth Pringle, *John Grisham: A Critical Companion* (Westport, CT: Greenwood Press, 1997), p. 87.

18. Ibid., p. 91.

19. Nick James, 'The Firm', *Sight and Sound*, vol. 8, no. 4 (NS) (October 1993), p. 45.

20. Ibid., p. 45.

21. Charles Derry, *The Suspense Thriller: Films in the Shadow of Alfred Hitchcock* (Jefferson, NC: McFarland, 1988), p. 62.

22. Ibid., p. 103. For 'governments', read organised crime, big business and corrupt or inefficient forces of law and order.

23. Ibid., p. 103.

24. Ibid., p. 217.

25. Ibid., p. 194.

26. Ibid., p. 270.

19

Film Parody and the Resuscitation of Genre

Dan Harries

Film parody has long been associated with the recitation and violation of rules: rules of character, rules of setting and rules of narrative – in essence, the rules of genre. And the breaking of rules has never been more popular and profitable in Hollywood. When *Austin Powers: The Spy Who Shagged Me* became 1999's fourth highest grossing release in the United States, it also became the thirtieth highest grossing film of all time with a box-office take of $205 million. Similarly, *Scary Movie* (2000) grossed over $42 million in its opening weekend, had the most successful three-day debut ever of any R-rated film and went on to become the highest grossing film in Miramax's history with a box-office gross of $156 million.[1] If box-office receipts are a guide, film parodies have struck a popular chord with contemporary audiences as the films become emblematic of Hollywood's heightened fascination with intertextuality.[2]

This contemporary impulse to repeat, deconstruct and reconstruct is alive and well in Hollywood cinema, as hybridity and genre intermixing eclipse more traditional demarcations of genre production and consumption. And at the locus of this activity is film parody as it recalls and critiques film canons and their established sets of rules and conventions. In fact, a cursory survey of recent film parodies confirms that few genres have been untouched by parody's targeting scope: science fiction – *Galaxy Quest* (1999), *Toy Story 2* (1999); detective films – *Loaded Weapon 1* (1993), *Wrongfully Accused* (1998); war films – *Hot Shots! Part Deux* (1993), *Small Soldiers* (1998); action-adventure – *Spy Hard* (1996), *Chicken Run* (2000); horror – *Dracula: Dead and Loving It* (1995), *Scary Movie*; Westerns – *Cannibal: The Musical* (1996), *Shanghai Noon* (2000).

Yet the most fascinating aspect of contemporary film parody is not so much its recitation and violation of genre codes, but rather its *resuscitation* of genre-based rules and conventions.[3] In this chapter, I examine how film parody in contemporary Hollywood cinema embodies a particularly charged actualisation of historical genre development (often signalling the latter phases of self-reflexive, generic development) by simultaneously critiquing established generic codes while also serving to sustain and reconstitute these codes and, therefore, the genre itself – creating what might arguably be the most condensed and crystallised instances of a given film genre today. In order to accomplish this, I will examine some of the ways in which film parody's critiquing activity embraces and often perpetuates the very codes it is spoofing – generating more or less a 'blueprint' of the targeted genre by laying bare the genre's structure and conventions. I will then turn to a specific analysis of contemporary horror spoofs and discuss many of the ways in which the conventions of the horror genre and the mechanisms of parody operate in tandem to both situate and subvert the viewing experience, therefore resulting in the perpetuation of a revised yet intact horror genre.

Traditional film genres have long been a favoured target of film parody, from Mack Sennett's 1916 Western spoof, *His Bitter Pill* (featuring a cross-eyed Ben Turpin spoofing cowboy star, William S. Hart), to the Wayans brothers' sequel to a parody of a parody, *Scary Movie 2* (2001). Film parody functions by taking pre-established and fairly stable semiotic structures (such as a genre, or the work of a particular director, or even a widely viewed single film) and recontextualising the structure through the oscillation between similarity to and difference from the targeted texts. Any given film genre and subgenre (such as the Western or the 'teen slasher' horror film), therefore, provides parody with a fairly stable model to both evoke and recontexualise.[4] In fact, one may argue that parody films are not only humorous critiques of genre, but also, indeed, *about* genre as they provide a meta-commentary on the genre while reiterating its rules and conventions.[5]

A film such as *Hot Shots!* (1991) not only operates as a 'comedy' in its own right, but also plays off of a number of different generic blueprints, including the war, superhero and action-adventure film genres. The expanding amount of generic blueprints in Hollywood encourages a proliferation of film parody productions in contemporary cinema as genres continue to dissolve into a number of related subgenres, cycles and hybrids. As one critic somewhat cynically remarks, 'studio executives love spoofs because they're quick and cheap to make, with predetermined characters, storyline and production design'.[6] While most Hollywood film parodies are, indeed, made on modest budgets and can return healthy gross receipts – *Austin Powers* was made for $9 million and grossed $53 million, while *Scary Movie* cost $19 million and has grossed more than $156 million – the real key to their proliferation and popularity is how they effectively harness a genre's 'predetermined' features to attract a particular audience. These films are not merely comedies and parodies; they are also directly connected to (and constituents of) the genre being spoofed. Spectators that go to see *Galaxy Quest* are more likely than not to be fans of the science-fiction genre, just as viewers of *Scary Movie* are likely to be fans of horror.

In this manner, film parody *relies* on the associated spectatorial activity that accompanies the watching of film genre. Typically, films that operate from within a particular genre execute their systems of iconography, narrative and style in a calculated and economic manner in order to ensure a strong identification with that genre. Altman adds that 'if spectators are to experience films in terms of their genre, films must leave no doubt as to their generic identity; instant recognisability must be assumed'.[7] One of the enduring principles of genre spectatorship is a previous knowledge of the genre and the pleasures that come from 'recognising' the genre's elements and codes across films.

Working off these established, yet never fixed, generic knowledges, film parody relies on the spectator's knowledge of the targeted text and on the ability to not only 'spot the reference', but also to notice any alteration to that reference. In this manner, the viewing of both genre and parody share the very important element of a certain level of 'insider knowledge'. One's experience of both a genre film and a parody film are often premised on previous knowledge of the target genre (and the ability to recall and apply such knowledge). In his review of *Scary Movie*, Philip French makes the telling point of how the laughter raised by the film's references to *Scream* and other horror films 'is occasioned less by witty invention than by mere recognition'.[8] Character's names in *Scary Movie* are often close replications ('Sidney' becomes 'Cindy', 'Dewey' becomes 'Doofy'), while, throughout most of the film, the killer's mask is an exact replication of the one seen in *Scream* (other than its alteration as the killer gets stoned with Shorty and his friends). It is this sense of insider knowledge (the narrative acknowledgment of a clever twist or the instance of audience laughter 'at the right moment') that makes Hollywood film parody so important in the understanding of contemporary culture and its varied routes of referential circularity.

Parody conducts its meta-commentary on genre through a process of recontextualisation that operates on the simultaneous creation of similarity to and difference from the targeted text. As expected, similar elements that reappear in the parody affirm the genre by restating recognisable codes and conventions. Yet any deviation from the target also inevitably ends up reaffirming that model with an unavoidable acknowledgment of the structure that parody is critiquing. When *Austin Powers: International Man of Mystery* (1997) adds a chase scene inspired by *A Hard Day's Night* (1964) into its spy caper narrative, it not only pokes fun at the extraneous inclusion of a scene that does not belong to the overall targeted genre (the spy caper), but also demonstrates and reaffirms the boundaries of that genre by including an element that does not reside within those boundaries. In other words, by evoking a genre to be spoofed, film parody not only uses the genre's structure to create difference through processes of exaggeration, extraneous inclusion, literalisation, inversion and misdirection, but also reiterates and reaffirms the conventions that constitute the genre's structure through these processes. As Thomas Schatz notes, 'we are most aware of a generic "contract" when it is violated'.[9] However, this activity of violation creates more than an 'awareness' of the codes, as it reaffirms and sustains the contract itself.

Let us next turn to some examples of how parody's difference-generating mechanisms also function to reaffirm canonical codes and conventions. Much like genre's reliance on a spectator's recognition that a particular genre is being evoked, film parody goes to great lengths to establish a clear connection to the genre(s) it is parodying. This is pursued through processes of reiteration and acts to increase the chances that the spectator will recognise both the blueprint and the deviations from that model. One of the areas where we see such activity operating is in the casting of actors who 'reappear' in parodies of genres or films that they are closely associated with. For example, the casting of Linda Blair in *Repossessed* (1990) to reprise her role in *The Exorcist* (1973) not only undercuts the necessary 'believability' of actors cast in horror films, but also reminds the viewer of her earlier horrific role as Regan in the parodied film. A similar example of creating linkages to the parodied texts is the casting of Charlie Sheen (who starred in the 1990 film *Navy Seals*) as Topper Harley in *Hot Shots! Part Deux* (as well

Scary Movie (2000): box office gross of more than $156 million

as the appearance in the film of his father, Martin Sheen, star of another military action-adventure film, *Apocalypse Now* [1979]).

Parodic exaggeration is another mechanism for generating difference that inevitably leads to reaffirmation of the object (and its relation to the parodied structure) that is being exaggerated. In the detective spoof *Wrongfully Accused*, Michael York's character, Hibbing Goodhue, is shot point-blank in a manner that is exaggerated even beyond today's violent cinematic standards. After the tenth gunshot, Hibbing states in a very understated manner, 'Ouch', and, after the thirtieth shot, asks the assailant, 'Have you quite finished?' Yet the sheer number of gunshots, while obviously exaggerated, is not too far from the barrage of gunfire from many contemporary Hollywood productions. In *Scary Movie*, one of the more interesting uses of special effects is a *Matrix*-inspired fighting sequence in which the battling characters stay floating in mid-air for karate kick after karate kick or become frozen in time while the camera rotates around them. This is exaggerated even more than the original in *Scary Movie*, with characters walking completely around the room in mid-air and even breaking into a sustained 'Riverdance'. Yet as a parody of both that film and the special effects associated with such science-fiction movies, the use of equally dazzling special effects only bolsters their place within the science-fiction canon.

Extraneous inclusion is another parodic process that is characterised by the addition of either a 'foreign' element into the film or the insertion of a narrative scenario typically located in other genres or formats. For example, in *Austin Powers: International Man of*

Mystery, the familiar US restaurant chain 'Big Boy' statue finds its way into the film's locale and violates what one would expect to see while watching a James Bond spoof set in London (and further twists this expectation by having the 'big boy' turn into Dr Evil's spaceship). In *Wrongfully Accused*, the narrative scenario of recently convicted criminals loading onto a prison-bound bus (a scene that fits comfortably within the confines of the detective genre) is altered by the addition of a scene typically played out on airlines: a guard stands at the front of the bus and gestures methodically with his hands as the voice over the speaker states: 'Seats in the upright position; handcuffs and ankle chains must be securely fastened, or you will be shot ...' We laugh at the incongruity of this scene not only because of its nonchalant lifting and revision of a stewardess's script, but also because it simultaneously reminds us of what 'should' happen in this scene.

Similarly, through the use of literalisation, parodies often employ the pun to both critique and evoke a targeted text. This often occurs by taking an object that fits within one narrative pattern and laterally converting it to another use. For example, in *Chicken Run*, the escaping hens use an eggbeater to tunnel out of their pen. Other film parodies create links to their targets through their condensed and pun-filled titles, such as *Plump Fiction* (1997) (based on *Pulp Fiction*) or *Fatal Instinct* (1993) (a combination of two erotic stalker films, *Fatal Attraction* and *Basic Instinct*). Other parody film titles literalise central narrative tropes found in the parodied genres, such as *Top Secret!* (1984), *Austin Powers: The Spy Who Shagged Me* and *Scary Movie*. Finally, parodies sometimes have titles that are so literalised that they are non-parodic and are so close to their targeted genre that one may mistake the film as just another film from that genre, such as the science-fiction spoof *Galaxy Quest*. By taking on titles that both recall and literalise their targets, film parodies end up reaffirming the presence of the films and genres being spoofed.

Inversion is yet another method used by film parody to critique target texts. While this method is often associated with the difference it generates (taking a narrative scenario or stylistic technique and turning it 'upside down'), such inversions also indicate the rules of what should stand 'right side up' within the genre. In *Small Soldiers*, the narrative scenario of attacking helicopters and soldiers accompanied by the blasting sounds of 'The Ride of the Valkyries' is directly lifted from *Apocalypse Now*, yet is inverted by featuring small toy soldiers riding toy helicopters chasing two frightened families throughout the interior of their house with the music coming from two large, commandeered household stereo speakers. In *Amazon Women on the Moon* (1987), the scene titled 'Son of the Invisible Man' features a *very visible* invisible man that inescapably underscores the way it 'should' be played out in the original series of 'Invisible Man' films. Similarly, the use of the superimposed location title, 'Somewhere in the Mediterranean', in *Hot Shots!* inverts our expectation that such titles should *add* greater geographic specificity to the scene, while also reinforcing the kind of title that would function 'correctly'.

Finally, parodic misdirection is not only an excellent technique for throwing the spectator off the genre's course, but also provides a road map on how to most likely get back on course. In *Fatal Instinct*, the famous shower scene from *Psycho* (1960) is evoked as the music, setting and actions faithfully replicate the scene from the original. But in an act of narrative misdirection, the killer continuously fails to stab the victim and turns to the use of a handgun to finish the job. Adding yet another layer to the level of misdirection, the round of gunshots misses the victim, prompting the killer to finally pull out a machine gun to complete the task. Although the twists in the narrative provide humorous detours from the original, the distinctive nature of the original scene is not far from memory.

By evoking the genre's codes and strategies of spectatorship, film parody also ends up being closely aligned to the genre it is spoofing to the point where the parody becomes a 'master map' of the genre. *Airplane!* (1980), therefore, embodies the 1970s disaster film cycle by evoking recognisable characters (ill-girl-in-transit, nuns), settings (aeroplane cockpit, control tower), narrative scenarios (disaster in the air, domestic problems) and iconography (aeroplane, radars) of the established cycle, while a viewing of *Scary Movie* provides insightful instruction on the functionings of the 'teen slasher' horror film. In fact, Wes Gehring suggests that parody can be thought of as an 'educational tool' that embodies a distilled version of the genre which 'might best be described as "creative criticism"'.[10]

This deconstructive display of a genre's components behind a veil of critical distance is exactly how film parody ends up embodying the 'master code' of a genre. Parody flaunts its command over the genre's codes and therefore becomes a form of authority on the targeted genre. A recognition of this 'authority' has been echoed in a number of recent reviews of film parodies as their ability to lay out, critique and reaffirm the rules of genre are lauded as nothing short of academic exercises. For example, in his review of *Scream 2*, Richard Williams characterises the film as a 'self-ironising slasher movie that even the theorists of *Cahiers du cinéma* couldn't resist'.[11] Similarly, *The Times* film critic Daniel Rosenthal relishes (or not?) the fact that *Scary Movie* essentially spoofs a spoof: 'If this weren't enough for film studies lecturers to chew on, the *Scream* series and *Scary Movie* were financed by the same studio: Miramax. Post-Modern; or what?'[12] These are, indeed, postmodern films operating within complex and layered forms of intertextuality. But if contemporary film parody does become some form of 'super film' of the genre, where does this leave the status of other contemporary films of the genre as they juggle their need to balance the standardisation of genre with the continuing introduction of novelty?

Parody has long been viewed as part of the evolutionary cycle of genre – typically occupying the 'late stages' of a genre's development. Within the context of contemporary Hollywood cinema, one might ask if the arrival of parody signals the end of a tired film genre or does it end up reinvigorating and extending the genre? Thomas Schatz sketches out a developmental trajectory of film genre, based on the writings of Henri Focillon, in which genre moves through four basic stages of development: experimental, classic, refinement and, finally, baroque.[13]

It is in the later 'baroque' stage that parody typically appears and is seen as 'a good indication of how we become familiar with a genre's conventions and appreciate seeing these conventions subverted'.[14] For example, a parody such as *Dead Men Don't Wear Plaid* (1982) appears thirty years after the peak of film noir and plays with both our recollection of the films being spoofed (conveniently assisted by the 'insertion' of scenes from those films) and our familiarity with film noir clichés (such as the use of internal voice-overs or the rapid-fire delivery of dialogue). Yet as Steve Neale correctly points out, moments of 'self-consciousness' in genre films are apparent in old Westerns as well as in new genres and therefore cannot be pegged to particular, singular moments in a genre's development.[15] For example, film parodies are often contemporaneous with the targeted film or genre, such as Buster Keaton's 1925 Western spoof, *Go West*, made during the 'classic' stage of the development of the genre or, in the case of highly idiosyncratic films that are recognisably unique in terms of their own semiotic structures, parodies can appear surprising quickly after the film's release. *The Blair Witch Project*, for example, was released in 1999 and inspired over seventeen parodies within a year of its release.[16] Nevertheless, contemporary Hollywood film parodies do typically appear after a period of generic supersaturation, albeit often within highly compressed developmental stages.

It takes very little time for parody to appear after a genre's 'baroque' stage becomes consumed by self-referentiality and hybridisation. In fact, many recent film parodies often target genres or subgenres that have already slipped into a highly self-reflexive and/or quasi-parodic stage, including the spy film, the 'commando action' film, the science-fiction film and the horror film. There is little parodic leap to be made from the ridiculously pumped and grunting Rambo shooting clip after clip of ammunition from machine guns in both hands to Charlie Sheen's Topper Harley in *Hot Shots!* doing exactly the same thing. Similarly, the films of James Bond or the television series of *The Saint* offer cohesive yet already quite parodic models to work off as parody, more or less, 'recalls' the parodic elements of the originals. As Adam Mars-Jones remarks in his review of *Austin Powers: The Spy Who Shagged Me*, 'should one type of film be deemed spoof-proof, so thoroughly inoculated with self-parody as to be immune to mockery from the outside, then it ought to be the 1960s spy caper'.[17] The parodying of genres and cycles that have already been through the parodic sieve creates less of an opportunity for critique and more of a chance for mere continuation of an already 'tired' genre.

Yet as parodies swoop in on more traditionally established genres, their critiquing activity also has a cultivating effect while serving the 'function of "weeding-out" clichéd conventions in order to allow for the canon's continued healthy growth'.[18] In this manner, 'parodic discourse seems to signal the end of a particular phase of a canon rather than an entire tradition through regenerating that tradition by working with the established system'.[19] In true Bakhtinian fashion, there is a form of 'rebirth' through death of the canon as the genre continues to be revised and reaffirmed. Yet this is not merely a process of 'reinstatement', but also a transmorphing process that reconfigures the genre while embracing core generic elements. Some even argue that contemporary Hollywood parodies not only resuscitate faltering genres, but also surpass them within the parameters of the genre itself. For example, as one critic notes, 'this year's *Galaxy Quest* . . . set out to mock "Star Trek" and its derivatives but ended up delivering moral dilemmas that matched, and special effects that outclassed, anything in the target films'.[20]

This can also be said about the status of contemporary horror movies as films such as *Scream* and *Bride of Chucky* (1998) constantly bounce between self-reflexive terror and reaffirming humour. In fact, the horror genre is particularly interesting as the iconographic and narrative excesses of the horror genre appear to be particularly suited, if not 'purpose built', for parodic critique. Over the years, the horror film genre has long been a target of film parody, from Laurel and Hardy's 1925 film *Dr. Pyckle and Mr. Pryde*, *Abbott and Costello Meet Frankenstein* (1948) and *Young Frankenstein* (1974) to the recent run of *Scream* and *Scary Movie* spoofs.[21]

One of the key features of the horror genre is a narrative structure based on suspense and thwarted expectations. For example, one of the more clichéd 'thwarted' expectations in contemporary Hollywood horror films involves the supposed death of the 'bad guy' who miraculously springs back to life for one more attempt at killing the 'good guy' (such as the many 'deaths' of Michael Myers in the *Halloween* films). This thwarted expectation was taken to its most extreme in *Friday the 13th* (1980). At the close of the film, the sole-surviving heroine has finally killed the 'bad guy' – an evil character bent on murdering a group of camp counsellors to avenge the death of her son, Jason. After killing Jason's mother, the heroine floats calmly in a canoe to the middle of a lake and we are quite confident that she has finally escaped danger. This expectation is thwarted when young Jason, who, it turns out, is not dead, leaps from the depths of the lake to attack the heroine in the movie's final scene. Such thwarted expectations take on many layers as the audience begins to believe that maybe this time their expectations will be up-ended in the reverse and the 'bad guy' will *not* come back to life. In fact, 'not only are horror movies filled with incoherent inanities but viewers expect those inconsistencies'.[22]

This form of narrative obviously plays well with parody as it works to both sustain and subvert established expectations. For example, in *Scary Movie*, Cindy (Anna Faris) receives a phone call from the killer who informs her: 'I'm in the house. Do you know where I am?' This is a narrative scenario borrowed directly from *Scream*, yet rather than panicking and hysterically running through the house, Cindy replies to the killer: 'Uh, you're behind the couch – I can see your feet,' as the killer scrambles to find another hiding place. This scene initially is set to be scary, but is humorously undercut by the parodic technique of inversion as the codes of the horror genre are laid bare.

In a similar vein, spectators of contemporary horror films are usually encouraged to take up viewing strategies that teeter between fright and funny. The film's narrative and aesthetics reflect a shifting nature of spectatorship: even the watching of older horror films evokes responses of laughter and the comic as we watch Dr Jekyll transform into Mr Hyde or an entire police force shooting at 'The Blob'. Some theorists suggest that older horror films evoked this response when they were initially released as well. Rhona Berenstein argues in her analysis of 1930s horror films that 'having a good time and *not* believing the content of the films were assumed to be elements of classic horror spectatorship'.[23] In this fashion, the contemporary textualisation of this response in film parody creates a strong, self-referential acknowledgment of viewing strategies that has a connection with the horror genre and continues the tradition of spectatorship centred on both gasping and laughing.

One of the horror subgenres that has had an extended life through parody is the 'teen slasher' film. Initiated through the release of such films as *The Texas Chain Saw*

Massacre (1974) and John Carpenter's *Halloween* (1978), this subgenre was fuelled by adolescent audiences' desire for increasingly gross and outlandish movies. This process has led to increasingly over-the-top special effects and narratives that seem to lead the subgenre further from terror and closer to humour. These increasingly over-the-top 'teen slasher' films include *Friday the 13th* (1980), *Friday the 13th Part VIII: Jason Takes Manhattan* (1989), *Halloween H20: 20 Years Later* (1998), *A Nightmare on Elm Street* (1984) and the seventh film in the 'Freddy Krueger' series, *New Nightmare* (1994), featuring director Wes Craven having nightmares about the script he is writing for a new *Nightmare* series film. All of these films are marked by an ever-increasing level of irony and self-reflexivity as the films became overtly evident in terms of 'knowing' and displaying their conventions, often slipping into quasi-parody. In fact, Linda Williams attributes contemporary 'fun' viewings of the once terrifying *Psycho* to the complex integration of traditional horror elements into the highly self-referential narratives of recent 'teen slasher' films. She writes that 'if today, it is becoming possible to recognize *Psycho* as fun, it is partly because the popular contemporary slasher film has taught us this lesson through generic repetitions of what was once so strikingly original in *Psycho*'.[24]

The release of *Scream* in 1996 (directed by Wes Craven, horror auteur who made his name with *Last House on the Left* [1972] and *A Nightmare on Elm Street* [1984]) has come to be recognised as another defining moment for the 'teen slasher' film. In fact, the quasi-parodic horror film has become a classic while also refining the subgenre. The film literalises this shift as the narrative overtly refers to the codes of the genre as it simultaneously subverts and reaffirms the codes. In one scene, the main character, Sidney (Neve Campbell), and her friends are watching a video of *Halloween* and Randy (Jamie Kennedy), the 'code-aware' friend of Sidney, pauses the tape in order to provide a brief lecture on the rules and codes of the contemporary horror film (and how to 'survive' through these codes): don't have sex, don't do drugs, and never, never say 'I'll be right back!' Of course, most of the teens in the film fail to heed his warnings and, as the rules require, are picked off one-by-one by the masked killer.

Because it constantly refers to previous horror films and motifs, *Scream* not only fits within the 'teen slasher' subgenre, but is also *about* the 'teen slasher' sub-genre. Even the press kit for *Scream* gets into the spirit, suggesting that 'genre buffs will be able to pick out familiar lines and set-ups in *Scream* from some of their most cherished flicks'.[25] *Scream* and its subsequent sequels became generic blueprints themselves as they generated a particular type of horror film – namely one that is both scary and humorously self-referential.

As examples of a unique fusing of both the refinement and baroque stages of horror genre development, the *Scream* films also effectively reinstated the horror 'teen slasher' films as a popular and profitable type of horror film, as evidenced by the number of non-parodic teen slasher films produced after the first *Scream* film, including *I Know What You Did Last Summer* (1997) (written by *Scream* screenwriter, Kevin Williamson) and its equally non-parodic sequel, *I Still Know What You Did Last Summer* (1998), *Urban Legend* (1998) and *Urban Legends: Final Cut* (2000).

By the time the third *Scream* film was released in 2000, the logics of compressed generic development were in full force as *Scary Movie* (more or less a parody of a parody) hit cinema screens. *Scary Movie* exposed, replayed and subverted a host of teen slasher generic codes as well as parodying a number of film and television references.[26] As with the *Scream* films, *Scary Movie* works hard to establish a close connection to its targets by evoking a number of recognisable character-types and narrative scenarios, as well as employing an overtly 'literal' title. In fact, we are lucky to have the abbreviated title of *Scary Movie*, as the film is the result of the combination of two working scripts that both took extreme pains to humorously make a connection to the referenced texts: 'Last Summer I Screamed Because Halloween Fell On Friday The 13th' and 'Scream If You Know What I Did Last Halloween'.

Scary Movie utilises a number of parodic techniques to recall and subvert the already-playful rules of the 'teen slasher' film. In one scene, Cindy tries to escape from the killer by running up the stairs of her house and throwing objects into his path – a common scenario found in a number of contemporary horror films, including *Scream 3*. Yet in the parody, this activity is exaggerated as she follows the throwing of a vase with a bicycle, her grandmother and finally a piano (which ends up flattening grandma at the bottom of the stairs). While the scene is humorous in the increasing exaggeration of objects being thrown down the stairs, the scene is also still frightful (the killer is still chasing her despite being hit with the first couple of objects) and reaffirms the scenario as one that can still induce feelings of fright and terror.

In another scene, reporter Gail Hailstorm (a play on 'Gale Weathers' in the original *Scream* films) and her cameraman are being chased into the woods by the killer, complete with jerky hand-held camera movements and muffled audio. As the lights suddenly turn off, we next see a very frightened Gail looking into a camera (with a recognisable 'up-the-nostrils' angle) and speaking in a quivering voice. While this scene and the style it is shot in immediately recall *The Blair Witch Project,* the subsequent action of her runny nose becoming excessively runny into the camera's lens undercuts most of the suspense and scariness that might have built up just prior to this shot. In fact, most spectators probably focus more on the fact that this is a direct parody of *The Blair Witch Project* (and the successful recognition of this) than on the exaggerated nature of her runny nose.

Yet probably the best example of a parodic *tour de force* of the 'teen slasher' rules in *Scary Movie* features Buffy (Shannon Elizabeth) as she describes the narrative of a helpless woman being murdered in a 'teen slasher' movie step by step at the same time as she is, indeed, being murdered by the killer. Believing that she is being set up for some kind of joke, Buffy confronts the masked killer in an empty locker room by first telling the killer to 'lose the cape, it's way too 90s horror'. This is followed by her sarcastic request: 'Can I be the helpless cheerleader?' When the killer stabs her in the stomach, she replies: 'So is this when I'm supposed to bleed?' After 'pretending' to run away from the killer, she then informs the killer: 'Now I'm going to fall and break my leg, leaving me helpless.' Most surprising about this scene is that she then does, indeed, fall and graphically break her leg, at which the killer looks away in shock. It is this odd inversion of horror that doubly functions to subvert expectation (although she, in fact, told us this is what would next happen) while reaffirming a very clichéd narrative moment found in countless contemporary horror films.

Scary Movie, like most contemporary film parodies, therefore becomes an ironic yet faithful blueprint of not only the 'teen slasher' subgenre, but also the contemporary horror genre in general. Parody's simultaneous violation and reconstitution of genre codes and conventions, as well as its overt display of a 'mastery' of these codes, not only functions to critique the structures and parameters of Hollywood film genres, but also works to sustain these conventions in altered and novel ways. As an effective and humorous agency for ironic play, film parody continues to merge long-term cinematic traditions (such as classic film genres) with contemporary references (typically popular television shows and commercials) within the context of 'knowing' and intertextual strategies of spectatorship. In other words, recent film parodies manage to be both hip and staid guardians of Hollywood's genre-based past.[27]

When *Scary Movie* was being promoted as quite possibly the 'last word' on the 'teen slasher' horror film, its tagline confidently announced: 'No mercy. No shame. No sequel.' Yet Hollywood typically ignores such easy exits and a sequel to *Scary Movie* was, indeed, produced. Adding an ironic twist that hints at contemporary culture's chronic obsession with clever self-referentiality, the tagline for *Scary Movie II* simply states: 'We lied.'

Notes

1. Box-office figures from 'The Box Office Guru', www.boxofficeguru.com.
2. Such popularity is evident in the increasingly important sector of Hollywood ancillary merchandising, with children continuing to ask for Freddy Krueger pyjamas while the 'Munch-inspired' mask featured in the *Scream* films (and further parodied in *Scary Movie*) remains a bestselling Halloween item. Even the two *Austin Powers* films are now referred to as a Hollywood 'franchise', with the production and marketing of action dolls, candles, talking key chains ('Oh, behave!') and even a Swedish penis enlarger.
3. There has been a limited yet increased amount of scholarly work centred on film parody and its critique of film canons in recent years, most notably Robert Stam, *Subversive Pleasures: Bakhtin, Cultural Criticism, and Film* (Baltimore, MD: Johns Hopkins University Press, 1989); Wes Gehring, *Parody as Film Genre: 'Never Give a Saga an Even Break'* (Westport: Greenwood Press, 1999); and my own *Film Parody* (London: BFI, 2000).
4. As Rick Altman notes, genre is a 'blueprint' that precedes industry production and provides a structure for the film, a label for distributors and exhibitors to use, and a contract with spectators of the film. *Film/Genre* (London: BFI, 1999), p. 14.
5. This point is rightly emphasised in Steve Neale, *Genre and Hollywood* (London: Routledge, 2000), p. 27.
6. Daniel Rosenthal, 'Take the Mickey and Run', *The Times*, Section 2, 7 September 2000, p. 18.
7. Altman, *Film/Genre*, p. 18.
8. Philip French, 'Other Films', *The Observer*, 10 September 2000, p. 9
9. Thomas Schatz, *Hollywood Genres: Formulas, Filmmaking, and the Studio System* (New York: Random House, 1981), p. 17.

10. Gehring also notes that parodies tend to be useful for the teaching of film genre in terms of highlighting the genre's structure and conventions. In fact, I've used *Airplane!* on many occasions to walk students through the basic elements of the disaster film. Gehring, *Parody as Film Genre*, p. 3.

11. Richard Williams, 'Review: *Scream 2*', *The Guardian*, Section 2, 1 May 1998, p. 7.

12. Rosenthal, 'Take the Mickey and Run', p. 18.

13. Tag Gallagher offers a sustained critique of Schatz's developmental stages, particularly in relation to the Western genre, in his essay titled 'Shoot-out at the Genre Corral: Problems in the "Evolution" of the Western', in Barry Keith Grant (ed.), *Film Genre Reader* (Austin: University of Texas Press, 1986).

14. Schatz, *Hollywood Genres*, p. 39.

15. Neale, *Genre and Hollywood*, p. 212.

16. *The Blair Witch Rejects* (1999), *The Wicked Witch Project* (1999), *The Blair Clown Project* (1999), *The Blair Fish Project* (1999), *The Blair Princess Project* (1999), *The Blair Witch Rejects* (1999), *Deep Blue Sea* (1999), *The Morgan Sex Project* (1999), *The Ninja Spirit Project* (1999), *The Oz Witch Project* (1999), *The Bare Wench Project* (1999), *Da Hip Hop Witch* (2000), *The Bunk Witch Project* (2000), *The Tony Blair Witch Project* (2000), *'The Bogus Witch Project'* (2000), *Scary Movie* (2000), *The Colored Star* (2001).

17. Adam Mars-Jones, 'He's Double Oh No, Licensed to Shoot Blanks', *The Times*, Section 3, 29 July 1999, p. 39.

18. Harries, *Film Parody*, p. 122.

19. Ibid., p. 123.

20. Adam Mars-Jones, 'That *Is* Scary', *The Times*, Section 2, 7 September 2000, p. 15.

21. One must also consider the amount of extra-cinematic, yet connected, parody of the horror genre that occurred in the 1950s and 1960s, including Vampyra's schlocky presentation of old Universal horror films on TV in 1954, Bobby Pickett's number-one hit song in 1962, 'Monster Mash', and the successful 'monster' TV programmes *The Munsters* and *The Addams Family* in 1964.

22. Rhona J. Berenstein, *Attack of the Leading Ladies: Gender, Sexuality, and Spectatorship in Classic Horror Cinema* (New York: Columbia University Press, 1996), p. 63.

23. Ibid., p. 22.

24. Linda Williams, 'Discipline and Fun: *Psycho* and Postmodern Cinema', in Christine Gledhill and Linda Williams (eds), *Reinventing Film Studies* (London: Arnold, 2000), p. 358.

25. Press Kit, Dimension Films, 2000.

26. In fact, *Scary Movie* casts a very wide parodic net as it spoofs over forty-seven films and television programmes, including: *The Waltons* (1972), *The Exorcist* (1973), *Laverne & Shirley* (1976), *Halloween, Trapper John, M.D.* (1979), *Friday the 13th, Friday the 13th Part 2* (1981), *Friday the 13th Part 3: 3D* (1982), *The Dead Zone* (1983*), A Nightmare on Elm Street, Lifeforce* (1985), *Girls Just Want to Have Fun* (1985), *Emmanuelle 5* (1987), *Die Hard* (1988), *Baywatch* (1989), *Twin Peaks* (1990), *Robin Hood: Men in Tights* (1993), *The Stand* (1994), *Pulp Fiction* (1994), *The Usual Suspects* (1995), *Clueless* (1995), *Scream, Thinner* (1996), *Buffy the Vampire Slayer* (1997), *Titanic* (1997), *Scream 2, Amistad* (1997), *Gridlock'd* (1997), *I Know What You Did Last Summer, Can't Hardly Wait* (1998), *Halloween H20: 20 Years*

Later, *Urban Legend*, *Lola rennt* (1998), *I Still Know What You Did Last Summer*, *Dawson's Creek* (1998), *Election* (1999), *Fight Club* (1999), *Drop Dead Gorgeous* (1999), *The Blair Witch Project*, *American Pie* (1999), *Harlem Aria* (1999), *American Beauty* (1999), *The Matrix* (1999), *The Sixth Sense* (1999), *Teaching Mrs. Tingle* (1999), *Scream 3*, *Final Destination* (2000). 'Internet Movie Database', <us.imdb.com/Title?0175142>.

27. In fact, the making of short parodies as film 'pitches' to demonstrate a mastery of Hollywood conventions as well as a 'hip sensibility' has become a particularly fashionable calling card for young, budding directors trying to break into big-time Hollywood film-making. Two recent success stories include UCLA graduate Craig Moss's 1999 short *Saving Ryan's Privates* and USC film school grad Joe Nussbaum's *George Lucas in Love* (1999). Subsequently, both film-makers have landed Hollywood contracts.

20

'Gone with the Wind Plus Fangs': Genre, Taste and Distinction in the Assembly, Marketing and Reception of *Bram Stoker's Dracula*[1]

Thomas Austin

Bram Stoker's Dracula (1992) is a particularly overt example of contemporary Hollywood's 'commercial aesthetic' of aggregation.[2] The film is a combination of diverse textual components subsequently disaggregated and promoted through marketing, media exposure and merchandising. These procedures mobilised a series of sometimes conflicting promises about the film. It was variously advertised, reviewed and consumed as the latest creation of an auteur, a star-vehicle (for any of four stars), a reworking of a popular myth, an adaptation of a literary 'classic', as horror, art film or romance, or as a mixture of these genres. In other words, *Bram Stoker's Dracula* was organised as what I have termed a 'dispersible text'. This is a package designed to achieve commercial, cultural and social reach, by both facilitating and benefiting from promotional and conversational processes of fragmentation, elaboration and diffusion. The dispersible text is not unstructured or infinitely open to interpretation, but its multiple address to a coalition of audience fractions is readily amplified through advertising, publicity and merchandising.[3] The dissemination of images, characters, songs, stars and interpretations of the film extends its presence in the social arena of potential viewers.[4] With no single, unified identity in the marketplace, *Bram Stoker's Dracula* was designed and positioned to 'touch base with all the sectors of the audience'.[5] Its industrially motivated hybridity and ultimate commercial success foreground issues of genre and taste.[6] In this article I interrogate how discursive formulations and categorisations of audiences are produced, and how distinctions are made between them, in three imbricating fields of activity: industrial practices, publicity and media commentary, and the behaviours of film viewers. In the process, I shall reconsider some assumptions of orthodox genre theory as it has developed in film studies.

The procedures of film assembly and marketing target audiences by anticipating patterns of consumption and 'piggybacking' on established tastes, including those for stars, story properties, music and visual styles. The production and advertisement of generically identifiable films constitutes one such attempt to manage demand, minimise risk and secure a stable market by promising 'guaranteed' pleasures.[7] Genre typologies also

Bram Stoker's Dracula (1992): Hollywood's aesthetic of aggregation

facilitate the segmentation and classification of film audiences according to perceived spending habits and the standardisation of product via a system of regulated difference.[8] For genres to function successfully, not only does the industry have to 'institutionalise . . . expectations, which it will be able to fulfil',[9] but audiences have to play – and pay – their part in such 'contractual' propositions as well. In this way, the genre system operates in the circuit of production, distribution and consumption by mediating between industry and audiences. However, as my research will demonstrate, there is no guaranteed fit between business intent and consumer response, despite the tacit assumptions to this effect which underpin many studies of film genres.[10]

I concentrate on taste conflicts fought out over the generic classification of *Bram Stoker's Dracula* and its corresponding assumed audiences, which were variously championed and disparaged by industry representatives, published observers and viewers. I track two conflicting tendencies in the marketing of the film: first, the commercial aim of disseminating it across multiple taste formations and, second, the hierarchisation of textual components, and the audiences for which they bid, according to their perceived economic significance. These procedures of dispersal and stratification were mediated and sometimes contested by the actions of commentators and individual viewers.

In 1984, Alan Williams asserted that: 'Genre studies' notion of the film audience will not stand up to examination: audiences are not uniform masses, reacting with uniformity and consistency.'[11] Despite two significant interventions, to which I shall soon turn, Williams's reproach remains apposite. Audiences' participation in the genre system is too often taken for granted, rather than subjected to sustained scrutiny. One of my aims is to address this blind spot by demonstrating how film viewers make use of ideas of genre, in part to construct their own discursive distinctions between audience groups. Rather than argue that genre is an invalid or redundant concept, I investigate its usages for a range of different agents engaged in the processes of formulating cultural and social categorisations. I consider the contingent and fluid nature of genres as collective understandings and the power relations that structure the demarcation and circulation of genre taxonomies. In taking this approach, I am building on James Naremore's concept of the 'genre function', which foregrounds the discursive productivity of genre naming.[12] Naremore shows how generic labels can be reworked according to critical and industrial imperatives. Rick Altman has developed this line of inquiry in his seminal analysis of 'genrification' – that is, the ongoing discursive construction and reconstruction of film genres. Altman shows how genres are always in process and subject to the interventions of producers, critics (both popular and academic) and (potentially) audiences.[13] However, Naremore focuses exclusively on institutional factors in the naming and policing of genres, and Altman's work on audience engagements with genre remains largely speculative. By contrast, I investigate both how genre headings and hierarchies are mobilised through commercial procedures and how they are reproduced or rewritten not only by press commentators, but also by individual viewers. The restoration of the audience enables a fuller understanding of the role which genre plays in the production, distribution and consumption of popular film, not least by facilitating a comparison between industrial, critical and 'ground-level' perspectives on audiences for particular genres.

Differentiating *Bram Stoker's Dracula* from previous versions of the vampire myth

Bram Stoker's Dracula was the first release in a short-lived Hollywood production cycle of big-budget 'classic' costume horrors which included *Mary Shelley's Frankenstein* (1994) and *Mary Reilly* (1996). *Bram Stoker's Dracula* was made for Columbia Pictures, while the other two films – both commercial disappointments – were made for its sister studio, TriStar Pictures.[14] Warner Bros.' successful adaptation of Anne Rice's cult novel *Interview with the Vampire* (1994) can also be seen as part of the cycle.[15] All three later films followed the lead of *Bram Stoker's Dracula* in targeting 'mainstream' and infrequent cinemagoers, especially women, beyond a 'core' horror audience perceived as predominantly male. This strategy can itself be seen as an attempt to replicate the success of *The Silence of the Lambs* (1990), an Oscar-winning 'upmarket' horror/crime thriller hybrid featuring a 'strong' female protagonist.[16]

As 'quality' films, costume horrors were aimed at broader markets than the 'low horror' slashers and gore films which served the video sector in the late 1980s and early 1990s. The new cycle consisted of opportunistic combinations of pre-sold literary properties, familiar horror character-types, expensive production values and major stars associated with non-horror genres such as Robert De Niro in *Mary Shelley's Frankenstein* and Julia Roberts in *Mary Reilly*. Despite Warners' success with *Interview with the Vampire*, the relative failure of TriStar's two costume horrors, and of other updated horror properties such as *Wolf* (1994) and *Vampire in Brooklyn* (1995), presaged the end of the cycle.[17]

I have been tracing here moments in the continual redefinition of the horror genre – in this instance, via the decisions of film producers. Subsequent rewritings of horror from producers' perspectives have included the boom in teen horrors which followed the success of *Scream* (1996) and the popularisation of documentary stylings initiated by the *Blair Witch Project* (1999). The fluidity of genres does not make them simply interchangeable, however. The genre system still functions to demarcate different film types, even if the boundaries between such categories are mobile and variously defined. Thus the concept of a genre hybrid as a recognisable combination of distinct genres still has theoretical and practical validity, as will become clear. The point is that a genre needs to be recognised as such by some agents in the process of genrification. By writing about a 'costume horror cycle', I am of course acting as just such an agent myself, constituting a filmic category by including certain titles and excluding others. It is such acts of generic definition, their conditions of production, their implications, their reproduction and their contestation, that I trace around *Bram Stoker's Dracula*.

Production, marketing and reception contexts for *Bram Stoker's Dracula* were complicated by the sedimentation of previous incarnations of the vampire and Dracula myths. More than 600 films and a hundred television programmes from around the world were listed in *The Illustrated Vampire Movie Guide*, itself published to coincide with the UK release of *Bram Stoker's Dracula*.[18] Accordingly, the film had to be differentiated from the extensive constellation of Dracula and vampire texts. Jon Anderson, director of advertising and publicity at the UK distribution arm of Columbia/TriStar Films, acknowledged this: '*Dracula* was in many respects a "Pre-Sold" title, so our job was making it a special event that people would want to see.'[19] In this way, *Bram Stoker's Dracula* provides a particularly clear case of Hollywood's simultaneous standardisation and variation of its products.

The title presented *Bram Stoker's Dracula* as a faithful adaptation of the novel and distinguished it from its predecessors. (Screenwriter and co-producer James Hart's script was originally subtitled 'The Untold Story'.) The film was also sold as unique via its allegedly unprecedented inclusion of the novel's gothic romance (a claim disputed by some commentators on the grounds of both fidelity and novelty). As Altman has argued, the production of popular film is a process of innovation and imitation shaped in part by producers assaying previous hits and recombining their components in new forms that they hope will be successful.[20] In interviews Hart declared just such an intention, to reproduce the broad appeal of the book and so capture a hitherto untapped audience of women:

> For *Dracula* to be done right on the screen, it needed a magnificent production on an epic scale, and a reading that reached to the heart of the character's seductiveness. Women more than men have tended to read *Dracula* and other vampire stories, and to understand the vampire's attraction.[21]

> To me, it's like *Gone with the Wind* with sex and violence.[22]

The claim to distinction made on behalf of the film here is rhetorical rather than reliable, however. Hart exaggerates the romance elements in the book and effectively rewrites a number of earlier screen versions. In fact, the film merely amplifies romantic and erotic elements already present in pictures such as *Dracula* (1958), *Count Dracula* (1973) and *Dracula* (1979). Nevertheless, the commercial opportunity presented by the female audience can be seen as a crucial reason why Hart's script – initially due to be filmed as a cable television movie – was picked up and developed by Coppola's company American Zoetrope and by Columbia. From the outset of the production, the strategy of widening the film's address was envisaged in terms of a generic and gendered mixture. Lester Borden, vice president of merchandising at Columbia's parent, Sony Pictures, commented: 'It's a very exciting story to tell, and it's also a male/female thing – a very romantic love story.'[23] Thus, to quote Robert E. Kapsis, 'which genres finally get made depends on how organizational gatekeepers at various stages of the film production process assess the potential product in relation to their perception of the audience's future tastes'.[24]

In the event, industry figures suggest that 50 per cent of the film's cinema audience in Britain was female.[25] The assumption that all these women were attracted to the film simply because of its high-profile romantic elements must be avoided, however. As will become clear, some of the female audience were habitual consumers of horror, who did indeed enjoy *Bram Stoker's Dracula*, but not because it was safely 'beyond' the horror category.

Hart's script rewrites the novel by introducing a prologue in which Romanian knight Vlad the Impaler (Gary Oldman) becomes a vampire following his wife's suicide. More than 400 years later, as Dracula, he finds that Mina (Winona Ryder), the fiancée of Jonathan Harker (Keanu Reeves), bears a strong resemblance to his wife, and he comes to London in the guise of Prince Vlad to find her. Employing Rick Altman's terminology, it is possible to trace in the film syntactic and semantic elements traditionally associated with both horror and romance.[26] Any such analysis effectively assumes more agreement on the recognition of 'romance' and 'horror' codings than is likely to exist among real, heterogeneous audiences, however. As Altman notes, 'disparate viewers may perceive quite disparate semantic and syntactic elements in the same film'.[27] It is nevertheless clear that the development of a romance between Dracula and Mina provided Columbia with a counterbalance to the story's well-known horror content that could be pushed aggressively in the advertising campaign. The poster tagline 'Love Never Dies' was intended to attract women viewers to a genre traditionally perceived as selling to male audiences.[28] The complex generic identity of the film was thus established not just by (nor is it simply readable from) its intratextual components. It was also constructed via extratextual advertising, publicity and merchandising. For example, the range of publicity stills put into circulation foregrounded codings of horror and romance, period costumes and settings, spectacular monster effects and a number of star images.

Casting decisions extended the appeal of *Bram Stoker's Dracula* across age, gender and taste boundaries. A roster of stars supplemented the uncertain commercial potential of the adaptation. The presence of pin-ups Winona Ryder (as Mina) and Keanu Reeves (as Harker) was intended to hook into a mixed-gender youth market labelled the 'MTV audience'.[29] In the role of the vampire hunter Van Helsing, Anthony Hopkins combined a background in British theatre and art-house cinema with a mass-market profile gained from *The Silence of the Lambs*. As Dracula, Gary Oldman was the source of some anxiety at Columbia, never having played the romantic lead in a major Hollywood production before. However, the familiar story and strong star line-up ensured that his name did not have to carry the film alone. The presence of Coppola as star-director added to the list of attractions: 'The legend appeals to the broad market; the Coppola name appeals to the sophisticates.'[30] Thus, rather than standing in opposition to commercialism in popular cinema, the discourse of auteurism is readily incorporated within industry logics.[31]

Released in the United States to tap into the 1992 Thanksgiving and Christmas market, *Bram Stoker's Dracula* opened in Europe the following January and February. In Britain, Columbia/TriStar made multiple promises about the film across a range of satellite texts. The narrow horror market remained in some ways taken for granted, while mainstream audiences were targeted more enthusiastically. Beyond the specialist horror press, cast and crew members took steps to distance *Bram Stoker's Dracula* from the genre. In the press pack circulated to journalists, Ryder categorised the film as 'very romantic and sensual and epic, a real love story ... It's not really a vampire movie.'[32] Questioned on *The South Bank Show*, Hart commented: 'This is not Freddy Krueger Goes to Transylvania.'

The bid to win incremental markets risked upsetting horror enthusiasts, but for Columbia this was a risk worth taking to reach a wider audience. However, the campaign did take some steps to persuade horror fans that the thrills they wanted had not been entirely displaced. Production information, personnel interviews and publicity stills were made available to horror and fantasy publications, which gave the film extensive coverage even while often expressing doubts about its overall quality. The reassurance of horror fans was also attempted through the bloody lettering of the ubiquitous title. The main poster mixed generic codings, however, showing Oldman and Ryder in an embrace below a gargoyle and combining the film's rubric with the romantic tagline.

The diversity of market segments that *Bram Stoker's Dracula* was intended to capture was echoed in its spread of licensed merchandising. In the publishing sector, the UK rights to the title logo and artwork were sold to Pan Books, which used them for a range of products: a novelisation of the script, a 'moviebook' containing script, behind-the-scenes information and lavish illustrations, and a paperback edition of *Dracula*. Further merchandise in the United Kingdom included an 'official graphic novel',[33] a licensed board game, a video game and a music soundtrack. The last two items are examples of the much-touted synergy which consumer electronics giant Sony enjoyed after its $3.4 billion purchase of Columbia and TriStar Pictures in 1989.[34] While Columbia Pictures made the film, Sony Imagesoft brought out the video game and Columbia Records released the soundtrack album.

Judging by both cultural profile and commercial performance, the assembly, marketing and merchandising of *Bram Stoker's Dracula* were largely successful in making the film an 'event' and encouraging a proliferation of possible avenues of access to it. Such strategies of dispersal also brought about some audience disappointments and clashes between disparate taste publics, however. These conflicts can be traced in both published accounts of the film and through audience research, and they were often played out via the discursive construction of generic taxonomies.

Distinctions in press commentary

Press commentary mediated *Bram Stoker's Dracula* by inserting it into a number of different interpretive frames and writing its generic identity in various ways. Reviews discriminated between the film's heterogeneous components and the diverse implied audiences addressed by these elements. While the details vary, the rhetorical strategy of differentiation and the selective ratification of taste fractions is a common one.

One vector of the film's multiple address was towards a 'cultured' audience. Borrowings from literature and painting, and the use of costumes designed by Japanese artist Eiko Ishioka endowed it with an aura of 'good taste'.[35] High art references to Klimt and Cocteau, in particular, were flagged in the press pack and 'moviebook'.[36] These gestures towards elite culture were largely ignored by the youth press and popular tabloids, but were picked up and elaborated upon in the so-called 'quality' press.[37] Coppola's status as an auteur – certified in 'middle-market' and 'up-market' publications – further elevated the cultural standing of the film.[38] On occasions, commentators asserted distinctions between 'knowing' audiences who could recognise the film's high-art citations and the 'base' tastes of less elevated viewers. In a *Sunday Telegraph* review freighted with a number of assumptions and judgments, Anne Billson wrote: '[The film] runs aground on the lovey-dovey scenes, which are not just inept but boring. By turning the bogeyman into a Mills & Boon heart-throb, screenwriter James V. Hart has drained the story of most of its plasma.'[39] The film's romance elements are rejected here through their association with a culturally denigrated 'female' genre, that of 'lowbrow' romantic fiction. Billson erected a second axis of distinction in rejecting another 'common' taste formation, that of an implicitly Americanised youth culture: 'Those of you with deliciously shivery memories of Christopher Lee or Bela Lugosi will not be disposed to look favourably upon *Bram Stoker's Dracula* ... Coppola's film is a Dracula for the Nineties, aimed not at classicists but at a fang-de-siècle generation weaned on MTV.' The inclusion of Lee, a star of the often-derided Hammer horror cycle, under the heading of 'classic horror' testifies to the flexible borders of such critical categories across time. When Billson considered positive effects of the film's 'feminisation', she mobilised an 'up-market' image of the female spectator: 'This has all the makings of a classic Accessory Film: one ought never to underestimate the cumulative aesthetic effect of all those nice scratchy fountain pens, pebble-lensed spectacles and pearly earrings.' In this (admittedly playful) review, three target audiences are stratified and only one is legitimated – that made up of adult, middle-class, art-loving, female spectator-consumers. Whereas Columbia's strategy was to appeal to both teenagers and adults, to 'elite' and 'common' tastes,[40] Billson makes a clear distinction between the terms of each couplet. This is an instance of the 'refusal' of the preferences of the 'other' which, according to Bourdieu, places tastes in mutual opposition.[41] Those who share Billson's taste draw on cultural capital provided by education and class background, and are thus differentiated from the 'masses'.

In the specialist horror press, commentators often took on the role of gatekeepers of the genre, judging the film by its fidelity or otherwise to the norms of horror. Those deeming *Bram Stoker's Dracula* successful allowed it entry to the generic corpus as a worthwhile innovation sometimes labelled 'epic' horror.[42] Other writers rejected the film because it was too different, citing the incursion of romance. Oppositions between an informed horror audience and ordinary cinemagoers ignorant of the genre structured reviews in the British horror magazines *The Dark Side* and *Samhain*. In contrast to Hart's approving comparison, the reference to *Gone with the Wind* (1939) here stands as a measure of the film's failings:

> Instead of Murnau's 'symphony of Horror' we have Coppola's pop promo of Horror, or even, a rather unwieldily modified *Gone with the Wind* plus fangs.[43]

> It's a horror movie that never once exudes or creates fear, menace or terror. It's a love story without a remotely believable scenario . . . Mills and Boon Gothic at best.[44]

Like *The Sunday Telegraph*, these reviews characterised the film through its association with juvenile and 'lowbrow female' tastes. All three commentaries rejected perceived commercial priorities in proposing alternative taste hierarchies. To unpack further the differentiations made in the horror press, I shall draw on Sarah Thornton's theory of 'subcultural capital'.[45] This modification of Bourdieu's model of cultural capital is designed to take account of the accumulation of 'additional' cultural resources beyond those derived from education and family background. Displayed in record collections, fashionable haircuts – or knowledge about films – subcultural capital 'confers status on its owner in the eyes of the relevant beholder'.[46] Its differential distribution under-pins taste distinctions such as 'cool' youth's disparagement of 'mainstream' culture. In opposing sanctioned versions of the Dracula myth with Columbia's offering, horror reviewers display subcultural capital (implicitly held by their readers, too) and establish dichotomies between an authentic horror culture and 'mainstream' Hollywood, which sells inferior products to easily pleased audiences. The horror fan subculture in which publications such as *Samhain* and *The Dark Side* circulate is commercial, but often represents itself as less so than the 'blind commercialism' of 'mass-market' Hollywood. Horror fans are at the very least differentiated as more discerning consumers than the cinemagoing crowd, whose preferences render them 'taste-less'. In all the reviews considered so far, 'average' and 'inauthentic' audiences are characterised as 'inferior' not just through their tastes, however, but also via marks of age, gender and/or class. In the process, *Bram Stoker's Dracula* is implicitly infantilised, feminised and/or banalised in contrast to tastes ratified by cultural or subcultural capital. The critical reception of the film thus foregrounds the articulation of taste conflicts with social and cultural identities. It succeeded commercially not by resolving these ongoing conflicts and assembling a unified or homogeneous mass audience, but by selling to an aggregation of different taste formations. This objective is not endangered by taste disputes, as long as enough audience segments find that a part of the film package speaks to them.

Audience responses

How did viewers respond to the multiple address of the dispersible text? How did they classify the film generically? In what terms was its perceived success or failure expressed? What distinctions did individuals make between its different audiences? In this section, I draw on questionnaires handed out to cinemagoers attending my local multiplex shortly after the film's first screening on terrestrial television.[47] The questionnaire included both open-ended and more specific questions. Of 250 questionnaires given out, a total of forty-nine were returned. The vast majority of this self-selected sample was white, with ages ranging from sixteen to forty-eight. Twenty women and eleven men had seen the film in some format.

I asked respondents to state their preferences for, and dislikes of, film types and genres. Gender is the sociological factor that is usually assumed by industry personnel and commentators to correlate most closely with genre preferences, and on occasion it was employed here as a mark of difference in taste. The correspondence between gender identity and genre preference was not always as neat as stock assumptions would imply, however. While some favoured films did conform to stereotyped 'female' and 'male' tastes, others confounded these and sometimes cut across 'incompatible' genre categories. For instance, one woman listed as her favourites 'Disney, true stories, murder, action'. Some respondents did not adhere to received genre typologies at all, but organised films under more idiosyncratic headings such as (for likes) 'clever', 'well directed' and 'intelligent cool films' or (dislikes) 'stereotyped' or 'most British films after 1970'. This kind of taxonomy appears to coexist with an awareness of more familiar classifications, while effectively overwriting them. I have been tempted to employ a 'public'/'private' dichotomy here, but it is somewhat problematic. What I might have termed 'private' typologies are less likely to be picked up by the media or otherwise endorsed in the public domain and so lack the institutional consolidation which marks and constitutes a film genre. But they, too, contribute to viewers' self-perceptions and can be 'converted' into a limited social currency through peer group interaction.[48] Moreover, all (institutionally sanctioned) genres are 'privatised' to the extent that individuals are able to recognise and deploy them. Indeed, genres rely on such shared recognitions to function successfully – even while viewers variously refashion, reconfigure and valorise or denigrate them in the process. It is clear that established film genres may also be entirely rewritten into idiosyncratic groupings such as those above. Some such groupings are even endorsed more publicly. Although 'clever', 'well directed' and 'intelligent cool films' are not as yet installed as fully fledged genres, similar categories are often proposed in critics' top tens or in scheduling decisions for televised film strands such as BBC 2's *Moviedrome*. By employing these terms, informants may be drawing upon such public discourses and presenting themselves as 'experts' with knowledge, taste and the ability to evaluate films across a range of genres. Viewers and commentators will of course disagree about the films to be included and excluded from any such corpus, but, as this article demonstrates, similar border skirmishes occur around more familiar, established genres.

Audiences approached *Bram Stoker's Dracula* anticipating pleasures that were shaped both by prior viewing experiences and awareness of diverse attractions flagged through advertising, publicity and ancillary products. There was no simple consensus about the film's generic status. Instead, it was ascribed various identities, including 'sensual, sad, romantic', a 'gothic-horror-love story', 'a thriller' and a 'normal Dracula movie with a bit more sex'. Horror fans[49] of both genders judged the film against favoured examples of the genre. Some rejected *Bram Stoker's Dracula* as a 'mainstream' mishandling of horror, so prioritising generic fidelity over mass appeal and implying alternatives to Columbia's operative taste hierarchy. The primary complaint was a failure to frighten. In characterising the film's ideal audiences as lacking in generic knowledge and subcultural capital, the following informants implicitly distinguished themselves from these less 'educated' taste publics, much as press commentators had done:

> Why I watched the film – the story is a classic, scary ... [The film was] Crap. I simply was not scared enough.
> [Who do you think *Bram Stoker's Dracula* appeals to most?] Those uneducated in film.
> (*17: anon. female. Charity worker, age 22. Part two; Q.35.)

> [Who do you think *Bram Stoker's Dracula* appeals to most?]
> People who mistakenly believe that Hammer = hammy. Fans of style over content.
> (*3: anon. male. Media worker, age 26. *Samhain* sample. Q.35.)

Some respondents had strategically lowered their expectations in anticipation of concessions to 'other' tastes:

> Didn't want to see it because I was sure they'd butcher it. Saw ½ of it on TV recently.
> [Who do you think *Bram Stoker's Dracula* appeals to most?]
> 13-year-olds, girls who wear itty bitty backpacks, fools.
> (* 19: anon. male. Student, age 23. Part two; Q.35.)

Not all horror fans were so disappointed, however:

> I thought the Gothic atmosphere was portrayed excellently. The make-up effects on Gary Oldman were good, and his portrayal of dracula was quite moving.
> The 'long lost love' angle ... was more interesting than the usual blood and gore type of vampire film.
> (* 10: anon. female. Biomedical scientist, age 33. Part two.)

This account evinces a dislike of 'gratuitous' gore, an enjoyment of involving characterisation and a sympathy for the dilemma of the vampire, all of which echo some of Brigid Cherry's findings about female horror fans.[50] Cherry's research points to women's pleasurable investments in the relationships between vampires and to a wider affinity for the monsters and 'outsiders' portrayed in the horror genre. While no simple and clear-cut gendered division emerged in my project, such pleasures were less likely to be mentioned by men in the sample.

Some informants' statements effectively corroborated Hart's claims about the sexual appeal of the film for female viewers. It is notable that these women also enjoyed being scared:

I'm an avid fan of horror – books and films alike, so there was no way I was going to miss *Dracula* ... I do remember getting the impression that the film was rather sexual in a subtle way. I think I got a bit aroused by it!
(*11: Evonne. Female student, age 21. Part two.)

I watched it because I quite like horror films and I thought it would be quite erotic and beautifully filmed. I was interested in the type of imagery used. I like being scared.
(*9: Anon. female. Student, age 21. Part two; Q.35.)

Brigid Cherry's suggestion that vampire films may function as a 'form of erotica for some women',[51] providing the opportunity for sexual fantasy along with pleasurable tension and suspense, is borne out here. Among respondents, more women than men found the film erotic. In a rare admission of sexual pleasure, a male *Samhain* reader wrote:

I appreciate the way Hart and Coppola attempted to give the novel more resonance by adding the 'eternal love' aspect ... by trying to appeal to two separate audiences: the horror fan, who wants to be scared, and those who find the vampire idea sexy as hell, there were two disparate avenues it could have explored. Unfortunately, Coppola tried both, and fell between them. As a viewer who wanted both aspects in my film, I was a bit happier than most ... I loved it.
(*3: anon. male. Media worker, age 26. Part two.)

What is striking here is the coexistence of a conception of the film-makers' commercial imperatives (the appeal to two markets) alongside a high degree of personal investment in the film. Such a dual perspective on the valued artefact has been located in other studies of fans' engagements with mass-media products.[52] Elsewhere in the sample, viewers less happy with the film typically attributed its failure to 'Hollywood-isation' – a phrase used to imply crass commercialism, Americanisation and simplification of the original material. Whatever their final opinion, many horror fans evaluated *Bram Stoker's Dracula* according to their 'rules' of the genre and favourite instances of this film type. Such judgments were similar, but less public, than those made in specialist publications. In this way, generic regimes may be policed privately by audience members as well as publicly by reviewers.

Despite attempts to sell the film to audiences wary of horror, it was expressly defined as such by some people – particularly women – for whom the term was clearly pejorative. The following account draws upon a popular 'folk theory' of media influence to express concern about horror films:

Disliked it. Not my kind of film. I get nightmares very easily. I think horror films (cinema or TV) deaden one's sensibilities and make one less sensitive to, and hence less caring about, the real horror in the real world.
(*21: Anon. female. Tax consultant, age 35. Part two; Q.12.)

By contrast, enthusiastic viewers often perceived the film to be addressed to audiences shaped in their own self-images:

[Who do you think *Bram Stoker's Dracula* appeals to most?]
Young, imaginative people.
(*11: Evonne. Female student, age 21. Part two; Q.35.)

Audiences are able to read markers of genre in advertising and publicity as one set of a series of 'publicly distributed orientations'[53] offering patterned ways of preparing for and responding to a film. They may participate in the contractual transactions which film genres propose (to which they bring payment and knowledge, and from which they expect a pleasurable combination of the familiar and the novel). Or they may read generic markers not as incitements to consume, but as reasons to avoid a film. In all cases, potential viewers are mediating industrial procedures of production, advertising and publicity, mobilising assumptions about the nature of a film and its target audience by drawing on extratextual materials and their experience of films similarly classified. Exactly how (non)viewers perceive a genre – its value, boundaries, pleasures and audience – will vary according to their different competencies, repertoires and orientations. As Gemma Moss puts it, the exact places users construct for a genre are shaped by their socially specific 'histories of engagement'.[54] In the process, they are also asserting something about themselves. In watching a film or declining invitations to do so, individuals use markers of cultural preference to negotiate their own sense of self. Identity is constructed and (re)asserted both through positive self-images (as 'imaginative', knowledgeable or tasteful, for instance) and by distinguishing oneself from those with 'invalid' tastes – for example, 'girls', 'boys', 'fools' or horror consumers with deadened sensibilities.

Conclusion

Accounts of genre in film studies need to examine in more detail audiences' differentially distributed knowledges of, and participations in, the generic regimes of Hollywood and other popular cinemas. As a first step, I hope to have demonstrated how this turn to the audience can produce new understandings of the interplay between industrial and critical logics and audience activities of discrimination and self-definition. Viewers may enjoy belonging to taste publics (commonly invoked in reviews and advertising campaigns) based on shared patterns of consumption, such as a preference for horror films or for appearances by Keanu Reeves or Winona Ryder. These communities are more often imagined or implied, rather than convened in a literally shared space.[55] But they can nevertheless offer consumers a powerful sense of identity. So can the symbolic rejection of such taste formations. Both positions were evinced in the affiliations and distinctions found in informants' accounts. In deploying generic markers, audiences are not simply accepting commercially and critically recognised categories in a passive fashion, but are taking them up and making them work for their own purposes. In the process, they shape the meaning, value and frontiers of established genres according to their diverse tastes and motives. Respondents' decisions about whether or not to classify *Bram Stoker's Dracula* as 'horror' suggest some variance over the definitions and contents of traditional genre categories. It seems that individuals can maintain ensembles of preferences which are not necessarily coterminous with industrial and critical typologies, while simultaneously knowing that they are addressed as members of institutionally constituted and demarcated constituencies through production, marketing and reviewing strategies. Such personal 'taste maps' may incorporate institutionalised categories such as horror, as well as groupings such as 'intelligent cool films' which cut across more established generic headings. It is not time to jettison the familiar taxonomies proposed by film genres. But it is necessary to recognise that they are subject to constant rewriting – by audiences in addition to producers and reviewers – and that they exist alongside, and their members are always being (re)arranged into, discursive categories which are yet to attain institutional consolidation.

Notes

1. An earlier version of this argument appeared in *Framework, The Journal of Cinema and Media*, vol. 41 (1999). An extended version is included in Thomas Austin, *Hollywood, Hype and Audiences* (Manchester: Manchester University Press, 2002). Thanks to those involved in both publications for permission to reproduce this piece here. Thanks also to Mark Jancovich, Matthew Hills and Charlotte Adcock for their helpful comments.

2. The term is Richard Maltby's. See Richard Maltby and Ian Craven, *Hollywood Cinema: An Introduction* (Oxford: Blackwell, 1995), pp. 30–5. The extent of textual aggregation does, of course, vary from film to film.

3. My concept of the dispersible text builds on the work of Barbara Klinger in her 'Digressions at the cinema: reception and mass culture', *Cinema Journal*, vol. 28, no. 4 (1989), pp. 3–19.

4. Assembling films as composite goods targeted at diverse audiences is not new. However, this mechanics of aggregation has intensified since the 1970s, driven by developments in Hollywood's economic organisation and operational procedures.

5. Duncan Clark, Columbia/TriStar's senior vice president of international marketing, quoted in Ana Maria Bahiana, 'Tooth and nail', *Screen International*, 13 November 1992, p. 12.

6. *Bram Stoker's Dracula* grossed $82 million in the United States and Canada, and $110 million in overseas markets.

7. See Steve Neale, *Genre and Hollywood* (London: Routledge, 2000), pp. 231–42.

8. See Steve Neale, *Genre* (London: BFI, 1980), pp. 22–3; Richard Maltby, '"Sticks, hicks and flaps": Classical Hollywood's generic conception of its audiences', in Melvyn Stokes and Richard Maltby (eds), *Identifying Hollywood's Audiences: Cultural Identity and the Movies* (London: BFI, 1999), pp. 23–41.

9. Neale, *Genre*, p. 54.

10. See also Rick Altman, *Film/Genre* (London: BFI, 1999), p. 16.

11. Alan Williams, 'Is a radical genre criticism possible?', *Quarterly Review of Film Studies*, vol. 9, no. 2 (1984), p. 124.

12. James Naremore, 'American film noir: the history of an idea', *Film Quarterly*, vol. 49, no. 2 (1995/6), pp. 12–28.

13. Altman, *Film/Genre*, especially pp. 30–82.

14. *Mary Shelley's Frankenstein* grossed $22 million in the US. *Mary Reilly* grossed a mere $6 million in the US.

15. The film grossed $105 million in the US.

16. See Mark Jancovich, 'Genre and the audience: genre classifications and cultural distinctions in the mediation of *The Silence of the Lambs*', in Melvyn Stokes and Richard Maltby (eds), *Hollywood Spectatorship: Changing Perceptions of Cinema Audiences* (London: BFI, 2001), pp. 33–45. The film grossed $130 million in the US.

17. *Wolf* grossed $65 million in the US, on a budget of $70 million. *Vampire in Brooklyn* grossed $20 million in the US.

18. Stephen Jones, *The Illustrated Vampire Movie Guide* (London: Titan Books, 1993).

19. Jon Anderson, letter to the author, 19 July 1993.

20. Altman, *Film/Genre*, pp. 41–7. Of course, this process cannot guarantee success.

21. James V. Hart, 'The script that wouldn't die', in Francis Ford Coppola and James V. Hart, *Bram Stoker's Dracula: The Film and the Legend* (New York and London: Newmarket Press/Pan Books, 1992), pp. 6–7.

22. Suzi Feay, 'Staking reputations', *Time Out*, 28 October 1992, pp. 18–19.

23. Bahiana, 'Tooth and nail', p. 12.

24. Robert E. Kapsis, *Hitchcock: The Making of a Reputation* (Chicago: University of Chicago Press, 1992), p. 6.

25. Cinema Advertising Association.

26. The 'semantics' of a genre are its 'building blocks': familiar settings, props, costumes and character-types. 'Syntax' refers to the meaning-bearing structures in which semantic elements are arranged. See Rick Altman, 'A semantic/syntactic approach to film genre', *Cinema Journal*, vol. 23, no. 3 (1984), reprinted in Altman, *Film/Genre*.

27. Altman, *Film/Genre*, p. 207.

28. Anderson, letter to the author.

29. Bahiana, 'Tooth and nail', p. 12.

30. Anderson, letter to the author.

31. See Timothy Corrigan, 'Auteurs and the new Hollywood', in Jon Lewis (ed.), *The New American Cinema* (Durham, NC: Duke University Press, 1998), pp. 38–63.

32. Columbia Pictures, *Bram Stoker's Dracula: Production Notes*, 1992, p. 5.

33. Roy Thomas, Mike Mignola and John Nyberg, *Bram Stoker's Dracula* (London: Pan, 1993).

34. Sony acquired CBS Records for $2 billion in 1987.

35. The film won an Oscar for best costume design.

36. See Coppola and Hart, *Bram Stoker's Dracula*, pp. 39, 70.

37. Anthony Quinn, 'Absolutely ravishing', *Independent on Sunday*, 31 January 1993, p. 19.

38. Ibid.; Jonathan Romney, 'At the court of Coppola', *The Guardian*, 21 January 1993, G2, pp. 2–3.

39. Anne Billson, 'Vlad the Mills & Boon hero', *The Sunday Telegraph*, 31 January 1993, Arts section, p. xv.

40. Cinema Advertising Association figures suggest that 54 per cent of the film's British cinema audience were from classes ABC1 and 46 per cent were from classes C2DE. 44 per cent of the audience were under twenty-four, and 22 per cent were over thirty-five.

41. Pierre Bourdieu, *Distinction: A Social Critique of the Judgement of Taste*, trans. Richard Nice (London: Routledge, 1984), especially pp. 31–4.
42. Frederick S. Clarke, editorial comment, *Cinefantastique*, vol. 23, no. 4 (December 1992), p. 3.
43. Ian Calcutt, '*Bram Stoker's Dracula*', *Samhain*, 37, March-April, 1993, p. 38.
44. Stefan Jaworzyn, '*Bram Stoker's Dracula*', *The Dark Side*, 29, February 1993, p. 9
45. Sarah Thornton, *Club Cultures: Music, Media and Subcultural Capital* (Cambridge: Polity Press, 1995).
46. Ibid., p. 11.
47. ITV, Saturday, 24 October 1996, 10 p.m. *Samhain* magazine had already published a request for readers to write to me. The reaction was disappointing: three letters and one subsequent questionnaire.
48. On 'conversion', see Roger Silverstone, *Television and Everyday Life* (London: Routledge, 1994), pp. 130–1.
49. By this term, I mean respondents who identified themselves as such or listed horror among their favourite genres.
50. Brigid Cherry suggests that women fans may not reject gore or violence per se, but that they are more often concerned with the way these elements are used in horror. Cherry, 'Refusing to refuse to look: female viewers of the horror film', in Stokes and Maltby (eds), *Identifying Hollywood's Audiences*, p. 196.
51. Ibid., p. 196.
52. See for example, Daniel Cavicchi, *Tramps Like Us: Music and Meaning among Springsteen Fans* (New York: Oxford University Press, 1998), pp. 83–5. Thanks to Matt Hills for pointing me towards this book.
53. The phrase is from Martin Barker and Kate Brooks, *Knowing Audiences: Judge Dredd, Its Friends, Fans and Foes* (Luton: University of Luton Press, 1998) p. 142.
54. Gemma Moss, 'Girls tell the teen romance: four reading histories', in David Buckingham (ed.), *Reading Audiences: Young People and the Media* (Manchester: Manchester University Press, 1993), pp. 119, 133.
55. See Altman, *Film/Genre*, pp. 156–65.

Index

Page numbers in *italics* denote illustrations; *n* = endnote; *t* = table

Abbott and Costello Meet Frankenstein (1948) 288
ABC/Cinerama 17
The Absent-Minded Professor (1961) 172
Ace Ventura: Pet Detective (1994) 122, 175–6
Ace Ventura: When Nature Calls (1995) 176
action/adventure films 2, 4, 15, 23, 29, 65, 77, 131, 174–5
  overlap with other genres 124, 134
  parodies 281, 282, 287
adaptations
  novels/(auto)biographies 5–6, 36–7, 251, 256–7, 260–1, 262–3, 269, 272–8, 279n4
  stage works 24, 148–60
The Addams Family (1991) 175
The Addams Family (TV) 292n21
Adventures in Babysitting (1987) 227–8
advertising 149–50, 160–1n5, 248, 291, 298
Aerosmith 84
An Affair to Remember (1957) 140, 146n34
Affleck, Ben 151
Affliction (1997) 178
African-American roles/culture 5, 82, 228, 274
  biopics 3, 92–5, 102–3, 104n23
  comedy 124, 135–6
  gangster/ghetto films 36, 39–40, 236–48
  misconceptions 247–8
After Dark, My Sweet (1990) 251, 260, 262–3
Agee, James 129n13
Airplane! (1980) 177, 286, 292n10
Airport (1970) 16, 19–20
Aladdin (1992) 167t, 171, 195
Albino Alligator (1997) 39
Alcott, Louisa May 84–5, 89n19
Aldrich, Robert 64
Alexander, Scott 96
Ali (2001) 93, 102–3

Alice Doesn't Live Here Anymore (1974) 79
Alien (1979) 23, 106
All Over the Guy (2001) 136
All the President's Men (1974) 39
Allen, Robert C. 137
Allen, Tim 171, 172
Allen, Woody 125, 139
Allied Artists 17
Ally McBeal (TV) 151, 270
Altman, Rick 5, 78, 91, 94, 185, 201–2, 203, 209, 213, 215n12, 255, 291n3, 296, 297, 298
Amadeus (1984) 96
Amazon Women on the Moon (1987) 285
Ambrose, Stephen 70
Ameche, Don 124
American Beauty (1999) 171, 178, 182
American Dreamer (1984) 134
American Film Institute (AFI) 18, 19
The American Girl (1917) 77
American Graffiti (1973) 20, 64, 119, 120
American Hot Wax (1978) 49, 53
An American in Paris (1951) 52
American International Pictures 15, 17
American Me (1992) 39
American Pie (1999) 123, 125, 176, 219, 220, *221*
The American President (1995) 135
An American Tale: Fievel Goes West (1991) 33
Anaconda (1997) 170
Analyze This (1999) 38, 133
Anastasia (1956) 26n32
Anastasia (1997) 24, 26n32
Anders, Alison 82
Anderson, Carolyn 3, 92
Anderson, Eric 32
Anderson, Jon 297
Anderson, Laurie 96
animated features 4, 24, 135, 171–2, 194–5, 199n50, 200n54, 200n57

Aniston, Jennifer 136
Anna and the King (1999) 92, 98
Annaud, Jean-Jacques 211
Annie (1982) 24
Annie Hall (1977) 139
The Anniversary Party (2001) 133
Antz (1998) 171, 182, 194
Anywhere But Here (1999) 79
Apocalypse Now (1979) 18, 22, 64–5, 70, 284, 285
Apollo 13 (1993) 174
The Apple Dumpling Gang (1975) 189
Arabian Nights (1979) 215n16
Arenas, Reinaldo 96–7
The Aristocats (1970) 189
Armageddon (1998) 167t, 168, 203
Armstrong, Gillian 84
Around the World in Eighty Days (1956) 13
Arrighi, Luciana 155
As Good as It Gets (1997) 131, 136, 137, 178
As You Like It (play) 139
The Asphalt Jungle (1950) 38
Astaire, Fred 51–2, 53
audiences, composition/targeting 18–20, 44–5n51, 204–6, 215n12, 295–6, 305–6, 306n4
  age 19, 28–9, 35, 136–7, 146n25, 165–6, 185, 190, 192, 203, 238–9, 302, 305, 307n40
  gender 28, 134, 297–8, 302–4, 308n50
  race 136, 239, 241
  sexuality 136
  social/cultural status 198–9n42, 300, 307n40
Austen, Jane 85–6, 139, 145n9
Austin, Thomas 6
Austin Powers: International Man of Mystery (1997) 6, 176, 282, 283, 284–5, 291n2
Austin Powers: The Spy Who Shagged Me (1999) 167t, 176, 281, 285, 287
auteurism 95–8, 148
Avary, Roger 39

Avco-Embassy 17
Avnet, John 180
The Awful Truth (1937) 128, 146n36
Aykroyd, Dan 124
'B' movies 23, 28, 169
Babe (1995) 173
Babe: Pig in the City (1998) 173
Baby Boom (1987) 125, 137
The Babysitters' Club (1995) 80
Back to the Future (1985) 23, 179, 193, 232–3, 235n8
Back to the Future III (1990) 33
Backer, Brian 226
Bacon, Kevin 59, 230
Bad Girls (1994) 33
Bad Lieutenant (1992) 212
The Bad News Bears (1976) 172
Bailey, Steve 5
Baker, Chet 263
Bakhtin, Mikhail 287
Balides, Constance 69, 70
Balio, Tino 1, 4, 14
Ball of Fire (1941) 133, 134
The Ballad of Gregorio Ortez (1982) 28
The Ballad of Little Jo (1993) 33
Banderas, Antonio 136
Bar Girls (1994) 81, 136
Bara, Theda 160
Barbarossa (1982) 28
Bardem, Javier 96, 104n24
Barrie, J.M. 173
Barrymore, Drew 111, 230
Bartlett, Keith 5–6
Basic Instinct (1992) 157, 180, 212, 213, 285
Basil the Great Mouse Detective (1986) 199n50
Basinger, Janine 77, 78
The Basketball Diaries (1995) 151
Basquiat (1996) 96–7
Bassett, Angela 93
Batman (1989) 23, 174
Bay, Michael 168
Bazin, André 27
Beaches (1988) 80
The Beatles 117–18
Beautiful Thing (1998) 136
Beauty and the Beast (1991) 23, 137, 171, 195, 200n57
Bedknobs and Broomsticks (1971) 189
Bedrooms and Hallways (1998) 136
The Bee Gees 53, 57
Beerbohm, Max 150
Beerbohm Tree, Sir Herbert 150–1, 152–3, 154–5, 159–60, 161n7
Before Night Falls (2000) 92, 96–7, 102, 104n24

Being John Malkovich (1999) 127, 128
Bella Mafia (1997) 35
Bellamy, Ralph 124, 146n36
Belushi, John 121
Ben Hur (1925) 12
Ben Hur (1959) 24, 155, 198n41
Bening, Annette 152, 178, 263
Benji (1974) 192
Benton, Robert 44n50
Berenstein, Rhona 288
Bergman, Ingrid 140
Berkeley, Busby 50–1
Bernstein, Matthew 219, 230
The Best Man (1999) 135
The Best Years of Our Lives (1946) 12
Better Than Chocolate (1999) 136
The Beverly Hillbillies (1995) 175
Beverly Hills Cop (1984) 124
Beyond the Valley of the Dolls (1970) 205
Big (1988) 125, 135
Big Daddy (1999) 176
Big Eden (2000) 136
Big Jake (1971) 28
The Big Parade (1925) 11–12
The Big Red One (1980) 72
Biggs, Jason 220
Biko, Steve 94
Billson, Anne 300
Billy Bathgate (1991) 35, 263
Billy Hollywood's Screen Kiss (1998) 136
Billy Jack (1971) 20–1, 26n22
Billy Madison (1994) 230
Billy the Kid 31
biopics 3, 91–103, 103–4n9, 104n12
  'duelling' 98–102
  of ethnic subjects 92–5, 102–3, 104n23
  overlap with other genres 91–2, 101
Bird on a Wire (1990) 133
The Bishop's Wife (1947) 146n34
Black, David A. 271–2, 273
The Black Cauldron (1985) 199n50
The Black Hole (1979) 192–3
Black Robe (1991) 33
Blackadder series (TV) 156
The Blackboard Jungle (1955) 232, 235
Blair, Linda 283
The Blair Witch Project (1999) 107, 170, 297
  parodied 287, 290, 292n16
Blast From the Past (1999) 135
blaxploitation 39, 47n78, 234, 237–8

The Blob (1961) 288
Block, Lawrence 258
blockbusters 2, 11–26, 28, 101–2, 167t
Blood Guts Bullets and Octane (1998) 39
Blood River (1991) 33
Bloom, Harold 153–4
Blue Diner/La Fona Anzul (2001) 136
Body Heat (1981) 256
Body of Evidence (1992) 212
Bogart, Humphrey 140
Bonanza (TV) 28, 31
Bond films 15, 117, 129n7, 174, 285, 287
The Bonfire of the Vanities (Wolfe) 269
Bonnie and Clyde (1967) 17, 34–5, 44n50, 45n51, 64
Bonnie and Clyde: The True Story (1992) 44n50
Boomerang (1992) 135
Boone, Herman 94
Booty Call (1997) 135
Bordwell, David 1
Born on the 4th of July (1989) 97
Born Yesterday (1950/93) 146n34
Boucher, Anthony 251, 252
Boulevard Nights (1979) 34
Bounce (2000) 133
Bound (1996) 35
Bound by Honor (aka *Blood in Blood Out*) (1993) 40
Bourdieu, Pierre 300, 301
Bowen, Kevin 67
Bowerman, Bill 99–100
The Bowery Boys 117
Bowie, David 96
box office 17, 22, 24, 25n2, 166, 167t, 189, 194–5, 197n24, 199–200nn51–3, 278–9n1, 281
Boxing Helena (1993) 212
Boys and Girls (2000) 137
Boys Don't Cry (1999) 102
The Boys in Company C (1979) 64
Boys on the Side (1995) 80, 81–2
Boyz N the Hood (1991) 39, 40, 236, 241, 242, 243, 245, 246
The Brady Bunch Movie (1995) 175
Brain Damage (1987) 107
Bram Stoker's Dracula (1992) 6, 107, 170, 294–306, 295
  audience composition/targeting 294–5, 297–9, 300
  audience responses 302–5
  generic status 294–6, 300–1, 305–6
Branagh, Kenneth 87, 107, 148, 155, 158, 160–1n5

Brandon, Teena 102
Braveheart (1995) 23, 175
The Breakfast Club (1985) 222–3, 224
Bride of Chucky (1998) 287–8
Bridget Jones's Diary (2001) 132
Bringing Up Baby (1938) 142–4, 147*n*40
Bristol, Michael 160–1*n*5
Broadcast News (1987) 126–7, 129*n*14, 178
Broadway Damage (1997) 136
Broccoli, Barbara 174
Broderick, Matthew 123, 126, 171, 220
Broken Blossoms (1919) 77
The Broken Chain (1993) 33
Broken English (1996) 212
Broken Hearts' Club — A Romantic Comedy (1999) 136
Bronco Billy (1980) 28, 41*n*9
The Bronx War (1990) 39
Brooks, Albert 126
Brooks, James L. 129*n*14, 177, 178
Brosnan, Pierce 174
The Brotherhood (1968) 44*n*48
The Brothers (2001) 135
Browne, Nick 185
Bruckheimer, Jerry 168
Brynner, Yul 26*n*32
'buddy films' 118–19
  female 79–81, 82–3
The Buddy Holly Story (1978) 2, 49, 53, 54–5
Buffalo Soldiers (1997) 34
Bugsy (1991) 35, 38, 45 n. 64, 46*n*64, 263
Bull Durham (1988) 134
Bulletproof Heart (1995) 38
Bullitt (1968) 17
Bullock, Sandra 126, 141, 278–9*n*1
Bulworth (1988) 135
Buñuel, Luis 157
The Burden of Proof (TV) 279*n*4
Burgoyne, Robert 31
Burnett, W.R. 252
Burton, Tim 102
Buscombe, Edward 1, 27
Busey, Gary 54
Bush, George (sr.) 270
Bushman, Francis X. 160
But I'm a Cheerleader (2000) 137
Butch Camp (1997) 136
Butch Cassidy and the Sundance Kid (1969) 118, 197*n*29
Bye Bye Love (1995) 137

The Cable Guy (1996) 122–3, 124
Caddyshack (1980) 121, *122*

Cage, Nicolas 126, 226
Cagney, James 157
Cain, James M. 251, 256–7, 258, 264*n*6
Cameron, James 166
Campbell, Neve 289
Campbell, Richard 31
Canby, Vincent 68
Candyman I/II (1992/95) 106
Cannibal: the Musical (1996) 281
Can't Buy Me Love (1987) 137
Can't Hardly Wait (1998) 137, 221–2
Cantwell, Robert 254
Capone, Al 36
Capone's Enforcer (1985) 35, 45 n. 57
Capra, Frank 144
Caputo, Phillip 67
Car Wash (1975) 119
Carlisle, Kitty 118
Carlito's Way (1993) 38
Carpenter, John 289
Carrey, Jim 4, 122–3, 124, 125, 128, 175–6
Carroll, Noel 105
cars, role in teen films 229–30
Carter, Jimmy 270
Carter, Rubin 94
Cartland, Barbara 139
Carvey, Dana 176
Casablanca (1942) 140
Casino (1995) 37, 45*n*64, 46*n*64
Caspar (1995) 112, 173
Cassady, Neal 102
Cassell, R.V. 251, 257–8
Castellano, Paul 36
Catch 22 (1970) 72
Cates, Phoebe 222
Caton-Jones, Michael 175
Cattle Annie and Little Britches (1981) 28
Cave, Nick 265*n*15
Caviezel, James 71
Cawelti, John 27, 41–2*n*17
The Cell (2000) 203
The Chamber (1994) 269, 272, 273, 274, 275, 278–9*n*1
Chances Are (1989) 135
Chandler, Raymond 251, 256
Chaplin, Ben 71, 138, 141
Charlie's Angels (2000) 23
Chase, Chevy 121
Chasing Amy (1999) 136, 145*n*11
Cherry, Brigid 303, 308*n*50
Cherry Falls (2000) 107, 113
Cheyenne Warrior (1994) 33
Chicken Run (2000) 281, 285
Child's Play series (1988-91) 106

Chinatown (1974) 256, 263
Christopher, Nicholas 254, 256
Christopher Columbus: The Discovery (1992) 98
Cimarron (1960) 28
Cimino, Michael 44*n*50, 65
Cin Cin/A Fine Romance (1991) 137
Cinderella (1950) 172
Cinema Center 17
city environment 227–9
City of Industry (1997) 39
The Civil War (1990) 33
Clancy, Tom 175
classification *see* ratings
Clear and Present Danger (1994) 175
Cleopatra (1963) 198*n*41
The Client (1994) 179, 269, 272–3, 274, 277–8, 278–9*n*1
Cliffhanger (1993) 174
Clinton, Bill 270
Clisby, Heather 154
Clockers (1993) 40
A Clockwork Orange (1971) 205, 216*n*29
Clooney, George 72
Close, Glenn 172
Close Encounters of the Third Kind (1977) 187, 190, 192
Clueless (1995) 83, 85–6, 136, 137, 145*n*9, 219, 220, 222, 226–7, 229
Coal Miner's Daughter (1980) 49
Cobb (1994) 102
Cochran, David 267*n*64
Cocktail (1988) 215*n*12
Cocteau, Jean 300
Code (later Classification) and Ratings Administration (CARA) 202–3, *204*, 205, 206, 208–13
Coleman, Baoan 62
Collins, Patricia Hill 247
Color of Night (1994) 212
The Color Purple (1985) 82
Columbia Pictures 17, 85, 87, 168
Columbus, Chris (director) 172–3, 196, 227
Columbus, Christopher (explorer) 98
comedy 117–28, 175–8
  overlap with other genres 3–4, 28, 31–2, 35, 39, *107*, 110–13, 118
  sub-genres 4, 119–20, 125–6, 128–9*nn*1–2, 129*n*7, 129*n*14, 175, 178 (*see also* romantic comedy)
Comes a Horseman (1978) 28
Coming to America (1988) 124, 135
Connery, Sean 174
Conrad, Joseph 258

Conspiracy Theory (1997) 175
Contact (1997) 169
The Conversation (1974) 271
Coolidge, Martha 226
Coppola, Francis Ford 107, 170,
    278–9n1, 298, 299, 300, 301, 304
Corinna, Corinna (1994) 132
Corliss, Richard 157, 251, 262–3
Corr, Eugene 99
Corrigan, Timothy 83
Costellano, Paul 36
Costner, Kevin 102, 175, 179
The Cotton Club (1984) 36
Count Dracula (1973) 298
Coup de Torchon (1981) 259
Courage Under Fire (1995) 72, 73
Coursen, H.R. 157
Cowie, Elizabeth 255
The Craft (1996) 221
Craig, Edward Gordon 160
Crash (1996) 212
Craven, Wes 106, 110, 289
Crazy Horse (1995) 33
Crazy Joe (1974) 35
Crichton, Michael 169, 180
Crowe, Cameron 178, 231
Crudup, Billy 99
Cruel Intentions (1999) 145n9
Cruise, Tom 99, 170, 174, 175, 178,
    179, 219, *271*, 278–9n1
Cruising (1980) 209–10, *211*,
    216n45
Crush (2001) 144–5n8
Cruz, Adriana 73
Cry Freedom (1987) 94
Cryer, Jon 230
Crystal, Billy 133, 177
Culkin, Macaulay 172–3
Cummings, John 36
Curtis, Richard 144–5n8
Cusack, John *261*
Custen, George F. 3, 91, 92–3,
    96–7, 103n2
The Cutting Edge (1992) 134
Cyrano de Bergerac (Rostand) 141,
    145n9

Dahl, John 256
Dalton, Timothy 174
Damage (1992) 212
Damon, Matt 71, 73, 180, 278–9n1
Dances with Wolves (1990) 23, 33,
    179
Danes, Claire 151, 152
Dangerous Game (1993) 212
Daniels, Jeff 176
Dante's Peak (1997) 168
The Dark Side (magazine) 301
Dash, Stacey 229

Dave (1992) 135
Davis, John H. 36
Davis, Miles 140
Dawn of the Dead (1979) 225, 226
Day, Doris 79
The Day the Earth Stood Still (1951)
    168
Dazed and Confused (1994) 223
De Bont, Jan 170
De Laurentiis, Dino 26n28
De Mornay, Rebecca 228
De Niro, Robert 133, 296
De Vito, Danny 38, 278–9n1
Dead Again (1991) 87
Dead Man (1995) 33
Dead Men Don't Wear Plaid (1982)
    256, 286–7
Dead Presidents (1995) 46n64
Deep Cover (1992) 39, 40
The Deer Hunter (1978) 18, 64–5
del Toro, Benicio 96
Delameter, Jerome 51–2
Delany, Dana 142
Delta of Venus (1995) 212
DeMille, Cecil B. 12, 130
Demme, Jonathan 179–80
Dench, Judi 155–6
DePalma, Brian 244
Depardieu, Gerard 141
Depp, Johnny *37*, 96
Derry, Charles 278
Desi's Looking for a New Girl (2000)
    136
Desperate Hours (1955/90) 256
Desperately Seeking Susan (1985) 80,
    134
Deutch, Howard 224
The Devil Thumbs a Ride (1947)
    262
Di Novi, Denise 84
Diaz, Cameron 126, 127, 145n22, 176
DiCaprio, Leonardo 151, 152, *154*,
    159, 166
Dick Tracy (1990) 263
Die Hard I/II (1988/90) 23, 174
digital imaging 92
Dillinger (1991) 44n50
Dillon, Matt 176
Dirty Dancing (1985) 49, 58
The Dirty Dozen (1967) 64, 168
disaster films 2, 4, 19–20, 166–8
Disclosure (1994) 180
Disney 4–5, 17, 24, 99, 102, 137,
    165, 166, 171–2, 181–2, 187,
    188–96, 199n47, 199n50
    finances 188–9, 194–6
    response to competition 189–90,
    192
    response to ratings system 191–4

Disturbing Behaviour (1998) 224
Dixon, Wheeler Winston 7
Doane, Mary Anne 77, 78
Doctor Zhivago (1965) 22
Dog Park (1998) 145n11
Doherty, Thomas 238
The Don Is Dead (1973) 35
Donaldson, Roger 268n79
Donnie Brasco (1997) 36–7, *37*, 38,
    46n64
*Don't Be a Menace to South Central
    While Drinking Your Juice in the
    Hood* (1996) 236
Don't Change Your Husband (1919)
    130
Doonan, Mark 99
The Doors (1991) 60, 97
Doran, Lindsay 86–8
Dostoyevsky, Fyodor 258
Double Indemnity (1943) 264n6
Douglas, Michael 180
Down to You (2000) 137
Downey, Robert, Jr. 152
Dr. Dolittle (1998) 124
Dr Jekyll and Mr Hyde (early films)
    288
Dr Pyckle and Mr Pryde (1925) 288
Dr Quinn, Medicine Woman (TV)
    33, 34
*Dr Seuss' How the Grinch Stole
    Christmas* (2000) 196
Dr Strangelove (1966) 157
Dracula (1958/79) 298
Dracula: Dead and Loving It (1995)
    281
Dragon: the Bruce Lee Story (1993)
    93
Dragonslayer (1981) 192–3
drama 4, 23, 37, 129, 178–81
Dream a Little Dream (1989) 135
Dream for an Insomniac (1998) 136
DreamWorks 24, 215n15
Dreyfuss, Richard 122
Drive Me Crazy (1999) 137, 219
Driving Miss Daisy (1989) 180
Drummond, Lee 129n7
Duel in the Sun (1946) 12, 14
Dumb and Dumber (1994) 128,
    175–6
Duncan, Paul 254
Dunne, Irene 128
Dyson, Michael Eric 249n7

Earp, Wyatt 31
Eastwood, Clint 28, 30, 41n9, *9*, 179
Easy Rider (1969) 17, 19
Ebert, Roger 152, 153–4, 179
Eco, Umberto 139, 140
Ed Wood (1994) 96, 102

Eddie Murphy Raw (1987) 124
Edge of Seventeen (1998) 136
Edwards, Blake 118, 125
8 Heads in a Duffel Bag (1997) 38
84 Charlie Mopic (1989) 65
Eilbacher, Lisa 124
Eisner, Michael 188
The Electric Horseman (1979) 28
Elizabeth, Shannon 290
Ellroy, James 268*n*79
Elsaesser, Thomas 64, 66
Emma (1996) 132
The English Patient (1996) 23, 181
Ephron, Nora 177–8
Erin Brockovich (2000) 101–2
Ermey, R. Lee 100
Escape to Witch Mountain (1974) 189
Estevez, Emilio 172
Eszterhas, Joe 157
E.T.: The Extra-Terrestrial (1982) 20, 129*n*2, 186–7
Everett, Rupert 127, 151
Everything Relative (1996) 136
Evil Dead II (1987) 107
Evita (1996) 24, 60, 97
Excess Baggage (1997) 134
The Exorcist (1973) 20, 23, 189, 283
The Exploits of Elaine (1914–15) 77

The Faculty (1998) 107, 223
The Fall of the Roman Empire (1964) 24
Fallen Angels: Six Noir Tales for Television (TV) 268*n*79
A Family Affair (2001) 136
'family' films 4–5, 18–20, 172–4, 185–96, 199*n*49
  audience appeal/targeting 165–6, 187, 189–90, 193–6, 198–9*n*42
The Family Man (2000) 137
Fantasia (1940) 190, 195
fantasy 23, 129*n*2, 135
Far and Away (1992) 33
Farber, Manny 256
Farewell My Lovely (1975) 256
Fargo (1995) 38, 46*n*69, 178
Faris, Anna 288
Farmer, Gary 32
Farrelly, Peter and Bobby 176–7
Fast Food, Fast Women (2001) 137
Fast Times at Ridgemont High (1982) 85, 119, 219, 222, 226, 230–1
Fatal Attraction (1987) 147*n*39, 180, 285
Fatal Instinct (1993) 285–6
Father of the Bride (1991) 125, 137
Faulkner, William 258
Feldman, Corey 229

Fellini, Federico 158
Ferris Bueller's Day Off (1986) 219, 220, 221, 223, 227, 229, 235*n*6
A Few Good Men (1992) 179
Fiddler on the Roof (1971) 17–18, 191
Field, Sally 173
Fierstein, Harvey 173
Fievel: An American Tail (1986) 199*n*50
film noir 253–7, 260, 265*n*27, 266*n*42
Finding Fish (2002, projected) 94
Fire on the Track (TV) 99
The Firm (1993) 179, 269, 270, 271, 273, 274, 276, 277, 278–9*n*1
First Blood (1982) 65–6
First Wives' Club (1996) 137
Firth, Colin 156
Fisher, Antwone 94
Flashdance (1983) 23, 49, 61*n*11, 241
The Flintstones (1994) 23, 173, 181, 182
Flockhart, Calista 151
Flubber (1997) 172
Flynt, Larry 102
Focillon, Henri 286
Foley, James 261, 278–9*n*1
Fools Rush In (1997) 136
Footlight Parade (1933) 51
Footloose (1984) 2, 49, 53, 58–60, 230
Forces of Nature (1999) 126
Ford, Harrison 174, 175
Forever, Lulu (1987) 134
Forman, Milos 96
Forrest Gump (1994) 92, 167*t*, 178–9, 235*n*8, 278–9*n*1
48 Hours (1982) 124
42nd Street (1933) 51, 61*n*6
Foster, Harold 224–5
Foster, Jodie 179–80
Four Weddings and a Funeral (1994) 131, 132, 144–5*n*8
1492: Conquest of Paradise (1992) 98, 102
Fox (studio) 16, 22, 24, 32, 85–6, 165, 168
Fox, Michael J. 233
Foxes (1980) 221, 222
Frank, Sam 211
Frank, Thomas 263
Frankenstein (1931) 108
Frankie and Johnny (1991) 136
Frears, Stephen 260, 261
Freddy Got Fingered (2001) 214
Free Willy (1993) 173–4
Freed, Alan 53

Freedman, Barbara 157
Freeman, Morgan 180
French, Philip 283
Friday the 13th series (1980–93) 106, 288, 289
Fried Green Tomatoes at the Whistle-Stop Café (1991) 81, 180
Friedkin, William 62–3, 64, 74, 209
Friends and Family (2000) 134, 136
Fright Night I/II (1985/88) 106
Fritz the Cat (1972) 200*n*54
The Front Page (1931) 146*n*34
The Fugitive (1993) 23, 175
Full Metal Jacket (1987) 65
The Full Monty (1997) 165
Fuller, Sam 72, 75*n*31, 259
The Funeral (1995) 35
Fussell, Paul 67, 68–9, 71

Galaxy Quest (1999) 281, 282, 285
Gallafent, Edward 256
Gallagher, Peter 141
Gallagher, Tag 292*n*13
The Gangster Chronicles (TV) 35
gangster films 2, 27, 34–40, 44*n*46, 90
  book-based 36–7, 45*n*60
  dialogue 46–7*n*70
  ethos 46*n*64
  sub-genres 5, 34–6, 39–40, 134
  target audience 35, 44–5*n*51
  television 44*n*48, 45*n*57
The Gangster Wars (1981) 35
Gardner, Erle Stanley 269
Garfield, John 261
Garmendia, Olatz Lopez 96
Garner, James 31
Garofalo, Janeane 138, 141
Garr, Teri 129*n*2
Gates, Bill 182
gay themes 81–2, 136, 209–10
Gehring, Wes 286, 292*n*10
General Cinema Corporation 210, 216*n*45
genre theory 1–2, 6–7, 27, 91, 113–16, 144*n*3, 148, 185–6, 201–2, 218, 253–6, 281, 291*n*3, 294–6, 307*n*26
  and age ratings 202–3, 213–14
George Lucas in Love (1999) 293*n*27
Gere, Richard 127, 128, 177
Geronimo: An American Legend (1993) 33, 93
Gershwin, George and Ira 53
Get Over It (2001) 137
Get Real (1998) 136
Get Shorty (1995) 38, 46*n*66
The Getaway (1972) 257, 268*n*79
The Getaway (1994) 268*n*79

Getting Gotti (1994) 35
Gettysburg (1993) 33
ghetto films 5, 39–40, 47*n74*,
    47*n78,* 236–48
  audience appeal 238–9, 240,
    241–2
  cultural background 239–40, 241,
    242–3, 249*n2,* 249*nn6–7*
  ethos 238, 242–7
  'realism' 247–8
Ghost (1990) 167*t,* 177
Ghost Dog: the Way of the Samurai
    (1999) 38
Ghostbusters (1984) 193
Giant (1956) 78
Gibson, Mel 155, 174, 175
Giddens, Anthony 115
Gifford, Barry 256, 267*n72*
Gilbert, Lewis 109
Girlfriends (1978) 79
Gladiator (2000) 23, 24
Gledhill, Christine 77, 78
Glenn, Scott 73
Gloria (1980) 35, 45*n56*
Gloria (1999) 35
Glory (1989) 32, 94
Go Fish (1994) 81, 136
Go Tell the Spartans (1978) 64
Go West (1925) 287
Godard, Jean-Luc 158
The Godfather (1972) 2, 20, 21,
    34–5, 36, 45*nn51–2,* 157, 189,
    190
The Godfather Part III (1990) 35
Godzilla (1998) 170
Gold Diggers of 1933 (1933) 50
Goldberg, Whoopi 81–2, 171, 177
Goldblum, Jeff 144–5*n8*
Goldeneye (1995) 174
Goldman, William 68–9
Goldwyn, Samuel 12
Gone with the Wind (1939) 12, 14,
    297, 301
The Good Mother (1988) 79
The Good Old Boys (1995) 33
Good Will Hunting (1997) 151, 180
Goodfellas (1990) 37–8, 46*nn63–4,*
    96
Gooding, Cuba, Jr. 93
Goodis, David 252, 253, 256, 257
Gorney, Karen Lynn 56
Gotti, John 36
Gotti (1996) 35
The Graduate (1967) 17
Grant, Barry Keith 185
Grant, Cary 128, 140, 143,
    146–7*n38*
Grant, Hugh 87, 132, 177
Granville-Barker, Harley 160

Grease (1978) 3, 24, 48, 49, 50, 52–3
Great Expectations (1998) 145*n9*
The Great Gatsby (1974) 18
The Great Race (1965) 118
The Green Berets (1968) 64
Green Card (1990) 132, 134, 141
Green on Red (band) 265*n15*
Greenaway, Peter 148
Greenwald, Maggie 260, 267*n56*
Greenwood, Lee 73
Griffith, D.W. 77
The Grifters (1990) 251, 260–1, *261,*
    262–3
Grisham, John 6, 179, 269–78,
    278–9*n1,* 279*n4*
Grist, Leighton 256
Grosse Pointe Blank (1997) 38, 134
Groundhog Day (1993) 122, 135
Grumpier Old Men (1995) 137
Grumpy Old Men (1993) 137
Guerrero, Ed 47*n78*
Gulf & Western 15
Gun Shy (2000) 38
Guns of Honor (1993) 33
Gunsmoke (TV) 31
Gypsy Boys (1999) 136

Hackman, Gene *271,* 278–9*n1*
Haim, Corey 229
Hair (1979) 50
Halberstam, David 66, 67
Hall, Sheldon 2
Halloween (1978) 108, 111, 288,
    289
Halloween 8 (2001) 106
Halloween H20: Twenty Years Later
    (1998) 289
Hamburger Hill (1987) 65, 66
Hamlet (Olivier, 1948) 155
Hamlet (Zeffirelli, 1990) 155,
    160–1*n5*
Hamlet (Branagh, 1996) 149, 155,
    160*n3,* 161*n9*
Hammett, Dashiell 36, 251
Hammett (1982) 256
Hammond, Michael 2, 3
The Hand That Rocks the Cradle
    (1992) 83
Handmade Films 32
Hanks, Tom 64, 126, 171, 174,
    177–8, 179
Hannah and Her Sisters (1986) 125
The Happiest Millionaire (1967) 189
Happy Accidents (2000) 135
A Hard Day's Night (1964) 117–18,
    283
Harrelson, Woody 181
Harries, Dan 6
Harris, Ed 98

*Harry Potter and the Philosopher's
    Stone* (2001) 196
Hart, James V. 297, 299, 300, 301,
    304
Hart, William S. 32, 282
Harvey, Stephen 30
Haskell, Molly 77, 118
Haunted (1995) 109
The Haunting (1999) 170
Hav Plenty (1997) 135
Havana (1990) 263
Hawks, Howard 142
Hawn, Goldie 142
Hay, James 5
Hayek, Salma 136
Hays Code *see* Production Code
Hayslip, Le Ly 96
Heartbreak Ridge (1986) 65
Heartbreakers (2001) 133
Heartburn (1986) 133
Heat (1995) 39, 46*n64*
Heathers (1989) 223
Heaven and Earth (1993) 96, 97
Heaven Help Us (1985) 119
Heaven's Gate (1980) 18, 28, 34,
    41*n7*
Heckerling, Amy 85–6
Heffner, Richard 209
Heineman, Larry 67
'heist' films 38–9, 46*n64,* 72–3
Hello, Dolly! (1969) 17, 191
Hellraiser series (1987-95) 106
Hell's Kitchen N.Y.C. (1999) 39
Hemdale 32
Henderson, Brian 132, 140
Henry, Portrait of a Serial Killer
    (1986) 107
Henry and June (1990) 96, 203
Henry V (1944) 148, 150
Henry V (1989) 87, 148, 158,
    160–1*n5*
Henry VI (Shakespeare) 150
Henry VIII (Shakespeare) 150,
    154–5
Henson, Jim 172
Hepburn, Katherine 143
Her Alibi (1989) 134
Herbie series (1969-77) 189
Hercules (1958) 14–15
Hercules (1997) 24
Hercules Unchained (1959) 14–15
The Hi-Lo Country (1999) 34
Hiding out (1987) 230–1
Higashi, Sumiko 130–1
Hill, Henry 36, 45*n59*
Hill, Walter 268*n79*
Hillier, Jim 1
Himes, Chester 256, 266*n42*

Hinson, Hal 157
Hirsch, Foster 256
His Bitter Pill (1916) 282
His Girl Friday (1940) 146*n34*, 146*n36*
The Hitch-Hiker (1953) 262
Hitchcock, Alfred 278
Hoffa (1992) 46*n64*, 102
Hoffman, Abbie 102
Hoffman, Dustin 129*n2*
Hoffman, Michael 151–2, 155
Holden, William 157
Hollinger, Karen 3
Holly, Buddy 54–5
Holly, Lauren 128
Home Alone 2: Lost in New York (1992) 173
Home Alone (1990) 126, 167*t*, 172–3
Home for the Holidays (1995) 133, 137
Honey, I Shrunk the Kids (1989) 125, 126
Honeymoon in Vegas (1992) 134
Hoodlum (1997) 35, 36, 40
Hook (1991) 125, 173
hooks, bell 248
Hoop Dreams (1994) 99
Hopkins, Anthony 170, 179–80, 295, 298–9
Hopper, Dennis 96, 253, 257, 260, 267*n54*
horror 3–4, 23, 105–16, 169–71, 201, 296–7
    audience expectations/responses 300–5
    and postmodernism 105–6, 113–16, 286
    secure *vs.* paranoid 106, 108–10, 115
    self-referential/parodic 107, 110–13, 281, 283, 286, 287–91, 292–3*n26*
Hot Shots! (1991) 282
Hot Shots! Part Deux (1993) 281, 283–4
The Hot Spot (1990) 253–4, 256, 257, 260, 263, 267*n54*
House I/II (1986/87) 106
House Party (1990) 241
Housekeeping (1987) 80
Housesitter (1992) 134, 142, 142–4, 147*n39*
Houston, Whitney 136
How I Spent My Summer Vacation (1997) 135
How the West Was Lost (1995) 33
How the West Was Won (1963) 28
How to Make an American Quilt (1995) 80

Howard, Ron 174
Howe, Desson 158
Hudson, Rock 79
Hughes, Allen and Albert 241, 243–5
Hughes, John 126, 222–3, 224, 227
Hugo, Chris 24
The Hunchback of Notre Dame (1996) 24
Hunt, Helen 168, 178
Hunt, Howard 98, 104*n20*
Hunt, Linda 30
The Hunt for Red October (1990) 174
Hunter, Holly 126
The Hurricane (1999) 94
Hurt, William 126, 177
Huston, John 24
Hynes, Samuel 75*n24*

I Know What You Did Last Summer (1997) 113, 223, 289
I Like it Like That (1994) 136
I Love Trouble (1994) 134
I Married a Witch (1942) 133
I Shot Andy Warhol (1996) 102
I Spit on Your Grave (1978) 112
I Still Know What You Did Last Summer (1998) 289
I Think I Do (1997) 136
The Ice Storm (1997) 178
An Ideal Husband (1999) 132
I'm Gonna Git You Sucka (1988) 39
Imitation of Life (1959) 79
In & Out (1997) 132, 136
In Living Color (TV) 122, 175
In the Boom Boom Room (2000) 134, 136
The Incredibly True Adventure of Two Girls in Love (1995) 81, 136
Indecent Proposal (1993) 167*t*
Independence Day (1996) 167*t*, 168, 195
Indian Summer/Alive and Kicking (1996) 136
Indiana Jones and the Temple of Doom (1984) 187
Interview with the Vampire (1994) 170, 296
Invaders From Mars (1953) 168
The Iron Giant (1999) 200*n54*
Ishioka, Eiko 300
Isn't She Great (2000) 102
It Happened One Night (1934) 133, 180
It Takes Two (1988) 137
It's a Wonderful World (1939) 133
It's in the Water (1998) 136

Jackson, Russell 149
Jackson, Samuel L. 62, 63, 63, 278–9*n1*
Jakubowski, Maxim 265*n11*
James, Frank and Jesse 31
James, Steve 99, 100
Jane Austen's Mafia! (1998) 35
Jarman, Derek 148
Jason X (2001) 106
Jaws (1975) 21, 23, 187, 189
Jeffrey (1995) 136
Jenkins, Henry 155
Jeopardy (1953) 262
Jeremiah Johnson (1972) 28, 198–9*n42*
Jerry Maguire (1996) 131, 135, 178
Jewel of the Nile (1985) 134
JFK (1991) 92, 97, 98, 102
Jingle All the Way (1996) 173
Joe MacBeth (1955) 46*n62*
Joe Versus the Volcano (1990) 134
John, Elton 101
Johnny Dangerously (1984) 35
Johnny Ryan (1990) 36
Johnson, William 261
The Jolson Story (1946) 54
Jones, Allan 118
Jones, James 70
Jones, Tommy Lee 62, 168, 278–9*n1*
Jordan, Neil 170
Jorgens, Jack 148
Judge Dredd (1995) 214
Judgment Night (1993) 228
Juice (1992) 39, 236
Julia (1977) 79
The Jungle Book (1967) 189
Juno, Andrea 257
Jurassic Park (1993) 21, 21, 23, 69, 70, 167*t*, 169–70, 171, 182, 195, 278–9*n1*
Just One More Time (1999) 136

Kama Sutra: A Tale of Love (1996) 212
Kansas City (1986) 36
Kaplan, E. Ann 256
Kapsis, Robert E. 298
Karaszewski, Larry 96
Kardong, Don 99
Karloff, Boris 170
Kasdan, Lawrence 30
Kaufman, Andy 123
Kaufman, Phillip 96
Ke Huy Quan 187
Keaton, Buster 287
Keeler, Greg 58, 61*n14*
Keener, Catherine 127
Kehr, Dave 118

Kelley, Robin D.G. 249*n6*
Kelly, Gene 49–50, 52, 53, 61*n11*
Kemp, Will 156
Kennedy, Burt 268*n79*
Kennedy, Jamie 289
Kennedy, John F. 44*n48*, 256
Kern, Jerome 53
Kerr, Deborah 140
Keyishian, Harry 155
Kids (1995) 221
Kill Me Again (1989) 256
The Kill Off (1990) 251, 260,
    267*n56*
The Killer Inside Me (1976) 268*n79*
The Killing (1956) 38
The Killing of Sister George (1968)
    205
Killing Zoe (1994) 38–9
Kilpatrick, Jacquelyn 31
Kimberley, Nick 259
Kind Hearts and Coronets (1949)
    157
King, Rodney 95
King, Stephen 251
The King and I (1956) 26*n32*
The King and I (1999) 24, 26*n32*, 98
King Kong (1976) 22
King Lear (1916) 160
King of New York (1990) 37
Kiss Me Deadly (1955) 258–9
Kiss Me Guido (1997) 136
Klimt, Gustav 300
Kline, Kevin 151–2
Klinger, Barbara 306*n3*
Knight, Arthur 210–11
Knights of the City (1985) 39
Koteas, Elias 71
Kovic, Ron 97
Kozloff, Sarah 46–7*n70*
Krämer, Peter 4–5
Kronman, Anthony T. 270
Krutnik, Frank 3, 4, 256–7
Kubrick, Stanley 216*n29*
Kudrow, Lisa 133
Kundun (1997) 96, 98
Kurins, Andrew 36
Kurosawa, Akira 148

La Cava, Gregory 132
LA Confidential (1997) 263,
    278–9*n1*
LA Law (TV) 270
LA Story (1991) 134, 135
Lady Mobster (1988) 35
The Land Before Time (1988)
    199*n50*
Landis, John 124
Lane, Nathan 171
Lang, Fritz 278

Lange, Jessica 129*n2*
Lansing, Sherry 86
Lara Croft: Tomb Raider (2001) 23
Last Action Hero (1993) 174
The Last Days of Chez Nous (1992)
    84
*The Last Days of Frank and Jesse
    James* (1986) 30
The Last Don I/II (1997/98) 35
The Last House on the Left (1972)
    107, 289
The Last of the Mohicans (1992) 33,
    175
The Last Outlaw (1993) 33
The Last Seduction (1994) 256
The Last Time I Committed Suicide
    (1997) 102
The Last Waltz (1978) 49, 53, 59–60
Late Bloomers (1996) 136
Latino films 40
Laughlin, Tom 20
Laurel and Hardy 288
A League of Their Own (1992) 175
Leather Jacket Love Story (1998) 136
Lee, Ang 86, 87–8, 178
Lee, Christopher 300
Lee, Harper 269
Lee, Jason Scott 93
Lee, Spike 93, 94–5
Lefebvre, Henri 234
legal thrillers 6, 179, 269–78, 279*n3*
The Legend of the Lone Ranger
    (1981) 28
Leigh, Jennifer Jason 222
Leonard, Elmore 264*n6*
Lepke (1975) 35
Less Than Zero (1987) 220–1
Lester, Richard 117
Lethal Weapon I/II (1987/89) 23,
    174
Leto, Jared 99
Levine, Joseph E. 14–15, 21, 26*n28*
Lewinsky, Monica 270
Lewis, Jerry 123, 124
Lewis, Jon 204–5, 207
Les Liaisons Dangereuses (Laclos)
    145*n9*
Lianna (1983) 81
Liar, Liar (1997) 123, 125
Licence to Kill (1989) 174
License to Drive (1988) 229
Lieberman, Joseph, Senator 214
A Life Less Ordinary (1997) 145*n22*
Linklater, Richard 223
The Lion King (1994) 167*t*, 171,
    172, 194, 199–200*n53*, 200*n64*
Liotta, Ray 37–8
Lipnicki, Jonathan 178
litigation 205, 208

Little Big Man (1970) 28
The Little Mermaid (1989) 137, 171,
    199*n47*, 203
Little Odessa (1994) 38
Little Women (1994) 83, 84–5, *85*,
    88, 89*nn19–20*
Lloyd, Harold 124, 129*n13*
Loaded Weapon I (1993) 281
Los Locos (1998) 34
Loehlin, James 157
Loews 207–8
Loncrane, Richard 150, 151, 157
Lone Star (1996) 34
Lonesome Dove (novel/TV) 29–31,
    42*nn28–9*
The Long Goodbye (1973) 256
The Long Riders (1980) 28
The Longest Day (1962) 75*n15*
Look Who's Talking series (1989-93)
    85, 125, 137
Lopez, Jennifer 93, 136
Loser (2000) 137
The Lost World: Jurassic Park (1997)
    167*t*, 169–70
Love Affair (1939/94) 146*n34*
Love and Basketball (2000) 135
The Love Bug (1969) 189
Love Jones (1997) 135
Love Potion No 9 (1991) 135
Love Story (1970) 20, 25*n19*
Love! Valor! Compassion! (1997) 136
The Lover (1992) 211, 213
Love's Labour's Lost (2000) 132,
    145*n9*
Loy, Myrna 118
Lubitsch, Ernst 132, 177–8
Lucas, George 168, 187, 189–90,
    192, 193, 199*n50*
Luciano, Lucky 36
Lugosi, Bela 300
Luhrmann, Baz 158
Lupo, Jon 3
Lust in the Dust (1985) 30
Lutz, John 99
Lyons, Arthur 254
Lyotard, Jean-Francois 105

Macbeth (1916) 153, 160, 161*n7*
MacDowell, Andie 132, 141,
    144–5*n8*, 177
Mad Dog and Glory (1993) 124
Made in Heaven (1987) 135
Madonna 136
Madsen, Virginia 263
Mafia Cop (1993) 36
Making Mr Right (1987) 135
Malcolm X (1992) 94–5, *95*
Malick, Terrence 71–2, 75*n24*
Malkovich, John 127

Mall Rats (1995) 225–6

Maltby, Richard 204, 258–9, 306*n2*

Man Bites Dog (1992) 107

Man of La Mancha (1972) 17

Man on the Moon (1999) 96, 123

Mandela, Nelson 95

Mann, Michael 39, 103, 175

Mannequin (1987) 135

Marcus, Greil 265*n15*

Margolyes, Miriam 152

Marlowe (1969) 256

Married to the Mob (1988) 35, 134

Mars-Jones, Adam 287

Martin, Steve 142

Martinez, Oliver 96

Marx, Groucho 123

Marx Brothers 117–18

Mary Poppins (1964) 171, 189, 191

Mary Reilly (1996) 296, 307*n14*

Mary Shelley's Frankenstein (1994) 107, 296, 307*n14*

*M*A*S*H* (1970) 17, 64, 72, 119, 120

The Mask (1994) 123

Maslin, Janet 171

Masterson, Mary Stuart 180

The Mating Habits of the Earthbound Human (1999) 135

The Matrix (1999) 23, 169, 284

Matthau, Walter 172

Maverick (1994) 33

McArthur, Colin 27

McCabe and Mrs Miller (1971) 28

McCarthy, Andrew 220, 223

McCarthy, Todd 33, 38

McConaughey, Matthew 278–9*n1*

McCoy, Horace 252

McKellen, Ian 150, 151, 152, 157

McMillan, Terry 82

McMurtry, Larry 29, 30–1

Me, Myself & Irene (2000) 123

Mean Streets (1973) 2, 34, 37

Meatballs (1979) 119, 121

Meet the Parents (2000) 137

Men in Black (1997) 167*t*, 168, 182, 195, 278–9*n1*

Men of Honor (2000) 93

Men of Respect (1991) 46*n62*

Menace II Society (1993) 40, 236, 241, 243–5, 248

merchandising 188–9, 193, 195–6, 240, 291*n2*, 299

Merchant/Ivory films 155

The Merchant of Venice (Shakespeare) 150, 159–60

Mermaids (1990) 137

Mernit, Billy 133–5, 138, 145*n12*, 145*n15*

The Mexican (2001) 134

MGM 11–12, 16, 52–3

Mi Vida Loca (1994) 40, 81, 82

Miami Blues (1990) 256

Michael (1996) 135, 177

Mickey Blue Eyes (1999) 134

Midler, Bette 79, 102

Midnight Cowboy (1969) 17, 205

A Midsummer Night's Dream (play) 124

see also *William Shakespeare's A Midsummer Night's Dream*

The Mighty Ducks (1992) 172

Milestone, Lewis 258

Miller, Barry 56

Miller, George 173

Miller, Ron 192

Miller's Crossing (1990) 35, 46*n64*, 263

Miss Congeniality (2000) 132

Missing in Action I/II (1984/85) 65

Mission: Impossible (1996) 23, 175

Mittel, Jason 215*n18*

Mob Boss (1990) 35

Mobs and Mobsters (1992) 35

Mobsters (1991) 35, 263

Modleski, Tania 78, 105

The Money Pit (1994) 132

Monty Python's Flying Circus (TV) 156

Moonlight and Valentino (1995) 80

Moonstruck (1987) 125, 126–7

Moore, Demi 177, 179, 180, 181

Moore, Kenny 99

Morrison, Jim 97

Mortal Kombat (1994) 23

Mortal Thoughts (1991) 81, 83

Moss, Craig 293*n27*

Moss, Gemma 305

Motion Picture Association of America (MPAA) 202–3, 204, 205–10, 213–14

Moulin Rouge (2001) 60

Moviedrome (TV) 302

Moving Violations (1985) 229

Mrs Dalloway (1997) 83

Mrs Doubtfire (1993) 125, 167*t*, 173, 278–9*n1*

Mrs Soffel (1985) 84

Much Ado About Nothing (1993) 132

Mulan (1998) 24

Mulroney, Dermot 127

The Mummy (1999) 23, 170

The Munsters (TV) 292*n21*

The Muppets Take Manhattan 185

Murder One (TV) 151, 270

Muriel's Wedding (1995) 132

Murnau, Friedrich Wilhelm 301

Murphy, Brittany 222

Murphy, Eddie 4, 122, 123–5, 129*n13*, 136

Murphy's Romance (1986) 134, 137

Murray, Bill 4, 121–3, *122*, 125

music, role of 47*n74*, 73, 96, 140, 146*n35*, 159, 171, 226, 228, 239–40, 241

musicals 2–3, 16, 23, 24, 48–61, 90, 201, 202

My Best Friend's Wedding (1997) 127, 131, 136, 145*n22*, 177

My Bodyguard (1980) 230

My Boyfriend's Back (1993) 135

My Brilliant Career (1978) 84

My Girl I/II (1991/94) 137

My Man Adam (1986) 137

My So-Called Life (TV) 99, 151

My Stepmother Is an Alien (1988) 135

Myers, Mike 176

Myrick, Daniel 170

Mystic Pizza (1988) 80

Nabokov, Vladimir 258

Naked Lunch (1991) 102

Naremore, James 254, 255, 258, 296

Narrow Margin (1952/90) 256

National Association of Theater Owners (NATO) 18, 204, 205, 206–10, 213, 214, 215*n19*

National General 17

National Lampoon's Animal House (1978) 117, 118–19, 120, 121, 124

National Lampoon's European Vacation (1985) 85

Native Americans, portrayal of 31–2, 34, 179

Native Americans (1994) 33

Natural Born Killers (1994) 210

Naturally Native (1998) 34

Navy Seals (1990) 283

Neale, Steve 2, 77, 78, 83, 91, 92, 115, 144*n4*, 185, 253, 254, 255, 287

The Neon Empire (1989) 35

Never Again (2001) 137

Never Been Kissed (1999) 137, 139, 224, 230–1

Nevins, Francis M., Jr. 265*n11*

'New Hollywood' 2, 15, 19–24, 27, 29, 115, 218

New Jack City (1991) 39, 40, 236, 241

'New Romance' see romantic comedy: modernisation

Newirth, Mike 262

Newman, Paul 118

News Corp 165
The Next Best Thing (2000) 136
Nicholas and Alexandra (1971) 17
Nicholson, Jack 102, 178, 179
Night of the Living Dead (1968) 107
Nightmare on Elm Street series
    (1984–94) 106, 110, 289,
    291*n2*
9 to 5 (1980) 81
Nixon (1995) 97–8, 102, 104*n19*
Nolte, Nick 71
Noonan, Chris 173
Norris, Chuck 65
Not Just Another Girl on the IRT
    (1994) 246
Notting Hill (1999) 132, 134,
    144–5*n8,* 177
novels *see* adaptations
Now and Then (1995) 80
Nunez, Victor 178
Nussbaum, Joe 293*n27*
The Nutty Professor (1996) 124–5,
    278–9*n1*

Oates, Joyce Carol 256–7
The Object of My Affection (1998)
    136, 140
O'Brien, Geoffrey 252–3, 254, 258,
    259–60, 262
O'Brien, Joseph F. 36
O'Brien, Tim 66, 67
O'Donnell, Chris 278–9*n1*
Oedipus the King (1969) 210–11
Old Bill Through the Ages (1926)
    162*n29*
The Old Dark House (1932) 170
Old Wives for New (1918) 130
Oldman, Gary 96, 298, 299, 303
Oliver! (1968) 191
Olivier, Laurence 148, 150, 155
On the Town (1949) 52
Once Around (1991) 133
Once Upon a Honeymoon (1942)
    146–7*n38*
Once Upon a Time In America (1984)
    35
Ondaatje, Michael 181
One Crazy Summer (1986) 137
101 Dalmations (1961/96) 172
One Fine Day (1996) 134
One Flew Over the Cuckoo's Nest
    (1975) 180
O'Neill, Ed 99
The Opposite of Sex (1998) 133
Original Gangstas (1996) 39
Orion Pictures 180
Oscar awards 23, 94, 171, 175, 177,
    178, 179, 180, 200*n57,* 307*n35*
Osment, Haley Joel 170–1

The Other Sister (1999) 133
Otto, Miranda 71
The Out-of-Towners (1999) 137
Outrageous Fortune (1987) 81
Over the Edge (1979) 221, 222
Overboard (1987) 134
Owen, Wilfred 74

Pacino, Al *37,* 209
Paint Your Wagon (1969) 17
Pakula, Alan J. 278–9*n1*
Pale Rider (1985) 29–30
Palookaville (1997) 39
Paltrow, Gwyneth 133, 151, 156
Pantoliano, Joe 228
The Parallax View (1974) 271
Paramount 15, 16, 22, 86
Consent Decree 202, 204, 206
Parenthood (1989) 125
Parker, Alan 24
Parker, Mary-Louise 180
parody 6, 28, 35, 236, 281–91,
    293*n27*
The Party (1968) 118
Pascal, Amy 103
Pasolini, Pier Paolo 215*n16*
Patch Adams (1998) 101
Patric, Jason 261
Patriot Games (1992) 175
Patton (1970) 16
Paul, William 3, 4
Paula, Chris 263
Paxton, Bill 168
Payback (1999) 175
Pearl Harbor (2001) 24
Pearson, Roberta E. 4
Peckinpah, Sam 257, 268*n79*
Peeping Tom (1960) 108
Peggy Sue Got Married (1986) 135
The Pelican Brief (1993) 179, 269,
    270, 272–3, 276–7, 278–9*n1*
Penn, Sean 71, 96
The People vs. Larry Flynt (1997) 96,
    97, 102
The Perez Family (1995) 136
Permanent Record (1988) 223
Perry Mason novels 269
Peter Pan (Barrie) 173
Pete's Dragon (1977) 189
Pfeiffer, Michelle 151
Philadelphia (1993) 179
Picker, Eugene 18
Pickett, Bobby 292*n21*
Pileggi, Nicholas 36, 37, 45*n59,*
    46*n63*
Pinedo, Isabel Cristina 105–6,
    114–15
Pink Floyd: The Wall (1983) 223
The Pink Panther (1964) 118, 192

Pinocchio (1940) 172, 190
The Pirate (1948) 52
Pistone, Joseph D. 36
Pitt, Brad 102, 170
Platoon (1986) 64, 65, 66–8
Pleasantville (1998) 178, 235*n8*
Plump Fiction (1997) 39, 285
Pocahontas (1995) 33, 195
Poel, William 160
Poetic Justice (1993) 246
Poitier, Sidney 94
Polito, Robert 251, 252, 253, 259,
    262
Pollack, Sidney 278–9*n1*
Poorman, Charlie 207
Popeye (1980) 192–3
Porky's (1981) 117, 120, 125
pornography 205, 207–8
Porter, Cole 138
The Portrait of a Lady (1996) 83,
    155
The Poseidon Adventure (1972)
    19–20
Posey, Parker 223
Posse (1993) 33
Poste, Melville Davisson 269
Postlethwaite, Pete 152
The Postman Always Rings Twice
    (1981) 256
postmodernism 3–4, 105–6,
    113–16, 286
Potter, Dennis 157
Powell, William 118
Powwow Highway (1989) 31–2
Practical Magic (1998) 135
Pratt, David 219, 230
The Preacher's Wife (1996) 135,
    146*n34*
Prefontaine (1997) 98–101
Prelude to a Kiss (1992) 135
Presumed Innocent (1990) 279*n4*
Pretty in Pink (1986) 137, 223–4,
    235*n3*
Pretty Woman (1990) 127, 128, 134,
    177
Prince, Stephen 65
The Prince of Egypt (1998) 24,
    26*n32,* 194
Prizzi's Honor (1985) 35, 134
Production Code 5, 64, 191, 205
Administration (PCA) 202, 204
Psycho (1960) 108, 285–6
Psycho (1998) 106
Psycho III (1986) 106
Pullman, Bill 141
Pulp Fiction (1994) 38, 178,
    278–9*n1,* 285
Purgatory (1999) 34
Purple Rain (1984) 49

The Purple Rose of Cairo (1985) 135
Puzo, Mario 34, 44*n50*

Qualls, D.J. 230
Queenie in Love (2001) 137
Quest for Camelot (1998) 24
The Quick and the Dead (1995) 33
Quick Change (1990) 122
Quills (2000) 96
Quo Vadis? (1951) 12, 13

Rafter, Nicole 37, 38
A Rage in Harlem (1990) 256
Raiders of the Lost Ark (1981) 23,
   28, 187
The Rainmaker (1995) 269, 270,
   273, 274, 275, 278–9*n1*
Rambo: First Blood Part II (1985)
   23, 65–6, 287
Rank Organisation 19
Ransom (1996) 175
rap music 239–40, 241, 249–50*n9*,
   249*nn6–7*
ratings system 5, 64, 191–2, 193–4,
   198*n37*, 198*n39*, 198*n41*,
   199–200*n53*, 202–3, 215*n11*
   criteria (sex/nudity) 210, 212–13
   'R' (*vs.* 'X') 203, 204–14, 215*n18*
Re-Animator (1985) 107
Read, Rex 154
Reagan, Ronald 233, 270
Rebel Without a Cause (1955) 59
Red Dawn (1986) 65
Red Rock West (1992) 256
Red Salute (1935) 133
Redford, Robert 39, 118, 181
Reed, Lou 96
Reeves, Keanu 169, 220, *295*, 298,
   305
Reinhardt, Max 148
Relax … It's Just Sex (1998) 136,
   145*n23*
Remember the Titans (2000) 94, 101,
   104*n23*
Repossessed (1990) 283
The Rescuers (1977) 189
Reservoir Dogs (1992) 38
The Return of Eliot Ness (1991) 35,
   36
The Return of Superfly (1990) 39
The Revenge of Al Capone (1989) 35
Rice, Anne 170, 296
Rich, Matty 236–7, 245
Richard III (1995) 4, 149, 150, 151,
   152, 154, 157–8, 162*n31*
Richardson, Robert 97
Richter, Jason James 174
Ride With the Devil (1999) 34
Riders in the Storm (1995) 33

Riders of the Purple Sage (1996) 34
Riefenstahl, Leni 157
Rifkin, Julian 206
The Right Stuff (1983) 96
Ringwald, Molly 224
Risky Business (1983) 219–20, 221,
   224, 228, 229–30
River's Edge (1986) 220
Road House (1948) 262
The Road to El Dorado (2000) 194
Road Trip (2000) 229–30
'roadshows' 12–15, 17–19, 21
Rob Roy (1995) 175
Robbins, Tim 75*n31*
Roberts, Julia 101–2, 126, 127, 128,
   132, 136, 177, 179, 181,
   278–9*n1*, 296
Robin Hood (1973) 189
Robin Hood: Prince of Thieves (1991)
   175
Robson, Peter *273*
Roebuck, Daniel 220
Rogers, Ginger 50–1, 146–7*n38*
Romancing the Stone (1984) 134
romantic comedy 4, 117, 118, 122,
   126–8, 129*n2*, 129*n15*, 130–44
   defined 132–3, 144*nn3–4*, 145*n15*
   modernisation 131–2, 138–41,
   176–8
   overlap with other genres 133–6
Romanus, Robert 226
Romeo and Juliet (1916 films) 160
   see also *William Shakespeare's
   Romeo + Juliet*
Romero, George A. 225, 226, 227
Romero, Joanelle Nadine 32
A Room with a View (1986) 155
Rooster Cogburn (1975) 28
Rose, Brian 198–9*n42*
The Rose (1979) 49
Rosenthal, Daniel 286
Ross, Gary 178
Ross, Katharine 118
Ross, Steve 73
Rothwell, Kenneth 157, 158, 159
Rourke, Mickey 278–9*n1*
Roxanne (1987) 145*n9*
Rubin, Martin 271
Ruby (1992) 98
Ruck, Alan 220
The Rugrats Movie (1998) 171
Rules of Engagement (1999) 62–4,
   63, 72, 74*n5*
Rum and Coke (1999) 136
Runaway Bride (1999) 134, 140,
   146–7*n38*, 177
Rush, Geoffrey 151, 155–6
Russell, David O. 73
Russell, Ken 158

Rustler's Rhapsody (1985) 29–30
Ruth of the Rockies (1920) 77
Ruthless People (1986) 177
Ryall, Tom 1, 27
Ryan, Meg 73, 126, 138, 177–8
Ryder, Winona 84, *85,* 170, 223,
   298, 299, 305

Sabrina (1954/95) 146*n34*
Sagan, Carl 169
The Saint (TV) 287
Salkind, Alexander 26*n28*
Salvador (1986) 65
Samhain (magazine) 301, 304,
   308*n47*
Samson and Delilah (1949) 12, 13
Sanchez, Eduardo 170
Sandler, Adam 176
Sandler, Kevin 5
The Santa Clause (1994) 125, *172*
Sante, Luc 258, 259
Sarandon, Susan *85,* 181, 278–9*n1*
Sartre, Jean-Paul 258
Saturday Night Fever (1977) 2, 49,
   53, 55–8, *57,* 59–60, 61*n14*
Saturday Night Live (TV) 121, 123,
   176
Saving Private Ryan (1998) 23, 63,
   64, 66, 69–72, 75*n24*, 167*t*, 174,
   177, 182
Saving Ryan's Privates (1999) 293*n27*
Say Anything (1989) 137
Scarface (1983) 35, 36
Scary Movie (2000) 6, 107, 112–13,
   281, 282–3, 284, *284,* 285, 286,
   287–8, 290–1, 291*n2*, 292–3*n26*
Scary Movie 2 (2001) 282, 291
Schatz, Thomas 1, 18, 27, 93,
   129*n8*, 255, 283, 286, 292*n13*
Scheurer, Timothy 48–9
Schickel, Richard 190–1, 192
Schindler's List (1993) 23, 70, 101,
   180, 182
Schnabel, Julian 96–7
school (as setting) 222–5, 230–1
Schrader, Paul 91, 103*n1,* 178
Schultz, Dutch 36
Schumacher, Joel 278–9*n1*
Schwarzenegger, Arnold 169, 173,
   174
science fiction 2, 4, 23, 168–9, 281
Scorsese, Martin 37, 46*n63,* 96,
   102, 244
Scott, Ridley 102
Scream (1996) 6, 106, 110–13, *112,*
   170, 218, 223, 283, 286, 288,
   289–90, 291*n2,* 297
Scream 2 (1997) 107, 170, 286
Scream 3 (2000) 290

'screwball' comedy 139–44, 146n36

Secret Admirer (1985) 137

Selena (1997) 93

Selznick, David O. 12, 14, 15, 20–1

Sennett, Mack 282

Sense and Sensibility (1995) 83, 86–8, 132

sequels 3–4, 23, 106, 112, 174, 288

Sergeant Pepper's Lonely Hearts Club Band (1978) 48

serials 23, 77

Série Noire (1979) 259

Set It Off (1996) 39, 40, 46n64

Seven Arts 15

Seven Minutes to Heaven (1986) 137

Seven Years in Tibet (1997) 98, 102

Sevigny, Chloe 102

Shag (1989) 137

Shainberg, Steven 268n79

Shakar, Martin 58

Shakespeare, William
   early films 153, 160, 161n7, 162n29
   modern screen adaptations 4, 132, 148–60
   stage productions 150–1, 152–3, 154–5, 159–60, 162n40
   updatings of 139, 145n9

Shakespeare in Love (1998) 4, 131, 132, 133, 149, 151, 154, 155–7, 158, 177

Shall We Dance? (1937) 51

Shanghai Noon (2000) 281

Sheen, Charlie 64, 283–4, 287

Sheen, Martin 284

Shephard, Ben 70

Sher, Antony 156

She's All That (1999) 137, 224

She's Gotta Have It (1986) 135

Shine (1996) 151

Shirley Valentine (1989) 144n7

Shivers (1975) 107

The Shootist (1976) 29

The Shop Around the Corner (1940) 146n34, 177–8

A Shot in the Dark (1964) 118

Showgirls (1995) 203, 212

Shrek (2001) 195, 196, 200n65

Shue, Elisabeth 228

Shyamalan, M. Night 170

The Sicilian (1987) 44n50

The Silence of the Lambs (1991) 179–80, 296, 299

Silver, Alain 254–5, 256

Silver, Ron 103

Silverado (1985) 29–30

Silverstone, Alicia 86, 220

Since You Went Away (1944) 14

Singer, Bryan 38

Singer, Lori 59

Singin' in the Rain (1952) 140

Single White Female (1992) 83

Singleton, John 245

Six Days, Seven Nights (1998) 134

Sixteen Candles (1984) 137, 221, 224

The Sixth Sense (1999) 109, 167t, 170–1

Skye, Ione 220

Slagrow, Michael 144

Slater, Christian 223

Sleep With Me (1994) 145n11

'sleepers' (surprise hits) 17, 20–1, 165, 170–1

Sleepless in Seattle (1993) 140, 177

Sliding Doors (1998) 132, 135

Sliver (1993) 212

Small Soldiers (1998) 200n54, 281, 285

Smith, Dwight D. 34

Smith, Kevin 225, 226

Smith, Maggie 152

Smith, Will 93, 102–3, 168

Smoke Signals (1998) 34

Sneakers (1993) 39

Snow White and the Seven Dwarfs (1937) 172, 194

Solanas, Valerie 102

Soldier Blue (1970) 28

Solomon, Stanley 61n3

Solondz, Todd 178

Some Kind of Wonderful (1987) 137, 224

Some Like It Hot (1959) 134

Something Wild (1986) 134

Sommers, Stephen 170

Son of the Morning Star (1991) 33

Sonnet, Esther 40

Sony 103

The Sopranos (TV) 38

Sorkin, Aaron 179

The Sound of Music (1965) 16, 191

South Central (1992) 39, 236

South Park: Bigger, Longer, Uncut (1998) 200n54

Spacey, Kevin 178

Spader, James 223

Spartacus (1960) 24

Speechless (1994) 134

Spielberg, Steven 4, 70, 71–2, 74, 82, 101, 168, 169, 173, 180, 182, 186–7, 189–90, 192, 193, 199n50

Splash (1984) 129n2, 135, 199n47

sporting themes 98–101, 104n23, 134–5, 249n2

Sprung (1997) 135

Spy Hard (1996) 281

spy thrillers 6, 129n7, 174, 175
   parodied 117, 281, 283, 284–5, 287

Squanto: a Warrior's Tale (1994) 33

Staiger, Janet 1

Stallone, Sylvester 174

Stanfield, Peter 5–6

Star Trek: First Contact (1996) 169

Star Trek: the Motion Picture (1979) 22, 23

Star Wars (1977) 20, 23, 26n26, 187, 192, 203

Star Wars: The Empire Strikes Back (1980) 28, 187

Star Wars: Return of the Jedi (1983) 187

Star Wars Episode I: The Phantom Menace (1999) 167t, 168, 193

Star Wars Episode II: Attack of the Clones (2002) 24

State of Grace (1990) 37

Steal This Movie (2000) 102

The Steel Helmet (1980) 72

Steel Magnolias (1989) 80

Stella (1990) 79

Stella Dallas (1937) 79

Stepmom (1998) 137, 181

Stern, Howard 102

Stewart, Patrick 169

Stiller, Ben 126, 127, 176

The Sting (1973) 20

Stone, Oliver 3, 68, 96, 97–8, 102, 104n19

Stone, Sharon 180

Stoppard, Tom 156

The Story of Vernon and Irene Castle (1939) 54

Straight out of Brooklyn (1991) 39, 236–7, 245

Street of No Return (1990) 256

Strictly Ballroom (1993) 132

Strictly Business (1991) 135

Stripes (1981) 119

Sugar and Spice (2001) 134

Sugar Hill (1994) 40

Sugartime (1995) 35

Summer Catch (2001) 137

Sunset (1988) 31, 32

Superman (1978) 22, 23, 28

The Sure Thing (1985) 137

Susann, Jacqueline 102

Sutherland, Donald 100

Swank, Hilary 102

Swayze, Patrick 177

Swicord, Robin 84–5, 86, 89n19

Switch (1991) 135

Switching Channels (1988) 134, 146n34

Swoon (1992) 102

The Taking of Pelham One, Two, Three (1974) 38
The Tall Guy (1989) 144–5n8
The Taming of the Shrew (Shakespeare) 145n9
Tandy, Jessica 180
Tarantino, Quentin 38, 39
Tarzan (1999) 24
Tasker, Yvonne 65
teen films 5, 85–6, 110–12, 137, 218–35
  locations 219–29
  'slasher' films 288–91
  social/cultural milieu 218–19, 232–5
  target audience 137, 165–6, 170, 203
Teenage Mutant Ninja Turtles (1990) 172
Telotte, J.P. 2–3
The Tempest (Shakespeare) 159–60
The Ten Commandments (1956) 12, 13, 24, 26n32, 155
10 Things I Hate About You (1999) 137, 145n9
Terminator 2: Judgement Day (1991) 22, 23, 167t, 169
Terms of Endearment (1983) 79, 178
Test Pilot (1938) 133
Tetsuo: the Iron Man (1991) 107
The Texas Chainsaw Massacre (1974) 107, 288–9
That's Life! (1986) 125
Thelma and Louise (1991) 80–1, 83
There's Something About Mary (1998) 127, 128, 131, 145n22, 176–7
Thief (1981) 39
The Thin Man (1934) 133
The Thin Red Line (1998) 23, 69, 70–2, 75n24
Things to Do in Denver When You're Dead (1995) 39, 46n64
This World, then the Fireworks (1998) 263
Thompson, Emma 86, 87–8
Thompson, Jim 5–6, 251–64, 265n15
  European appeal 258, 259
  film adaptations 251, 260–3, 268n79
  and *film noir* tradition 253–7, 260
  literary background/qualities 251–3, 257–60, 263–4, 264n6, 266n42, 266n47, 267n64
Thompson, Kristin 1
Thomson, David 257–8
Thornton, Sarah 301
Thousand Pieces of Gold (1991) 33
3 Days of the Condor (1975) 39

Three Kings (1999) 72–3
Three Little Words (1950) 54
Three Men and a Baby (1987) 125, 137
Three of Hearts (1993) 136
The Three Stooges 117
Three to Tango (1999) 136
Threesome (1994) 145n11
Thurman, Uma 141
Till the Clouds Roll By (1946) 54
A Time to Kill (1996) 179, 269, 272, 273, 274, 275, 276, 278–9n1
Tin Cup (1996) 134–5, 175
Titan A.E. (2000) 200n54
Titanic (1997) 22, 23, 166–8, 167t, 194
Titus (1999) 149, 160n3
To Kill a Mockingbird (Lee) 269
Tom Horn (1980) 28
Tombstone (1993) 33, 98
Tomcats (2001) 214
Tomorrow Never Dies (1997) 174
Too Hot to Handle (1938) 133
Tootsie (1982) 129n2
Top Gun (1986) 65
Top Hat (1935) 51
Top Secret! (1984) 285
Tora! Tora! Tora! (1970) 17, 24
Tortilla Soup (2001) 136
Total Recall (1990) 169
Touch of Evil (1958) 256
The Towering Inferno (1974) 22
Town and Country (2001) 137
Towne, Robert 99, 100
Toy Story (1995) 167t, 171, 195
Toy Story 2 (1999) 167t, 171, 193, 194, 281
Trading Places (1983) 124
Travolta, John 38, 46n66, 53, 55, 57, 177
Tree, Sir Herbert Beerbohm *see* Beerbohm Tree
Tremors (1989) 107
Triangle Pictures 153
Trick (1999) 136
Tristar 32
The Triumph of the Will (1935) 157
Tron (1981) 192–3
True Grit (1969) 28
True Heart Susie (1919) 77
True Romance (1993) 39
The Truman Show (1998) 123
The Truth About Cats and Dogs (1996) 138, 141–2, 147n39
Tucci, Stanley 151
Tudor, Andrew 1, 3–4, 27
Tuff Turf (1985) 230
Tumbleweeds (1999) 79
Turan, Kenneth 169, 174

Turner, Tyrin 244
Turow, Scott 269–70, 279n4
Turpin, Ben 282
20,000 Leagues Under the Sea (1954) 192
Twice Upon a Yesterday (1998) 133
Twister (1996) 167t, 168, 182
2001: A Space Odyssey (1968) 16, 18, 22
Two Can Play That Game (2001) 135
2 Days in the Valley (1997) 38
Two for Texas (1998) 34
Two Girls and a Guy (1998) 145n11
The Two Jakes (1990) 256
Two Much (1996) 136
Two of a Kind (1983) 135

Ulee's Gold (1997) 178
Uncle Buck (1989) 125
Uncommon Valor (1983) 65
Undercover Blues (1993) 134
The Underneath (1995) 39
Unforgiven (1992) 33, 179
Union City (1980) 256
United Artists 15, 16, 41n7, 209–10
Universal 21, 166, 173
An Unmarried Woman (1979) 79
The Untouchables (1987) 35–6, 263
The Untouchables (TV) 35–6
Uphill All the Way (1985) 30
Urban Legend (1998) 289
Urban Legends: Final Cut (2000) 289
Used People (1992) 137
The Usual Suspects (1995) 38

Vale, V. 257
Valenti, Jack 74n3, 204, 205, 207–8, 211–12
Valley Girl (1983) 226, 227, 229
Vampire in Brooklyn (1995) 296, 307n16
Vampyra 292n21
Van Sant, Gus 180
Velvet Goldmine (1998) 102
Vendetta (1991) 35
Verhoeven, Paul 212
Verne, Jules 192
Vernet, Marc 254–5
Viacom 165
Vibe magazine 249–50n9
video, social/financial significance of 22, 194, 218–19, 265n27
Vietnam war
  depictions on screen 3, 62–8, 74, 74n5, 97
  influence on US cinema 63, 64–5, 70, 71, 72–3, 74
  'Westerns' 28, 29

Viren, Lasse 100–1
The Virginian (TV) 28
Voight, Jon 278–9n1
Volcano (1997) 168
Volkman, Ernest 36

Wachowski, Larry and Andy 169
Wagons East! (1994) 33
Waiting to Exhale (1995) 82
Walken, Christopher 65
Walker, Alexander 67, 147n39
Walker, Alice 82
Walker, Gerald 209
Walker, Justin 226
Walker, Texas Ranger (TV) 34
war films 3, 23, 31, 62–74, 120, 281
War Party (1989) 31, 32
Ward, Elizabeth 255, 256
Ward, Rachel 263
Warde, Frederick 160
Warhol, Andy 102
Warner Bros (AOL Time Warner)
    15, 20, 22, 24, 32, 50–1, 73, 95,
    99, 102, 165
The Warriors (1979) 39
Warshow, Robert 27
Washington, Denzel 3, 73, 93–4, 95,
    101, 278–9n1
Washington Square (1997) 83
Wasko, Janet 188
The Waterboy (1998) 176
Watkins, Craig 5, 39
Way Down East (1920) 77
The Way West (1995) 33
Wayans, Damon/Marlon 282
Wayne, John 29, 64
Wayne's World (1992) 176
Webb, James 74n5
Webster, John 156
The Wedding Banquet (1993) 136
The Wedding Planner (2001) 134,
    136
The Wedding Singer (1998) 131
Welcome to the Dollhouse (1996)
    178
Wells, H.G. 168
Wells, Paul 113–14
Wes Craven's New Nightmare (1994)
    106, 110, 289
Westerns 2, 27–34, 201, 202
    decline 23, 27–29, 117
    parodies 281, 287
    revival 29–32
    sub-genres 15, 28–29, 32–34,
    43n38, 179
    television 28, 29, 30–1, 33, 34
Whale, James 170
What About Bob? (1991) 122–3

What Did You Do in the War, Daddy?
    (1966) 118
What Lies Beneath (2000) 109
What Planet Are You From? (2000)
    135
Whatever It Takes (2000) 137
What's Eating Gilbert Grape? (1993)
    151
What's Love Got to Do with It (1993)
    93
When Harry Met Sally... (1989) 134,
    138, 140, 177
When the Chickens Come Home to
    Roost (play) 94
Where the Boys Are (1984) 137
While You Were Sleeping (1995)
    131, 134, 141, 142, 147n39
Whitaker, Forest 82
White Heat (1948) 157
White Men Can't Jump (1992) 175
Who Framed Roger Rabbit? (1988)
    179, 199n50
The Whole Nine Yards (2000) 38,
    134
Why Change Your Wife? (1920) 130
Wide Sargasso Sea (1992) 212
The Wild, Wild West (1999) 33–4
Wild at Heart (1990) 256
Wild Bill (1995) 33
The Wild Bunch (1969) 28, 33, 63,
    64, 74n3, 157
Wild Things (1998) 221
Wilde, Oscar 130, 144n1
Wilder, Billy 264n6
wilderness (as location) 192,
    198–9n42
The Wilderness Family (1975) 192
Willeford, Charles 252, 256, 257,
    266n42
William Shakespeare's A Midsummer
    Night's Dream (1999) 149, 151,
    153–4, 155
William Shakespeare's Romeo + Juliet
    (1996) 4, 145n9, 149, 151, 153,
    154, 154, 158–9, 160n4
Williams, Alan 295
Williams, Charles 253
Williams, Linda 77
Williams, Richard 286
Williams, Robin 101, 171, 172, 173,
    180
Williamson, Kevin 113, 289
Willis, Bruce 31, 168, 170
Willy/Milly (1986) 137
Wilson, Michael 174
Windwalker (1980) 28
Winslet, Kate 166
Wise Guys (1986) 38

Wiseguy: Life in a Mafia Family
    (1985) 36–7
Without a Stitch (1970) 207–8
Without Limits (1998) 98–101
Witness to the Mob (1998) 35
The Wiz (1978) 48, 49, 52–3
Wolf (1994) 296, 307n16
Wolfe, Tom 269
The Woman Who Dared (1910) 77
women
    in biopics 92, 103n8
    in comedy 126–8, 134
    as directors/producers 83–8
    in gangster/ghetto films 35,
    45n56, 47n80, 246–7
    in (legal) thrillers 179, 180, 272–3
    'women's films' 3, 77–88, 180–1
    defined 77–8
    renaissance/sub-genres 79–83, 88
Woo, John 157, 158
Woo (1999) 135
Wood, Edward D., Jr. 102
Wood, Michael 48, 51, 52
The Wood (1999) 135
Woodstock (1970) 17
Woolrich, Cornell 252, 253, 265n11
The World Is Not Enough (1999)
    174
World War II 3, 68–72, 75n15, 78
Wright, Jeffrey 96
Written on the Wind (1957) 78
Wrongfully Accused (1998) 281, 284,
    285
Wyatt, Justin 72
Wyatt Earp (1994) 33, 98, 102

X-Men 160n3
Xanadu (1980) 3, 48

Yeats, W.B. 140
York, Michael 284
You Can't Hurry Love (1988) 137
Young, Harrison 69
Young Frankenstein (1974) 288
Young Guns (1988) 31, 32
Young Guns II (1990) 33
The Young Riders (TV) 33
Young Winston (1972) 17
You've Got Mail (1998) 133, 134,
    139, 146n34, 177–8

Zeffirelli, Franco 155, 160–1n5
Zellweger, Renee 178
Zemeckis, Robert 178–9
Zorro the Gay Blade (1981) 28
Zucker, Jerry 177